Lecture Notes in Computer Science 11578

Commenced Publication in 1973
Founding and Former Series Editors:
Gerhard Goos, Juris Hartmanis, and Jan van Leeuwen

Gabriele Meiselwitz (Ed.)

Social Computing and Social Media

Design, Human Behavior and Analytics

11th International Conference, SCSM 2019
Held as Part of the 21st HCI International Conference, HCII 2019
Orlando, FL, USA, July 26–31, 2019
Proceedings, Part I

 Springer

Editor
Gabriele Meiselwitz
Computer Science
Towson University
Towson, MD, USA

ISSN 0302-9743   ISSN 1611-3349 (electronic)
Lecture Notes in Computer Science
ISBN 978-3-030-21901-7   ISBN 978-3-030-21902-4 (eBook)
https://doi.org/10.1007/978-3-030-21902-4

LNCS Sublibrary: SL3 – Information Systems and Applications, incl. Internet/Web, and HCI

This Springer imprint is published by the registered company Springer Nature Switzerland AG
The registered company address is: Gewerbestrasse 11, 6330 Cham, Switzerland

Foreword

The 21st International Conference on Human-Computer Interaction, HCI International 2019, was held in Orlando, FL, USA, during July 26–31, 2019. The event incorporated the 18 thematic areas and affiliated conferences listed on the following page.

A total of 5,029 individuals from academia, research institutes, industry, and governmental agencies from 73 countries submitted contributions, and 1,274 papers and 209 posters were included in the pre-conference proceedings. These contributions address the latest research and development efforts and highlight the human aspects of design and use of computing systems. The contributions thoroughly cover the entire field of human-computer interaction, addressing major advances in knowledge and effective use of computers in a variety of application areas. The volumes constituting the full set of the pre-conference proceedings are listed in the following pages.

This year the HCI International (HCII) conference introduced the new option of "late-breaking work." This applies both for papers and posters and the corresponding volume(s) of the proceedings will be published just after the conference. Full papers will be included in the *HCII 2019 Late-Breaking Work Papers Proceedings* volume of the proceedings to be published in the Springer LNCS series, while poster extended abstracts will be included as short papers in the HCII 2019 *Late-Breaking Work Poster Extended Abstracts* volume to be published in the Springer CCIS series.

I would like to thank the program board chairs and the members of the program boards of all thematic areas and affiliated conferences for their contribution to the highest scientific quality and the overall success of the HCI International 2019 conference.

This conference would not have been possible without the continuous and unwavering support and advice of the founder, Conference General Chair Emeritus and Conference Scientific Advisor Prof. Gavriel Salvendy. For his outstanding efforts, I would like to express my appreciation to the communications chair and editor of *HCI International News,* Dr. Abbas Moallem.

July 2019   Constantine Stephanidis

HCI International 2019 Thematic Areas and Affiliated Conferences

Thematic areas:

- HCI 2019: Human-Computer Interaction
- HIMI 2019: Human Interface and the Management of Information

Affiliated conferences:

- EPCE 2019: 16th International Conference on Engineering Psychology and Cognitive Ergonomics
- UAHCI 2019: 13th International Conference on Universal Access in Human-Computer Interaction
- VAMR 2019: 11th International Conference on Virtual, Augmented and Mixed Reality
- CCD 2019: 11th International Conference on Cross-Cultural Design
- SCSM 2019: 11th International Conference on Social Computing and Social Media
- AC 2019: 13th International Conference on Augmented Cognition
- DHM 2019: 10th International Conference on Digital Human Modeling and Applications in Health, Safety, Ergonomics and Risk Management
- DUXU 2019: 8th International Conference on Design, User Experience, and Usability
- DAPI 2019: 7th International Conference on Distributed, Ambient and Pervasive Interactions
- HCIBGO 2019: 6th International Conference on HCI in Business, Government and Organizations
- LCT 2019: 6th International Conference on Learning and Collaboration Technologies
- ITAP 2019: 5th International Conference on Human Aspects of IT for the Aged Population
- HCI-CPT 2019: First International Conference on HCI for Cybersecurity, Privacy and Trust
- HCI-Games 2019: First International Conference on HCI in Games
- MobiTAS 2019: First International Conference on HCI in Mobility, Transport, and Automotive Systems
- AIS 2019: First International Conference on Adaptive Instructional Systems

Pre-conference Proceedings Volumes Full List

1. LNCS 11566, Human-Computer Interaction: Perspectives on Design (Part I), edited by Masaaki Kurosu
2. LNCS 11567, Human-Computer Interaction: Recognition and Interaction Technologies (Part II), edited by Masaaki Kurosu
3. LNCS 11568, Human-Computer Interaction: Design Practice in Contemporary Societies (Part III), edited by Masaaki Kurosu
4. LNCS 11569, Human Interface and the Management of Information: Visual Information and Knowledge Management (Part I), edited by Sakae Yamamoto and Hirohiko Mori
5. LNCS 11570, Human Interface and the Management of Information: Information in Intelligent Systems (Part II), edited by Sakae Yamamoto and Hirohiko Mori
6. LNAI 11571, Engineering Psychology and Cognitive Ergonomics, edited by Don Harris
7. LNCS 11572, Universal Access in Human-Computer Interaction: Theory, Methods and Tools (Part I), edited by Margherita Antona and Constantine Stephanidis
8. LNCS 11573, Universal Access in Human-Computer Interaction: Multimodality and Assistive Environments (Part II), edited by Margherita Antona and Constantine Stephanidis
9. LNCS 11574, Virtual, Augmented and Mixed Reality: Multimodal Interaction (Part I), edited by Jessie Y. C. Chen and Gino Fragomeni
10. LNCS 11575, Virtual, Augmented and Mixed Reality: Applications and Case Studies (Part II), edited by Jessie Y. C. Chen and Gino Fragomeni
11. LNCS 11576, Cross-Cultural Design: Methods, Tools and User Experience (Part I), edited by P. L. Patrick Rau
12. LNCS 11577, Cross-Cultural Design: Culture and Society (Part II), edited by P. L. Patrick Rau
13. LNCS 11578, Social Computing and Social Media: Design, Human Behavior and Analytics (Part I), edited by Gabriele Meiselwitz
14. LNCS 11579, Social Computing and Social Media: Communication and Social Communities (Part II), edited by Gabriele Meiselwitz
15. LNAI 11580, Augmented Cognition, edited by Dylan D. Schmorrow and Cali M. Fidopiastis
16. LNCS 11581, Digital Human Modeling and Applications in Health, Safety, Ergonomics and Risk Management: Human Body and Motion (Part I), edited by Vincent G. Duffy

http://2019.hci.international/proceedings

11th International Conference on Social Computing and Social Media (SCSM 2019)

Program Board Chair(s): **Gabriele Meiselwitz, *USA***

- Rocío Abascal-Mena, Mexico
- Francisco Alvarez, Mexico
- James Braman, USA
- Adheesh Budree, South Africa
- Adela Coman, Romania
- Panagiotis Germanakos, Germany
- Tamara Heck, Germany
- Sara Hook, USA
- Hung-Hsuan Huang, Japan
- Carsten Kleiner, Germany
- Erick López-Ornelas, Mexico
- Joon Suk Lee, USA
- Marilia S. Mendes, Brazil
- Takashi Namatame, Japan
- Hoang D. Nguyen, Singapore
- Kohei Otake, Japan
- Daniela Quinones, Chile
- Cristian Rusu, Chile
- Christian W. Scheiner, Germany
- Simona Vasilache, Japan
- Giovanni Vincenti, USA
- Kathy Wang, USA
- June Wei, USA
- Brian Wentz, USA

The full list with the Program Board Chairs and the members of the Program Boards of all thematic areas and affiliated conferences is available online at:

http://www.hci.international/board-members-2019.php

HCI International 2020

The 22nd International Conference on Human-Computer Interaction, HCI International 2020, will be held jointly with the affiliated conferences in Copenhagen, Denmark, at the Bella Center Copenhagen, July 19–24, 2020. It will cover a broad spectrum of themes related to HCI, including theoretical issues, methods, tools, processes, and case studies in HCI design, as well as novel interaction techniques, interfaces, and applications. The proceedings will be published by Springer. More information will be available on the conference website: http://2020.hci.international/.

General Chair
Prof. Constantine Stephanidis
University of Crete and ICS-FORTH
Heraklion, Crete, Greece
E-mail: general_chair@hcii2020.org

http://2020.hci.international/

Contents – Part I

Human Behaviour in Social Media

Social Network Analysis

Community Engagement and Social Participation

Contents – Part II

Social Media in Education

Digital Marketing and Consumer Experience

Social Media Design and Development

Wajeez: An Extractive Automatic Arabic Text Summarisation System

Abrar Al Oudah[1], Kholoud Al Bassam[1], Heba Kurdi[1],
and Shiroq Al-Megren[2]([⊠])

[1] Computer Science Department, King Saud University, Riyadh, Saudi Arabia
{436203175,437202894}@student.ksu.edu.sa, hkurdi@ksu.edu.sa
[2] Information Technology Department, King Saud University, Riyadh, Saudi Arabia
salmegren@ksu.edu.sa

Abstract. The volume of Arabic information is rapidly increasingly nowadays, and thus, access to the corrects is arguably one of the most difficult research problems facing readers and researchers. Text Summarisation Systems are utilised to produce a short text describing significant portions of the original text. That is by selecting the most important sentences, following several steps: preprocessing, stemming, scoring, and summary extraction. Nevertheless, summarisation systems remain still in their infancy for the Arabic language. Therefore, this paper proposes an automatic Arabic text summarisation systems, entitled Wajeez, that introduces a new inclusive scoring formula that generates a final summary from several top-ranking sentences. Wajeez was applied on two different datasets: the Essex Arabic Summaries Corpus (EASC) and a manual summary to assess its performance using the Recall-Oriented Understudy for Gisting Evaluation (ROUGE) set of metrics. In comparison to two other competitions systems, Wajeez performed comparatively well when a title is provisioned to support summarisation.

Keywords: Natural language processing · Text summarisation · Extractive approach · Arabic language · Sentence scoring methods · Ranking

1 Introduction

As research on text summarisation is becoming a hot topic in Natural Language Processing. There is a big demand for automatic text summarisation systems which automatically retrieves the data from documents that minimising our precious time. The benefits of automatic Arabic text summarisation appear on some applications and fields such as the first page of the newspaper is a brief summary of next pages, sending news by SMS that helps in keeping the time of users. Eduard Hovy defines a summary as: "a text that is produced from one or more texts, which contains a significant portion of the information in the original text(s), and that is no longer than half of the original text(s)" [13].

© Springer Nature Switzerland AG 2019
G. Meiselwitz (Ed.): HCII 2019, LNCS 11578, pp. 3–14, 2019.
https://doi.org/10.1007/978-3-030-21902-4_1

Text summarisation can be classified according to different criteria; one of these criteria is summarisation method. The summarisation methods can be classified into abstractive and extractive summarisations [11]. Extractive Text Summarisation (ETS) uses classical approaches to generate summaries by cropping important segments of the original text and combining them to build a consistent summary. In Abstractive Text Summarisation (ATS), the document will be generated from scratch without being restrained to phrases from the original text. This is like the human-written sentences to generate summaries.

The Arabic language is the native language for more than 300 million people worldwide and one of the six official languages used at the United Nations. The Arabic languages includes 28 letters and is written from right to left. The letters change forms according to their position in the word. Furthermore, Arabic short vowels do not appear as letters it appears as diacritical marks, which are marks written on the top. In addition, the Arabic language has no capitalisation. In written Arabic, if the vowels omitted then the result will have a higher level of ambiguity. This ambiguity will be a problem in information retrieval, in the fact that an Arabic word can have several meanings. In addition to the ambiguity, there is another problem of the plural form of irregular nouns, also called broken plural. In this case, a noun in plural takes another morphological form different from its initial form in singular [16].

There is a need of Arabic text summarisation as the number of texts written in Arabic rapidly increases. Users cannot manually handle a large amount of text, and thus there is a necessity to have an automated system to generate a summary to give the reader the main idea of the text. Therefore, the need to automate Arabic text summarisation was a desirable goal. Text summarisation (TS) aims to generate a new document (summary) which consisting of a few sentences capture the most important content of an input document or a set of documents.

This paper proposes a new system, Wajeez, that automatically generates summarisation of Arabic text to balance both information scores and readability. That is by extracting sentences of the highest scores to help understand the general meaning of the original text. The main objectives of this work is examine the effect of combining many features of text extraction that generate an automatic Arabic summary text depending on the extraction of the most salient sentences of a text that help to understand the general meaning of the whole text. The performances of Wajeez is comparatively assessed against two established systems using the Recall-Oriented Understudy for Gisting Evaluation (ROUGE) set of metrics. The findings support the usefulness of Wajeez at producing valid summarisation when an adequate title is provided with the text to be summarised.

The remainder of this paper is organised as follows. First, the related work section reviews work for extractive text summarisation system for both Arabic and English languages. Third, the following sections describes Wajeez, the proposed extractive Arabic text summarisation systems. Fourth, the experimental set-up is descried and the results are presented and discussed. The final section summarises and concludes the paper and briefly draws future directions.

2 Related Work

The past few years have seen many works proposing text summarisation techniques for various languages. In this section, a review of the literature on extractive text summarisation system for English and Arabic language will be presented. First, we will present many related works for the English language. Then some Arabic text summarisation system will be shown in the second part.

Since 1950's, a lot of researches have been conducted on text summarisation using a variety of and languages. For an English language system, a computer program that used machine learning and natural language processing developed approaches to automatically generate summaries of full-text scientific publications [8]. This program uses an extractive approach to generate the summery. The summaries of the sentence and fragment levels were evaluated in finding common clinical systematic review (SR) data elements.

A novel word-sentence co-ranking model named CoRank was proposed [12]. This CoRank model combines sentence scoring techniques by combine the word-sentences relationship with the graph-based unsupervised ranking model. The actions of CoRank are also supplemented with a redundancy elimination techniques. Two real-life datasets were used to assess the performance of CoRank with nearly 600 documents. The findings confirm the effectiveness of the proposed approach in producing short summaries.

A model for automatic text summarisation was introduced and was based on fuzzy logic system evolutionary algorithms and cellular learning automata [1]. First, the proposed approach extracts the most important features. A linear combination of these features shows the importance of each sentence. A combined method based on artificial bee colony algorithm and cellular learning automata are then used to calculate similarity measures. Furthermore, a new method is proposed to set the best weights of the text features using particle swarm optimisation and genetic algorithm. This method assigns weights to all text by discovering more important and less important text features. In the end, a fuzzy logic system is used to perform the final scoring.

A topic modeling approach to extractive automatic summarisation was presented to achieve a good balance between compression ratio, summarisation quality, and machine readability [18]. The approach goes through many steps, the first step is extracting the candidate sentences associated with topic words from a preprocessed novel document. Then, select the most important sentences from the candidate sentences to generate an initial novel summary. The last step is the summary smoothing to improve the summary readability by overcomes the semantic confusion caused by ambiguous or synonymous words.

Text summarisation field has not been studied enough for Arabic language and currently, only a few related works are available. The first system designed for Arabic text summarisation, uses a combination of many statistical features (terms frequency, the position of the sentence, etc.) [9]. Extractive Arabic Text Summarization based on graph theory and semantic similarity between sentences to calculate importance of each sentence in the document so to extract the most important sentence was also developed [6]. For a final extractive summary, they used the ranking algorithm in combination with Maximal Marginal Relevance method instead of selecting top-ranked sentences. For experimentation, they had been building their own corpus of Arabic articles, a total number of documents is 25 were the summaries produced manually by an expert in the Arabic language. Their approach evaluated using Precision, Recall, and F-measure and obtained by the following values 79.0%, 71.8% and 75.22% respectively.

An Arabic text summarisation system that combines statistical and semantic approaches to achieve the summarisation task implemented was more recently proposed [5]. The system goes through three steps; preprocessing, computes P the similarity between each pair of sentences, then converts the text into a graph model using PageRank algorithm. Then, the score of each sentence is improved by adding other statistical features such as TF.IDF and sentence position. Including the top-ranked sentences from the input, document forms the summary, and an adapted version of maximal marginal relevance (MMR) algorithm is applied to remove information that is redundant and enhance the quality of the result summary.

Text summarisation relies heavily on human-engineered features. Therefore, a generic extractive Arabic Single-Document summarisation approach using the hybrid graph and statistical approaches integrated with the Genetic Algorithm that depends on the semantic relationship between sentences was proposed [14]. The evaluation of this approach using EASC corpus, and ROUGE evaluation method to determine the accuracy. With compression ratio equal to 40% of the original text size, the F-measure equal to 0.5476 for ROUGE-1 and 0.4465 for ROUGE-2. In another paper, an approach for using Practical Swarm Optimisation (PSO) algorithm for summary extraction for single Arabic document was produced [2]. In the research, EASC corpus used as a dataset and evaluated the result using ROUGE tool. PSO approach combined informative scoring with semantic scoring to find the optimal summary.

In conclusion, it is notable that each of the above-mentioned approaches has its own advantages towards single-document summarisation. However, there are some issues and limitation. From this section, we can see that there is no approved benchmark for the Arabic language used in the evaluation process neither gold standard corpora and the different measures used to assess text summarisation. This gap is address in this works and its exploration of appropriate techniques for the Arabic text summarisation.

3   Extractive Arabic Text Summarisation System

In this section, the processes and structure of our proposed Extractive Automatic Arabic Text Summarization System, Wajeez, are presented. The system is easy to use and has the feature of enabling the user to determine the size of the summary through a number of sentences, a number of words and a percentage of the original. It also allows the user to enter a query to enhance the summary. i.e. the user can enter a specific word or a list of words. First, we divide the text to set of sentences. We then assign a score to each sentence based on seven scoring functions calculated for each sentence. At the end, we pick sentences that have a maximum score while satisfying the constraint set by the user in terms of length of the summary and the query if it had entered Otherwise the system will generate the default summary size which is 30% as some other system [5,6]. Wajeez processes on five main subsystems: data acquisition, preprocessing, stemming, sentence scoring, and finally we generate the summary within the user determined size. The following subsections summarises each subsystems, with a particular concentration on the scoring function.

3.1 Data Acquisition

The data acquisition subsystem describes the inputs of the system and it is required structure. Text, query, and size of the text are the main inputs of the system. The user then selects either support the system with a query to satisfy a requested summary, which would be a sentences, word, or a collection of words. The user would then specify the size of the summary as a generated ratios, a specified number of sentences or number of words.

3.2 Preprocessing

The preprocessing subsystem is a structured representation of the original text. Preprocessing has six main steps: sentence segmentation, tokenisation, removing sentence noise word, and removing stopwords, and extracting strong words. The task of preprocessing is to segment a text into a set of sentences then filter the sentences from undesirable additions such that: numbers, symbols, punctuation, diacritics, define article and stop words.

Sentence Segmentation. Texts segmentation is the process of dividing input text into meaningful units called a sentence. This task involves identifying sentence boundaries between words in different sentences [15]. Most written languages, including Arabic language, have main punctuation marks which occur at sentence boundaries such as the period, question mark, and exclamation mark. One sentence segmentation issue occurs with a period, where it can be used for terms such as Dr. in the English language. To deal with this issue we proposed a list of Arabic abbreviations that end with or contain period, which contributed to an increased level of performance.

Tokenisation. Tokenization is a text term number which is a count measure used in calculating a number of words in text input to be text's size. It is used in generating a summary if a user specified a desired size of summary by words number. In addition, it is important in the coming preprocessing steps, which deals with each word individually.

Removing Sentence Noise Word. The noise of sentence means the additions to a sentence or to individual words that not needed in next processes. It includes filtering each sentence from numbers, punctuations, and diacritics and defines articles.

Removing Stopwords. Stop words are non-meaning words appear mostly in the text to conjunction other words. There are categories of stop words: prepositions, pronouns, relative pronouns, demonstrative pronouns, etc. Stop words filtered out before or after processing of natural language data to make the process easier. In Wajeez, an open source list of Arabic stopwords is used [7].

Extracting Strong Words. Strong words in Arabic are word with a strong meaning that needs to be considered when calculating the scoring function to increase the importance of a sentence that appears with one or more strong words. It is a statistical technique to identify and increase the strong word counter value if one of the strong words appears in a sentence.

3.3   Stemming

The stemming subsystem is converting each word to its stem, which the past verb forms. All words are derived from the stem, and there are several kinds of derives: verb derivation, noun derivation, and infinitive derivation. Summarisation systems need to stem process because it works with the meaning of the words, not the forms, the system then will calculate the frequency of stems and compute the similarity of two sentences, the similarity with title or query if it exists. In Wajeez, three stemmers were investigated: Khoja, ISRI, and Tashaphyne light stemmer.

3.4   Sentence Scoring

In the process of identifying important sentences, determining the factors that affect the relevance of sentences. Our proposed system uses the following seven factors to calculate scoring function for each sentence: Position (Ps) also known as the Location of Sentence, Length of Sentence (L), Frequencies (F) for each word on sentence, Similarity (SI) to determine whether this sentence related to other sentences, existence of Strong Word that commonly used on Arabic (SW), existence of Title Matching Stems (TM) and user entered Query Matching Stems (QM).

To analysis scoring function first, we had tested the factors separately on some text to calculate how much each factor affects summarisation by using standard evaluation measures for each factor. Compute the factors for each sentence by using following equations.

Let Ps be a position of the sentence that calculated using a counter that retains the appearance position of each sentence in the original text. Then:

$$Ps(s(i)) = \frac{Ns - Ps}{Ns} \tag{1}$$

Where Ns is the number of sentences in original text and P is the position of sentence $s(i)$.

Let L be the length of sentence which computed by calculating the number of stems in a sentence $s(i)$ divided by the number of words in the sentence that has the highest length.

$$L(s(i)) = \frac{Number\ of\ stems}{Number\ of\ words\ of\ the\ highest\ length\ of\ sentence} \tag{2}$$

The frequency of a word or word frequency Fw is count repetition of each word individually in a whole text. Then divide by total text words.

$$Fw(w(i)) = \frac{count(w(i))}{Nw} \tag{3}$$

Where $count(w(i))$ is the number of occurrence of word $w(i)$ and Nw is the total number of words in the document. Then, frequency F for each sentence $s(i)$ is calculated below where k is the number of words in sentence $s(i)$.

$$F(s(i)) = \frac{\sum_{i=1}^{k} Fw(w(i))}{k} \tag{4}$$

Once you are reading the title you will get the idea of that text. Sentence $s(i)$ will be classified as important if there exists intersection with title stems. The similarity with the title will be calculated by:

$$TM(s(i)) = \frac{stem(s(i)) \cap stem(t)}{stem(s(i)) \cup stem(t)} \tag{5}$$

Where $stem(s(i))$ is the stem of words in a sentence $s(i)$ and $stem(t)$ is the stem of words in the title t.

The sentence $s(i)$ is more important than other sentences if its stems commonly appear in other text sentences. The similarity with text sentences will be calculated below where $stem(ts)$ represent words stems of all text sentences and $stem(s(i))$ be as described previously.

$$SI(s(i)) = \frac{stem(s(i)) \cap stem(ts)}{stem(s(i)) \cup stem(ts)} \tag{6}$$

Hence this system is built to serve user as much as possible, it asks the user to enter a query that includes desirable words or complete sentence which the user prefer to appear on the generated sentences. Query matching will be calculated for sentences $s(i)$ as:

$$QM(s(i)) = \frac{stem(s(i)) \cap stem(q)}{stem(s(i)) \cup stem(q)} \tag{7}$$

Where $stem(s(i))$ is the stem of words in a sentence $s(i)$ and $stem(q)$ is the stem of words in the user entered a query.

The Arabic language includes some words that make the sentence a strong meaning which are preferable in summary. The sentence $s(i)$ which has strong words will be assigned a score by:

$$SW(s(i)) = \frac{Number \ of \ strong \ word \ in \ s(i)}{length \ of \ sentence \ s(i)} \tag{8}$$

After calculating a scoring function for each sentence using the equations above, the sentences should be sorted according to its scoring function value and its weight in a decreasing order. The proposed scoring function is a function based on the linear combination of all factors, then multiplying the score for each sentence by a scale value to normalise fluctuated factor values of each factor to improve the summary extracted result.

$$Score(s(i)) = Ps(s(i)) + L(s(i)) + F(s(i)) + SI(s(i)) + TM(s(i)) + QM(s(i)) \tag{9}$$

$$S(i) = \sum_{k=1}^{N} S(k) \cdot Score(s(i)) \tag{10}$$

Where $S(k)$ is the scale to normalise fluctuated feature values of each factor and N represents the number of factors and i is represented the number of sentences which entered by the user. To calculate this scale, take the average values of factor F respect to all sentences and repeat this with all factors. Pick the largest average of these factors then divides it by factor value as:

$$S = \frac{Largest \ average}{Average \ factor \ value} \tag{11}$$

3.5   Summary Generation

This is the last step in our system, which produce the output (summary) to the user according to the entered size either by ratio, number of sentence or number of words. If the user chooses to summarise the text based on "sentences number", then the extraction process done by ranking the sentences based on their scores, after that extract the highest ith sentences. If the size unit is ratio or number of words Wajeez system using LengthController algorithm which is based on the 0/1-Knapsack problem to generate the final summary which ensures it has a highest possible score and not exceed the size [10]. Finally, order these extracted sentences depending on the priority of their position as they appear in the original text.

4   System Evaluation

Wajeez was developed using Python 2.7.x programming language. In our system, we used two datasets to evaluate our system: EASC and manual summaries. EASC is used to evaluate the proposed approach. The corpus includes

153 documents and has five summaries for each document; with a total of 765 Arabic human-made summaries generated using Mechanical Turk (Mturk) [10]. Ten subjects are embedded in EASC corpus: art, music, environment, politics, sports, health, finance, science and technology, tourism, religion, and education. In Wajeez System, we select 3 articles from each subject. Manual summaries we provide 12 texts from different sources: sites, newspapers, and e-book that are in different scopes type: science, news, research, general Articles, hadith, and health.

Evaluating the summarisation approaches face a challenge with Arabic text summarisation systems, it can be done manually, automatically, or semi-automatically [4]. However, it appears that one of the main problems in Arabic text summarisation is the absence of Arabic gold standard summaries. Moreover, the difficulties of evaluation for Arabic summarisation is due to the lack of Arabic benchmark corpora, lexicons and machine-readable dictionaries make automatic [3].

In the evaluation, we will measure the actual quality of the machine summaries generated by our system. The summary will be produced based on one of three units either percentage, a number of sentences or number of words that user specify it. We will combine two based of the summary techniques: Generic and Query to improve the quality of the machine summary.

We ran our algorithm to generate summaries for sample texts in different sizes: 20%, 25%, 30%, 35%, and 40% which are the ratios of the summary length to the original document length. To evaluate the system generated summaries, three measures were used: precision, recall, and F-measure. F-measure (F) balances recall and precision using a parameter β, where $\beta = 1$. This means precision and recall are given equal weight. More formally, we assume that S_{manual} is the set of sentences in the manual summary and S_{auto} is the sentences in the auto-generated summary, therefore:

$$P = \frac{|S_{manual} \cap S_{auto}|}{S_{auto}} \tag{12}$$

$$R = \frac{|S_{manual} \cap S_{auto}|}{S_{manual}} \tag{13}$$

$$F = \frac{2PR}{P + R} \tag{14}$$

Table 1 displays the performance results of Wajeez using the EASC dataset at varying summary sizes. We then compare our system with two competitive approaches, Arabic Summarisation based on Graph Theory (ASGT) and Arabic Summarisation based on the statistical and semantic analysis. ROUGE toolkit [7,17] had been used to evaluate our automatically generated summaries that are a widely used evaluation metric. We choose to take the summary size equal to 30% in the comparison. The results of comparing our system with the other two systems are shown in Table 2.

Table 1. Wajeez's evaluation results on the EACS dataset at varying summary sizes

Summary size	F-measure
20%	0.27
25%	0.29
30%	0.32
35%	0.33
40%	0.34

Table 2. Wajeez's evaluation results on the EACS dataset in comparison with ASGT and SSAS.

Summary size	F-measure
ASGT	46.75
SSAS	58.2
Wajeez	31.5

Table 2 shows that Wajeez has the lowest performance over the other two systems. We conclude that this may occur because our system has the best performance when the text contains a title. SSAS system has the highest F-measure with 58.2%.

On the other hands, we had tested the quality of the machine summary using the manual dataset. We provide 12 texts from different sources (Sites, Newspapers, and E-book that are in different scopes type: Science, News, Research, General Articles, Hadith and Health) to an expert to get human summaries and experience of these texts. Then we auto-generate the summary for these texts using Wajeez system in different sizes. The summaries were evaluated to get Precision (P), Recall (R) and F-measure (F) measures for untitled text and title text as well. Table 3 shows the average results of the manual summary results. After evaluating many tests, the system performance with F measures is equal to 0.59 with title feature calculation and 0.58 without title calculation, which considered as a high performance compared to some other Arabic systems. In addition, Wajeez system gives greater value for its performance at 40%, and this performance will increase up when percentage increases.

Table 3. Wajeez's evaluation results on the manual text summary

Summary size	P	R	F-measure
15%	0.422	0.422	0.422
25%	0.551	0.678	0.607
30%	0.583	0.582	0.578
40%	0.630	0.600	0.639
15% (with title)	0.472	0.500	0.482
25% (with title)	0.644	0.737	0.687
30% (with title)	0.575	0.617	0.593
40% (with title)	0.676	0.753	0.710

5 Conclusion and Future Work

This paper proposed a new Extractive Arabic text Summarisation, entitled Wajeez. The main contribution of this work is the investigation of a preprocessing methods, preprocessing for a light stemmer Tashaphyne [16] to enhance its performance and scoring function. Testing was done to measure the performance of the system for the EASC corpus dataset as well as the manual dataset. Rouge toolkit was used, in addition to EASC corpus; the system has a low performance comparing with ASTG and SSAS with F-measure equal to 31.5% for our system and 46.75% and 58.2% respectively. After perform testing on the manual dataset, the performance of the system with F-measures is equal to 59% with title feature calculation and 58% without title calculation. In addition, Wajeez system gives greater value for its performance at 40%, and this performance will increase up when parentage increases.

For future work, we will allow the system to categorise the text and to generate a title for a non-title text. Also, we will enable the user to enter text by entering a URL of a web page and to send the summary by email. We will improve the system performance by summarising the generated summary if the user chose a different size on the same text.

References

1. Abbasi-ghalehtaki, R., Khotanlou, H., Esmaeilpour, M.: Fuzzy evolutionary cellular learning automata model for text summarization. Swarm Evol. Comput. **30**, 11–26 (2016)
2. Al-Abdallah, R.Z., Al-Taani, A.T.: Arabic single-document text summarization using particle swarm optimization algorithm. Proc. Comput. Sci. **117**, 30–37 (2017)
3. Al Qassem, L.M., Wang, D., Al Mahmoud, Z., Barada, H., Al-Rubaie, A., Almoosa, N.I.: Automatic Arabic summarization: a survey of methodologies and systems. Proc. Comput. Sci. **117**, 10–18 (2017)
4. Al-Saleh, A.B., Menai, M.E.B.: Automatic arabic text summarization: a survey. Artif. Intell. Rev. **45**(2), 203–234 (2016)

5. Alami, N., El Adlouni, Y., En-nahnahi, N., Meknassi, M.: Using statistical and semantic analysis for Arabic text summarization. In: Noreddine, G., Kacprzyk, J. (eds.) ITCS 2017. AISC, vol. 640, pp. 35–50. Springer, Cham (2018). https://doi.org/10.1007/978-3-319-64719-7_4

6. Alami, N., Meknassi, M., Ouatik, S.A., Ennahnahi, N.: Arabic text summarization based on graph theory. In: 2015 IEEE/ACS 12th International Conference of Computer Systems and Applications (AICCSA), pp. 1–8. IEEE (2015)

7. Arabic Stop Words. Sourceforge (2018). http://arabicstopwords.sourceforge.net/

8. Bui, D.D.A., Del Fiol, G., Hurdle, J.F., Jonnalagadda, S.: Extractive text summarization system to aid data extraction from full text in systematic review development. J. Biomed. Inform. **64**, 265–272 (2016)

9. Douzidia, F.S., Lapalme, G.: Lakhas, an Arabic summarization system. In: Proceedings of DUC 2004 (2004)

10. El-Haj, M., Kruschwitz, U., Fox, C.: Using mechanical Turk to create a corpus of Arabic summaries (2010)

11. Evans, D.: Identifying Similarity in Text: Multi-Lingual Analysis for Summarization. Columbia University, New York (2005)

12. Fang, C., Mu, D., Deng, Z., Wu, Z.: Word-sentence co-ranking for automatic extractive text summarization. Expert Syst. Appl. **72**, 189–195 (2017)

13. Hovy, E.: Text summarization. In: The Oxford Handbook of Computational Linguistics, 2nd edn (2003)

14. Jaradat, Y.A., Al-Taani, A.T.: Hybrid-based Arabic single-document text summarization approach using genetic algorithm. In: 2016 7th International Conference on Information and Communication Systems (ICICS), pp. 85–91. IEEE (2016)

15. Palmer, D.D.: Tokenisation and sentence segmentation. In: Handbook of Natural Language Processing, pp. 11–35 (2000)

16. Reddy, P.V., Vardhan, B.V., Govardhan, A.: Corpus based extractive document summarization for Indic script. In: 2011 International Conference on Asian Language Processing (IALP), pp. 154–157. IEEE (2011)

17. RxNLP/ROUGE-2.0. GitHub (2018). https://github.com/RxNLP/ROUGE-2.0/tree/master/versions

18. Wu, Z., et al.: A topic modeling based approach to novel document automatic summarization. Expert Syst. Appl. **84**, 12–23 (2017)

Arabic Speech Recognition with Deep Learning: A Review

Wajdan Algihab, Noura Alawwad, Anfal Aldawish,
and Sarah AlHumoud[(✉)]

College of Computer and Information Science,
Al-Imam Mohammad Ibn Saud Islamic University (IMSIU),
Riyadh, Saudi Arabia
{Waghaihb, Naawad, Anaduweish}@sm.imamu.edu.sa,
Sohumoud@imamu.edu.sa

Abstract. Automatic speech recognition is the area of research concerning the enablement of machines to accept vocal input from humans and interpreting it with the highest probability of correctness. There are several techniques to implement speech recognition models. One of the emerging techniques is using neural networks with deep learning for speech recognition. Arabic is one of the most spoken languages and least highlighted in terms of speech recognition. This paper serves as a brief review on the available studies on Arabic speech recognition. In addition, it sheds some light on the services and toolkits available for Arabic speech recognition systems' development.

Keywords: Automatic speech recognition (ASR) ·
Arabic Automatic Speech Recognition (AASR) · Deep learning ·
Artificial neural networks (ANN) · Deep neural network (DNN) ·
Recurrent neural network (RNN)

1 Introduction

Arabic is one of the most widely spoken languages around the world with an estimated number of over 313 million speakers with 270 million as a second language speaker of Arabic ranked as the forth after Mandarin, Spanish and English [1]. Moreover, it is the language of the Islamic holy book "Quran" with 1.8 billion Muslims around the world in 2015 and projected to increase to 3 billion in 2060 [2]. There have been relatively little speech recognition researches on Arabic compared to other languages [3].

The Arabic language has three types: classical, modern, and dialectal. Classical Arabic is the language Quran. Modern Standard Arabic (MSA) is based on classical Arabic but with dropping some aspects like diacritics. It is mainly used in modern books, education, and news. Dialectal Arabic has multiple regional forms and is used for daily spoken communication in non-formal settings. With the advent of social media, dialectal Arabic is also written. Those forms of the language result in lexical, morphological and grammatical differences resulting in the hardness of developing one Arabic NLP application to process data from different varieties.

G. Meiselwitz (Ed.): HCII 2019, LNCS 11578, pp. 15–31, 2019.
https://doi.org/10.1007/978-3-030-21902-4_2

Al-Anzi and AbuZeina in [4] addressed challenges in speech recognition such as different acoustic conditions, different accents, and the variety of expressing words. Meanwhile, they introduce Arabic speech recognition challenges such as the Arabic script discretization. The authors claimed that the Arabic language is in the early stages compared to English.

Deep learning is a branch of machine learning that inspired by the act of the human brain in processing data based on learning data by using multiple processing layers that has a complex structure or otherwise, composed of multiple non-linear transformations that is capable of unsupervised learning from unstructured or unlabeled data. Deep learning research has been successful in the last few years and it is used in various fields such as in computer vision, speech recognition, natural language processing, handwriting recognition. Deep learning is one of the promising areas in machine learning for the future tasks involved in machine learning especially in the area of the neural network [5].

The published research on models, techniques and applications on English speech recognition based on deep learning is comparably higher than that of Arabic. For Arabic, the literature is limited and scattered. This review serves as pivot point aiming at shedding the light on the available literature on Arabic speech recognition using deep learning.

In later sections, we will introduce the following: Sect. '2' Review methodology. Then, in Sect. '3', the background and related work presented and discussed. After that, in Sect. '4' Application of Arabic Automatic Speech Recognition (AASR) is presented. Further, Sect. '5', discusses the techniques used for deep learning with AASR. Finally, Sect. '7' is the conclusion.

2 Review Methodology

In developing this review, we are inspired with the methodology described by [6, 7]. Additionally, the focus of this review is depicted in the following research questions:

  RQ1: what are the techniques for ASR
  RQ2: what are the studies on Arabic ASR using deep learning
  RQ3: what are the available services and frameworks for developing Arabic ASR.

The databases we did search in are ACM, IEEE, Springer, Sage journals and Science Direct. The keywords used are: "Deep learning", "Arabic automatic speech recognition", "Speech recognition", "Arabic speech recognition", "Neural Networks", "Deep neural networks", "Recurrent neural networks", "Voice recognition". Moreover, timeframe of the review focused on published papers from year 2000 until now. After eliminating papers that does not answer the research questions, we are let with 17 papers. Figure 1 shows the distribution of the papers across the different databases.

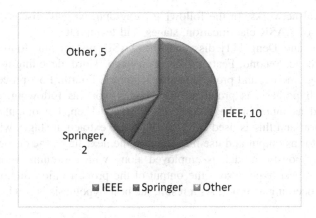

Fig. 1. Research paper results based on the publisher

3 Background and Related Work

The aim of speech recognition is to enable machines to accept sounds and act based on it. Automatic speech recognition is the ability for a machine to recognize "receive and interpret" the speech and convert it into readable form or text and performing an action based on the instructions defined by the human [8].

Speech analysis is the process of analyzing voice and different speech patterns. Speech analysis techniques are divided into segmentation analysis, sub-segment analysis, and surpa segmental analysis [9]. Meanwhile, speech feature extractions are done using Linear predictive coding (LPC) and Mel frequency cepstral coefficients (MFCC).

In addition, the approaches of speech recognition are the Template-Based approach, Knowledge-based approaches, Neural network based approaches, Dynamic time warping (DTW) based approaches and Hidden Markov model (HMM) based speech recognition [10].

Template based approach is the process of matching unknown spoken word and then comparing them with speech patterns templates (pre-recorded words) to find the best match. While the Knowledge-based approach deals with acoustic aspects of spoken words. It analyses sound wave properties based on observed features and then incorporate them with the knowledge of the relationship between the acoustic feature and phonetic symbol. The spoken words are decoded to obtain a sequence of phonemes and other linguistic units. Moreover, Dynamic Type Warping approach is based on an algorithm for measuring the similarity between two sequences, to find the optimal match between a given sequence that may be varied in time or speed. Finally, Hidden Markov Model which is widely used in the stochastic approach, where the Hidden Markov model is characterized using a set of distribution outputs and finite state Markov model. Word and phone boundaries are automatically determined in the training process.

In this paper, we will focus on neural network-based approaches that are represented as an important class of discriminative techniques and as it inspired the biological neural networks. In the following paragraph, we will discuss the literature based in terms of AASR classification, stages, and techniques.

Authors Yu and Deng [11] dissected the AASR system into four stages. First, preprocessing stage. Second, Feature extraction stage. Third, decoding using Acoustic model, Language model, and pronunciation dictionary. Fourth, Post-processing results were the best hypothesis is produced. The stages work as following: First, speech waveform used as input in the preprocessing stage. Then, the output is processed speech waveform and this is used as input in feature extraction stages where we have the feature vector as output and use it as input in the next stage, the decoding stage. In this stage, the Acoustic model, is employed along with a pronunciation dictionary. After that, the n-best hypothesis - the output of the pronunciation dictionary stage is used in post-processing as input. As a result, the best hypothesis is produced from this work operation.

Turab, Khatatneh, and Odeh in [12] discussed the phoneme recognition as it is related to speech recognition. The techniques used are as follows: Gaussian Low Pass filtering algorithm along with the neural network in the pre-processing stage to have an improvement on the results. Furthermore, the stages of phoneme recognition are: catching a signal, sampling, quantization and setting energy. After that, a neural network is used to enhance the results. Moreover, this paper shows the enhanced impact in results after applying the Gaussian Low Pass filter in voice signals hence, the noise was reduced. After that, in the training phase, the neural network has been used to train the system in order to recognize the speech signals.

Ahmed and Ghabayen in [3] proposed three approached to enhance the AASR. The paper started with the first approach which is the punctuation modeling, in this approach Ahmed and Ghabyaen proposed a decision tree with variant pronunciation generation. After that, a hybrid approach proposed and used to adapt the native acoustic model with another native acoustic model. Finally, the language model is enhanced and improved using a processed text. The model efficiency was measured by Word Error Rate (WER) which is a metric to measure the performance of speech recognition and calculates misrecognitions at the word level. Consequently, the pronunciation model reduced WER by 1%, The acoustic modeling reduced the WER by 1.2% and the language model reduced WER by 1.9%.

Emami and Mangu [13], examine the neural network usage for Arabic speech recognition using a distributed word representation. Furthermore, the model of the neural network allows robust generalization and enhance the ability to fight the data sparseness problem. Also, the investigation process includes different configuration neural probabilistic model, n-gram order parameter experiment, output vocabulary, the method of normalization, model size and parameters. The experiment has been done on the Arabic news broadcast, and conversation broadcast. As a result, some improvement has been achieved using the optimized neural network model over the 4-gram baseline model resulting in up to 0.8% absolute reductions and 3.8% relative WER. However, different parameters do not have a significant impact on model performance. The paper was based on analyzing first. Then, feature extraction. After that, modeling and finally, testing.

Based on Desai, Dhameliya, and Desai [14], the proposed speech recognition system contains four stages. First, feature extraction. Second, database. Third, network training. Fourth, testing or decoding.

In [4] Al-Anzi and AbuZeina used WER metric to evaluate the performance of isolated-word recognition and continuous speech recognition. The evaluation of continuous speech was presented for seven papers based on the improvement of WER. The results were as follow: Kirchhof, Bilmes and Stolcke in [15] performed performance evaluation using a language model for morphology and the improvement of WER for two different test sets is 1.8% and 1.5% respectively. In [16], Emami, Ahmad and Lidia use two different configurations of neural probabilistic models and the improvement of WER is 0.8% and 3.8% respectively. The authors in [17] used broadcast news corpus and improve the WER by 13.66%. Hyassat and Abu Zitar in [18] used the holy Quran corpus and WER improved by 46.182%. In [19] Elmahdy and Mohamed used Egyptian Colloquial Arabic and reached 99.34% of recognition accuracy. Selouani, Sid Ahmed and Malika Boudraa in [20] used MSA continues speech corpus and reach an accuracy rate of 91.65%. In [21] the authors Jurafsky and Martin used MSA continues speech corpus and the improvement of WER using diacritical marks and without resulting 11.27% and 10.07% respectively.

4   Arabic Automatic Speech Recognition with Deep Learning

Some popular techniques used in ASR and AASR are artificial neural networks, dynamic time warping and Hidden Markov modeling. In this review, we are going to focus on artificial neural network techniques. Moreover, speech recognition systems can be classified in different classes based on what type of utterances they can recognize. Those are of four types: isolated words, connected words, connected speech, and spontaneous speech. Those are discussed in more detail in the following subsections.

4.1   Isolated Words

Isolated word recognizers require to have Listen/Not-Listen states between each utterance, it processes the words during the "not listen" state [22].

The authors in [23] show a comparison between general regression neural network (GRNN) algorithm and the traditional multi-layer perceptron in the recognition of a large set of Arabic words. The results show that the GRNN gives better results than those based on the feedforward backpropagation in the recognition rate. The proposed architecture consists of two parts: pre-processing phase which consists of segmental normalization and feature extraction and a classification phase which uses neural networks based on nonparametric density estimation. Using MLP the error rate was respectively 8%, 8% and 12% for the digit "2", "3" and "8" pronounced by male speakers. It is less significant when they used the non-parametric regression (respectively 2%, 6% and 6%). The GRNN gives better recognition rate and it was the faster algorithm when having a large dimension of input vectors.

The authors in [24] designed a speech recognition system that investigates Arabic digits based on a recurrent neural network. They implement it as a multi-speaker mode and a speaker-independent mode. The system in the case of a multi-speaker mode achieved 99.5% correct digit recognition, and in the case of the speaker-independent mode, the system achieved 94.5%.

A novel approach was presented in [1] describing the implementation of Arabic isolated speech recognition system by modular recurrent Elman neural networks (MRENN). The authors claimed that the results have shown that this new neural network approach can compete with the traditional HMM-based speech recognition approaches. They show a table with the obtained results of 6 speakers some of them with a noise background and other with clean background. The recognition rate for the different speakers was around 85% and 100%.

4.2   Connected Words

Connected word systems are similar to isolated words but allow separate utterance to be run together with "minimum pause between them" [22].

In [25] the author introduces a "simple and effective time alignment" for spoken Arabic digit recognition systems. The algorithms are simple and low in computational power, and in the understanding of the algorithm also. The speech recognition system designed based on an artificial neural network tested with automatic Arabic digit recognition and implemented in a multi-speaker mode. The authors used the time alignment algorithm to compensate for the differences in the utterance and the misalignment of the phoneme the time alignment algorithm. The algorithm was tested on a MLP neural network based recognizer; the overall system performance for Arabic digit recognition was 99.49%.

The authors aimed in [26] to observe the differences in the 29 letters of the Arabic alphabet. They proposed a system based on a fully-connected recurrent neural network with a backpropagation through time learning algorithm. The purpose was to improve the knowledge of the Arabic alphabet. They compared the LPCCC and MFCC performance with different hidden node (40, 50 and 60) for different 4 speakers, overall the LPCCC outperform the MFCC performance by 0.7%.

An approach in learning to deal with a non-uniform sequence length of the speech utterances have been proposed in [27] based on Long Short-Term Memory (LSTM). The system consists of two phases: feature extraction with the Mel Frequency Cepstral Coefficients algorithm (MFCC), and then process the features with a deep neural network. They used a recurrent LSTM or GRU architecture to encode sequences of MFCC features like a fixed size vector to feed a multilayer perceptron network to perform the classification.

4.3   Continuous Speech

Continuous speech recognizers allow the user to speak almost naturally. Due to the utterance boundaries, it uses a special method, which is why it considered as one of the most difficult systems to create [22].

The authors in [28] present three different system structures. They manually constructed an Arabic phoneme database. The Mel Frequency Cepstral Coefficients algorithm (MFCC) was used to extract the features from the input signal. The normalized dataset was used to train and test the three different systems. The performances of these systems were 47.52%, 44.58% and 46.63% frame recognition for single MLP identification system, category-based phonemes recognition system and individual Phoneme classifier system respectively.

Also, an argument in the improvement of the performance of speech recognition in mobile communication system has been shown in [29], the authors used in the feature extraction phase the Multitaper Frequency Cepstral Coefficients features and the Gabor features, and in the processing phase they have investigated three different systems: Continues Hidden Markov Models (CHMM), Deep Neural Network (DNN) and HMMDNN hybrid. They focused on HMMDNN and claimed that it can get consistently almost 8% of clean speech, 13% of AMR-NB coder and 8.5% of DSR coders.

A novel approach [30] where the authors combines the benefits of the morpheme-based LMs and feature-rich modeling with the DNN-LMs for the Egyptian Arabic. A result have been shown when a single hidden layer, 2 hidden layers, 3 hidden layers and 4 hidden layers. The most improvement was obtained in the single hidden layer. Incorporating the conventional n-gram LM, the DNN-LM and the feature-rich DNN-LM achieve the best performance.

An AASR system was developed in [31] with a 1,200-h speech corpus. The authors modeled a different DNN topologies including: Feed-forward, Convolutional, Time-Delay, Recurrent Long Short-Term Memory (LSTM), Highway LSTM (H-LSTM) and Grid LSTM (GLSTM). A table with all the models and its result has been shown. The best performance was from a combination of the top two hypotheses from the sequence trained GLSTM models with 18.3% WER.

A comparison for some of the state-of-the-art speech recognition techniques was shown in [32]. The authors applied those techniques only to a limited Arabic broadcast news dataset. The different approaches were all trained with a 50-h of transcription audio from a news channel "Al-jazirah". The best performance obtained was the hybrid DNN/HMM approach with the MPE (Minimum Phone Error) criterion used in training the DNN sequentially, and achieved 25.78% WER.

An Arabic broadcast news speech recognition system was built using the KALDI toolkit in [33]. The system was trained with 200 h broadcast news database. They build a broadcast news system with 15.81% WER on Broadcast Report (BR) and 32.21% WER on Broadcast Conversation (BC) with a combined WER of 26.95%.

A LIUM ASR system win the second position in the 2016 Multi-Genre Broadcast (MGB-2) Challenge in the Arabic language [34]. Their main idea was to combine the GMM derived features for training a DNN with the use of time-delay neural networks for acoustic models for automatically phonetic the Arabic words. The key features was the training data selection approach, where a five neural network AMs of different types with a various acoustic features and also a different techniques for speaker adaptation and two types of phonetization. The final system was a combination of a five systems where the result obtained succeeded the best single LIUM ASR system with a 9% of WER reduction and also succeeded the baseline MGB system that was provided by the organizers with a 43% WER reduction.

Also in the same 2016 Multi-Genre Broadcast (MGB-2) Challenge in the Arabic language, The lowest WER was achieved among the nine participating teams by [35] with 14.2%. They built a system that is a combination of three LF-MMI trained models; TDNN, LSTM and BLSTM. Before combinations, The models were rescored using a four-gram and RNNME LM. The system was trained using 1,200 h audio with lightly supervised transcription.

4.4 Spontaneous Speech

It is a speech that is natural sounding and not rehearsed. An ASRS should be able to handle a variety of natural speech features like words being run together [22].

An approach that integrates into adverse acoustic conditions multiple components to improved speaker identification in spontaneous Arabic speech has been presented in [36]. They used two acoustic speakers models the maximum likelihood linear regression support vector machine (MLLR-SVM) and the Cepstral Gaussian Mixture Models (GMM) models and a neural network combiner. A result of the Arabic portion of the NIST (National Institute of Standards and Technology) mixer data is shown. The authors apply noises like babble and city traffic, in both they found an equal error rate reductions over the no-compensation condition. Which gave a complementary gain for both acoustic models. The authors show different tables with the result, Surprisingly, they found the combiner that trained in clean conditions gives a similar performance to the one that trained in matched conditions.

The authors in [37] presented a comparative study between two identification engines to identify speakers automatically from their voices when speaking spontaneously in Arabic. The continuous hidden Markov models (CHMMs) was used in the first engine, and in the second engine, they used artificial neural networks (ANNs). In the feature extraction phase of the signal, the Mel frequency cepstral coefficients (MFCCs) were used. They used the general Gaussian density distribution HMM, as for the ANN-based engine they used the Elman network. The identification rate was found to be 100% for both engines during text dependent experiments. However, for text-independent experiments, the performance for the CHMM-based engine outperformed that of the ANN-based engine. The identification rates for the CHMM- and the ANN-based engines were found to be 80% and 50% respectively.

5   AASR Deep Learning Techniques

Deep learning has different techniques which can be applied on AASR. In this paper we focus on the artificial neural network technique. We cover the main types of ANN. Table 1 cover the summary of the main types of ANN.

5.1   Neural Networks

It is more convenient to use NN for speech recognition than serial programming which execute only one operation at a time. In this section, we review the three available papers for AASR using NNs.

Emami and Mangu [20] showing the use of distributed representations and neural network for AASR. They used the AASR decoder to generate a set of lattices with an average link density. The training samples were 7 M words collected from Arabic broadcast news and broadcast conversations. This paper used a baseline 4-gram model which helped in improving the NN by reducing up to 0.8% absolute and 3.8% relative in WER. Experimented the parameters of NN language models (LMs) with different configurations of NN LMs which concluded that the performance of NN LMs was not affected by parameters. The size of the NN has no effect on the performance.

Ettaouil et al. [19] used a hybrid model ANN/HMM for AASR to determine the optimal codebook generated by Kohonen network Self Organizing Maps (SOM). The Optimal codebook used to the classification of the Arabic digits this leads to optimization of Kohonen approach. The numerical results are satisfactory showing that the classification was affected by the size of the dictionary. The codebook vectors are with size 34, 36, and 48 they had a recognition rate 84%, 85%, and 86% respectively.

Wahyuni in [20] used Mel-Frequency Cepstral Coefficients (MFCC) based on feature extraction and ANN to distinguish between the pronounce of three different letters (sa, sya, and tsa) by Indonesian speakers which have the same sound for those different letters which is (sa) according to their usual using Bahasa. The result showing that the usage of

MFCC with ANN gave the better recognize the three letters average accuracy of 92.42%.

5.2 Recurrent Neural Networks

Recurrent Neural Networks (RNN) is one of the best models applied for sequential data [21]. It allows for both feedforward and feedback paths. For AASR only two papers used the Elman RNN which is the type of RNN. Elman has an advantage when compared with fully RNN [4]. It can use backpropagation to train the network.

Alotaibi in [5] show the usage of recurrent ANN namely recurrent Elman network for AASR to the recognition of ten Arabic digits (from Zero to nine). Asking 17 male Arabic native speakers to repeat the digits ten times. This created the database with 1700 token, that is, 170 samples for every digit. Operating the system in two different modes. The first mode is a multi-speaker mode which used the same speakers sound for both training and testing phases. The training tokens set has 340 tokens. That is 17 speakers, 2 repetitions and 10 digits. Where the test set used 1700 tokens. The system performance was 99.47% in this mode. The second mode is speaker-independent mode which used the different speaker sounds for training and testing phases. The training tokens set has 400 tokens, that is 4 speakers, 10 repetitions, and 10 digits. Where the testing set using 1,300 tokens that is 13 speakers, 10 digits, and 10 repetitions. The system performance was 96.46% in this mode. The system in both modes cannot recognize the digit 9 that according to the dissimilarity of this digit and the other digits. Digit 1, 4 and 8 have high error rates, particularly in the second mode.

Choubassi et al. [4] used small RNN and their recognizer has recognized a limited set of isolated words there were: "manzel" (house), "hirra" (cur), "chajara" (tree), "tariq" (road), "ghinaa" (singing), "zeina" (zeina). All those words have individual RNN to detected only the specific word. Training has two phases first is consistent of consistent training then discriminative training. Consistent training used the different utterances of the dedicated word. In discriminative training use utterances of other words not only the dedicated word. This paper used 4 female speakers in a clean environment without any noise for training. For testing they used one women speaker and one-male speaker both in a clean environment. They used back-propagation with momentum and variable learning rate as a training algorithm. This paper used MATLAB to simulate the result. They took a slot of output curves to determine the classification of an utterance over other dedicated words by comparing its result slope s with minimum slope sm. The result of the paper indicated that the usage of RNN gives the same recognition rate matching as the HMM-based approach as mention in Sect. '4'.

5.3   Deep Neural Networks

Deep Neural Networks (DNNs) have reached to suitable performance. DNNs have three advantage when used over other NN [22]. First, DNNs can extract robust and significant features of the input data via several non-linear hidden layers. Second, DNNs can merge multiple extracted feature vectors efficiently. Third, DNNs can prevent overfitting problem by using dropout technique. We find only one paper use this method for AASR.

AbdAlmisreb et al. [22] presented the DNN with three hidden layers, 500 Maxout units with 2 neurons for the unit and used Mel-Frequency Cepstral Coefficients (MFCC) for feature extraction. This approach was trained and tested over a corpus which consisted of 20 Malay speakers of consonant Arabic phonemes recorded. The training set consisted of 5 waveforms and the tested set contained 15 waveforms. The result show that the Maxout based deep structure gave better performance with lowest error rate than other deep networks such as Restricted Boltzmann Machine (RBM), Deep Belief Network (DBN), Convolutional Neural Network (CNN), the conventional feedforward neural network (NN) and Convolutional Auto-Encoder (CAE) which had error rate between 2800 and 3000 (numbers).

Table 1. Summary of the main types of ANN

Approach	Aims	Preprocessing	Type of NNs	Used datasets	Result
Emami and Mangu [20]	Showing the use of distributed representations and neural network for AASR	Used the AASR decoder to generate a set of lattices with an average link density Use different order of neural probabilistic model by taking those parameters:	Neural Networks (NN)	The training samples were 7M words collected from Arabic broadcast news and broadcast conversations	This paper used a baseline 4-gram model which helped in improving the NN by reducing up to 0.8% absolute and 3.8% relative in WER. Experimented the parameters of NN language models (LMs) with different

(*continued*)

Table 1. (*continued*)

Approach	Aims	Preprocessing	Type of NNs	Used datasets	Result
		- N-gram order - Output vocabulary - Normalization method - Model size			configurations of NN LMs which concluded that the performance of NN LMs was not affected by parameters. The size of the NN has no effect on the performance
Ettaouil et al. [19]	Determine the optimal codebook generated by Kohonen network Self Organizing Maps (SOM)	Used a hybrid model ANN/HMM for AASR. By generate three dictionaries with three neural networks the first with 34 neurons, the second with 36 and the third with 48 neurons	Neural Networks (NN)	Consists of 8800 tokens for Arabic digits Dataset divide to: 1–75% of the samples for training set 2–25% of the samples for test set	The classification was affected by the size of the dictionary. The codebook vectors are with size 34, 36, and 48 they had a recognition rate 84%, 85%, and 86% respectively
Wahyuni in [20]	Distinguish between the pronounce of three different letters (sa, sya, and tsa) by Indonesian speakers which have the same sound for those different letters which is (sa) according to their usual using Bahasa	They extract feature by using Mel-Frequency Cepstral Coefficients (MFCC) then use ANN for classification	Neural Networks (NN)	738 data of three letters as: 248 data of sa (س), 254 data of sya (ش), 236 data of tsa (ث) Collect them by recording human voice with pronounces letters sa (س), sya (ش), tsa (ث), by depending on the *makhraj* pronunciation of hijaiyah	The usage of MFCC with ANN gave the better recognize the three letters average accuracy of 92.42%
Alotaibi in [5]	Show the usage of recurrent ANN namely recurrent Elman network for AASR to the recognition of ten Arabic	- Extract feature by using (MFCC) - Used VECTOR QUANTIZATION technique to compression data	Recurrent Neural Networks (RNN)	Asking 17 male Arabic native speakers to repeat the digits ten times. this created the database with	The system performance was 99.47% The system performance was 96.46% The system in both modes cannot

(*continued*)

Table 1. (*continued*)

Approach	Aims	Preprocessing	Type of NNs	Used datasets	Result
	digits (from Zero to nine)			1700 token, that is, 170 samples for every digit Operating the system in two different modes 1-multi-speaker mode which used the same speakers sound for both training and testing phases The training set has 340 tokens. And the test set used 1700 tokens 2-Speaker-independent mode which used the different speaker sounds for training and testing phases The training set has 400 tokens. And the testing set using 1,300 tokens	recognize the digit 9 that according to the dissimilarity of this digit and the other digits. Digit 1, 4 and 8 have high error rates, particularly in the second mode
Choubassi et al. [4]	To recognize a limited set of isolated words there were: "manzel" (house), "hirra" (cur), "chajara" (tree), "tariq" (road), "ghinaa" (singing), "zeina" (zeina)	- Used small RNN and their recognizer - All those words have individual RNN to detected only the specific word - used back-propagation with momentum and variable learning rate as a training algorithm	Recurrent Neural Networks (RNN)	Two phases for Training: 1st phase consistent training which used the different utterances of the dedicated word 2nd phase discriminative training which use utterances of other words not only the dedicated word. This paper used	This paper used MATLAB to simulate the result. They took a slot of output curves to determine the classification of an utterance over other dedicated words by comparing its result slope s with minimum slope sm. The result of the paper indicated that the usage of RNN gives the same recognition rate

(*continued*)

Table 1. (*continued*)

Approach	Aims	Preprocessing	Type of NNs	Used datasets	Result
				4 female speakers in a clean environment without any noise for training. For testing they used one women speaker and one-male speaker both in a clean environment	matching as the HMM-based approach as mention in Sect. 4
AbdAlmisreb et al. [22]	Test performance of DNN based on Maxout	Use: 1-Mel-Frequency Cepstral Coefficients for feature extraction 2-Maxout Deep Neural Network by using Maxout algorithm with dropout function to improve the efficiency	Deep Neural Networks (DNN)	The training set consisted of 5 waveforms and the tested set contained 15 waveforms	The result show that the Maxout based deep structure gave better performance with lowest error rate than other deep networks such as Restricted Boltzmann Machine (RBM), Deep Belief Network (DBN), Convolutional Neural Network (CNN), the conventional feedforward neural network (NN) and Convolutional Auto-Encoder (CAE) which had error rate between 0. 2800 and 0.3000

6 AASR with Deep Learning Services

Speech recognition using deep-learning is a huge task that its success depends on the availability of a large repository of a training dataset. The availability of open-source deep-learning enabled frameworks and Application Programming Interfaces (API) would boost the development and research of AASR. There are multiple services and frameworks that provide developers with powerful deep-learning abilities for speech recognition.

6.1 API Services

One of the marked applications is Cloud Speech-to-Text service from Google [35] which uses a deep-learning neural network algorithm to convert Arabic speech or audio file to text. Cloud Speech-to-Text service allows for its translator system to directly accept the spoken word to be converted to text then translated. The service offers an API for developers with multiple recognition features.

Another service is Microsoft Speech API [36] from Microsoft. This service help developers to create speech recognition systems using deep neural networks.

IBM cloud provide Watson service API for speech to text recognition [37] support modern standard Arabic language until now there is not any work use this API with Arabic.

6.2 Toolkits

The Kaldi [38]. It is a toolkit for speech recognition using deep neural network and support Arabic language as Ali et al. in [37] showing the usage of Kaldi to build Arabic broadcast news speech recognition system. They use all Kaldi conventional models. The result showing that the building of broadcast news system on broadcast report take 15.81% WER and 32.21% WER on broadcast conversation.

Manohar et al. in [40] use Kaldi toolkit for Arabic Multi-Genre Broadcast (MGB-3) challenge which deal with dialectal Arabic of Egyptian. For their study, they take 80 different video from YouTube for seven genres. Their comparative study for the efficiency of using Kaldi by take multi-reference word error rate (MR-WER) to measure the efficiency. The system first, built with Minimum Bayes Risk (MBR) system combination of sMBR and nonsMBR system and produce the MR-WER of 32.78% on the MGB-3 test set. They conclude that the Kaldi improve the efficiency of MR-WER.

Additionally, is the Microsoft Cognitive Toolkit (Microsoft's CNTK) [41] which is an open-source toolkit that trains the deep learning algorithm. This toolkit enables using more than one model like DNN, CNN, and RNN. There is no paper that developed AASR with this tool kit.

6.3 Frameworks

one of the main frameworks offering deep-learning capabilities for developers is Tensorflow [42] which is a library that provides accuracy when used with other models to produce speech recognition. Sim et al. [17] used Tensorflow to improve the efficiency of Forward-backward algorithm with English speech recognition.

7 Conclusion

This paper presented a review on Arabic speech recognition using deep-learning Neural Networks. The literature covered seventeen papers and presented according to the recognized entity and according to the learning technique. Recognized entities are of four types: isolated word, connected word, continues word and Spontaneous speech.

Furthermore, Deep learning techniques have three main types, Neural networks, recurrent neural networks, and deep learning networks. This paper presented the state of the art frameworks and services that aid in the ASR system development.

References

1. El Choubassi, M.M., El Khoury, H.E., Alagha, C.E.J., Skaf, J.A., Al-Alaoui, M.A.: Arabic speech recognition using recurrent neural networks. In: Proceedings of the 3rd IEEE International Symposium on Signal Processing and Information Technology (IEEE Cat. No. 03EX795), Darmstadt, Germany, pp. 543–547 (2004)
2. Lipka, M., Hackett, C.: Why Muslims are the world's fastest-growing religious group. Pew Research Center (2017). http://www.pewresearch.org/fact-tank/2017/04/06/why-muslims-are-the-worlds-fastest-growing-religious-group/. Accessed 14 Nov 2018
3. Ahmed, B.H.A., Ghabayen, A.S.: Arabic automatic speech recognition enhancement. In: 2017 Palestinian International Conference on Information and Communication Technology (PICICT), Gaza, Palestine, pp. 98–102 (2017)
4. Al-Anzi, F., AbuZeina, D.: Literature survey of Arabic speech recognition. In: International Conference on Computing Sciences and Engineering (ICCSE) (2018)
5. Rana, C.: A review: speech recognition with deep learning methods, p. 8 (2015)
6. Kitchenham, B.: Procedures for performing systematic reviews. Joint Technical report, Keele University Technical report (TR/SE-0401) and NICTA Technical report (0400011T.1), July 2004 (2004)
7. Heckman, S., Williams, L.: A systematic literature review of actionable alert identification techniques for automated static code analysis
8. Nasereddin, H.H.O., Omari, A.A.R.: Classification techniques for automatic speech recognition (ASR) algorithms used with real time speech translation. In: 2017 Computing Conference, London, pp. 200–207 (2017)
9. Shanbhogue, M, Kulkarni, S., Suprith, R.: A study on speech recognition, vol. 4, p. 6 (2016)
10. Pdfs.semanticscholar.org (2012). https://pdfs.semanticscholar.org/04c8/b7668hc09eebcb56d54ba221a26d8fd174d7.pdf. Accessed 14 Nov 2018
11. Yu, D., Deng, L.: Automatic Speech Recognition: A Deep Learning Approach, pp. 13–21. Springer, London (2015). https://doi.org/10.1007/978-1-4471-5779-3
12. Turab, N., Khatatneh, K., Odeh, A.: A novel Arabic Speech Recognition method using neural networks and Gaussian Filtering. (IJEECS) Int. J. Electr. Electron. Comput. Syst. **19** (01) (2014)
13. Emami, A., Mangu, L.: Empirical study of neural network language models for Arabic speech recognition. In: 2007 IEEE Workshop on Automatic Speech Recognition & Understanding (ASRU), The Westin Miyako Kyoto, pp. 147–152 (2007)
14. Desai, N., Dhameliya, K., Desai, V.: Feature extraction and classification techniques for speech recognition: a review, **3**(12), 5 (2013)
15. Kirchhoff, K., Vergyri, D., Bilmes, J., Duh, K., Stolcke, A.: Morphology-based language modeling for conversational Arabic speech recognition. Comput. Speech Lang. **20**(4), 589–608 (2006)
16. Emami, A., Mangu, L.: Empirical study of neural network language models for Arabic speech recognition. In: IEEE Workshop on Automatic Speech Recognition & Understanding, ASRU. IEEE (2007)
17. Alghamdi, M., Elshafei, M., Al-Muhtaseb, H.: Arabic broadcast news transcription system. Int. J. Speech Technol. **10**(4), 183–195 (2007)

18. Hyassat, H., Abu Zitar, R.: Arabic speech recognition using SPHINX engine. Int. J. Speech Technol. **9**(3–4), 133–150 (2006)
19. Elmahdy, M., et al.: Modern standard Arabic based multilingual approach for dialectal Arabic speech recognition. In: Eighth International Symposium on Natural Language Processing, SNLP 2009. IEEE (2009)
20. Selouani, S.A., Boudraa, M.: Algerian Arabic speech database (ALGASD): corpus design and automatic speech recognition application. Arab. J. Sci. Eng. **35**(2C), 15 (2010)
21. Jurafsky, D., Martin, J.: Speech and Language Processing. Prentice Hall, Upper Saddle River (2000)
22. AbdAlmisreb, A., Abidin, A.F., Tahir, N.: Maxout based deep neural networks for Arabic phonemes recognition, p. 6 (2015)
23. Amrouche, A., Rouvaen, J.M.: Arabic isolated word recognition using general regression neural network. In: 2003 46th Midwest Symposium on Circuits and Systems, Cairo, Egypt, vol. 2, pp. 689–692 (2003)
24. Alotaibi, Y.A.: Spoken Arabic digits recognizer using recurrent neural networks. In: Proceedings of the Fourth IEEE International Symposium on Signal Processing and Information Technology, Rome, Italy, pp. 195–199 (2004)
25. Alotaibi, Y.: A simple time alignment algorithm for spoken Arabic digit recognition. J. King Abdulaziz Univ.-Eng. Sci. **20**(1), 29–43 (2009)
26. Ahmad, A.M., Ismail, S., Samaon, D.F.: Recurrent neural network with backpropagation through time for speech recognition. In: IEEE International Symposium on Communications and Information Technology, ISCIT 2004, Sapporo, Japan, vol. 1, pp. 98–102 (2004)
27. Zerari, N., Abdelhamid, S., Bouzgou, H., Raymond, C.: Bi-directional recurrent end-to-end neural network classifier for spoken Arab digit recognition. In: 2018 2nd International Conference on Natural Language and Speech Processing (ICNLSP), Algiers, pp. 1–6 (2018)
28. Hmad, N., Allen, T.: Biologically inspired continuous Arabic speech recognition. In: Bramer, M., Petridis, M. (eds.) SGAI 2012, pp. 245–258. Springer, London (2012). https://doi.org/10.1007/978-1-4471-4739-8_20
29. Bouchakour, L., Debyeche, M.: Improving continuous Arabic speech recognition over mobile networks DSR and NSR using MFCCs features transformed, **12**, 8 (2018)
30. El-Desoky Mousa, A., Kuo, H.-K.J., Mangu, L., Soltau, H.: Morpheme-based feature-rich language models using deep neural networks for LVCSR of Egyptian Arabic. In: 2013 IEEE International Conference on Acoustics, Speech and Signal Processing, Vancouver, BC, Canada, pp. 8435–8439 (2013)
31. AlHanai, T., Hsu, W.-N., Glass, J.: Development of the MIT ASR system for the 2016 Arabic multi-genre broadcast challenge. In: 2016 IEEE Spoken Language Technology Workshop (SLT), San Diego, CA, pp. 299–304 (2016)
32. Cardinal, P., et al.: Recent advances in ASR applied to an Arabic transcription system for Al-Jazeera, p. 5
33. Ali, A., Zhang, Y., Cardinal, P., Dahak, N., Vogel, S., Glass, J.: A complete KALDI recipe for building Arabic speech recognition systems. In: 2014 IEEE Spoken Language Technology Workshop (SLT), South Lake Tahoe, NV, USA, pp. 525–529 (2014)
34. Tomashenko, N., Vythelingum, K., Rousseau, A., Esteve, Y.: LIUM ASR systems for the 2016 multi-genre broadcast Arabic challenge. In: 2016 IEEE Spoken Language Technology Workshop (SLT), San Diego, CA, pp. 285–291 (2016)
35. Khurana, S., Ali, A.: QCRI advanced transcription system (QATS) for the Arabic multi-dialect broadcast media recognition: MGB-2 challenge. In: 2016 IEEE Spoken Language Technology Workshop (SLT), San Diego, CA, pp. 292–298 (2016)

36. Graciarena, M., Kajarekar, S., Stolcke, A., Shriberg, E.: Noise robust speaker identification for spontaneous Arabic speech. In: 2007 IEEE International Conference on Acoustics, Speech and Signal Processing, ICASSP 2007, Honolulu, HI, pp. IV-245–IV-248 (2007)

37. Tolba, H.: Comparative experiments to evaluate the use of a CHMM-based speaker identification engine for Arabic spontaneous speech. In: 2009 2nd IEEE International Conference on Computer Science and Information Technology, Beijing, China, pp. 241–245 (2009)

38. Ettaouil, M., Lazaar, M., En-Naimani, Z.: A hybrid ANN/HMM models for arabic speech recognition using optimal codebook. In: 2013 8th International Conference on Intelligent Systems: Theories and Applications (SITA), Rabat, Morocco, pp. 1–5 (2013)

39. Wahyuni, E.S.: Arabic speech recognition using MFCC feature extraction and ANN classification. In: 2017 2nd International conferences on Information Technology, Information Systems and Electrical Engineering (ICITISEE), Yogyakarta, pp. 22–25 (2017)

40. Venkateswarlu, R., Kumari, R., JayaSri, G.: Speech_recognition_by_using_recurrent_neural_networks, **2**(6), 7 (2011)

41. Cloud Speech-to-Text. https://cloud.google.com/speech-to-text/. Accessed 18 Feb 2019

42. Speech-to-Text. https://azure.microsoft.com/en-us/services/cognitive-services/speech-to-text/. Accessed 18 Feb 2019

43. IBMWatsonSpeech-to-Text. https://www.ibm.com/watson/services/speech-to-text/. Accessed 18 Feb 2019

44. KALDI. http://kaldi-asr.org/. Accessed 18 Feb 2019

45. Ali, A., Zhang, Y., Cardinal, P., Dahak, N., Vogel, S.: A complete KALDI recipe for building Arabic speech recognition systems. In: Presented at the 2014 IEEE Spoken Language Technology Workshop (SLT), pp. 225–229 (2014)

46. Manohar, V., Povey, D., Khudanpur, S.: JHU Kaldi system for Arabic MGB-3 ASR challenge using diarization, audio-transcript alignment and transfer learning. In: 2017 IEEE Automatic Speech Recognition and Understanding Workshop (ASRU), Okinawa, pp. 346–352 (2017)

47. The Microsoft cognitive toolkit. https://www.microsoft.com/en-us/cognitive-toolkit/. Accessed 18 Feb 2019

48. An open source machine learning framework for everyone. https://www.tensorflow.org/. Accessed 18 Feb 2019

49. Sim, K.C., Narayanan, A., Bagby, T., Sainath, T.N., Bacchiani, M.: Improving the efficiency of forward-backward algorithm using batched computation in TensorFlow. In: 2017 IEEE Automatic Speech Recognition and Understanding Workshop (ASRU), Okinawa, Japan (2017)

The State of the Awareness of Web Accessibility Guidelines of Student Website and App Developers

Shiya Cao[✉] and Eleanor Loiacono

Worcester Polytechnic Institute, Worcester, MA 01609, USA
{scao2, eloiacon}@wpi.edu

Abstract. Websites and applications (apps) have become so ingrained in society, it is important that everyone, regardless of their disability, has equal access to websites and apps. However, Web accessibility continues to be an issue. One of the reasons often cited for inaccessible websites and apps is lack of training. Many developers are not educated, or even exposed, to accessibility guidelines in their college preparations. Thus, understanding the extent to which current student website and app developers are exposed to accessibility is a critical first step in determining how to increase their use of accessibility guidelines. This mixed method study is a first step to understand the awareness of Web accessibility guidelines of student website and app developers. The survey questions have been developed to understand student website and app developers' education, experience, and perceptions of accessibility guidelines. The interview data collected has been used to explain the quantitative results and explore to narrow the gaps in the perceptions and implementation of accessibility guidelines.

Keywords: Web accessibility · Accessibility guidelines ·
Student website and app developers

1 Introduction

Web accessibility continues to be an issue (Loiacono 2004; Loiacono et al. 2005, 2009). The Business Disability Forum has been assessing the accessibility of websites since 2008 and has found that 70% of websites reviewed have lacked accessibility (Rocca 2016). Another assessment (Castro et al. 2017) conducted by Information Technology & Innovation Foundation (ITIF) in 2016 and 2017, indicated that 42% of the 260 most popular federal government websites in the US failed the accessibility test for people with disabilities.

Because websites and applications (apps) have become so ingrained in society, it is important that everyone, regardless of their disability, has equal access to websites and apps. That is what World Wide Web Consortium (W3C) Accessibility Guidelines aim to accomplish. Those guidelines help encourage website and app developers to make more accessible websites and apps. For example, one recommendation contained in the newly released Web Content Accessibility Guidelines (WCAG) (version 2.1, released June 5, 2018) is to "provide text alternatives for any non-text content so that it can be

G. Meiselwitz (Ed.): HCII 2019, LNCS 11578, pp. 32–42, 2019.
https://doi.org/10.1007/978-3-030-21902-4_3

changed into other forms people need, such as large print, braille, speech, symbols or simpler language" (https://www.w3.org/TR/2018/REC-WCAG21-20180605/). This recommendation ensures that people with different disabilities, such as deafness or blindness, can access online materials.

However, many developers are not educated on, or even exposed to accessibility guidelines. Thus, a critical first step is to understand the extent to which current student website and app developers are exposed to accessibility guidelines in their college preparations. In this initial study, as a first step of our research, we used a mixed method to survey and interview student website and app developers to understand their awareness of Web accessibility guidelines.

2 Literature Review

Previous research (Lawton 2005; Lawton et al. 2017) indicated that Web accessibility provides benefits, not only to people with disabilities, but to society as a whole. Web accessibility guidelines are a key resource to incorporate accessibility in websites and apps (Loiacono 2004; Rouse 2018). Research has shown that legislation can compel companies to increase their adherence to accessibility guidelines (Loiacono et al. 2013). Pervious research (Lazar et al. 2004; Abou-Zahra 2017) showed that education, training, and awareness of diverse disabilities help enhance the understanding of Web accessibility.

2.1 Web Accessibility Is Beneficial to Everyone

In its simplest form, Web accessibility means that all people can use websites and apps, regardless of their disability. This includes people with temporary or changing disabilities and means that everyone must be able to perceive, understand, navigate, and contribute to websites and apps (Lawton 2005). Making websites and apps accessible is socially responsible (Lawton 2005); it is a human right for everyone to have equal access and equal opportunity (Lawton et al. 2017). Web accessibility provides benefits to entire society. For example, people from any background or situation can contribute to a worldwide online community, and those with disabilities should have access to this. Accessible websites and apps can also hugely benefit companies. A website or app that is well designed and accessible provides better search-engine optimization (SEO) and usually requires less maintenance (Lawton et al. 2017). Inaccessible websites and apps hinder usage for people with disabilities while also being inconvenient to people without disabilities. For instance, under the WCAG, ensuring that there are definitions for idioms, jargon, or abbreviations used on websites and apps, can not only help those with cognitive issues, but also those unfamiliar with the topic of the website or app. Therefore, Web accessibility can benefit everyone.

2.2 Web Accessibility Guidelines Are Essential to Design Accessible Web

The Web Accessibility Initiative (WAI) was founded by the W3C in 1996. The WAI has developed guidelines in place to incorporate Web accessibility in every aspect of the Web. The initial WCAG version 1.0 was developed in 1999 and the WAI updated to WCAG version 2.1 in 2018. This new version includes 4 guiding principles (perceivable, operable, understandable, and robust) and 13 guidelines to ensure website page content such as text, images, forms, and sounds accessible to people with disabilities (https://www.w3.org/TR/WCAG21/#conformance). In addition, the United States government provides guidelines and tools in the Section 508 initiative (https://www.section508.gov/), requiring that all electronic and information technology must be accessible to people with disabilities (Rouse 2010). Moreover, the Americans with Disabilities Act (ADA), enacted by the United States Congress in 1990, has been expanded to cover the accessibility of websites, requiring that websites must be prepared to offer communications through accessible means (Kaplan 2000).

2.3   Awareness Disabilities Helps People Understand Various Demands of Web Accessibility

Different types of disabilities present unique barriers to users and unique challenges to website and app developers because users need different accessibility features. For example, those with visual disabilities may require an alternative to audio media, while those with cognitive disabilities can be assisted by logical and consistent design and simpler text to use websites and apps. Even people with the same category of disability may require different demands depending on the degree of their disability. For instance, for those who are just hard of hearing, good audio quality and the ability to change the volume of media is an acceptable starting point; however, for those who are completely deaf, an alternative to audio is necessary–usually addressed by using captions for videos or by supplying a separate transcript (Abou-Zahra 2017).

2.4   Education and Training Help Form the Perceptions of Web Accessibility

Lazar et al. (2004) found that societal foundations, such as education and training, influence website and app developers on their awareness and decision of whether a website or app will be built for accessibility or not. Education and training play an important role in the perceptions of Web accessibility, especially for student website and app developers because they acquire knowledge mainly from the classroom and related projects.

3   Research Method

This research uses a mixed method to survey and interview student website and app developers to understand their awareness of Web accessibility guidelines. We have collected and analyzed the quantitative and qualitative data[1]. The reason for collecting

---

[1] Three undergraduate students collected part of the quantitative and qualitative data in their Interactive Qualifying Project (IQP) from September 2017 to December 2017.

both quantitative and qualitative data is to provide a comprehensive and deep understanding of the awareness of Web accessibility guidelines of student website and app developers.

3.1 Quantitative Data

The survey questionnaire, consisting of 15 questions, was developed by the researchers and reviewed by experts in website and app development and accessibility. Except for the demographic questions, all questions focused on student website and app developers' education, experiences, and perceptions of Web accessibility guidelines. These questions contained various types of questions, including multiple choice and open-ended questions. The questionnaire was pilot tested by researchers and random subjects (not include in the survey data). Institutional Review Board (IRB) approval was obtained for the study (both survey and interview protocol). Advertisements to faculty who taught website and app development or design courses in various universities in the Northeastern US. Faculty who were willing to promote this research sent the study promotion email and survey link to their students. Using this approach, we made sure that participants had a background knowledge of Web accessibility. Participants were solicited through Qualtrics.

3.2 Qualitative Data

To enhance our understanding of the quantitative data, at the end of the survey questionnaire, we asked participants if they were willing to sign up for interviews or not. If they were willing to participate in interviews, they would click a link provided in the questionnaire, which leaded to a time-slot sheet for signing up for interviews by Slottr. Signing up for a time-slot required the participant's email. Then researchers contacted participants through email to check interview dates and times and sent participants the consent form approved by IRB. An approved protocol, which was also reviewed by the experts, was used to conduct the interview. The interview consisted of 14 questions. Overall, the interviews were about respondents' experiences and perceptions of accessibility guidelines. In addition, some questions delved into respondents' experiences in implementing Web accessibility in their work. Interviews lasted around 15 min. For those who agreed to it, interviews were audio recorded and transcribed to ensure accuracy of notetaking. Participants who finished both survey and interview were awarded $5 Amazon gift cards.

3.3 Demographics of Participants

As of today, we have collected a total of 76 surveys and 34 interviews. The number of participants in each gender was 54 in male (71.1%), 20 in female (26.3%), 1 in other identification (1.3%), and 1 in preferred not to answer (1.3%). The sample consisted of 56 undergraduate students (73.7%) and 20 graduate students (26.3%). The number of participants in each major was 36 in computer science (47.4%), 21 in information technology (27.6%), 17 in other majors (22.4%), and 2 students did not state their majors (2.6%). The interview sample consisted of 23 male (67.6%) and 11 female (32.4%), 24 undergraduate students (70.6%) and 10 graduate students (29.4%), as well as 18 in computer science (52.9%), 6 in information technology (17.6%), and 10 in other majors (29.4%).

4 Initial Quantitative Results

4.1 Education and Training

There are two items to measure education and training of accessibility—the number of website and app development or design courses a student has taken, and whether or not a student has taken courses that discussed accessibility.

It is noted that the majority of participants reported to have taken one website and app development or design course (55%) or have not taken any relevant courses (28%), as can be seen in the graphic at Fig. 1.

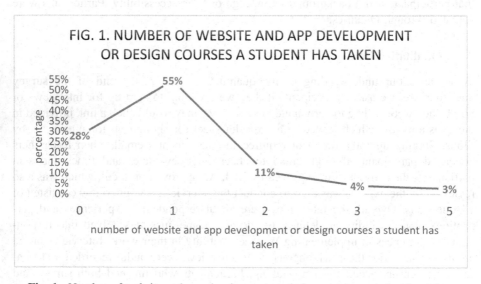

Fig. 1. Number of website and app development or design courses a student has taken

Not every website and app development or design course discusses accessibility. As it can be observed in Fig. 2, 55% of the participants stated that they have not taken courses that discussed accessibility.

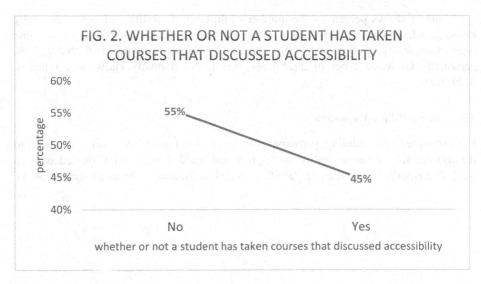

Fig. 2. Whether or not a student has taken courses that discussed accessibility

4.2 Disabilities Awareness

The item used to measure awareness of diverse disabilities is the number of different disabilities a student website and app developer personally knew people who have.

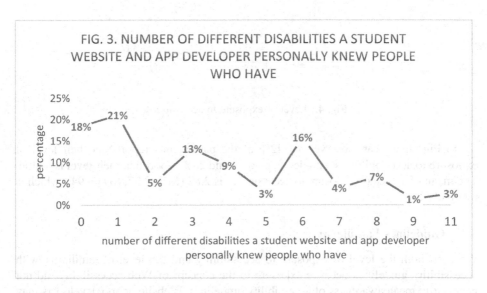

Fig. 3. Number of different disabilities a student personally knew people who have

Figure 3 shows percent of the number of different disabilities students personally knew people who have varied. 82% of the participants at least personally know one type of disability, among which 21% personally know one type of disability, 16% personally know six types of disabilities, and 13% personally know three types of disabilities.

4.3   Accessibility Exposure

For exposure to accessibility, participants were asked to report their level of exposure to the concept of "Web accessibility" as "a great deal" (coded as 5), "a lot" (coded as 4), "a moderate amount" (coded as 3), "a little" (coded as 2), and "none at all" (coded as 1).

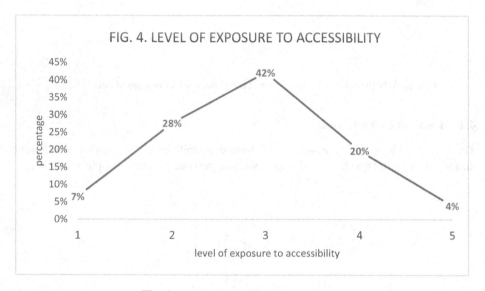

Fig. 4. Level of exposure to accessibility

In Fig. 4, we can observe that 42% of the participants report that their level of exposure to accessibility is a moderate amount and 28% report that their level is a little. The mean of scores of exposure to accessibility is 2.87 (M = 2.87, SD = .94), which is relatively low.

4.4   Guidelines Familiarity

We used both the level of exposure to accessibility and the level of familiarity with accessibility guidelines because exposure to the concept of Web accessibility did not necessarily mean awareness of accessibility guidelines. Website or app developers may know the concept of Web accessibility that everyone should have equal access to the

Web (Lawton et al. 2017), however, to accomplish Web accessibility, they need to know and apply specific guidelines to create accessible features for website and app content.

In the survey questions, participants were asked whether or not they were familiar with any of the three main accessibility guidelines or laws (ADA, Section 508, and WCAG) in the US. If a case reported to be not familiar with any guidelines, it was coded as 0; if a case reported to be familiar with one guideline, it was coded as 1; if a case reported to be familiar with two guidelines, it was coded as 2; if a case reported to be familiar with three guidelines, it was coded as 3.

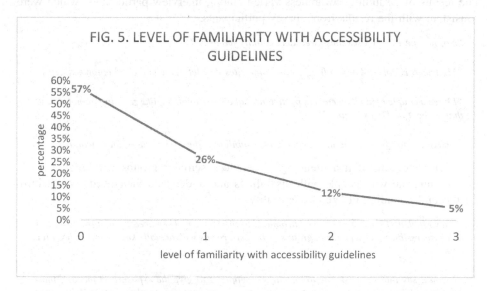

Fig. 5. Level of familiarity with accessibility guidelines

In Fig. 5, it is observed that many of the participants are not familiar with accessibility guidelines at all (57%) and only 26% are familiar with one accessibility guideline. The mean of scores of familiarity with accessibility guidelines is .66 (M = .66, SD = .89), which is quite low.

5   Initial Qualitative Results

5.1   Education and Training

In general, interview participants said that course discussions could make them more aware of Web accessibility, but some courses taught accessibility guidelines briefly, so they were still not familiar with those guidelines.

> *"In my web design class, we focus a lot on user experience and part of it is to make it more accessible."*

"It's kind of in general. Like there is a guideline on YouTube for how to use technology and using those features on our computers to use technology. It's sort of that exposure."

"As far as the (school name) courses, I've taken HCI, the mobile development one, mobile computing and so there I learned briefly about accessibility standards..." "I think if we talk about the more in classes, no brief for it because that was all like how human interacted with computers but how do we make that easy for them?"

5.2   Disabilities Awareness

The results of disabilities awareness varied among interview participants, which were consistent with the results from survey participants.

"No, no one I know uses these web accessibility features."

"My friend is color blind, so he goes on some sites that let him change the color settings."

"I have a couple of family members particularly about eyesight. So, like zooming in on text and, that's about as far as it goes."

"I have a good friend. She has a couple of disabilities. She uses some of these features."

Interviewees mentioned attending conferences, seminar, groups, and bigger crowds to communicate with people with disabilities and understand their needs was helpful for the understanding of Web accessibility.

"They (students) really need to be introduced to the concept. They need to be introduced to it (Web accessibility) in seminar in groups or bigger crowds who actually know to what level it is being used."

"I would say that the best way to encourage people is to give the exposure of meeting those people and understanding ..." "... get attending these conferences about accessibility every year."

5.3   Accessibility Exposure

Most interviewees reported to know a moderate amount of accessibility, which were consistent with the survey data.

"I'm not sure if I know too much. As I understand, it's more about making sure the websites there easy to understand, all the tools and all the features they use are users need from product end."

"I assume it has to do with like, you know, disability accident. Yeah. So basically, the only real web accessibility stuff that I know about would be subtitles close captioning that kind of stuff."

5.4   Guidelines Familiarity

Most interviewees reported that they were not familiar with accessibility guidelines, which were consistent with the survey data.

"No, I'm not aware of them."

"I know they exist. I don't know exactly how...what they are."

"I just don't think they are very much informed at all. Almost like they are optional goal."

Interviewees said that check lists and suggestions for how to implement guidelines as well as open resources and tools or plugins could make guidelines easier for them to understand and implement guidelines.

"One thing is just having a quick reference list..."

"I think if there are a set of guidelines and if there's some way that you've actually tell them, if there's some kind of journal that tells about how you should be doing things."

"They are not very easy to find for instance, I wouldn't know where I start to look for resources to find to make my website more accessible."

"Basically, if there is something that, um, was a tool specifically tasked for each of the individual features. So, like I know that there is, um, I know that there's apps that are on your computer that can magnify screen the independent of the browser...."

Interviewees also indicated that projects' requirements and showing business values could enhance their intentions to use accessibility guidelines.

"If the students are provided with a project and the professor gives them these guidelines that needs to be strictly followed, they'll follow that."

"My boss would already be interested in the numbers; he'd be interested in money. So, I try to appeal to him by saying that, you know, maybe we're missing a whole chunk of people who could, who could be a target audience for our website, but I've been not able to do because they don't, they cannot, it's not very accessible to them. So, by making a page very accessible and all inclusive, maybe we can get more hits and people to visit our website...."

6 Discussion

The initial analysis of the survey and interview data showed a couple of key findings:

(1) Participants showed a relatively low level of exposure to accessibility and familiarity with accessibility guidelines.
(2) Participants pointed out that deep course discussions, various events exposure, projects' requirements, open resources, check lists, or tools to implement the guidelines, and business awareness could be helpful to make them understand and use accessibility guidelines.

7 Conclusions and Future Research

This first step of our research utilized a mixed method to survey and interview student website and app developers to understand their awareness of Web accessibility guidelines. Preliminary results of the quantitative and qualitative data analysis indicated that student website and app developers had a relatively low level of exposure to accessibility and familiarity with accessibility guidelines. The future research will use statistic modeling to investigate whether or not education and training play a role in enhancing the awareness of accessibility guidelines of student website and app developers and use qualitative analysis to further explore how to help students better understand and implement those guidelines. Together, we hope that this research benefits society as a whole by increasing the accessibility of websites and apps for everyone. We plan to present more of our findings at the conference next July.

References

Abou-Zahra, S.: Diversity of Web Users (2017). https://www.w3.org/WAI/intro/people-use-web/diversity. Accessed 16 Nov 2018

Castro, D., Nurko, G., McQuinn, A.: Benchmarking U.S. Government Websites. Information Technology & Innovation Foundation, 60 (2017)

Kaplan, F.M.: Designing a Website that is ADA-compliant, p. 34. NREI (2000)

Lazar, J., Dudley-Sponaugle, A., Greenidge, K.: Improving web accessibility: a study of webmaster perceptions. Comput. Hum. Behav. **20**, 269–288 (2004)

Lawton, H.: Essential Components of Web Accessibility (2005). https://www.w3.org/WAI/intro/components.php. Accessed 16 Nov 2018

Lawton, H., Liam, M.: Web Design and Accessibility (2017). https://www.w3.org/standards/webdesign/accessibility. Accessed 16 Nov 2018

Loiacono, E.: Cyberaccess: web accessibility and corporate America. Commun. ACM **47**, 83–87 (2004)

Loiacono, E.T., Djamasbi, S.: Corporate website accessibility: does legislation matter? Univers. Access Inf. Soc. **1**, 115–124 (2013)

Loiacono, E., McCoy, S.: Website accessibility: a cross-sector comparison. Univ. Access Inf. Soc. **4**, 393–399 (2005)

Loiacono, E., Romano, N., McCoy, S.: The state of corporate website accessibility. Commun. ACM **52**, 128–132 (2009)

Rocca, D.: Seventy Percent of Websites are Breaking the Law on Accessibility - Here's How and Why That Needs to Change. https://www.huffingtonpost.co.uk/damiano-la-rocca/website-accessibility_b_9931304.html?guccounter=1&guce_referrer_us=aHR0cHM6Ly93d3cuZ29vZ2xlLmNvbS8&guce_referrer_cs=san1gOKPPficWO8ejmeEZg. Accessed 16 Nov 2018

Rouse, M.: Section 508. https://searchcio.techtarget.com/definition/Section-508. Accessed 16 Nov 2018

Using a Social Media Inspired Optimization Algorithm to Solve the Set Covering Problem

Broderick Crawford[1(✉)], Ricardo Soto[1], Guillermo Cabrera[1],
Agustín Salas-Fernández[2], and Fernando Paredes[3]

[1] Pontificia Universidad Católica de Valparaíso, Valparaíso, Chile
{broderick.crawford,ricardo.soto}@pucv.cl
[2] Universidad Tecnológica de Chile INACAP, Santiago, Chile
jsalasf@inacap.cl
[3] Universidad Diego Portales, Santiago, Chile
fernando.paredes@udp.cl

Abstract. Currently, researchers have focused on solving large-scale and non-linear optimization problems. Metaheuristics as its prefix indicates, are superior heuristics that aim to deliver acceptable results to optimization problems in a short period of time, trying to achieve a correct balance between exploration and exploitation in the search for solutions. In this paper we present the application of a metaheuristic technique called Social media optimization algorithm for the resolution of the Set Covering Problem (SCP). This technique is inspired by the behavior of users of social networking platforms such as Twitter. The users through different interactions manage to make a *Tweet* more relevant than others. The user who generates the best Tweet, is recognized as a *celebrity*. This process of social relationship is precisely what allows us to find better solutions given the experiments and results presented in this document.

Keywords: Twitter Optimization · Social media · Metaheuristics · SCP

1 Introduction

Finding an optimal solution for an optimization problem is often a very challenging task [1], depending on the choice and the correct use of the correct algorithm. The choice of an algorithm may depend on the type of problem, the availability of algorithms, computational resources and time constraints. For large-scale, non-linear global optimization problems, there is often no agreed guideline for the choice of algorithm and, in many cases, there is no efficient algorithm. Several algorithms can be used to solve optimization problems. The conventional or classical algorithms are mostly deterministic.

© Springer Nature Switzerland AG 2019
G. Meiselwitz (Ed.): HCII 2019, LNCS 11578, pp. 43–52, 2019.
https://doi.org/10.1007/978-3-030-21902-4_4

Metaheuristics is another major field devoted to solving optimization problems. They are useful when finding the best solution is computationally very expensive. The key is to provide a way of finding a *good-enough* solution in a fixed amount of time. Metaheuristics, as the suffix says, are upper level heuristics. They are intelligent strategies to design or improve general heuristic procedures with high performance. In their original definition, metaheuristics are general purpose approximated optimization algorithms; they find a good solution for the problem in a reasonable time (not necessarily the optimal solution). They are iterative procedures that smartly guide a subordinate heuristic, combining different concepts to suitably explore and operate the search space.

Over time, these methods have also come to include any procedures that employ strategies for overcoming the trap of local optimality in complex solution spaces, especially those procedures that utilize one or more neighborhood structures as a mean for defining admissible transitions from one solution to another, or to transform solutions in a constructive process [2]. To get good solutions, any search algorithm must establish an adequate balance between two overlayed process characteristics:

Intensity is a mechanism that explores more throughly the portions of the search space that seem promising in order to make sure that the best solution in these areas is indeed found (space exploitation).

Diversity is a mechanism that forces the search into unexplored areas of the search space (space exploration). This balance is needed to quickly identify regions with good quality solutions and do not waste time in promising or visited regions. The metaheuristics are categorized in: Constructive heuristics: they start from an empty solution and continue adding components until a solution is built. (i.e.: GRASP [3], Ant Colony Optimization [4] and Intelligent Water Drops [5]). Trajectory methods: they start from an initial solution and then, iteratively, try to replace it with a better one from their neighborhood. (i.e.: Local Search [6], Tabu Search [7], Simulated Annealing [8]). Population-based methods: they iteratively evolve a population of solutions (i.e.: Genetic Algorithms [9,10], Particle Swarm [11]).

Metaheuristic optimization algorithms are often inspired from nature. According to the source of inspiration of the metaheuristic algorithms they can be classified into different categories. The main category is the biology-inspired algorithms which generally use biological evolution and/or collective behavior of animals. Science is another source of inspiration for the metaheuristics.

These algorithms are usually inspired physic and chemistry. Moreover, art-inspired algorithms [12] have been successful for the global optimization. They generally inspired from artists behavior to create artistic stuffs (such as musicians and architectures). Socially inspired algorithms can be defined as another source of inspiration and the algorithm simulate the social trying to extract the "swarm intelligence". In this paper, we use a social media inspired optimization algorithm: Twitter Optimization (TO) originally developed by Lv et al. on [13]. TO is able to solve combinatorial optimization problems by imitating human's social actions on Twitter: following, tweeting and retweeting.

As the most intelligent biological system, human society is considered very worthy of investigation. By observing the daily routine of humans, we surprisingly discovered that we ourselves, as individuals in human society, were actually performing some unconscious optimization tasks on the Internet, or more specifically on Twitter. This is because when we use Twitter, we tend to publish the Tweet (a term similar to Twitter) that is considered more valuable. For example, if someone receives two Tweets, separately on the local climate and the presidential elections, he would be more willing to share this last message on Twitter because it is worth mentioning. Similar filtering behavior occurs in all Twitter users. Everyone receives the Tweets filtered by others and publishes the Tweets filtered by himself.

Tweets that can be widely disseminated among users have been filtered millions of times and would be considered the most valuable Tweets at that time. This explains why Twitter users can always catch up with the access point. Inspired by this phenomenon, the algorithm called Twitter Optimization (TO) was created.

To create an effective algorithm for the phenomenon mentioned above, TO introduces three metaphors on Twitter. First, each Tweet is considered as a solution vector x composed of D real value parameters. And to minimize the optimization mission of the objective function F, the smaller the value $F(x)$, the more valuable the Tweet will be. Secondly, when a person publishes a Tweet, he will send the content to all his followers (a Twitter term represents a unidirectional relationship). This means that he produces a solution and shares it with the specific crowd connected to him.

Finally, each person must retweet (a Twitter term means to republish) the most valuable Tweet of the people who followed, implying that it is helping the best solution to spread more. The realization of the three metaphors makes TO look for the global optimum.

2   Social Media Optimization

The inspiration of this metaheuristic is taken from the interaction of people in social media, more specifically the behavior of people on Twitter. In order to define the behavior of the algorithm, it is imperative to detail the central elements that configure it. To do this, in the next section will delve into the formal definition of each of this elements.

Objective Function. Mathematical expression representing the problem to solve. In this case we apply the TO to solve the SCP.

Fitness. Represent the value of a solution or in this case a Tweet, evaluated in the objective function $(F(x))$. For example, if we are working with a minimization problem and evaluate two solution vectors: $F(x_1)$ and $F(x_2)$ with the objective function, you get the values 100 and 200 respectively, you could say that the vector x_1 is better, because it has a lower value than x_2.

Tweet. A tweet in case of this metaheuristic, corresponds to a feasible solution of the search space. A tweet represent vector of n columns. In binary case, possible values are 0 and 1 in each columns. Formally we define a new tweet as: $x_{new} = \{x_1, x_2, \ldots, x_n\}, \forall i \in \{1, 2, \ldots, n\}$ and $x_i \in \{0, 1\}$. Some metaheuristics work with binarization functions for the generation of solution vectors as shown in [14], however in TO, the formulas are presented in a general way but the decision variables (x_i), just can take the values $\{1, 0\}$.

Following. This behavior mimics human relations given in the context of tweeter. Initially the algorithm generates a direct graph between each of the people or tweeter users. Each user is allowed to follow only F users. Then, in each round, each user will update or optimize the following set through the operations of follow or unfollow. He will select the tweet with the best fitness received in this round and will follow his original author, if he does not follow it already. After this operation has been carried out correctly, the user who has the tweet with the worst fitness must be eliminated in such a way that F is preserved. The presented method makes the direct graph adjust as each round passes. This methodology ensures that p will be following the users that generate the best tweets, that is, the solutions closest to the global optimum.

Initialization of Algorithm. The process of tweeting involves generating a new solution and sharing it with the followers. During the initiation of the search algorithm, each user issues a tweet. The formal procedure is described in Eq. (1):

$$x_i^k = min_i + (max_i - min_i) * rand() \tag{1}$$

where x^k is the current solution of user k and x_i^k is the value of x^k in i-th dimension. min_i and max_i represent lower and upper value of solution value in i-th dimension.

The random retweet consists of the initialization process where a person k randomly selects a person p from $following_k$ and proceeds to retweet the p solution. Formally we can say $y_i^k = x_i^p$, where y^k is the solution that the user k will share and x^p is the current solution found by the user p.

Tweeting and Retweeting. The process of retweeting corresponds to the imitation of the process of sharing with followers, content that the user recognizes as valuable. This behavior ensures that a good solution is shared by as many users as possible. The TO algorithm adds two disturbance operators which are discussed below. When the user k decides to retweet the user's Tweet p, the user k randomly selects one of the following operations:

Comments:

$$x_{i\,new}^p = x_i^p + Character^k * rand(-1, 1) \tag{2}$$

Participation:

$$x_{i\,new}^p = x_i^k \tag{3}$$

When user decides to *comments* the Eq. (2) is calculated, for each dimension i, there is the possibility that the new solution is better than the current one, given that case, the new solution should replace the current one.

When a user decides to *participate*, he will contribute his own share to the activity. Given the above, Eq. (3) is used to simulate this behavior.

Publishing New Tweet. This specific operation consists of discarding a current solution to generate a new one. Additionally, users called *celebrity* are chosen in each round if they are ranked within the best 1% of all users and classified as *averageman* otherwise.

For the celebrity a new behavior is introduced which takes into consideration if its solution has not been updated during the last W times, given this case generates a new solution. Where W corresponds to the number of followers of k in the current round.

The behavior for *averagemen* in each round, will consist in generating a new Tweet according to the Eq. (4). The *celebrity* will choose the Tweet with better fitness and will own it.

$$x_i^k = x_{new_i} + \delta * rand(-1, 1) \tag{4}$$

where x_{new} is the best solution found so far, δ is the scan radius. The Eq. (4) is able to generate solutions near the best available solution. TO will stop when the number of iterations is greater than the upper limit N.

Hottest Tweet. The Hottest tweet or global optimum is defined as a solution $s^* \in S$ and it has a better fitness than all solutions of the search space, i.e., $\forall s \in S, f(s^*) \leq f(s)$.

A complete flow chart of the TO algorithm can be reviewed in the Fig. 1.

3   Set Covering Problem

SCP Formulation. The SCP is a well-known mathematical problem, which tries to cover a set of needs at the lowest possible cost. The SCP was included in the list of 21 $\mathcal{NP}$-*complet* problems of Karp [15]. There are many practical uses for this problem, such as: airline crew scheduling [16,17], location of emergency facilities [18], vehicle routing [19], network attack or defense [20], traffic assignment in satellite communication systems [21], the calculation of bounds in integer programs [22], assembly line balancing [23], political districting [24], among others. The SCP can be formulated as follows:

$$\text{Minimize} \quad Z = \sum_{j=1}^{n} c_j x_j \tag{5}$$

Subject to:

$$\sum_{j=1}^{n} a_{ij} x_j \geq 1 \quad \forall i \in I \tag{6}$$

$$x_j \in \{0, 1\} \quad \forall j \in J \tag{7}$$

Let $A = (a_{ij})$ be a $m \times n$ 0-1 matrix with $I = \{1, \ldots, m\}$ and $J = \{1, \ldots, n\}$ be the row and column sets respectively. We say that column j can be cover a row

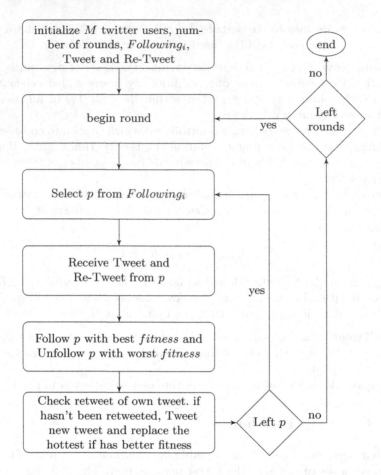

Fig. 1. Social media optimization workflow.

i if $a_{ij} = 1$. Where c_j is a nonnegative value that represents the cost of selecting the column j and x_j is a decision variable, it can be 1 if column j is selected or 0 otherwise. The objective is to find a minimum cost subset $S \subseteq J$, such that each row $i \in I$ is covered by at least one column $j \in S$.

4   Experiments

In order to test the correct execution of the T.O. metaheuristics, 30 independent executions were made of each instance of the benchmark. The metaheuristic T.O. measured its effectiveness against the instances of the library or benchmark OR (Beasley, 1990). T.O. was programmed in language Python 3.6, making use of the libraries Numpy and Scipy. GIT was used as source code repository. As a persistence, text files and in memory Data Base were used and as processing, a virtual machine with a 2.0 GHz (64 bit) dual-core CPU, 12 GB of RAM, 80 GB

Table 1. Solutions of SCP4.1 through T.O.

Instance	Optimum	Min	Max	Avg	RPD
SCP4.1	429	451	456	453.5	1.10
SCP4.2	512	611	675	643	19.34
SCP4.3	516	522	565	543.5	7.61
SCP4.4	494	514	548	531	6.20
SCP4.5	512	520	581	550.5	10.50
SCP4.6	560	566	648	607	12.65
SCP4.7	430	446	475	460.5	6.11
SCP4.8	492	499	526	512.5	5.13
SCP4.9	641	644	748	696	13.90
SCP4.10	514	543	580	561.5	6.38

of Hard Disk and Ubuntu 18.04 as operating system. In the table presented in this section, the RPD column reports the relative percentage deviation between the lowest experimentally obtained value (best fitness) and the global optimum for that instance (s *). The RPD is calculated by Eq. (8).

$$RPD = 100\frac{(Min - Optimum)}{Optimum} \tag{8}$$

As we can see in Table 1, the values of RPD are maintained between 1% and 19% for all evaluated instances. The instance with the best result was SCP4.1, obtaining an RPD of 1.10%, with a minimum value of 461. The worst result was obtained in the instance SCP4.2, where the value of the RPD was 19.34%. The regular behavior of the algorithm without changes in its parameters was around 6%. In terms of RPD evaluation, the algorithm behaved consistently in all evaluated instances.

If we look at Fig. 2, a fast convergence of the algorithm towards the global optimum is verified, achieving an asymptotic behavior to y axis, managing to escape from local optima successfully. The behavior of the algorithm before the benchmark has demonstrated its functionality and effectiveness.

Additionally, a comparison of the results obtained when solving the SCP was made, with two known algorithms. Specifically, TO is compared with Harmony Search (HS) in the work done by Salas et al. in [25] and with Black Hole in the work done in [26]. As can be seen in Table 2, the TO algorithm was superior in 9/10 instances, achieving an outstanding result.

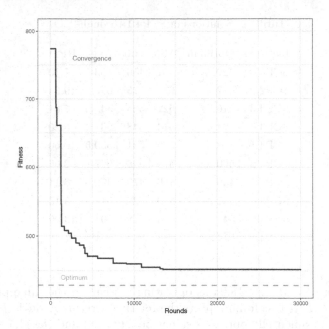

Fig. 2. Convergence to optimum, instance SCP41.

Table 2. Comparison of algorithms for SCP resolution

Instance	Optimum	TO	HS	BH	Best algorithm
SCP4.1	429	451	468	455	**TO**
SCP4.2	512	611	611	544	BH
SCP4.3	516	522	587	551	**TO**
SCP4.4	494	514	569	527	**TO**
SCP4.5	512	520	581	548	**TO**
SCP4.6	560	566	648	601	**TO**
SCP4.7	430	446	495	461	**TO**
SCP4.8	492	499	560	528	**TO**
SCP4.9	641	644	775	688	**TO**
SCP4.10	514	513	596	547	**TO**

5   Conclusion

Basically the social capacity to relate between people, allows us to be able to imitate their behavior to obtain relevant topics in their interaction. As indicated in the introduction to this paper, people are more willing to share information they consider valuable or important, rather than of little value. This very natural behavior allows to be applied in algorithms that behave in a good way in the resolution of problems like the SCP.

Our experiment results show good results solving SCP benchmark functions. Some improvements can be implemented taking ideas from other metaheuristic techniques, that introduce certain operators that better aspects such as exploitation and exploration. This is considered as future work. Finally It can be concluded that TO has a potential in solving optimization problems.

References

1. Talbi, E.: Metaheuristics: From Design to Implementation, vol. 74. Wiley, Hoboken (2009)
2. Beheshti, Z., Shamsuddin, S.: A review of population-based meta-heuristic algorithms. Int. J. Adv. Soft Comput. Appl. **5**(1), 1–35 (2013)
3. Festa, P., Resende, M.: GRASP: an annotated bibliography. In: Essays and Surveys in Metaheuristics. ORCS, vol. 15, pp. 325–367. Springer, Boston (2002). https:// doi.org/10.1007/978-1-4615-1507-4_15
4. Dorigo, M., Birattari, M., Blum, C., Clerc, M., Stützle, T., Winfield, A.F.T. (eds.): Ant Colony Optimization and Swarm Intelligence. LNCS, vol. 5217. Springer, Heidelberg (2008). https://doi.org/10.1007/978-3-540-87527-7
5. Shah, H.: The intelligent water drops algorithm: a nature-inspired swarm-based optimization algorithm. Int. J. Bio-Inspired Comput. **1**(1–2), 71–79 (2009)
6. Ishibuchi, H., Murata, T.: A multi-objective genetic local search algorithm and its application to flowshop scheduling. IEEE Trans. Syst. Man Cybern. Part C (Appl. Rev.) **28**(3), 392–403 (1998)
7. Nowicki, E., Smutnicki, C.: A fast tabu search algorithm for the permutation flowshop problem. Eur. J. Oper. Res. **91**(1), 160–175 (1996)
8. van Laarhoven, P.J.M., Aarts, E.H.L.: Simulated annealing. In: Simulated Annealing: Theory and Applications. MAIA, vol. 37, pp. 7–15, Springer, Dordrecht (1987). https://doi.org/10.1007/978-94-015-7744-1_2
9. Whitley, D.: A genetic algorithm tutorial. Stat. Comput. **4**(2), 65–85 (1994)
10. Glover, F., Laguna, M., Martí, R.: Scatter search and path relinking: advances and applications. In: Glover, F., Kochenberger, G.A. (eds.) Handbook of Metaheuristics. ISOR, vol. 57, pp. 1–35. Springer, Boston (2003). https://doi.org/10.1007/0-306-48056-5_1
11. Kennedy, J.: Particle swarm optimization. In: Sammut, C., Webb, G.I. (eds.) Encyclopedia of Machine Learning, pp. 760–766. Springer, Boston (2011). https://doi.org/10.1007/978-0-387-30164-8
12. Patnaik, S., Yang, X.-S., Nakamatsu, K.: Nature-Inspired Computing and Optimization, vol. 10. Springer, Heidelberg (2017). https://doi.org/10.1007/978-3-319-50920-4
13. Lv, Z., Shen, F., Zhao, J., Zhu, T.: A swarm intelligence algorithm inspired by Twitter. In: Hirose, A., Ozawa, S., Doya, K., Ikeda, K., Lee, M., Liu, D. (eds.) ICONIP 2016. LNCS, vol. 9949, pp. 344–351. Springer, Cham (2016). https://doi.org/10.1007/978-3-319-46675-0_38
14. Crawford, B., Soto, R., Astorga, G., García, J., Castro, C., Paredes, F.: Putting continuous metaheuristics to work in binary search spaces. Complexity **2017**, 8404231:1–8404231:19 (2017)
15. Karp, R.: Reducibility among combinatorial problems. In: Jünger, M., et al. (eds.) 50 Years of Integer Programming 1958–2008 - From the Early Years to the State-of-the-Art, pp. 219–241. Springer, Heidelberg (2010). https://doi.org/10.1007/978-3-540-68279-0_8

16. Marchiori, E., Steenbeek, A.: An evolutionary algorithm for large scale set covering problems with application to airline crew scheduling. In: Cagnoni, S. (ed.) EvoWorkshops 2000. LNCS, vol. 1803, pp. 370–384. Springer, Heidelberg (2000). https://doi.org/10.1007/3-540-45561-2_36

17. Housos, E., Elmroth, T.: Automatic optimization of subproblems in scheduling airline crews. Interfaces 27(5), 68–77 (1997)

18. Farahani, R.Z., Asgari, N., Heidari, N., Hosseininia, M., Goh, M.: Covering problems in facility location: a review. Comput. Ind. Eng. 62(1), 368–407 (2012)

19. Daskin, M.S., Stern, E.H.: A hierarchical objective set covering model for emergency medical service vehicle deployment. Transp. Sci. 15(2), 137–152 (1981)

20. Intanagonwiwat, C., Estrin, D., Govindan, R., Heidemann, J.: Impact of network density on data aggregation in wireless sensor networks. In: Proceedings 22nd International Conference on Distributed Computing Systems, pp. 457–458, July 2002. https://doi.org/10.1109/ICDCS.2002.1022289. ISSN: 1063-6927

21. Ribeiro, C.C., Minoux, M., Penna, M.C.: An optimal column-generation-with-ranking algorithm for very large scale set partitioning problems in traffic assignment. Eur. J. Oper. Res. 41(2), 232–239 (1989)

22. Fisher, M.L.: The Lagrangian relaxation method for solving integer programming problems. Manag. Sci. 27(1), 1–18 (1981)

23. Beasley, J.E.: An algorithm for set covering problem. Eur. J. Oper. Res. 31(1), 85–93 (1987)

24. Garfinkel, R.S., Nemhauser, G.L.: The set-partitioning problem: set covering with equality constraints. Oper. Res. 17(5), 848–856 (1969)

25. Salas, J., Mora, M., Barriga, H., Rubio, J., Broderick, C.: Study of population variation using harmony search for the resolution of set covering problem. Revista Científica de la UCSA 4(3), 20–33 (2017)

26. Rubio, Á.G., et al.: An binary black hole algorithm to solve set covering problem. In: Fujita, H., Ali, M., Selamat, A., Sasaki, J., Kurematsu, M. (eds.) IEA/AIE 2016. LNCS, vol. 9799, pp. 873–883. Springer, Cham (2016). https://doi.org/10.1007/978-3-319-42007-3_74

Toward RNN Based Micro Non-verbal Behavior Generation for Virtual Listener Agents

Hung-Hsuan Huang[1,2](✉), Masato Fukuda[1], and Toyoaki Nishida[1,2]

[1] RIKEN Center for Advanced Intelligence, Kyoto, Japan
[2] Graduate School of Informatics, Kyoto University, Kyoto, Japan
hhhuang@acm.org

Abstract. This work aims to develop a model to generate fine grained and reactive non-verbal idling behaviors of a virtual listener agent when a human user is talking to it. The target *micro* behaviors are facial expressions, head movements, and postures. The following two research questions then emerge. Whether these behaviors can be trained from the corresponding ones from the user's behaviors? If the answer is true, what kind of learning model can get high precision? We explored the use of two recurrent neural network (RNN) models (Gated Recurrent Unit, GRU and Long Short-term Memory, LSTM) to learn these behaviors from a human-human data corpus of active listening conversation. The data corpus contains 16 elderly-speaker/young-listener sessions and was collected by ourselves. The results show that this task can be achieved to some degree even with the baseline multi-layer perceptron models. Also, GRU showed best performance among the three compared structures.

Keywords: Virtual agent · Facial expression ·
Facial Action Coding System (FACS) · Multimodal interaction ·
Deep learning · Recurrent neural network (RNN) ·
Long Short-term Memory (LSTM) · Gated Recurrent Unit (GRU)

1 Introduction

The population of elderly people is growing rapidly in developed countries. If they do not maintain social life with others, they may feel loneliness and anxiety. For their mental health, it is reported effective to keep their social relationship with others, for example, the conversation with their caregivers or other elderly people. There are already some non-profit organizations recruiting volunteers for engaging "active listening" with the elderly. Active listening is a communication technique that the listener listens to the speaker carefully and attentively. The listener also ask questions for confirming or showing his/her concern about what the speaker said. This kind of support helps to make the elderly feel cared and to relieve their anxiety and loneliness. However, due to the lack of the number of volunteers comparing to that of the elderly who are living alone,

© Springer Nature Switzerland AG 2019
G. Meiselwitz (Ed.): HCII 2019, LNCS 11578, pp. 53–63, 2019.
https://doi.org/10.1007/978-3-030-21902-4_5

the volunteers may not be always available when they are needed. In order to improve the results, always-available and trustable conversational partners in sufficient number are demanded.

The ultimate goal of this study is the development of a computer graphics animated virtual listener who can engage active listening to serve elderly users at a level close to human listeners. In order to conduct successful active listening, it is considered essential for the listener to establish the rapport from the speaker (elderly users). Rapport is a mood which a person feels the connection and harmony with another person when (s)he is engaged in a pleasant relationship with him/her, and it helps to keep long-term relationships [8,9]. In order to realize this, like a human listener, the virtual listener has to observe the speaker's behaviors, to estimate how well the speaker is engaging the conversation [14], and then reacts to the user. The utterances of the speaker are obvious cues for the estimation of the speaker's engagement. However, due to the nature of active listening conversation, the speaker may utter in arbitrary contexts, It is difficult to utilize this information. Non-verbal behaviors are considered more general and more robust (less user-dependent). Previous works in generating the non-verbal behaviors of virtual agents usually adopt manually defined or machine learning rules to trigger predefined animation sequences [9]. When there is no attentional behavior being triggered, the character will stay steady or play so-called idling motions in a loop. Due to the fact that human body can never keep steady and always move slightly, though the movement may be neither meaningful nor attentional. Idling movements which are randomly generated or a looped replay of motion captured human movements are adopted. However, the character animation is still a repetitive replaying of exactly identical sequences or is not reactive to the user's behavior. These *repeated patterns* make the agent be perceived unnatural.

This work aims to develop a model to generate fine grained and reactive non-verbal behaviors of the virtual character when the human user is talking to it. The target *micro* non-verbal behaviors are facial expression, head movements, and postures. Then the following research questions emerge:

– Are the listener's behaviors learnable only from the speaker's behaviors? That is, the listener's behavior is only (mostly) dependent on the speaker.
– If the answer for the question above is true, which machine learning model will be appropriate? That is, which kind of regression model can achieve high precision in the learning task.

Deep neural networks have been proven to be effective in various learning tasks. Facial expressions, head movements, and postures involve dozens of parameters simultaneously, this is supposed to be an appropriate application for neural networks, which can generate multiple outputs in nature. In this paper, we presents our exploration on the use of recurrent neural networks (RNN) which is designed to capture time series data to learn the reactive behaviors to the human communication interlocutor's corresponding micro non-verbal behaviors. The generated animation is expected to be fine-grained both temporally and spatially, no identical sequences, and reactive to the user's behaviors. We compared two typical temporal models, Long Short-term Memory (LSTM) [6] and a simpler model, Gated Recurrent Unit (GRU) [3] which omits the forget and output gates with the classic non-temporal multi-layer perceptron as a baseline. This paper is organized as the follows: Sect. 2 introduces related works, Sect. 3 introduces the data corpus used in the machine learning experiment, Sect. 4 describes the neural network models compared, and Sect. 5 concludes the paper.

2   Related Works

Deep neural networks (DNNs) have been shown their performance in generalizing the learning process of complex contexts including the multimodal classification of human behaviors [1]. Despite of the time consuming process in the learning phase of DNNs which usually requires large dataset, the application of learned models is fast. Therefore, DNN is a suitable tool for the generation of multiple parameters with large number of input variables. DNNs have been shown their power in image or speech recognition and are also gradually getting popular in human-agent interaction and social computing fields. They are most often used in prediction and estimation of human state such as visual focus [12] or sentiment [2] by using low-level multimodal features. Recently, DNNs are also seen in the generation part such as utterance [15] and gesture [5]. A Generative Adversarial Networks (GAN) is used in generating photo-realistic facial expression images in reacting to another facial expression [10]. However, there is no direct previous work in generating facial expression parameters to animate virtual characters in active listening context yet.

3   Active Listening Data Corpus

3.1   Data Collection Experiment

In order to collect data closer to the situation as talking with a virtual agent on screen, the data corpus was collected in with tele-communication sessions via Skype. For elderly people (69 to 73 years old, 71 in average) were recruited for the speaker roles, and four college students (averagely 22 years old) were recruited for listener roles. The genders of the participants were balanced in each age group. Only two elderly subjects knew one young subject while the other subjects met each other for the first time. Each elderly participant talks with every young participants for at least 15 min. The experiment recorded 16 sessions of dyadic conversation with length up to 30 min. All participants are native Japanese speakers and the conversation was done in Japanese.

There was no determined topic in the conversation, and the participants could talk freely. The subjects were instructed to talk as they met for first time. The listener participants were instructed to actively listen to the speakers, that is, instead of talking about themselves, they should talk about the elderly speakers, try to motivate the disclosure of the speakers, and let them enjoy the talks. The results were, the two interlocutors in the conversation did not play equal roles, and the conversation sessions were usually conducted in interview style, i.e. the listener asks questions and the speakers answer them.

The monitor used at the elderly participant side is a large size TV (larger than 50″) while the video at young participant side is projected to a 100″ screen. In addition to the WebCams for Skype connection, two digital video camera with full HD resolution (1920 × 1080) at 29.97 fps were used to capture the participants from their front sides, camera positions were adjusted to cover their whole upper bodies (Fig. 1).

Fig. 1. Video recording of the active listening experiment. For the situation closer to face-to-face conversation, large size screens are used and the height of sitting position and screen is adjusted to align the heights of the subjects' eyes

3.2   Data Preparation

The video taken by the two video cameras were used for the extraction of multimodal features. Since the objective is the generation of listening behaviors while the speaker is talking, it is necessary to identify the time periods when the speaker is speaking. The behaviors of the speaker in those periods are then extracted as explanatory variables, and the behaviors of the listener in corresponding periods are extracted as response variables. Speakers' speech activities were automatically identified by the annotation software, ELAN [11] with additional manual corrections. The speaker of each utterance is manually labeled. Considering the balance of data length of each session, at most 20 min from the beginning are used in longer sessions.

The participants' facial expressions are extracted with an open source tool, OpenFace[1]. OpenFace estimates head posture, gaze direction, and 17 of 46 facial action units (AU) in accordance with Ekman's Facial Action Coding System (FACS) [4]. The posture information were extracted by using the open source tool, OpenPose[2]. Since OpenPose only generates two-dimensional coordinates

---

[1] https://github.com/TadasBaltrusaitis/OpenFace.
[2] https://github.com/CMU-Perceptual-Computing-Lab/openpose.

of the joints of human bodies, posture information (leaning in two axes, forward/backward and left/right) are approximated with the assumption that the widths of the participants' shoulder are the minimum values when they are sitting straight up (i.e. they only lean forward but backward). Prosodic features of speakers' voice were extracted by using the open source tool, OpenSMILE[3]. The 16 low-level descriptors (LLD) of the Interspeech 2009 Emotion feature set [13] were extracted at 100 fps. The features include root-mean-square of signal frame energy, zero-crossing rate of time signal, voicing probability, F0, and MFCC. All of the feature values are normalized to be within the range between 0.0 and 1.0.

Table 1 shows the overview of the prepared dataset. Despite the frames with partially invalid or missing data, totally there is four hours and 21 min of recorded data. Male listeners spoke less than female listeners. This coincides to the observation during the experiment, the two male listener participants performed relatively worse than the two females one. They were less skillful in motivating the speakers to talk more. Usually asked typical questions one by one and did not widen the topics in the answers from the speaker.

Table 1. Overview of the dataset. Data size is the set with two-second window

Listener	Speaking	Frame	Length (s)	Data size
Male	Yes	69,818	2,334	1.4 GB
	No	169,387	5,663	13.6 GB
Female	Yes	82,261	2,750	1.7 GB
	No	147,165	4,920	11.8 GB

4 RNN Models for Behavior Generation

4.1 Experiment Procedure

We formalize the purpose of this work as a regression problem from the speaker's facial expression (17 variables), gaze (8 variables), head movements (6 variables), and prosodic information of voice (16 variables) to the listener's (i.e. the agent) facial expression, head movements, and postures (2 variables). Since human behaviors are continuous activities of these parameters, the data frames are not independent to each other.

The dynamics of human behaviors are supposed to be better captured as time series data. Recurrent neural networks (RNN) which take the influence of previous input data into account are proposed for processing such time series data. Two variations of RNNs, Long Short-term Memory (LSTM) and Gated Recurrent Units (GRU), and the baseline multi-layer perceptron (MLP) were explored in this work. We designed a simple common three-layer network structure to run the evaluation experiments (Fig. 2). The first layer is separated into

---

[3] https://www.audeering.com/what-we-do/opensmile/.

two groups, one handles the input of video information (OpenFace), and the other one handles the input of audio information (OpenSMILE). The inputs are fed into LSTM/GRU layer with eight times units than the input, they then go trough a fully connected (dense) layer with 128 nodes, respectively. This absorbs the different frame rates in different modalities (30 fps v.s. 100 fps) and separates the temporal process of each modalities. The first fully connected layer has the same amount of nodes for each input group, this balances the influential power of the two input modalities (video and audio). They are then concatenated and go trough an additional fully connected layer that has 512 nodes before the output layer.

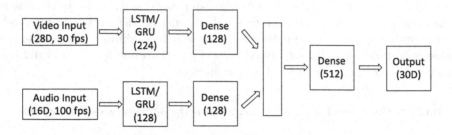

Fig. 2. Network architecture of the evaluation experiments

The same network structure is evaluated with LSTM and GRU units running on one-second and two-second long input data sequences. The raw data are transformed to trunks of time series with sliding window. In the cases of MLP models, the data trunks are reshaped to one-dimension arrays and are fed to the network in trunks by trunks. Therefore, the inputs for MLP with two seconds of data window will have $28 \times 30 \times 2 + 16 \times 100 \times 2 = 4,880$ dimensions. In addition to one-second and two-second windows, MLP was tested with zero-second window (i.e. the data of one frame only), too. The models are in seven combinations of the dataset, the whole dataset, male listeners, female listeners, and four individual listeners. All models are evaluated by leave-one-speaker cross validation, that is, the data when the listener(s) is/are interacting with one of the four speakers are extracted as the test dataset while the data of the other three speakers are used as training set. This procedure is repeated for four times so that the data of each speaker is used once as the test dataset. Then the average of the four trials is used as the final results. The experiment program is developed to use GPU computation where large amount of computation is done in parallel so that the reproducibility cannot be secured. Therefore, each experiment trial above was run for three times and the results are averaged. Each trial is trained for 200 epochs and the intermediate model which has best performance (lowest mean-squared-error (mse) upon the training dataset) is used for cross validation. mse is also adopted as the evaluation metric of the experiment. Since all data values are normalized to the range between 0 and 1, mse values can be interpreted regarding to this range.

4.2 Experiment Results

Experiment results are shown in Fig. 3. According to the evaluation results, we have the following findings:

- *mse* values of all temporal models except one-second LSTM one for male listeners are under 0.02. Considering the value range is up to 1.0, the errors are relatively low. This implies that the micron non-verbal behaviors of the listeners are indeed reactive to those of the speakers and therefore can be learned.
- The responsive behaviors are person dependent, individual models always perform better than gender-specific models and the whole-set model in the same setting. Among these, the models learned from female listeners generally perform better than male ones. This is probably because the female listeners were more skillful in communication, their reactions were more dynamic, and hence convey more characteristics which could be learned. On the contrary, male listener's reactions were more monotonous and were more difficult to be learned.
- GRU models generally perform better than corresponding LSTM ones on our dataset. Since GRU units have less parameters to be tuned, this may indicate that LSTM's additional parameters are over-killing and increase the difficulty of the learning task.
- As expected, MLP models generally perform worst, but surprisingly they still can be trained to some degree of precision even with the one-frame datasets.
- All models converges within 150 epochs, and there are no obvious impacts on the number of epochs in cross validation even though more epochs (we tried up to 500 epochs) tend to generate more precise models on the training set.
- Not always but two-second window size models often perform worse than their one-second counterparts. This may imply the listeners' reaction to the speaker does not require long period of perception (within one second). However, when actually apply the models to a realtime working agent system [7], the long-window version generates smoother (with less jittering) character animation from observation.
- Although there are only slight differences, two-second models perform better than one-second models on male listeners' datasets. On the other hand, one-second models perform considerably better than two-second ones on female listeners' datasets. This implies the different tendency in reacting to communication interlocutors for male and female subjects in our dataset.

Due to inherently different network structure, direct and completely fair comparison between the feature sets of different modalities is impossible in the case of neural networks. Out network settings were an approximation of comparable networks of multiple combinations of feature modalities and may not be the perfectly fair settings. Figure 4 depicts the comparison on the effectiveness of different combinations of modality features. Contrary to the priori expectation, multimodal models do not always perform better than uni-modal models. For

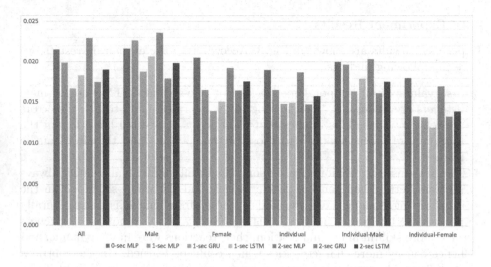

Fig. 3. Mean-squared-error values of compared models. "Individual" denotes the average of all individual listeners while "Individual-Male" and "Individual-Female" denotes the average values of male and female listeners, respectively

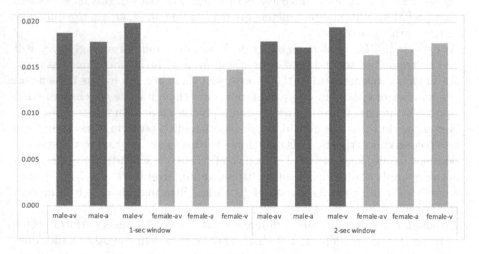

Fig. 4. Comparison of the leave-one-speaker-out cross validation results among different combinations of input modalities to GRU models using male and female listener datasets

male datasets, audio features perform best while the multimodal models perform best for female datasets. Comparing to video feature set, audio feature set is always more effective in cross validation measurements. On the other hand, from the learning curves depicted in Fig. 5, contrary to cross-validation results, video information is more active in network training itself. Video-only models converge faster and to a stable level with less errors. Jointly consider cross-

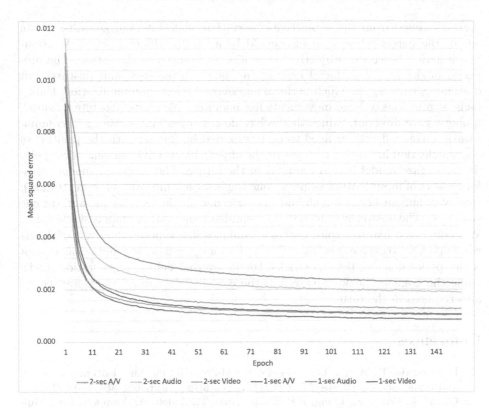

Fig. 5. Learning curves of the GRU models conducted from female listeners' dataset. The curves are depicted regarding to one and two second window as well as the combinations of audio/video features

validation results, it may imply that video information is more powerful, but it is more person-dependent. On the other hand, audio information contains more general characteristics among different subjects.

5 Conclusions and Future Work

This paper reports the exploration in using RNN models for the generation of micro listening behaviors for virtual agents. The models are trained on an active listening data corpus which features elderly speakers talking with young active listeners and was collected by ourselves. We compared the performance of MLP, GRU, and LSTM networks and the results show that the reactions of listeners can be trained to some degree merely from the speaker's behaviors. Also, GRU is confirmed to be most effective among the three.

The numeric-wise performance of tested models was not bad, however, it is hard to say that this performance is good or not. From the aspect in learning such person-dependent human behaviors, we would say the accuracy is quite high. However, from the subjective observation when interacting with such an agent, the perceived performance could be a totally different story. A serious investigation based on subjective perception is required in the future. The proposed model generates facial expressions, head movements, and postures but does not generate gaze which perform an essential role in communication. Unlike facial expressions or head movements like nodding which have absolute meaning, numeric gaze direction values themselves do not reveal any meaning in communication. Gaze directions need to be interpreted by linking with the position of communication interlocutor's eyes or the objects in the environment. A properly designed gaze model is also required in the future. The proposed model transforms a set of input feature values to one single set feature values (i.e. regression). However, human behaviors should not have one single "correct answer" in one situation. The answer should be an acceptable range rather than a single value. We would also like to explore other techniques like generative adversarial networks (GAN) to derive this "range". Finally, an agent who does not speak cannot really perform active listening tasks, the non-verbal behavior generation model while the agent is speaking as well as the model to determine its utterances are also required in the future.

References

1. Baltrusaitis, T., Ahuja, C., Morency, L.: Multimodal machine learning: a survey and taxonomy. CoRR abs/1705.09406 (2017). http://arxiv.org/abs/1705.09406
2. Chen, M., Wang, S., Liang, P.P., Baltrusaitis, T., Zadeh, A., Morency, L.P.: Multimodal sentiment analysis with word-level fusion and reinforcement learning. In: 19th ACM International Conference on Multimodal Interaction (ICMI 2017), Glasgow, UK, November 2017
3. Cho, K., et al.: Learning phrase representations using RNN encoder-decoder for statistical machine translation. CoRR abs/1406.1078, September 2014. http://arxiv.org/abs/1406.1078
4. Ekman, P., Friesen, W.V., Hager, J.C.: Facial Action Coding System (FACS). Website (2002). http://www.face-and-emotion.com/dataface/facs/description.jsp
5. Hasegawa, D., Kaneko, N., Shirakawa, S., Sakuta, H., Sumi, K.: Evaluation of speech-to-gesture generation using bi-directional LSTM network. In: Proceedings of the 18th International Conference on Intelligent Virtual Agents (IVA 2018), Sydney, Australia, pp. 79–86, November 2018
6. Hochreiter, S., Schmidhuber, J.: Long short-term memory. Neural Comput. 9(8), 1735–1780 (1997)
7. Huang, H.H., Fukuda, M., van der Struijk, S., Nishida, T.: Integration of DNN generated spontaneous reactions with a generic multimodal framework for embodied conversational agents. In: 6th International Conference on Human-Agent Interaction (HAI 2018), Southampton, UK, December 2018
8. Huang, H.H., et al.: Toward a memory assistant companion for the individuals with mild memory impairment. In: 11th IEEE International Conference on Cognitive Informatics & Cognitive Computing (ICCI*CC 2012), Kyoto, pp. 295–299, August 2012

9. Huang, L., Morency, L.-P., Gratch, J.: Virtual rapport 2.0. In: Vilhjálmsson, H.H., Kopp, S., Marsella, S., Thórisson, K.R. (eds.) IVA 2011. LNCS, vol. 6895, pp. 68–79. Springer, Heidelberg (2011). https://doi.org/10.1007/978-3-642-23974-8_8
10. Huang, Y., Khan, S.M.: DyadGAN: generating facial expressions in dyadic interactions. In: 2017 IEEE Conference on Computer Vision and Pattern Recognition Workshops (CVPRW), Honolulu, USA, pp. 11–18, July 2017
11. Lausberg, H., Sloetjes, H.: Coding gestural behavior with the NEUROGES-ELAN system. Behav. Res. Methods 41(3), 841–849 (2009)
12. Otsuka, K., Kasuga, K., Kohler, M.: Estimating visual focus of attention in multiparty meetings using deep convolutional neural networks. In: 20th ACM International Conference on Multimodal Interaction (ICMI 2018), Boulder, USA, pp. 191–199, October 2018
13. Schuller, B., Steidl, S., Batliner, A.: The INTERSPEECH 2009 emotion challenge. In: 10th Annual Conference of the International Speech Communication Association (INTERSPEECH 2009), Brighton, United Kingdom, September 2009
14. Tickle-Degnen, L., Rosenthal, R.: The nature of rapport and its nonverbal correlates. Psychol. Inq. 1(4), 285–293 (1990)
15. Wu, J., Ghosh, S., Chollet, M., Ly, S., Mozgai, S., Scherer, S.: NADiA: neural network driven virtual human conversation agents. In: Proceedings of the 18th International Conference on Intelligent Virtual Agents (IVA 2018), Sydney, Australia, pp. 173–178, November 2018

Recommendations for the Design of Digital Memorials in Social Web

Cristiano Maciel[1]([✉]), Aron Lopes[1], Vinicius Carvalho Pereira[1],
Carla Leitão[2], and Clodis Boscarioli[3]

[1] Universidade Federal do Mato Grosso (UFMT), Cuiabá, Brazil
crismac@gmail.com, aronlopes@gmail.com,
viniciuscarpe@gmail.com
[2] Pontifícia Universidade Católica do Rio de Janeiro (PUC-RIO),
Rio de Janeiro, Brazil
cfaria@inf.puc-rio.br
[3] Universidade do Oeste do Estado do Paraná (Unioeste), Cascavel, Brazil
boscarioli@gmail.com

Abstract. Nowadays, the cultural practices in our society are affected by fast technological innovation. Among those practices, there is mourning and the way we face death. In this context, our mortuary rites are being transferred to the digital world as well. Applications for online or digital memorials are increasingly common in the web. In order to help designers model applications of the like, we herein present practical recommendations to design digital memorials, considering the technical and cultural peculiarities of addressing death and mourning in digital environments. Designers should try to follow these recommendations with a view to: meeting users' expectations regarding this kind of social software; ensuring that all types of users will have a satisfactory interaction with the system; preserving the deceased user's reputation; and promoting awareness of the cultural diversity of death-related domain. We illustrate these recommendations with prototypes of a possible social network for digital memorials. Finally, we discuss challenges and future works concerning these applications.

Keywords: Digital memorials · Mourning · Users' sensations · Social web · Guidelines

1 Introduction

Death is an unavoidable event for any living being, but only humans are aware of their finitude, so they perform rites of passage and mourning. These rituals play a central role in all human cultures and in Western societies they usually include tributes to the dead by means of wakes, funerals, burials, prayers, and the construction of memorials.

These death-related cultural practices are also impacted by the fast technological innovation that we experience nowadays, which affects not only the way we live, but also how we die or face the death of our beloved ones. Therefore, expressions of grief and funeral rites in general are now beginning to be transferred to the virtual world. Applications that implement the concept of online memorials (herein called digital

G. Meiselwitz (Ed.): HCII 2019, LNCS 11578, pp. 64–79, 2019.
https://doi.org/10.1007/978-3-030-21902-4_6

memorials) are becoming increasingly common on the web. In these systems, users are empowered to create a memorial for someone who died and to pay him/her homage in the form of virtual messages, flowers, candles or even prayers [1–5].

However, there is still a lack of studies about technical, cultural and legal issues regarding death in the digital space. This includes the need for research on users' expectations and intentions when interacting with digital memorials. As stated by Brubaker, Hayes and Dourish [6] and Lopes, Maciel and Pereira [5], when these applications are incorporated into the Social Web, a network of living users created about a digital memorial, that is, a dead user's profile. Besides, digital memorials can also be connected to one another, so that living and deceased users compose a complex network, where posthumous interaction [3], i.e., interaction with deceased users' data, takes place.

Our literature review shows that there is current research on mourning practices mediated by technology and on the role of digital legacy; however, solutions that consider human aspects in their design are still required. This topic considers challenges in some communities, such as reported in the GranDIHC-BR Technical Report [7] and in the GranDSI-BR Technical Report [8].

In order to assist designers to project digital memorials, practical recommendations will be presented in this article considering the technical and cultural specificities of addressing death and mourning in the digital environment. Some of these recommendations will be illustrated by prototypes of a possible design of a social network for digital memorials.

2 Literature Review

The concept of digital memorials derives from the concept of memorials in the physical world, where concrete monuments are used to symbolize and honor the memory of a person or event [9]. According to Riechers [2], all personal memorials arise from common human needs: paying homage to the dead and comforting people in mourning.

Therefore, memorials in the physical world have many cultural purposes, especially those related to religious and ritualistic practices, far beyond the instrumental function of containing the body of a deceased person. One famous example of a memorial that plays different cultural roles, not only as a place for mourning and honoring, but also as a landmark for tourism and as a constant image for political speeches, is the National September 11 Memorial (see Fig. 1) in United States.

The practice of paying tributes to the dead is evidently also transposed to the virtual universe, because many users feel the need to express their feelings for deceased people through technologies [10]. The materiality of physical memorials plays a central role in the process of recollection and mourning: flowers, photos, candles and other objects used in real-world wakes and funerals metaphorically represent the absence of the deceased [11]. This also holds true in digital memorials, e.g. in the FindAGrave website [12], which allows users to leave virtual candles, flowers or messages to any deceased [1].

In posthumous interaction through digital memorials, the deceased becomes either the element around which users interact or the recipient of messages and tributes from

Fig. 1. Memorial for the victims of the 09/11 terrorist attack (New York). (Source: author's archive)

the living users. This kind of process can be seen both in web platforms created with other purposes and in those specifically created to support memorialization services.

Some social networks are now adding digital memorial profiles to their services. In Facebook, dead users' profiles can be changed into digital memorials either if the system automatically detects the user's death, or if other users notify the system. Campos et al. [13] pointed out some relevant elements of Facebook digital memorials, such as the possibility to name an heir or the request for the deletion of the deceased user's account.

In addition to the systems that were/are being adapted to support digital grief and digital memorialization, new web applications are being developed specifically focusing on services of this nature.

According to Riechers [2], digital memorial websites have been around since 1996, with the release of the Virtual Memorials platform [14]. According to Brubaker et al. [6], "these sites users can post slideshows, videos, texts, audios and buy gifts prints, like balloons and cake to celebrate a birthday. These practices of sharing memories allow the bereaved to preserve the postmortem identity of their loved ones". Thus, they create a kind of "digital limbo" between life and death [15], redefining interaction practices somehow involving the dead. The creation of specific platforms where living and dead coexist leads Brubaker and Vertesi [16] to consider deceased users not as a special subgroup, but rather as a case of "extreme users", whose needs pose special challenges for software design.

Results of a qualitative study of tombs, tombstones and physical memorials from four cemeteries from different cultures [17] identify expressive components that must be considered in the design process of digital memorials. Designers must explore the possibilities of representing: the religious identity of the deceased, their possible multiple identities (public and/or private ones), the significant temporal markers of their lives, and their social, political and economic status, among others. A culture-sensitive approach is also important during the design process, aiming at honoring the deceased's values and avoiding cultural taboos.

Some other studies on digital memorials have been carried out focusing on systems connected to QR-Code tags attached to tombstones. According to Cann [18], "QR codes transfer the dead from the cemetery to the realm of the living by giving the living a connection to the deceased that can be accessed anywhere." For Maciel et al. [19], "In general, QR codes in cemeteries permit the access to digital memorials, where different kinds of data about the deceased (photos, videos, textual information etc.) can be found". These authors analyzed users' perceptions of digital memorials linked to graves via QR Code technology in a cemetery space. One of the problems evidenced by their study was the lack of information in deceased users' profiles. Because data are not collaboratively inserted, depending on specific stakeholders to be available (e.g., the family, or the company that manages the software), the lack of information is commonly noticed. Additionally, the information architecture impacted negatively on navigability and accessibility on mobile devices—usability and/or communicability tests might help identifying and fixing such kind of problems. Additionally, the possibility of integrating these systems with other social tools could add value to memorials, promoting their adoption and usage.

Whereas the aforementioned studies analyze different general issues about digital memorials, our literature review found only a few studies presenting initial guidelines, scaffolds or recommendations for the design of these applications [4, 17]. Publications of that nature would be vital to lead designers to more satisfactory projects of this type of application, since it is necessary to consider issues such as users' beliefs and the different representations of death [20] espoused by different social groups.

In the following section, the research methodology of the present study is explained. Next, we show the recommendations developed and the prototypes created for the discussion of these recommendations.

3   Methodology

Firstly, a literature review was carried out on topics such as interaction with posthumous data [21, 22], beliefs and taboos related to death [10, 11, 20, 22–24], digital memorial pages on Facebook [5, 6, 13, 25] and specific environments for digital memorials [1, 2].

Next, we searched the Brazilian social web for digital memorials. The following platforms were found: iHeaven [26], Saudade Eterna [27], and Memorial Digital [28]. Due to technical problems in the latter, we registered in the first two platforms, and explored them to understand their basic operational procedures.

Then, two studies were carried out on iHeaven and Saudade Eterna. The first study consisted of an investigation of both systems in the light of social web elements [21, 29]. By means of Ethnography [30], we were able to collect data from the software and perform a qualitative analysis of the functional aspects proposed by Maciel [21], Maciel, Roque and Garcia [31], Smith [29].

The second study, in the iHeaven platform, consisted of interaction tests with users faced with digital memorials for the first time. The interaction tests aimed to understand how users feel when interacting with this type of application. 29 participants, from 18 to 30 years old, did the test. The tests were individually answered and were composed of two stages: first, a list of activities that the users should perform within the software; then, a questionnaire to be answered after the interaction with the digital memorials.

From the researchers' observations during the tests and users' replies to the questionnaires, it was possible to better understand how they feel when interacting with this type of application. Partial results of these studies are available in Lopes, Maciel and Pereira [3], Lopes et al. [4, 5].

As a final step, a semiotic inspection [32] of the communicative cultural perspectives in death-related interactive systems was carried out. Super Lachaise, an open-source application that supports visits to the French cemetery of Père-Lachaise and is available for download at Apple Store, was explored. Then, as a triangulation step of the research, the results were compared to those of a previous study on a Brazilian digital memorial – Memoriall [34] – a system connected to QR-Code tags attached to tombstones located at the Consolação Cemetery (São Paulo, Brazil) [19]. The main contributions of the paper are available in Leitão, Pereira and Maciel [33]) and aim at helping designers of death-related systems: a. define the interface mediation between users and contents from a foreign culture; and b. organize and express these contents.

From the investigation of death-related interactive systems and the data obtained through the qualitative analysis in the light of social web elements, together with the results obtained in the investigative tests, practical recommendations for the design of digital memorials were created, as presented in the next section. Such recommendations were prototyped using the software Balsamiq Mockups. These recommendations and the prototypes might help software engineers, system developers and HCI designers develop digital memorials with a view to technical and cultural aspects inherent to posthumous interaction.

4   Recommendations for the Design of Digital Memorials in the Social Web

This section presents recommendations for the design of digital memorials [5]. Designers should try to follow them with a view to: meeting users' expectations regarding this kind of social software; ensuring that all types of users will have a satisfactory interaction with the system; preserving the deceased user's reputation; and promoting awareness of the cultural diversity of death-related domain.

4.1   Modeling Social Networks Elements [6, 13, 17, 21, 29, 31, 33]

This section goes over the elements that characterize social networks, suggesting techniques to implement them in the realm of digital memorials.

- Identity: There must be a remarkable distinction between living users' profiles and digital memorials. In the case of a social network that deals with data of deceased users, differentiating the identities of the living and the dead is highly advisable for the sake of interaction. It is also important to considerer multiples identities of deceased users (e.g. names and nicknames used in professional and/or informal settings).

- Content: In a digital memorial, designers must decide how to balance data about the life of death users, information about their death and the space for expression of mourning. This balance generates different impacts on users' interaction, such as the more intense emotional effects involved in reading users' statements of grief when compared to those generated by reading the biography of the deceased.
- Relationships: In a social network involving profiles for living users and memorials, there must be relationships among users, among users and memorials, and among memorials. There can also be relationships among users, physical and digital memorials (e.g. QR code technologies tagged on tombs of cemeteries). Such modeling opens up a range of possibilities, such as the creation of tools that generate family trees from these relationships data, or the creation of digital tools to mediate users' physical or virtual experiences and interaction on physical memorials
- Chat: In purely scientific terms, dialogue can occur only among the living, so a chat tool only makes sense for conversations between living users' profiles. However, a functionality to privately send messages to a memorial can be implemented, considering that this one-way communication can have symbolic and sentimental value for some people.
- Groups: Digital memorials can be considered forms of grouping users who had some relationship with the deceased. Therefore, the modeling of digital memorials should be thought of as in "communities of interest". Users can also be interested in creating specific groups, such as members of a family, friends of a deceased user etc.
- Privacy Levels and Permissions: There must be a design project of users' and groups' permissions with a view to: generating content about the deceased, collaborating on the edition of the profile, posting data, files, statements, editing privacy of data, messages and statements, etc. Different or equal levels of privacy and of permissions can be implemented.
- Reputation: There must be ways to increase the reputation of a digital memorial through messages on its "wall" (i.e. a virtual space where messages can be posted and seen by other users), by adding pictures and videos of the deceased, or by adding events to its timeline. According to Brubaker et al. [6], such forms of tributes help preserve the post-mortem identity of the deceased. Besides, Lopes et al. [4] state that users value the possibility to increase a memorial's reputation.
- Recommendation: A social network of digital memorials should recommend to its users not only the profiles of other users they might be friends with, but also memorials they might want to connect with or pay homage to.
- Presence: This element should only be modeled for living users, as digital memorials cannot have an "online" status.
- Sharing: In this kind of social network, different elements can be shared, such as pictures and videos of the deceased, messages published on the wall of a memorial, or even a whole memorial itself. In addition to that, users should be able to share, in

other social networks, the interactions they participated in on the digital memorials network. Such sharing can be explicit, through network sharing buttons, or implicit, by exporting activities into other networks (but without open notification that data have been exported from one network to another).

- Volition: In a social network for digital memorials, the system should model volition, ensuring that, after the death of an account owner, his/her desires are fulfilled regarding the destination of his/her data and the management of his/her digital memorials. As suggested by Maciel [21], designing solutions for that problem is essential, and there are several options for dealing with posthumous data.

4.2 Ensuring the Honoring of the Deceased [4–6, 33]

This section draws attention to some precautions to take during the design process aiming to ensure the honoring of deceased users.

- Digital memorials should have a wall: in the interaction tests, we noticed that many users think that writing a message is the most appropriate way to pay tribute to the deceased. In the tests, several users were uneasy when interacting with other less conventional forms of homage.
- Consider content curation or moderation: although collaboration is a key factor on social networks, deceased's data are sensitive. Public exposure of personal information and inappropriate statements or photos posted on the interface are some of the problems that may threaten the honoring of the deceased. Defining different users' roles in the network and ensuring a curation process (even a collaborative one) can minimize negative effects.
- Be cautious when using buttons: in this type of social network, the keyword for a button that performs a direct interaction with a digital memorial should be chosen carefully. Users can find it weird to "like" a memorial (or any other frivolous manifestation of appreciation). Some also find it disrespectful to click on buttons to perform religious manifestations, such as to "pray" for the memorial.
- Allow the sharing of tributes in the social network or in other networks: users feel like publicizing that they have paid homage to a digital memorial, either by sharing this piece of information with their friends in the digital memorials social network, or in other social networks. If the system has been designed as a social network, this recommendation is related to the abovementioned possibility of "sharing".
- Design with users: designers should seek to understand users' expectations for the application, so that the system is responsive and sensitive to users' values.

4.3 Promoting Awareness of the Cultural Diversity of Death-Related Domain [4, 5, 20, 33]

This section stresses the central role of culture on death-related interactive systems, such as digital memorials.

- Bring culture into the design since the beginning of the process: as death, its representations, practices and rituals are variable and strongly dependent on culture, designers must consider digital memorials as culture-sensitive systems. Designers must previously reflect on which cultural variables they will model and how they will do that. Language is a key variable; religious symbols, funeral and burial rituals, and communicative condolence protocols are other relevant cultural variables in digital memorials.

- Design for diversity: in this type of application, designers should consider that users have very different profiles [2, 35] and different conceptions of death [20]. It is also important to avoid that designers' beliefs and taboos on death limit the solutions for the system (although beliefs always mediate our perceptions and influence our solutions). The customization of the system by users is highly recommended.

- Explore possibilities, and, then, make choices: there are many possibilities to represent, express and communicate cultural content about death to users. So, there are also many different ways to engage users in multicultural experiences of dealing with death and mourning. However, there are limits to explore diversity. Only a few cultural perspectives can be anticipated and communicated within the interface. Sometimes, less is more. The risk of trying to embrace every cultural factor and perspective might lead to a system that fits no one. Designers should make intentional choices about how to deal with cultural dimension.

- Communicate cultural perspective to users: since a system cannot be culturally comprehensive, it is important to make users aware of the cultural nature of the domain and of the cultural contexts available in the interactive system. Communicate through the interface what cultural perspective is therein adopted [36]. By doing so, designers can give users the cultural context they need for social interaction. For instance, a digital memorial can be available in many languages and can provide a high level of customization (e.g. different religious icons), aiming at cultural diversity. In this case, users can choose their own cultural context among many possibilities anticipated on the interface. On the other hand, a digital memorial could also express only a specific cultural perspective (a Buddhist digital memorial, for example), with cultural markers expressing how a specific social group represents death, with limited customization options. In this case, information about the cultural perspective adopted could help users to understand another culture, providing cultural context for the social interaction. In both cases users should be aware of cultural diversity.

- Avoid vocabulary limited to a specific religion: In a system aimed at people with the most diverse religious affiliations (or even no religion at all), using vocabulary limited to specific religions may hinder the interaction. The noun "heaven", for example, is not associated to post-mortem in many religions. If a limited vocabulary is used, users should be aware of the reasons behind these limits.

- Allow users to customize the interface with icons of their religion: according to Maciel and Pereira [20], the symbols that represent death and death-related phenomena vary across different religions and creeds. For example, while Catholic users tend to ascribe symbolic meaning to tombs, Protestant users tend to assign higher significance to coffins, as analyzed by these authors. On the other hand, a Protestant user may feel like clicking a button to "pray" for a memorial, a form of interaction that maybe would not make sense for an atheist. Systems must be designed to allow users to change the symbols of the interface, especially when they relate to religious beliefs.

5 Prototyping

This section presents the prototypes made based on the aforementioned practical recommendations for the design of digital memorials. These prototypes can help human-computer interaction designers and software designers achieve a clearer vision of solutions for this type of application. Notice that the prototypes herein presented do not cover all the functionalities proposed in the recommendations.

Firstly, designers must reflect on the top-level culture-sensitive design strategy, considering, among others: (i) users' profiles, needs and cultural backgrounds; and (ii) the cultural perspective to be adopted (the aimed scope of cultural diversity and the cultural variables involved) [17, 33]. In the prototypes presented, English is the language adopted, aiming to embrace a more cultural diversity of users, as it is more commonly used in cross-cultural social network communication. 'Places' are key cultural variables to provide contextual information about users: place of birth, places of death and burial, places visited, etc. On the other hand, 'religion' is not explicitly elicited as a variable. These options are not the only design choice, although they impact the ways users will be engaged in culture-sensitive interaction.

After the definition of the cultural perspective, systems functionalities can be prototyped. Figure 2 illustrates some of the prototype functions, so as to help the reader understand the figures that are next presented.

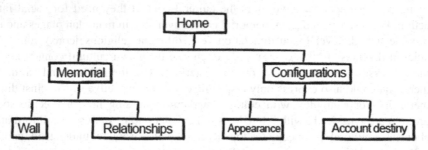

Fig. 2. A script of the prototype's visualization.

5.1 Products Generated

The first prototype generated was the user's "Home" page, shown in Fig. 3. The interface consists of a section composed of "reminders" of important dates, such as friends' birthdays or deceased users' death anniversaries (memorial) (1); then, there are the updates and news about friends' interactions with other users and memorials (2). At the end of the page, there are suggestions of digital memorials (3) and friends (4) to add, based on memorials and friends in common. The question mark icons (5) refer to help tabs, supposed to assist the user in case of questions about the tools. Item (6) concerns the area of system settings.

This interface also shows applications of practical recommendations presented in the previous section. The social networking element "recommendation" can be identified in (3) and (4), where the user receives recommendations from the system about

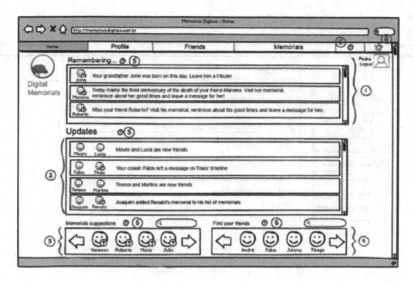

Fig. 3. The "Home" interface

memorials and profiles with which their friends have interacted. In addition to that, the element "sharing" and the recommendation "Allow the sharing of tributes in the social network or in other networks" are represented in (2), where the system allows the user to share public interactions he/she had with digital memorials or with other users.

Figure 4 presents the interface of a memorial that shows basic information about the deceased (1), such as data about places and dates of birth and death. A memorial has also general information about the deceased (2), such as places where he/she worked/studied, and hobbies, similar to a user's profile in other social networks. Information in (1) and (2) was considered by the designers as important cultural variables to mediate cross-cultural interactions. Those pieces of information are inserted by the user who created it, or by the honored whom the memorial pays homage to, in case he/she is still alive (this particular situation will be analyzed in the paper later). Besides, a memorial may contain various pieces of data about the deceased, such as his/her timeline, his/her relationships, photos, videos, among others, listed from (4) to (10).

In accordance with the aforementioned recommendations, the element "identity" plays an essential role in distinguishing digital memorials from ordinary users. In our prototype, all digital memorials have the symbol of a cross (3) in the lower right corner of the profile photo, which tells them apart from ordinary users. Notice that the option of a cross as a symbol is more frequently used to express death in many Christian religions [17]. However, in a more detailed prototype where "Religion" could be considered as a cultural variable, other symbols should be offered as customized options to express death.

The features (5), (7) and (8) should also be implemented in the memorial to ensure the social network element "reputation", as detailed in the previous section. The "timeline" (5) should show great events in the deceased user's life, while "pictures"

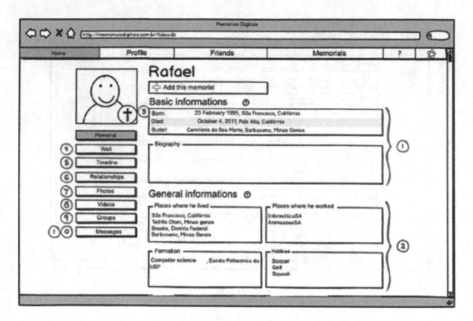

Fig. 4. The "Memorial" interface

(7) and "videos" (8) would be areas where multimedia files could be found in the memorial. To implement the social network element "groups", there must be a space where users connected to the memorial can interact among themselves; in our prototype, we called this area a "circle of grief" (9). Refined prototyped versions should include permission and privacy administration functionalities in this area.

The implementation of a tool to send private messages to the memorial is also desirable, because, as seen in the recommendations section, users may want to send private messages to memorials, in a one-way chat (10). Elements (4) and (6) of this interface will be discussed in the analysis of the next prototype, since they can be found in both interfaces.

The next prototype to be created was the "wall" (Fig. 5), a space where users can write public tributes to the memorial, or publish photos, videos and links on it. This interface consists of the site where users can add their tributes (1) and the space where they can view the interactions performed by other users (2). The wall can be interpreted as a tool where users can increase the reputation of the memorial, by sharing stories, memories, or multimedia files. Refined prototyped versions could consider if the administrator should also moderate the wall content. In addition to that, this prototype follows the practical recommendations "Digital memorials must have a wall" and "Allow the sharing of tributes in the social network or in other networks". We can see in (3) and (4) the sharing options in the digital memorials network and in other networks.

The prototype in Fig. 6 shows an interface for the relationships of a digital memorial: family relationships (1), and the "friends of the memorial" (2), i.e. people who added that memorial to their own list of memorials. This interface follows the

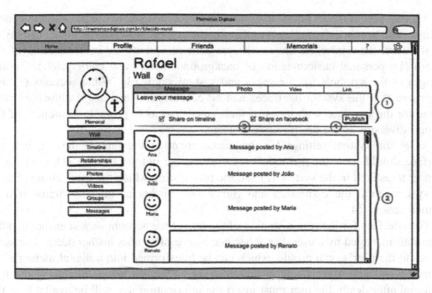

Fig. 5. The "Wall" interface

recommendations proposed for the design of the element "relationship" in social networks of this type, including a genealogical tree for the deceased user's family. In this tree, the dead should also be identified with a "cross" and, in case they were also users of this social network, they should be linked to the tree. It is important to remember that the administrator of a memorial inserts data about some relatives in the tree, but the system can also suggest other relatives based on the connections between users' profiles. The relatives can also be displayed in a list, as in (3).

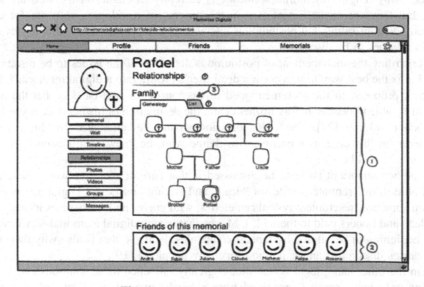

Fig. 6. The "Relationships" interface

Another part of the recommendations, not prototyped yet, has to do with the system settings. The first interface related to them is the configuration of the visual display of the software. This interface shows the pre-defined options for customization of the system (1); personal customization of background images and color palette (2); and changes in the symbols for messages and system status (3). While sections (1) and (2) ensure that the system interfaces can be customized, section (3) allows users to customize the interface with icons of their creeds, so as to promote awareness of the cultural diversity of the death-related domain.

As to the system settings for the management of the fate of the account, the interface should show the memorials the user has the right to manage (1), the heirs to the user registered in the system (2) and the time during which the user can stay out of the system, until the ownership and rights over his/her account are transferred to another person (3).

The interface for the administration of the fate of the account should ensure that the memorials managed by a user do not become inaccessible after his/her death. The same applies to the user's own profile, which can be transformed into a digital memorial (if the user wants to). After stating his/her wish for having his/her profile changed into a memorial after death, the user must insert the information that will be available in the future memorial.

In future steps of the research, the prototypes presented above will be tested, in order to assess usability and communicability and verify whether such design is appropriate.

6 Final Considerations

Digital memorials provide users with new forms of mourning and honoring those who passed away. Digital memorial applications currently available on the web are still new, but they are an important step in the process of developing software for this domain, demonstrating that posthumous interactions and postmortem digital legacy are relevant issues to be discussed.

Regarding the management of posthumous data, one of the issues to be discussed is: what is the best way to transform a dead user's profile into a digital memorial? The solution proposed in the aforementioned discussion of the interfaces is that the user should be able to decide, before his/her death, the destination of his/her data, according to his/her volition [21]. Then, this decision should be automated by the system. However, in this case it is necessary to define who the "new" administrator of this memorial would be.

Another important issue to be discussed is that current social networks have not been able to differentiate profiles of "dead" and "living" users yet. Digital memorials should somehow resemble physical cemeteries, with graves and tombstones identifying the dead and honors paid to them [33]. Maybe that is why digital memorial services are now beginning to be offered by funeral companies. Perhaps, that is also why their use still causes discomfort and is a taboo for many people [4, 19].

On the other hand, legal issues should greatly influence these solutions and some actions only make sense if proposed from a legal perspective. "Terms of use" and "privacy policies" of applications are usually intended to protect users' data, but they must be carefully adapted in terms of cultural diversity and legal systems to meet users' needs in this domain. Otherwise, terms of use and privacy policies are no more than mere formalities.

In the case of digital memorials created by users (rather than automatically created by the system after a user's death), the information present in the memorial is entirely inserted by its administrator. It is not possible to verify if the information is true, so that digital memorials become hostages of a single source of data. A possible solution would be if the deceased user's friends and family could make suggestions or changes in the data of the memorial, in a sort of collective administration. To provide transparency to this administration, the page should show information like: "Administered by [name1] [name2] … [nameN]".

Moreover, how could such applications work with specific "groups" of users and not only with individual profiles? For example, how could we have a specific "sub-memorial" for each deceased person within a collective memorial (common for people who died in wars and in natural catastrophes)?

Other tools could be created for that kind of application, such as a map in the memorial indicating where the deceased user had resided, worked, studied or been buried. In the field of digital memorials, various applications can be created, meeting users' expectations to repute the image of the deceased and undergo digital mourning.

In this research, we have only studied some ideal characteristics for digital memorials, especially aiming at practical issues in the design of these applications. However, many social networks [37] allow users to change profiles into memorials. These solutions are limited, but interesting, as discussed by Campos et al. [13].

Investigating how to deal with death and designing multidisciplinary solutions to digital legacy systems in the light of technical, cultural, legal, ethical, and affective principles is comprehensive and challenging. According to Maciel and Pereira [19] highlight some challenging research questions for this area that will enable us to draw up guidelines to conceive systems that consider the fate of digital legacy embedded in software and to inform normative institutions on the discussion of those issues. Finally, this is also an opportunity for the software industry to obtain important inputs to develop systems that deal with the mortality of human beings.

References

1. Braman, J., Dudley, A., Vincenti, G.: Death, social networks and virtual worlds: a look into the digital afterlife. In: Proceedings of the SERA 2011, pp. 186–192. IEEE Computer Society, Washington (2011)
2. Riechers, A.: The persistence of memory online: digital memorials, fantasy, and grief as entertainment. In: Maciel, C., Pereira, V. (eds.) Digital Legacy and Interaction, 1st edn, pp. 49–61. Springer, Cham (2013). https://doi.org/10.1007/978-3-319-01631-3_3
3. Lopes, A.D., Maciel, C., Pereira, V.C.: Memoriais digitais na web social sob a perspectiva dos usuários. In: Proceedings of the IHC 2013, pp. 323–324. Brazilian Computer Society, Porto Alegre (2013)

4. Lopes, A.D., Maciel, C., Pereira, V.C.: Virtual homage to the dead: an analysis of digital memorials in the social web. In: Meiselwitz, G. (ed.) SCSM 2014. LNCS, vol. 8531, pp. 67–78. Springer, Cham (2014). https://doi.org/10.1007/978-3-319-07632-4_7

5. Lopes, A.D., Maciel, C., Pereira, V.C.: Recomendações para o design de memórias digitais na web social. In: Proceedings of the 13th Brazilian Symposium on Human Factors in Computing Systems, pp. 275–284. Sociedade Brasileira de Computação, Foz do Iguaçu (2014)

6. Brubaker, J.R., Hayes, G.R., Dourish, J.P.: Beyond the grave: Facebook as a site for the expansion of death and mourning. Inf. Soc. 29(3), 152–163 (2013)

7. Baranauskas, M.C.C., de Souza, C.S., Pereira, R.: I GranDIHC-BR Grand Research Challenges in Human-Computer Interaction in Brazil. Human-Computer Interaction Special Committee (CEIHC) of the Brazilian Computer Society (SBC), Porto Alegre/BR (2015). ISBN 9788576692966

8. Boscarioli, C., Araujo, R.M., Maciel, R.S.P.: I GranDSI-BR – Grand Research Challenges in Information Systems in Brazil 2016–2026. Special Committee on Information Systems (CE-SI). Brazilian Computer Society (SBC), Porto Alegre/BR (2017). ISBN 978-85-7669-384-0

9. American Heritage Dictionary of the English Language. https://www.ahdictionary.com/word/search.html?q=memorial. Accessed 10 Feb 2019

10. Mims, C.: When We Die: The Science, Culture, and Rituals of Death. St. Martin's Press, New York (1998)

11. Hallam, E., Hockey, J.: Death, Memory, and Material Culture. Oxford, New York (2001)

12. Find a Grave. http://www.findagrave.com. Accessed 15 Dec 2018

13. Campos, K.L., Justi, T., Maciel, C., Pereira, V.C.: Digital memorials: a proposal for data management beyond life. In: XVI Brazilian Symposium on Human Factors in Computational Systems (IHC 2017), Joinville, SC, pp. 218–227. SBC, Porto Alegre (2017)

14. Virtual Memorials. http://www.virtual-memorials.com. Accessed 08 Jan 2019

15. Kern, R., Abbe, E.F., Gil-Egui, G.: R.I.P.: Remain in perpetuity. Facebook memorial pages. Telemat. Inf. 30(1), 2–10 (2013)

16. Brubaker, J.R., Vertesi, J.: Death and the social network. In: CHI 2010 Workshop on HCI at the End of Life: Understanding Death, Dying, and the Digital. Atlanta, GA/USA (2010)

17. Pereira, V.C., Maciel, C., Leitão, C.F.: The design of digital memorials: scaffolds for multicultural communication based on a semiotic analysis of tombs. In: Proceedings of the 15th Brazilian Symposium on Human Factors in Computing Systems (IHC 2016). Brazilian Computer Society, Porto Alegre (2016)

18. Cann, C.K.: Tombstone technology: deathscapes in Asia, the U.K. and the U.S. In: Maciel, C., Pereira, V. (eds.) Digital Legacy and Interaction, pp. 101–113. Springer, Cham (2013). https://doi.org/10.1007/978-3-319-01631-3_6

19. Maciel, C., Pereira, V.C., Leitão, C., Pereira, R., Viterbo, J.: Interacting with digital memorials in a cemetery: insights from an immersive practice. In: Proceedings of Federated Conference on Computer Science and Information Systems (FedCSIS), pp. 1251–1260 (2017)

20. Maciel, C., Pereira, V.C.: Social network users' religiosity and the design of post mortem aspects. In: Kotzé, P., Marsden, G., Lindgaard, G., Wesson, J., Winckler, M. (eds.) INTERACT 2013. LNCS, vol. 8119, pp. 640–657. Springer, Heidelberg (2013). https://doi.org/10.1007/978-3-642-40477-1_43

21. Maciel, C.: Issues of the social web interaction project faced with afterlife digital legacy. In: Proceedings of the IHC+CLIHC 2011, pp. 3–12. ACM Press (2011)

22. Maciel, C., Pereira, V.C.: Digital Legacy and Interaction: Post-Mortem Issues, 1st edn. Springer, Heidelberg (2013). https://doi.org/10.1007/978-3-319-01631-3

23. Becker, S.H., Knudson, R.M.: Visions of the dead: imagination and mourning. Death Stud. **27**, 691–716 (2003)
24. Massimi, M., Baecker, R.M.: Dealing with death in design: developing systems for the bereaved. In: Proceedings of the CHI 2011, pp. 1001–1010. ACM Press, New York (2011)
25. Facebook Special Request for Deceased Person's Account. https://www.facebook.com/help/contact/228813257197480. Accessed 15 Dec 2018
26. Iheaven. http://www.iheaven.me. Accessed 15 Dec 2018
27. Saudade Eterna. http://www.saudadeeterna.com.br. Accessed 05 Feb 2019
28. Memorial Digital. http://www.memorialdigital.com.br. Accessed 22 Nov 2018
29. Smith, G.: Social software building blocks. http://nform.com/blog/2007/04/social-software-building-blocks/. Accessed 16 Nov 2018
30. Pressman, S.R., Lowe, D.: Engenharia Web, 1st edn. Livros Técnicos e Científicos (2009)
31. Maciel, C., Roque, L., Garcia, A.C.B.: Interaction and communication resources in collaborative e-democratic environments: the democratic citizenship community. Inf. Polity **15**, 73–88 (2010)
32. de Souza, C.S., Leitão, C.F.: Semiotic Engineering Methods for Scientific Research in HCI. Morgan Claypool (2009)
33. Leitão, C.F., Maciel, C., Pereira, V.C.: Exploring the communication of cultural perspectives in death-related interactive systems. In: Proceedings of the 16th Brazilian Symposium on Human Factors in Computing Systems, pp. 247–256. SBC, Porto Alegre (2017)
34. Memoriall. http://Memoriall.com.br/. Accessed 22 Nov 2018
35. Massimi, M., Baecker, R.R.: A death in the family: opportunities for designing technologies for the bereaved. In: Proceedings of the CHI 2010, pp. 1821–1830 (2010)
36. Salgado, L.C.C., Leitão, C.F., de Souza, C.S.: A Journey Through Cultures: Metaphors for Guiding the Design of Cross-Cultural Interactive Systems. Springer, London (2012). https://doi.org/10.1007/978-1-4471-4114-3
37. Trocha, G., Maciel, C., de Souza, P.C., Arruda, N.A.: Análise dos termos de uso e políticas de privacidade de redes sociais quanto ao tratamento da morte dos usuários, In: VII Workshop on Aspects of Human-Computer Interaction in the Social Web (WAIHCWS 2017), Joinville, SC, pp. 82–93 (2017)

How "Friendly" Integrated Development Environments Are?

Jenny Morales[1,3](✉) ⓘ, Federico Botella[2] ⓘ, Cristian Rusu[3] ⓘ,
and Daniela Quiñones[3] ⓘ

[1] Facultad de Ingeniería, Universidad Autónoma de Chile, Temuco, Chile
jmoralesb@uautonoma.cl
[2] Universidad Miguel Hernández de Elche, Elche, Spain
federico@umh.es
[3] Pontificia Universidad Católica de Valparaíso, Valparaíso, Chile
{cristian.rusu,daniela.quinones}@pucv.cl,
jenny.morales.b@mail.pucv.cl

Abstract. Programmers and software developers are using different Integrated Development Environments (IDEs) to perform their daily work. IDEs are often complex applications, not friendly for novice programmers, with a learning process of several weeks and with usability and satisfaction of use not always as good as expected. The Programmer eXperience (PX) is a particular case of User eXperience (UX), based on the use of the IDEs and other artifacts. We have found studies about the programmer's behavior and work, and also articles addressed the usability and new tools proposals for IDEs. In this work, we conducted a survey to evaluate the usability of several IDEs. The survey was based on the System Usability Scale (SUS), which we adapted for the purpose of our research. We focus the study on popular IDEs such as Dev-C++, Eclipse and NetBeans. The survey was conducted in two Chilean universities and one Spanish university, with students enrolled in two undergraduate programs in Informatics Engineering. The results obtained show that the IDEs evaluated have several issues related to the usability perceived by our participants. An interview was conducted with six experienced programmers that are working in different programming environments, in order to consult them on what aspects they would like to improve the IDEs. Their comments indicate that IDEs should incorporate connection with other programmers, and also, they claim for more intuitive interfaces and understandable error messages.

Keywords: Usability · User eXperience · Programmer eXperience · Integrated Development Environment · Survey · Interview

1 Introduction

The programming environment plays a very important role in the software development. Learning to program is a difficult process that requires several months or years. Students and practitioners interact with the different interfaces that provide the different programming environments or languages. Most of programming environment

G. Meiselwitz (Ed.): HCII 2019, LNCS 11578, pp. 80–91, 2019.
https://doi.org/10.1007/978-3-030-21902-4_7

interfaces do not accomplish with the basic principles of usability and/or accessibility, so the result is an environment difficult to learn and difficult to handle for users.

In this work, we present a study of the usability perceived by user of programming environments centered in three of them: Dev-C++, Eclipse and NetBeans. We selected these Integrated Development Environments (IDEs) because they are used in the Informatics Engineering program of the three universities where we conducted this study: Universidad Autónoma de Chile, Pontificia Universidad Católica de Valparaíso (Chile), and Universidad Miguel Hernández de Elche (Spain). We conducted a survey to students of these three universities and we performed several interviews to professionals working in different computer programing Chilean enterprises.

The results show in general low usability in the IDEs. Eclipse is the IDE that obtained the best score. Both NetBeans and Dev-C++ are considered as IDEs with a low degree of usability, obtaining the lowest score Dev-C++. The interviews provide interesting results on the preference of the participants and aspects to improve in the IDEs.

This work is organized as follows: in Sect. 2 we describe the background, in Sect. 3 we introduce the methodology used, in Sect. 4 results obtained are presented, and finally, Sect. 5 contains conclusions and future work.

2   Background

The work carried out by a programmer are challenging and allows the programmer to interact with various elements such as programming environments and other development artifacts. Usability is one of the important aspects of the programmer work. However, usability aspects are not enough, and some models of User eXperience explain more complete aspects that influence in the programmer experience. Some of these aspects can be the interaction of the programmer with systems, languages and programming environments to reach a more pleasant programming experience.

2.1   Usability

Usability is defined by the International Organization for Standardization (ISO) 9241-11 of 2018 as: "Extent to which a system, product or service can be used by specified users to achieve specified goals with effectiveness, efficiency and satisfaction in a specified context of use" [1]. Usability has specific attributes that allow its assessment, such as: Learnability, facility to be learned and very important to reach for novice users; Efficiency, related to the speed in which the user can reach their objectives; Memorability, related to the ability of users not frequent to remember how the system is used; Errors, related to the number of errors that a user commits when performing a task; and Subjective Satisfaction, a subjective attribute that measures the subjective impression that the user has of the system [2].

2.2   User eXperience

Nowadays the User eXperience (UX) has become the concept very important for the systems, products or services. ISO 9241-210 of 2010 defines the UX as: "person's perceptions and responses resulting from the use and/or anticipated use of a product, system or service" [3]. There are several models that explain the user experience, one of them is Honeycomb, proposed by Morville [4]. This model considers that UX has seven aspects that go beyond of the usability. In this work, we take this model as a reference for systems such as IDEs. The aspects defined in Honeycomb model are:

- Valuable, the system must deliver value and contribute to the customer satisfaction.
- Usable, the system should be simple and easy to use. The usability is necessary but is not sufficient.
- Useful, the system or product must be useful and satisfy a need, otherwise there is no justification for the product.
- Desirable, the visual aesthetics of the product or system must be attractive and easy to interpret.
- Findable, the information should be easy to find and easy to navigate. The users can find what they need.
- Accessible, the system should be designed so that even users with disabilities can have the same user experience as others.
- Credible, the company and its products or services need to be reliable.

2.3 Programmer eXperience

Programmers use IDEs and several development artifacts, so UX concept may be particularized as Programmer eXperience (PX). Due to the complexity of the programmers' tasks, and the fact that they interact with several artifacts of diverse nature, we may consider programmers as customers. The Customer eXperience (CX) concept is therefore relevant in the software development process.

In the review of articles that address the programmer's experience, researches were found on the benefits of programming languages and graphic environments. These articles show that readability of the codes can be improved, presenting advantages over other that are textual and positively impacting the development of software [5, 6]. Development environments that implement graphic aspects can improve and facilitate various tasks of the programmer, such as the finding information in programming environments during software maintenance [7] and the monitoring and understanding of the code [8].

Software maintenance is an arduous task. Programmers requires to read and to analyze programmed codes. We found several works related to software maintenance: (1) how facilitate the reading of codes [9]; (2) how instructions can be more predictable by the reader [10]; (3) and how codes can be implemented in a more readable way [11, 12].

Two interesting studies about programmers were found. The first one evaluates whether the programmer's experience influences the quality of the code he writes, obtaining as a result that years of experience are not a good predictor of programmer performance. A good predictor could be the academic background and the specialization [13]. The second study address on the productivity of the programmer, specifying new metrics to measure productivity for both for lonely programmers and programmers in pairs, these metrics are applicable to the entire life cycle of development [14].

2.4   Integrated Development Environments

IDE usually contains a source code editor, a debugger, automatic building tools, and some of them also have IntelliSense, a tool that helps programmers to fill automatically the code. One IDE can have a compiler, an interpreter or both. Examples of the most used IDEs are Eclipse, NetBeans and Visual Studio. It is worth to mention that an IDE can usually support several programming languages and also has a graphical interaction interface in which the tools available are displayed.

Several articles reviewed about IDEs showed the interest to improve the interaction of the programmer with the IDEs and to facilitate the work of the programmer. We identify: (1) the incorporation of complements to facilitate editing and changes in the codes [15, 16]; (2) the incorporation of social aspects and the benefits that brings for programmers [17, 18]; (3) the improvement of specific aspects of debugging that IDEs do not cover today [19]; (4) the incorporation of users that can define usability experiments integrated into the environments [20]; and (5) the implementation of a specific tool for IDE that was also analyzed in order to make programming easier and minimize errors [21].

We found studies about the usability of the programming environments, one of them show the need for a multitouch environment which contributes to ease of use [22]. Other studies explain that overloaded assistive features in environment present difficulties for the programmer [23].

One of the elements that programmers use in their work is Application Programming Interfaces (APIs). Studies on usability of APIs were found in relation to (1) the relevance of documentation about ease of use [24]; the most important element in the API is providing easy communication, which would favor and minimize the errors that can be generated in the development [25]; and (3) the ease of the use and implementation which indicates that their use is not as simple as expected [26].

3   Methodology

This study has two parts: (1) one survey about usability perceived by users of different IDEs based on the System Usability Scale (SUS) and (2) several interviews performed to different professional programmers in order to complement the answers obtained on the survey.

3.1   Survey

We conducted a survey to evaluate the usability of several IDEs. The survey was based on the SUS, which we adapted for the purpose of our research. SUS is a general tool developed by Brooke [27], (arguably) applicable to any type of interactive system. SUS includes 10 questions that allows to obtain a general measure of usability perceived by users that could cover several aspects of usability like effectiveness, efficiency and satisfaction. Each item of SUS consists of 5-point Likert Scale: 5 means "strongly agree" whereas 1 means "strongly disagree". In all odd items, the result will be obtained by subtracting 1 from the participant's response. The result of the even items will be obtained by subtracting to 5 the answer of the participant. So, the scale for each item is from 0 to 4. The original total score of the survey is in the range [0–40] that will be converted to [0–100] by multiplying by 2.5 each item score. One system is considered "usable" when scores above 68. Table 1 shows the adapted survey applied in our study.

Table 1. Survey applied in our study.

No	Questions
Q1	I think I would like to use this IDE frequently
Q2	I found the IDE unnecessarily complex
Q3	I thought the IDE was easy to use
Q4	I think I would need the support of a technical person to be able to use this IDE
Q5	I found that the various functions in this IDE were well integrated
Q6	I thought there was too much inconsistency in this IDE
Q7	I would imagine that most people would learn to use this IDE very quickly
Q8	I found the IDE very cumbersome to use
Q9	I felt very confident using the IDE
Q10	I needed to learn many things before I could work with this IDE

Among the most used programming languages are C/C++ and Java [28]. We focus the study on popular IDEs that support these languages: Dev-C++, Eclipse and NetBeans.

The survey was carried out in two universities in Chile: Universidad Autónoma de Chile and Pontificia Universidad Católica de Valparaíso, and one university in Spain, Universidad Miguel Hernández de Elche. Participants were selected from students enrolled in undergraduate programs in Informatics Engineering.

The study involved 140 participants and was conducted from June to October 2018 in Chile and in January 2019 in Spain. Students participated in the survey voluntarily. In both countries, students from 1st year were asked to conduct the survey about Dev-C ++ IDE. Since C is the initial language in the teaching of programming in the participating universities of the study. Other students with more experience in Chile from 2nd to 5th year answer a randomly about NetBeans, Eclipse and Dev-C++. In the case of Spain, students of the 2nd year were asked to fill the survey to evaluate Eclipse IDE, as they are working with Java in their second year. Moreover, students of 4th year were asked to fill both Dev-C++ IDE and Eclipse IDE as they have worked with both IDEs and have experience with more IDEs when they arrive at their last degree year; we split the group in two parts to get responses to both surveys.

The survey was conducted in the classrooms of the different universities, in students' usual environment. Mainly we want them to answer about the IDEs that they have usually had the opportunity to work this semester and the previous semesters. The time allotted to answer the survey was 10 min maximum. Generally, the students responded in less time. The data was collected through a printed form in Chile, and a digital form in Spain (we used Google Forms).

3.2   Interviews

The purpose of the interview was to collect relevant information about the opinions of professionals who are users of development environments. The type of interview used was partially structured, in which six open-ended questions were considered, in which there is the possibility of deepening in some of them if necessary. The reason for selecting this type of partially structured interview allows to collect more information than the users and in turn to guide the interview process towards the points of interest.

The interview is composed of two initial questions that characterize the user. The third question is a general question about the environments they have used. The fourth question is focused on the advantages and disadvantages of IDEs. The two last questions are devoted to what they would like to improve in the environments.

The six questions defined in the interview are:

1. What IDE have you used?
2. What functionalities of the IDEs have you used?
3. Referring to the IDEs used Which one do you like best and which one less?
4. You can tell us three favorable things and three unfavorable things of the IDEs that you have used.
5. If you had to recommend an IDE, what would it be and why?
6. What would you like to improve in IDEs?

We contact professional informatics engineering graduates that have experience in software development (experience over 3 years) in Chilean enterprises. The interviewees were all male between 25 and 35 years old. They freely decided to participate in the interview. They were anticipated that the interview has six questions, so it would be short enough. The interviews were conducted in their offices directly and notes were collected in notebooks manually. Although the interview has well-defined questions, it was intended that the interviewee feel comfortable. The interviews last between 10 and 15 min.

4   Results

The analysis of the results of the survey will be carried out by interpreting single items from the SUS proposed by Sauro [29]. Five grades are detailed for SUS, from A to F, being A the highest grade and F the lowest. It also provides a description of scores for each question based on previous studies, which allows establishing whether the scores obtained are related to average scores or good scores. The analysis of the answers of the interviews will be carried out through a qualitative analysis for each question.

4.1   Dev-C++

This IDE was initially developed by Bloodshed Software until 2005 and then by Orwell since 2011. Its latest version available is from 2015. Dev-C++ allows programming in languages C/C++. This environment is used in the first year at all universities that participated in this work [30].

The total number of participants who answer about Dev-C++ in Chile is 35, of which 23 are first-year students. The general score obtained is 53.0, which places it in grade D of SUS, which means that it is very low as expected to be considered usable.

The lowest scores are in questions Q4 and Q10, what shows that students consider it difficult to use and complex to work. The highest scores were obtained in questions Q5 and Q6. The score obtained in Q5 does not reach to be average. In the case of Q6, his score places him in grade A, that is, a good score. This means that students consider Dev-C++ very consistency.

The total student that answered in Spain is 22, 13 of them are students of first year. The score obtained in general is 47.5 which is very low, considering it very unsatisfactory on the part of the students, this score places it in an F grade of SUS. The lowest scores were obtained by Q7 and Q10, which means that students consider that Dev-C++ is difficult to learn and difficult to use. The highest scores were obtained in Q2 and Q3, but only Q2 achieves an average score. In Fig. 1, we can see the results obtained in both countries.

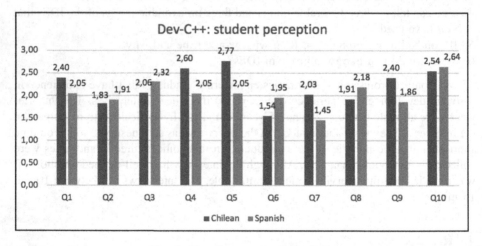

Fig. 1. Dev-C++: results (scale 0–4).

In both results we can see that the perception of students about the IDE is quite negative, especially in the case of Spanish students. Whereas Dev-C++ is complex, difficult to use and to learn. All the above indicates that the satisfaction of the students is very low.

4.2   Eclipse

Eclipse is an open source platform with a worldwide known IDE that allows to work with Java programming language and can be extended to other languages, such as the programming languages C/C++ and Python. Its latest version is from 2018 [31].

Eclipse was evaluated by 36 students in Chile in the 2nd, 4th and 5th years. The result obtained is of 60.9, which places it in grade D, so it has important aspects to improve. The lowest scores were obtained in Q4 and Q10, being perceived by students as difficult to use and difficult to work. Questions Q1 and Q5 obtained the highest scores, but neither of them reached a minimum average score, so they are relevant to highlight as positive aspects perceived by the students.

In total 27 students from Spain belonging to 2nd and 4th year answered the Eclipse survey. The score obtained is 67.8 so the IDE is considered as usable by the students. The lowest scores are in Q4 and Q10, both reach an average score, this means that students consider moderately difficult to use and complex to work. The highest scores were obtained in Q1 and Q6. Only Q6 reaches a good score. So, the students consider that Eclipse is a consistent environment.

The results obtained show that Spanish students perceive that Eclipse is a usable IDE unlike Chilean students. In both cases the lowest scores were obtained in questions Q4 and Q10, with Chilean students evaluating it with the lowest results. In Fig. 2, we can see the results obtained.

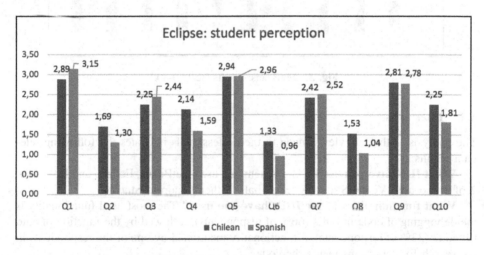

Fig. 2. Eclipse: results (scale 0–4).

4.3 NetBeans

NetBeans is developed by Apache Software Foundation and it is a free multiplatform IDE programmed in Java. Mainly for Java language developments, it can be extended to other languages. Its latest available version is from December 2018 [32].

NetBeans was only evaluated by 20 Chilean students in 3rd year. Spanish students have a transition from Dev-C++ to Eclipse directly, without using NetBeans, as is the case of Chilean students who follow the sequence, Dev-C++, NetBeans, and then Eclipse.

The results show that the total score obtained is 59.6. This result places NetBeans in a D grade, that is, it has aspects to improve to be more usable. The questions that have lower scores are Q4 and Q10, which means that students consider the complex to use and to work. The highest score was obtained in Q5, however it is not enough to obtain an average score, so it could not be considered as a positive aspect in the students' perception. In Fig. 3, we can see the results.

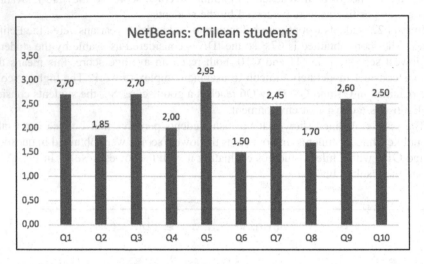

Fig. 3. NetBeans: results (scale 0–4).

4.4   Interviews

The analysis of the interviews made to the professionals indicates the following relevant results:

What IDE have you used? All of them had used NetBeans, Eclipse and Dev-C++. 2 of 3 had used Visual Studio whereas half of them Android Studio.

What functionalities of the IDEs have you used? The most used functionality is the debugging of code in IDEs (66% of respondents), followed by the function of auto fill code (33% of respondents), a functionality mentioned by one of the respondents in the search for definitions inside the code.

Referring to the IDEs used: Which one do you like more and which one less? The IDEs most liked by respondents are NetBeans and Visual Studio, each one with two preferences, followed by Eclipse and Visual Studio with one preference. As for the less preferred, Dev-C++ is mentioned twice, because they consider it is a very basic IDE that is rarely used in the work they do.

Can you can tell us three favorable things and three unfavorable things of the IDEs that you have used? About NetBeans, the interviewees mentioned how fast the speed to create projects, besides supporting several languages. In the case of Eclipse, ease of use and speed to find errors stand out were the more mentioned favorable aspects. Favorable aspects of Visual Studio like familiarity and ease of use were also mentioned. In case of Android Studio, interviewees mentioned the speed of compilation and debugging. No participant referred to positive aspects of Dev-C++. About unfavorable aspects of Eclipse and NetBeans IDEs, the interviewees (50% of them) stated that they use many resources of the computer which makes them slow in their performance. Others stated that IDEs in general have non-visible functionalities and that error messages are not understandable.

If you had to recommend an IDE, what would it be and why? In this question the interviewees responded in some cases with more than one recommendation. The most recommended IDE by the interviewees was NetBeans, recommended by 50% of them, due to the easiness to create projects and availability of complements. Followed by Visual Studio, recommended twice for its ease of use and documentation. Finally Eclipse, Android Studio and Dev-C++, were recommended only by one interviewee; in the case of Dev-C++ only for the use of programming in C language.

What would you like to improve in IDEs? Although this question is quite broad and general, it seeks to identify the functionalities that the users experienced considered necessary to implement. The answers show that what they would like to improve in the IDEs is access to forums internally, without having to leave the environment to communicate with the other programmers (50% of them considered it). It was also considered important to improve the generation of more documentation and in other languages besides English for beginning programmers (this is because the native language in Chile is Spanish). These answers about the social interaction with forums and the outside had already been found in a recent work of Astromskis et al. where the behavior of the programmers is monitored [33].

5 Conclusions and Future Work

In relation to the surveys conducted, the total number of students surveyed is 140, composed of 91 Chilean students and 49 Spanish students. This is a significant number for this study. As for Dev-C++, students perceive it as a system with low usability; especially Spanish students are more critical about it. Dev-C++ was considered complex, difficult to learn and difficult to use. The previous results were obtained with students from different courses of their degrees. The lowest results of the study were obtained by Dev-C++.

In relation to NetBeans, the results show that it is an IDE with important aspects to improve, being considered by the students as complex and difficult to work. This IDE obtained the average score of the three IDEs.

Clearly, the results of Eclipse were better, obtaining the best perception of usability by students both in Chile and in Spain. Eclipse achieved a score of 67.8 and was considered as an IDE quite usable by the Spanish students. It is also considered that it has aspects to improve such as the difficulty of use and the complexity to work it.

The interviews offered interesting conclusions about the most used aspects of IDEs, such as debugging and auto-filling code functionalities. In addition to the consideration that Dev-C++ is the least used in the work that the interviewees perform. The ease of creating projects appears also as a relevant aspect of NetBeans. As well Eclipse and NetBeans are considered slow IDEs and they require too many resources of the computer. An interesting finding is the need for programmers to connect with others through the programming environment.

As future work, the segmentation of the students and the comparison of the obtained results will be considered. This study could be refined by considering equivalent years of the degree of the participants. In Chile, surveys have been conducted between students of 5 different levels (1st, 2nd, 3rd, 4th and 5th year courses) and in the case of Spain surveys have been conducted by students of only 3 different levels (1st, 2nd and 4th year course), so it would be interesting to establish a more equitable relationship in terms of the course studied.

In the interviews arise new IDEs that programmers use in their work such as Visual Studio and Android Studio. These two IDEs will also be included in surveys of our future works. In addition, we will complement the interviews with more professionals from both Chile and Spain to find more interesting and comparable results.

Acknowledgment. We are grateful the all the students that have participated in the surveys and interviews from the Universidad Autónoma de Chile, Pontificia Universidad Católica de Valparaíso (Chile) and Universidad Miguel Hernández de Elche (Spain). Jenny Morales is a beneficiary of one INF-PUCV doctoral scholarship.

References

1. ISO 9241-11: Ergonomics of human-system interaction- Part 11: Usability: Definitions and concepts (2018)
2. Nielsen, J.: Usability Engineering. AP Professional (1993)
3. ISO 9214-210: Ergonomics of human system interaction-Part 210: Human-centred design for interactive system, Switzerland (2010)
4. Morville, P.: User experience honeycomb. http://semanticstudios.com/user_experience_design/. Accessed 14 Jan 2019
5. Hollmann, N., Hanenberg, S.: An empirical study on the readability of regular expressions: textual versus graphical. In: 2017 IEEE Working Conference on Software Visualization (VISSOFT), Shanghai, China, pp. 74–84. IEEE (2017)
6. Zhang, Y., Surisetty, S., Scaffidi, C.: Assisting comprehension of animation programs through interactive code visualization. J. Vis. Lang. Comput. 24(5), 313–326 (2013)
7. Athreya, B., Scaffidi, C.: Towards aiding within-patch information foraging by end-user programmers. In: 2014 IEEE Symposium on Visual Languages and Human-Centric Computing (VL/HCC), Australia, pp. 13–20. IEEE (2014)
8. Karrer, T., Krämer, J.P., Diehl, J., Hartmann, B., Borchers, J.: Stacksplorer: call graph navigation helps increasing code maintenance efficiency. In: Proceedings of the 24th Annual ACM Symposium on User Interface Software and Technology, USA, pp. 217–224. ACM (2011)
9. Beelders, T.R., du Plessis, J.P.L.: Syntax highlighting as an influencing factor when reading and comprehending source code. J. Eye Mov. Res. 9(1) (2015)
10. Stefik, A., Siebert, S.: An empirical investigation into programming language syntax. ACM Trans. Comput. Educ. (TOCE) 13(4), 19 (2013)
11. Sedano, T.: Code readability testing, an empirical study. In: 2016 IEEE 29th International Conference on Software Engineering Education and Training (CSEET), USA, pp. 111–117. IEEE (2016)
12. Kraeling, M.: Embedded software programming and implementation guidelines. In: Software Engineering for Embedded Systems, pp. 183–204 (2013)

13. Dieste, O., et al.: Empirical evaluation of the effects of experience on code quality and programmer productivity: an exploratory study. Empirical Softw. Eng. **22**(5), 2457–2542 (2017)
14. Solla, M., Patel, A., Wills, C.: New metric for measuring programmer productivity. In: 2011 IEEE Symposium on Computers & Informatics (ISCI), Malaysia, pp. 177–182. IEEE (2011)
15. Vakilian, M., Chen, N., Zilouchian Moghaddam, R., Negara, S., Johnson, R.E.: A compositional paradigm of automating refactorings. In: Castagna, G. (ed.) ECOOP 2013. LNCS, vol. 7920, pp. 527–551. Springer, Heidelberg (2013). https://doi.org/10.1007/978-3-642-39038-8_22
16. Yoon, Y., Myers, B.A.: Supporting selective undo in a code editor. In: 2015 IEEE/ACM 37th IEEE International Conference on Software Engineering (ICSE), vol. 1, pp. 223–233. IEEE (2015)
17. Hundhausen, C.D., Carter, A.S.: Supporting social interactions and awareness in educational programming environments. In: Proceedings of the 5th Workshop on Evaluation and Usability of Programming Languages and Tools, USA, pp. 55–56. ACM (2014)
18. Bravo, C., Duque, R., Gallardo, J.: A groupware system to support collaborative programming: design and experiences. J. Syst. Softw. **86**(7), 1759–1771 (2013)
19. Salvaneschi, G., Mezini, M.: Debugging for reactive programming. In: Proceedings of the 38th International Conference on Software Engineering, pp. 796–807. ACM (2016)
20. Humayoun, S.R., Dubinsky, Y., Catarci, T.: UEMan: a tool to manage user evaluation in development environments. In: Proceedings of the 31st International Conference on Software Engineering, pp. 551–554. IEEE Computer Society (2009)
21. Coblenz, M., Nelson, W., Aldrich, J., Myers, B., Sunshine, J.: Glacier: transitive class immutability for Java. In: 2017 IEEE/ACM 39th International Conference on Software Engineering (ICSE), Argentina, pp. 496–506. IEEE (2017)
22. Bellucci, A., Romano, M., Aedo, I., Díaz, P.: Software support for multitouch interaction: the end-user programming perspective. IEEE Pervasive Comput. **15**(1), 78–86 (2016)
23. Dillon, E., Anderson, M., Brown, M.: Comparing feature sets within visual and command line environments and their effect on novice programming. In: Proceedings of the 43rd ACM Technical Symposium on Computer Science Education, USA, p. 675. ACM (2012)
24. Endrikat, S., Hanenberg, S., Robbes, R., Stefik, A.: How do API documentation and static typing affect API usability? In: Proceedings of the 36th International Conference on Software Engineering, India, pp. 632–642. ACM (2014)
25. Bastos, J.A., Afonso, L.M., de Souza, C.S.: Metacommunication between programmers through an application programming interface: a semiotic analysis of date and time APIs. In: 2017 IEEE Symposium on Visual Languages and Human-Centric Computing (VL/HCC), USA, pp. 213–221. IEEE (2017)
26. Gonçalves, R., Amaris, M., Okada, T., Bruel, P., Goldman, A.: OpenMP is not as easy as it appears. In: 2016 49th Hawaii International Conference on System Sciences (HICSS), USA, pp. 5742–5751. IEEE (2016)
27. Brooke, J.: SUS-A quick and dirty usability scale. Usability Eval. Ind. **189**(194), 4–7 (1996)
28. Parsons, D., Susnjak, T., Mathrani, A.: Design from detail: analyzing data from a global day of coderetreat. Inf. Softw. Technol. **75**, 39–55 (2016)
29. Sauro, J.: Interpreting single items from the SUS. https://measuringu.com/sus-items/. Accessed 15 Jan 2019
30. Dev-C++ Blog. http://orwelldevcpp.blogspot.com/. Accessed 15 Jan 2019
31. Eclipse Foundation. https://www.eclipse.org/. Accessed 15 Jan 2019
32. Netbeans. https://netbeans.org/. Accessed 14 Jan 2019
33. Astromskis, S., Bavota, G., Janes, A., Russo, B., Di Penta, M.: Patterns of developers behaviour: a 1000-hour industrial study. J. Syst. Softw. **132**, 85–97 (2017)

Construction of Support System for Demand Driven Design of Cocktail Recipes by Deep Learning

Soichiro Ota[1]($\boxtimes$), Kohei Otake[2]($\boxtimes$), and Takashi Namatame[3]($\boxtimes$)

[1] Graduate School of Science and Engineering, Chuo University,
Hachioji 112-8551, Japan
a14.dxte@g.chuo-u.ac.jp
[2] Department of Information and Communication Technology, Tokai University,
Shibuya City 108-8619, Japan
otake@tsc.u-tokai.ac.jp
[3] Faculty of Science and Engineering, Chuo University, Hachioji 112-8551, Japan
nama@indsys.chuo-u.ac.jp

Abstract. Cooking recipes have become available by various ways. However, there are not always recipes that can satisfy any request. In order to reliably provide recipes that can meet his or her needs, it is necessary to newly produce recipes that meet requirements as needed. In addition, a support system is necessary for people who do not have much knowledge to easily devise their favorite recipe. We propose a decision support system for demand driven design of cocktail recipes, that is systemized using Deep Learning due to diversity of ingredients and combinations, differences in taste, etc.

Keywords: Cocktail recipe · Deep learning · Deep neural network

1 Introduction

Cooking recipes have become available by various means. However, despite the huge number of recipes, there are not always dishes that perfectly match each individual's preference. Also, even if they exist, it is not always easy to find them. It is also clear that too many choices can cause problems [6]. For example, it can be a cause of inhibition of motivation to the selection, a decrease of satisfaction to the selected object, and so on. Likewise, because of huge combination of cocktails made from multiple liquors, beverages, etc., there are not always recipes that can satisfy any request. In order to reliably provide recipes that can meet his or her needs, it is necessary to newly produce recipes that meet requirements as needed. In this study, we focus on cocktails where recipes are simpler than general cuisine and devise a method to generate recipes based on requests. Since combinations of ingredients are complicated, we make a support system by deep learning. A support system is necessary for people who do not have much knowledge to easily devise their favorite recipe.

© Springer Nature Switzerland AG 2019
G. Meiselwitz (Ed.): HCII 2019, LNCS 11578, pp. 92–108, 2019.
https://doi.org/10.1007/978-3-030-21902-4_8

2   Dataset

We used 3110 recipes obtained from the website [5] that posted cocktail recipes. The variables contain the quantities of 645 different ingredients (treated as different ingredients if units of quantity are different) (Table 1).

Table 1. An example of dataset.

Amaretto [Part]	Apple Juice [Part]	Cherry [Whole]	⋯	White Cacao Liqueur [Part]	Tonic Water [Part]	Strawberry [Whole]	Strawberry [Piece]
0.25	1.00	0.00	⋯	0.00	0.00	0.00	0.00
0.00	0.50	0.00	⋯	0.00	0.00	0.00	4.00
1.00	0.00	1.00	⋯	0.00	0.00	0.00	0.00
0.00	0.00	0.00	⋯	1.00	0.00	0.00	0.00
0.00	0.00	0.00	⋯	0.00	2.00	0.00	0.00
0.00	0.00	0.00	⋯	0.00	0.00	1.00	0.00
0.00	0.00	0.00	⋯	0.00	0.00	0.00	0.00

3   Method

First of all, our system takes as inputs a collection of required ingredients, a collection of forbidden ingredients and whether "surprise" is necessary. Required ingredients are always used in recipes to be output finally, while forbidden ingredients are never used. "surprise" is like an indicator of a level of a concept close to the term serendipity used in the field of marketing. Regarding this part, we almost follow the work of Grace et al. [1,2]. However, there is only one point difference, which is that the input on "surprise" is not at that level and whether it is necessary or not.

On the other hand, our system consists of two processes: the generation of sets of ingredients and the generation of ingredient quantities (Fig. 1).

3.1   The Generation of Sets of Ingredients

In the generation of sets of ingredients, two deep learning models are used. One is a multilayer perceptron [3]. It takes as input a vector representation of a part of ingredients contained in a recipe and outputs levels of co-occurrence relation that each ingredient is included in the recipe. Another is a variational autoencoder [4] that encodes a vector with information such as which ingredient is included in a recipe into a vector of multidimensional normal distribution. First, the system receives a request in the form of a collection of required ingredients, a set of forbidden ingredients, and whether "surprise" is necessary. Next, using the multilayer perceptron, excluding forbidden ingredients, add an ingredient with the highest levels of co-occurrence relation of entering recipe or "surprise"

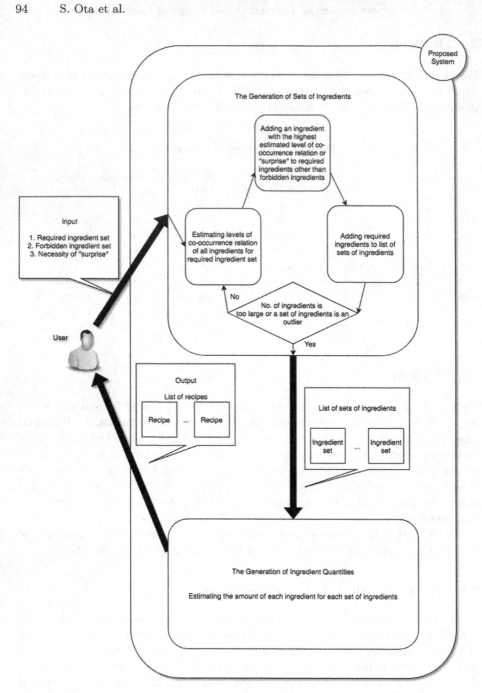

Fig. 1. Image of the proposed system.

estimate to the required ingredient set. The definition of "surprise" here [1,2] is as follows. When a set of other ingredients is given in multilayer perceptron and it estimates levels of co-occurrence relation P_θ of entering recipe of different ingredients, s expressed by the following equation is called "surprise".

$$s(f|c) = -\log_2 \frac{P_\theta(f)}{P_\theta(f|c)} \tag{1}$$

where f is an ingredient and c is context of set of ingredients. Considering computational ease of use, the length of the combination at training is up to 3.

For a recipe to which a selected ingredient is added for an required ingredient set, outlier detection with the Mahalanobis distance and the chi-squared distribution [4] is performed on the vector coded by the variational autoencoder. If there is no outlier, a process such as addition of ingredient and processing of outlier detection is repeated. If it is judged as outlier or the number of ingredients exceeds the maximum value of the data set, this algorithm ends. We output a list including all the collections of ingredients from the required ingredient set to the final set of the repetition (however, those whose ingredient set size is 1 or 0 are removed from the candidates).

3.2   The Generation of Ingredient Quantities

The generation of ingredient quantities receives as input a list of ingredients outputted in the process of the generation of sets of ingredients. The following processing is performed on each set of ingredients. First, using the regression by multilayer perceptron [3], the system estimates amounts of each ingredient contained in the set of ingredients. Information on the estimate of quantity is added to the set of ingredients. A set of all ingredient sets subjected to the above processing is regarded as a final output result.

Loss Function in Learning of Multilayer Perceptron (MLP). When existing functions such as Mean Squared Error, Mean Absolute Error and MAPE are used as the loss function in learning of Multilayer Perceptron (MLP) for ingredient quantity generation, a problem that extremely small amounts (value close to 0) is output since the train data is sparse (amounts of ingredients that are not used is 0) arises. Therefore, in this study, we have defined the loss function L_N uniquely (2).

$$L_N = \frac{1}{NP} \sum_{n=1}^{N} \sum_{p=1}^{P} \frac{\text{sign}(y_p^{(n)})|y_p^{(n)} - \hat{y}_p^{(n)}|}{\max(y_p^{(n)}, \epsilon)} \tag{2}$$

$$0 \le y_p^n \le 1, 0 \le \hat{y}_p^{(n)} \le 1, \epsilon > 0$$

where, N is the number of data, P is the dimension of data. ϵ is a tiny positive number to prevent division by 0, such as 10^{-7} is used. In MAPE, the loss for each sample is multiplied by the sign of the true value y_p^n. When y_p^n is 0, the loss is fixed to 0.

Evaluation Function in Validating of Multilayer Perceptron (MLP). If the proposed loss function 2 is used as an evaluation function in validating, there is a problem that it is easier to output a better evaluation value (lower value) as the number of ingredients used is smaller, that is, data with a lot of $y_p^{(n)}$ where sign($y_p^{(n)}$) takes zero. Therefore, we also uniquely defined the evaluation function (3).

$$L_N = \frac{1}{\sum_{n=1}^{N} \sum_{p=1}^{P} \text{sign}(y_p^{(n)})} \sum_{n=1}^{N} \sum_{p=1}^{P} \frac{\text{sign}(y_p^{(n)})|y_p^{(n)} - \hat{y}_p^{(n)}|}{\max(y_p^{(n)}, \epsilon)} \tag{3}$$

$$0 \leq y_p^n \leq 1, 0 \leq \hat{y}_p^{(n)} \leq 1, \epsilon > 0$$

By replacing NP with the sum of sign($y_p^{(n)}$), it becomes equivalent to MAPE for $y_p^{(n)}$ which take positive values.

4   Experiment

Based on our method, we constructed a support system for recipe design on WEB application. Below are two screens of the application screen.

If you enter information on "required ingredients", "forbidden ingredients" and "surprise", you will transition to the result page (Fig. 2).

The input information is described at the top. A recommended recipe is displayed under that. Below it a plurality of recipes generated by the algorithm are displayed (Fig. 3).

First, We also generated recipes by our method using requests of randomly generated. After that, we took and analyzed a questionnaire including question items on the generated recipes.

In the questionnaire, the main questions are roughly divided into two types. One type is the question "Which of the following two recipes do you feel more than wanting to drink?" Another type is the question "Which of the following two recipes do you think is "a cocktail recipe created by a computer algorithm"?". Ten questions were prepared for each question type. The two recipes presented in one question are the recipe generated by the algorithm based on a certain request and the known recipe that most closely matches the same request. Furthermore, we asked questions such as taste for alcoholic beverages and drinking habits. A questionnaire survey was conducted for 37 males and females aged from 20 to 43. Using the data obtained from the questionnaire, we analyzed the probability of wanting to drink the recipe of the algorithm, the probability of discrimination between a recipe of the algorithm and a known recipe, respectively by logistic regression.

4.1   Procedure

Two patterns of analysis by logistic regression are carried out based on the questionnaire result. One is modeling the probability that the recipe of the algorithm is preferred, and another is modeling the probability that the recipe of the algorithm is distinguished.

Fig. 2. The page for entering a query.

Fig. 3. The page displaying a result.

First, modeling the probability that the recipe of the algorithm is preferred is explained. The objective variable is set to 1 if the algorithm recipe is selected as the recipe that the user prefers, and 0 if not selected. We prepared the following variables as explanatory variable candidates.

- Type of alcohol drink preference (True: 1, False: 0)
  - The most popular alcohol drink (whisky or wine or beer, plum wine)
  - Popular alcohol drink (liqueur or jin or shochu or sake)
  - Unpopular alcohol drink (brandy or spirits or vodka oe rum)
  - None
- Question
  - Question 1
  - Question 2
  - Question 3
  - Question 4
  - Question 5
  - Question 6
  - Question 7
  - Question 8
  - Question 9
  - Question 10
- Use of "surprise" in algorithm (True: 1, False: 0)
- Alcohol preference (True: 1, False: 0)
- Cocktail preference (True: 1, False: 0)
- Age (normalized)
- Sex (Male: 1, Female: 0)
- Alcohol drink preference (True: 1, False: 0)
  - Whisky
  - Jin
  - Beer
  - Liqueur
  - Wine
  - Sake
  - Plum wine
  - Shochu
- Experience equivalent to work of making cocktail (True: 1, False: 0)
  - Experienced
  - Not experienced
- Frequency of drinking cocktail
  - No drinking
  - Few (About 2 days or less per month)
  - Normal (About 1 to 3 days per week)
  - Frequent (About 4 days or more per week)
- Frequency of drinking alcohol
  - No drinking
  - Few (About 2 days or less per month)

- Normal (About 1 to 3 days per week)
- Frequent (About 4 days or more per week)
- Drinking amount on drinking alcohol
  - No drinking
  - Small (It is equivalent to beer medium bottle (1 bottle) or sake (1 go) or whisky single (2 cups) or less)
  - Normal (It is equivalent to beer medium bottle (1 to 2 bottles) or sake (1 to 2 go) or whisky single (3 cups))
  - Large (It is equivalent to beer medium bottle (3 bottles) or sake (3 go) or whisky double (3 cups)) or more
- Maximum value of "surprise" at the time of ingredient selection (normalized)

Variables are selected from the above variables using the variable increment method of the stepwise method based on AIC criterion and the resulting model is treated as an official model in this study.

We describe the modeling the probability that the recipe of the algorithm is distinguished. The objective variable is 1 if the recipe of the algorithm is selected as the recipe which is thought to have been created by the algorithm, and 0 if it is not chosen. For explanatory variables, we use the same variables as those used for modeling the probability that the recipe of the algorithm is preferred. However, note that the variables of the question correspond to different questions. In the same way as modeling the probability that the recipe of the algorithm is preferred, the variable selection is also done, and the model obtained from the result is handled as an official model in this study.

4.2   Results

Crosstabulation on whether or not each respondent like alcohol and whether or not each respondent like cocktails is shown below (Table 2).

Table 2. Crosstabulation on whether or not each respondent like alcohol and whether or not each respondent like cocktails.

	No. of respondent who like cocktails	No. of respondent who do not like cocktails	Total
No. of respondent who like alcohol	21	6	27
No. of respondent who do not like alcohol	7	3	10
Total	28	9	37

Crosstabulation of preference of existing recipe vs. recipe created by algorithm and presence of "surprise" is shown below.

Table 3. Crosstabulation of preference of existing recipe vs. recipe created by algorithm and presence of "surprise."

	"surprise"	No "surprise"	Total
Existing recipe	66	115	181
Recipe created by algorithm	45	144	189
Total	111	259	370

As shown in Table 3, the recipe of the algorithm seems to prefer to drink is about 51%.

The result of modeling the probability that the recipe of the algorithm is preferred is shown in the following table (Table 4).

Table 4. The result of modeling the probability that the recipe of the algorithm is preferred.

Coefficient	Estimate	z value	p value
Intercept	−0.2644	−1.210	0.22629
Use of "surprise" in algorithm	0.6280	2.682	0.00733
Alcohol drink preference (liqueur)	0.6640	2.356	0.01846
Alcohol drink preference (beer)	−0.4654	−2.099	0.03586
Type of alcohol drink preference (unpopular alcohol drink)	−0.6522	−1.825	0.06807

Crosstabulation of the recipe which was thought to be a recipe created by the algorithm and the presence of "surprise" is shown below (Table 5).

Table 5. Crosstabulation of the recipe which was thought to be a recipe created by the algorithm and the presence of "surprise."

	"surprise"	No "surprise"	Total
Recipe created by algorithm (Correct)	113	47	160
Existing recipe (Incorrect)	146	64	110
Total	159	111	370

From the result, the rate at which the recipe of the algorithm is perceived is about 57%.

The result of modeling the probability that the recipe of the algorithm is distinguished is shown in the following table (Table 6).

Table 6. The result of modeling the probability that the recipe of the algorithm is distinguished.

Coefficient	Estimate	z value	p value
Intercept	1.0116	2.450	0.01428
Alcohol drink preference (whisky)	−0.7336	−3.006	0.00265
Alcohol drink preference (liqueur)	0.8870	2.775	0.00553
Cocktail preference	−1.1172	−3.086	0.00203
Frequency of drinking alcohol (few)	−0.6893	−0.836	0.40330
Frequency of drinking alcohol (normal)	−1.4085	−1.786	0.07407
Frequency of drinking alcohol (frequent)	−1.7200	−2.027	0.04271
Experience equivalent to work of making cocktail (experienced)	1.1330	2.548	0.01082
Type of alcohol drink preference (popular alcohol drink)	1.4128	2.002	0.04531

5   Discussion

In this study, it is desirable that we proposed a system with the following properties. One is to make people want to drink cocktails of recipes generated by the algorithm. Another is that recipes generated by the algorithm is indistinguishable from existing recipes.

As an overall tendency, there are more cases where people want to drink a cocktail of recipes generated by the algorithm, and there are more cases that a recipe generated by the algorithm is distinguished from an existing recipe by a person. However, neither of these trends is prominent.

In order to make more appreciate recipe which is match to individual person's favorite, the following factors are important. First of all, it is better to use "surprise". In the system proposed in this study, it is left to the user whether or not to use "surprise", but we should always use "surprise" to reduce the elements that the user must select. By reducing the number of elements that must be selected, motivation for user selection and improvement in satisfaction after selection can be expected. Also, the features of users suitable for the proposed system are as follows.

– Person who likes liqueurs
– Person who does not like beer
– Person who does not like unpopular alcohol drink

People who can not distinguish between recipe generated by algorithm and existing recipe have the following features.

– Person who does not like liqueurs
– Person who likes cocktails

- Person who frequently drinks alcohol
- Person who has no experience equivalent to work making cocktails
- Person who likes popular alcohol drink

To summarize the discussions in the above two viewpoints, we point out following matters.

The likes and dislikes of liqueur in the features of users suitable for the proposed system are opposite, however, people who like liqueurs are thought to want to drink cocktails of algorithm recipes after distinguishing them from existing recipes. Therefore, liqueur lover is appropriate as a target user image. Even people who do not like popular alcohol drinks or unpopular alcohol drinks, some people prefer cocktails. Such people are suitable as users of our system. Such people are considered people who does not like drinking alcohol drink as it is. In other words, they are suitable people as a target for providing cocktails. People who do not like popular drinks and have no experience equivalent to a cocktail job match the user image. It is thought that such people are not familiar with alcohol drink or cocktail. Therefore, it should be assumed that the user does not have much knowledge. People with a high frequency of alcohol drinking are not only difficult to discriminate through recipes generated by algorithms or not, but also they should consume a large amount of alcohol. It can be said that these people can be promising customers from a commercial point of view.

6   Conclusion

We proposed a support system for demand driven design of cocktail recipes.

As an overall tendency, there were more cases where people want to drink a cocktail of recipes generated by the algorithm, and there were more cases that a recipe generated by the algorithm is distinguished from an existing recipe by a person. However, neither of these trends was prominent.

In addition, as a result of analyzing the questionnaire, the features of people ideal for users and the points to be improved of the system were also clarified.

At the present study, we adopted a system that allows users to select ingredients. However, in the present system, there are too many choices and it may become a burden to the user. Therefore, instead of letting users choose ingredients, we should allow users to enter rough information such as taste. Also, since we found "surprise" to be preferable, we will change to specifications that always use "surprise".

Furthermore, we would like to conduct an evaluation experiment that people actually drink cocktails made based on recipes made by the proposed method.

Appendix: Questionnaire

In questions whose types are "Which of the following two recipes do you feel more than wanting to drink?" or "Which of the following two recipes do you think is "a cocktail recipe created by a computer algorithm"?", a recipe generated by the algorithm and an existing recipe are presented in a paired comparison format. Ten kinds of different recipe pairs were prepared for each of the two types of questions.

Next, questions of the questionnaire is shown with the answer format.

- Sex
  - Male
  - Female
- Age
An integer of 20 or more
- Do you like alcohol?
  - Yes
  - No
- Frequency of drinking
  - 7 days per week
  - 6 days per week
  - 5 days per week
  - 4 days per week
  - 3 days per week
  - 2 days per week
  - 1 day per week
  - 1 or 2 days per month
  - Many months I do not drink
  - I do not drink at all
- Drinking amount per day of drinking alcohol
  - It is equivalent to beer medium bottle (1 bottle) or sake (1 go ($\fallingdotseq$ 200 ml)) or whisky single (2 cups) or less
  - It is equivalent to beer medium bottle (1 to 2 bottles) or sake (1 to 2 go) or whisky single (3 cups)
  - It is equivalent to beer medium bottle (3 bottles) or sake (3 go) or whisky double (3 cups)
  - It is equivalent to beer medium bottle (4 to 6 bottles) or sake (4 to 6 go) or whisky double (5 cups)
  - It is equivalent to beer medium bottle (7 to 10 bottles) or sake (7 go to 1 sho) or whisky bottle (1 bottle)
  - It is equivalent to beer medium bottle (over 10 bottles) or sake (over 1 sho) or whisky bottle (more than 1 bottle)
  - I do not drink at all
- What kind of alcohol drink you like
  - Whisky
  - Vodka
  - Gin
  - Spirits
  - Beer
  - Brandy
  - Lamb

- Liqueur
- Wine
- Sake
- Plum wine
- Shochu
- Other
- Do you like cocktails?
  - Yes
  - No
- Frequency of drinking cocktails
  - 7 days per week
  - 6 days per week
  - 5 days per week
  - 4 days per week
  - 3 days per week
  - 2 days per week
  - 1 day per week
  - 1 or 2 days per month
  - Many months I do not drink
  - I do not drink at all
- Do you have cocktail making work or equivalent experience?
  - Yes
  - No
- Which of the following two recipes do you feel more than wanting to drink?
  - Question 1
    * Bourbon 1.50[Part]/Orange Juice 2.00[Part]
    * Flowers (Edible) 1[Flower]/Bourbon 1.25[Part]/Blue Curacao 0.50[Part]
  - Question 2
    * Bourbon, Peach Flavored 1.50[Part]/Raspberry Rum 0.50[Part]/Raspberry 2.67[Whole]
    * Bourbon, Peach Flavored 2.00[Part]/Lemon 1[Twist]
  - Question 3
    * Brandy 1.00[Part]/Galliano 1.00[Part]
    * Williams Pear Liqueur 0.33[Part]/Brandy 1.00[Part]/Almond Liqueur 0.50[Part]
  - Question 4
    * Gin 1.50[Part]/Ginger Beer 5.00[Part]
    * Tamarind Juice 0.50[Part]/Milk, Frozen In Cubes 0.67[Part]/Mint Leaf 1[Sprig]
  - Question 5
    * Maraschino Cherry 1.00[Whole]/Agave Nectar 0.33[Part]/Lime Juice 0.67[Part]
    * Absolut Vodka 2.00[Part]/Campari 1[Dash]/Maraschino Cherry 1.00[Whole]

- Question 6
  * Apple Juice 1.00[Part]/Butter 1.00[Teaspoon]/Dark Rum (Aged) 1.00[Part]/Lemon 1.00[Slice]
  * Absolut Vodka 1.50[Part]/Apple Juice 5.00[Part]/Blue Curacao 0.75[Part]/Lemon 1[Wheel]
- Question 7
  * Absolut Peppar 1.50[Part]/Tomato 1.00[Slice]
  * Pink Peppers 10.75[Whole]/Tomato 1[Quarter]/Olive Juice 0.25[Part]
- Question 8
  * Cherry 1.00[Whole]/Pineapple Liqueur 0.25[Part]/Cream Of Coconut 0.50[Part]
  * Cherry 1.00[Whole]/Light Rum 2.00[Part]/Soda Water 4.00[Part]
- Question 9
  * Absolut Vanilia 0.75[Part]/Calvados 0.75[Part]/Cinnamon Syrup 2[Dash]
  * Lemon Popsicle 0.75[Whole]/Tea 1.50[Part]/Simple Syrup 0.33[Part]
- Question 10
  * Star Anise 1.00[Slice]/Chocolate 1.00[Whole]/Simple Syrup 0.33[Part]/Light Rum 1.00[Part]
  * Chocolate 1.00[Whole]/Dark Cacao Liqueur 0.33[Part]/Port, Red 1.00[Part]/Yellow Chartreuse 0.33[Part]
- Which of the following two recipes do you think is "a cocktail recipe created by a computer algorithm"?
  - Question 1
    * Milk 4.00[Part]/Pastis 1.00[Part]
    * Pastis 1[Dash]/Bitter Lemon 0.75[Part]/Lemon 1[Twist]
  - Question 2
    * Elderflower Liqueur 0.50[Part]/Tomato Juice 1.25[Part]/Absolut Cilantro 1.25[Part]
    * Absolut 100 1.50[Part]/Lemon Juice 2[Dash]/Tomato Juice 5.00[Part]
  - Question 3
    * Bourbon 1.00[Part]/Maraschino Liqueur 3[Dash]/Triple Sec 0.50[Part]
    * Falernum 0.25[Part]/Watermelon Juice 1.33[Part]/Melon 1.00[Slice]
  - Question 4
    * Dry Vermouth 2.00[Part]/Pastis 2[Dash]
    * Coffee Beans 3.00[Whole]/Pastis 1[Dash]/Dark Rum Of Jamaican Type 0.75[Part]
  - Question 5
    * Absolut Apeach 1.50[Part]/Lemon-Lime Soda 5.00[Part]/Lime 1[Wedge]
    * Banana 1.00[Slice]/Absolut Apeach 1.00[Part]/Cream 0.67[Part]
  - Question 6
    * Bourbon 1.00[Part]/Cognac 1.00[Part]/Milk, Frozen In Cubes 4.00[Part]/Milk 4.00[Part]

* Milk, Frozen In Cubes 0.75[Part]/Amontillado Sherry 0.25[Part]/Bourbon 0.50[Part]/Cognac 0.50[Part]
* Question 7
  * Orange Juice 0.67[Part]/Apricot 1.25[Whole]/Dry Vermouth 0.33[Part]
  * Champagne 3.00[Part]/Orange Juice 2.00[Part]
* Question 8
  * Saffron Sugar Syrup 0.25[Part]/Canadian Whisky 1.33[Part]/Orange Juice 1[Dash]
  * Canadian Whisky 1.00[Part]/Cordial Medoc 1.00[Part]/Dry Vermouth 1.00[Part]
* Question 9
  * Absolut Vodka 0.33[Part]/Almond Liqueur 0.50[Part]/White Cacao Liqueur 0.50[Part]
  * Green Apple Liqueur 0.50[Part]/Garlic Salt [To Taste]/Balsamico Vinegar 0.25[Part]
* Question 10
  * Absolut Vodka 1.50[Part]/Cucumber 1.00[Slice]/Sake 0.50[Part]
  * Cinnamon Cane 1.00[Whole]/Vanilla Pod 1.00[Whole]/Honey 0.33[Part]

In Question 2, Question 5, Question 6, Question 8, and Question 10, whose type is "Which of the following two recipes do you feel more than wanting to drink?" and Question 2, Question 7 and Question 8, whose type is "Which of the following two recipes do you think is "a cocktail recipe created by a computer algorithm"?", the recipes created by the proposed algorithm is arranged above, other than the recipe created by the algorithm is placed below. Also, in Question 2, Question 3, Question 5, Question 6, Question 7, Question 9 and Question 10, whose type is "Which of the following two recipes do you feel more than wanting to drink?" and Question 5, Question 7 and Question 10, whose type is "Which of the following two recipes do you think is "a cocktail recipe created by a computer algorithm"?", "surprise" is used for the recipes created by the algorithm.

Second, we describe a method of preparing a pair of recipes. First, a virtual user's request is generated by random number. For this request, a pair of a recipe generated by an algorithm and an existing recipe is prepared. For the recipe generated by the algorithm, the user's request is given as input of the proposed system. However, since multiple recipes are generated in the proposed system, one recipe selected by random number from recipes of an output of the system is set as a recipe generated by the algorithm. For existing recipes, we chose a recipe that is most suitable for an user's request by the method described later from the existing recipes we have.

Third, the generation of user's requests is described. Regarding ingredients, the number of elections is decided for each required or forbidden ingredient by random number, and required ingredients and forbidden ingredients are selected as many as the determined number. For "surprise" as well, we decide whether or not to use it by random number.

Lastly, the selection of an existing recipe is described. The selection of an existing recipe uses only the information related to the ingredients of the user's request. Specifically, it selects based on values of an index d that is disimilarity to the user's request based on the distance from the required ingredients entered, plus the penalty based on the set of forbidden ingredients. We defined the index by the following equation.

$$d(A, B, C) = 1 - \text{Dice}(A, B) + |A \cap C| \tag{4}$$

where, A is a set of ingrediens used for one existing recipe, B is a set of required ingredients in request, C is a set of forbidden ingredients in request, $Dice(\cdot, \cdot)$ is Dice coefficient.

References

1. Grace, K., Maher, M.L., Wilson, D.C., Najjar, N.A.: Combining CBR and deep learning to generate surprising recipe designs. In: Goel, A., Díaz-Agudo, M.B., Roth-Berghofer, T. (eds.) ICCBR 2016. LNCS (LNAI), vol. 9969, pp. 154–169. Springer, Cham (2016). https://doi.org/10.1007/978-3-319-47096-2_11
2. Grace, K., Maher, M.L.: Surprise-triggered reformulation of design goals. In: AAAI, pp. 3726–3732 (2016)
3. LeCun, Y.A., Bottou, L., Orr, G.B., Müller, K.-R.: Efficient BackProp. In: Montavon, G., Orr, G.B., Müller, K.-R. (eds.) Neural Networks: Tricks of the Trade. LNCS, vol. 7700, pp. 9–48. Springer, Heidelberg (2012). https://doi.org/10.1007/978-3-642-35289-8_3
4. Kingma, D.P., Welling, M.: Auto-encoding variational bayes. arXiv preprint arXiv:1312.6114, 14 p. (2013)
5. Absolut Drinks: Discover the best cocktails and drink recipes. https://www.absolutdrinks.com/en/. Accessed 23 Dec 2018
6. Iyengar, S., Lepper, M.: When choice is demotivating: can one desire too much of a good thing? J. Pers. Soc. Psychol. **79**, 995–1006 (2000)
7. Filzmoser, P.: A multivariate outlier detection method. In: Aivazian, S., Filzmoser, P., Kharin, Y. (eds.) Proceedings of the Seventh International Conference on Computer Data Analysis and Modeling, vol. 1, pp. 18–22. Belarusian State University, Minsk (2004)

Methodologies and Trends in Multimedia Systems: A Systematic Literature Review

Carlos Alberto Peláez[1]([✉]), Andrés Solano[1], Toni Granollers[2], and Cesar Collazos[3]

[1] Universidad Autónoma de Occidente, Kmt. 2 Vía Cali-Jamundí, Cali, Colombia
{capa, afsolano}@uao.edu.co
[2] Universitat de Lleida, Pza. Víctor Siurana, 1, 25003 Lleida, Spain
antoni.granollers@udl.cat
[3] Universidad del Cauca, Cl. 5 #4-70, Popayán, Colombia
ccollazo@unicauca.edu.co

Abstract. The studies about systematic literature review (SLR) related with Multimedia and produced between 2011 and early of 2018, we found that are focused in the Multimedia Systems (MS) development for health sciences mainly. No SLR results were found centered in studies about methodologies or frameworks used for their development, practices and tools applied for this purpose, or the study about validation processes. Neither are research focused on the characterization, and recent formulation, of taxonomies about MS.

This findings led to the realization of the present study in order to identify, which methodological approaches or frameworks are focused with the development of MS, Interactive and Multimodal Systems (IS and MMS, respectively). Due to the large number of results, we made the revision of 1506 studies found in 7 consulted databases, focusing the SLR in 32 documents closely related with five research questions.

This research evidences a limited number of methodologies or frameworks related specifically with the development of MS; and the wide use of generic practices for its development, mainly influenced by System Engineering, Software Engineering and Human-Computer Interaction disciplines, through the use of Interactive System (IS) development methodologies, where the attributes and specificities of the MS are not covered at all.

Keywords: Multimedia systems methodologies · Multimedia Systems · Interactive systems · Multimodal Systems

1 Introduction

The digital media industry is one of the main sectors showing a highest contribution growth, in the economy of the leading countries, producing increasing benefits to its gross domestic product (GDP). This is a trend evidencing the way how the digital media are displacing the traditional media, being not exclusive direction for the first world economies: Latin America has been registered as the region with the highest

© Springer Nature Switzerland AG 2019
G. Meiselwitz (Ed.): HCII 2019, LNCS 11578, pp. 109–127, 2019.
https://doi.org/10.1007/978-3-030-21902-4_9

global growth in the digital media industry with 12.8%, followed by the Asia-Pacific region with 7.9% [1].

In Colombia, for example, the information provided by PriceWatherHouseCoopers [2] related with the advertising through multiple digital media, reports a growth in digital advertising investment of 30.2% between 2016 and 2017, although its contribution to the national economy is still significantly lower, than the one offered by the traditional mass media. In consequence, the country must be continue making efforts towards the development of its digital media industry.

In the other hand, the survey produced by Lang and Barry [3], although it is not a recent research, reveals several trends since early the 2000's acting as a barrier to achieve this purpose: one of them, the predominant use of methodologies and practices "in-house" for MS development in the industry of the first world economies, phenomenon that feeds the increasing gap and affects the competitiveness of the digital media industries belonging to the third world countries.

This trend about "in-house" practices for MS development in the industry, can be an influence for found a limited number of published methodologies focused in MS development currently, according with the findings of this SLR. Most of these methodologies are outdated compared with the new trends about several practices and standards of the industry. Actually, this has produced the use and adaptation of generic methodologies centered in IS development, to guide the MS development, leaving several gaps in their design process.

The objective of this work, is to carry out a research using a SLR method, focusing in methodologies and frameworks, practices and tools used, validation processes produced and trends, related with the MS development, including the research about studies centered in the characterization, differentiation and relationship between the MS, IS and MMS.

2 Background

The term "multimedia" was used for first time in July 1966 by music writer and artist Bob Goldstein, referring to the nature of the technological argument used to present his show "LightWorks at L'Oursin" in New York, being popularized in the publication of magazines like Variety [4]. However, Smith et al. [5] appropriated the phrase of MS, to refer to the use of different media, such as audiovisual media, as being part of a teaching-learning method, where both the teacher and the student are active participants.

Meanwhile, the IS concept emerges to differentiate up-and-coming interactive computing by early the 1960s [6], including user interfaces for the first time, from the batch processing. With the interactive computing, a human can interact with the system using a command line console, producing a difference from the batch processing systems, where a series of tasks are executed, without user intervention along the computing process [7].

In the 1980s, with the dawn of the personal computer and the possibility of accessing the Internet as a global public network, the conditions for moving towards a convergence of the Information and Communication Technologies industry (ICT) are met [8], leading to the mass media industry - represented by radio, film, television and photography - to access an ideal scenario for producing the multimedia convergence [9].

This digital media convergence led to the development of IS which make use of interactive multimedia information, by different kind of hardware and software interfaces. This allowed the generation of new digital products and services, where the MS are commonly defined as systems that lets the deployment in an integrated way, of different sorts of interactive digital media, allowing storage, capture, generation, recovery, processing, transmission and presentation of multimedia information [10].

Meanwhile, the IS are defined as technologies based on computer systems and peripherals that, through the user interaction, performs a set of tasks [11]. This is a broader concept than the MS, however, the relationship and differences between both systems, it is not widely studied in the related literature.

A third kind of system related with the MS are the MMS, which foundations are based on the modality concept. The modality concept comes from the psychology, where Charwart's definition [12] were referenced, specifying it, as a perception that proceeds through one of the three channels: visual, auditory or tactile. This is the basis for technocentrism MMS definitions, such as the proposed by Möller et al. [13], which defines it, as a system in which Human-Machine Interaction is enabled, through the media, using different sensorial channels.

The deployment of interactive experiences generated through the development of MS, has traditionally allowed the integration of digital media based on audio, video and images as we can see in [14] and [15], offering at the user, to access at multimedia content focused on visualization techniques, for example, experiences based on projection mapping and augmented reality as recognized in [16].

In the 1980s, Shavelson and Salomon and Hawes in their works, coined the term "interactive multimedia" [17–19], referring, not only to the options that a MS can offer for visualization of multiple digital media, but also, for possibilities of interaction between the system user and the multimedia content. This multimedia content interaction, is one of the most important attributes in the design of MS, having an important role in the process development as a set of requirements for the system [20].

3   Research Methodology - SLR Justification

This paper is based on a methodology suggested by Kitchenham and Charters [21], for performing systematic literature review in software engineering, following a procedure to identify, analyze and summarize the information which has been documented, about previous research in Multimedia, specifically on aspects concerning with methodologies or frameworks formulated for the development of Multimedia, Multimodal and Interactive Systems, the tools, practices and validation processes performed along the MS development, trends in MS involving emerging technologies; and previous studies related with the characterization, differences and relationships between MS/IS/MMS.

The terms Multimedia, Interactive and Multimodal, were included in the search patterns of the SLR, due the wide use of these terms by many authors in its publications, related with systems that supports the deployment of multimedia content for the user.

Thanks to the previous study about SLR produced between 2011 and early 2018, were found publications related with MS and IS; and its application in different case studies in sectors like the Health Care [22–30], Education [31], Telecommunications [32] and Sports [33]. We concluded that about the 75% of the articles presented as systematic reviews related to multimedia and interactive systems and its applications, are closely related with the Health Sciences, without evidence of SLRs produced, focused on methodologies, practices and trends about MS development.

The subsequent steps to carry out this SLR are presented as follow:

3.1 Research Questions

The research questions and their basis against the study, are presented in Table 1.

Table 1. Research questions for the SLR.

Number	Question	Basis
RQ1	¿What methodologies or frameworks have been used or are susceptible to being adapted for the development of Multimedia Systems?	This RQ is the basis for this SLR, since it allows us to study the references related with studies that have been proposed previously, being a requirement to study those methodologies or frameworks related to Multimedia System and its relationship with methodologies for the development of IS and MMS
RQ2	¿What practices and tools are the most commonly used to guide a process of development for Multimedia, Multimodal and Interactive Systems?	The scope of this RQ require the recognition about the practices and tools that supports the different methodologies or frameworks studied in the previous question, in order to study their approaches in relation to the Multimedia field
RQ3	¿What are the trends related with the development of Multimedia Systems based on emerging technologies?	This RQ is necessary to know if there have been validation processes recognized in the methodologies and practices studied
RQ4	¿What are the trends related with the development of Multimedia Systems based on emerging technologies?	This RQ wants to recognize some of the main trends in MS development based in emerging technologies and, in the other hand, to contrast them with the scope of the methodologies and practices studied
RQ5	¿What studies are related with the characterization, foundations, relationship and differences between the concepts of Multimedia, Multimodal and Interactive Systems?	This last RQ is focused on the foundations about the MS, IS and MMS, studying aspects about its relationship and differentiation, in order to understand the scope of the methodologies and frameworks studied

3.2   Information Resources and Search Strategies

The search protocols were created through the literature review of different papers and book chapters, both in English and Spanish, produced in the last fourteen years (2004-early quarter 2018), with the purpose of achieving the greatest coverage possible related with methodologies, trends and foundations about MS, MMS and IS development.

The following are the databases consulted during the review process, in English:

- SCOPUS (https://www.scopus.com/home.uri)
- IEEEXplore (http://ieeexplore.ieee.org)
- ACM Digital Library (http://dl.acm.org)
- Springer (http://link.springer.com)
- Science Direct (http://www.sciencedirect.com)

The sources in Spanish:

- e-libro (http://www.e-libro.com/)
- Redalyc (http://www.redalyc.org/)

In the produced searches, the root terms used were: "multimedia system*", "interactive system*", "multimodal system*"; "mulsemedia", and "cyber-physical multimedia system*" were included for question RQ4, as result of previous searches produced in the chosen databases, using the root term: "multimedia research" protocol and whose findings are included in the analysis of results.

These root terms were associated with words as "design", "framework", "develop*", "method*" and "process", as second terms that must be associated in the recovered documents with MS, IS and MMS development methodologies and its validation process.

Therefore, the inclusion of these chains in the search protocols, together with the root terms, offers an articulated approach between the concepts of methodologies, frameworks, validation processes, practices and tools; allowing to examine, through an integrated approach, the research questions RQ1, RQ2 and RQ3.

For question RQ5, the words: "definition", "classification" and "taxonomy" were used in order to look for documents centered in foundations about MS, IS or MMS, which can create a connection between concepts.

SCOPUS

This database allows the search by title, abstract and by keywords in the document. The search was made by title, summary and keywords.

Once the search protocol was designed using the root terms and the keywords, a total of 317 documents were found for the search protocols related with the questions RQ1, RQ2 and RQ3.

With the given results obtained in the e-libro database, we proceeded to search in SCOPUS for documents by abstract, title and keywords with the term "MPIu+a" as a development methodology focused on IS under usability and accessibility practices. With this search criteria, we found a total of 4 additional documents.

For question RQ4 a total of 84 documents were retrieved, using searching by title, summary and keywords, due to the small amount of existing publications recovered in the preliminary search. For question RQ5, 44 documents were recovered.

Springer

Following the same criteria defined in the search protocol for questions RQ1, RQ2 and RQ3, we used the words "multimedia system*" or "interactive system*" in the title, and making sure that in the document it contained the words "design", "framework", "method*", "process or develop*" since this database does not allow searches by title and abstract, recovering 337 documents.

For question RQ4, three searches protocol was produced as follow: the first one, with the word "mulsemedia"; the second, using the exact phrase "multiple sensorial media"; and the third, "cyber physical system*" in its title; and including the word "multimedia" within the document. A total of 40 documents were retrieved.

In question RQ5, 2 documents were recovered using the search protocol: "multi-media system*", "interactive system*" and "multimodal system" in the title.

IEEE Xplore

Using the command search option in the advanced settings, 144 related documents were retrieved for the questions RQ1, RQ2 and RQ3, where the keywords were found at the title level of the document and words contained in the summary.

For question RQ4, the search was divided into two parts: the first, including the terms "multiple sensory media" and "mulsemedia" by document title, recovering 9 documents. The second search included the term "cyber physical system*" by document title and the term multimedia by summary, without returning search results. For question RQ5, 7 documents were recovered.

ACM Digital Library

An advanced search was produced for questions RQ1, RQ2 and RQ3, which included the terms "multimedia system *" or "interactive system *" in the title and any of the terms described in the search protocols showed below, in the whole content of the document, recovering a total of 126 documents.

For question RQ4, a search was designed by document title, with the word "mulsemedia" and the term "multiple sensorial media". Likewise, it was carried out with the term "cyber physical system*" and the search for the word "multimedia" in the entire document. A total of 35 documents were recovered. No results were found for question RQ5.

Web of Science

Due to the few results obtained using the terms defined for questions RQ1, RQ2 and RQ3, a broader search was carried out using the terms "multimedia system", "inter-active system" or "multimodal system" at the title level, without the associated words defined for these questions in order to access as many possible documents related to the subject in this database. We found a total of 326 documents.

For question RQ4, searching protocols were applied at the title, summary and keywords level, recovering 11 documents.

Finally, and for question RQ5, a search protocol was designed according to the established terms, without finding documents that met the search criteria at the level of title, summary or keywords.

e-libro

For the search related with questions RQ1, RQ2 and RQ3, in e-libro in Spanish language, the search protocol was designed with the terms "sistema multimedia" and "sistema interactivo" in the title; in addition to: "diseño", "desarrollo", "modelo", "metodología", "proceso" and "framework", as words to be searched in text fields and key fields. Three results were obtained, without results for "sistema multimodal".

For question RQ4, we included the terms "mulsemedia", "sistemas ciberfísicos" and "sistemas multisensoriales", at the text level, document title and search in all fields respectively, in order to expand the search as much as possible, without results.

For question RQ5, we proceeded with a search protocol that linked the words "definición", "clasificación" and "taxonomía" within text fields and key fields of the document, as well as the terms "sistemas multimedia" and "sistemas interactivos" in their titles, recovering 2 documents.

Redalyc

Because the database does not allow searches with filters or use operators such as AND/OR, it was decided to search through the Google engine, where filters can be applied by site and file type. Through the applied search protocol, which on this occasion did not include the words "metodología" and "proceso" for the questions RQ1, RQ2 and RQ3, since they are usually included within the word "desarrollo" (for example, "metodología para el desarrollo de sistemas multimedia"), a total of 6 documents were recovered. For question RQ4, we found 9 documents using the Google engine.

In question RQ5, the words "definición", "clasificación" and "taxonomía" were applied to each of the terms: "sistemas interactivos", "sistemas multimedia" and "sistemas multimodales", without obtaining documents that met the search criteria.

3.3   Management of Studies and Inclusion/Exclusion Criteria

For classification purposes of the documentation retrieved, some exclusion criteria are established to determine which of the found studies will not be included in the review. These exclusion criteria are:

- EC1: Document not available for download.
- EC2: Document not available in English or Spanish language.
- EC3: The document describes the development of a multimedia/multimodal/ interactive system, with not focusing on the process methodology or practices for its development.
- EC4: The document describes the development of interactive or multimodal system, without any relationship with multimedia systems.

Likewise, the studies selected for the SLR meet the following including criteria:

- IC1: The study was published between 2004 and early quarter 2018.

– IC2: The study is focused on the proposal of a methodological process or practice related with the design or development of multimedia/multimodal/interactive systems, or its use for the development of a specific solution.
– IC3: If the document focuses on aspects related with the IC2, even if it is in a language other than English or Spanish.
– IC4: Studies related with the state of the art, about emerging technologies in MS.
– IC5: The document is related with fundamentals of Multimedia/Multimodal/ Interactive Systems and its relationship.

3.4   Data Retrieving

For the data extraction, an instrument in excel was used for preserving relevant information about main papers. After applying the inclusion and exclusion criteria to the base of the consulted sources, the classification of the documents is produced with the following information: (a) Database name, (b) Search term, (c) Inclusion criteria, (d) Research question(s) related to the document (e) Document ID, (f) Authors, (g) Document title, (h) Keywords, (i) DOI, (j) ISBN, (k) Year of Publication, (l) Name of the conference or journal from which the study proceeds, (m) Source of Publication such as book chapter, journal paper or conference paper.

The search for the systematic literature review was conducted between June 2017 and March 2018. A total of 1,506 results were retrieved from all the databases, subsequently filtered by title and abstract revision. Once the exclusion and inclusion criteria were applied, only 32 documents of interest were chosen for the review process, which are closely related to the research questions.

After reviewing the documents, 3 of them are related with the same methodology for the IS development: the first, related with the approach of the MPIu+a as methodology for IS development [34], the second, which offers a variant in the proposed methodology, describes the integration of practices focused on the development of user interfaces, focusing on usability and accessibility [35]; and the third, about a validation process for educational software in the treatment of children with disabilities [36].

The same happens in the studies presented by Basnyat et al. and Navarre et al., because the first one [37], is the basis that leads the formulation of the GIMF framework, which is discussed in the second document [38]. Table 2 presents the summary of the results.

Table 2. Search results summary.

Database	Search results	Duplicated documents	Relevant documents
SCOPUS	449	4	14
Springer	379	–	5
IEEE Xplore	160	4	7
ACM Digital library	161	2	4
Web of Science	338	1	–
e-Libro	5	–	2
Redalyc	15	–	–
Total	1506	11	32

4 Results Analysis

After reviewing the selected documents, a classification was made based on the research questions:

The recently paper produced by Olivera et al. [39], is a good reference for beginning the result analysis, mainly those related to the research questions RQ1, RQ2 and RQ3 and IS development methodologies, because their study is not only focused on the analysis of different proposals and approaches formulated by different authors related with the design, specification and verification of IS; and also makes an study about the fundamentals of those proposals, offering a classification related to informal, semi-formal and formal methods for IS development.

The study privileged an analysis centered, mainly, on the evaluation of the quality of IS, through the use of different formal techniques for modeling the system and its properties, evaluating the strengths and weaknesses of each described proposal. The application of these models is highly dependent on the experience and knowledge of the designers in relation to the protocols used in each model. This can be seen in the verification of models, the theorems proofing and the verification of equivalence, where the use of specialized software tools for such verification, is usual in the majority of proposals exposed in the paper.

Related with questions RQ1, RQ2 and RQ3, we find the papers [34–36], based on the same methodological proposal of MPIu+a, for IS development.

Some remarkable aspects of MPIu+a are related with its formulation under a generic approach based in an adapted evolutionary and iterative lifecycle process from Software Engineering based in prototypes. The user is involved from early stages of the process development, with special emphasis on practices related with the evaluation and the prototyping of the solution. The practices centered in Usability and Accessibility, are permeated along all the lifecycle process of the methodology.

MPIu+a flexibility has allowed different adaptations in its core, for example, the adaptation done by Villegas et al. [35], using OpenUP as a development process framework and a specification language as SPEM 2.0, for merge a methodology for User Interfaces development (CIAF) and the MPIu+a methodology for IS development. On the other hand, the use of the methodology has made possible its application for the development of multimedia educational software, in the treatment of children suffering of dyslexia, using a tablet as a deployment device of the experience [36].

Cuevas et al. in [40] exposes his life-cycle for MS development based in a process model using prototyping techniques from the Software Engineering discipline and adapting it, with a set of practices from the User Centered Design (UCD). The author makes a special emphasis, about the importance of having a "multidisciplinary" work team to guide the MS development process, for example, anthropologists, psychologists and sociologists, between others, but not specify the involved roles and who, how, where and when intervene in the process development for MS.

The Model-Based Design (MBD) based in the "V" process model is used by Boy in [41], for both, the development of tangible and mission critical IS in the aerospace industry, and MS development for Human-In-the-Loop-Simulations. In the design process, the model refers at the Human – Systems Integration as a key concept, consequence of the merge between the Human – Centered Design and the Technology – Centered Engineering.

This model involves the stakeholder's participation from the early stages of solution planning, which increases the use of resources at the beginning of the project, in contrast with the traditional MBD model from System Engineering. However, the use of resources are significantly reduced in the final stages of the process development, as result of the adapted model, optimizing the project resources and the risk management.

Another example of using MBD for MS development, is the job presented by Leonard in [42], related with the development of embedded systems for in-flight entertainment (IFE) at low cost. In this paper, the methodology is used to produce the design of the hardware-software architecture model for the embedded MS. The hardware subsystem includes the LCD touch screen and the used microcontroller (Arduino). A key point to choose the MBD process in this research, is related with the verification of the required standards by the authorities responsible for certifying the design of any type of system, where MBD adheres to strict compliance to the set normativity, DO-331 and DO-178C, related with the critical systems of the aerospace industry.

Same situation is presented in the design model for the development of mission critical IS showed by Navarre et al. in [38], named Generic Integrated Modeling Framework (GIMF) and also based in MBD, represented by a set of six phases, using a series of techniques and software tools based on IS modeling, including within its design, the UCD practices and the errors detection, when the user interacts with the IS, using the Security Modeling Language described by Basnyat et al. in [37]. The paper exposes the fact that interaction techniques applied to critical systems, increases the possibility of incidents or accidents when the user interact with them.

Centered in MMS, Barricelli et al. in [43] exposes a method for Ubiquitous Web-based Multimodal Interactive Systems development, using the Software Shaping Workshop (SSW) and including rapid prototyping as a task that must be carried out throughout the life cycle process development. The paper describes the use of the methodology for MS development with a graphical interface using images and text for medical diagnose; and a visual and auditory experience for geographical maps using a text-to-speech tool.

A hexagonal model for IS design based on the theory of activity, is presented by Döweling et al. in [44]. The development is guided along an iterative prototyping process, in which a regular evaluation about the solution applicability on different types of systems takes place through the combination of physical and technical elements, as well as human and social, mixed together with an integral perspective. The model not specify considerations about hardware-software, or interface's design. The model presented, has a high level of abstraction, given the conceptual application of the activity theory to produce its description.

Related with the MMS development, the Vilimek work in [45] describes a generic procedure that guides the developer through a process of eight phases, highlighting those related with the interaction design, defined by the choice of the modalities that must be included in the system in the phase 3 and the merge of these modalities in relation with the user interaction in phase 4, highly dependent of the modalities chosen before. This paper is relevant, because should suggest the need from a design process for MS development, where includes phases for choice the kind of media content needed by the user and the multimedia content integration related with the user interaction with the system.

In contrast with previous authors, dealing with all the stages of the MS/IS/MMS process development, Bowen in [46] exposes a set of techniques and tools grouped in a semi-formal framework, focused in the Interaction Design (ID) in IS specifically, for interaction spaces design provided by the system and for the user.

Similar to Bowen and based on an MBD approach, the practice described by Brajnik in [47], for measure the ID before building the system using a software tool, representing different models of behavior in a User Interface by the use of a UML based graph, facilitating the specification and use of possible system-use scenarios, employing ID techniques. The tool allows the calculation of possible interaction pathways through a series of metrics based on possible routes that may, or may not, include user navigation errors. The practice suggested and applied through the use of this software tool, offers the possibility of producing the described design analysis, without the need to create system prototypes and a manual monitoring of the user's actions, allowing to improve the design before any type of User Interface (UI) proto-type is built. However, it should not be used to draw final conclusions about the usability of the system, because the methodological practice is not aimed to examine all the scope involved in a complete Usability analysis of the system.

Hashim in [48] presents the evaluation method about factors involved along the process design for Immersive MS, but does not make reference to a methodology for MS development. The evaluation method describes a cube model with three dimensions interrelated with the system: usability measurement, evaluation techniques and measurement of realism of the immersive experience.

Both, Bandung in [49] and Sun in [50] presents studies related with the MS development. Bandung shows a description of practices that guide a specific process for the development of solutions and emphasis is placed on the Hardware-Software design necessary for the creation of an embedded system and its graphical user interface. Sun exposes an architecture for the deployment of audio and video experiences using streaming techniques. However, neither Bandung nor Sun describes methodologies for MS development.

Related with trends about MS based in emerging technologies, the job presented by Moreno et al. [51], introduce a set of challenges of Multimedia, related with decision-making processes based on cognitive computing, suggesting a merge between Multimedia and other areas as machine learning, as a trend. In the dimension related with knowledge consumption, the concept of Mulsemedia (Multiple-Sensorial-Media) is mentioned as a key for the deployment of interactive experiences on behalf of the cognitive processes of the user, taking advantage of the multiple sensorial media offered by the System. This is consistent with the development of new haptic devices for Human-Computer Multisensory Interaction, allowing the multiple sensorial media integration in the emerging Mulsemedia Systems (MSS) [52], based in a system architecture like MPEG-V [53], for the interoperability between virtual and real worlds, enabled through the use of sensors and actuators and supporting a Sensorial Effects Description Language (SEDL), based on XML.

The third challenge, is focused in capturing the intention of the user as decision maker, involving knowledge fields and technologies based on Internet of the Things (IoT) and Cyber Physical Systems (CPS), where the SLR has lead us to authors like Kaeri et al. [54], recognizing advances in a novel trend related with the Internet of Multimedia Things (IoMT) architectures, supporting remote collaboration with video stream and storage services, involving basic IoT elements and devices such as sensors, cameras, microphones and multimedia communication lines.

The works presented by Duchon [55], Liu [56] and Akpınar in [57], are examples about the merge of areas as multimedia with the CPS and IoT respectively, bringing in the first reference, the Cyber-Physical Multimedia System (CPMMS) term, related with a solution using sensorial-auditory perceptions, for auditory experiences between users which are located in different geographical regions, feeling a proximity perception. The second reference, related with the development of an adaptive multimedia recommender system, using feedback control frameworks in CPSs, and the last one, related with a multimedia collaborative environment represented by a table, where both: virtual objects and functional representations of real objects can be shared remotely. All these works are foundations from which the IoMT paradigm is emerging.

The trends in Multimedia, evidences a transition from traditional Multimedia to Multisensory Multimedia such as described by Sulema [58], opening new possibilities for exploiting other human senses, such as olfactory, thermoception and kinesthetic, among others. The author describes a set of hardware devices that have been used for Multisensory MS development. These devices allow the information capture and the deployment of system's sensorial effects directed towards the User Experience.

Ghinea et al. [59], exposes an analysis about the importance of making progress in the Quality of Experience (QoE), particularly on the development of mathematical models that allow the user to obtain more realistic experiences during the deployment of the mulsemedia interactive experience offered by the system. This is corroborated in recent publications dealing with different approaches and designs to improve the QoE, mainly in experiences integrating auditory, visual and olfactory perceptions, as the works showed by Murray et al. in [60] and Monks et al. in [61], where in the last one, the model is used for integration with a 3D-based video experience. In these studies, the proposed mathematical models are linear, in contrast with the work of Jalal and Murroni [62], which proposes a non-linear pattern for QoE evaluation in the MSS, obtaining a better precision and performance, in relation with the traditional linear models.

Only Sousa et al. in [63] deals with a model based in Model Driven Architecture (MDA) for MSS development, integrating software, media and sensory effects, centered on solutions based on digital TV. The model describes a set of layers adapted from MDA: the computation independent model (CIM) for the requirements specification of the application through artifacts from the sensory multimedia and software development area, a platform-independent model (PIM) receiving the artifacts generated by the CIM and performs the design activity supported by the Multimedia Modeling Language (MML) offering a set of views: (i) the scene model and the (ii) presentation model, responsibility of the media team. The (iii) structural model and the (iv) interaction model, responsibility of the software team. Finally, the platform-specific models (PSM) makes the transformation to one specific mulsemedia digital TV application model.

The studied trends suggest an important evolution around the multimedia and its merge with new systems and emerging technologies, giving a reason to lead efforts in this SLR, towards the research about the evolution and changes of multimedia foundations, mainly those related with the MS and its relationship and differences with the IS and MMS. We found few evidence in the consulted databases about recently MS foundations, involving the relationship and differences between them, the IS and MMS. However, we found recent studies about MMS fundamentals in the work of Wechsung [64], with no evidence of its relationship and difference with the MS and IS, except by the Oviatt definition cited by Wechsung for MMS, involving the MS term. As Wechsung, the work of Caschera et al. [65] offers an analysis about the MMS development and focused in the evolution of the methodologies applied between 2005 and 2015, showing a solid background about its foundations and trends.

4.1 Findings Regarding About Research Questions

RQ1. ¿What methodologies or frameworks have been used or are susceptible to being adapted for the development of Multimedia Systems?

The 28% of the all selected documents in the SLR described some type of methodology for MS/IS/MMS development. The works studied in [34] through the validated experience in [36, 40] showing a life cycle process and a set of practices for MS development, [41] through the MS development for Human-In-the-Loop-Simulations, [42] with the MS development for IFE, and [63] for multiple sensorial development system based in Digital TV experience, are related or have some evidence of been used for MS development. However, in [40] there is not a validation evidence about the practices suggested for MS development.

In the other hand, the work studied in [43] describes a methodology centered in MMS development, using some case studies as validation, for a system design with multimedia content deployment; and [45], where authors exposes a methodology with 8 phases for MMS development, without evidence about validation process, but taking account an adapted model for the design of the interaction modalities of the system.

The methodology exposed in [38] for IS development, is strongly centered on mission critical systems and use the model-design approach, from the system engineering and its merge with practices from software engineering. The IS development methodology studied in [44], it's a conceptual process model, based in activity theory for merge subject-tool-object in a model; and centered in prototyping and UCD practices, without evidences about a validation process until now.

We observe the methodology studied in [34] for IS development, based on Usability, Accessibility and Software Engineer, offers flexibility to be adapted for multiple purposes, such the case studied in [35].

Finally, we found a set of generic methodologies adapted for MS development; and methodologies based in IS and MMS development that has been used for MS development. However, in both cases, we do not find a methodology specifically designed from its basis and foundations, for MS development, in contrast with the studied methodologies for IS and MMS development.

RQ2. ¿What practices and tools are the most commonly used to guide a process of development for Multimedia, Multimodal and Interactive Systems?

Almost 47% of the documents selected for review, are related with practices and tools used for MS, IS and MMS development, where cases studied in [46–49] and [50], do not specify any kind of methodology related with their practices. Software Engineering, Systems Engineering and HCI are the dominant disciplines for the model process development and practices used, using mostly, evolutive and iterative cycles. Prototyping and evaluation practices are recurrent in each of the phases of the iterative cycle being a necessary strategy to involve the user from the initial stages of the solution design. These practices are also adapted for the "V" model process, in cases where the MBD methodology is applied, as studied in [38, 41] and [42]. Only those techniques used from MBD describe processes related with both, software and hardware design.

Only in studies discussed in [38] and [47], describes a set of software tools for support different activities and processes that are involved within the IS development life cycle.

RQ3. ¿What validation processes of the methodology or framework studied has been used, as evidence of their effectiveness to drive the developing process of Multimedia, Multimodal or Interactive Systems?

The works involving the use or adaptation of the MPIu+a methodology, are validated through the application of case studies, mainly for Web-based applications solutions, without any other evidence about validations related with hardware-software systems, which would imply validation processes designing other kind of interfaces. The studies based on MBD makes its validations, in cases related with the aeronautical industry mainly. In [42], the validation offers more detailed evidence about its obtained results in the process development, but not describes teams or UCD practices involved along the process. The study cases exposed in [38] and [41], are supported by an industry antecedents in the aerospace and aeronautical industry mainly, but documents not describes a specific validation process.

RQ4. ¿What are the trends related with the development of Multimedia Systems based on emerging technologies?

From discussed studies in [55, 56] and [57] developing multimedia experiences based in IoT and CPS principles and cited by some authors as CPMMS, we found the basis for evolve towards a novel paradigm where the smart and heterogeneous multimedia things, can interact with another things in a network, named as IoMT.

The trends in MS development evidences an evolving merge with machine learning and its influence in emerging services as the IoMT, or for the QoE optimization related with the multimedia experience, not just for multiple-sensorial media experiences and new interaction possibilities for the user, as we can see in [59], but also, for improve the QoE of IoMT services for networks users.

The MSS open new possibilities beyond those offered by traditional MS limited in visual and auditory perception, offering new experiences involving sensory perceptions, such as kinesthetic, olfactory and thermoception, among others. However, the development of algorithms for improve the QoE is one of the current challenges for both: the MSS development and IoMT service networks.

RQ5. ¿What studies have taken place regarding the characterization, relationship and differences between the concepts of Multimedia, Multimodal and Interactive Systems?

In contrast with the studies related about the MMS fundamentals in [64] and [65], there are few recent studies related with methodologies and trends involving fundamentals about MS, not just as a basis that we consider relevant for establishing the scope and boundaries from a well-defined methodology for MS development, but also, about the new possibilities that can offer for the User Experience, trends as multiple sensorial media design and the growing multimedia services omnipresence, thanks to emerging paradigms as the IoMT.

5 Conclusions and Future Work

There has been produced a SLR, with a set of papers chosen in a wide window of time publication (2004 and early quarter of 2018); taking into account a diversity of concepts about fundamentals, methodologies, frameworks and trends, related with the MS development process.

It covered 1506 studies and found 32 relevant documents for the SLR that have been selected following the exclusion and inclusion criteria and a set of search protocols for each database, related with the research questions. Of these 32 documents, 12 deals with aspects directly related with methodologies or frameworks for MS, IS and MMS development; and 1 about MSS development. However, only 3 are focused specifically on practices and a methodologies related with MS development.

In none of the methodologies or framework studied we observed practices for choose the media contents more suitable for the user needs and expectations, or practices and process related with a specific process for the design of the multimedia experience to be supported through the MS. Neither practices nor process design were recognized, for the design of interfaces or interaction techniques more suitable, according to the type of multimedia content that want to be deployed.

Only the study presented by de Sousa in [63], deals with a process design from the adapted MDA, for the development of multiple sensorial media experiences systems. However, this approximation is restricted for multimedia experiences based in interactive digital TV experiences. Also, for wind, vibration and light sensorial experience design restricted to a software system design, without taking account, practices and process related with hardware design for objects and devices as sensors or actuators, according to user needs and expectations.

On the other hand and related with emerging trends as the IoMT, we identify that are not covered by any scope of the studied methodologies and frameworks for MS development, being an opportunity for the development of new methodologies, that innovate the design process of these systems, with novel practices and tools, dealing with trends as IoMT, or mulsemedia experiences and machine learning for MS development.

However, we observe "hundreds" of new MS developed by the industry making the multimedia an omnipresent resource for the people, using different devices and peripherals. This would suggest an increasing of "in-house" practices, as part of the "know-how" and value strategy of the involved companies, to ensure its competitiveness and productivity. Maybe, a new and recent survey following a similar methodology as worked by Lang and Barry in [3], could offer a better clarity about the current trends and behaviors of the multimedia industry.

References

1. Mckinsey & Company: Global Media Report Global Industry Overview (2016)
2. Publicidad Colombia: Reporte Ejecutivo Publicidad Digital en Colombia (2017)
3. Lang, M., Barry, C.: Techniques and methodologies for multimedia systems development: a survey of industrial practice. In: Russo, N.L., Fitzgerald, B., DeGross, J.I. (eds.) Realigning Research and Practice in Information Systems Development. ITIFIP, vol. 66, pp. 77–86. Springer, Boston, MA (2001). https://doi.org/10.1007/978-0-387-35489-7_6
4. Albarino, R.: Goldstein's LightWorks at Southhampton. Variety 213(12) (1966)
5. Smith, M.D., Schagring, M., Poorman, L.E.: Multimedia systems: a review and report of a pilot project. AV Commun. Rev. 15(4), 345–369 (1967)
6. Sherwood, F.: Interactive Computing: International Computer State of the Art Report. Infotech Information Limited (1972)
7. Michigan UO: The Computing Center: Coming to Terms with the IBM System/360 Model 67. Research News University of Michigan (1969)
8. Blackman, C.R.: Convergence between telecommunications and other media: how should regulation adapt? Telecommun. Policy 22, 163–170 (1998)
9. Eduardo, V.: Convergencia multimedia: más allá de la Internet. In: Encuentro de la Federación Latinoamericana de Facultades de Comunicación Social, Sao Paulo (2000)
10. Sampaio, P.N.M., Rodello, I.A., Peralta, L.M.R., Bressan, P.A.: Customizing multimedia and collaborative virtual environment. In: Encyclopedia of Networked and Virtual Organizations. Information Science Reference (animprint of IGI Global), Hershey, New York, pp. 377–384 (2008)
11. Ficarra, F.V.C.: Web 2.0 and interactive systems: aesthetics cultural heritage for communicability assessment. In: Handbook of Research on Technologies and Cultural Heritage: Applications and Environments. IGI Global (2011)
12. Charwart, H.J.: Lexikon der Mensch-Maschine-Kommunikation. Oldenbourg (1992)
13. Möller, S., Engelbrecht, K.-P., Kühnel, C., Wechsung, I., Weiss, B.: A taxonomy of quality of service and quality of experience of multimodal human-machine interaction. In: Proceedings of the First International Workshop on Quality of Multimedia Experience (QoMEX 2009), pp. 7–12 (2009)
14. Chang, S., et al.: Multimedia classification. In: Data Classification Algorithms and Applications, pp. 338–356. CRC Press, New York (2015)
15. Mitra, S., Bhatnagar, G.: Introduction to Multimedia Systems. Elseiver (2001)
16. Raskar, R., Welch, G., Chen, W.-C.: Table-top spatially-augmented realty: bringing physical models to life with projected imagery. In: Proceedings of the 2nd IEEE and ACM International Workshop on Augmented Reality, (IWAR 1999) (1999)
17. Shavelson, R.J., Salomon, G.: Information technology: tool and teacher of the mind. Educ. Res. 14, 4 (1985)
18. Hawes, K.S.: Comment of information technology: tool and teacher of the mind. Educ. Res. 15, 24 (1986)
19. Shavelson, R.J., Salomon, G.: A reply. Educ. Res. 15, 24–25 (1986)

20. Müller, J., Alt, F., Schmidt, A., Michelis, D.: Requirements and design space for interactive public displays. In: Proceedings of the ACM Multimedia 2010 International Conference, MM 2010, Firenze, Italy (2010)
21. Kitchenham, B., Charters, S.: Guidelines for Performing Systematic Literature Reviews in Software Engineering (2007)
22. Raaff, C., Glazebrook, C., Wharrad, H.: A systematic review of interactive multimedia interventions to promote children's communication with health professionals: implications for communicating with overweight children. BMC Med. Inform. Decis. Making **14**, 8 (2014)
23. Nehme, J., El-Khani, U., Chow, A., Hakky, S., Ahmed, A., Purkayastha, S.: The use of multimedia consent programs for surgical procedures: a sistematic review. Surg. Innov. **20** (1), 13–23 (2013)
24. Palmer, B., Lanouette, N., Jeste, D.: Effectiveness of multimedia aids to enhance comprehension of research consent information: a systematic review. IRB Ethics Hum. Res. **34**(6), 1–15 (2012)
25. Strauss, E., et al.: The arthroscopic management of partial-thickness rotator cuff tears: a systematic review. Arthroscopy: J. Arthroscopic Related Surg. **27**(4), 568–580 (2011)
26. Wang, Q., Markopoulos, P., Yu, B., Chen, W., Timmermans, A.: Interactive wearable systems for upper body rehabilitation: a systematic review. J. NeuroEng. Rehabil. **14**(1), Artículo Número 20 (2017)
27. McLendon, S.: Interactive video telehealth models to improve access to diabetes specialty care and education in the rural setting: a systematic review. Diab. Spectr. **30**(2), 124–136 (2017)
28. Bleakley, C., Charles, D., Porter-Armstrong, A., McNeill, M., McDonough, S., McCormack, B.: Gaming for health: a systematic review of the physical and cognitive effects of interactive computer in older adults. J. Appl. Gerontol. **34**(3), 166–189 (2015)
29. dos Santos Nunes, E.P., Lemos, E.M., Maciel, C., Nunes, C.: Human Factors and Interaction Strategies in Three-Dimensional Virtual Environments to Support the Development of Digital Interactive Therapeutic Toy: A Systematic Review. In: Shumaker, R., Lackey, S. (eds.) VAMR 2015. LNCS, vol. 9179, pp. 368–378. Springer, Cham (2015). https://doi.org/ 10.1007/978-3-319-21067-4_38
30. Blackburn, S., Brownsell, S., Hawley, M.: A systematic review of digital interactive television systems and their applications in the health and social care fields. J. Telemed. Telecare **17**(4), 168–176 (2011)
31. Ganan, D., Caballe, S., Conesa, J., Barolli, L., Kulla, E., Spaho, E.: A systematic review of multimedia resources to support teaching and learning virtual environments. In: Proceedings - 2014 8th International Conference on Complex, Intelligent and Software Intensive Systems, CISIS 2014, Birminghan City, UK (2014)
32. Costa Segundo, R., Saibel Santos, C.: Systematic review of multiple contents synchronization in interactive televesion scenario. ISRN Commun. Netw. **2014**, Article no. 127142 (2014)
33. Neumann, D., Moffitt, R., Thomas, P., Loveday, K.W.: A systematic review of the application of interactive virtual reality to sport. Virtual Reality **22**, 1–16 (2017)
34. Granollers i Saltiveri, T., Lorés Vidal, J., Cañas Delgado, J.: Diseño de sistemas interactivos centrados en el usuario, Barcelona: UOC (2005)
35. Villegas, M.L., Giraldo, W.J., Collazos, C.A., Granollers, T.: Software process implementation method with eclipse process framework composer MPiu+a case, pp. 1–6. IEEE (2013)

36. Rodríguez Martínez, K., Díaz Quintero, M.d.J., Quintero Fuentes, N.: Development of an educational software for the treatment of children with dyslexia in Panama applying MPIu+a for the design of user interfaces. In: 11th Ibero-American Conference on Systems, Cybernetics and Informatics, CISCI 2012, Jointly with the 9th Ibero-American Symposium on Education, Cybernetics and Informatics, SIECI 2012, Orlando (2012)
37. Basnyat, S., Palanque, P., Schupp, B., Wright, P.: Formal socio-technical barrier modelling for safety-critical interactive systems design. Saf. Sci. **45**, 545–565 (2007)
38. Navarre, D., Palanque, P., Martinie, C., Winckler, M.A., Steere, S.: Formal description techiniques for human-machine interfaces: model-based approaches for the design and evaluation of dependable usable interactive systems. In: The Handbook of Human-Machine Interaction. A Human-Centered Design Approach, Ashgate, pp. 235–266 (2011)
39. Oliveira, R., Palanque, P., Weyers, B., Bowen, J., Dix, A.: State of the art on formal methods for interactive systems. In: Weyers, B., Bowen, J., Dix, A., Palanque, P. (eds.) The Handbook of Formal Methods in Human-Computer Interaction. HIS, pp. 3–55. Springer, Cham (2017). https://doi.org/10.1007/978-3-319-51838-1_1
40. Cuevas, I., et al.: Sistemas Multimedia: Análisis, Diseño y Evaluación, Madrid: Editorial UNED - Universidad Nacional de Educación a Distancia (2004)
41. Boy, G.A.: Tangible Interactive Systems. Springer, Heidelberg (2017)
42. Leonard, S., Olszewska, J.I.: Model-based development of interactive multimedia system. In: 2017 3rd IEEE International Conference on Cybernetics (CYBCON) (2017)
43. Barricelli, B., Mussio, P., Padula, M., Marcante, A., Provenza, L., Scala, P.: Designing pervasive and multimodal interactive systems: an approach built on the field. In: Multimodal Human Computer Interaction and Pervasive Services, pp. 243–264. IGI Global (2009)
44. Döweling, S., Schmidt, B., Göb, A.: A model for the design of interactive systems based on activity theory. In: ACM 2012 Conference on Computer Supported Cooperative Work, CSCW 2012, Seattle, WA; United States (2012)
45. Vilimek, R.: More than words: designing multimodal systems. In: Vilimek, R. (ed.) Usability of Speech Dialog Systems, pp. 123–145. Springer, Heidelberg (2008). https://doi.org/10.1007/978-3-540-78343-5_6
46. Bowen, J., Dittmar, A.: A semi-formal framework for describing interaction design spaces. In: 8th ACM SIGCHI Symposium on Engineering Interactive Computing Systems, EICS 2016, Brussels, Belgium (2016)
47. Brajnik, G., Harper, S.: Measuring interaction design before building the system: a model-based approach. In: 8th ACM SIGCHI Symposium on Engineering Interactive Computing Systems, EICS 2016, Brussels, Belgium (2016)
48. Hashim, A., Romli, F., Osman, Z.: Research on evaluation techniques for immersive multimedia. In: International Conference on Graphic and Image Processing (2012)
49. Bandung, Y., Tanuwidjaja, H., Subekti, L., Mutijarsa, K.: Development of multimedia system for supporting education in rural areas. In: 2015 International Symposium on Intelligent Signal Processing and Communication Systems, ISPACS 2015, Bandung, Indonesia (2015)
50. Sun, L.: The design of interactive multimedia system in wireless environment. In: 2014 IEEE Workshop on Advanced Research and Technology in Industry Applications, WARTIA 2014, Ottawa, Canada (2014)
51. Moreno, M., Brandão, R., Cerqueira, R.: Challenges on multimedia for decision-making in the era of cognitive computing. In: 18th IEEE International Symposium on Multimedia, ISM 2016, San Jose, USA (2017)
52. Ghinea, G., Andres, F., Gulliver, S.: Multiple Sensorial Media Advances and Applications: New Developments in MulSeMedia. IGI Global (2011)

53. Yoon, K., Kim, S.-K., Han, J., Han, S., Preda, M.: MPEG-V: Bridging the Virtual and Real World. Elseiver (2015)
54. Kaeri, Y., Moulin, C., Sugawara, K., Manabe, Y.: Agent-based system architecture supporting remote collaboration via an internet of multimedia things approach. IEEE Access **6**, 17067–17079 (2018)
55. Duchon, M., Schindhelm, C., Niedermeier, C.: Cyber physical multimedia system: a pervasive virtual audio community. In: International Conference on Advances in Multimedia, Munich (2011)
56. Liu, C.H., Zhang, Z., Chen, M.: Personalized multimedia recommendations for cloud-integrated cyber-physical systems. IEEE Syst. J. **11**(1), 106–117 (2017)
57. Akpınar, K., Ballard, T., Hua, K.A., Li, K., Tarnpradab, S., Ye, J.: COMMIT: a multimedia collaboration system for future workplaces with the internet of things. In: Proceedings of the 8th ACM on Multimedia Systems Conference (2017)
58. Sulema, Y.: Multimedia vs. mulsemedia: state of the art and future trends. In: The 23rd International Conference on Systems, Signals and Image Processing, Bratislava, Slovakia (2016)
59. Ghinea, G., Timmerer, C., Lin, W., Gulliver, S.R.: Mulsemedia: state of the art, perspectives, and challenges. ACM Trans. Multimed. Comput. Commun. Appl. (TOMM) **11**, 17 (2014)
60. Murray, N., Lee, B., Qiao, Y., Miro-Muntean, G.: The impact of scent type on olfaction-enhanced multimedia quality of experience. IEEE Trans. Syst. Man Cybern.: Syst. **47**, 2503–2515 (2017)
61. Monks, J., Olaru, A., Tal, I., Muntean, G.-M.: Quality of experience assessment of 3D video synchronised with multisensorial media components. In: 2th IEEE International Symposium on Broadband Multimedia Systems and Broadcasting, BMSB 2017, Cagliari, Italy (2017)
62. Jalal, L., Murroni, M.: A nonlinear quality of experience model for high dynamic spatio-temporal mulsemedia. In: 9th International Conference on Quality of Multimedia Experience, QoMEX 2017, Erfurt, Germany (2017)
63. de Sousa, M.F., Kulesza, R., Guimarães Ferraz, C.A.: A model-driven approach for MulSeMedia application domain. In: Proceedings of the 22nd Brazilian Symposium on Multimedia and the Web (2016)
64. Wechsung, I.: What are multimodal systems? Why do they need evaluation?—theoretical background. In: Wechsung, I. (ed.) An Evaluation Framework for Multimodal Interaction. TSTS, pp. 7–22. Springer, Cham (2014). https://doi.org/10.1007/978-3-319-03810-0_2
65. Caschera, M., D'Ulizia, A., Ferri, F., Grifoni, P.: Multimodal systems: an excursus of the main research questions. In: On the Move to Meaningful Internet Systems: OTM 2015 Workshops, Rhodes, Greece (2015)

A Set of Usability and User eXperience Heuristics for Social Networks

María-Josée Saavedra⬦, Cristian Rusu⬦, Daniela Quiñones⁽✉⁾⬦,
and Silvana Roncagliolo⬦

Pontificia Universidad Católica de Valparaíso, Valparaíso, Chile
mariiajoseesc@gmail.com,
{cristian.rusu,daniela.quinones,
silvana.roncagliolo}@pucv.cl

Abstract. Social networks have existed in all stages of the human history. Digital systems only helped to globalize their use. Usability refers to the efficacy, efficiency, and satisfaction in achieving user's goals through a product, system or service. User eXperience (UX) extends the usability concept to the whole range of user's perception when using (or even intend to use) a product, system or service. Heuristic evaluation is one of the most popular usability evaluation methods. Generic or specific heuristics may be used. Generic heuristics are familiar to evaluators and therefore easy to apply, but they can miss specific usability issues. Specific heuristics can detect relevant domain related usability issues. Evaluating social networks usability and UX is challenging. General usability heuristics, as Nielsen's, cannot detect specific, domain-related, usability problem. There are relatively few sets of specific usability heuristics for social networks. Moreover, heuristics rarely focus on UX aspects, other than usability.

For this work we used the methodology proposed by Quiñones et al. [7], which includes 8 stages, and can be applied iteratively. Finally, we developed a set of 11 heuristics oriented to UX in social networks, applicable for both mobile devices and websites versions. Heuristics were refined based on experts' feedback, and validation's results. As future work we pretend to further validate (and possible improve) the set of 11 heuristics based on new case studies.

Keywords: Social media · User eXperience · Usability · Heuristic evaluation

1 Introduction

We can say that today digital social networks are already part of a person's daily routine. Everyone who owns an electronic device, whether it's a computer or a smartphone, uses a social network to keep in touch with friends or relatives. The social media has achieved great versatility today as not even age is an impediment to use them. However, it is important to note that the use of social networks should not be confused with their correct use. When a user is using some medium to communicate with someone or keep in touch with people it does not imply that they are alienated from frustrations by how the information or content is presented to them on the website.

© Springer Nature Switzerland AG 2019
G. Meiselwitz (Ed.): HCII 2019, LNCS 11578, pp. 128–139, 2019.
https://doi.org/10.1007/978-3-030-21902-4_10

The User eXperience (UX) is responsible for evaluating the emotions and sensations generated in users by the use of a system, product or service [1]. These perceptions can be negative or positive because they can generate frustration when the way the information is delivered confuses users; or a certain sense of success and achievement when what is shown by the device is as expected.

Our research aimed to define a set of heuristics to evaluate UX in social networks. The set of heuristics was validated through expert's judgement and experiments. Our study focused on two of the most popular social networks in Chile in recent months, based on the intelligent tool SimilarWeb [2]: Twitter and Facebook.

The paper is organized as follows. Section 2 presents some theoretical background that is important for understanding concepts approached by the research. Section 3 shows the set of usability/UX heuristics for Social Networks, documenting their development process. Section 4 highlights conclusions and future work.

2 Theoretical Background

2.1 User eXperience (UX)

Directly or indirectly every website causes sensations, and these can be positive or negative. The first impressions in the human are important, since in a short period of time we decide if something pleases us or not [3]. Therefore, the first time a user accesses an application or website is paramount. This generates in us a judgment of whether we will give that website a chance to perform the same action in the future, or we will choose to find other alternatives that could be more pleasant and comfortable for the same purpose.

There are many accepted definitions of what is known as UX, according to the ISO 9241-11:2018 standard is "user's perceptions and responses that result from the use and/or anticipated use of a system, product or service" [1]. Several authors propose models of UX. Among others, Morville explains each of the attributes of the UX through his 'honeycomb' model [4]:

- Usable: The site should be easy to use, without users having to think too much about how an activity or action is performed.
- Useful: Facilitate the user to reach his goals and satisfy some need.
- Desirable: It must create content in order to evoke emotion and appreciation from users to achieve their desire to interact with the product.
- Findable: It must be impossible for users not to find your content.
- Accessible: The content must be designed for everyone, including people with specific needs.
- Credible: The user must have confidence in the product being offered and therefore in the person offering it.
- Valuable: The product, system or service must be valuable.

2.2 Usability

According to the ISO9241-11:2018 [1], this concept is understood as "extent to which a system, product or service can be used by specified users to achieve specified goals with effectiveness, efficiency and satisfaction in a specified context of use", presenting three main features:

- Effectiveness: accuracy and completeness with which users achieve specified goals.
- Efficiency: resources used in relation to the results achieved.
- Satisfaction: extent to which the user's physical, cognitive and emotional responses that result from the use of a system, product or service meet the user's needs and expectations.

2.3 Social Networks

Social networks have been developing for decades. Currently, computer systems have served as a tool to complement and promote this term that has always existed. Today we can learn more about the social networks that surround us, and these can constantly change in order to satisfy the needs of its users. These changes may or may not go hand in hand with the experience they manage to deliver to users. There are social networks that give a lot of emphasis to the emotions that their users could experience with the use of their platforms, as well as there are others that prefer to give preference to their usability.

Identifying the beginnings of social networks is complex, since they were not born in a digital way, but this medium complemented them later. Similarly, we can say that a social network is what we know as a group of friends, a family, or co-workers. They have always existed but not with the help of computer systems. Highlighting the words of Ponce [5], who indicates that a social network is a social structure formed by people or entities connected and joined together by some kind of relationship or common interest.

There are many social networks throughout the world, in some countries some are used more than others and the popularity of some comes at different times. But one thing that all social networks should have in common is the UX they apply at the time of their concession. A social network is the means by which people communicate, inform, keep in touch and express through the Internet. For this reason, they require a platform that supports them in the most comfortable, pleasant and safe way possible with a correct organization of the delivery of their information and its functionalities, among other factors.

Therefore, social networks are sites that are accessed through the Internet, which allow users to connect to each other virtually, share experiences and content, and even create new ties or friendships, but it should always be borne in mind that users who interact through these media also share their personal information with the confidence that it will not be disclosed or exposed to others, so achieving credibility is a primary factor for the responsible for the system.

As a result of the observation of different social networks, it was possible to identify six characteristics that any system of this type, current or future, should satisfy:

- Security: users must be able to trust the system, refers to everything related to login and logout, registration of a new account and or close any user account.
- Connectivity: users can manage their contacts within the social network, refers to everything related to follow, add, delete, block and report users.
- Interaction: users can interact with the system and the rest of the users of it, refers to everything related to the activity between contacts within the network, either send and delete messages, create instant messaging groups, and share, view, evaluate, comment and report content.
- Customization: users can adjust various settings of the social network, refers to the customization of profile and configure notifications that are received, the permissions granted and language, among others.
- Management of content: users add, create and delete content within their space in the network, regardless of whether other users of the network will interact with it or not.
- Help Center: users will be given a help service to resolve frequent or concerns related to the system.

2.4 Heuristic Evaluation

According to the website Allaboutux, there are currently 86 known methods for evaluating UX [6], including inspections, heuristic evaluations and experiments. This research relied on the heuristic evaluation method to validate the set proposed.

A heuristic evaluation is a type of usability inspection in which a small number of evaluators look for problems within an individual system, and then compile the results along with the rest of the evaluators (ideally). The recommended number of evaluators ranges from three to five and the experience of each will influence the number of problems encountered.

The evaluators are provided with a set of heuristics to evaluate the usability/UX of a website; it is important to emphasize what [7] mentions about the existence of generic heuristics and specific heuristics. General heuristics are applicable to a wide range of applications, usually detecting general problems; they are known by most evaluators. Specific heuristics detect both general and specific problems, but are domain-oriented, applicable only to specific applications.

Heuristic evaluation as probably the best-known evaluation; usually applied when evaluating usability, but Quiñones et al. [7] suggest it could be used to evaluate UX attributes others than usability.

3 Methodology

In this research we used the methodology to develop usability/UX heuristics for specific domains proposed by Quiñones et al. [7], its 8 stages are explained below:

- Exploratory stage: performing a literature review.
- Experimental stage: analyzing data obtained through experiments.
- Descriptive stage: selecting and prioritizing the most important topics of all information that was collected in the previous stages.

- Correlational stage: matching the features of the specific application domain with the usability/UX attributes and existing heuristics (and/or other relevant elements).
- Selection stage: keeping, adapting and/or discarding the existing sets of usability/UX heuristics that were selected during the descriptive stage.
- Specification stage: formally specifying the new set of usability/UX heuristics.
- Validation stage: validating the set of heuristics.
- Refinement stage: refining and improving the new set of heuristics based on the feedback that was obtained in the validation stage.

3.1   How the Set of Heuristics Was Developed

Our research included three iterations; none of these were performed the 8 stages of the methodology. Figure 1 shows how we worked in each iteration.

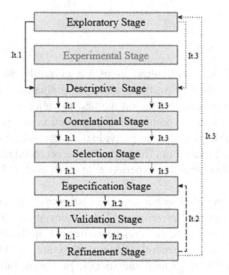

Fig. 1. Iterative process used in the research.

In the first iteration, all stages of the methodology were performed except the experimental stage; In the second iteration, only the last three stages of the methodology were completed, since details of the specifications had to be improved and the feedback was not critical with respect to the set proposed. Finally, some initial definitions were corrected, and most of the initial stages of the methodology were revisited.

Evolution of Heuristics. Thanks to the first stage of the methodology, which included a review of previous literature in order to find any research related articles that might be useful for creating or adapting a set of heuristics focused on UX in social networks. There were three investigations directly related to the domain of the problem. As the main base of this work was the set of heuristics proposed by Arancibia and Gonzalez [8] listed below (Table 1):

Table 1. Heuristics on which the set is based.

Id	Name
HRS1	Visibility of system status
HRS2	Visibility of the elements and important information of the system
HRS3	User availability
HRS4	Coincidence between the system and the real world
HRS5	Consistency and standards between system elements
HRS6	Consistency in web symbology and design
HRS7	User control and freedom
HRS8	Error prevention
HRS9	Minimize user memory load
HRS10	Flexibility and efficiency of use
HRS11	Aesthetic and minimalist design
HRS12	Help the user to recognize, diagnose and recover from errors
HRS13	Help and documentation
HRS14	Privacy and exposure control
HRS15	Control of published content
HRS16	Security and user account recovery

Although their work delivers a set of sixteen heuristics oriented to usability/UX in social networks and after analyzing each of them, we concluded that there are certain characteristics of social networks that might not be addressed by his work, in addition to not involving mobile platforms.

Table 2. Action to take, first filter.

Id	Name	Action
HRS1	Visibility of system status	Adapt
HRS2	Visibility of the elements and important information of the system	Discard
HRS3	User availability	Keep
HRS4	Coincidence between the system and the real world	Discard
HRS5	Consistency and standards between system elements	Discard
HRS6	Consistency in web symbology and design	Discard
HRS7	User control and freedom	Adapt
HRS8	Error prevention	Adapt
HRS9	Minimize user memory load	Adapt
HRS10	Flexibility and efficiency of use	Discard
HRS11	Aesthetic and minimalist design	Discard
HRS12	Help the user to recognize, diagnose and recover from errors	Adapt
HRS13	Help and documentation	Adapt
HRS14	Privacy and exposure control	Adapt
HRS15	Control of published content	Keep
HRS16	Security and user account recovery	Adapt

Document Changes. The proposed set went through a series of modifications along its conception, which are documented below. In the first instance, the base set was adapted to work on this research; creating, modifying and eliminating specific heuristics from the Arancibia and Gonzalez set [8].

As shown in Table 2, only ten heuristics were used to develop the new set. The justification for the action that was carried out with each heuristic is presented below.

- HRS1 - It is important that the user always has a notion of what happens on the site or application given their actions.
- HRS2 - It is not considered relevant to the wide range of social networks available on the market today.
- HRS3 - It is relevant to satisfy the features: customization, connectivity and interaction.
- HRS4 - It is considered that each social network has its own symbology with which it tries to set trends. Therefore, coincidence with the real world is not considered relevant.
- HRS5 - It is not understood what is sought to evaluate with this heuristic, if the reference were between its mobile versions and its web versions would make more sense.
- HRS6 - It is considered that each social network has its own symbology with which it tries to set trends. Therefore, coincidence with the real world is not considered relevant.
- HRS7 - It is relevant to satisfy the features: management of content and interaction.
- HRS8 - It is relevant for satisfy the customization's feature.
- HRS9 - It is relevant to satisfy the features: management of contents, customization and interaction.
- HRS10 - The purpose of heuristics is not clear enough, and its purpose is not understood.
- HRS11 - The design of a social network will vary depending on its purpose, therefore, it is not considered necessary to evaluate this topic.
- HRS12 - It is relevant to satisfy the features: help center and customization.
- HRS13 - Relevant for satisfy the help center's feature.
- HRS14 - It is relevant to satisfy the features: management of content, customization and interaction.
- HRS15 - It is important to satisfy the feature "management of content".
- HRS16 - It is important to satisfy the safety feature.

After this preliminary version of the set (Table 3), a second version of the set was obtained (Table 4); which aimed to complete the template proposed by the methodology of Quiñones et al. [7] for the specification stage along with all its attributes.

Finally, and after applying inspections to the set, it was considered that the heuristics of the set still did not have a definition that included the UX as expected from the research. So, in the third iteration we modify all definitions and explanations of heuristics to give them a focus on UX, and not just usability.

Table 3. SNUXH "Social Network User eXperience Heuristics", version 1

Id	Name	Heuristic's updates
SNUXH1	Visual feedback and system status	Base heuristics are adapted to the set, with all its attributes
SNUXH2	Ergonomic interface (Applies to smartphones)	Base heuristics are adapted to the set
SNUXH3	User perception and status	Base heuristics are kept to the set, with all its attributes
SNUXH4	Minimize user memory load	Base heuristics are adapted to the set, with all its attributes
SNUXH5	Prevention and recovery of errors	Base heuristics are adapted to the set, with all its attributes
SNUXH6	User control and freedom	Base heuristics are adapted to the set, with all its attributes
SNUXH7	Control of published content	Base heuristics are kept to the set, with all its attributes
SNUXH8	Control of notifications and alerts	Base heuristics are adapted to the set, with all its attributes
SNUXH9	Privacy and exposure control	Base heuristics are adapted to the set, with all its attributes
SNUXH10	User account security and recovery	Base heuristics are adapted to the set, with all its attributes
SNUXH11	Help center	New heuristic creates
SNUXH12	Consistent multiplatform	Base heuristics are adapted to the set, with all its attributes

3.2 A Set of Usability and User eXperience Heuristics for Social Networks (SNUXH)

- (SNUXH1) Visual feedback and system status: The social network must inform the user of the status of the system after any action taken by the him or her.
- (SNUXH2) User control and freedom: The social network should allow the user undo and redo actions; user should always feel in control.
- (SNUXH3) Consistency and standards in multiplatform: There should be no visual or functional differences between the various platforms delivered by the same social network, to the extent that user interaction is influenced.
- (SNUXH4) Prevention and recovery from errors: The social network must prevent and avoid errors in use of the system through warning messages that deliver the right information, without too much technicality that may confuse the user.
- (SNUXH5) Minimize user memory load: User should not have to remember information that he/she already provided.
- (SNUXH6) Aesthetic and minimalist design: The social network must show an aesthetic design that includes only the elements relevant to the user in a certain context of use.

Table 4. SNUXH "Social Network User eXperience Heuristics", version 2

Id	Name	Heuristic's updates
SNUXH1	Visual feedback and system status	Add checklist
SNUXH2	User perception and status	Add checklist; explanation was improved; add problems
SNUXH3	Minimize user memory load	Add checklist; explanation was improved; add problems
SNUXH4	Prevention and recovery of errors	Add checklist; definition and explanation were improved
SNUXH5	User control and freedom	Add checklist
SNUXH6	Control of published content	Add checklist; explanation was improved
SNUXH7	Control of notifications and alerts	Add checklist; explanation was improved
SNUXH8	Privacy and exposure control	Add checklist; explanation was improved
SNUXH9	User account security and recovery	Add checklist; definition and explanation were improved
SNUXH10	Help center	Add checklist; add benefits
SNUXH11	Consistent multiplatform	Add checklist
SNUXH12	Aesthetic and minimalist design	New heuristic on the set. Adaptation of traditional heuristics
SNUXH13	Consistency and standards between system elements	New heuristic on the set. Adaptation of traditional heuristics
SNUXH14	Customization and direct access	New heuristic creates
SNUXH15	Ergonomic interface	Add checklist

- (SNUXH7) Help center: The social network must have a space where users can resolve their doubts about the system; the help information must be brief, accurate and user-centered.
- (SNUXH8) User perception and status: The system must allow user to configure, at any time, whether he/she is available (or not) to communicate; user must easily perceive other users' availability.
- (SNUXH9) Control of published content: The social network must control the content that publishes so as not to affect the sensitivity of users, through filters and regulations; the user must be able to denounce/report content published by other users on the network, indicating the reason (Table 5).
- (SNUXH10) Customization and configuration settings: The user must be able to adjust the different settings provided by the social network and customize the space it provides.
- (SNUXH11) Security and user account recovery: The social network must include security measures, protection of the user's account and personal data; it must also provide an account recovery option.

Table 5. Example of a complete heuristic: SNUXH9 – Control of published content.

Id	SNUXH9
Priority	(3) Critical
Name	Control of published content
Definition	The social network must control the content that publishes so as not to affect the sensitivity of users, through filters and regulations; the user must be able to denounce/report content published by other users on the network, indicating the reason
Explanation	Users expect to enjoy social network content without inconvenience or annoyance. For this reason, the site must allow users to indicate that published content is not suitable for everyone. Also, it must allow users to report content, indicating the reasons why they believe that the publication is not suitable for anyone on the site
Application feature	Customization, Management of content, Interaction
Example	• The social network has the option "Report this publication". If you press it, you will see a pop-up window that requires you to indicate the reason for the complaint • As a user, I want to have among my contacts only certain users, but I am not interested in the content they publish within my social network, therefore, users can 'unfollow' that kind of people, without prejudicing the relationship
Examples with images	Examples of heuristic's compliance are shown in Figs. 2 and 3
Benefits	Users will be able to avoid viewing unpleasant content for them, so their surfing through the system will not be affected
Problems	An expert might confuse the approach with SNUXH10: Customization and configuration settings. And SNUXH2: User control and freedom
Checklist	• The user has the possibility to denounce publications, justifying why • The social network responds in reasonable waiting times to complaints reported by users • The social network constantly monitors the content that is published inside it • Content considered offensive or violent is presented with a symbology indicating what it means to access it
Usability attribute	Satisfaction
UX attribute	Credible, Findable
Set of heuristics related	Arancibia and González [8]

3.3 Preliminary Validation

The set of heuristics was preliminary validated using three evaluation methods: expert judgement, heuristic evaluation and user test.

The expert judgement involved eight experts, all of them had participated in at least one heuristic evaluation. The method consisted of subjecting the experts to a survey

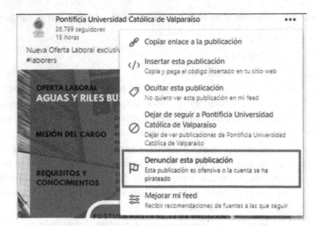

Fig. 2. With this screenshot to the social network 'LinkedIn', we can see an example of heuristic compliance.

Fig. 3. With this screenshot to the social network 'Facebook', we can observe another example of heuristic compliance.

that aimed to obtain feedback from them. The heuristics were evaluated in three dimensions (clarity, usefulness and ease of use). The results were mostly favorable, reflecting minimal modifications to the set.

The usability tests aimed to evaluate the set through the interactions that real users had using the system. Although social networks are a product that is used alone, this time it was decided to perform the co-discovery method as a test, in which users express aloud their opinion, feelings and thoughts while surfing the site. Finally, the experiment demonstrated that important heuristics were left aside within the set, and confirmed the usefulness of certain heuristics.

The last method was a heuristic evaluation, which was previously explained. There were six evaluators with similar experience, three people qualified and looked for problems based on the control set [8], while the other three used the SNUXH set. Each collaborator evaluated the study case "Twitter" in its web and mobile versions individually. In this opportunity the results were quite even, the evaluators of the sets found a similar number of problems. In addition, it was considered, based on the experience of the evaluators, that there could have been an overestimation on the part of the control group. Finally, this last validation reflects that the proposed set does not exceed the control set in all aspects evaluated.

4 Conclusion

Social networks have always existed and will continue to exist even when computer systems become extinct. Because people are what make them up. Although with the simple use of the Internet these have broken down borders that people could not cross so freely before, it should also be kept in mind that this tool is only that, and it depends on the users themselves the use they are given.

This research sought to provide a set of heuristics to evaluate the UX when using this type of systems, attempting to present a set that encompasses other aspects beside usability. After having established the attributes of usability and UX relevant to this research, accessibility was discarded, since at this moment there is not enough time to achieve a complete and correct validation of this aspect that freezes more than a simple heuristic can deliver. Finally, after applying the methodology for the development of domain-specific heuristics, it was possible to establish eleven heuristics. A preliminary validation of the set of heuristics was made.

As future work we expect to further validate the set of heuristics and check how useful it is for the evaluation of UX in social networks. We also pretend to refine the set, if necessary.

References

1. ISO 9241-210: Ergonomics of human-system interaction—Part 210: Human-centered design for interactive systems. International Organization for Standardization, Geneva (2018)
2. SimilarWeb LTD Top Websites Ranking. https://www.similarweb.com/top-websites/chile/category/internet-and-telecom/social-network. Accessed 21 Apr 2018
3. Iam, M.: La importancia de la primera impresión. https://ismaelcala.com/la-importancia-de-la-primera-impresion/. Accessed 20 Mar 2018
4. Morville, P.: User Experience Design. http://semanticstudios.com/user_experience_design/. Accessed 28 Mar 2018
5. Monográfico: Redes sociales. http://recursostic.educacion.es/observatorio/web/ca/internet/web-20/1043-redes-sociales?start=3. Accessed 20 Mar 2018
6. All About UX. https://www.allaboutux.org/. Accessed 10 Jan 2019
7. Quiñones, D., Rusu, C., Rusu, V.: A methodology to develop usability/user experience heuristics. Comput. Stand. Interfaces **59**, 109–129 (2018)
8. Arancibia, D., González, S.: Heurísticas de Usabilidad y Experiencia del usuario en redes sociales, Undergraduate Thesis, Pontificia Universidad Católica de Valparaíso, Chile (2017)

Infer Creative Analogous Relationships from Wikidata

Mei Si[✉]

Department of Cognitive Science, Rensselaer Polytechnic Institute,
Troy, NY 12180, USA
sim@rpi.edu

Abstract. Making analogies is an important rhetorical device. Analogies can not only help explain new concepts, but also make the expressions more interesting and creative. In our previous work, we explored an automated approach for making analogies using data from knowledge graphs where concepts are connected by their relationships. The algorithm computes how analogous two relationships are to each other based on the structural similarity of their adjacent concepts and relationships. The analogous relationships are then used to construct analogies between two concepts. In this work, we study how people's impressions of the analogies are affected by how the analogies are presented. We hypothesized that the analogy between a pair of relationships will be perceived as stronger when it is presented in a group of analogous relationship pairs for supporting making an analogy between two concepts than when it is presented alone. This hypothesis is confirmed by our empirical study. In addition, we found that people's impressions of how creative the analogy between a pair of relationships is not affected by how they are presented.

Keywords: Analogy · Computational creativity · Knowledge graph

1 Introduction

Analogies describe comparative relationships between two sets of concepts. According to the Stanford Encyclopedia of Philosophy, "An analogy is a comparison between two objects, or systems of objects, that highlights respects in which they are thought to be similar" (Bartha 2013), e.g. "Life is like a box of chocolates, you never know what you're gonna get". Here, an analogy is made between the uncertainty of what happens in life and the flavor of chocolates one may get by randomly picking one from a box. Scientific analogies often compare one system to another, such as Rutherford's atomic model which compares the atomic system to the solar system. Making analogies is a common and important rhetorical device. Analogies can not only help explain new concepts, but also make the sentences more interesting and creative.

With the rapid development of computational technologies in recent years, creating conversational agents that can communicate with people in task orientated dialogue or small talk has received increasing interest in recent years. Intelligent conversational agents, such as Alexia, Google assistant, and Siri have become a more and more integral part of people's everyday lives. Enabling conversational agents to use

© Springer Nature Switzerland AG 2019
G. Meiselwitz (Ed.): HCII 2019, LNCS 11578, pp. 140–151, 2019.
https://doi.org/10.1007/978-3-030-21902-4_11

analogies in their speech will enhance their ability to communicate or develop a social relationship with the users.

1.1 Cognitive Theories on Analogy-Making

Many cognitive theories have been proposed for explaining how people form analogies, such as LISA (Kubose et al. 2002), CAB (Larkey and Love 2003), Structure-Mapping Theory (SMT) (Gentner 1983; Gentner and Smith 2012), and (Winston 1980; Kline 1983; Kedar-Cabelli 1985; Greiner 1988; Holyoak and Thagard 1989; O'Donoghue and Keane 2012; Grootswagers 2013). Common to most existing work, the central idea behind analogy-making involves mapping hierarchical relationship structures among the concepts in two different domains. For example, according to the Structure-Mapping Theory (SMT), analogical mapping is created by establishing a structural alignment of the relationships between two sets of concepts. The closer the structural match is, the more optimal the inferred analogy will be. The Structure-Mapping Engine (SME) is a computational system that implements SMT (Falkenhainer et al. 1989). For producing the analogy between the solar system and the Rutherford model, SME can computationally determine that maximum structural mapping happens when the Sun is mapped to the nucleus and the planets are mapped to the electrons. This mapping is resulted from the structural mapping of the relationships among these concepts. In the solar system, the Sun attracts the planets and has a greater mass than the planets; as a result, the planets revolve around the Sun, i.e. the attract and the greater-than relationships together cause the revolve relationship. Furthermore, the attract relationship is caused by both the Sun and the planets have mass and therefore have gravity. The same relationship structure exists for explaining how the nucleus attracts the electrons and makes the electrons revolve around it. Figure 1 shows SMT's models of the solar system and the Rutherford model. The relationship structures are also often expressed in predicate calculus.

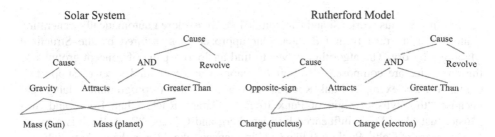

Fig. 1. Relationship structures of the solar system and the Rutherford model.

1.2 Create Analogies Without Hierarchically Structured Data

A major challenge of adapting existing theories on analogy-making to generate dialogue for conversational agents is acquiring appropriate input data. In most cases, existing theories rely on the input data containing structural information about concept relationships, such as the relationship structures shown in Fig. 1. Automatically gathering data with such hierarchal structure is almost impossible. Manually created input data tend to be small scaled which will significantly limit the amount and variety of analogies a dialogue agent can make.

In this work, we explore automatically creating analogies using contents from knowledge graphs. Semantic web such as DBpedia (Bizer et al. 2009) and Wikidata (Erxleben et al. 2014) contain a massive amount of structured data, which can be used to construct knowledge graphs easily. In knowledge graphs, concepts are connected by links which represent the relationships among the concepts. Knowledge graphs, therefore, intuitively provide a good basis for automatically generating analogies. On the other hand, the concept-relationship structure is flat in knowledge graphs. There is no hierarchical relationship structure, and therefore we cannot directly use content from knowledge graphs to infer relationship structural mappings for analogy-making. Figure 2 provides an example knowledge graph crawled from Wikipedia. Sun was used as the seed node, and we only included concepts that are within two steps from the Sun. We used the Seealsology tool (Seealsology) for generating this graph. For generating analogies in this work, we wrote our own crawler for gathering data which will be explained in Sect. 2.

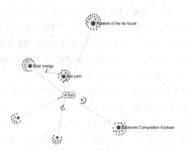

Fig. 2. Sun and related concepts in Wikipedia.

In our previous work (Si and Carlson 2017), we explored automatically generating analogies using data from DBpedia. Our approach was inspired by the Structural Mapping Theory. The algorithm strives to find analogous pairs of concept groups and the analogies are composed of a pair of mapping concepts and a set of supporting evidences. For example, Punk Rock is analogous to LPC (a programming language) because "the stylistic origin of Punk Rock is Garage Rock, Glam Rock, and Surf Music, just like LPC is influenced by Lisp, Perl, and C," and "Punk Rock is a music fusion genre of Celtic Punk, just like LPC influences Pike." Here, the analogy between Punk Rock and LPC is supported by mapping the "stylistic origin" of a music genre to the "influenced by" relationship among programming languages, and the "fusion genre" relationship among music genres to the "influence" relationship among programming languages.

An important step in the algorithm is inferring pairs of analogous relationships. The algorithm computes how analogous two relationships are to each other based on the structural similarity of their adjacent concepts and relationships. For example, if on average, the concepts where relationship r is linked from are always associated with more relationships than the concepts where r is targeting at, then r is more similar to other relationships which also have this pattern than to those that have a different pattern, e.g. the concepts where the relationship is linked from are always associated with the same relationships as the concepts where the relationship is targeting at. In our algorithm, we computed four sets of relationship differences between the linked-from concept and the targeting concept:

1. Gain – what relationships are associated with the targeting concept but not the linked-from concept;
2. Loss – what relationships are associated with the linked-from concept but not the targeting concept;
3. Same – what relationships are associated with both the targeting concept and the linked-from concept;
4. Diff – the combination of the gain and the loss sets.

Section 2 provides the details of the algorithm for computing the structural similarity between two relationships. After we have obtained the similarities between each pair of relationships in a domain or two different domains if we septate the source and the target domains, the relationships are then used to construct analogies between concepts. If two concepts have many relationships that are analogous/similar to each other, the two concepts are regarded as being analogous.

1.3 Evaluations of the Generated Analogies

Though the process of computing how analogous two relationships are to each other leverages on the idea of computing structural similarity, the results produced by (Si and Carlson 2017) are different from results produced by SME or other theories that infer analogies purely based on structural similarities. Using SME, a relationship is mapped to another, e.g., the revolving relationship in a planet revolves around the Sun and the revolving relationship in an electron revolves around the nucleus because of the structural alignment between the two groups of concepts and does not have anything to do with what the relationships are. Two relationships both named involving does not make them more analogous to each other than two relationships with different names.

In our previous work as well as in this work, we aim at creating analogies where the relationship mapping itself is analogous. Using the analogy example between programming languages and music genres, we believe Punk Rock is analogous to LPC exactly because "stylistic origin" is analogous to "influenced by" and "fusion genre" is analogous to "influence." When interpreting analogies created by our system, people's perception of how much two concepts seem analogous to each other are dependent on how much they think each of the related relationship pairs are analogous to each other. Here, "influence" and "sub-genre" are mapping relationships. They are not synonyms but have similar meanings in their respective domains. We can similarly say Python influenced many other programming languages just like Jazz has many sub-genres. Without the supporting evidences, Python and Jazz are largely not related. However, the influenced relationship and the sub-genre relationship may still read analogous to each other. Further, unlikely presenting the analogy itself where the supporting evidences must be included, the analogous relationships can be presented alone, and without additional supporting information. This property makes it very convenient to use analogous relationship in dialogue generation.

In this work, we study how people's impressions of the analogies and in particular the analogous relationships are affected by how the analogies are presented. (Kubose et al. 2002) showed that when multiple propositions can jointly provide a stronger structural support for an analogy and are presented together, people understand the mappings in the analogy more accurately than when the propositions are presented individually. Our hypothesis is inspired by this finding. We hypothesized that the analogy between a pair of relationships will be perceived as stronger when it is presented in a group of analogous relationships for making an analogy between two concepts than when it is presented alone. In addition, we want to find out whether people can differentiate the mapping between two concepts or two relationships is analogous or is creative.

2 Make Analogies Using Knowledge Graphs

2.1 Information from Wikidata

In this work, we explored using contents from Wikidata for generating analogies. Knowledge graphs such as DBpedia or Wikidata contain huge sets of connected concepts. In (Si and Carlson 2017), we used information from DBpedia as the base for generating analogies. In this work, we want to explore using information from Wikidata. The main benefit of switching to Wikidata is that the relationships in Wikidata are all uniquely identifiable. This eliminates the need for dealing with relationships with similar names such as "influence" and "influences." It turned out to be a challenging task to decides what relationships can/should be merged when using data from DBpedia. For getting information from Wikidata, we wrote a web crawler using Python, which stores concepts and their relationships in a network structure that can be directly used by the analogy building algorithm.

2.2 Find Analogous Relationship and Concepts

When computing mapped relationships, we used the topological similarity between the groups of relationships related to the source and target concepts as a multi-dimensional embedding for each relationship. Algorithm 1 is taken from (Si and Carlson 2017). It is the main algorithm for computing a unique index for each relationship in a domain. As mentioned in Sect. 1.2, for each pair of concepts connected by a given relationship r, we computer four sets of relationship differences between the linked-from concept and the targeting concept: gain, loss, same and diff. These four sets are aggregated over all the concept pairs connected by the relationship. We then compute the Jaccard index between each pair of the sets and generate an embedding for the relationship with six dimensions. These embeddings are used to compute the similarity between two relationships. Because there are no concept or relationship names in the embedding, the relationships from different domains can be compared with each other, and thus enable us to generate analogies between concepts from different domains. The details of the analogy-making algorithms can be found in (Si and Carlson 2017).

Another difference between this work and (Si and Carlson 2017) is that we are using much larger domains now. In our previous work, the sizes of domains are ranging between having hundreds of to thousands of concepts. In this work, we expanded the domains to have more than 20k concepts. As a result, the aggregated gain, loss, same and diff sets may become very large. We capped the sizes of these sets to 5000. When the sets grow beyond the limit, we down sample the set by randomly deleting items in it.

Algorithm 1 Index_Relationship_Type (*domain*):

loss, gain, same, diff, index = {} # empty dictionaries
# n: concept; r: relation; d: destination node of r
for each *n* in *domain* **do**
    for each *r, d* of *n* **do**
        # compare n's relations with d's relations
        loss[r] += *n.relations - d.relations*
        gain[r] += *d.relations - n.relations*
        same[r] += **Common** (*n.relations, d.relations*)
        diff[r] += **Difference** (*n.relations, d.relations*)
    end for
end for
for each *r* in *domain* **do**
    index[r] = (**Jaccard_index**(*loss[r], gain[r]*),
                    Jaccard_index(*loss[r], same[r]*),
                    Jaccard_index(*loss[r], diff[r]*),
                    Jaccard_index(*gain[r], same[r]*),
                    Jaccard_index(*gain[r], diff[r]*),
                    Jaccard_index(*same[r], diff[r]*]))
end for
return *index*

2.3 Example Outputs

The example output from our system consists of a pair of mapping concepts and a number of supporting evidence, which are the mapping relationships and their targeting concepts. An example analogy created by our system between The Source (a famous painting) and OS/2 (an operating system) is provided below:

- The Source → OS/2
- instance of painting → instance of operating system
- country France → language of work or name English
- location Musée d'Orsay → platform x86
- genre figure painting → programming language C

This example reads like "The Source is analogous to OS/2. This is because The Source is an instance of paining just like OS/2 is an instance of operating system. The Source's country is France just like OS/2's language of work is English, etc. Another example is provided below. An analogy is made between the state Vermont and (2970) Pestalozzi – an asteroid.

- Vermont → (2970) Pestalozzi
- instance of state of the United States → instance of asteroid
- located in time zone Eastern Time Zone → parent astronomical body Sun
- country United States of America → minor planet group asteroid belt
- head of government Peter Shumlin → discoverer or inventor Paul Wild (2970) Pestalozzi

We created these analogies by forcing the system to look for analogous concepts from different domains, i.e., the two concepts are not the same type of instance. Both of these two examples were used in the evaluation study described in Sect. 3.

3 Experiment Design and Materials

In this study, we want to evaluate how the presentations of the analogies affect people's impressions of them. In particular, we hypothesized that the analogy between a pair of relationships will be perceived as stronger when it is presented in a group of relationship pairs for making an analogy between two concepts than when it is presented alone. In addition, we want to find out whether people can differentiate the mapping between two concepts or two relationships is analogous or is creative.

3.1 Experiment Design

For evaluating the hypothesis, we designed a between group study with three conditions:

1. Full: the full analogy is presented with both the concept pairs and the supporting evidences which are composed of corresponding relationships and their targeting concepts, such as the analogy example given in Sect. 2.3.
2. R+D: only the relationship and targeting concept pairs are presented, e.g., country France → language of work or name English.
3. R: only the relationship pairs are presented, e.g. country → language of work.

The study was conducted on Amazon's mTurk. We recruited 50 subjects for each condition.

3.2 Materials and Procedure

The experiment material consists of 16 analogies generated by the system. Just like the examples provided in Sect. 2.3, each analogy contains four pieces of supporting evidence. The first one is always the mapping between each concept's instance-of relationship. Except for the instance-of relationship, the rest of the mapping relationships do not have the same name. In general, our algorithm is capable of generating analogies with more supporting evidence, and it is not necessary for the mapping relationships to have different names. We enforced these rules when generating the analogy examples for this study.

During the study, the subjects need to read the analogies with their supporting evidences if provided, and rate how analogous and how creative each item is. If the full analogy is presented, the subject needs to rate each supporting evidence first before rating the analogy between the two concepts. Each question is given a Likert scale of 1 to 7 (1 = Strongly Disagree, 7 = Strongly Agree). In the R+D and R conditions, the analogy between the two instance-of relationships is excluded from being rated. In addition, in the R condition, if the same relationship mapping appears in multiple analogies, we only asked the subjects to rate it once.

The overall time for the study is less than 5 min for most subjects.

4 Results and Discussion

Figures 3 and 4 compares the ratings of the same relationship mapping when being presented within a full analogy (the Full condition), separately with the targeting concept (the R+D condition) and alone (the R condition). The x-axis shows the question IDs. The first digit of the ID indicates the index of analogy example the question belongs to. Each analogy contains 10 questions. The first 8 questions are about how analogous and creative each supporting evidence is, with odd-numbered questions asking about how analogous an item is, and the even-numbered questions asking about how creative an item is. The 9th and the 10th questions are about the concept mapping itself. Even though in the R+D and R conditions subjects do not see the mapping concepts, we keep the same naming convention. So, question ID 13 means it is the 3rd questions about Analogy example 1. Whether it is about the relationship and targeting concepts or just the relationship alone is dependent on which experimental group the subject belongs to. Questions 1 and 2 are about the instance-of relationship. Because both the R+D and R conditions do not rate this relationship, the answers to these questions are excluded from the plot. Similarly, the answers to the 9th and the 10th questions are excluded. We also excluded a few questions where we didn't collect enough data because of technique problems.

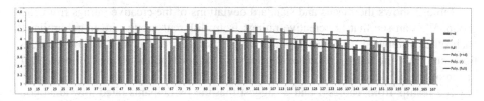

Fig. 3. Analogous ratings. The x-axis shows question IDs. (Color figure online)

From Fig. 3, we can see that the analogous ratings from the R+D group (blue bars) are usually the highest, and the ratings from the R group and the Full group are compatible. The polynomial trend lines indicate there is a constant decrease in the subjects' ratings in the Full group. This trend is not apparent for the other two groups.

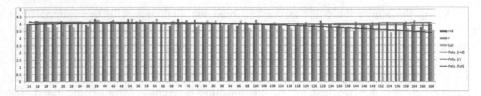

Fig. 4. Creative ratings. The x-axis shows question IDs.

We suspect the trend in the Full group is caused by the fatigue factor. The subjects in this group need to rate more items than the subjects from the other two groups.

In contrast, for ratings about how creative the items are, we cannot see clear differences among the three groups. There is a similar trend that the Full group's ratings gradually decrease over time.

Table 1 shows the means and standard deviations of the analogous ratings from each group. We report both the statistics for the entire sequence, and for the first half, i.e., the first 7 questions for ruling out the potential impact of the participants' fatigue factor. We performed two-tailed paired sample T-tests between the ratings from different. As we can see in Table 1, the R group gave the highest ratings in general. The ratings from the R group and the Full group are significantly higher than the ratings from the R+D group. The R group and the Full group gave similar ratings when only consider the first half of the questionnaire.

Table 1. Means, standard deviations, and T-tests for analogous ratings.

Group	Full sequence (mean/SD)	First half (mean/SD)	T-test full sequence		T-test first half
Full	3.9/0.2	4.1/0.2	Full vs. R+D	<.01	<.01
R+D	4.0/0.1	4.0/0.1	R+D vs. R	<.01	<.01
R	4.1/0.1	4.2/0.1	R vs. Full	<.01	.08

Table 2 shows the means and standard deviations of the creative ratings from each group. We can see that the creative ratings from different groups are more similar to each other compared to the analogous ratings. Looking at the first half of the questionnaire, only the ratings from the R group are higher than the ratings from the R+D group at the .05 level.

The results from Tables 1 and 2 suggest that the participants rated how analogous and how creative a mapping is in different ways. Based on the results in Fig. 4 and Table 4, we suspect that people could not meaningfully rate the creativity of the mappings generated from our algorithm. However, people can tell how analogous they are. Our hypothesis is confirmed that a relationship mapping is rated as being more analogous when it is presented within an analogy than when it is presented alone with an example of its targeting concept. We consider the R+D condition as providing an example of the relationship R's targeting concept because typically each relationship can point to multiple targeting concepts. A somewhat surprising result is the R group

Table 2. Means, standard deviations, and T-tests for creative ratings.

Group	Full sequence (mean/SD)	First half (mean/SD)	T-test full sequence		T-test first half
Full	3.9/0.3	4.1/0.2	Full vs. R+D	<.01	.20
R+D	4.0/0.2	4.1/0.1	R+D vs. R	.85	.05
R	4.0/0.1	4.0/0.1	R vs. Full	.01	.67

received the highest ratings for how analogous the mappings are. This suggests that supplying examples, i.e., the R+D group may not always help people understand the concepts better – in this case supplying a concrete example of the targeting concept, in fact, hurts people's ability to see the analogous relationship between the two relationships.

Fig. 5. Heat map comparing the creative and analogous ratings. (Color figure online)

The difference between the ratings on being creative and being analogous is further illustrated in Fig. 5. Figure 5 is a heat map of the differences between ratings from different groups. The first line contains the difference between the Full and the R+D group. To obtain this difference, we simply used the ratings from the Full group to minus the corresponding ratings from the R+D group. Similarly, the second line contains the difference between the R and the R+D group. The third line contains the difference between the Full and the R group. The last line is the question's ID. We only took results from the first half of the questionnaire. The odd column in Fig. 5 are associated with the analogous ratings, and the even columns are associated with the creativity ratings. We can see that there is no clear pattern in the difference between the Full and the R groups. Further, there is no clear pattern in the creative ratings as well. There are green bars in the alternative columns indicating that both the Full and R groups are receiving higher ratings on how analogous the presented items are than the R+D group.

5   Conclusion and Future Work

Making analogies is a common and important rhetorical device. Analogies can not only help explain new concepts, but also make the expressions more interesting and seem more creative. In this work, we explored creating analogies using information crawled from Wikidata. We also conducted an empirical study for investigating how people's impressions of the analogies are affected by how the analogies are presented. Our results show that both presenting the analogous relationships just by themselves and within an analogy between two concepts work better than showing the relationships along with a targeting concept the relationship can point to. Our study also shows that people's impressions of how creative the analogy between a pair of relationships is not affected by how they are presented. We also suspect though people can judge how analogous the generated analogies are, it is hard for them to judge how creative the analogies are.

Our future work lies in two main directions. One is improving the algorithm of analogy generation for creating more interesting and sound analogies. In particular, even though data coming from knowledge graphs typically do not contain hierarchical relationships, leveraging on semantic and network analysis tools, we may be able to build a hierarchical relationship structure in an ad hoc fashion and using it to aide our reasoning on analogy building. Related to this goal, we also plan to explore creating analogies that are more similar to those appearing in literature, rather than for explaining scientific concepts. Secondly, we are interested in conducting more experiments like the one presented in this work and study how we can use the automatically generated analogies more effectively in conversations.

Acknowledgement. This work is partially supported by the Rhino-bird visiting professor program from Tencent, and part of the research was conducted at Tencent AI Lab, Bellevue, WA.

References

Bartha, P.: Analogy and analogical reasoning. In: Zalta, E.N. (ed.) The Stanford Encyclopedia of Philosophy, Spring 2019 (forthcoming). https://plato.stanford.edu/archives/spr2019/entries/reasoning-analogy/

Bizer, C., et al.: DBpedia-a crystallization point for the web of data. Web Semant.: Sci. Serv. Agents World Wide Web 7(3), 154–165 (2009)

Erxleben, F., Günther, M., Krötzsch, M., Mendez, J., Vrandečić, D.: Introducing wikidata to the linked data web. In: Mika, P., Tudorache, T., Bernstein, A., Welty, C., Knoblock, C., Vrandečić, D., Groth, P., Noy, N., Janowicz, K., Goble, C. (eds.) ISWC 2014. LNCS, vol. 8796, pp. 50–65. Springer, Cham (2014). https://doi.org/10.1007/978-3-319-11964-9_4

Falkenhainer, B., Forbus, K., Gentner, D.: The structure-mapping engine: algorithm and examples. Artif. Intell. **41**, 1–63 (1989)

Forbus, K., Oblinger, D.: Making SME greedy and pragmatic. In: Proceedings of the 12th Annual Conference of the Cognitive Science Society, pp. 61–68 (1990)

Gentner, D., Markman, A.B.: Structure mapping in analogy and similarity. Am. Psychol. **52**, 45–56 (1997)

Gentner, D., Smith, L.: Analogical reasoning. In: Ramachandran, V. (ed.) Encyclopedia of Human Behavior, 2nd edn, pp. 130–136. Elsevier, Oxford (2012)

Gentner, D.: Structure-mapping: a theoretical framework for analogy. Cogn. Sci. **7**(2), 155–170 (1983)

Greiner, R.: Learning by understanding analogies. Artif. Intell. **35**(1), 81–125 (1988)

Grootswagers, T.: Having your cake and eating it too: towards a fast and optimal method for analogy derivation. Master dissertation, Radboud University, The Netherlands (2013)

Holyoak, K., Thagard, P.: Analogical mapping by constraint satisfaction. Cogn. Sci. **13**(3), 295–355 (1989)

Kedar-Cabelli, S.T.: Purpose-directed analogy. In: Proceedings of the Cognitive Science Society Conference, pp. 150–159 (1985)

Kline, P.J.: Computing the similarity of structured objects by means of a heuristic search for correspondences. Doctoral dissertation, University of Michigan (1983)

Kubose, T.T., Holyoak, K.J., Hummel, J.E.: The role of textual coherence in incremental analogical mapping. J. Mem. Lang. **47**(3), 407–435 (2002)

Larkey, L.B., Love, B.C.: CAB: connectionist analogy builder. Cogn. Sci. **27**(5), 781–794 (2003)

O'Donoghue, D., Keane, M.T.: A creative analogy machine: results and challenges. In: Proceedings of the International Conference on Computational Creativity (2012)

Seealsology. http://tools.medialab.sciences-po.fr/seealsology/. Accessed 3 Jan 2019

Si, M., Carlson, C.: A data-driven approach for making analogies. In: Proceedings of the Cognitive Science Society Conference, pp. 3155–3160 (2017)

Winston, P.H.: Learning and reasoning by analogy. Commun. ACM **23**(12), 689–703 (1980)

Research on O2O Product Design of Beautiful Rural Tourism in the We-Media Era

Congyao Xu[1(✉)] and Xiwen Xu[2]

[1] Nanguang College, Communication University of China,
Nanjing 210071, China
xucongyao@126.com, xucongyao@me.com
[2] Institute of Arts, Southeast University, Nanjing 211189, China

Abstract. This paper analyzes the present situation and development trend of rural tourism, and puts forward the idea of developing tourism-like O2O products by using We-Media communication effect. By deconstructing the three functions of We-Media era, tourists' experience behavior and O2O products, a beautiful village from the We-media era is constructed with the breakthrough of tourists' experience mode and the function mode of O2O products. The design method and concrete measures of tourism O2O product system are introduced, and the design practice of Tangshan Village in Nanjing City is taken as an example to verify the method. It provides a reference for the innovative construction of the beautiful countryside in the mobile Internet era.

Keywords: Rural tourism · We-media communication ·
O2O product function · Experiential behavior mode · Virtual image design

1 Introduction

Since the 19th National Congress, the rural revitalization strategy centered on the issues of agriculture, rural areas and farmers has been raised to an unprecedented height. At present, the research results on beautiful countryside are mainly focused on policy interpretation, research and analysis in a certain region, information services and the construction of rural complex ecosystem, but the research achievements in the field of product design are very rare. At a time when the number of free travelers is constantly rising, beautiful countryside has great potential for developing its characteristic products. Therefore, tourism, as a green, high-quality industry that can effectively boost consumption, has become the entry point for beautiful countryside's development. The media environment has changed in the mobile Internet era, and the We-media communication platform has formed a momentum of large user base, sufficient content creativity and great communication power. Because of the low utilization rate of mobile phone applications, more and more traditional brands have abandoned the application development model and tried to explore new models and create new products on the We-media platform. Therefore, in the mobile Internet era, it is urgent to carry out practical research on how to make full use of the advantage of We-media communication to design and develop characteristic products in beautiful countryside.

G. Meiselwitz (Ed.): HCII 2019, LNCS 11578, pp. 152–165, 2019.
https://doi.org/10.1007/978-3-030-21902-4_12

2   The Current Situation and Development of Tourism in Beautiful Countryside

2.1   The Present Situation of Beautiful Countryside and Its Tourism Development

In the process of rapid urbanization, confronted with the problems of declining traditional agriculture and deteriorating ecological environment, villages are facing marginalization and hollowing-out, the concept of "beautiful countryside" has been put forward: a sustainable development village with scientific planning, production development, comfortable living, civilized rural style, clean and tidy village, democratic management, as well as livable and suitable industry [1].

In the 1970s, Japan's "village building movement" has exerted great efforts to build up the characteristics of rural industry and humanistic charm, which has a profound impact on its rural revitalization and development. One of the most representative "One Village, One Product" campaign is a typical case of comprehensive development of rural resources for high quality, leisure, diversity and other needs of the city. In recent years, a number of good examples of beautiful countryside construction have also emerged in our country, such as Wuyuan in Jiangxi and Anji in Zhejiang, both of which have become "the most beautiful countryside in China" by virtue of their natural environmental resources and superior geographical conditions and relying on diversified publicity and tourism products. Rural tourism is the fastest growing sector in China's tourism investment. In 2017, the number of tourists received exceeded 2.5 billion, and the tourism consumption scale increased to 1.4 trillion, driving 9 million farmers to benefit [2]. It can be seen that tourism, as an industry that can realize the all-round development of economy, environment and humanities, has become a breakthrough in the development of beautiful countryside.

2.2   Beautiful Countryside's Tourists Demand Escalates

Statistics released by the National Tourism Administration in 2017 show that free travel is the main way of rural tourism, and self-driving is another major trend. Specific to the travel time and distance, the tourists' two-day tour is generally between 150 and 300 km, and the three-day tour is generally within 600 km [3]. This means that most tourists with a certain consumption ability will freely choose the rural tourism route on weekends or small holidays. Besides, they have a certain consumption ability and aesthetic judgment, and the choice of destination mostly comes from the Internet. If the rural tourism projects are still only on the same performance and the same small commodity display, it is already difficult to meet their needs. Therefore, under the surface geographical environment characteristics, the deeper and differentiated rural connotation and customs display have become the new demand of tourists, and the creation of its core experience content has become particularly important.

2.3   Tourism Development of Beautiful Countryside with the O2O Model

With the development of mobile Internet and Internet of Things intelligent technology, beautiful countryside's tourism products rely on intelligent information technology to complete data acquisition, identification, storage, analysis and feedback through VR (Virtual Reality) technology, thus constituting a complete industrial chain. The beautiful countryside tourism under O2O (Online to Offline) mode is to use online display and interaction to expand the offline tourism space, enable consumers to delete and pay for products and services online through the Internet, and then use vouchers to go to offline destinations to experience relevant tourism services. With the popularization of mobile terminals and the Internet, Online to Offline has three typical characteristics of socialization, localization and mobility, which can effectively use its social communication effect to gather popularity for the development of local rural tourism and promote its consumption upgrade so as to boost the development of local related agriculture.

2.4   We-Media Communication Effect and Beautiful Rural Tourism

We Media as a way to begin to understand how ordinary citizens,empowered by digital technologies that connect knowledge throughout the globe,are contributing to and participating in their own truths, their own kind of news [4]. This concept breaks the traditional mode of one-way information dissemination, including microblog, WeChat, short video social networking sites and other types. The user's subjective consciousness is enhanced; the content of the dissemination is fragmented and personalized, and it can cause instant public opinion effect [5]. Therefore, combining with Online to Offline design and innovation of tourism products from the media era, it will become the engine for industrial development, transformation and upgrading of beautiful rural industries.

3   Construct a Tourism O2O Product System in Beautiful Countryside from the We-Media Era

The construction of beautiful countryside's tourism O2O product system in the era of We-media is divided into three parts: First, the construction of tourists' experience mode, which mainly refers to the integration of tourists' experience behavior, sharing behavior and consumption behavior. The second is the construction of O2O product function, which mainly refers to the exchange and transformation of information data between the virtuality and reality. The third is to propose specific product design measures under the prototype of constructed method.

3.1   Construction of Tourist Experience Mode

Since the media era, the mode of tourists' access to information has changed dramatically: the mobile convenience of mobile phones has promoted a high degree of integration between social networks and real life, and to a large extent has affected tourists' purchase and consumption behavior. On the one hand, the channels and carriers of tourism information dissemination are combined through the We-media platform and tourists' way of life. Then O2O products become an important node connecting tourism destinations and users' needs, bearing the role of experience acquisition and sharing diffusion. On the other hand, every tourist is a relatively independent and complete individual. They make up a virtual community through the We-media platform owing to a certain life link or interest. What's more, they also have real social activities, obtain and share information with each other. Therefore, the most valuable construction in O2O product system is the integration of tourists' experience behavior, sharing behavior and consumption behavior. The experience consumption behavior of tourists is interpreted into five stages of AIVSA, and the experience mode in O2O product system is constructed according to the sharing characteristics of the We-media era. As shown in Fig. 1:

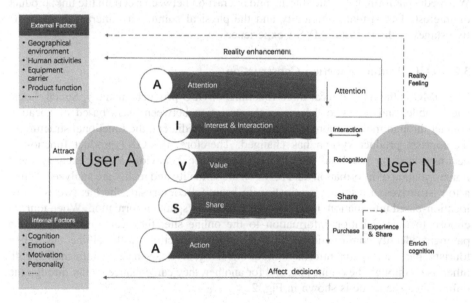

Fig. 1. Tourist experience pattern map

1. The external factors (geographical location, cultural activities, equipment carriers and product performance, etc.) of rural tourism destinations are concerned by the internal factors (cognition, emotion, motivation and personality, etc.) of tourists User A, which is the first stage of the experience model A that is attracted and recognized.
2. User A starts product interaction in the second phase of experience I (INTEREST & INTERACTION), including interaction with other users(User N), and interaction between User A and the tourism external environment through AR(Augmented Reality) technology in O2O products to form a reality enhancement.

3. Usually go through the first two stages to enter the third stage V(Value)-value recognition, and then enter the fourth stage S(Share) to share their feelings with other users(User N) on the basis of this recognition.
4. User A directly enters the final stage of experience mode A(Action) after V(Value) is approved to buy or consume and then returns to the fourth stage S(Share) to share the good experience to other users(User N).
5. Other users(User N) who share information can influence each other's internal factors during the interaction with User A, and can also feel their external factors simultaneously in O2O product system through the interaction of both sides, respectively, to enhance their real experience.

Therefore, the external factors that attract tourists involve people, culture, production, land and scenery, which constitute the local community entities in beautiful countryside. Tourists User A and other users(User N) form a virtual community through We-media platform due to the sharing and interaction between a certain life link, product or interest. The virtual community and the physical community interact through the five stages of the tourists' AIVSA experience.

3.2   O2O Product Function Construction

SOLOMO is the most typical three functions of O2O products, namely, Social, Local and Mobile, and refers to the regional interaction between users based on location contact through mobile phones [6]. Since the We-media era, the functional structure of the tourism product system has changed. Therefore, the O2O product function is deconstructed on the basis of tourists' experience behavior, as the exchange and transformation of information data between the virtuality and reality are analyzed. When a tourist arrives at a tourist destination in beautiful countryside, he has two types of location-based information: location information and spatial information. When tourists choose to share location information to the online site, they can match the online payment, identity confirmation, Chink-in and other functions at the offline site. When tourists share their spatial information, for one thing, they can share the information with other users through the online site, and for another, they can enhance reality through the online site. The mode is shown in Fig. 2.

1. Tourists (User A) have two kinds of information based on the tourist location: location information and spatial information when they reach the destination of the tour, that is, the offline of O2O system. Location information usually includes: geographic location, equipment carrier, environmental route, etc. Spatial information usually includes: landscape, theme activities, product appearance, etc.
2. User A's location information is authenticated and matched through personal information with Offline account login, enabling to use online booking, online payment, Check-in, Check-out, GPS, traffic and weather queries and other functions at the Online;
3. User A's spatial information can make him show his own pictures, short videos and playing experience through the system's We-media online, or also share experiences, display pictures and exchange with other users(User N), etc.

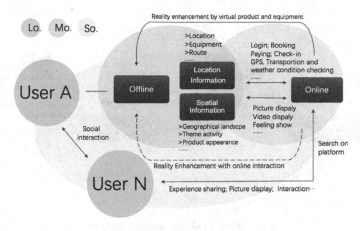

Fig. 2. O2O product function diagram

4. User A's spatial information directly enhances the real environment at Offline of O2O system by interacting with products at Online;

5. The spatial information of User A enhances the real environment of Offline again through the interaction between the Online and other users(User N).

6. Other users(User N) can search for User A's location information at the Online through direct social communication with User A, thus realizing sightseeing activities at the Offline of the destination.

7. Other users(User N) make online reservation and payment through the spatial information display of User A on the online to reach the aimed offline of the destination for sightseeing.

Therefore, the aimed offline of the tour destination and its location information and spatial information belong to the Local function of the whole O2O product system. The online terminal of the user's mobile equipment belongs to the Mobile function of O2O product system. During this period, the information sharing and interaction between User A and User N was realized by using the We-media platform, which belongs to the Social function of the entire O2O product system.

3.3   Product Design Initiatives

Entering the era of We-media of information interconnection, the traditional top-down industry model of traditional product design has been broken, and the design chain has gradually penetrated into the upstream market analysis, product research and development and downstream product marketing.

As shown in Fig. 3, stage A is the responsibility of the traditional product design. with the optimization of information and internet technology, product designers participate in the user demand analysis of the market research and development department, and then product design enters stage B. Since the media era, product design has extended to the stage C: it is a step closer to users. In addition to making use of big data to obtain potential demand more conveniently, it can also participate in product

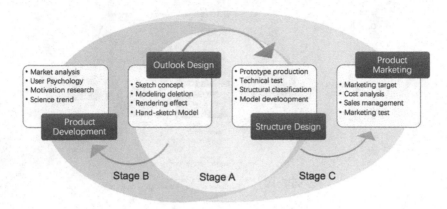

Fig. 3. Product design process diagram

marketing more directly and obtain experience feedback of user interaction in a timely manner. Therefore, the product design in the We-media era shows the new features of expanding the design chain, shortening the development cycle, demanding the core content of the product, cross-border integration of teams, and innovation of marketing model [7]. Through the constructed product system, the following four specific measures for the design and development of tourism O2O products in beautiful countryside are provided:

(1) **Pay attention to the design of brand virtual image and explore its cultural transmission.** According to the experience model of tourists in the system, we can see that since the We-media era, tourists have been no longer blindly guided by commercial advertisements but actively have started collecting relevant information, and the content with relevance and sense of identification is more likely to attract the attention of tourists' internal elements and be actively accepted and disseminated. At the same time, the product brand of the We-media platform has the function of media: it can become a provider of content, even design and produce high-quality media content, and then release it directly to target customers through the We-media platform. Therefore, User A in the system is not only a real individual tourist, but also a virtual image of a product brand. It makes the brand have the characteristics of image specificity and personification, makes its design concept concrete into a virtual image, and enables tourists to understand the valuable information behind its products and arouse their recognition and resonance through personalized interaction with other users from the We-media platform.

(2) **Making use of the community effect to create customized services.** In the system model, users gradually form a virtual community in the We-media platform because of their living environment or interests. They gather together to share life, work or entertainment information without geographical restrictions, constituting another interest community among themselves and emerging new consumption demands. At the same time, the external factors that attract tourists in the system involve people, culture, production, land and scenery, constituting

the local community entity in beautiful countryside [8]. They influence each other through the AIVSA experience phase of tourists. Therefore, the development of the real community in beautiful countryside needs to analyze the target user's information data in the virtual community, explore the potential demand matched with its cultural connotation, create customized services, and achieve a higher degree of integration of virtual reality through hardware equipment.

(3) **Design the theme of products and focus on experience and interaction.** In accordance with the interest interaction and sharing mode in the experience system, tourists are no longer satisfied with offline single-line consumption but prefer online interactive participation to experience local culture. Therefore, in developing products, we should not only tap the value of local products, but also focus on the sensory experience that users get in the whole O2O product interaction: designing the routes, services and derivatives of rural themes, and creating their relevant visual, auditory, tactile, taste, smell and other experiences according to users' demands, not only staying in the product development at the "object" level, but also building tourists' using logic, behavior trajectory, scene space and even lifestyle [9]. Taking advantage of the sharing features in the experience mode, tourists can spread the experience through the We-media platform to attract more potential groups to understand, share and feel the beautiful village in person. In the meantime, the secondary processing and creation of this information has also become an important part of the whole system, realizing the value creation of both users and products.

(4) **Activation of rural resources and diversification of product forms.** The primary factor attracting tourists' attention in the constructed system is the external factors of the tourist destination, so it is essential to realize the activation of rural resources: to develop the main rural resources and pillar industries in depth and at multiple levels so that they can operate independently and effectively in good order to attract local villagers to return to their homes, and to participate in the refactoring and construction of rural resources, and make their homes truly "beautiful countryside" [10]. Hence, in the process of carrying out this experiential design, the design forms of the products are diversified: compared with the traditional products, the tourism O2O products in beautiful countryside lay more stress on expressing their regional cultural characteristics through diversified technical means, creating a more novel and unique sensory experience, and enhancing their realistic expression through the interaction of the mobile end of the network to satisfy tourists' artistic imagination and experience new feelings.

4 Design Practice

4.1 Designing Background and Research on Current Situation

Tangshan Village in Nanjing is the east gate of Nanjing, covering a total area of 172 km^2, and consisting of 133 natural villages in 16 communities of Tangshan, with an agricultural population of 50241. There are now two golden flower villages and a modern leisure agriculture park [11]. As a world-renowned hot spring town, Tangshan

Village has abundant tourism resources: natural resources dominated by hot springs, Ming culture represented by Yangshan monument materials, ape-man cave ruins, Jiang's villa and Canglong Temple, etc. Meanwhile, Tangshan Village was led by the government to create new rural communities such as Tangjiajia and Qifang, combining tourism development with local agricultural production. On this basis, as the representative of beautiful countryside, Tangshan Village has the natural conditions and opportunities to develop tourism O2O products. After on-the-spot investigations and surveys, three manifest problems were found: First, hot spring tourism has a single theme, a great deal of redundancy and strong seasonal dependence. Second, the conceptual hysteresis of industrial development, the single mode of business, the serious homogenization, and the weak chain aggregation effect with local agriculture. Third, the new rural community has lower participation, lack of brand management concept and weak promotion.

To sum up, according to the constructed O2O product system design framework, under the background of Tangshan hot spring tourism development with a single theme, attention should be paid to the experience design of surrounding scenic spots with humanistic connotation, and brand management should be strengthened on the basis of new rural communities, so as to promote the active participation of local farmers on the one hand and enhance interaction with tourists on the other.

4.2   Design Proposal I: Design Virtual Image and Concentrate on Product Content Communication

The site of the ancient ape man cave on the northern slope of Tangshan village in Nanjing was selected for design practice: in the Leigong mountain of Tangshan Village, there is a huge cave group with a total area of tens of thousands of square meters. The skull fossils of Nanjing ape man unearthed in the cave are about 300,000 years ago, confirming that the Yangtze river basin is one of the birthplaces of the Chinese nation and has great archaeological significance. At present, Leigong Cave and Hulu Cave are open to tourists, but the actual tourist visited-rate is low. Besides, the landscape development is roughly the same as that of similar attractions. As shown in Fig. 4, the whole journey can take about 15 min to get out of the cave entrance, and the view of the cave entrance is wide enough to see Tangshan Village.

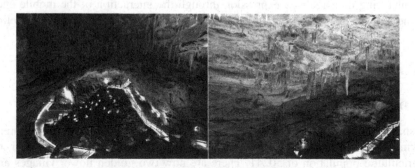

Fig. 4. Picture taken in the cave of ape man

In view of the practical problems, under the background of the development of Tangshan hot spring tourism with a single theme, attention should be paid to the experience design of surrounding scenic spots with humanistic connotation. According to the structured O2O product system design framework, virtual images are designed for the ape-man cave route to enable users to better obtain tourism from the perspective of product content dissemination. As shown in Fig. 5, the experiential design of the hominid cave is conducted from four aspects: online publicity, enhanced interaction, routes expansion and derivative products.

First of all, in the form of comics, draw the experience story version of the whole tour route from the perspective of tourists User A, and publish it through We-media platforms such as microblog and We-chat, as shown in Fig. 6. In the era of time-fragmented picture reading, the Online terminal arrests users' attention in a more vivid and direct way, and uses the social cluster effect to convey tourist routes and relevant products vividly to potential users through comics.

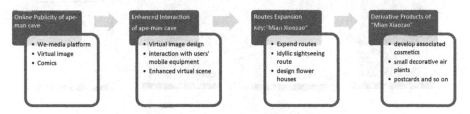

Fig. 5. Sketch map of ape man cave design process

Fig. 6. The cartoon excerpts of Visitors User A's experience

As shown in Fig. 7, take We-chat platform as an example to push popular science and activity information of relevant scenic spots on Tangshan public number homepage from time to time. The ape-man cave route is designed with a virtual image of "ape-ape" to serve tourists with functions such as scenic spot navigation, introduction to ape-man cave, and stalactite encyclopedia. At the same time, in the process of visiting ape-man cave, we can use image recognition and voice input and output technologies to vividly realize virtual reality enhancement with the image of "ape-ape".

Fig. 7. The excerpts of interactive interface of product

According to the actual investigation, there is a typical herb in Tangshan Village: Mian Zaoer, which has the medicinal effects of promoting blood circulation, detoxifying, detumescence and relieving pain in addition to its good ornamental value. On this basis, the brand image of "Mian Xiaozao" is designed, and at the same time, develop associated cosmetics, decorative air plants and postcards. As shown in Fig. 8, taking advantage of the wide view of the cave entrance and the unique geographical position around the ape man cave, we designed and expanded an idyllic sightseeing route, planned to plant related plants, designed flower houses and post stations, and opened online purchase and distribution channels simultaneously with product introductions. In the meantime, it also connects the scenic spots such as the flower house post station expanded on offline into the tourist route of the ape-man cave through the way of online drainage.

4.3   Design Proposal II: Substitution Theme Design with Emphasis on Immersion Experience and Interaction

The Ming Culture Village in the northern part of Tangshan Village is selected for design practice: Nanjing Ming Culture Village is located in Guquan Village in Tangshan, Nanjing, and consists of Ming Culture Village, Yangshan Guaishi Forest and Yangshan Beilin Wenwu District. It is a cultural tourism and sightseeing area

Fig. 8. "Mian Xiaozao" brand image and product sample map

based on Yangshan Xiaoling Tomb tablet materials and featuring the historical scenes of the Ming Dynasty, as shown in Fig. 9. However, the actual number of tourists per day is less than 100. The main reasons for this are: remote location, low popularity, slightly higher ticket price (48 yuan/person), single tour mode, low interaction of scenic spots, and idle tourist attractions, etc.

Fig. 9. The Pictures of General route of scenic spot, scenic entrance and the Imperial Drug Institution

In response to the actual problems, a substitute experience theme was designed for the route of Ming Culture Village to strengthen the interaction between tourists and scenic spots. First off, the way to collect tickets for the tour is designed as a mode of identity authentication: you can top up 100 yuan in cash or online in exchange for the entry token, and with this entity token, you can visit and consume in the scenic area. If the actual overspend, it can be recharged online or exchanged in cash at the pawnshop. The token will be returned when leaving the scenic spot, and RMB will be exchanged when it is not used up. The entire scenic spot browsing uses a physical product to complete the identity conversion and substitution, and can inspire tourists' consumption desire and tourist achievement, as shown in Fig. 10.

Fig. 10. The role experience design of Ming Culture Village

In addition, all the scenic spots with closed doors will be opened, and the staff will restore the real life of Ming people through clothing and scenes, and also set up some tourist experience links. For example, the staff in the royal pharmacy personifies the shopkeeper and page, and tourists can come here to watch the cleaning and drying of medicinal materials, experience the links in the process, and buy the relevant medicinal derivatives. Then, some scenes of life in Ming Dynasty will be combined with modern life. For example, the escort agency can perform the function of modern express delivery and provide packaging and shipping services for goods purchased by tourists in other shops, as shown in Fig. 11.

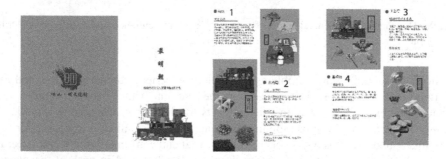

Fig. 11. The design plan for scenic spots of Ming Culture Village

5   Conclusion

This paper takes beautiful countryside's tourism O2O products as the research object, proposes the design method of constructing its product system under the background of the We-media era. It also puts forwards the measures and guidelines of system design through the construction of tourists' experience mode and O2O product function mode. What's more, it comes up with the concrete design scheme for the field investigation and design practice of Tangshan Village in Nanjing. Grasping the core of user experience and paying attention to the characteristics of communication and interaction in the era of We-media, we apply online to offline design method to the development of tourism products in beautiful countryside, which is practical and innovative. More importantly, it is a new trend in beautiful countryside research in the era of mobile Internet, which deserves further practical exploration.

Acknowledgements. The authors are grateful for the financial support provided by the 2018 Jiangsu Province Cultural Research Project (18YB09): Research on O2O Product Design of Tourism in beautiful countryside in the Age of We-media—A Case Study of Tangshan Village, Nanjing City.

References

1. Qiuhong, Q., Faiwen, Y.: Summary of the research and practice of beautiful countryside construction. Learn. Pract. (6), 107–116 (2014)
2. National Development and Reform Commission: Action plan to promote rural tourism development and upgrading, pp. 07–16 (2017)
3. Junlou, L., Jun, Z.: The development and Countermeasures of rural tourism O2O integration in the era of "Internet plus". Mod. Serv. Ind. (6), 107–116 (2014)
4. Bowman, S., Willis, C.: We media how audiences are shaping the future of news and information. The American Press Institute, p. 9 (2003)
5. Jinxia, S.: Analysis of the characteristics of information dissemination from the we-media. Today's Mass Media, 94–96 (2012)
6. Yuchen, P., Desheng, W., Olson, D.L.: Online to offline (O2O) service recommendation method based on multi-dimensional similarity measurement. Decis. Support Syst. **08**(003), 116 (2017)
7. Congyao, X.: Characteristic product design of beautiful countryside in Nanjing from the We-media age. In: Asian Design Cultural Society (ADCS), pp. 114–125 (2018)
8. Baosheng, W.: Open design for rural development based on local community. Packag. Eng. (02), 95–101 (2018)
9. Fangliang, W., Liquan, L.: Product design innovation: from tradition to "Internet+". Hundred Sch. Arts. (5), 69–72 (2017)
10. Shihui, H.: Japan's experience in sustainable rural areas: the use of the original resources in rural areas. In: The Third Asian Design Conference, China Japan Korea Symposium, pp. 123–130 (2001)
11. Haiqin, W., Chuan, Z.: Exploring the planning of the beautiful countryside in the suburbs of Metropolis – a case study of Tang Shan village in Nanjing. Small Town Constr. (11), 74–79 (2015)

Human Behaviour in Social Media

User Characteristics of Vaguebookers versus General Social Media Users

Chloe Berryman[1(✉)], Bridget McHugh[2], Pamela Wisniewski[3],
Chris Ferguson[4], and Charles Negy[1]

[1] Department of Psychology, University of Central Florida, Orlando, FL, USA
ceberryman333@knights.ucf.edu, charles.negy@ucf.edu
[2] Center for Education and Training for Employment,
The Ohio State University, Columbus, OH, USA
mchugh.159@osu.edu
[3] Department of Computer Science, University of Central Florida,
Orlando, FL, USA
pamwis@ucf.edu
[4] Department of Psychology, Stetson University, DeLand, FL, USA
cjfergus@stetson.edu

Abstract. Using the Unified Theory of User Acceptance and Use of Technology (UTAUT), we examined how user traits predict both general acceptance of social media as well as vaguebooking, an understudied subtype of problematic social media use. Past research has suggested that general acceptance of social media platforms and problematic social media use may be linked to different user traits. Based on a sample of young adults ($N = 467$), general acceptance and use of social media platforms were associated with a need to belong, while vaguebooking was associated with loneliness and histrionic symptoms. Histrionic users also had a higher acceptance of social media platforms.

Keywords: Social media · Loneliness · Histrionic · User acceptance ·
Vaguebooking · Problematic internet use · Need to belong

1 Introduction

As social media's popularity has grown, there has been increasing concern over the possible negative effects of these emerging technologies on users. 79% of adults with internet access have a Facebook profile, and 70% of those users use the platform everyday [1]. Both popular press outlets [2] and research communities [3] have suggested that social media may be linked to problematic internet use [4], leading to higher rates of depression [5], increased social isolation [6], and narcissistic behavior [7]. On the other hand, other researchers have suggested that negative emotional experiences or poor mental health may actually motivate certain individuals to use and accept these technologies or use these technologies to engage in maladaptive behaviors at a great rate than their healthier counterparts [8]. Using the Unified Theory of Acceptance and Use of Technology (UTAUT), the present study examines how various healthy,

© Springer Nature Switzerland AG 2019
G. Meiselwitz (Ed.): HCII 2019, LNCS 11578, pp. 169–181, 2019.
https://doi.org/10.1007/978-3-030-21902-4_13

unhealthy, and demographic user characteristics may contribute to user acceptance and use of social media. Since certain user characteristics, such as narcissism [7] and other personality traits [9], have already been examined as predictors of social media use, we focus our examination on user traits that have been less examined in the literature: histrionic personality disorder, loneliness, and the need to belong. To distinguish from general acceptance of social media, we also examine how these traits are related to vaguebooking, a type of problematic social media use that has been under-examined in the literature.

2   Related Literature

One of the greatest concerns surrounding social media is its possible link to problematic internet use [10]. Problematic internet use is a broad term that can refer to any sort of pathological internet use, and often includes maladaptive or psychologically unhealthy behaviors, such as internet dependency [11] and internet addiction [12]. Some of these behaviors are equivalent to unhealthy or maladaptive offline behaviors, such as using the internet to engage in procrastination [13] and practicing poor impulse control [14]. Many of these behaviors may be motivated or exacerbated by mental health issues such as anxiety, depression [15] and social isolation [6]. Internet use is also especially problematic when users perceive themselves as having few connections that are not virtual or feel uncomfortable interacting with others offline [16]. It has also been suggested that problematic internet use may include attention-seeking behaviors and may be used by individuals who have mental illnesses that encourage attention-seeking [17].

3   Research Framework

3.1   Social Media and Problematic Internet Use

Many popular press outlets suggest that problematic social media use in general can lead to negative mental health outcomes. However, the directional relationship between mental health and social media use remains unclear. Some research suggests that more time spent on social media may lead to depression and other negative emotions [18]. On the other hand, individuals who spend more time online may also use social media more because they have mental health issues [19], and that maladaptive online behaviors, not overall use is more related to mental health [20]. This research suggests that poor mental health may actually lead certain users to engage in problematic social media use as a means of coping with mental health issues in a maladaptive way. For example, individuals who are lonely may use online communication to reduce loneliness in a way that decreases more healthy in-person contact [6]. Thus, while users may use social media to engage in unhealthy coping behaviors, social media use is not necessarily used to engage in maladaptive behaviors.

Social media use and acceptance may also be motivated by nonpathological needs, such as a desire to expand one's social network [21] or to strengthen bonds formed offline [22]. Indeed, social media can be used to strengthen communications by opening up new forms of communication with family and friends [23] and help individuals from marginalized groups find support groups they cannot find in offline contexts [24]. Therefore, when examining predictors of problematic internet use, many researchers separate problematic internet use from more neutral or positive use and acceptance of online platforms [25], often focusing on specific categories of problematic internet use [16], such as online gambling [26], cyberloafing [27], and social media addiction [28]. In our case, the present study focuses specifically on vaguebooking, an understudied but prevalent type of problematic social media use [29]. However, we also examine a users' need to belong as a potential nonpathological need for using social media.

3.2 Vaguebooking on Social Media

Like offline communities, online communities such as social media websites also have their own norms that must be followed by users. These social media norms dictate what content or information is appropriate to share on social media platforms [30]. These norms are usually implicit [31] and are an extension of norms usually observed in offline contexts [32]. Some of these norms mirror offline norms, with some social media specific context. For example, users are expected to tailor information shared on social media to whichever users may see this information [33]. Social media norms also dictate whether information that is overly emotional or personal should be shared in private communication channels (e.g., messaging) versus public communication channels (e.g., Facebook timeline posts, public tweets) [34].

One type of potentially maladaptive online behavior, which violates social media norms is vaguebooking. Vaguebooking refers to posts on Facebook or other social media sites that are intentionally vague and ambiguous [35]. These ambiguous posts are seen as norm violations in part because they appear to be private messages that are shared with public audiences [33]. They are also considered norm violations because they may contain overly emotional or dramatic wording [34]. Users who engage in vaguebooking may do so in an effort to protect their privacy from people who may have access to their social media profile, but are not the intended target of the message [29]. However, research that examines specific motivating factors for these posts suggest that most users engage in vaguebooking as a means of eliciting emotional support or gaining attention from other users [35]. Users may vaguebook as a means of gaining comfort from other users without making a direct request for help [35]. These vaguebooking posts, while seemingly innocuous, can often be passive aggressive, as they allow the vaguebooking user to avoid speaking to someone who has caused them emotional distress directly [36]. Since they violate social media norms, they may also strain and damage relationships with people who view these messages [37], as well as create stress for receivers who are confused or frustrated by the ambiguity of these posts [38]. For these reasons, vaguebooking is generally seen as an unhealthy or maladaptive behavior [39] that is associated with attention seeking [39]. Though vaguebooking has already been studied in past research [33–35], there is no research to date on the antecedents of vaguebooking. In the following sections, we describe our research framework for examining vaguebooking behaviors and social media use.

3.3   Histrionic Personality Symptoms

Histrionic personality disorder is a clinical disorder recognized by the Diagnostic and Statistical Manual of Mental Disorders [40]. This disorder is characterized by a need to be the center of attention. Individuals with histrionic personality disorder often fulfill this need for attention through overdramatic expressions of emotion [41]. Histrionic individuals may feel frustrated when people do not notice them [42]. Histrionic individuals also have trouble gauging how intimate relationships are, and may seek out emotional support from people they are not close to [43]. Though histrionic personality disorder is relatively prevalent, with 2–3% of the population experiencing clinically diagnosable symptoms [44], it is underresearched in comparison to similar personality disorders [42].

As vaguebooking is usually an attention-seeking and overdramatic behavior [39] and often used to indirectly bid for emotional support or interaction from other users [29], users who engage in vaguebooking may have traits that are associated with these behaviors. Since vaguebooking is characterized by emotional and melodramatic bids for attention [40], individuals who exhibit histrionic personality symptoms may be more likely to vaguebook. However, while narcissistic personality symptoms and problematic social media use have been thoroughly examined in the literature [7], histrionic personality symptoms has not been examined in relation to problematic internet use. Therefore, the current study examines the relationship between vaguebooking and histrionic personality symptoms.

> **H1:** *Users who exhibit histrionic personality symptoms will be more likely to vaguebook.*

4   Loneliness

Like histrionic personality symptoms, loneliness also may prompt individuals to seek out emotional support [45]. Loneliness may arise from a perceived lack of social support or a perceived discrepancy between one's desired and actual social support [46]. Loneliness can be acute (e.g., feeling lonely during a solitary holiday) or chronic (e.g., feeling lonely for several months) [47]. While loneliness is a negative experience [48], it is not considered pathological. Instead, loneliness is considered a negative emotional experience that occurs when someone has an unmet need for social connections [49].

Social media acceptance and use may be motivated by a desire to connect with others [50]. It is possible that individuals may be more likely to engage with and use social media in part because it allows them to create new connection with other users or maintain relationship with offline friends and family [51]. Lonely individuals may be particularly drawn to online communication forms where they feel they can gain the connections they lack [52]. Previous content analyses of vaguebooking posts suggest that this behavior is based on a need for emotional support or social interaction [35]. Problematic internet use that is meant to elicit emotional and social support is common

[53] and is often motivated by users' loneliness [54]. Therefore, it is also probable that loneliness is also related to vaguebooking behaviors.

H2: *Loneliness will be directly related to vaguebooking behaviors.*

4.1 Need to Belong

Another trait that is related to a desire to connect to other is the need to belong (NTB). NTB is defined by the need to form attachments and feel a sense of intimacy with others [55]. Individuals who have a greater sense of belonging tend to have a higher sense of self-competence and worth [56]. Individuals who have a greater need to belong tend to seek out and strengthen interpersonal attachments [57]. For this reason, individuals who have a greater need to belong are more likely to engage in activities that allow them to forge new friendships. They are also able to maintain stronger friendships [58], in part because they are better able to follow group norms [57].

Though NTB has not been studied in the context of problematic social media use, it is generally related to more positive social behaviors offline [59]. Moreover, previous research suggests that NTB does motivate online behaviors that are related more to non-problematic internet use meant to strengthen, maintain, or form new social bonds [60]. Moreover, individuals with a greater NTB tend to observe social cues and norms at a higher rate in online contexts [61]. As vaguebooking is considered a violation of social media norms [29], individuals with a greater need to belong may engage in vaguebooking less.

H3: *Users with a greater NTB will be (a) more likely to use and accept social media and (b) be less likely to engage in vaguebooking.*

4.2 Demographics and User Acceptance

Demographic variables are one of the more widely studied predictors of user acceptance. The unified theory of acceptance and use of technology (UTAUT) [62] suggests that demographics are one of the key predictors of adoptions of new technology. Gender in particular determines which types of technology users tend to accept. Males may use the internet more heavily for entertainment purposes, such as gaming [63]. Females tend to use the internet for communication or social reasons [64], and are therefore more likely to integrate social media into their lives [65].

H4: *Females will have a higher rate of social media use and acceptance when compared to males.*

Another demographic variable included in the UTAUT is age. Age has been shown to be a strong predictor of technology acceptance and adoption [66]. Past national surveys indicate that younger people tend to be heavy users of social media sites [1], in part because younger individuals have spent a larger portion of their lives with the internet [67].

H5: *Younger user will accept and use social media at a higher rate.*

5 Materials and Methods

Analyses were based on archival data from a previous study that examined different research questions [68]. Undergraduate students from a university in the America southeast were invited to complete an online survey for extra credit. 471 undergraduate students elected to take part in the study. Of these participants, 467 completed enough of the survey to be included in the analyses. The majority of the remaining participants identified as female (71.7%), were young adults ($M = 19.66$, $SD = 3.92$), and identified as White or Caucasian (60.2%; 16.5% Hispanic or Latinx; 10.1% African American or Black; 6.6% Asian American; 6.2% Other).

5.1 Measures

Social Media Acceptance and Use. Since the present study examines social media acceptance and use, we utilized a measure that captured the extent to which users integrate and embed social media into their daily lives. The Social Media Use Integration Scale (SMUIS) [69] is a ten item scale that measures emotional investment in social media as well as preference for social media over other communication technologies. Example items include, "Using social media is part of my everyday routine" and "Social media plays an important role in my social relationships." Respondents rate their level of agreement for each statement on a scale of 1 (strongly disagree) to 6 (strongly agree) point scale. Scores on the SMUIS were relatively high for this sample ($M = 3.05$, $SD = 0.80$) and had acceptable reliability (Cronbach $\alpha = .90$).

Vaguebooking. Vaguebooking was measured using three items included in the survey: "I post vague updates that allude to something else on my social networking account," "I post social networking updates that prompt friends to ask me what is going on," and "I speak my mind on my social networking account without talking about what I am referencing directly." These items were based on formal and informal definitions found in past literature on vaguebooking [29, 35]. All items were answered using a 1 (never) to 4 (frequently) point frequency scale. The scale had acceptable reliability in this sample (Cronbach $\alpha = .79$) and a low mean ($M = 1.83$, $SD = 0.75$).

Loneliness. Participants completed the UCLA Loneliness Scale Version 3.0 (UCLALon-3) [70] to measure loneliness. Participants completed the scale by rating the extent to which they agreed with twenty statements on a scale of 1 (never true) to 4 (always true) point scale. The mean for this sample was relatively low ($M = 2.18$, $SD = 0.51$) and had acceptable reliability (Cronbach $\alpha = .93$).

Histrionic Personality Symptoms. Histrionic personality symptoms were measured using an eleven item self-report scale of histrionic personality disorder (the Brief Histrionic Personality Scale or BHPS). [42] Participants rated the extent to which they agreed with each statement on a scale of 1 (never true) to 4 (always true) point scale. Example items include, "I like to be the center of attention" and "I get frustrated when people don't notice me." The mean score on the BHPS was 2.14 ($SD = 0.49$). The scale demonstrated acceptable reliability in this sample (Cronbach $\alpha = .81$).

Need to Belong. The Need to Belong scale or NTB [71] was used to assess participants' need to belong. Respondents fill out the NTB by indicating the extent to which they agree with ten statements on a 1 (strongly disagree) to 5 (strongly agree) point scale. The mean for the sample was 3.36 (*SD* = 0.70). The scale had acceptable reliability for this sample (Cronbach α = .80).

Other Variables. Two non-hypothesized variables were also included in our analyses. The first was social media use frequency, measured as the average number of hours a day spent using social media to communicate with others online. This was meant to distinguish social media use frequency (i.e., how often an individual is on a social media site) and overall acceptance and use of social media (i.e., the extent to which social media use is accepted as an integral part of the user's life). This variable was also included to account for the fact that participants who use social media for a longer period of time may be more likely to engage in vaguebooking because they spend more actual time on social media sites. We also included a socially desirable responding scale in the survey. Since vaguebooking is considered a negative behavior [35], it is possible that respondents who engage in socially desirable responding may be less likely to report engaging in vaguebooking. Using the Marlowe-Crowne Social Desirability Scale-Short Form [72], we assessed the extent to which participants respond to items in a way that portrayed them in a favorable light. All questions were answered in a true-false format. The mean of the sample was 0.51 (SD = 0.22) with acceptable internal reliability (Cronbach's α = .69).

6 Results

To examine the hypothesized relationships between variables, a path analysis was performed using SmartPLS, as shown in Fig. 1.

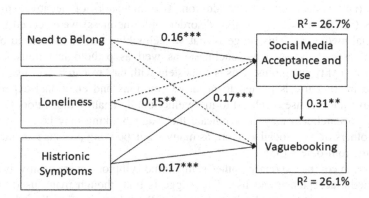

Control Variables: Gender, Age, Frequency of Use, and Social Desirability Response

Fig. 1. Path analysis of user characteristics, vaguebooking, and social media acceptance. SM = social media. SD = socially desirable. *$p < .05$. **$p < .01$. *$p < .001$.

6.1 Vaguebooking

As hypothesized, both loneliness ($\beta = 0.151$, $p < .05$) and histrionic symptoms ($\beta = 0.171$, $p < .001$) predicted vaguebooking, while NTB ($\beta = -0.082$, $p > .05$) did not [73]. For demographic variables, females tended to vaguebook more ($\beta = 0.099$, $p < .05$), while age was unrelated to vaguebooking ($\beta = -0.042$, $p > .05$). For control variables, socially desirable responders were not less likely to report vaguebooking ($\beta = -0.086$, $p > .05$), but people who spent more time online ($\beta = 0.083$, $p < .05$) and had a greater use and acceptance of social media ($\beta = 0.313$, $p < .001$) did report more vaguebooking.

6.2 Social Media Acceptance and Use

Consistent with H3, NTB ($\beta = 0.159$, $p < .001$) was related to social media acceptance and use. However, an unhypothesized relationship between histrionic symptoms ($\beta = 0.151$, $p < .001$) was also significant. In addition, it appears that people who accept social media are more likely to vaguebook ($\beta = 0.313$, $p < .001$), though this may merely be a reflection of the fact that people who have a higher acceptance of social media also spend more time on social media ($\beta = 0.288$, $p < .05$). Unlike vaguebooking, no demographics variables were related to social media acceptance and use. Socially desirable responders were also less likely to report social media acceptance ($\beta = -0.166$, $p < .001$), suggesting there may be a self-presentation bias to answers on this scale.

7   Discussion

Overall, most of our hypotheses were supported. NTB, a healthy motivation, was related to general social media acceptance, but unrelated to a type of problematic social media use (i.e., vaguebooking). In addition, two indicators of negative emotional experiences (i.e., histrionic personality disorder and loneliness) were related to problematic social media use. This suggests that vaguebooking can be influenced by non-pathological user traits, such as loneliness, as well as pathological traits, such as histrionic personality symptoms. This is consistent with past research that suggests that problematic internet use is related to negative emotions and emotional experiences, while positive internet use is related to more emotionally healthy motivators [74]. The relationship to loneliness may also indicate that vaguebooking may be an attempt to connect to others or gain social support, as many vaguebooking posts are an attempt to seek support from others [35].

However, in contrast to our hypothesis, histrionic symptoms were positively related to social media acceptance and use. This suggests that, though many users may be motivated to accept social media in order to fulfill healthy emotional needs such as forming stronger relationships and creating a sense of belonging, other users may also be drawn to social media because it helps them fulfill unhealthy needs. For example, social media can be used as a form of communication. However, social media can also be used feed an unhealthy need to be noticed and validated by other people [19].

Moreover, social media may also be used as a method to flirt with others, or to seek out romantic partners [75], in part because users have more control over the online image they present to potential partners [76]. These behaviors are typical of people with histrionic personality disorder. Therefore, our results may indicate that individuals with histrionic symptoms may accept and use social media in order to gain attention or to engage in flirting. Future research could examine these relationships more explicitly.

Our results for demographic variables were also not expected. Women were more likely to engage in vaguebooking, though gender was unrelated to social media acceptance and use. This may be a reflection of gender roles in our American sample. Vaguebooking posts are often a bid for emotional support from other users [35]. Traditional American gender roles discourage men from expressing emotional vulnerability [77] and seeking out emotional support [78]. Female vaguebooking may then be another form of this behavior, a possibility that could be explored by studying gender roles in relation to vaguebooking in future research. The relationship between age and social media use and acceptance was also inconsistent with past research [65]. However, this may be due to restriction of range, as the majority of our sample were young adults. It may also be due to self-selection bias; people who use social media more were probably more likely to elect to participate in a study about social media.

Socially desirable responders tended to report lower levels of social media acceptance and use. This may indicate that there is a stigma towards social media [2]. Also contrary to research, socially desirable responders were not less likely to self-report vaguebooking. This suggest that, though vaguebooking is considered a negative behavior that violates social norms [35], it is not considered socially unacceptable among the young adults who participated in the study.

7.1 Conclusion

Users who have a higher acceptance of social media tend to vaguebook more. However, it appears that there are several differences between a user who vaguebooks versus a user who has a higher acceptance of social media use. Typical social media acceptance and use may be motivated by a need to belong, whereas vaguebooking is linked to negative emotional experiences such as loneliness and histrionic symptoms.

References

1. Lenhart, A., Purcell, K., Smith, A., Zickuhr, K.: Social Media and Mobile Internet Use Among Teens and Young Adults. Millennials. http://files.eric.ed.gov/fulltext/ED525056.pdf
2. Stephens-Davidowitz, S.: Don't Let Facebook Make you Miserable (2017). https://www.nytimes.com/2017/05/06/opinion/sunday/dont-let-facebook-make-you-miserable.html
3. Barry, C.T., Sidoti, C.L., Briggs, S.M., Reiter, S.R., Lindsey, R.A.: Adolescent social media use and mental health from adolescent and parent perspectives. J. Adolesc. 61, 1–11 (2017)
4. Kittinger, R., Correia, C.J., Irons, J.G.: Relationship between Facebook use and problematic internet use among college students. Cyberpsychol. Behav. Soc. Netw. 15, 324–327 (2012)
5. Çerkez, Y., Kara, D.: Investigating the relationship between university students' use of social media, loneliness and depression. Eur. J. Educ. Stud. (2017)

6. Lee, E.-J., Cho, E.: When using Facebook to avoid isolation reduces perceived social support. Cyberpsychol. Behav. Soc. Netw. **21**, 32–39 (2017)
7. Andreassen, C.S., Pallesen, S., Griffiths, M.D.: The relationship between addictive use of social media, narcissism, and self-esteem: findings from a large national survey. Addict. Behav. **64**, 287–293 (2017)
8. Caplan, S.E.: Relations among loneliness, social anxiety, and problematic internet use. Cyberpsychol. Behav. **10**, 234–242 (2007)
9. Correa, T., Hinsley, A.W., De Zuniga, H.G.: Who interacts on the web?: the intersection of users' personality and social media use. Comput. Hum. Behav. **26**, 247–253 (2010)
10. DeJong, S.M.: Problematic internet use: a case of social media addiction. Adolesc. Psychiatry **4**, 112–115 (2014)
11. Odacı, H., Çelik, Ç.B.: Group counselling on college students' internet dependency and life satisfaction. J. Psychol. Couns. Sch. **27**, 239–250 (2017)
12. LaRose, R., Lin, C.A., Eastin, M.S.: Unregulated internet usage: addiction, habit, or deficient self-regulation? Media Psychol. **5**, 225–253 (2003)
13. Thatcher, A., Wretschko, G., Fridjhon, P.: Online flow experiences, problematic internet use and internet procrastination. Comput. Hum. Behav. **24**, 2236–2254 (2008)
14. Mazhari, S.: Association between problematic internet use and impulse control disorders among iranian university students. Cyberpsychol. Behav. Soc. Netw. **15**, 270–273 (2012)
15. Dalbudak, E., Evren, C., Aldemir, S., Coskun, K.S., Ugurlu, H., Yildirim, F.G.: Relationship of internet addiction severity with depression, anxiety, and alexithymia, temperament and character in university students. Cyberpsychol. Behav. Soc. Netw. **16**, 272–278 (2013)
16. Davis, R.A., Flett, G.L., Besser, A.: Validation of a new scale for measuring problematic internet use: implications for pre-employment screening. Cyberpsychol. Behav. **5**, 331–345 (2002)
17. Wu, J.Y.-W., Ko, H.-C., Lane, H.-Y.: Personality disorders in female and male college students with internet addiction. J. Nerv. Ment. Dis. **204**, 221 (2016)
18. Shensa, A., Escobar-Viera, C.G., Sidani, J.E., Bowman, N.D., Marshal, M.P., Primack, B.A.: Problematic social media use and depressive symptoms among U.S. young adults: a nationally-representative study. Soc. Sci. Med. **182**, 150–157 (2017)
19. Davenport, S.W., Bergman, S.M., Bergman, J.Z., Fearrington, M.E.: Twitter versus Facebook: exploring the role of narcissism in the motives and usage of different social media platforms. Comput. Hum. Behav. **32**, 212–220 (2014)
20. Harman, J.P., Hansen, C.E., Cochran, M.E., Lindsey, C.R.: Liar, liar: internet faking but not frequency of use affects social skills, self-esteem, social anxiety, and aggression. Cyberpsychol. Behav. **8**, 1–6 (2005)
21. Kraut, R., Patterson, M., Lundmark, V., Kiesler, S., Mukophadhyay, T., Scherlis, W.: Internet paradox: a social technology that reduces social involvement and psychological well-being? Am. Psychol. **53**, 1017–1031 (1998)
22. Moore, K., McElroy, J.C.: The influence of personality on Facebook usage, wall postings, and regret. Comput. Hum. Behav. **28**, 267–274 (2012)
23. Valkenburg, P.M., Peter, J.: Online communication among adolescents: an integrated model of its attraction, opportunities, and risks. J. Adolesc. Health **48**, 121–127 (2011)
24. Ybarra, M.L., Mitchell, K.J., Palmer, N.A., Reisner, S.L.: Online social support as a buffer against online and offline peer and sexual victimization among US LGBT and non-LGBT youth. Child Abuse Negl. **39**, 123–136 (2015)
25. Cooper, S.: Internet, social media, and television use: what effect does problematic use of technology have on one's psychological well-being, appreciation, and life satisfaction? (2017). https://login.ezproxy.net.ucf.edu/login?auth=shibb&url=http://search.ebscohost.com/login.aspx?direct=true&db=psyh&AN=2017-10860-186&site=ehost-live&scope=site

26. Floros, G.D., Siomos, K., Fisoun, V., Geroukalis, D.: Adolescent online gambling: the impact of parental practices and correlates with online activities. J. Gambl. Stud. **29**, 131–150 (2013)
27. Lim, V.K.G., Chen, D.J.Q.: Cyberloafing at the workplace: gain or drain on work? Behav. Inf. Technol. **31**, 343–353 (2012)
28. Andreassen, C.S.: Online social network site addiction: a comprehensive review. Curr. Addict. Rep. **2**, 175–184 (2015)
29. Child, J.T., Starcher, S.C.: Fuzzy Facebook privacy boundaries: exploring mediated lurking, vague-booking, and Facebook privacy management. Comput. Hum. Behav. **54**, 483–490 (2016)
30. Zhao, X., Lampe, C., Ellison, N.B.: The social media ecology: user perceptions, strategies and challenges. Presented at the Proceedings of the 2016 CHI Conference on Human Factors in Computing Systems (2016)
31. Hooper, V., Kalidas, T.: Acceptable and unacceptable behaviour on social networking sites: a study of the behavioural norms of youth on Facebook. Electron. J. Inf. Syst. Eval. **15**, 259 (2012)
32. McLaughlin, C., Vitak, J.: Norm evolution and violation on Facebook. New Media Soc. **14**, 299–315 (2012)
33. Cotter, C., Wanzer, M.: Facebook norms and expectancy violations. Presented at the National Communication Association Conference, San Diego, CA, November 2008
34. Choi, M., Toma, C.L.: Social sharing through interpersonal media: patterns and effects on emotional well-being. Comput. Hum. Behav. **36**, 530–541 (2014)
35. Buehler, E.M.: "You shouldn't use Facebook for that": navigating norm violations while seeking emotional support on Facebook. Soc. Media Soc. **3** (2017). https://doi.org/10.1177/2056305117733225
36. Edwards, A., Harris, C.J.: To tweet or 'subtweet'?: impacts of social networking post directness and valence on interpersonal impressions. Comput. Hum. Behav. **63**, 304–310 (2016)
37. Miller, K., Joseph, L., Apker, J.: Strategic ambiguity in the role development process. J. Appl. Commun. Res. **28**, 193–214 (2000)
38. McManus, T.G., Nussbaum, J.: Ambiguous divorce-related communication, relational closeness, relational satisfaction, and communication satisfaction. West. J. Commun. **75**, 500–522 (2011)
39. Carpenter, C.J., Tong, S.T.: Relational distancing and termination between online friends: an application of the investment model. In: Proceedings of the 2017 CHI Conference on Human Factors in Computing Systems, pp. 6925–6935. ACM, New York (2017)
40. American Psychiatric Association: Diagnostic and Statistical Manual of Mental Disorders-DSM-5 (2013)
41. AlaviHejazi, M., Fatehizade, M., Bahrami, F., Etemadi, O.: Histrionic women in Iran: a qualitative study of the couple interactive pathology of the women with symptoms of histrionic personality disorder (HPD). Rev. Eur. Stud. **9**, 18 (2016)
42. Ferguson, C.J., Negy, C.: Development of a brief screening questionnaire for histrionic personality symptoms. Personal. Individ. Differ. **66**, 124–127 (2014)
43. Cale, E.M., Lilienfeld, S.O.: Histrionic personality disorder and antisocial personality disorder: sex-differentiated manifestations of psychopathy? J. Personal. Disord. **16**, 52–72 (2002)
44. Kraus, G., Reynolds, D.J.: The "A-B-C's" of the cluster B's: identifying, understanding, and treating cluster B personality disorders. Clin. Psychol. Rev. **21**, 345–373 (2001)
45. Perlman, D., Peplau, L.A.: Theoretical approaches to loneliness. In: Loneliness: A Sourcebook of Current Theory, Research and Therapy, pp. 123–134 (1982)

46. Rubenstein, C., Shaver, P.: The experience of loneliness. In: Loneliness: A Sourcebook of Current Theory, Research and Therapy, pp. 206–223 (1982)
47. Johnson, D.P., Mullins, L.C.: Growing old and lonely in different societies: toward a comparative perspective. J. Cross-Cult. Gerontol. **2**, 257–275 (1987)
48. Wildschut, T., Sedikides, C., Cordaro, F.: Self-regulatory interplay between negative and positive emotions: the case of loneliness and nostalgia. In: Nyklíček, I., Vingerhoets, A., Zeelenberg, M. (eds.) Emotion Regulation and Well-Being, pp. 67–83. Springer, New York (2011). https://doi.org/10.1007/978-1-4419-6953-8_5
49. Cacioppo, J.T., Hawkley, L.C.: Loneliness. In: Handbook of Individual Differences in Social Behavior, pp. 227–240. Guilford Press, New York (2009)
50. Chen, G.M.: Tweet this: a uses and gratifications perspective on how active Twitter use gratifies a need to connect with others. Comput. Hum. Behav. **27**, 755–762 (2011)
51. Shamugam, L.: Aging society, loneliness and social support: is social media making them less lonely? (2015)
52. Morahan-Martin, J.: The relationship between loneliness and internet use and abuse. Cyberpsychol. Behav. **2**, 431–439 (1999)
53. Peng, S., Pandey, S., Pandey, S.K.: Is there a nonprofit advantage? Examining the impact of institutional context on individual-organizational value congruence. Public Adm. Rev. **75**, 585–596 (2015)
54. Kim, H., Markus, H.R.: Deviance or uniqueness, harmony or conformity? A cultural analysis. J. Pers. Soc. Psychol. **77**, 785–800 (1999)
55. Hornsey, M.J., Jetten, J.: The individual within the group: balancing the need to belong with the need to be different. Personal. Soc. Psychol. Rev. **8**, 248–264 (2004)
56. Pittman, L.D., Richmond, A.: University belonging, friendship quality, and psychological adjustment during the transition to college. J. Exp. Educ. **76**, 343–362 (2008)
57. Baumeister, R.F., Leary, M.R.: The need to belong: desire for interpersonal attachments as a fundamental human motivation. Psychol. Bull. **117**, 497 (1995)
58. Chipuer, H.M.: Dyadic attachments and community connectedness: links with youths' loneliness experiences. J. Community Psychol. **29**, 429–446 (2001)
59. Lambert, N.M., Stillman, T.F., Hicks, J.A., Kamble, S., Baumeister, R.F., Fincham, F.D.: To belong is to matter: sense of belonging enhances meaning in life. Pers. Soc. Psychol. Bull. **39**, 1418–1427 (2013)
60. Pickett, C.L., Gardner, W.L., Knowles, M.: Getting a cue: the need to belong and enhanced sensitivity to social cues. Pers. Soc. Psychol. Bull. **30**, 1095–1107 (2004)
61. Sun, T., Wu, G.: Traits, predictors, and consequences of Facebook self-presentation. Soc. Sci. Comput. Rev. **30**, 419–433 (2012)
62. Venkatesh, V., Morris, M.G., Davis, G.B., Davis, F.D.: User acceptance of information technology: toward a unified view. MIS Q. **27**, 425–478 (2003)
63. Winn, J., Heeter, C.: Gaming, gender, and time: who makes time to play? Sex Roles **61**, 1–13 (2009)
64. Borrero, J.D., Yousafzai, S.Y., Javed, U., Page, K.L.: Expressive participation in Internet social movements: testing the moderating effect of technology readiness and sex on student SNS use. Comput. Hum. Behav. **30**, 39–49 (2014)
65. Greenwood, S., Perrin, A., Duggan, M.: Social Media Update. http://www.pewinternet.org/2016/11/11/social-media-update-2016/
66. Venkatesh, V., Thong, J.Y., Xu, X.: Consumer acceptance and use of information technology: extending the unified theory of acceptance and use of technology (2012)
67. Kilian, T., Hennigs, N., Langner, S.: Do Millennials read books or blogs? Introducing a media usage typology of the internet generation. J. Consum. Mark. **29**, 114–124 (2012)

68. Berryman, C., Ferguson, C.J., Negy, C.: Social media use and mental health among young adults. Psychiatr. Q. **89**, 307314 (2017)
69. Jenkins-Guarnieri, M.A., Wright, S.L., Johnson, B.: Development and validation of a social media use integration scale. Psychol. Pop. Media Cult. **2**, 38 (2013)
70. Russell, D.W.: UCLA loneliness scale (version 3): reliability, validity, and factor structure. J. Pers. Assess. **66**, 20–40 (1996)
71. Leary, M.R., Kelly, K.M., Cottrell, C.A., Schreindorfer, L.S.: Individual differences in the need to belong: mapping the nomological network. Unpublished manuscript, Duke University (2007)
72. Reynolds, W.M.: Development of reliable and valid short forms of the Marlowe-Crowne social desirability scale. J. Clin. Psychol. **38**, 119–125 (1982)
73. Kim, J., LaRose, R., Peng, W.: Loneliness as the cause and the effect of problematic internet use: the relationship between internet use and psychological well-being. Cyberpsychol. Behav. **12**, 451–455 (2009)
74. Shaw, L.H., Gant, L.M.: In defense of the internet: the relationship between internet communication and depression, loneliness, self-esteem, and perceived social support. Cyberpsychol. Behav. **5**, 157–171 (2002)
75. Lenhart, A., Smith, A., Anderson, M.: Chapter 2: How teens meet, flirt with and ask out potential romantic partners (2015). http://www.pewinternet.org/2015/10/01/how-teens-interact-with-potential-romantic-partners/
76. Fullwood, C., Attrill-Smith, A.: Up-dating: ratings of perceived dating success are better online than offline. Cyberpsychol. Behav. Soc. Netw. **21**, 11–15 (2017)
77. Oransky, M., Marecek, J.: "I'm not going to be a girl": masculinity and emotions in boys' friendships and peer groups. J. Adolesc. Res. **24**, 218–241 (2009)
78. Ashton, W.A., Fuehrer, A.: Effects of gender and gender role identification of participant and type of social support resource on support seeking. Sex Roles **28**, 461–476 (1993)

The Digital Tools: Supporting the "Inner Lives" of Customers/Visitors in Museums

Adela Coman[✉], Ana-Maria Grigore, and Andreea Ardelean

The University of Bucharest, Bucharest, Romania
{adela.coman, andreea.ardelean}@faa.unibuc.ro,
anagrig27@gmail.com

Abstract. Few areas are so challenging/exciting as the world of museums. Although we are accustomed to look at the museum world in a rather romantic way, we must not forget that they are in fact service providers. Museums fulfill these roles today, especially with the help of digital tools. The digital channels and platforms used by museums shape the user's personal context, stimulating his/her behavior, interests, previous knowledge and personal commitment to art. The same channels and platforms support the formation of human and social interactions in museums but, at the same time, create the premises for new challenges for visitors and museums alike.

The aim of this paper is to answer the following questions: to what extent the digital tools used in museums change behaviors, satisfy interests and offer upgrades to their visitors' knowledge? What are the relevant experiences lived by the consumers likely to attract new audiences in the future?

In order to fulfill our purpose, we made a qualitative and quantitative analysis based on a questionnaire designed to investigate the visitor-museum relation. 341 (randomly chosen) visitors of four major museums located in Bucharest answered, providing a reasonable statistical base. The hypotheses of this study – most of them confirmed – converge towards the idea of the necessity to evaluate museums from the challenging perspectives of experiences the consumers have by using digital tools.

Keywords: Digital tools · Museums · Customer/visitor experience and behavior

1 Introduction

Today, museums are currently undergoing a process of negotiation of their own identity and of the role they have to play in the contemporary world (Johnson and Garbarino 2001). The "noble" character of the museum imposes respect and, most of the time, a silent admiration of the visitors towards objects/artifacts. The relation between object and public has been one of a strictly visual and static nature up to the apparition of the internet.

Latest research (Hein 1998) has tried to determine the role of objects within the museum, showing that objects/exhibits represent experience-generating "sites". Therefore, an emphasis movement has occurred regarding exhibits, as they were once seen as objects that could only be statically admired and contemplated, whereas now,

© Springer Nature Switzerland AG 2019
G. Meiselwitz (Ed.): HCII 2019, LNCS 11578, pp. 182–201, 2019.
https://doi.org/10.1007/978-3-030-21902-4_14

the exhibits are seen as cultural interconnectivity spaces (Sylaiou et al. 2010). Interactivity becomes a "tool" that promises experiences as the interaction with objects makes visitors react, challenging them towards participation and commitment. However, the subjectivity of experiences may endanger the authority of the museum, as the forum that is in control of the "monopoly" on professional interpretation of all forms of art (Hein 1998). This is one of the reasons why museums have assumed a completely new task for themselves, that is, to *create experiences* that trigger thoughts and emotions.

The adoption of informational technologies by museums promises a democratization of the learning process, contextualization of information regarding exhibits and, most of all, it promises a contribution to the increase of the number of visitors (Traxler and Griffiths 2009). The new technologies offer visitors the chance to make choices. Thus, the resulted experiences create the necessary space, so that as many voices as possible can be heard. The experiences a visitor has when she or he gets closer to an object or an artifact by using a digital tool, are not only of a cognitive and intellectual nature, but at the same time, of an intimate and a profoundly personal kind. In this context, *the digital technologies* have been presented by numerous specialized studies as being the key factor destined to *reconfigure the relation between museum and visitor* and to improve public experiences (vom Lehn and Heath 2005).

Hein (1998) argues that the learning experience and knowledge acquisition demand a person's *active participation*. Within the museum, active participation does not only mean to establish a direct relation with the exhibits, but rather the possibility to "play" with them – this also including the use of digital tools. Museums have responded to the need of progress by adopting new methods, tools and technologies destined to promote active participation and assimilation of new knowledge by visitors. Among the well-known tools used by visitors, we may mention: social media, Wikis, blogs, chat-rooms, user-generated contents (UGC), and among the interactive systems that mediate the relation between museum and visitor, we may mention: virtual reality (VR), mixed reality (MR) or tangible and multimodal user interfaces (TUI) (Kidd et al. 2011). All these tools facilitate the learning process and assimilation of knowledge and, at the same time, encourage people for action and social interaction.

Similarly, to other organizations, museums need to take into consideration the environmental factors in which they run their activity. Indeed, in comparison to the managers from the private sector, museum managers can choose not to take the environment into consideration. However, this may transform into a gradual degradation of the quality of activities carried out by the museum, thus leading to a defective accomplishment of the mission undertaken by the museum, and possibly, if prolonged for a long-term, even leading to its shutdown. No matter how much the scholars of museums despise economic principles and techniques, they must be aware of the fact that the accomplishment of their social, educational and artistic aims is directly proportional to their compliance with the rules that govern the market. Nowadays, museums exist within an environment where the skills acquired in using digital tools and the management oriented to proactive marketing are critical for their future.

Even if some of them own rich and attractive collections, there are only a few museums in Romania that have significantly renewed their museum discourse by using suitable modern techniques of presentation and promotion. However, according to the

National Institute for Research and Cultural Formation, within ten years (2007–2017), the number of visitors of Romanian museums increased over 3700000 (from 12.255.182 to 15.940.666), and the total number of museums and collections grew over 80 (from 679 to 762). In terms of number of visitors, the leader is Bucharest with 2 147 287 visitors of its 47 museums and public collections.

According to the Cultural Consumer Barometer for 2017, the most visited museums in the Romanian capital classified according to their type are: the art museums (46%); history museums (44%); ethnography and folklore museums (30%); natural sciences museums (24%). Thus, the leaders of the top according to general public preferences are: "Dimitrie Gusti" National Village Museum, The National Museum of Art of Romania and "Grigore Antipa" National Museum of Natural History.

Obviously, not every cultural act can be represented in numbers. We will never be able to either measure or weigh emotional experiences or emotions felt by a visitor at a museum exhibition (Plosnita 2014). However, we will always be capable of assuring the public quality of the museum. Usually, we immediately agree on the primacy of quality over quantity, primarily regarding the field to which we refer. We might not agree on the essence of quality, but the organizational quality is far more important than the quality of exhibits. A high quality managerial performance consistently applied to a long-term strategy will eventually constitute something as valuable as the exhibit itself: a peculiar image, a visual identity or a brand.

This paper is organized in three sections: in the first section, we review the specialized literature of the targeted field and we discuss the relation between visitor and museum in the context of the presence of new technologies in the world of museums; in the second section, we present the research methodology, namely the objectives and the researched hypotheses; in the third section, we discuss the results of the research. The paper ends with several conclusions and suggestions regarding strategies meant to support and improve the inner lives of both museums and visitors.

2   Museums and Consumers/Visitors: A Literature Review

According to the specialized literature, museums are cultural institutions that collect, preserve, research, restore, communicate and exhibit material and spiritual testimonies of the existence and evolution of human communities, as well as of the environment for the purpose of learning, education and recreation. However, museums are not only cultural institutions: they provide a wide range of services for the population. From the economic point of view, these services improve the urban infrastructure and create new jobs (Coman and Pop 2012).

Museum institutions, regarded as providers of services are, however, more difficult to evaluate than the companies producing assets. This occurs because the evaluation of services is based on different expectations from consumers (Zeithaml et al. 1993; Zethaml 1988). Therefore, in the case of services, the consumer's satisfaction is given by the fulfillment of the level of expectations: consumers compare initial expectations regarding the promised value to the perception of the actually provided value when she or he uses the service (Johnson et al. 1995). As consumers compare the two aspects (promised expectations compared to those actually verified), they can confirm or disconfirm how well the organization has managed on the aspect regarding the quality of the provided service (de Ruyter et al. 1997). The confirmation/disconfirmation theory is definitely applied in the case of the museum as well, towards which the consumer/visitor has certain expectations that can be confirmed or not by their experience. In other words, the visitor compares his or her initial expectations to the "state" of contentment (or frustration) they feel after visiting a museum. This "state" generates (or not) a specially-felt satisfaction, starting from the intensity of feelings and the experienced emotions (Oliver 1980).

2.1 Satisfaction

According to Harrison and Robin (2004), satisfaction is a "state" that the consumer experiences after buying the product and putting in balance its costs and benefits. If, in the case of products, satisfaction appears after they are bought, in the case of services – for instance, the ones provided by museums – *satisfaction may be evaluated continuously* during its delivery or consumption, rather than after buying and consuming the service (Gabbot and Hogg 1998). This means that researchers should evaluate both the satisfaction of the visit overall and the satisfaction offered by various key elements that constitute the experience (Danaher and Mattson 1994). Therefore, *satisfaction* should be evaluated as a *cumulative experience* and less as a transaction or a state specific to one single moment (Gabbot and Hendry 1999; Youngdahl and Kellogg 1994). Latest research has also introduced emotions felt by the consumer as a determining factor in defining satisfaction. Including *emotions* within the concept of satisfaction is important due to the fact that the favorable perception (or unfavorable) regarding services provided by museums is based on the consumer's participation and experiences (Szymanski and Henard 2001).

Moreover, the satisfaction only connected to one particular element of the experience is unlikely to lead to long-term loyalty whereas overall judgment based on multiple elements of the experience(s) at the museum could make the consumer come back to the museum or make the consumer recommend the museum to other people.

2.2 The Experiences of the Consumer/Visitors

According to Pine and Gilmore (1998), *an experience* occurs when an organization "intentionally uses services as the stage and goods as props, to engage individual consumers in a way that creates a memorable event" (p. 5).

The visitors of museums (the "purchasers" of experiences) value what the museum unfolds throughout time. Whereas offers for goods and services are exterior to the consumer, experiences are inherently personal, as they only exist within the mind of the person who has got emotionally, physically, intellectually and spiritually involved. Thus, two people cannot have the same experience because each experience derives from the interaction between the event (exhibition, artifact, etc.) and the individual's mood. If the material assets are tangible and services are intangible, then, experiences must be memorable (including the ones experienced in the world of museums) in order for them to be classified as such (Pine and Gilmore 1998). Therefore, we could say that museums, as well as firms, "stage" experiences every time this involves visitors/consumers in a personal and memorable way, and the new technologies especially encourage the apparition of new types of experiences by using interactive games, chat-rooms, virtual reality, etc.

A great way to think about experiences is to refer to their dimensions. The participative dimension of the experience differentiates consumers according to their level of involvement in the event. Thus, the *passive consumers* are those consumers who do not contribute in any kind of way to the event they attend. On the other hand, we have *active consumers* who play a key role in creating the experience or the event generating experiences. The second dimension is a constructivist one and refers to the connection between the consumers and the event, a connection mediated nowadays by the use of digital tools. From the point of view of the relation with the environment, we distinguish consumers absorbed by what happens to them when they get closer to an artwork and consumers who try the immersion feeling within the created event (Pine and Gilmore 1998). Both consumers absorbed by the created event and consumers who choose immersion within painting, atmosphere or generally art, are considered to be active consumers.

2.3 Digital Tools

Gradual integration of digital tools within traditional museums has completely transformed the inner lives of both museums and visitors. With new technologies, such as social networks, augmented reality (AR) or high resolution digital images, the visitor's experience in the museum has been completely redefined. Digital technologies have not only substantially improved the visitor's experience, but at the same time, they have created numerous applications. Starting from preservation and research operations of artifacts to familiarizing and educating people interested in history and, more than that, to maintaining certain important aspects of the contemporary world, the integration of digital tools within museums has profoundly transformed the relation between visitor and museum (Lohr 2014). Thus, the same author discusses the way in which digital technologies used within museums "enhance the physical experience of exploring the museum". One of these technologies is the augmented reality (AR) – a smart soft that provides additional information to an artwork on a computer or a tablet. Therefore, museums that adopt AR can replace the classical tours with a more detailed and more customized option, thus offering the visitor a (more) captivating experience. Another example of innovative technology is that of specialized cameras where the visitor can let their imagination and creativity freely work when visitors project background images on touch screen devices.

At their turn, visitors use a wide range of digital tools, such as: social networks, blogs, Wikis, chat-rooms, tagging (process consisting of users adding their own keywords to the description made by the museum on the exhibited objects) or UGC (user generated content – photos, comments, personal memories – uploaded by them on the webpage of the museum). A valuable digital tool that appears to become very popular in being used by visitors is *wiki* – that is, a site that permits users to upload and edit information by changing the content of the site at the same time. A visitor can use wiki during the visit to the museum, but also, when being outside of it. Therefore, wiki seems to be an ideal digital tool for creating a symbolic relation between the visitor and the museum by using an online application. Moreover, Loosely and Roberto (2009) suggest that one wiki connected to the webpage of the museum can challenge the authority and examination of the museum itself, by the visitor who wants to be heard within the public domain.

A valuable digital tool used on a large scale by visitors is, no doubt, the smartphone. However, the technologies specific for the mobile phone have not been included in the present research due to the large number of studies already existing on this topic.

3 Research Methodology

3.1 Objectives and Hypotheses

Our research is an exploratory one and has as main objective the identification of the way in which consumers use digital tools in relation to museums. According to statistics, the most visited museums in Romania are: "Grigore Antipa" National Museum of Natural History, the Village Museum, The National Museum of Art of Romania and the Bucharest Municipality Museum, all of them being situated in Bucharest and using digital technologies in their relation with the public. The large number of visitors and the use of digital tools by them determined us to select them in order to try and answer the following questions: in what way are the visitors of these museums specifically related to modern technology? Are there behavior changes among visitors when they use digital tools? Generally, to what extent can digital technology improve "the inner lives" of both museums and their visitors?

Therefore, we elaborated a questionnaire consisting of 16 questions to which 341 respondents, who had visited at least one of the mentioned museums, answered. The questionnaire was shared with the visitors of the 4 museums between July and August 2018 on the exit from the museum. The demographic structure of the respondents is presented, as follows: 40% women, 59% men, and 1% people who refused to have their sex declared; 59% of the visitors were from Bucharest, 29% were people coming from the province, 11% were foreigners, whereas 1% did not specify their residential environment. From the total number of respondents, 62% graduated a form of higher education, 27% graduated secondary studies, 10% graduated primary studies, and 1% did not declare the type of graduated studies. Regarding their occupation, 58% of the respondents were employed, 22% were university students, 10% were pupils, 2% were unemployed, 5% had other professions and 3% did not declare any occupation. The respondents who were between 26 and 39 years old were the majority – 37%, followed by young adults between the ages 19 and 25 – 26%. The adult respondents who were between 40 and 55 years old represent 20% from the total number of respondents whereas people between the ages 55–65 represent 5%. Only 1% from the total number registered by the statistics were people over 65 years old.

Museums have become a real presence within the digital world ever since webpages were made into important tools of exploration of collections by visitors and of information on museum activities and exhibitions (Giannini and Bowen 2018). The introduction of Web 2.0 domains on the websites of museums began in the United States where blogs, forums, wikis and social networks were seen as an opportunity to create online communities engaged in information/knowledge exchange (Proctor 2010; Simon 2010). According to Muniz and O'Guinn (2001), the participative evolution, respectively the constructivist one, on the webpage of the museum (Hellin-Hobbs 2010) was supported by the apparition of the cultural "prosumer" – that is, the visitor who does not only consume cultural content, but she or he reuses it and comments on it, bringing significance to it and creating derived types of media (Hinton and Whitelaw 2010). To the extent to which the "state" and digital identity change the visitors' behavior and their expectations, these also reconfigure the identity of the museum within and over its physical boundaries, as it unlocks new ways of perceiving the world and the life and new challenges to awaken the visitors' social and cultural consciousness (Giannini and Bowen 2018). From this perspective, the online users' participation to museum communities also has marketing implications (for instance, the use of the webpage by the museum as a necessary tool to be taken into consideration when the museum wants to awaken the potential visitors' curiosity and interest towards its exhibitions and artifacts, but at the same time, to build a capable brand that can evoke emotions and the sense of belonging, triggering implication and active participation) (Bonacini 2012).

The observations mentioned above led us to the formulation of the following hypothesis:

H1: As a means of information, the webpage of the museum constitutes the trigger of a visit to the museum.

The adoption of digital tools by museums has also a great impact outside the museum – in schools and universities. According to Wetterlund (2008), the new technologies have created the opportunity for museums to imagine, create and deliver a wide spectrum of educational resources from those provided by online multimedia to resources made by teachers while using digital tools. For example, modern museums like Metropolitan Museum of Art started to display their artifacts on their own websites and they even produced smartphone applications that list the works of art and provide explanations related to them. These approaches encourage students to find out more about exhibitions and exhibits, but these also encourage them to literally visit the museum. Therefore, digital images of collections function as a door for students, teachers and public in general to see what awaits them; like an invitation to step out of the class or from the workplace and to step into the world of art.

Nowadays, we know that visitors want more than an ordinary experience when they go to a museum. A study entitled "Do Museums Matter? Key Findings from the Museums R&D Research collaborative" (NEAM 2015) shows that only 12% of the large public perceives museums as being educational institutions. Other studies present similar figures. Thus, the study called "Impacts data on overall satisfaction" (Dilenschneider 2013) shows that "the educational experience" is only a minor factor in the review made by visitors to cultural organizations, whereas entertainment matters approximately one fifth in their reviews.

Entertainment may act as a door towards education. Even for the visitors who mainly come to the museum in order to learn something, they only become engaged and connected to the reality of the museum if what happens during the visit is also *entertaining*. However, the contrary is just as true: visitors who go to the museum for the entertainment usually learn more than they expect. No matter the main orientation of the museum (education or entertainment), we believe that museums can create the context that could invite visitors to participate at the creation of understanding of the experiences by using digital technologies. Thus, museums are no longer unique information providers. They become providers of means of entertainment for visitors, who later on, become creators of significances, and probably the most important of all, they become people who learn by using digital tools. These observations led us to the following hypothesis:

H2: Visitors use digital tools as a mediation instrument of a relation with the museum in order to enrich their knowledge (through unusual and non-traditional learning experiences) *and* entertainment.

Both museums and visitors use social networks to communicate with each other. Social media (SM) is especially used by museums as a tool to communicate with the public, but also to engage itself in the world. For instance, American museums appear to use social media for listing events, posting reminders, sharing promotions and announcements in order to get to a larger number of (potential) visitors (Fletcher and Lee 2012). However, latest research (Lazzeretti and Sartori 2015) shows that Facebook, Twitter and Youtube achieve a double objective in the case of museums: on the one hand, these networks are used in order to promote the museum and the events created by the museum; on the other hand, these are used in order to support and increase the visitors' interest towards these activities in time by initiating a bidirectional process of communication that may provoke discussions and debates. Thus, the museum does not only look for more loyalty, but it also seeks to obtain suggestions, feedback and critiques (if needed) regarding the visiting experience. According to this, it results that social networks and "live" events organized by the museum fulfill a *complementary and a mutual supporting/strengthening function*: the creation of a vivid and engaged dialogue with the public; a dialogue resulting, on the one hand, from the interaction between media channels and multiple digital channels, and on the other hand, from the visitors' initiatives.

On the other hand, consumers look for diversity in the digital tools found in relation to the museum: except social networks, visitors use wikis, personal blogs, mobile phones and chat-rooms when they want to post an impression or upload a photo. For instance, photos on Instagram get to a point when they acquire their own life which is in parallel with the life of a painting from the art gallery. In the gallery, the pleasure of regarding a painting is carried out over the time the visitor discovers within the painter's work of art, senses and elements less visible at first sight. However, the pleasure of regarding a painting online appears when the visitor "translates"/transforms the painting in something new that overpasses his or her expectations, provoking or surprising himself or herself. More than that, exhibits become "game partners" when the visitor recreates exhibited object by using a downloaded application on the tablet or they become film characters in a video made by a visitor with the staff's support.

In other words, using digital tools changes visitors' behavior in museums, which leads us to the following hypothesis:

H3: Using digital technologies by museums, but also by visitors, changes the users' behavior from predominantly passive (admiring or contemplating exhibits) to pre-dominantly active (interacting with exhibits, participating at games and activities or socializing, etc.).

The consumer's satisfaction is perceived within the specialized literature as a key factor in *maintaining the relation* between consumer and product (Chaudhuri and Holbrook 2001). In the museum field, satisfaction also influences loyalty and information transmission from one person to another (Harrison and Robin 2004). For visitors of museums, previous experiences in particular are the ones that determine satisfaction (Oliver 1980). On the other hand, one visitor's satisfaction is rather linked to delight, that is, the capacity of a "product" to generate a pleasant surprise. Therefore, the satisfaction of the visit to the museum results, in our case, from the capacity of works of art/exhibits/artifacts to overpass the visitors' expectations and thus, to surprise them.

The observations mentioned above lead us to the formulation of the following hypothesis, that is:

H4: The quality of the experiences a visitor has during the visit which are moderated by digital tools determine the general level of satisfaction, but also the premises for the visitors to come back to the museum.

4 Results and Discussion

The first question addressed to our respondents was related to their visitor status: 53.55% of the respondents declared that it had been their first visit to the museum whereas 46.5% confirmed that they were not visiting the chosen museum for the first time. The following Table 1 gives further information.

Table 1. Means of information used by visitors

The website of the museum	178	36.6%
The Facebook page of the museum	58	11.9%
The presentation brochure of the museum	30	6.2%
Recommendations coming from friends	157	32.2%
Traditional social media (radio, TV, journals, magazines, etc.)	64	13.1%

For the question referring to the digital tools used by visitors to get information before they actually visited the museum, most of our respondents – 36,6% – mentioned the webpage of the museum, which was closely followed by recommendations coming from friends – 32,2% – and to a smaller extent, traditional social media (radio, TV, press) or the Facebook page of the museum. Thus, we conclude that as a means of information, the webpage of the museum constitutes the trigger of a visit to the museum. On the other hand, the fact that the recommendations coming from friends are also taken into consideration shows that the experiences they had during the visit were powerful enough to further recommend the museum to those interested by this kind of experiences. The most looked up information on the webpage of the museum were especially connected to their visiting hours and their entry fee. At the same time, aspects regarding owned collections, organized events and accessing possibilities of online services are also important. Simultaneously, educational programs for children also arouse interest.

Therefore, hypothesis no. 1, starting from the premise that the website of the museum constitutes a trigger for a visit to the museum, is confirmed, taking into consideration the conditions in which more than a third from our total number of respondents consults the webpage to get information regarding the offer of the museum.

When asked what digital tools they use before/during/after the visit to the museum, the respondents particularly indicated tools like Wikis, social media, videos and films, as well as virtual tours. This result suggests that visitors of museums express an *active behavior*, one of connecting to the reality of the museum and one of participating to the interpretations of provided content. And the fact that they use digital tools before, during or after visiting a museum is evidence upon the *relation* that they establish *with the museum* – a relation that can later be cultivated by the museum itself in order to vividly maintain visitors' interest in the world of museums regarding future activities and events. The following Table 2 provides more information:

Table 2. Digital tools used by visitors

	Before the visit	During the visit	After the visit
Wikis	128	52	55
Blogs	49	10	34
Podcasting	16	11	15
RSS	12	1	16
Forums for discussions	52	12	28
Social media networks	130	42	76
Digital storytelling	38	19	32
Videos and films	110	34	66
Virtual tours	81	37	40

Then, the respondents were asked what activities drew their attention at most during their visit to the museum.

Table 3. Activities preferred by the visitors

	First choice	Last choice	Mean grade
Direct interaction with exhibits	250	4	1.37
Explanations provided by their guide	64	16	2.56
Audio explanations	53	16	2.89
Computer games	8	62	4.63
Video games	8	75	4.75
Films	31	26	3.30

According to Table 3 regarding the visitors' preferences, the hierarchy of activities for most people looks, as follows: on the first place, there is the direct interaction with exhibits; then, on the second place, we have the explanations provided by the guide; on the third place, there are the audio explanations. Then, according to the rank of preferences, films, computer and video games follow. However, if we apply the chi-square test, we notice how meaningful differences appear among museums regarding the hierarchy of possible answers (multiple choice).

Table 4. Activities preferred by visitors regarding the visited museum

	ANTIPA	BM	NMAR	VM
Direct interaction with exhibits	1.34	1.3	1.46	1.42
Explanations provided by the guide	2.97	2.77	2.39	1.86
Audio explanations	2.49	2.38	3.16	4.04
Computer games	3.04	4.56	5.31	4.89
Video games	4.23	4.74	5.06	5.14
Films	3.33	3.15	3.4	3.22

Thus, according to Table 4, the statistics regarding the direct interaction with exhibits is similar and it is maintained in the case of all the four museums, whereas when it comes to the other preferences expressed by visitors, we can notice slight differences. For instance, at the Village Museum (VM), visitors consider that the best explanations are provided by their guide; at Antipa, visitors rate audio explanations and computer/video games as best explanation-providers, and at the Museum of Bucharest, visitors consider that they find the best films. These differences may also be explained through the fact that these four museums belong to various fields (Science, History, Art, Ethnography and Folklore).

Table 5. Visitors' motivation

For me, visiting the museum meant an opportunity:	Very high	Above average	Average	Below average	Very low
-to improve my knowledge	144	137	40	8	2
-to socialize	35	101	97	46	33
-to connect with the past	89	136	62	20	18
-to improve my abilities	32	61	91	63	56
-to affirm my identity	31	57	73	63	72
-to live relevant experiences for personal development	49	83	90	42	40
-to understand better the world in which I live	108	112	50	20	22
-to entertain myself and spend quality leisure time	101	109	68	17	16

As seen from Table 5, for many respondents, visiting a museum means especially an opportunity to improve their knowledge, to understand better the world in which they live and to spend quality leisure time. Last but not least, visiting a museum also represents a good opportunity to socialize and connect with the past. Exactly as expected, education and entertainment do not mutually exclude themselves, and therefore, our calculations are made in accordance with older and more recent research (Goulding 1999; 2000) which claim that visitors want to improve their knowledge and spend quality leisure time when they choose to visit a museum. However, museum managers should understand better how each of these components contributes to the realization of relevant experiences for the visitor, and to the reputation of the museum overall so that later, they can create an appropriate strategy.

However, a (relatively) new element results from our data, as well: visitors want to understand better the world in which they live. Therefore, they look for information, participate and evaluate the experiences to which they have had access by also using digital tools. In other words, they explore the world of yesterday by using modern technology in order to understand better the world of today and its challenges.

In conclusion, we can state that the second hypothesis (H2), according to which visitors use digital tools as *a mediation instrument of a relation with the museum* in order to enrich their knowledge (through unusual and non-traditional learning experiences) *and* entertainment, is validated.

Table 6. Visitors' behavior

	Museums				Total
	ANTIPA	BM	NMAR	VM	
Active person	71	39	28	22	160
Passive person	76	41	24	37	178
Total	147	80	52	59	338

Regarding the visitors' behavior, 47.1% of our respondents consider themselves as being *active people* (they use digital technologies, involve themselves in activities, and experience new things directly) whereas the other 52.4% auto perceive themselves as being *passive people* (they listen, regard and meditate upon what they see/what they hear). From this point of view, we mention that there are no significant differences between the 4 museums even if taken separately. This was concluded after applying an adequate statistical test (the Chi-Square Test) that indicated this, with a p-value of 0.335 greater than 0.05. Nevertheless, there is a slight variation in the case of the Village Museum (there existing a higher number of respondents who perceived themselves as being passive) and The National Museum of Art of Romania (where more respondents perceive themselves as being active people) – as in Table 6.

Nevertheless, interesting differences appear when we analyze the way the respondents perceive themselves as active or passive, *related to the circumstances/the context* in which the visit has taken place. Thus, we notice a significant difference (indicated, by applying, again, the chi-square test, that in this case gives a small p-value of 0.008 < 0.05) considering the conditions in which the visit takes place: people going with friends perceive themselves as being more active in the relation to the museum, compared to people who visit the museum with their families or alone (Table 7).

Table 7. Visitors' behavior correlated with the context of the visit

	Alone	With family	With friends	Total
Active person	11	62	86	159
Passive person	22	88	67	177
Total	33	150	153	336

At the same time, what is interesting is that, in the relation to the museum, men perceive themselves as being more active than women (also being a significant difference from the statistical point of view with a p-value of 0.016 smaller than 0.05).

If we take into consideration the means of information used by the respondents, we may notice statistically significant differences: people who access the website of the museum seem to be more active (Table 8).

Table 8. Visitors' behavior correlated to weather they accessed the website or not

	Accessing the museum website		Total
	No	Yes	
An active person	64	96	160
A passive person	93	82	175
Total	157	178	335

Summarizing the observations mentioned above, we may state that the third hypothesis (H3) starting from the premise that the use of digital tools changes the users' behavior from *preponderantly passive* (admiring or contemplating exhibits) to *preponderantly active* (interacting with exhibits, sharing stories, socializing, participating at games, etc.), is not validated.

Notes: the difference between active and passive respondents is a very small one, that is, of only 17 people. In other words, there is a fragile balance between the two types of behavior, significant differences from the statistical point of view only being demonstrated in the case of men (more active than women) and in the case of accompanied people (more active than people visiting the museum alone).

Next, we investigated the level of satisfaction felt by the respondents after visiting the museum by using the classical grading system that is grading the satisfaction level from 10 – the highest level of satisfaction –, to 1 – lack of satisfaction. The average sum of the grades received by each of the 4 analyzed museums is presented as follows:

NMAR – 9, 17; Antipa – 8,8; BM – 8,87; VM – 9,05, and the general grade of satisfaction felt by visitors has an average sum of 8.92 with a standard deviation of 1.227.

From the histogram below (Fig. 1), we can notice that there is a negative asymmetry, high values being predominant in the evaluation.

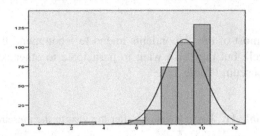

Fig. 1. Distribution of grades regarding visitors' satisfaction

What is interesting is that, even if there seems to be more people at their first visit to the museum, there is no significant difference between the number of newcomers and the number of those who have visited the museum before (182 of the respondents are at their first visit whereas 158 claim that they have visited the museum before). This can be positively interpreted, as we may conclude that the previous visit to the museum might have triggered their level of satisfaction.

Table 9. Satisfaction-generating elements

The experience of the actual visit	99
The satisfaction level felt as a result to direct interaction with exhibits/environment	70
The organized events by the museum at that particular moment	25
The possibility to experiment by involving in various activities	17
Other	12

Among those who have visited the museum before (question no. 2, multiple choice), the experience of the actual visit was the answer found in most visitors' cases, closely followed by the level of satisfaction felt as a result to the direct interaction with the exhibits/environment (Table 9).

The Chi-square test presented below (Table 10) shows that there is a very significant difference regarding the place of origin: most of the visitors who come back to the museum are usually from Bucharest (p-value/asymptotic significance equal to zero).

Table 10. Chi-Square tests

	Value	df	Asymp. sig. (2-sided)
Pearson Chi-Square	22.186	2	.000
Likelihood ratio	23.725	2	.000
Linear-by-linear association	21.759	1	.000
N of valid cases	338		

After the visit, most of the respondents intend to recommend the museum to their acquaintances as well, but they also want to participate to other activities and events organized by the museum (Table 11).

Table 11. Possible actions after the visit to the museum

-to recommend the museum to friends and colleagues (from school, from the workplace, from social media, etc.);	251
-to participate to activities organized by the museum in the near future;	34
-to attend the event called "The Night of the Museums";	40
-others	4

Therefore, the forth hypothesis (H4), according to which the quality of the experiences a visitor has during the visit which are moderated by digital tools determine the general level of satisfaction, but also the premises for the visitors to come back to the museum, is confirmed.

Note: In our case, the experience of the actual visit and the direct interaction with exhibits had been factors that determined the visitors to come back to the museum. What is interesting is the fact that the level of satisfaction remains high in the case of all the visitors (older and newer ones), which is confirmed by their intention of recommending the museum to their colleagues and friends. According to the specialized literature (Catoiu and Teodorescu 2006), recommendations coming from friends represent an important step in building up loyalty towards a particular brand.

5 Conclusions

Museums deliver not only a simple service: they deliver experience (Hui and Bateson 1991). The need to understand the *nature of experiences* offered by museums is imperative today because these cultural institutions face the successive budget reduction, but also new performance criteria based on the customer satisfaction management. Therefore, museums are "forced" to find new ways to attract new audience/consumers (Hooper-Greenhill 1996).

From the consumer's perspective, to really get to visit a museum, even if the visitor has wide access to information nowadays, continues to remain difficult: visitors seem to (still) have insufficient information regarding collections and artifacts that might make them interested. Then, what are the information sources used by the consumers when they choose to go visit a museum? From our research, it looks like, for visitors, *the webpage of the museum* remains the main information source regarding collections and events organized by the museum, as well as the trigger for a later visit. This simple observation should incite museums to supported, professional, and redesigning actions and permanent adaptation of the webpages, so that the information provided for the public is relevant and at the same time, contributes to a more accurate outlining of the identity of the museum.

We already know that there are countless reasons why people of all ages choose the museum as a place to spend their leisure time (Falk 2006). To educate the wide public is part of the mission of every museum institution. Even if there is a number of data that certifies the fact that entertainment represents the main reason of spending free time in a way or another, in the case of a visit to the museum, the dilemma between learning experience versus entertaining experience proves to be a false one: the results of our study show that visitors prefer *educational and entertaining experiences* at the same time. Or, if you want, an educational experience that has at least one entertaining component. Museums have the opportunity now due to digital technologies to reunite facts (and their history) with entertainment in ways that can be relevant for human experience at both personal and universal level. Providing the necessary *context,* museums can help visitors to create their own experiences, to learn while amusing themselves, but at the same time, to entertain themselves while learning. Thus, we believe that museums should prepare themselves better in order to carry out these two functions, or, even better, to think of a strategy of making educational experiences more entertaining for their visitors, but also more relevant for them, as these experiences are meant to make them understand better the world in which they live.

Recent theories regarding the learning process and the attribution of meanings and significances to exhibits tend to consider the visitor more than just a neutral and passive subject who assimilates information and knowledge from those perceived until recently as the unique authority within the field: the curators. Today, visitors bring their own knowledge to museums which could be considered as legitimate as those owned by the curators of the museum. More than that, visitors are rather active subjects and determinant factors in the process of creating new significances through the direct interaction with the exhibits/artifacts. However, our research shows that the *transition from the passive visitor to the active one* is not yet finished: there are relatively more people who perceive themselves as being passive in comparison to the number of people who see themselves as being active in their relation to the museum. Nevertheless, what is to be noticed is that the transition from passive to active is *mediated by the use of digital tools:* people who access the webpage of the museum are more active than those who visit the museum accompanied by their families or friends, men perceiving themselves as being more active than women, in general.

Creating and maintaining a *relation between visitor and museum* is, no doubt, a cornerstone for every museum institution. Visitors evaluate the museum through their experiences. If these experiences are memorable, then, the satisfaction will motivate the visitor to come back to visit the museum and to recommend the museums to friends as well. According to our data, the relation between visitors and museum is strengthened by everything related to modern technology: the use of digital tools makes it possible for the visitors to discover new senses, emotions and ideas, according to their own cultural and intellectual biographies. Therefore, the quality of the experience and the satisfaction are *mediated by technology,* this conferring the museum countless possibilities to "democratize" its own collections, to open a specific place for the purpose of dialogue and to promote experience and idea exchanges, whereas for visitors – unexpected ways to express themselves, emphasizing their imagination, creativity and intellect.

Hence, digital tools serve today for a multitude of purposes: they help visitors to get information, to enjoy more captivating experiences, to feel satisfied and to wish to come back to the museum. On the other hand, museums have the obligation to think of *strategies* to attract more recent and older visitors. Digital tools and technologies can help museums in this case. Here are a few suggestions:

The first step for museums would be to *know their visitors better.* Understanding their identities, interests and behaviors better, museums can offer visitors captivating experiences (educational experiences, entertaining ones, etc.), by making visitors feel involved before, after or even during the visit. From our observations, it results that the easiest starting point to collect data about visitors is the ticket booth at the entry of the museum. However, in order for this to be possible, museums should successfully operate the transition from selling paper tickets to selling tickets online or via smartphone. Information gathered in this way can later be linked to information resulting from their visiting tour – the visitor's choice of itinerary, the amount of time spent while admiring each exhibit, etc. For instance, Louvre Museum concluded a partnership with MIT Senseable City Lab in order to see how much time it takes for visitors to actually finish the tour of the museum, this being possible through the use of a Bluetooth signal used for pursuing. By combining the obtained observations, museums can develop more efficient and personal relations with their visitors.

The next step for every museum should be the orientation of museums to creating *captivating experiences* for the visitors' right on their webpage. If there are preliminary data about the visitors, these could be used by the museum in order to offer them a customized version of their visit to the museum by indicating them exhibits that are more likely to arouse their interest. If there are no such data, museums could offer predefined virtual tours, identified on categories of visitors according to profiles created through previous visits.

Last but not least, even more captivating experiences can be obtained by using multimedia solutions. For instance, Victoria & Albert Museum from London concluded a partnership with a company (Sennheiser) in order to create an extraordinary audio experience in immersion within the 2017 Pink Floyd exhibition. Other museums, such as history or natural sciences museums, experiment together with Google in order to permit visitors to explore exhibits in the augmented reality (AR).

All of these solutions are also fully applicable to Romanian museums discussed in the present paper. This leads us to the formulation of the *limits* of this research. Briefly, these would be the following: the reduced number of museums and respondents involved in the research which makes it difficult for us to apply the results on a national level; the impossibility to establish relevant correlatives, for instance, between the respondents' distribution by age or level of education and them using digital tools. Last but not least, the museums selected have different profiles, meaning that their public, as well, is probably a specialized one and/or exclusively interested in the field promoted by the museum.

Taking into account the mentioned limits, we believe that an interesting direction of research in the future may be towards a comparative perspective on museums according to their specificity. Our questions would be: are there significant differences between the increase of the numbers of visitors in the case of modern museums that use digital technologies and which are, at the same time, funded by the state, and private museums that do not benefit from such financing, and which register even a higher afflux of visitors? How much of this increase is owed to actual collections and how much is owed to the use of digital tools?

We believe that these directions of research are useful because the advanced technologies seem to have created numerous opportunities for museums: even if the transition from print to digital is not a very easy one, the museums that engaged themselves in this transition can already see a part from the final results: a higher visibility and understanding of their collections. However, it depends on the public so that the inner life of museums becomes richer, more intense and more connected to the realities beyond the walls. And a more numerous, more educated and more loyal public could be the key for anchoring the museums, by the use of technology, in the contemporary reality.

References

Bonacini, E.: The museum participation on the web: forms of user participation to the cultural production and the creation of cultural value. Cult. Cap. Stud. Value Cult. Herit. **5**, 93–125 (2012). https://riviste.unimc.it/index.php/cap-cult/article/view/201

Catoiu, I., Teodorescu, N.: Comportamentul consumatorului. Uranus Publishing House, Bucharest (2006)

Chaudhuri, A., Holbrook, M.B.: The chain of effects from brand trust and brand affect to brand performance: the role of brand loyalty. J. Mark. **65**(2), 81–93 (2001). www.gsb.columbia.edu/mygsb/faculty/research/pubfiles/593/The_Chain_of_Effects.pdf

Coman, A., Pop, I.: Why do museums matter? A case-study on the maramures county museums. In: Proceedings of the International Conference in Economics and Administration, ICEA-FAA 2012, Bucharest, pp. 121–133 (2012) www.researchgate.net/publication/299495008_Entrepreneurship_-the_key_for_a_successful_museum

Danaher, P.J., Mattson, J.: Customer satisfaction during the service delivery process. Eur. J. Mark. **28**(5), 5–16 (1994). https://www.emeraldinsight.com/doi/abs/10.1108/03090569410062005

Dilenschneider, C.: Entertainment vs education: how your audience really rates the museum experience (2013) http://www.colleendilen.com/2013/07/31/entertainment-vs-education-how-your-audience-really-rates-the-museum-experience-data/

Falk, J.H.: An identity-centered approach to understanding museum learning. Curator: Mus. J. **49**(2), 151–166 (2006). https://onlinelibrary.wiley.com/doi/abs/10.1111/j.2151-6952.2006.tb00209.x

Fletcher, A., Lee, M.: Current social media uses and evaluation in American Museums. Mus. Manag. Curator. **27**(5), 505–521 (2012). https://www.tandfonline.com/doi/abs/10.1080/09647775.2012.738136

Gabbott, M., Hendry, J.: A cross-cultural study of service quality using critical incidents. In: Cadeaux, J. (ed.) Proceedings of Australia and New Zealand Marketing Academy Conference. University of South Wales, Sydney (1999)

Gabbott, M., Hogg, G.: Consumers and Services. Wiley, Chichester (1998)

Giannini, T., Bowen, J.P.: Of museums and digital culture: a landscape view (2018). https://evic.bcs.org/upload/pdf/ewic.eva18_ma_paper2.pdf

Goulding, C.: Contemporary museum culture and consumer behavior. J. Mark. Manag. **15**(7), 647–671 (1999). https://www.tandfonline.com/doi/abs/10.1362/026725799785037003

Goulding, C.: The museum environment and the visitor experience. Eur. J. Mark. **34**, 261 (2000). https://www.emeraldinsight.com/doi/full/10.1108/03090560010311849

Harrison, P., Robin, S.: Consumer satisfaction and post-purchase intentions: an exploratory study of museum visitors. Int. J. Arts Cult. Manag. **6**(2), 23–32 (2004). https://dro.deakin.edu.au/eserv/DU:30002566/harrison-consumersatisfactionandpost-2004.pdf

Hellin-Hobbs, Y.: The constructivist museum and the web. In: Seal, A., Bowen, J.P., Ng, K. (eds.) Proceedings of the 2010 International Conference on Electronic Visualisation and the Arts, EVA's 2010, pp. 72–78. British Computer Society, Swinton (2010)

Hein, G.: Learning in the Museum, 1st edn. Routledge, London (1998)

Hinton, S., Whitelaw, M.: Exploring the digital commons: an approach to the visualisation of large heritage databases (2010). https://www.bcs.org/content/conWebDoc/30649

Hui, M., Baterson, J.: Perceived control and the effects of crowding and consumer choice on the service experience. J. Consum. Res. **18**(2), 174–184 (1991). https://doi.org/10.1086/209250

Hooper-Greenhill, E.: Museum and Their Visitor. Routledge, London and New York (1996)

Institutului Național pentru Cercetare și Formare Culturală. https://www.culturadata.ro/activitatea-de-cercetare/

Johnson, M.D., Anderson, E.W., Fornell, C.: Rational and adaptive performance expectations in a customer. J. Consum. Res. **21**(4), 695–707 (1995). https://academic.oup.com/jcr/issue/21/4

Johnson, M.D., Gabarino, E.: Customers on performing arts organizations: are subscribers different from nonsubscribers? Int. J. Nonprofit Volunt. Sect. Mark. **6**(1), 61–77 (2001). https://onlinelibrary.wiley.com/doi/abs/10.1002/nvsm.134

Kidd, J., Ntalla, I., Lyons, W.: Sensing the social museum. In: International Conference "Rethinking Technologies in Museums", Ireland (2011)

Lazzeretti, L., Sartori, A.: Museums and social media: the case of the museum of natural history of florence. Int. Rev. Public Nonprofit Mark. **12**, 267–283 (2015). https://doi.org/10.1007/s12208-015-0136-5

Lohr, S.: Museums morph digitally. The New York Times, 23 October 2014. Accessed 10 Jan 2019

Loosely, R., Roberto, F.: Museums & wikis: two case studies. In: Trant, J., Bearman, D. (eds.) Museums and the Web 2009: Proceedings. Archives and Museum Informatics, Toronto, Canada (2009)

Muniz Jr., A.M., O'Guinn, T.: Brand community. J. Consum. Res. **27**, 413–432 (2001). https://doi.org/10.1086/319618

New England Museum Association: Do museums matter? Key findings from the museums R&D research collaborative (2015). https://reachadvisors.com/past-presentations/2015-archive/

Oliver, R.L.: A cognitive model of antecedents and consequences of satisfaction decisions. J. Mark. Res. **17**, 460–469 (1980). http://www.sietmanagement.fr/wp-content/uploads/2017/12/Oliver.pdf

Pine, B.J., Gilmore, J.: Welcome to the experience economy. Harv. Bus. Rev. **76**(6), 3–12 (1998). www.researchgate.net/publication/299292969_The_Experience_Economy

Plosnita, E.: Marketingul și muzeele Republicii Moldova. Revista de Stiinta, Inovare, Cultura si Arta "Akademos" **2**(33), 136–141 (2014)

Proctor, N.: Digital: museums as platforms, curator as champion in the age of social media. Curator: Mus. J. **53**(1), 35–43 (2010). https://onlinelibrary.wiley.com/doi/abs/10.1111/j.2151-6952.2009.00006.x

de Ruyter, K., Wetzels, M., Lemmink, J., Mattson, J.: The dynamics of service delivery process: a value-based approach. Int. J. Res. Mark. **14**(3), 231–243 (1997). www.sciencedirect.com/science/article/abs/pii/S0167811697000049

Simon, N.: The participatory museum (2010). https://www.participatorymuseum.org/read/

Szymanski, D.M., Henard, D.H.: Customer satisfaction: a meta-analysis of the empirical evidence. J. Acad. Mark. Sci. **29**(1), 16–35 (2001). https://journals.sagepub.com/doi/pdf/10.1177/0092070301029001102

Sylaiou, S., Mania, K., Karoulis, A., White, M.: Exploring the relationship between presence and enjoyment in a virtual museum. Int. J. Hum.-Comput. Stud. **68**(5), 243–253 (2010). https://www.sciencedirect.com/science/article/abs/pii/S1071581909001761

Traxler, J., Griffiths, L.: IWB4D - interactive whiteboards for development. In: Proceedings of the Third International Conference on Information and Communication Technologies and Development, Doha, Qatar (2009). www.ictd2009.org/documents/ICTD2009Proceedings.pdf

Vom Lehn, D., Heath, C.: Accounting for new technology in museum exhibitions. Int. J. Arts Manag. **7**(3), 11–21 (2005). www.gestiondesarts.com/en/accounting-for-new-technology-in-museum-exhibitions/

Youngdahl, W., Kellogg, D.L.: Customer costs of service quality: a critical incident study. Adv. Serv. Mark. Manag. **3**(C), 149–173 (1994). https://doi.org/10.1016/S1067-5671(94)03017-0

Zeithaml, V.A.: Consumer perceptions of price, quality and value: a means-end model and synthesis of evidence. J. Mark. **52**, 2–22 (1988)

Zeithaml, V.A., Berry, L.L., Parasuraman, A.: The nature and determinants of customer expectations of service. J. Acad. Mark. Sci. **21**(1), 1–12 (1993). https://doi.org/10.1177/0092070393211001

Wetterlund, K.: Flipping the field trip: bringing the art museum to the classroom. Theory Pract. **47**(2), 110–117 (2008). https://www.academia.edu/5790434/Flipping_the_Field_Trip_Bringing_the_Art_Museum_to_the_Classroom

https://museumhack.com/our-first-twitter-poll/

http://culturadatainteractiv.ro/cartografierea-sectorului-cultural/numar-de-vizitatori-in-muzee-si-colectii-publice/?r=1

Netflix, Who Is Watching Now?

Cristóbal Fernández-Robin[1]([⊠]), Scott McCoy[2], Diego Yáñez[1],
and Rodrigo Hernández-Sarpi[1]

[1] Universidad Técnica Federico Santa María, Valparaiso, Chile
{cristobal.fernandez,diego.yanez}@usm.cl,
rodrigo.hernandes.13@sansano.usm.cl
[2] Mason School of Business, Williamsburg, VA, USA
scott.mccoy@mason.wm.edu

Abstract. The continuous development of new ICTs has promoted their penetration in all aspects of daily life. One of the ICTs with the highest growth in recent years is streaming. Since companies that use streaming to deliver their services are thriving, several telecommunication companies are adopting this distribution technology. However, few studies have focused on this industry. This study models the behavior of Netflix consumers using an extension of the UTAUT2 model that includes the latent variable trust (TR). The model was analyzed through SEM. The results show that the latent variables trust (TR), performance expectancy (PE) and hedonic motivation (HM) are significant for behavioral intention (BI). Additionally, the latent variables hedonic motivation (HM) and social influence (SI) determine trust (TR) in a significant way. Finally, a new model is proposed in which social influence (SI) not only affects trust, but also hedonic motivation (HM) and performance expectancy (PE), and trust (TR) also determines performance expectancy. We suggest that this model needs to be further tested on a new sample.

Keywords: Intention to use · Consumer behavior · Streaming · Internet · Netflix

1 Introduction

Information and communication technologies have developed exponentially in recent years, becoming one of the most important resources for society. This phenomenon has led to a boom in data transmission, exchange and knowledge [32]. Information and communication technologies (ICT) have revolutionized the means of communication since the early '90s. Since then, the Internet has moved from a specialized instrument used by the scientific community to an easy-to-use network that has transformed social interaction [7]. One of the information technologies that has witnessed the largest growth in this period is streaming, which consists in data compression and distribution of multimedia content (audio and video) by means of a continuous, real-time flow directed to a user's laptop [35]. The explosive development of streaming has caused several changes in entertainment companies. In 2000, 69 million Americans subscribed to cable television or satellite services; today, that number stands at 49 million [34]. In addition, between 2015 and 2016, the number of TV series with original scripts

© Springer Nature Switzerland AG 2019
G. Meiselwitz (Ed.): HCII 2019, LNCS 11578, pp. 202–216, 2019.
https://doi.org/10.1007/978-3-030-21902-4_15

produced by online streaming services increased substantially from 46 to 93 [19], marking the peak of this industry in recent years.

Netflix is a leading company in the streaming field. With more than 100 million subscribers all over the world, this service has been recognized as one of the most innovative companies in the industry. The latter characteristic is critical for success in the current complex and changing environment, since the survival of companies depends on their adaptive capacity [18, 30]. In this context, we wonder what factors lead people to watch content on Netflix.

2 Literature Review

Several studies have focused on the intention to adopt a particular information system. Due to the nature of Netflix, we conducted a review of the studies that used UTAUT2 or extensions of the same. Factors were identified that influenced the adoption of mostly hedonic information technologies in order to determine in which consumption and entertainment contexts the model was applied, the variations of the same and how these tests may or may not be applicable to this study.

Helkkula [22] carried out research on the intention to subscribe a music streaming service. In his study, the author extended the UTAUT2 model by adding the variable tangibility preference, which refers to the physical properties of the product and the extent to which it can be seen, felt, heard and smelled, among others [14]. The results of this model may be valuable for other innovative and highly hedonic industries like the video game industry. In addition, Baabdullah [5] researched the intention to adopt games in mobile social networks (M-SNG). In this case, the model included the variable trust, which is related to intention to use and, at the same time, is determined by the variables hedonic motivation and social influence. Vinnik [39] studied the adoption of mobile applications, incorporating the variables herd behavior and online rankings and reviews into the model. To understand the reasons that people tag photographs in social networks, Dhir [11] added variables based on the social cognitive theory [6] to the model proposed by UTAUT2. This way, the model comprises the variables social presence, social status and self-efficacy.

These models confirmed that the UTAUT2 model can be used in different hedonic contexts with high reliability and adding single variables related to the context of the study. Therefore, the UTAUT2 model can be applied to the streaming industry. We decided to apply the model developed by Baabdullah [5], as it includes the variable trust. This variable is relevant to prepaid media streaming service.

3 Model and Hypothesis

The extension of the model selected for this research is based on the study conducted by Baabdullah [5], which incorporates the construct trust (TR) into the UTAUT2 model. Trust is a latent variable that within information systems (IS) refers to the perception that one can trust another person [40]. In e-commerce, trust refers to the confidence that clients will be provided with the desired benefits and facilities under safe and trustworthy conditions [16]. According to Gefen [17] trust in a seller is associated with greater behavioral intention (BI), which is crucial for a paid sub-scription service like Netflix. Additionally, the relationship between TR and BI has not been studied in streaming services. Considering all of this, the model proposed for this study is shown in Fig. 1.

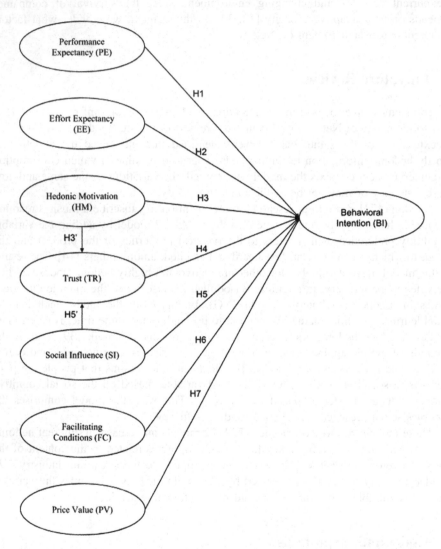

Fig. 1. UTAUT2 model extension applied to Netflix (Source: own elaboration)

3.1   Performance Expectancy (PE)

Performance Expectancy is defined as the degree at which the use of a technology will help consumers perform certain activities [38]. Consumers seem to be more motivated to use new technologies if they perceive that these are more useful in their daily lives [3, 10, 37]. Several studies have determined the importance of this construct out of the workplace [1, 5, 20]. From this, we believe that:

H1: PE has a positive effect on intention to use Netflix.

3.2 Effort Expectancy (EE)

Effort Expectancy is defined as the degree of perceived ease of use of the technology by the individual [38]. The behavioral intention of people varies if they feel that using a specific service is much easier and more convenient [5]. A number of studies have shown the influence of this construct on the intention to adopt new technologies [2, 25, 31]. Therefore, we propose the following hypothesis:

H2: EE has a positive impact on the intention to use Netflix.

3.3 Hedonic Motivation (HM)

HM is the fun or pleasure derived from the use of a technology. This variable has been proven to play an important role in acceptance and use of technology [38]. Netflix is a service classified as highly hedonic because its purpose is to entertain consumers who subscribe to its content. Studies on streaming have demonstrated that entertainment (closely associated with hedonic motivation) is related to intention to use [9, 22]. Therefore:

H3: HM has a positive effect on the intention to use Netflix.

HM increases people's trust in using this information technology. When individuals are highly motivated by hedonic factors, the trust in using this technology grows [3]. In online purchase systems, when consumers discover that buying can make them experience enjoyment and usefulness, they start to trust and adopt the online purchase system [16], which can be extrapolated to a paid subscription service. Therefore, we believe that:

H3': HM increases the role of trust of Chilean customers in using Netflix.

3.4 Trust (TR)

This construct refers to the perception inherent to humans of being able to trust another person [40]. Mayer [29] defines it as the will to be in a vulnerable state based on positive expectations of the future behavior of another person. Studies about online services have shown that trust affects intention to use [4, 13, 21, 23]. As a paid subscription service, Netflix needs users to trust that the company is acting in good faith. Therefore, the following hypothesis is proposed:

H4: TR has a positive impact on intention to use Netflix.

3.5 Social Influence (SI)

Social Influence is defined as the extent to which individuals perceive that other people important to them believe they should use the new information system [37]. This construct is also denominated as a social norm in models such as TAM, TAM2 and TRA.

Social influence proved to be significant in music streaming, games and mobile purchase services [12, 24, 42]. This way, we believe that:

H5: SI has a positive effect on intention to use Netflix.

SI plays an invaluable role in the level of trust on a service. Therefore, through different opinions, potential users could voice their intention to use or not a service [27]. When people know their peers and the society prefer to user a technology like Netflix, people tend to believe that the use of such a technology can bring them benefits and similar values. Research has already indicated the importance of social influence to trust [5, 33]. Consequently, it is believed that:

H5': SI influences trust in Chilean Netflix users.

3.6   Facilitating Conditions (FC)

Facilitating Conditions are defined as the extent to which individuals believe that there is an organizational and technical infrastructure that supports the use of the system [37]. In a consumer context, this variable can be defined as the perceptions users have of the resources and support available to perform a specific behavior [38].

Netflix requires some technological elements such as a laptop, mobile phone or Smart TV, as well as an Internet connection with enough speed for the platform to work properly. Users with access to a favorable set of facilitating conditions will have greater intention to use a new technology, as demonstrated by Zhou [43]. Therefore, it is believed that:

H6: FC has a positive impact on intention to use Netflix.

3.7   Price Value (PV)

Price Value is the cognitive calculation users make between the benefits perceived from an information system and the monetary cost of using it [38]. Price value is positive when the benefits of using an information system are perceived as higher than its monetary cost, which makes users more enthusiastic about adopting a new technology [38]. Netflix is a service for which consumers pay. Therefore, PV is expected to have a significant impact on the selection of the service. According to Venkatesh [38], individual consumers are more sensitive to price than people who use a service paid for by their company, because the cost of the new technology is paid by the same consumer. Several studies on technologies used outside of the workplace have pointed to the importance of price value for intention to use [28, 41]. Therefore, we believe that:

H7: PV has a positive impact on the intention to use Netflix.

4   Methodology

In this study, a confirmatory approach for the structural theory was undertaken. The survey applied to Netflix use in Chile was an adaptation of the questionnaire created by Baabdullah [5]. The instrument was validated by an exploratory text in which 15 people were first surveyed and asked for feedback on the questionnaire. This way, ambiguous questions were removed, while the wording of others was changed for clarity. Subsequently, an expert gave a final opinion about the duration, simplicity and clarity of language the language used in the questionnaire. A 7-point Likert scale was used, in which scores ranged from totally agree (value 1) to totally disagree (value 7) (See Table 1).

Table 1. Survey used in this study (Source: own elaboration based on Baabdullah [5])

Construct	Item
Performance expectancy (PE)	PE1. Using Netflix will increase my chances of achieving things that are important to me
	PE2. Using Netflix will help me accomplish things more quickly
	PE3. Netflix will be useful in my daily life
	PE4. Using Netflix will increase my productivity
Effort expectancy (EE)	EE1. Learning how to use Netflix will be easy for me
	EE2. My interaction with Netflix will be clear and understandable
	EE3. Netflix will be easy to use
	EE4. It will be easy for me to become skillful at using Netflix
Social influence (SI)	SI1. People who are important to me think that I should use Netflix
	SI2. People who influence my behavior think that I should use Netflix
	SI3. People whose opinions that I value prefer that I use Netflix
Facilitating conditions (FC)	FC1. Netflix is compatible with other technologies I use
	FC2. I have the resources necessary to use Netflix
	FC3. I have the knowledge necessary to use Netflix
	FC4. I can get help from others when I have difficulties using Netflix
Hedonic motivation (HM)	HM1. Using Netflix will be fun
	HM2. Using Netflix will be enjoyable
	HM3. Using Netflix will be very entertaining
Price value (PV)	PV1. Netflix is reasonably priced
	PV2. Netflix is good value for the money
	PV3. At the current price, Netflix provide good value
Trust (TR)	TR1. Netflix is trustworthy
	TR2. Netflix provide good services
	TR3. Netflix know their market
	TR4. Netflix care about customers
	TR5. Netflix is honest
	TR6. Netflix is predictable
Behavioral intention (BI)	BI1. I will use Netflix in the future
	BI2. I will always try to use Netflix in my daily life
	BI3. I will plan to use Netflix frequently

Afterward, the questionnaire was published through SurveyMonkey on different social networks. Therefore, sampling was by convenience. Four hundred and fifteen surveys were filled in, all of them 100%. In addition, a demographic information section was included, with questions regarding age and gender, as well as questions about the frequency of use and consumption of Netflix.

The software Statistics v24 and SPSS Amos v24 were used to obtain the statistics and conduct the confirmatory analysis by SEM. Additionally, a reliability analysis was conducted using Cronbach's alpha.

5   Results

5.1   Profile and Characteristics of Respondents

Out of the 415 people surveyed, 53.5% were men and 47.5% were women. The age of the respondents ranged from 15 to 65 years, with a mean of 24 years. The age group 21–29 made up 75.9% of participants, followed by people under 20 years of age, who represented 15.4%, and by the 30–39 age group with 7.0%. In the last place were people 40 or over, who made up 1.7% of the sample.

Regarding the characteristics of the use of Netflix mentioned by participants, 98.6% has used Netflix before, while 87.2% currently use it. As for frequency of use, most participants use Netflix several times per week (35.2%), followed by those who use the service once per week (21.7%). Additionally, most respondents use the service for 1 to 2 h per time of use (43.9%), and 26.0% for 2 to 4 h per time of use.

5.2   Scale Reliability

To ensure the reliability of the model's constructs, Cronbach's alpha was analyzed. According to Loewnthal [26], the limit value for this indicator is 0.6, as these constructs have fewer than 10 items. The results are presented in Table 2.

Table 2. Cronbach's Alpha by construct (Source: own elaboration)

Construct	Cronbach's Alpha
EE	.886
PE	.673
FC	.610
HM	.895
PV	.880
SI	.906
TR	.800
BI	.828

As can be seen, all the constructs have a Cronbach's Alpha value above the cutoff point (0.6), which ranges between 0.610 (FC) and 0.906 (SI). Therefore, the constructs are above the acceptance limit and variables do not need to be eliminated.

5.3 Confirmatory Analysis Results

The results of the model regressions indicate that the R^2 of intention to use is 0.493; that is, 49.3% of variance in the errors of this latent endogenous variable is explained by the latent exogenous variables.

Table 3 indicates that 396 degrees of freedom are obtained. This means that the model is over identified and (i.e. more equations than unknown parameters). Therefore, there is no exact solution and more than one set of parameter estimates is possible.

Table 3. SEM degrees of freedom (Source: own elaboration)

Number of distinct sample moments:	465
Number of distinct parameters to be estimated:	69
Degrees of freedom (465 - 69):	396

5.4 Standardized Regression Coefficients

Table 4 shows the standardized regression coefficients of intention to use and its associated exogenous variables. The significance of these relationships is also provided.

Table 4. Standardized regression coefficients and significance for each latent variable (Source: own elaboration)

	Estimate	S.E.	C.R.	P-value	Significance
TR ← SI	.237	.026	4.451	***	Significant
TR ← HM	.617	.050	7.802	***	Significant
BI ← HM	.281	.050	4.068	***	Significant
BI ← SI	.029	.027	.593	.553	Not significant
BI ← TR	.325	.093	3.993	***	Significant
BI ← FC	.094	.065	1.717	.086	Not significant
BI ← PV	.055	.029	1.205	.228	Not significant
BI ← EE	.015	.050	.337	.736	Not significant
BI ← PE	.423	.070	5.824	***	Significant

The results indicate that the factors for trust (TR), performance expectancy (PE) and hedonic motivation (HM) are significant in the prediction of the intention to use Netflix, since they have a p-value lower than 0.05. In contrast, the factors for social influence (SI), facilitating conditions (FC) and price value (PV) were not significant. Additionally, social influence (SI) and hedonic motivation (HM) were found to be latent variables that affect trust (TR) significantly. These results are of the utmost importance for the conclusions of this study, as they show which are the variables that predict behavioral intention (BI) with acceptable significance. Thus, hypotheses H1, H3, H3', H4 and H5' are accepted, while hypotheses H2, H5, H6 and H7 are rejected. The results of the structural equation model can be seen in Fig. 2.

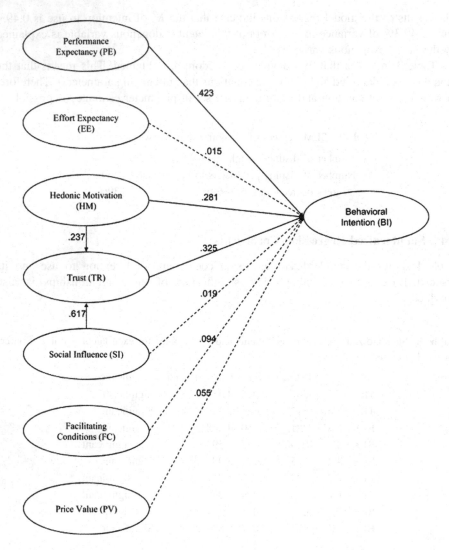

Fig. 2. Results of the structural equation model (Source: own elaboration)

Goodness-of-Fit Statistics

Below, Table 5 shows the final results of the goodness-of-fit statistics as well as the criteria considered.

Table 5. Goodness-of-fit statistics of final model (Source: own elaboration)

Statistics	Value	Criteria
CMIN	1650.824	
Probability level CMIN	.000	<.05
CMIN/DF	4.169	<3
GFI	.769	>.90
NFI	.762	>.90
CFI	.807	>.90
RMSEA	.087	<.06

The results of the fit indexes indicate that CMIN was 1650.824 with a significance below 0.05, which equals an acceptable model. The other statistics are not within the respective criteria for good adjustment of the model: RMSEA, CFI, NFI, GFI and CMIN/DF are below the acceptance limit. Based on these results, a new model will be proposed for assessment on a new sample. This model will be presented in Sect. 7.

6 Conclusions

In this study, we conducted different analyses to determine the factors that influence the adoption of paid subscription streaming services by Chilean users. The results indicate that the latent variables trust (TR), performance expectancy (PE) and hedonic motivation (HM) are significant for the behavioral intention (BI) of Netflix. Additionally, the latent variables hedonic motivation (HM) and social influence (SI) affect trust (TR) significantly.

The performance expectancy associated with Netflix is the factor that most determines the intention to use this service (0.423). This expectancy is related to the possibility of watching multimedia content faster, as well as to the personal perception that Netflix is useful for everyday life. Considering that Chile is a country with high stress rates in the population [8, 15], the need for distractive and hedonic elements is very high. At the same time, these elements need to be fast to avoid lost or dead time, which is often associated with loading or downloading times for multimedia elements. As such, a fundamental aspect for the intention to use Netflix is the avoidance of elements that delay entertainment; that is, the perceived speed of the service. Another relevant aspect is the importance a person gives to audiovisual media.

The second factor most significant for the intention to use Netflix is trust (TR) (0,325); that is, the perception of the honesty, reliability and quality of the service is crucial for the intention to use this service in Chile. Being a paid service that requires the use of a credit card to subscribe, Netflix needs a high perception of trust for users to be willing to provide their personal information to use the service, especially taking into account the sometimes-unreliable credit card security systems.

Hedonic motivation is the third factor that directly affects the intention to use Netflix (0.281). Therefore, for people to use Netflix, they need to find the service entertaining, fun or amusing, which reassures the hedonic nature of this streaming service. Other studies about hedonic information systems have already demonstrated this phenomenon [22, 36]. This indicates that the content of a streaming service influences the intention of users to subscribe to the same, because if the service catalogue does not satisfy the requirements of users, they will not feel entertained when they access the platform.

In addition, we determined that hedonic motivation influence trust significantly. In other words, when a service is perceived as entertaining, this translates into an increase in the trust of users. Consequently, when users feel comfortable using a service, their trust in the same will grow. This point highlights the importance of digital content within a streaming service, since hedonic motivation not only directly impacts intention to use, but also trust, which is the second major predictor of intention to use.

7 Recommendations

From the results, we can see that the variables performance expectancy, trust, hedonic motivation and social influence were fundamental for the intention to subscribe to Netflix in the Chilean context. This means that Netflix and other companies from the streaming sector should focus on having higher service speed, as speed is directly associated with performance expectancy. Therefore, brands need to be positioned as high-performance services targeting the functions the user needs. In advertisement, it should be underscored that Netflix and other streaming service are much faster than buying, renting or downloading a movie, and that these services allow users to enjoy multimedia content without having to move from home to go to the cinema. Additionally, streaming platforms should emphasize that content can be watched without interruptions, even if the Internet speed of the user is slow.

Another fundamental aspect to bear in mind is the content of the streaming service, which directly and indirectly affects intention to use through hedonic motivation. It is necessary that advertisement reinforces the concept of fun when using the application. At the same time, companies need to continue creating their own content to give users personalized content based on their preferences and needs, creating different libraries for series, movies and documentaries to satisfy the needs of all user segments. Advertising the awards won for original content goes in this same line.

A third point is that companies should invest in security systems to protect user data, since trust directly influences intention to use. Streaming companies should constantly improve their security systems in order to provide maximum confidence to the people who trust them with their personal data. Thus, companies need to effectively communicate their efforts to maintain cybersecurity, as well as to implement high level post-sales service that allows users to reach them quickly and efficiently in case of any questions or problems with the service or payment.

Based on the fit indicators of the model and the significance of factors that affect the intention to use Netflix, we propose a new research model. This model does not include the latent variables whose regression coefficients were non-significant. Consequently, the constructs effort expectancy, facilitating conditions and price value are removed from the relationship between SI and BI.

In the model proposed (Fig. 3), social influence not only affects trust but also influences hedonic motivation and performance expectancy. Furthermore, trust determines the performance expectations of Netflix, because users who trust the company tend to think the service will have better performance than users who do not trust it. Thus, the model proposed is the following:

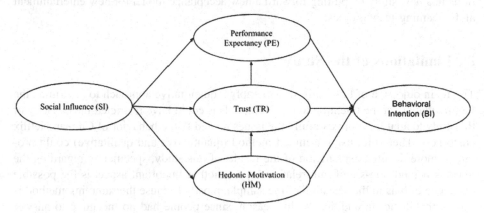

Fig. 3. Model proposed for new study on the intention to use Netflix (Source: own elaboration)

The new model does not consider the observable variables with regression coefficients below the cut-off value (0.5). Therefore, TR6, PE1 and PE2 are not part of this model. The survey proposed for this new model is presented in Table 6.

Table 6. Survey proposed for new study on the intention to use Netflix (Source: own elaboration based on Baabdullah [5])

Construct	Item
Performance expectancy (PE)	PE2. Using Netflix will help me accomplish things more quickly
	PE3. Netflix will be useful in my daily life
Social influence (SI)	SI1. People who are important to me think that I should use Netflix
	SI2. People who influence my behavior think that I should use Netflix
	SI3. People whose opinions that I value prefer that I use Netflix
Hedonic motivation (HM)	HM1. Using Netflix will be fun
	HM2. Using Netflix will be enjoyable
	HM3. Using Netflix will be very entertaining
Trust (TR)	TR1. Netflix is trustworthy
	TR2. Netflix provide good services
	TR3. Netflix know their market
	TR4. Netflix care about customers
	TR5. Netflix is honest
Behavioral intention (BI)	BI1. I will use Netflix in the future
	BI2. I will always try to use Netflix in my daily life
	BI3. I will plan to use Netflix frequently

Another aspect to consider is that although the UTAUT2 model focuses on consumption, its questionnaire is associated to the observable variables and therefore does not completely fit the context of streaming and Netflix. This is because Netflix is a service exclusively devoted to entertainment and some questions do not match 100% what users expect from this type of service. Thus, we propose to adjust these limitations in a new study by putting forward a new acceptance model for new entertainment and streaming technologies.

8 Limitations of the Study

The main objective of this study was to apply a quantitative approach to determine the factors that affect the intention to use Netflix. This could have restricted the capacity of the study to analyze more carefully the issues related to the behavior of Chilean Netflix customers. Therefore, using a mixed method (quantitative and qualitative) could provide a more detailed explanation of the results of this study, specifically regarding the reasons behind non-significant relationships. Another important aspect is the possible existence of bias in the selection of the sample, mostly because the sampling method is non-probabilistic. In addition to this reason, since people had no incentive to answer the survey, they might have responded quickly and without complete awareness of their own answers.

References

1. AbuShanab, E., Pearson, J.: Internet banking in Jordan: the unified theory of acceptance and use of technology (UTAUT) perspective. J. Syst. Inf. Technol. **9**(1), 78–97 (2007). https://doi.org/10.1108/132872607
2. Alalwan, A., Dwivedi, Y., Rana, N., Algharabat, R.: Examining factors influencing Jordanian customers' intentions and adoption of internet banking: extending UTAUT2 with risk. J. Retail. Consum. Serv. **40**, 125–138 (2018). https://doi.org/10.1016/j.jretconser.2017.08.026
3. Alalwan, A., Dwivedi, Y., Rana, N., Williams, M.: Consumer adoption of mobile banking in Jordan: examining the role of usefulness, ease of use, perceived risk and self-efficacy. J. Enterp. Inf. Manag. **29**(1), 118–139 (2016). https://doi.org/10.1108/JEIM-04-2015-0035
4. Alalwan, A., Dwivedi, Y., Rana, N.: Factors influencing adoption of mobile banking by Jordanian bank customers: extending UTAUT2 with trust. Int. J. Inf. Manag. **37**(3), 99–110 (2017). https://doi.org/10.1016/j.ijinfomgt.2017.01.002
5. Baabdullah, A.M.: Consumer adoption of mobile social network games (M-SNGs) in Saudi Arabia: the role of social influence, hedonic motivation and trust. Technol. Soc. **53**, 91–102 (2018). https://doi.org/10.1016/j.techsoc.2018.01.004
6. Bandura, A.: Social Learning Theories. Prentice-Hall, Englewood Cliffs (1977)
7. Calandra, P., Araya, M.: Conociendo las TIC. Libro lanzado por la Universidad de Chile en cooperación con INOVA Chile y Corfo, Facultad de Ciencias Agronómicas, Santiago (2009)
8. Canales-Vergara, M., Valenzuela-Suazo, S., Paravic-Klijn, T.: Condiciones de trabajo de los profesionales de enfermería en Chile. Enfermería Universitaria **13**(3), 178–186 (2016). https://doi.org/10.1016/j.reu.2016.05.004

9. Chen, C., Lin, Y.: What drives live-stream usage intention? The perspectives of flow, entertainment, social interaction, and endorsement. Telemat. Inform. **35**(1), 293–303 (2018). https://doi.org/10.1016/j.tele.2017.12.003

10. Davis, F., Bagozzi, R., Warshaw, P.: User acceptance of computer technology: a comparison of two theoretical models. Manag. Sci. **35**(8), 982–1003 (1989). https://doi.org/10.1287/mnsc.35.8.982

11. Dhir, A., Kaur, P., Rajala, R.: Why do young people tag photos on social networking sites? Explaining user intentions. Int. J. Inf. Manag. **38**(1), 117–127 (2018). https://doi.org/10.1016/j.ijinfomgt.2017.07.004

12. Dörr, J., Wagner, T., Benlian, A., Hess, T.: Music as a service as an alternative to music piracy? Bus. Inf. Syst. Eng. **5**(6), 383–396 (2013). https://doi.org/10.1007/s12599-013-0294-0

13. Featherman, M., Pavlou, P.: Predicting e-services adoption: a perceived risk facets perspective. Int. J. Hum.-Comput. Stud. **59**(4), 451–474 (2003). https://doi.org/10.1016/S1071-5819(03)00111-3

14. Freiden, J., Goldsmith, R., Takacs, S., Hofacker, C.: Information as a product: not goods, not services. Mark. Intell. Plan. **16**(3), 210–220 (1998). https://doi.org/10.1108/026345098

15. Fundación Chile: Chile saludable, vol. 5. oportunidades y desafíos de innovación para el aumento de consumo de productos del mar (2016)

16. Gefen, D., Karahanna, E., Straub, D.: Trust and TAM in online shopping: an integrated model. MIS Q. **27**(1), 51–90 (2003)

17. Gefen, D.: E-commerce: the role of familiarity and trust. Omega **28**(6), 725–737 (2000). https://doi.org/10.1016/S0305-0483(00)00021-9

18. Giesen, E., Riddleberger, E., Christner, R., Bell, R.: When and how to innovate your business model. Strat. Leadersh. **38**(4), 17–26 (2010). https://doi.org/10.1108/10878571011059700

19. Goldberg, L.: Scripted originals hit record 455 in 2016: FX study finds. The Hollywood Reporter, 21 December 2016. http://www.hollywoodreporter.com/live-feed/scripte doriginals-hit-record-455-2016-fx-study-finds-958337

20. Gupta, A., Dogra, N.: Tourist adoption of mapping apps: a UTAUT2 perspective of smart travellers. Tour. Hosp. Manag. **23**(2), 145–161 (2017). https://doi.org/10.20867/thm.23.2.6

21. Hanafizadeh, P., Behboudi, M., Koshksaray, A.A., Tabar, M.J.S.: Mobile-banking adoption by Iranian bank clients. Telemat. Inform. **31**(1), 62–78 (2014). https://doi.org/10.1016/j.tele.2012.11.001

22. Helkkula, A.: Consumers' intentions to subscribe to music streaming services. Master's thesis, Department of Marketing, Aalto University (2016)

23. Lee, M., Turban, E.: A trust model for consumer internet shopping. Int. J. Electron. Commer. **6**(1), 75–91 (2001). https://doi.org/10.1080/10864415.2001.11044227

24. Leong, L.Y., Ooi, K.B., Chong, A.Y.L., Lin, B.: Modelling the stimulators of the behavioral intention to use mobile entertainment: does gender really matter? Comput. Hum. Behav. **29**(5), 2109–2121 (2013). https://doi.org/10.1016/j.chb.2013.04.004

25. Lin, H.F.: An empirical investigation of mobile banking adoption: the effect of innovation attributes and knowledge-based trust. Int. J. Inf. Manag. **31**(3), 252–260 (2011). https://doi.org/10.1016/j.ijinfomgt.2010.07.006

26. Loewnthal, K., Lewis, C.: An Introduction to Psychological Tests and Scales. UCL Press, London (1996)

27. Luo, X., Li, H., Zhang, J., Shim, J.P.: Examining multi-dimensional trust and multi-faceted risk in initial acceptance of emerging technologies: an empirical study of mobile banking services. Decis. Support Syst. **49**(2), 222–234 (2010). https://doi.org/10.1016/j.dss.2010.02.008

28. Martins, C.I.: Exploring digital music online: user acceptance and adoption of online music services. Aalto University School of Business (2013)
29. Mayer, R., Davis, J., Schoorman, F.: An integrative model of organization trust. Acad. Manag. Rev. **20**(3), 709–734 (1995). https://doi.org/10.5465/amr.1995.9508080335
30. Morris, L.: Business model innovation the strategy of business breakthroughs. Int. J. Innov. Sci. **1**(4), 191–204 (2009). https://doi.org/10.1260/1757-2223.1.4.191
31. Muñoz-Leiva, F., Climent-Climent, S., Liébana-Cabanillas, F.: Determinants of intention to use the mobile banking apps: an extension of the classic TAM model. Span. J. Mark.-ESIC **21**(1), 25–38 (2017). https://doi.org/10.1016/j.sjme.2016.12.001
32. Prieto, D.V., et al.: Impact of the information and communication technologies in education and new paradigms in the educational approach. Rev. Cubana de Educación Médica Superior **25**(1), 95–102 (2010)
33. Shareef, M.A., Dwivedi, Y., Kumar, V., Kumar, U.: Content design of advertisement for consumer exposure: mobile marketing through short messaging service. Int. J. Inf. Manag. **37**(4), 257–268 (2017). https://doi.org/10.1016/j.ijinfomgt.2017.02.003
34. Sims, D.: Could YouTube TV mean the end of cable? The Atlantic, 1 March 2017. https://www.theatlantic.com/entertainment/archive/2017/03/does-youtube-tv-mean-the-endof-cable/518346/?utm_source=feed
35. Sosa, L.: Los nuevos medios en la era digital: Convergencia e industrias del Streaming. 10° Congreso Redcom (2008)
36. Van der Heijden, H.: User acceptance of hedonic information systems. MIS Q. **28**(4), 695–704 (2004). https://doi.org/10.2307/25148660
37. Venkatesh, V., Morris, M., Davis, G., Davis, F.: User acceptance of information technology: toward a unified view. MIS Q. **27**(3), 425–478 (2003). https://doi.org/10.2307/30036540
38. Venkatesh, V., Thong, J., Xu, X.: Consumer acceptance and use of information technology: extending the unified theory of acceptance and use of technology. MIS Q. **36**(1), 157–178 (2012). https://doi.org/10.2307/41410412
39. Vinnik, V.: User adoption of mobile applications: extension of UTAUT2 model. Master thesis, Norwegian School of Economics, Bergen (2017)
40. Wong, C.C., Hiew, P.L.: Drivers and barriers of mobile entertainment: empirical study from a Malaysian survey. In: Proceedings of 2005 International Conference on Services Systems and Services Management, ICSSSM 2005, vol. 2, pp. 1325–1330. IEEE (2005)
41. Xu, X.: Understanding users' continued use of online games: an application of UTAUT2 in social network games. In: MMEDIA 2014: The Sixth International Conferences on Advances in Multimedia, pp. 58–65 (2014)
42. Yang, K.: Determinants of US consumer mobile shopping services adoption: implications for designing mobile shopping services. J. Consum. Mark. **27**(3), 262–270 (2010). https://doi.org/10.1108/07363761011038338
43. Zhou, T., Lu, Y., Wang, B.: Integrating TTF and UTAUT to explain mobile banking user adoption. Comput. Hum. Behav. **26**(4), 760–767 (2010). https://doi.org/10.1016/j.chb.2010.01.013

From Belief in Conspiracy Theories to Trust in Others: Which Factors Influence Exposure, Believing and Sharing Fake News

Daniel Halpern[1]([⊠]), Sebastián Valenzuela[1,2], James Katz[3], and Juan Pablo Miranda[1]

[1] School of Communications, Research Center for Integrated Disaster Risk Management (CIGIDEN), Pontificia Universidad Católica de Chile, Alameda 340, Santiago, Chile
{dmhalper,savalenz,jpmiranda}@uc.cl
[2] Millennium Institute for Foundational Research on Data (IMFD), Santiago, Chile
[3] Emerging Media Studies, College of Communication, Boston University, Boston, USA
katz2020@bu.edu

Abstract. Drawing on social-psychological and political research, we offer a theoretical model that explains how people become exposed to fake news, come to believe in them and then share them with their contacts. Using two waves of a nationally representative sample of Chileans with internet access, we pinpoint the relevant causal factors. Analysis of the panel data indicate that three groups of variables largely explain these phenomena: (1) Personal and psychological factors such as belief in conspiracy theories, trust in others, education and gender; (2) Frequency and specific uses of social media; and (3) Political views and online activism. Importantly, personal and political-psychological factors are more relevant in explaining this behavior than specific uses of social media.

Keywords: Misinformation · Social media · Fake news

1 Introduction

1.1 Current Theories in Literature

Since 2009, Social Network Sites (SNS) have gained attention not because of their function of creating and exchanging user-generated content but also because they have emerged as a main channel for information-seeking and news distribution. One indicator of this shift may be seen in Pew Research Center data: In 2018 68% of U.S. adults got their news via social media [1], whereas in 2012 only 49% did so [2]. Complementing the rise of SNS is the ever-increasing oceans of information available online, which can become a special problem if some of this information is misleading, intentionally wrong or falsely promotional [3]. Research on natural disasters, for instance, has shown that while on average 30% of total tweets posted about an event contained situational information about the event [4]. This percentage is even higher in

© Springer Nature Switzerland AG 2019
G. Meiselwitz (Ed.): HCII 2019, LNCS 11578, pp. 217–232, 2019.
https://doi.org/10.1007/978-3-030-21902-4_16

health-related issues: of all anorexia-related videos posted in YouTube, 30% misinformed viewers about several aspects of this eating disorder [5]. In coverage of the HPV vaccine, one-third of the videos did not present accurate information [6]. Subsequent paragraphs, however, are indented.

Scholars who investigate the internet's role in promoting misperceptions have offered a variety of explanations for user's finding and sharing false information and news. One views is that online news facilitates politically biased news consumption [7], leaving partisan audiences with a deficit in their knowledge. This promotes inaccurate beliefs and the formation of "echo chambers" or "filter bubbles" [8]. Another view holds that misperceptions are the result of the psychological processes through which information is interpreted and then perceptions formed [9–11]. Additionally, researchers have looked at the phenomena as being influenced by political factors (e.g. strength of partisanship); derived from technical characteristics (e.g.. algorithms or social media use) and psychological-attitudinal (e.g., trust in media or conspiracy mentality) [12].

However, to the best of our knowledge, there are no comprehensive efforts to integrate these different dimensions into a single model in order to understand the relative weight and relevance of these factors. Accordingly, our study aims to assess which types of variables influence users to be exposed to, believe in, and share the misinformation they find online. We start our analysis by positing that in order to share fake news (i.e., that which the users interpret as "news" and not as an instance of irony or repudiation), users first need to believe in, or at least be open to, the general orientation represented by the false item and also be exposed to the specific item's content. Thus, we suggest that social media qualities, political behavior/ideology, trust and psychological factors have an indirect effect on sharing fake news, mediated by exposure and credibility. We test our model through a Structural Equation Model (SEM), which integrates the above (operationalized) variables, on a two-wave Chilean panel data collected in 2017 and 2018.

1.2 Social Media Affordances

Used in the human-computer interaction, design, and communication fields [13], the term "affordance" refers to the perceived—and actual—properties of an object that allow people to do something with it. The literature suggests that SNS like Twitter or Facebook incorporate at least three set of affordances that facilitates the generation and spread of fake news through internet [10, 12, 14, 15]. First, platforms like Facebook or Twitter allow any users produce and share information at little or no cost. Second, given the vast amount of information produced via these platforms and the limited time users have to process the data they encounter, SNS are creating an environment where information exceeds the capability of users to reflexively analyze the news that they are exposed to. This is especially the case when they use their phones to interact with this content, further limiting their ability to evaluate the veracity of the shared information. Third, as several authors have argued, SNS are ideologically segregated by algorithms that filter information to which users are exposed based on their preferences and online behavior. Thus, saturated information spaces, low cost of information production, and algorithms, facilitate SNS's role in circulating fake news.

Following this line of argument, we can hypothesize that those individuals who use SNS more frequently would also tend be more exposed to information through these platforms, and consequently, more exposed to fake news and, given the above factors, may be more likely to believe the fake news. On this basis, we argue:

H1: Frequency of social media use is positively related to (a) exposure to fake news, and (b) holding misperceptions (i.e., incorrectly believing false news are accurate).

H2: News consumption through social media is positively related to (a) exposure to fake news, and (b) holding misperceptions.

1.3   Political Participation and Identification

A second set of variables used to explain the proliferation of fake news is related to political behavior and ideology. Several studies have found a positive relationship between actively participating in politics and being exposed or believing in fake news [16, 17]. They hold that as users participate more actively in politics, they develop a political or party identity, which is linked to cognitive biases [18, 19]. Thus, political participation has been traditionally associated to the formation of closed groups that function as news filters that generate a selective exposure of information [20, 21].

Most of this literature draws on the cognitive theory developed by Kunda concerning confirmatory biases [22]. This perspective holds that individuals with marked political preferences tend to orient their conclusions to confirm prior political beliefs. More, Kunda found that while individuals seek to reach conclusions that coincide or reinforce their positions, they are not free to take any path to the conclusions they wish. Rather, that to reach certain conclusions, individuals must reasonably justify their positions, maintaining an "illusion of objectivity".

Consequently, it may be more difficult for politically active individuals to distinguish the veracity of different media due to their cognitive biases that filters the type of news to which they are exposed. And, when it challenges their beliefs, cognitive bias also prevents them from considering corrective information in a balanced way.

Further, the relationship between political participation and sharing misinformation is affected by the level of misperception in individuals [23]. Researchers show that in explaining the individuals' support in US for the Iraq war in 2003 for instance, in addition to party identification, it was also relevant what information they had about the possession or absence of weapons of mass destruction by the Iraqi government. Yet it was the mistakenly informed people who were most likely to share their opinion online. Drawing on their finding, it seems that, unlike people who are totally uninformed about a topic, misinformed individuals are more likely to share inaccurate information on SNS, especially when they are politically active. Given that this research seeks to compare the relevance of different types of variables, we include hypotheses of both participation and political ideology to evaluate the impact of political factors compared to other types of variables.

H3: Frequency of online political participation is positively related to (a) exposure to fake news, and (b) holding misperceptions.

H4: Extremity of political opinions is positively related to (a) exposure to fake news, and (b) holding misperceptions.

1.4   Trust in Media, Contacts and Conspiracy Mentality

The third set of possible explanations we consider assume that fake news proliferation through social media is a consequence of attitudes [24] and psychological factors [25], especially those associated with trust. Trust, which is understood for the purpose of this paper, is an element that allows people to overcome the vulnerability derived from uncertainty through competence, reliability, integrity and security of other people and systems [26]. The reason is simple: confidence works as an affiliative conduit that allows individuals to discern between sources of information, peoples or institutions, reliable or unreliable [14].

Yet confidence in institutions is declining in many areas of social life, such as traditional media, which can facilitates exposure to misinformation and its propagation [10, 14]. Three reasons have been advanced by researchers for this spread of misinformation/fake news. First, has to do with news media: Traditional news media are becoming indistinguishable from other forms of news dissemination, collectively called alternative news media, whose rigor is difficult to verify [11, 21, 26]. Following this logic, we propose the following hypotheses:

> H5: Mistrust in traditional news media is positively related to (a) exposure to fake news, and (b) holding misperceptions.

A second area has to do with trust in social media contacts. These help define how users share and interact with content posted by other users [27]. If users trust their contacts, they (almost by definition) would trust the information shared by them. Further, studies have shown that the interactions that occur in platforms like Facebook work in a similar way to face-to-face interactions, as these interactions promote intimacy, confidence, and participation [28]. Consequently, it is expected that the more confidence users of social networks have in their contacts, the more credibility they will have in the information shared by them, including fake news. Therefore, given the increased circulation of fake news via SNS, it is expected:

> H6: Trust in information shared by contacts is positively related to (a) exposure to fake news, and (b) holding misperceptions.

Third, psychological variables affect the proliferation of misinformation through social media, particularly the influence of conspiracy mentalities, which refer to claims that seek to explain some event or practice by reference to the machinations of powerful people, who attempt to conceal their role [29]. According to Flynn et al. [16] they are distinctive insofar as they focus on the behavior of powerful people and may be rooted in stable psychological predispositions. Others suggest that conspiracy mentality can be defined as a belief system related to a rejection of what is perceived as power groups who are covertly responsible for negative political or economic events [30]. Conspiracy theories have been a common topic among fake news studies [10, 14, 25]. Drawing on them, we expect that people who have a greater conspiracy-oriented mentality will be more likely to believe in rumors (or facts) unsupported by the standards of evidence, regardless their political ideology or partisanship. Taking this into account we propose the following hypothesis:

H7: Having a conspiracy mentality is positively associated with (a) exposure to fake news, and (b) holding misperceptions.

2 Methods

2.1 Data and Context

A two-wave panel survey was conducted to examine the hypotheses, during April 2017 and June 2018 respectively. A national panel was employed following the Chilean National Socioeconomic Characterization Survey (CASEN) in order to assure a more accurate national representation. Three variables were used to generate a representative sample: gender, age, and geography. Of the 8840 participants who received the initial email with the survey's URL, 1007 respondents ended up participating in the first wave (2017) and of those 1007, 45% participated a year later in the second wave (451). To correct for demographic biases, we used a model-based strategy, which means that we entered as a control any variable that could be used to construct a post-stratification weight [31].

Concerning the country were the data was collected, it is relevant to mention two aspects. First, after Chile's last political election (November 2017), the fake news issue became a subject of national media attention, which warned the public, inter alia, that fake news was seen 3.5 million times during the year 2017 [32]. Second, Chile has a high use of social networks such as Twitter, Facebook or WhatsApp, all of which serve as a source of information and news (64%) compared to the world average (23%) [33], and a growing distrust in traditional media such as television and newspapers [34]. Consequently, it is possible to argue that Chile also experiences the symptoms of informational disorder observed in the global North [35].

2.2 Analysis

We used a lagged dependent variable model estimated with OLS regression where exposure, credibility, and sharing fake news variables in wave two are the main outcome variables. This type of model is used under the assumption that the variable of interest, in this case exposure, credibility and sharing of fake news of wave 2, are strongly explained by their past (wave 1). Therefore, the exclusion of the lagged variables of wave 1 can lead to biases of omitted variable and reduce the reliability of the coefficients of the rest of the independent variables. The inclusion of lagged variables absorbs a large portion of the variance of the model, while the remaining coefficients can be interpreted as the predicted change in dependent variable compared with the value it could have taken knowing its previous value [36, 37].

We are aware that the inclusion of lagged dependent variables could reduce the contribution of other independent variables and increase standard errors. However, this quality makes our models conservative when estimating the coefficients, which gives more robustness to our conclusions.

We also use as a complement tools of structural equations (SEM) to identify direct and indirect effects of the independent variables in the three variables of interest separately. The data also presented a small proportion of missing values. So as not to bias the coefficients, we decided to impute these cases with the mean (N = 423).

Finally, all independent and dependent variables considered in the analysis except for lagged variables correspond to wave 2 of the survey. Figure 1 shows the theoretical model with proposed causal relations in which social media qualities, political behavior and ideology, and trust and psychological variables impact directly exposure and credibility to fake news. Of course, both variables then explain sharing fake news. So, in this article we do not focus in the direct relation between the first three groups of variables and sharing fake news, but in their indirect relation mediated by exposure to and credibility of fake news.

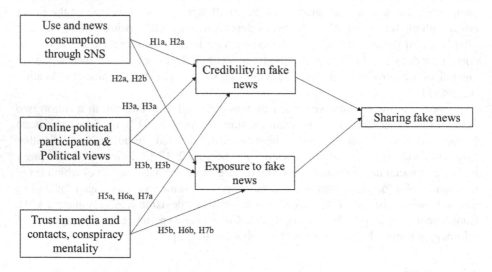

Fig. 1. The hypothesized variables included in the model

2.3   Dependent Variables

Exposure to Fake News. Respondents were exposed to a set of 14 fake news stories that circulated in Chile in the preceding 15 months and then were asked if they were aware of them (respondents were not told that news were false). The list of fake news included misinformation about natural disasters, health, politics and immigration (e.g., "Some vaccines can produce autism in children," "The President of Venezuela, Nicolás Maduro, called for support of the candidate for the Presidency, Alejandro Guillier"). These so-called news stories had circulated in the authors' own social media accounts, were fact-checked by El Polígrafo and found to be false. Based on this question we built an exposure variable (range = 0 [not aware of any story] to 14 [aware of all stories]; Cronbach's α = .70, M = 8.13, SD = 2.76).

Sharing Fake News. Respondents were also asked if they had shared any of the 14 fake news stories. From their answers we created a variable of sharing fake news (range = 0 [no story was shared] to 14 [shared all stories]; Cronbach's α = .69, M = .953, SD = 1.50).

Credibility in Fake News. Subsequently, respondents were asked if they believed in any of the news stories we had shared, regardless of whether they had heard them before or if they had shared them (range = 1 ["not believable at all"] to 5 ["Very credible"]). Based on this question we built a credibility variable of fake news (Cronbach's α = .85, M = 2.58, SD = 0.67).

2.4   Social Media Use

Frequency of SNS Use. Participants were asked how much time they spent on four social networks platforms (Facebook, Twitter, Instagram, and WhatsApp) (range = 0 [do not use that social network] to 7 [use more than 6 h per day]; (Cronbach's α = 0.62, M = 3.45, SD = 1.25).

News Consumption in SNS. Respondents were asked how many days per week they consumed news on SNS using an 8-point scale, ranged from "I do not see news or do not have news service" to "Every day of the week" (M = .6, SD = 2.57).

2.5   Political Views and Participation

Online Political Participation. A battery of 8 questions with different examples of political involvement in social networks was used (e.g., "Change profile picture or status in a social network or WhatsApp in support of a political or social cause"). Respondents were asked about the frequency of such activities using a 5-point scale ranging from "Never" to "Always" (Cronbach's α = .86, M = 1.97, SD = .72).

Strength of Political Views. We used a 7-point scale for political ideology ranging from "Very left" to "Very right." To create the variable for strong political identification, the item was folded into a 4-point scale, ranging from weak to strong political views (M = 0.29, SD = 0.45).

2.6   Trust and Physiological Variables

Trust in Traditional Media. Respondents were asked about 9 statements concerning trust in traditional media (press, radio and television) such as "They are reliable sources of information" or "They present all the sides of a news equally" using a 5-point scale ranging from "Strongly Disagree" to "Strongly Agree" (Cronbach's α = .86, M = 2.88, SD = .68).

Confidence in Information Shared by Contacts. Participants were asked about their level of agreement with the statement, "I trust most of the news shared by my social network contacts" using a 5-point scale ranging from "Strongly disagree" to "Strongly agree" (M = 2.31, SD = .83).

Conspiracy Mentality. Based on Bruder et al. [38], respondents were asked about their level of agreement with 4 conspiracy statements, such as "many very important things happen in the world, which the public is never informed about" and "there are secret organizations that greatly influence political decisions" (Cronbach's α = .76, M = 3.46, SD = .71).

2.7 Control Variables

Three demographic variables were considered: sex (M = 1.57; SD = .46), age (range = 20 to 71; M = 35.02; SD = 12.32) and educational level (range = 1 [Elementary school incomplete] to 7 [Postgraduate]; M = 5.93, Mdn = 6 [university completed], SD = .72). We also included a variable related to the attention of the respondents to different type of news (Politics, Crime, International news, Economy and business, Food and health, Environment, Technology and Science, Sports and Sports) (range = 1 [no attention to news] to 5 [a lot of attention to news]; Cronbach's α = .67, M = 3.06, SD = .56). A scale of political ideology ranged from 1, "Very Left", to 7 "Very Right" was also included (M = 3.8, SD = 1.32). Given that several studies have shown the relevance of online self-efficacy in explaining social media use and behavior [39], we also considered individuals' perception of their ability to influence their online environment through their skills to understand online information [40]. Thus, participants were asked their level of agreement with 7 statements (e.g., "I can discern between relevant information" or "It is easy to be well informed about important issues") (range = 1 [Total disagreement] to 5 [Total agreement]) (Cronbach's α = .74, M = 3.99, SD = .51).

3   Results

3.1   Descriptive Analysis

Before reviewing the proposed hypotheses, we observed the prevalence of exposure, credibility and the propensity to share fake news in the Chilean case using the latest wave of the study, namely 2018. According to table No. 1, we can see the high proportion of familiarity with the fake news revealed in the survey (most respondents had between 30.5% and 84.4% of familiarity). This familiarity is contrasted to fake news about tolerance towards multiculturalism (No. 3, No. 9, and No. 11) and fake news about politics that are not related to the last presidential elections of 2017 (No. 3, No. 10, and No. 2), where participants showed lower levels of familiarity. However, it is important to note that for respondents none of the news stories exceeds 50% of credibility, although 4 of them reach 30% or more. Nevertheless, the highest levels of credibility were found in news about politics and those related to health (No. 6, No. 5 and No. 8). Finally, only a few percentage of respondents said that they had shared fake news. (The range goes from 0.5% to 18.2%.) Thus, except for the news N 4, we see that those fake news stories about politics were less shared than those about health, natural disasters and tolerance to multiculturalism.

3.2   Direct Effects

Returning to our hypothesis, we seek to identify which type of variables are the most relevant in explaining why social media users are exposed, believe, and share fake news through the internet. Figures N1, N2 and N3 presents the SEM models with the direct effects between variables (Fig. 2).

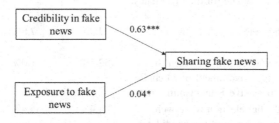

Fig. 2. Direct effects of exposure and credibility of fake news on sharing fake news

First, Figure N2 presents the relation between sharing fake news and both variables credibility in fake news and Exposure to fake news. The relation between these variables was tested including the rest of independent and control variables in the model. According with Figure N1 we find a significant and positive relation between sharing fake news and being exposed to fake news (b = .041, p < .01), and sharing fake news stories and believing in them (b = .630, p < .001). This means that the more individuals are exposed to and the more they believe in fake news, the more they will share them in social media (Table 1).

Regarding the direct effects between the selected variables and credibility of fake news, Fig. 3 shows a negative effect between the frequency of SNS use and credibility in fake news (b = −0.049, p < 0.05). This means that, contrary to what was proposed in hypothesis 1a, the more individuals use the social media, the less they believe in fake news. We also find a positive effect between the confidence in information shared by contacts (b = 0.058, p < 0.5) and holding a conspiracy mentality (b = 0.245, p < 0.01), which allows us to support hypothesis 6a and 7a respectively. We did not find support for hypothesis 2a, 3a, 4a and 5a. This means that in order to explain credibility in fake news, the variables related to trust and physiological factors are more relevant than the political aspects and those related to social media use.

Regarding the role of these variables in exposure to fake news, only online political participation is related significantly to exposure to fake news, which confirms H3b (b = 0.245, p < 0.01). However, none of the others variables have an impact, as Fig. 3 shows.

We also find relevant effects in control variables. Holding strong political beliefs does not seem to explain credibility in fake news, holding more Right-leaning political ideology does have a positive effect in the believing of misinformation in social network (b = 0.071, p < 0.01). This indicates that the orientation of political thought is relevant, with Right-leaning people being more prone to believe in fake news than Left-leaning people. Age also has a significant and negative effects (b = 0.004, p < 0.05),

Table 1. Prevalence of misinformation exposure, beliefs, and sharing

Claim	Exposure to claim	Believes claim is accurate	Has shared claim
	%	%	%
1. The President of Venezuela, Nicolás Maduro, called to support the candidate for the Presidency, Alejandro Guillier	66.2%	40.9%	2.4%
2. President Sebastián Piñera suffers from Parkinson's	7.3%	7.8%	0.5%
3. There was a secret agreement between the United Nations and the government of Michelle Bachelet for Chile to receive Haitian immigrants	52.5%	21.0%	5.7%
4. In the last presidential election there were several votes marked in favor of the candidates Alejandro Guillier and Beatriz Sánchez	84.4%	36.4%	10.6%
5. The consumption of animal milk does not feed and, in certain circumstances, is even harmful to health	65.2%	29.6%	10.6%
6. The consumption of genetically modified foods, such as Monsanto seeds, is harmful to health	69.7%	46.8%	18.2%
7. Some vaccines can produce autism in children	72.3%	17.5%	5.0%
8. Some vaccines have side effects that may be worse than the same disease they are trying to prevent	75.4%	26.7%	8.7%
9. Israeli agents have bought large tracts of land in Patagonia	45.6%	20.1%	5.2%
10. President Michelle Bachelet suffered depression and alcohol abuse at certain stages of her government	30.5%	13.5%	3.3%
11. In Santiago operates a band of Colombian origin that kidnaps minors in parks and school exits	40.0%	25.1%	5.0%
12. Mapuche groups began the mega-fire that occurred in the summer of last year	77.3%	16.3%	8.5%
13. The forestry companies started the mega-fire last year to collect the insurance and reduce the losses due to the drop-in exports caused by the election of Donald Trump	71.4%	26.7%	8.7%
14. Members of the FARC of Colombia together with Mapuche groups burned the forests of the south last summer to destabilize the country	55.1%	8.5%	2.8%

Percentage that believes the story is accurate is the sum of participants who find it "very credible" and "extremely credible".

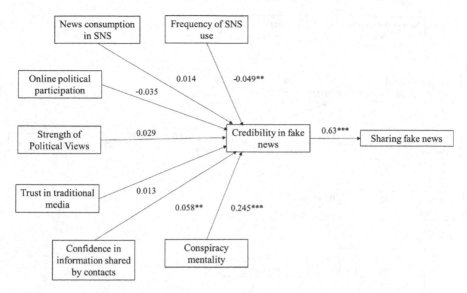

Fig. 3. Direct effects of the hypothesized variables on credibility in fake news and sharing fake news

which indicate that older individuals tend to believe less in fake news. Finally, the gender is also relevant with women being more prone to believe in fake news than men (b = 0.089, p < 0.1).

3.3   Mediation Effects

Together with the direct effects described in previous section, we also analyzed indirect effects mediated by the variables "exposure to fake news" and "credibility in fake news." We found three variables mediated by credibility in fake news: social media use (b = −0.0307, p < 0.5) confidence in information shared by contacts (b = 0.0366, p < 0.5) and conspiracy mentality (b = 0.1542, p < 0.01). These results show that the three variables do have an effect in sharing fake news, but only through the credibility of fake news. So, according to the results, the more the individuals use social platforms, the less they share fake news, mainly because they trust this information less. Similarly, the more individuals hold a conspiracy mentality, the more they share fake news. However, unlike credibility, none of de variables have an indirect effect mediated by exposure.

These results allow us to assume that the variable of credibility in fake news is a relevant variable to explain the indirect relation between several variable and sharing fake news. Also, Fig. 4 shows the importance of trust and psychological variables in explaining the spread of fake news through social media. It again, shows theoretically contradictory evidence about the assumed positive relation between the use of social media and the spread of misinformation through internet (Fig. 5).

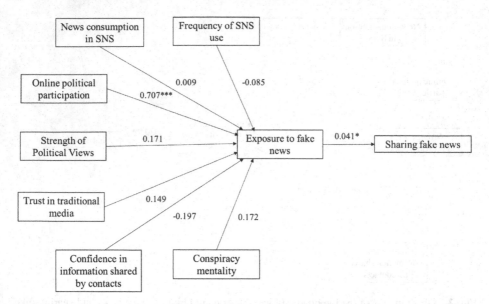

Fig. 4. Direct effects of the hypothesized variables on exposure to fake news and sharing fake news

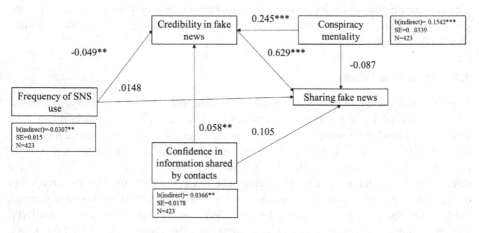

Fig. 5. Indirect effects and mediation

4 Discussion

Due to its rapid spread in social networks and the harmful effect, the topic of fake news has become a major issue for the public and researchers alike. Justifiable fears exist for the risk fake news poses to democracy, comity, and informed debate. Responsive to this growing concern, we used a panel data to study the topic. To understand the proliferation of fake news in social networks, we compared the effect of different types of factors on three key variables: exposure, credibility and sharing fake news. The findings are discussed below.

First, researchers have consistently argued that the rise of fake news is attributable to the emergence of new digital platforms that facilitate the production and propagation of misinformation. They also suggest that the medium in which public debate takes place makes it difficult for users to discriminate between truthful information and information created for other purposes, including misleading ones. However, our results show that controlling for other variables, the use of social network seems to be negatively associated with believing in fake news. Thus, one possible implication is that more connected users may have developed a sense of awareness about the information quality in social media, and would be less exposed to these types of news.

Second, we outlined that variables related to political identification and participation would have an impact on exposure to fake news, as suggested by previous investigations [11, 16–21]. Our results show that individuals who most identify with the political Right are those who are more likely to believe fake news compared to the people identified with the Left. This, however, can be explained by the type of fake news about which the respondents were consulted, which refer to the past government of Michelle Bachelet, president identified with center-left spectrum of politics. In other words, much of the beliefs that researchers themselves hold about who accepts and propagates fake news may be an artifact of the topics chosen as fake news and the specific platforms and aspects they choose to investigate. They would be an ironic and inadvertent demonstration perhaps of Kunda's earlier findings concerning her cognitive analysis about how people seek to reinforce their prior views and commitments.

Third, as several authors point out, the confidence of users is important in explaining the proliferation of fake news on social networks [17, 21, 24]. Coherently, we find that both confidence in information shared by contacts and conspiracy mentality are important variables to understand why people believe in fake news. However, the relevance of these variables was not significant in predicting exposure to fake news. A plausible explanation could be that trust in contacts and holding a conspiracy mentality make people more susceptible to believe in fake news, but that does not translate into actively seeking out misinformation or engaging with sources that promote them.

And this finding is relevant for two reasons. On the one hand, the fact that users trust the information shared by their contacts may enhance filter bubbles or echo chambers within platforms such as Twitter or Facebook, either by the algorithms of these networks or by a natural tendency of groupings based on similar interests. This aspect is central, because it may augment the disinformation effects of the fake news, since it prevents users engaging with others who will present them with counter-acting dissonant information.

On the other hand, we also find support for the idea that there are certain types of individuals who, due to personality traits (e.g., lack of confidence, paranoia, low self-esteem), constitute ideal victims of fake news. This was shown in the relationship between conspiracy mentality and believing in fake news.

Finally, we found three relevant indirect effects mediated by credibility in fake news, which are social media use, conspiracy mentality and confidence in formation shared by contacts. The presence of this indirect effect underscores the need to analyze with more detail and complexity the relation between different factors that influence misinformation in internet and social media. The indirect effects found in this research allow us to asseverate that using social media, holding a conspiracy mentality or trust in information shared by contacts are not enough on their own to explain why people spread misinformation through internet. Even in the presence of these variable, if individuals do not believe in the information to which they are exposed, based on our data, we cannot expect that they will share these pieces of information.

In short, the literature on fake news has provocatively addressed several theories. In this study, we have tried to take the most important variables offered by the literature and observe how they operate when they are included within a single integrated and longitudinal model. Our intention was to advance our understanding of a long-standing phenomenon, such as fake news, which today has commanded still greater attention due to social media. We know much about how each dimension works separately, but in literature there is a lack of analyses that integrate different dimensions. Our effort here is to respond to this vacuum by conducting (what we believe to be) the first longitudinal study in the area.

However, much remains to be done. In this article we analyze the case of a Latin American country, Chile. Even though many of our conclusions may be useful for current debates among scholars, there may be no reason to expect that other region around the globe behave in the same way regardless misinformation passing through the internet. However, it is relevant to note that one of the limitations of this study is the fact that more than half of the users surveyed in the first wave were not included in the second wave. One reason that may explain this lower participation is the time elapsed between the first and second waves (15 months). Another limitation is related to the fact that we analyzed several fake news stories without considering if they refer to political, health, migration or tolerance themes. Further investigation can separate fake news stories based on topics and may find different patterns between variables. In spite of the limitations, we hope that this article could help as an initial step for more comprehensive and multidimensional studies about fake news and misinformation in the internet.

Acknowledgements. This work was funded by Chile's National Commission of Scientific and Technological Research (CONICYT) through grants CIGIDEN/Fondap/15110017 and Fondecyt/ 1181600.

References

1. Matsa, K.E., Shearer, E.: News Use Across Social Media Platforms. Pew Research Center's Journalism Project (2018)
2. Rainie, L., Smith, A., Schlozman, K.L., Brady, H., Verba, S.: Social media and political engagement. Pew Internet & American Life Project (2012)
3. Thorson, E.: Belief echoes: the persistent effects of corrected misinformation. Polit. Commun. **33**, 460–480 (2016). https://doi.org/10.1080/10584609.2015.1102187

4. Gupta, A., Kumaraguru, P.: Credibility ranking of tweets during high impact events. In: Proceedings of the 1st Workshop on Privacy and Security in Online Social Media, pp. 2–12. ACM, Lyon (2012). https://doi.org/10.1145/2185354.2185356
5. Syed-Abdul, S., Fernandez-Luque, L., Jian, W.S., Li, Y.C., Crain, S., Hsu, M.H., et al.: Misleading health-related information promoted through video-based social media: anorexia on YouTube. J. Med. Internet Res. **15**, 2 (2013). https://doi.org/10.2196/jmir.2237
6. Briones, R., Nan, X., Madden, K., Waks, L.: Sorting through search results: a content analysis of HPV vaccine information online. Health Commun. **27**, 478–485 (2012). https://doi.org/10.1016/j.vaccine.2011.10.025
7. Garrett, R.K., Weeks, B.E., Neo, R.L.: Driving a wedge between evidence and beliefs: how online ideological news exposure promotes political misperceptions. J. Comput.-Mediat. Commun. **21**(5), 331–348 (2016). https://doi.org/10.1016/j.vaccine.2011.10.025
8. Conover, M.D., Gonçalves, B., Flammini, A., Menczer, F.: Partisan asymmetries in online political activity. EPJ Data Sci. **1**, 1–6 (2012). https://doi.org/10.1140/epjds6
9. Tsai, C.I., Klayman, J., Hastie, R.: Effects of amount of information on judgment accuracy and confidence. Organ. Behav. Hum. Decis. Process. **107**(2), 97–105 (2008). https://doi.org/10.1016/j.obhdp.2008.01.005
10. Del Vicario, M.: The spreading of misinformation online. Proc. Natl. Acad. Sci. **113**(3), 554–559 (2016). https://doi.org/10.1073/pnas.1517441113
11. Lazer, D., et al.: The science of fake news. Science 8–10 (2018). https://doi.org/10.1126/science.aao2998
12. Allcott, H., Gentzkow, M.: Social media and fake news in the 2016 election. J. Econ. Perspect. **31**, 211–236 (2017). https://doi.org/10.1257/jep.31.2.211
13. Ellison, N.B., Vitak, J.: Social network site affordances and their relationship to social capital processes. In: Sundar, S.S. (ed.) The Handbook of the Psychology of Communication Technology, pp. 205–227. Wiley, Malden (2015). https://doi.org/10.1002/9781118426456
14. Bode, L., Vraga, E.K.: In related news, that was wrong: the correction of misinformation through related stories functionality in social media. J. Commun. **65**, 619–638 (2015). https://doi.org/10.1111/jcom.12166
15. Knoll, J., Matthes, J., Heiss, R.: The social media political participation model. Converg.: Int. J. Res. New Media Technol. **22**, 1–22 (2018). https://doi.org/10.1177/1354856517750366
16. Flynn, D.J., Nyhan, B., Reifler, J.: The nature and origins of misperceptions: understanding false and unsupported beliefs about politics. Polit. Psychol. **38**, 127–150 (2017). https://doi.org/10.1111/pops.12394
17. Greenhill, K.M., Oppenheim, B.: Rumor has it: the adoption of unverified information in conflict zones. Int. Stud. Q. **2**, 660–676 (2017). https://doi.org/10.1093/isq/sqx015
18. Levendusky, M.S.: Why do partisan media polarize viewers? Am. J. Polit. Sci. **57**, 611–623 (2013). https://doi.org/10.1111/ajps.12008
19. Reedy, J., Wells, C., Gastil, J.: How voters become misinformed: an investigation of the emergence and consequences of false factual beliefs. Soc. Sci. Q. **95**, 1399–1418 (2014). https://doi.org/10.1111/ssqu.12102
20. Schaffner, B.F., Luks, S.: Misinformation or expressive responding? What an inauguration crowd can tell us about the source of political misinformation in surveys. Public Opin. Q. **82**, 135–147 (2018). https://doi.org/10.1093/poq/nfx042
21. Stroud, N.J.: Niche News: The Politics of News Choice. Oxford University Press, Oxford (2011)
22. Kunda, Z.: The case for motivated reasoning. Psychol. Bull. **108**, 480–498 (1990). https://doi.org/10.1037/0033-2909.108.3.480
23. Hochschild, J.L., Einstein, K.L.: Do facts matter? Information and misinformation in American politics. Polit. Sci. Q. **130**, 585–624 (2015). https://doi.org/10.1002/polq.12398

24. Miller, J.M., Saunders, K.L., Farhart, C.E.: Conspiracy endorsement as motivated reasoning: the moderating roles of political knowledge and trust. Am. J. Polit. Sci. **60**, 824–844 (2016). https://doi.org/10.1111/ajps.12234

25. Vosoughi, S., Roy, D., Aral, S.: The spread of true and false news online. Science **359**, 1146–1151 (2018). https://doi.org/10.1126/science.aap9559

26. Tandoc, E.C., Ling, R., Westlund, O., Duffy, A., Goh, D., Zheng Wei, L.: Audiences' acts of authentication in the age of fake news: a conceptual framework. New Media Soc. (2017). https://doi.org/10.1177/1461444817731756

27. Halpern, D., Valenzuela, S., Katz, J.E.: We Face, I Tweet: how different social media influence political participation through collective and internal efficacy. J. Comput.-Mediat. Commun. **22**, 320–336 (2017). https://doi.org/10.1111/jcc4.12198

28. Bode, L.: Facebooking it to the polls: a study in online social networking and political behavior. J. Inf. Technol. Polit. **9**, 352–369 (2012). https://doi.org/10.1080/19331681.2012.709045

29. Uscinski, J.E., Parent, J.M.: American Conspiracy Theories. Oxford University Press, Oxford (2014)

30. Imhoff, R., Bruder, M.: Speaking (un-) truth to power: conspiracy mentality as a generalised political attitude. Eur. J. Pers. **28**, 25–43 (2014). https://doi.org/10.1002/per.1930

31. Gelman, A.: Rejoinder: struggles with survey weighting and regression modeling. Stat. Sci. **22**, 184–188 (2007). https://doi.org/10.1214/088342307000000203

32. Arriagada, C., Velasco, I.: Noticias falsas sobre Chile fueron vistas o compartidas 3,5 millones de veces en redes sociales durante este año [Fake news about Chile were seen or shared 3.5 million times in social networks during this year]. El Mercurio (2017). http://impresa.elmercurio.com/Pages/NewsDetail.aspx?dt=26-11-20170:00:00&NewsID=532717&dtB=26-11-20170:00:00&BodyID=3&PaginaId=8

33. Newman, N., Fletcher, R., Kalogeropoulos, A., Levy, D., Nielsen, R.: Reuters institute digital news report 2017. Reuters Inst. Study Journal. **53**(8), 1 (2017). https://doi.org/10.1080/21670811.2012.744561

34. González, R.: La creciente desconfianza en los medios de comunicación [The increasing mistrust on mass media]. La Situación (2017). http://lasituacion.cl/2017/10/17/la-creciente-desconfianza-en-los-medios-de-comunicacion/

35. Wardle, C., Derakhshan, H. Information Disorder: Toward an interdisciplinary framework for research and policy making Council of Europe report DGI, France (2017). https://rm.coe.int/information-disorder-toward-an-interdisciplinary-framework-for-researc/168076277c

36. Eveland, W.P., Thomson, T.: Is it talking, thinking, or both? A lagged dependent variable model of discussion effects on political knowledge. J. Commun. **56**, 523–542 (2006). https://doi.org/10.1111/j.1460-2466.2006.00299.x

37. Chamberlain, A.: A time-series analysis of external efficacy. Public Opin. Q. **76**, 117–130 (2012). https://doi.org/10.1093/poq/nfr064

38. Bruder, M., Haffke, P., Neave, N., Nouripanah, N., Imhoff, R.: Measuring individual differences in generic beliefs in conspiracy theories across cultures: conspiracy mentality questionnaire. Front. Psychol. **4**, 225 (2013). https://doi.org/10.3389/fpsyg.2013.00225

39. Velasquez, A., LaRose, R.: Youth collective activism through social media: the role of collective efficacy. New Media Soc. **17**, 899–918 (2015). https://doi.org/10.1177/1461444813518391

40. Livingstone, S., Helsper, E.: Balancing opportunities and risks in teenagers' use of the internet: the role of online skills and internet self-efficacy. New Media Soc. **12**, 309–329 (2010). https://doi.org/10.1177/1461444809342697

Fifteen Seconds of Fame: A Qualitative Study of Douyin, A Short Video Sharing Mobile Application in China

Xing Lu[1] and Zhicong Lu[2(✉)]

[1] School of Information Engineering, Ningxia University, Yinchuan, China
lxncs@nxu.edu.cn
[2] Department of Computer Science, University of Toronto, Toronto, Canada
luzhc@cs.toronto.edu

Abstract. The proliferation of short video sharing mobile applications like Douyin and Kuaishou in China has led to new forms of entertainment and information sharing practices. Even the huge live streaming industry in China has been influenced by these popular video sharing mobile applications, because some people are drawn away from watching live streams to watching short videos. However, little research has looked into why and how people use Douyin, what engages users, and what concerns and negative experiences users have with Douyin. Through interviews with 28 regular Douyin users, we identify several unique motivations of using Douyin compared to other social media, reveal several different categories of content that engaged them, and present several challenges and concerns they have when using Douyin. We show that people use Douyin not only for entertainment, but also for keeping up with "fashion" and for informational and practical needs. We situate our findings with prior research on social media use in China, and provide design implications for future video-based social media.

Keywords: Short video sharing · Uses and gratifications · User engagement · Social computing · Online community

1 Introduction

Douyin (抖音 or Tik Tok, for its international version) is a short video and music video sharing mobile application that was launched in autumn 2016. It allows users to produce and browse quick-fire video clips lasting from 15 s to one minute, to share funny and even nonsense videos widely online, similar to how Vine [2] was used. With over 500 million global monthly active users [1] and over 250 million daily active users in China [21], Douyin (Tik Tok) has been the most downloaded non-game app of iOS App Store globally since the first quarter of 2018 [16]. Douyin's influence has even extended offline, as many users identify

The two authors contributed equally to this work.

© Springer Nature Switzerland AG 2019
G. Meiselwitz (Ed.): HCII 2019, LNCS 11578, pp. 233–244, 2019.
https://doi.org/10.1007/978-3-030-21902-4_17

themselves as 'Douyiner' ("抖音人") and socialize with each other using jargons in real life. Many songs have garnered tractions because many content creators on Douyin used them as background music of their videos.

One of the key differences between Douyin and Vine is its editing functions, which allow the users to have add-ons, stickers, special visual effects, and animations easily when they are creating videos. Douyin also emphasizes the role of music in the creation of videos, allowing users to easily align special visual effects of videos to the chosen music. Besides, it adopts recommendation algorithms to customize what is shown to different users when they are browsing videos. These features enable end users to easily produce short videos that are of high production values, and enable viewers to freely explore many videos of interest. These features could also indicate a new genre of affordances in video-based social media, especially those built around video sharing (Vine, Instagram, and YouTube), though little work has been done to explore and understand the motivations, practices, challenges, and opportunities of this emerging style of short video watching and sharing.

This paper aims to answer these questions by an interview-based study with active Douyin users. We use uses and gratifications as a lens to explore motivations, user engagement, and potential challenges and concerns of using short video sharing social platforms, relate our results to prior research in video interaction and video sharing platforms, live streaming, and social computing theories, and discuss its design and social implications from our investigation in the situated cultural context of China.

2   Background and Related Work

There are many online platforms and communities which support video sharing. YouTube is the largest platform for sharing video content online. It does not have constraints on topics or time limits, and hosts billions of public accessible archived videos. Vine was a public short video sharing platform operated by Twitter but shut down in 2017, which had a 6-second time limit for videos. Instagram, now owned by Facebook, began as a photo-sharing platform, but has recently started to support videos of 3 to 15 s. While all of these platforms are popular, Douyin has some unique features, such as emphasizing on background music and special visual effects, and the aforementioned platforms are currently not available to Chinese users. We chose to focus on Douyin to understand the specific uses and gratifications of short video sharing platforms, and to investigate the affordances of such platforms in the unique social media landscapes and social contexts of China.

Prior work has investigated public video sharing platforms such as YouTube, Vine, and Snapchat. For example, a survey of online videos conducted by Pew Research in 2013 found that 18% of adult users produce videos and share them online [10]. The survey also found that adult content producers mostly post videos of family and friends doing everyday things (58% of the content producers), themselves or other people behaving in funny ways (56%), and events they

Fig. 1. User interface of Douyin (Tik Tok). Left: a video showing a dynamic wallpaper for mobile phones. Right: a video showing a love letter with narrations

attend (54%). Ding et al. examined Youtube authorship through measuring and analyzing video uploaders of YouTube, and found that 63% of the most popular uploaders were mostly sharing user-copied (rather than original) video content [5]. Farnham et al. found that people maintain faceted lives in online spaces, choosing presentation of their identity based on the affordances and constraints of various social technologies [6]. Yarosh et al. studied youth video authorship on YouTube and Vine, and found that youth authors treat online video sharing platforms as a stage to perform, tell stories, and express their opinions and identities in a performative way [24]. McRoberts et al. studied how Snapchat users perceive and use the Stories feature, and relate their findings to theories of self-presentation and identity curation in social media [15]. Cavalcanti conducted an interview-based study to understand the affordances of ephemeral communications of Snapchat, and found that Snapchat users experienced media, meaning, and context loss, and they developed workarounds to deal with these losses through preemptive action and collaborative saving [3]. Though relevant, Douyin has several unique design features and different demographics of users, and it should be an important part of research agenda for understanding video interaction, similar to Vine [9]. Douyin also supports in-app live streaming functionality with gamification elements which allows viewers to send virtual gifts to their favorite content providers, and we will situate our results with prior work on live streaming of video gaming [18], information behavior on social live streaming services [18], mobile live streaming [20], live streaming in China [11,13,14], and gamification in live streaming [17]. To the best of our knowledge, this paper is one of the first to examine the uses and gratifications of short video sharing practices on Douyin.

3   Method

Inspired by the popularity and impact of Douyin, our study is motivated by the following research questions:

RQ1: Why are people using Douyin and how are they using it?
RQ2: What engage the users when watching the videos shared on Douyin?
RQ3: What are concerns, challenges and negative experiences using Douyin?

3.1   Interviews and Participants

To address these questions, we conducted 28 semi-structured interviews with active Douyin users in China, 5 of whom were also active content creators (Table 1). Our participants were 50% female, aging 16–31 (M = 23, SD = 4) They were recruited through snowball sampling, and were mostly located in Beijing, Shanghai, and Yinchuan. The interviews were conducted remotely using video or audio calls from October 2018 to January 2019. Each interview lasted approximately 40 min, and participants were volunteers who did not receive any honorarium. Interviews included questions about their motivations to watch short videos on Douyin, what types of content they enjoyed watching on Douyin, what they liked or disliked about using Douyin, how they interacted with other users on Douyin, and concerns and negative experiences they had with Douyin. During the interviews, participants were also asked to share with us some video clips they recently saw and thought as engaging or interesting, and we asked them to elaborate on why they enjoyed watching the videos. Interviews were conducted in Mandarin, audio-taped, and transcribed by the author who conducted the interviews.

3.2   Data Analysis

The transcripts of all the interviews were analyzed using an open coding methods [4]. The authors who are both native Mandarin speakers first coded the transcripts individually, and met to gain consensus on the codes. Then the authors discussed about the codes using affinity diagramming as a modified version of grounded theory analysis, to find and group the themes that emerged.

4   Findings

Our analysis revealed several different user motivations of using Douyin, users' practices of using Douyin, what content engaged users, and negative experiences, concerns, and challenges of using Douyin.

Table 1. Summary of Douyin users interviewed. P8, P9, P16, P22, P26 were also active content creators.

ID	Sex	Age	Location	Occupation	Months using Douyin	ID	Sex	Age	Location	Occupation	Months using Douyin
P1	M	19	Yinchuan	Student	10	P15	F	27	Beijing	Manager	6
P2	M	21	Yinchuan	Student	15	P16	M	26	Shanghai	Programmer	15
P3	F	17	Yinchuan	Student	12	P17	M	19	Beijing	Student	9
P4	M	23	Beijing	Student	18	P18	F	20	Yinchuan	Student	16
P5	F	22	Beijing	Office worker	11	P19	M	21	Beijing	Student	15
P6	F	16	Yinchuan	Student	8	P20	F	24	Yinchuan	Accountant	13
P7	M	24	Shanghai	Programmer	20	P21	F	23	Shanghai	Student	5
P8	F	25	Beijing	Doctor	10	P22	M	31	Shanghai	Programmer	18
P9	M	21	Shanghai	Student	24	P23	M	22	Beijing	Student	15
P10	M	26	Beijing	Programmer	8	P24	F	25	Yinchuan	Student	10
P11	F	23	Shanghai	Accountant	6	P25	M	29	Yinchuan	Manager	8
P12	M	18	Yinchuan	Student	11	P26	F	27	Yinchuan	Office worker	15
P13	F	24	Yinchuan	Student	16	P27	F	26	Beijing	Programmer	12
P14	F	22	Beijing	Office worker	10	P28	M	18	Shanghai	Student	6

4.1   User Motivations

For Entertainment and Sociality. All of the interviewees reported that they watch videos on Douyin to relax and have fun. Killing time, making more friends from strangers online, communicating with others and sharing personal life stories, sharing their point of view, and finding an appropriate community were also reported as important motivations for using Douyin. These motivations align with findings about live streaming practices in China [14], which may explain why Douyin is influencing the popularity of live streaming services in China – people use both Douyin and live streaming for entertainment and sociality, and the two types of media certainly compete for time.

"A Fashionable Lifestyle". We found that 21 interviewees use Douyin for following the perceived stylish and up-to-date lifestyle, because they consider using Douyin as "fashionable lifestyle". Further, 16 interviewees reported that they used Douyin to be able to talk with people around them with interesting and trending topics, because peer students or workers often talk about content on Douyin. This is especially true for young Douyin users. As noted by P3, a female high school student:

> "Over 90% of students in my class are using Douyin. We often talk about interesting videos we saw on Douyin and even produce funny videos together. They often share the information of some fancy items they get to know about from some videos on Douyin, like some cute bags or nice cosmetics, and even buy them on the Internet once they become super popular. That seems cool for most of us. I cannot imagine what it will be like if I do not use Douyin. It would be like an outlier, I guess, that I could

not understand what others are happily talking about. I use Douyin to keep up with the trend in my class."

We also found that, especially for young Douyin users (those under 20 years old), their attitudes toward those who do not use Douyin aligned with Social Identity Theory [19] that they will discriminate those who were not using Douyin. They thought non-Douyin users were *"uncool and outdated"*, and tend to socialize less with such people in real life. Two interviewees (P6 and P28) even mentioned that they did not usually use it when they were alone, because they wanted to focus on study or their hobbies in their own time, but would use Douyin when they were together with close friends who enjoyed using Douyin, because they wanted to present themselves as *"being up-to-date and knowledgeable"* about using Douyin to their peers. The fear of being discriminated by peers is another reason driving the use, which adds to the motivations of using Douyin for most of the young interviewees.

Engaging in a Virtual Intimate Relationship. Our interviewees also reported that they used Douyin to feel as if in a virtual "intimate" relationship with their favorite content providers, especially with those who often post videos of them narrating lover's prattle to their fans (Fig. 1). They enjoyed hearing these prattles and imagined being in a pleasant virtual relationship without having to be heavily committed to it. They also learn from such prattles and use them in their real life for romantic relationship, as noted by P6, a female high schooler:

"I really enjoy watching this Douyiner. His voice is nice, and he always posts videos in which he is narrating beautiful prattles to us. I feel as if I am in love with him. And the background musics he uses are great, too. I will listen to them again and again. I also share some prattles he wrote with my close friends, and we take notes about these prattles. I think we can use them to our beloved ones one day."

This reflects a pattern of para-social interaction [8] that fans extend their emotional energy, interest and time to their favorite content providers on Douyin, while content providers may not respond to the devoted energy and interest directly. However, as the content providers on Douyin constantly post new short videos which may partly respond to each fan's voice, the emotional needs of fans may be satisfied and they in turn pay more attention to the content of their favorite content providers.

Informational and Practical Purposes. Interviewees also reported that they enjoyed watching short videos that have practical values to them in real life. Videos related to work and study were most liked, such as sharing learning notes, dealing with *guanxi* (the ties between people fostered through exchanges of social capitals [23]), and self-improvement tips. For example, P3 noted:

I like watching other students sharing their learning notes about Maths on Douyin. Some notes are really of high quality and easy to understand, because they know what we as students are confused about. I watch them to learn how I can improve my note-taking skills.

Interestingly, several young users reported that they like watching and sharing videos in which the creator is sharing good-looking profile images for them to adopt for their social accounts, fancy nicknames for online social accounts, and creative animated mobile phone wallpapers for individuals or couples (Fig. 1). This shows a trend that the content of some short videos can be easily "materialized" and adopted in other social channels, and the videos penetrate into users' real life. As noted by P28, a male student who was in a relationship:

"My girlfriend really likes to adopt the profile images recommended by a content provider as her WeChat account. She says that those profile images are beautiful and can fit with her personality well. She also likes to adopt animated mobile phone wallpapers shared on Douyin. Sometimes those wallpapers are for a couple, which are very creative in that two phones can create a holistic story when put together, and she always urges me to adopt those wallpapers together with her. It is a way to show to her friends that we are in a sweet relationship."

4.2 Categories of Engaging Content

We found several different categories of content that users are engaged in. Due to the limitations of the qualitative studies, the results we report here are not intended to provide a representative sample of content that is perceived engaging, but to highlight the unique genres that were not usually presented in prior research. We intentionally leave out some common genres of videos that were intensively studied and reported in prior research, such as movie clip remix, selfie style videos, creative dance, important life moment, etc, which are often reported in prior research [15, 24].

Positive Energy. Twenty two interviewees mentioned that they enjoyed watching short videos that show positive emotions or prosocial behaviors, for example, showing kindness to homeless people or strangers who need help, donating money to those in need, showing the efforts of soldiers when they are training, etc. Several interviewees noted that such content is well curated, and make them feel confident about humankind and humanity, e.g., as noted by P11,

"I think there should be more content about positive energy on Douyin. I remember one video which the content provider performed singing on the street to raise money for one of his classmate who got cancer. I was so touched about this video and even donated some money to him."

Knowledge Sharing. All the interviewees reported some content that was intended for sharing knowledge from the content providers. Such knowledge was often shared in a comprehensive way, with each short video only covering one or two key points of certain knowledge. Animation or slide style presentation were usually adopted by the content providers, with their narrations aligned with closed captions of the video. The types of knowledge shared via short creative videos on Douyin covered a wide range, and the commonly mentioned topics included:

Popular Science: Popular natural science (physics, chemistry, biology, etc.), popular social science (history, geography, etc.), health, safety, law, etc.

Education: K12 education, undergraduate education (e.g., Spoken English, learning tips, etc.), graduate education (e.g., how to prepare for Chinese Graduate School Entrance Exam), etc. Such content is more of interest to students.

Arts and Skills: Singing, calligraphy, dancing, handicraft, painting, photography, etc. Our interviewees enjoyed the high production value and the creative stories that showcased the arts and skills in a comprehensive and attractive way. Some interviewees also noted that some videos stimulate their interest in arts and encouraged them to practise or learn more about certain skills. Some arts and crafts related videos were actually about intangible cultural heritage in China, for example, Chinese calligraphy, Peking Opera, Shadow Play, Dough Figurines, etc., which were mostly used for promoting traditional cultural practices by these cultural practitioners. Apart from short creative videos, livestreams were also adopted by these content providers for engaging more viewers with cultural practices, as previously studied by Lu et al. [12].

Profession Related: Self improvement, professional skills, social skills, investment, etc. Our interviewees noted that a lot of such content was rarely seen in books or on other websites, and that "it is better conveyed through videos than words alone". Such content was especially perceived useful by interviewees who were working. Videos about social skills, or even office politics, were especially mentioned by several interviewees, and they noted that such videos were very useful for Chinese society, where *guanxi* played an essential role in social and professional life [23].

Life Hacks: Life tips, cooking, body building, makeup, pets, home decoration, gardening, etc. Such content was often mentioned by young adults (e.g., P5, P20) who just graduated from universities and started their careers, and began to live in apartment and equip their own 'home'. Such young adults could benefit from the life hacks shared in these videos, which helped them improve their quality of life without having to do extensive searching on the Internet or bothering older people who had more experience for advice.

Baby Related: Baby raising, early education, parenting, etc. The educational baby-related videos were more attractive for those who were raising or expecting babies, while other baby-related videos, which were about showing off how talented the babies were, or what fun it was to have a baby do creative things, were attractive for most people.

It is interesting that interviewees noted that they typically did not search for specific information actively when using Douyin. Instead, most of the time, they watched such informative videos because these videos were 'pushed' to them by the recommendation algorithms of Douyin. This differs from watching informative videos on YouTube, where most people seek information actively. Such 'effortless' encountering with educational videos made watching knowledge sharing short videos attractive and engaging for Douyin users. As noted by P22, a male software engineer in Shanghai, who used Douyin mostly for watching beautiful girls dancing or creative content.

> "I enjoy watching knowledge sharing videos because although I do not use Douyin directly for acquiring knowledge, but more for killing time, I can still gain some useful and practical knowledge from those knowledge sharing videos recommended to me, so that I won't feel too guilty. For example, I learnt from Douyin how to make Douyin meal (抖音饭)), which is super easy for us office workers to cook for dinner."

Traveling and Tourism. Our interviewees also noted that they saw many videos that were about traveling to places of interest. Many cities, not only in China, but also all over the world, were covered by such creative videos, and typically they were not like official promo videos of a city, but rather, more like a well-produced video clips of representative views of the city. Asian cities outside of China were mentioned more than cities in America, Europe, or other continents, but it might be due to few content providers had access to those cities outside of Asia. Several interviewees noted that watching such videos can inspire them of potential travel destinations in the future.

Several young interviewees also mentioned some videos that were about traveling, but shot in a way as telling a story of how the content providers finally made up their minds to quit their jobs and planned a trip with a limited budget to a foreign place of interest. These interviewees noted that such videos inspired them of alternative lifestyles, that could relieve themselves from the chore of their family and social life to pursue their "dreamed" life. As noted by P24:

> "After watching these people who give up something, like their jobs, in real life, for a trip to their dreamed places, I really admire them and begin to think about how should I pursue my dream in a more practical and meaningful way. Their story reminds me that I am still young, and I should try to pursue my dream even with limited resources."

The Effects of Music. All the interviewees mentioned that the background music of videos played a great role in their engagement with Douyin. They really enjoyed some well-produced original pieces of music that were adopted by many popular videos, and sometimes they even browsed videos using the same piece of music if they really like that piece of music. Several interviewees even mentioned that they sometimes even intentionally skim videos to keep up with the trend of popular music, as noted by P22,

"I get to know many new songs just from Douyin. Without Douyin, maybe I won't be able to know so many trendy pop songs. Douyin trendy songs (抖音神曲) can be heard almost everywhere in my life, on the street, on music apps, or even other people's mobile ringtones."

4.3   Concerns, Challenges, Negative Experiences, and Implications

Our interviewees mentioned several concerns, challenges, and negative experiences using Douyin.

Several interviewees noted that it was hard for them to find what exactly they needed when they used Douyin for learning, especially when the topic was a little too complicated and there are many relevant videos. They had trouble filtering out short videos that really fit their needs, and most of the time they have to search from other resources, such as searching on the Internet, if they really want to know more about the topic. Future design of such creative short video sharing mobile applications should consider how to facilitate information seeking behaviors for serious learners.

Some interviewees reported that some videos on Douyin were so negative for emotions, that they made them hopeless about real life, and even brought contagion of negative emotions within friends if they shared the video with each other. Recommendation algorithms might make the situation worse, as noted that sometimes they kept seeing negative content being recommended to them. Future design should consider assessing the negativity of videos, and to give interventions to viewers when risks of negative emotional contagion were detected. The design of the recommendation engine should also be improved to avoid accumulating negative emotions for viewers.

Privacy issues were another concern, as some interviewees noted that Douyin could recommend very relevant ads to them, which made them concern about the fact that Douyin knows too much about them, because it has so much data about their preferences for video content. Future research should look into how to better protect user's privacy while balancing the convenience brought by the recommendation system for video sharing mobile applications.

Some interviewees were concerned about addiction to Douyin, and its potential impact on younger generations, as they felt that many adolescents were sharing and watching videos intensively using Douyin. Future work must investigate how to mitigate user's addiction, and how to make Douyin a safer place for adolescents. Douyin provides valuable knowledge sharing videos which can benefit adolescents in acquiring knowledge that is not easy to gain from other sources, but the addiction to Douyin and its negative content might do more harm to the students.

5   Discussion

Living in a society where *guanxi* is highly valued and keeping face is important in daily life, Chinese people's use of social media platforms is deeply influenced by these cultural elements and social media landscapes [11,14,23], which also emerged from our results. Some users adopt Douyin partly because they want to present themselves as leading a "fashionable" lifestyle, and they do not want to be looked down upon by those who already adopted, which aligns with theory of the presentation of self [7], that people present their perfect selves at the front stage of their social life. For Douyin users, using Douyin intensively and interacting with creative videos, content providers, and other viewers actively on Douyin become a social norm that should be presented at the front stage of daily life. Douyin users are willing to actively present themselves as Douyin users at the front stage, using jargons to socialize with each other in offline life. Further, they also have to manage their impression while using the app, that they have to present themselves through creative videos, likes, or comments on Douyin. Sharing videos on Douyin requires larger amount of self-disclosure than text or image, and they may struggle with a coherent presentation of self in this sphere. Future work should delve deeper into this question, to investigate how Douyin users negotiate the presentation of self between video and non-video modality, and between online and offline social life.

Our results also echo previous research that Chinese people, especially those from rural China, use social media for pursuing a "dreamed" life [22], and we argue that the form of short videos makes such "dreamed" life feel closer to real life, with increased exposure to creative visual stimuli, social features, and interactivity. Although the fate of Douyin is still unknown at this stage, it shows a trend of the changing culture in our society afforded by convenient and effortless video sharing platforms, which should be further investigated to inform the design of better social media platforms.

References

1. Short video sharing platform Tik Tok spreads to over 150 countries. http://www.xinhuanet.com/english/2018-06/22/c_137273901.htm
2. Vine. https://www.vine.co/
3. Cavalcanti, L.H.C., Pinto, A., Brubaker, J.R., Dombrowski, L.S.: Media, meaning, and context loss in ephemeral communication platforms: a qualitative investigation on snapchat. In: Proceedings of the 2017 ACM Conference on Computer Supported Cooperative Work and Social Computing, CSCW 2017, pp. 1934–1945. ACM, New York (2017). https://doi.org/10.1145/2998181.2998266
4. Corbin, J., Strauss, A.: Basics of Qualitative Research: Techniques and Procedures for Developing Grounded Theory. Sage Publications, Inc., Thousand Oaks (1998)
5. Ding, Y., et al.: Broadcast yourself: understanding YouTube uploaders. In: Proceedings of the 2011 ACM SIGCOMM Conference on Internet Measurement Conference, pp. 361–370. ACM (2011)
6. Farnham, S.D., Churchill, E.F.: Faceted identity, faceted lives: social and technical issues with being yourself online. In: Proceedings of the ACM 2011 Conference on Computer Supported Cooperative Work, CSCW 2011, pp. 359–368. ACM, New York (2011). https://doi.org/10.1145/1958824.1958880
7. Goffman, E.: The Presentation of Self in Everyday Life. Doubleday, New York (1959)

8. Horton, D., Richard Wohl, R.: Mass communication and para-social interaction: observations on intimacy at a distance. Psychiatry **19**(3), 215–229 (1956)
9. Juhlin, O., Zoric, G., Engström, A., Reponen, E.: Video interaction: a research agenda. Pers. Ubiquit. Comput. **18**(3), 685–692 (2014)
10. Kristen Purcell: Online Video 2013—Pew Research Center. http://www.pewinternet.org/2013/10/10/online-video-2013/
11. Lin, J., Lu, Z.: The rise and proliferation of live-streaming in china: insights and lessons. In: Stephanidis, C. (ed.) HCI 2017. CCIS, vol. 714, pp. 632–637. Springer, Cham (2017). https://doi.org/10.1007/978-3-319-58753-0_89
12. Lu, Z., Annett, M., Fan, M., Wigdor, D.: "I feel it is my responsibility to stream": streaming and engaging with intangible cultural heritage through livestreaming. In: Proceedings of the 2019 CHI Conference on Human Factors in Computing Systems, p. 229. ACM (2019)
13. Lu, Z., Heo, S., Wigdor, D.J.: StreamWiki: enabling viewers of knowledge sharing live streams to collaboratively generate archival documentation for effective in-stream and post hoc learning. In: Proceedings of the ACM on Human-Computer Interaction, vol. 2, no. CSCW, p. 112 (2018)
14. Lu, Z., Xia, H., Heo, S., Wigdor, D.: You watch, you give, and you engage: a study of live streaming practices in china. In: Proceedings of the 2018 CHI Conference on Human Factors in Computing Systems, p. 466. ACM (2018)
15. McRoberts, S., Ma, H., Hall, A., Yarosh, S.: Share first, save later: performance of self through snapchat stories. In: Proceedings of the 2017 CHI Conference on Human Factors in Computing Systems, CHI 2017, pp. 6902–6911. ACM, New York (2017). https://doi.org/10.1145/3025453.3025771
16. Nelson, R.: The top mobile apps for November 2018 TikTok reached a new high, December 2018. https://sensortower.com/blog/top-apps-november-2018
17. Scheibe, K.: The impact of gamification in social live streaming services. In: Meiselwitz, G. (ed.) SCSM 2018. LNCS, vol. 10914, pp. 99–113. Springer, Cham (2018). https://doi.org/10.1007/978-3-319-91485-5_7
18. Scheibe, K., Fietkiewicz, K.J., Stock, W.G.: Information behavior on social live streaming services. J. Inf. Sci. Theory Pract. **4**, 6–20 (2016)
19. Tajfel, H., Turner, J.C.: An integrative theory of intergroup conflict. In: Organizational Identity: A Reader, pp. 56–65
20. Tang, J.C., Venolia, G., Inkpen, K.M.: Meerkat and periscope: i stream, you stream, apps stream for live streams. In: Proceedings of the 2016 CHI Conference on Human Factors in Computing Systems, CHI 2006, pp. 4770–4780. ACM, New York (2016). https://doi.org/10.1145/2858036.2858374
21. Toutiao: Douyin big data report, January 2019. https://index.toutiao.com/report/download/ff024b54a032bc14b5a837398b25cdec.pdf
22. Wang, X.: Social Media in Industrial China. UCL Press, London (2016)
23. Yang, J., Ackerman, M.S., Adamic, L.A.: Virtual gifts and guanxi: supporting social exchange in a Chinese online community. In: Proceedings of the ACM 2011 Conference on Computer Supported Cooperative Work, pp. 45–54. ACM (2011)
24. Yarosh, S., Bonsignore, E., McRoberts, S., Peyton, T.: YouthTube: Youth video authorship on youtube and vine. In: Proceedings of the 19th ACM Conference on Computer-Supported Cooperative Work & Social Computing, CSCW 2016, pp. 1423–1437. ACM, New York (2016). https://doi.org/10.1145/2818048.2819961

Understanding Appropriation Through End-User Tailoring in Communication Systems: A Case Study on Slack and WhatsApp

Ana Paula Retore[✉] and Leonelo Dell Anhol Almeida

Postgraduate Program in Technology and Society (PPGTE),
Federal University of Technology - Paraná,
Av. Sete de Setembro, 3165, Curitiba-PR, Brazil
aretore@alunos.utfpr.edu.br, leoneloalmeida@utfpr.edu.br

Abstract. People appropriate technologies in order to make them more suitable to their needs. Technology appropriation is related to assigning new meanings and can be achieved in a variety of ways. Among many possibilities there are functionalities within computational systems, such as end-user tailoring. This research seeks to investigate how people appropriate communication systems through end-user tailoring. Two communication systems were object of study, one directed to the personal context, WhatsApp, and another to the professional context, Slack. We conducted interviews and applied questionnaires to 12 users. Evidence was found that contextual factors motivate and condition appropriation through end-user tailoring in communication systems. We identified four cases that people used end-user tailoring to appropriate the systems. In addition, this research provides an understanding of the context, motivations and circumstances in which people appropriate.

Keywords: Appropriation · End-user tailoring · Context ·
Collaborative communication systems · Slack · Whatsapp

1 Introduction

When people use technologies, they tend to adapt these artifacts to their reality, assigning new meanings and making the technology their own. Dourish [1] defines appropriation as the process by which people adopt and adapt technologies, fitting them into their working practices. According to the author, the starting point to understand appropriation is not with technology but with practice. Practice reflects the set of meanings that can be attributed to objects and actions on them as part of a community.

People can appropriate technologies in a variety of ways, from sticking notes on the computer screen to programming new codes. Among these possibilities there is end-user tailoring. Tailoring is defined as the activity of modifying a

© Springer Nature Switzerland AG 2019
G. Meiselwitz (Ed.): HCII 2019, LNCS 11578, pp. 245–264, 2019.
https://doi.org/10.1007/978-3-030-21902-4_18

computational application in the context of its use [2]. Mørch [4] distinguishes three levels of tailoring, which are customization, integration, and extension. Customization is the act of modifying the appearance of objects or editing values by selecting among a set of predefined options. Integration is creating or recording a sequence of program executions that results in new functionality which is stored with the application. Extension is an approach in which the functionality of an application is improved by adding new code [4]. The scope of this research is at the level of customization, which means predefined tailoring options that are executed under user commands. We use the term end-user tailoring here as a reference for this scope.

End-user tailoring assumes an even more specific quality when it comes to the context of communication systems. Communication systems allow interaction between multiple users, within groups, organizations or communities, which broadens the social, political and cultural contexts where these systems are used. In this sense end-user tailoring is, among other aspects, an option to provide end-users with resources to appropriate a system. Two applications were used as study objects, one with functionalities focused in the professional context (Slack) and another with functionalities focused in the personal context (WhatsApp). These applications were selected because they are widely adopted by people and companies in Brazil, where this research was conducted. Once both are used for communication between individuals and groups, it is possible to make comparisons based on context indicators where they are inserted. In this sense, the choice for applications with large adoption supports a diverse sampling in data collection, making it easier to find appropriation cases.

This research seeks to investigate how people appropriate communication systems through end-user tailoring. Appropriation emerges in contexts of use and, although it is not possible to clearly bound professional and personal spheres, this work aims to understand how technology appropriation occurs in different social contexts and groups.

2   Theoretical Framework

Dourish [1] argues that to understand appropriation, we should not start by the technology itself, but by practice. The practice is more than simply how things get done, but reflects the sets of meanings that can be ascribed to objects and actions over those objects as part of a larger enterprise. In this sense, we understand that appropriation is concerned both with the ways in which technology comes to play a role in this set of meanings and with the ways in which people influence and change this set of meanings. Tchounikine [5] argues that appropriation happens when users assign functional values to a system.

Appropriation sometimes requires improvement in system settings, what may demand the system to be changed, if such means exist. Lindtner, Anderson and Dourish [6] state that the notion of appropriation can easily be understood as user empowerment. Through end-user tailoring people will make the changes that they consider necessary in the systems. End-user tailoring is defined as the activity in which users modify a computational application according to their specific usage practices or personal preferences [7,8]. Appropriation materializes changes in several spheres, from the object itself to the way in which people interact with it. Trigg and Bødker [9] argue that the traditional binary (and technocentric) division of people into designers and users is becoming nebulous. Increasingly, we recognize a rich spectrum of people having a variety of skills from applying technology from a routine use to designing new technologies.

It is recognized that creators, designers, and developers imprint purposes, meanings, and values on technology. As Feenberg [10] argues, technical choices mark the horizons of everyday life. These choices define a "world" within which the specific alternatives we think about—as purposes, goals, uses—emerge. In this sense, it can be understood that technology is often the materialization of the subjective perceptions of its creators. In addition, it is understood that technology does not necessarily brings benefits in the context of its use. Appropriation is, in this sense, a way for people to adapt and make their own technologies when they do not fit properly in the context where they are. Balka and Wagner [11] confirm the mutual shaping of technology and contexts resemble an ongoing design process that end-users perform largely without any involvement of professional developers.

Appropriation, when contextualized in communication systems, must take into account not only the individual preferences but also the needs of the group as a whole. Communication systems allow interaction of multiple users, within groups, organizations or communities and can be used in real time or be asynchronous [12]. Pipek [13] reports that collaboration between users helps significantly in appropriation. When viewing the activity level of the collaborations, the author realized that it was not tailoring itself that helped users to decide in favor (or against) alternative uses, but the action of explaining, demonstrating and discussing it. Still considering the professional context, Tchounikine [5] argues that appropriation is often related to the role of work practices. According to the author, in respect to appropriation, this means that the way users perceive and use technology find explanations in the characteristics of the professional activity.

End-user tailoring has proven to be a great ally in the development and use of collaborative systems. Greenberg [14] in his study of personalizable groupware states that a prerequisite for a successful groupware is that it must be acceptable to most or all members of the group. In this sense, the author argues that these systems can be modified to match the specific needs of the individuals and the particular needs of the group as a whole.

The understanding of appropriation as a reflection of contextual factors is related to the interests of the third wave of Human Computer Interaction (HCI). Harrisson, Tatar and Sengers [15] cite it is a matter of interest in the third wave to understand how people appropriate technologies and how we can support these appropriations. It is in the context where people realize the technology is not suited to their intentions or desires and, by different means, they make it appropriated and attribute new meanings to it. Among the different ways in which people can appropriate, end-user tailoring is an alternative where technology provides resources for people to adapt it as they wish or need.

3   Method

Figure 1 summarizes the method developed for this research. Each step is described below in order to contextualize its role within the scope of this research.

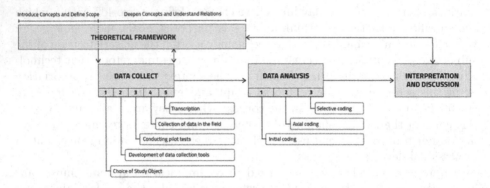

Fig. 1. Research method

3.1   Theoretical Framework

In the first step of this research we contextualized the concepts and the theoretical approaches concerning the themes addressed in this research: Appropriation, End-user Tailoring and Communication Systems. Even though it was the first step in this work, this step was extended in parallel and was revised after the conclusion of the same. The literature read before data collection aimed to define a more limited scope for data collection. The theoretical framework studied parallel to and after data collection aimed deepening concepts and understanding how the relations between them are established. According to results of data analysis, the theoretical framework was also revisited during the interpretation and discussion.

The construction of the theoretical framework began by reading texts about tailoring, which was the initial focus proposed for this work. However, the readings pointed out that end-user tailoring was inserted within a larger conjuncture. From this understanding, the authors referenced in the texts as well as the theoretical basis of Science and Technology Studies (STS) and third wave HCI studies, extended the understanding to the context where the "non-predicted" activities took place, who were the users and what their motivations could be.

3.2   Data Collect

The first part of the theoretical framework helped to define a scope for data collection, which aimed to observe how people appropriate collaborative systems by end-user tailoring. We used triangulation of methods, combining analysis by specialist, semi-structured interview, and questionnaire for data collection. Lakatos and Marconi [16] commented that triangulation is intended to cover the maximum extent in the understanding of a fact studied. Following, we list the 5 steps of the data collection process are listed.

1. **Choice of Study Object**
   Selection of two communication systems: one with work-oriented functionalities, Slack[1], and another more personal-oriented, WhatsApp[2]. It should be emphasized that, naturally, the division between personal and professional contexts is not clear and there is interference from both sides. Bødker [17] argues that there are connections between work and leisure and the technologies that mediate relationships between people end up going through such situations.
   The choice of these communication tools aimed to deepen the analysis of practices of use and sharing of information by individuals and groups either in real time or asynchronously. Because both tools are widely adopted by individuals and companies, their comprehensiveness was a motivating factor in their choice. The goal is that, with two applications used for communication between people and groups, it would be possible to draw comparisons due to the distinction of context in which they are inserted. In this sense, selecting tools with broad adoption allows for a more diverse sampling in data collection, making it more likely to find appropriation examples.
   The analysis by specialist consisted in the researcher's work on identifying end-user tailoring functionalities in both systems. These features were listed according to the criteria of Mørch [4] for the third level of end-user tailoring: customization which consists of "Modifying the appearance of presentation objects, or editing their attribute values by selecting among a set of predefined configuration options."

2. **Development of data collection tools**
   After selecting the communication systems, we developed two data collection tools: questionnaires and protocols for semi-structured interviews. The end-user tailoring functionalities identified in the analysis by specialist were the basis for the questionnaire. The protocols for the semi-structured interviews were based on questions related to the context and motivations for end-user tailoring. We chose semi-structured interview because it provided conditions for a deeper understanding of the issues of interest, and we chose the questionnaire as a method to assist in the expansion of the data collected.

3. **Conduction of Tests**
   Two tests were performed with interview and questionnaire, being one test

---

[1] https://slack.com/.
[2] https://www.whatsapp.com/.

with a Slack user and another with a WhatsApp user. The purpose of the tests is to highlight possible flaws, such as: complexity of issues, imprecision in the essay, unnecessary questions, and constraints to the participant [18]. In both tests, participants suggested improvements for both the semi-structured interview protocol and the questionnaires. From the revisions made, a version was defined that would be applied in field data collection.

4. **Field Data Collection**
Data collection covered 12 individual semi-structured interviews and the application of the questionnaires in sequence, being 6 interviews for Slack users and 6 interviews for WhatsApp users. All participants gave an interview and answered the questionnaire voluntarily and by accepting a free and informed consent form. Interviews were conducted mostly in person and, depending on availability, through videoconference. Each interview lasted 45 min in average.

The sampling was intentional and followed as strategy criteria the diversity of interviewees' profiles. WhatsApp participants were from different ages, professions and experience of use of the application. Slack participants were employees of companies from different areas of activity: Food, Financial, Educational, and Administrative. Given the qualitative nature of this research, sampling is also characterized as accessibility sampling, since people contacted to participate were known or indicated by people close to the researcher.

5. **Transcription**
Collected data was recorded and later transcribed, taking the necessary precautions to preserve anonymity of the participants and the companies involved. The next step in methodology, data analysis, used the transcriptions of semi-structured interviews as the basis material for coding.

3.3 Data Analysis

In order to analyze data collected in the interviews, we used the method of coding, based in Grounded Theory. Although this research is not classified as Grounded Theory itself, coding was one of its methods adopted in this research for data analysis. According to Strauss and Corbin [19], coding is the fundamental process used by the researcher for analysis. In research on Grounded Theory, there are three basic types of coding: initial, axial, and selective. For this research the three types of coding were used as described below:

1. **Initial Coding** Coding is the process in which data is fragmented, analyzed, and interpreted [19]. The first stage of coding process consisted in a careful reading, sentence by sentence of interviewees' answers. For each sentence, codes were created conceptualizing the ideas expressed in answers. As coding progressed, previous transcripts were revisited, and some codes were renamed or replaced. It was noticed that the last transcripts were the ones that generated less new codes, since a great part of the codes used had previously been generated.
A total of 84 codes were initially generated. All generated codes went through

a first refinement, where similar codes were grouped and others were removed. According to Gibbs [20], refining codes helps the author to revisit the text to see if it can be coded differently, either by using different codes in longer passages, or by checking for examples elsewhere in the same transcript that need to be coded with new codes, or making the initial descriptive codes more analytical. After refinement, we came to the number of 79 codes that were also grouped by similarity, as suggested by [20]. The author comments that grouping facilitates the creation of a hierarchy of codes, where the researcher looks for patterns, makes comparisons, and constructs models. We created 18 groups of code, also called subcategories, that were later used for axial coding.

2. **Axial Coding**

   According to Charmaz [21] axial coding relates subcategories to categories, specifies the properties and dimensions of a category, and brings together the data that has been fragmented during initial coding to give coherence to the emerging analysis. We made the relation of subcategories to a category through the "Coding Paradigm" that considers aspects such as conditions, context, strategies (action/interaction) and consequences.

   To facilitate the relation of subcategories to the coding paradigm, subcategories were grouped following hierarchy degrees. Gibbs [20] argues that a long list of codes is not very useful and therefore it makes sense to organize them into a hierarchy in which relations can be clearly seen. The three groups of subcategories created respected the order in which they were reported in the interviews. Thus Axial Coding was done by means of a relationship of subcategories within each respective group with the four elements of the coding paradigm: Causal Conditions, Context, Action/Interaction Strategies and Consequences. This relationship in axial coding resulted in four categories: (Sect. 4.1) Elements of Context, (Sect. 4.2) Experience with the System, (Sect. 4.3) Factors to end-user tailoring, and (Sect. 4.4) Implications Reported. These categories were the basis for selective coding.

3. **Selective Coding**

   Finally, selective coding is the process by which all categories are unified around a "central" category, and categories that need further explanation are filled with descriptive details [19]. In selective coding, categories resulting from axial coding were revisited in order to result in a central category. This central category has assumed a more abstract level since it contains and represents the others.

   Strauss and Corbin [19] comment that a central category may emerge from the categories already identified or a more abstract term may be needed to explain the main phenomenon. Other categories will always be related to the main category as conditions, actions, strategies or consequences. With this targeting as a basis, keywords were selected within each category and after several attempts relating these keywords came, ultimately, to the central concept. After a series of possibilities raised, words replaced and terms combined the central code we found was: (Sect. 4.5) Contextual factors motivate and condition appropriation through end-user tailoring in communication systems.

3.4   Interpretation and Discussion

Data collected and coded from semi-structured interviews and questionnaire responses were interpreted and discussed based on the literature studied in the Theoretical Framework. The categories resulting from axial coding as well as the central category resulting from selective coding served as the basis for structuring the analysis. Data interpretation used the perspectives of the STS studies and the third wave of HCI. These two conceptual approaches broadened the understanding of evidence found among the data analyzed. The main contributions of the two approaches lie in the understanding of contextual influences and appropriation practices, since both take as their starting point the understanding of relation between people and artifacts as mutually influenced and contextualized.

4   Results

Considering that the objective of this research is to broaden the discussion on appropriation articulated through end-user tailoring in communication systems, the next section discuss data collected from the theoretical perspective of this work. To organize the sections, we used the emergent categories of axial codings ((Sect. 4.1) Elements of Context, (Sect. 4.2) Experience with the System, (Sect. 4.3) Factors to end-user tailoring, and (Sect. 4.4) Implications Reported) along the central category that emerged from selective coding (Sect. 4.5) "Contextual factors motivate and condition appropriation through end-user tailoring in communication systems." Each section therefore addresses aspects of each one of the four categories, in addition to the central category. Data presented in each section are based not only on the semi-structured interviews, but also include answers obtained in the questionnaires.

4.1   Elements of Context

The theoretical framework adopted in this research had already approached the influence of the context as both motivator and inhibitor in the use of collaborative systems. Dix [22] comments that users work within a social and organizational context, which broadens the interaction context and can influence the activities and motivation of the user.

About 66% of both, WhatsApp and Slack respondents stated that they started using the applications under the influence of someone, because the company requested (in the case of Slack), or because in one way or another someone made them aware of the existence of the applications. In the case of Slack the influence to use the system is especially connected to context, which assumes a characteristic of the work environment. Out of the 6 Slack participants, 5 commented that they started using the system since it was the internal communication tool already adopted by the company. Leo[3] comments that he does not

---

[3] All names mentioned here are pseudonyms in order to guarantee people's and companies' privacy.

remember how he started using Slack, but that "Probably someone discovered in the office, said to us, and... we are using it." Priscilla reports that Slack "was already the communication mechanism of the company," a very similar response from other interviewees. Robert was the only respondent who reported that having discovered Slack on his own. He reported: "I was looking for a platform for the development team where we would centralize the software discussions."

In the case of Slack, motivation to use the system is often tied to a requirement or determination. This is because most companies or teams already use the tool and asked the new members to use it as well. In this sense, the hierarchy and levels of power within the company are clearly defined. In Priscilla's case, it was an imposition, a requirement for her to use. In Leo's case, it was not a requirement, but an influence by some colleague. In Robert's case, he ordered that the development team would use Slack. It was noticed that the dynamics of use in the companies studied is related to the determinations of people in positions with power of decision.

In the case of WhatsApp, the influence of the social group on the knowledge of the system is quite expressive. Many respondents did not even remember how they had heard about the platform, but when asked about why this application was being used and not another one, it was emphasized that most people in their social sphere already joined the system.

For example, Marcela attributes the use of WhatsApp to "The fact that most of my friends already use WhatsApp and not other platforms, so it turns out that I have more contacts in that application than in others." The social group involves friends, family, classmates, work colleagues, neighbors, and other people with whom there was some kind of relationship. The fact that most contacts already joined WhatsApp proved to be a convenience issue, firstly because it allows for free communication with someone or a group. Once the contacts were already using the platform, it would be possible to make calls, send messages or files without paying for it. Secondly, it was a matter of belonging, of not being outside. Louise comments that she uses WhatsApp "Because it is the application that almost everyone uses" as John reports "I started to use it after a large group of people came to use it."

We noticed that, in addition to the regular habits of use, there are singular situations in which people use the system in different ways than usual. These situations can stimulate the use of unexplored resources in unexpected situations or even the creation of new purposes. Example of this is Marcela, who reports "I end up not using the audio call too much because the quality of WhatsApp is very bad, so I really only use it when I need to make a call to someone who is not in my city." In addition to exceptions to regular use, many situations like these are motivating for end-user tailoring.

The influence of context as a motivator for end-user tailoring is clear in the case of WhatsApp. All the WhatsApp's respondents reported having configured the non-automatic saving of media because, by default, the app saves all shared media in smartphone's storage. Excessive sharing of files that are not relevant to users in their social groups, along with storage limitation on smartphones were both determining factors for the system to be adapted to people's reality. For example, during the interview, Marcela assumed that tailoring could be done by more people besides her, reporting that: "Image and video auto-save settings everyone does, I think. There is so much irrelevant content." Since the application was automatically saving all images and videos in devices' storage, it was necessary later manually discard files in order to free up space. After disabling auto-save, files are saved only according to user commands. That is, the end-user tailoring was triggered by both a technological limitation, low storage space in the device, and a contextual situation, the user having to constantly delete irrelevant contents. Here we can draw a parallel with the destabilizing factor pointed out by Spinuzzi [23]. In this sense, it is after a destabilization that the need to make a change in the system becomes clearer.

Another point observed in the interviews were the intersections between work and personal contexts. In fact, in a perspective aligned with the third wave of HCI, Bødker [17] argues that there are connections between work and leisure, and that technologies that mediate relationships between people end up going through such situations. In this sense, we found evidence that there is no rigid separation between these contexts. Two characteristics were perceived in this intersection: the purpose and the moment of use. The purpose is consistent with the issues addressed in each system, that is, people who also dealt with personal matters via Slack and people who also dealt with work matters via WhatsApp. In the case of WhatsApp, 100% of interviewees reported that they used it to communicate with suppliers, customers, bosses and co-workers. In Slack's case, only half of respondents reported using the system for personal matters but involving co-workers. Priscilla commented that she and her colleagues use Slack for a variety of subjects: "Oh... For happy hours, and personal things, okay... that happens. We don't just use it to work."

The second characteristic that articulates the intersections between work and personal life, is the moment of use. In general, people deal with personal matters at working hours, and work matters at personal moments. In the case of Slack, five respondents reported responding messages in Slack after working hours. In the case of WhatsApp, this distinction is even more uncertain, as they all use WhatsApp for work purposes. In this sense, in fact, work and personal life intersect, since they are social positions attributed to the same person. According to Woodward [24] it is difficult to separate some of our identities and to establish boundaries between them.

4.2 Experience with the System

In general, in both Slack and WhatsApp, people use the apps to send and receive messages, which obviously is according to the purpose for which both systems have been developed: communication. In both cases, communication with other people happens on a daily basis, even in the case of Slack, where it is assumed that it is only used during working hours. Leo, for example, when asked if he answered Slack messages outside of working hours he replied: "(Laughs) Are there working hours?" Frequency of use of WhatsApp was also seen as a disadvantage by some respondents. When asked if they perceived any disadvantage with the use of WhatsApp, Louise replied: "The addiction (laughs)" and Mary: "Waste of time. (...) if you do not know how to filter a little, you end up getting involved with it [the WhatsApp] almost all the time."

Another feature that both systems provide is file sharing. In fact, Grudin [12] argues that information sharing is a human behavior that contributes to collaboration along with communication and coordination. However, file sharing takes on different meanings when using WhatsApp and Slack. In Slack scenario, approximately 67% of respondents said to send files only weekly, while WhatsApp 100% replied that they send files daily. The nature of the files that the systems allow sharing is quite similar and includes images, links, and files in general, such as PDFs, audios, videos, among others (in addition, Slack allows the creation of texts and snippets of code directly on the platform). What makes the purpose of file-sharing assume different frequencies are not differences in the functionalities of the systems (which are similar) but the differences of contexts in which these systems are used.

In Slack, shared files are generally somewhat related to work matters, for example file versioning, large file submissions, formal record of who sent or received[4]. In practice, this may mean that companies use other means for files to be shared between teams: email or file manager in the cloud. In WhatsApp, many of the shared files are related to social context: pictures and videos of friends and family, jokes, advertisements, news, motivational messages, and a large number of materials of different types. It means that in this diversity of shared content, many things are not of people's interest. In fact, one of the few settings that 100% of respondents ever did at WhatsApp was to disable automatic saving of files on smartphone. In Slack, 83% of respondents reported never having set file download options. It can be understood since, in Slack, files are downloaded according to user's commands, and not automatically as WhatsApp's default setting.

These examples make it clear that the practices of using technologies assume meaning in context of use, and not only in the features available in the technology itself. The functionalities provide conditions for people to assign a certain purpose to technology. File sharing is much more used in WhatsApp than in Slack, but it is being used so often that it is intrusive, leading all people interviewed to disable auto-save on their smartphones.

4.3 Factors to End-User Tailoring

This section addresses factors involved in end-user tailoring, from familiarity or knowledge about the possibilities, influences of/on other people and the use of tailoring functionalities. Both in WhatsApp and in Slack people become aware of many end-user tailoring functionalities by learning from others. It was noticed that, especially in WhatsApp, people preferred to ask someone how to tailor

---

[4] In free version, Slack archives history when it reaches a specific limit of storage.

rather than to search the application itself or in the Frequently Asked Questions, for example. Mary, for example, reporting her experience performing end-user tailoring said, "Yes, I did [tailored] to not automatically save the images and take the sound off the keyboard. My daughter did that." Louise comments that: "My friend showed me on her phone how to hide the blue checks and I made it on mine." In fact, approximately 67% of both Slack and WhatsApp respondents, reported that people close to them stimulate execution of end-user tailoring.

This knowledge sharing is inherent of users' social context, since interviewees reported learning or teaching to do certain end-user tailoring with friends, relatives or people with a minimum level of intimacy. And even if the person was not close, we realized that people only asked for help from someone with whom they had some degree of confidence. In line with the understanding of the third wave of HCI, Bødker [17] comments that sharing becomes a matter of engaging with other users through common artifacts and it is in this multiplicity that people participate by building meaning, creating results, appropriating, and developing the uses.

Another perspective to analyze are tailorings that affect the whole group, regardless of whether or not people have consented to it. Some tailorings have a direct or indirect effect on all group members who use the app. Regardless of whether people have requested, agree or dislike the change, their own experience of use is modified. For example, in the case of Slack, tailoring has a general effect on group members, especially in integrations with other systems. Michael, as a member of the development team, reports that he did an integration that affected his colleagues: "Yes, I did it for myself and my team. I did the integrations using the Zapier[5] and shared with my colleagues." Priscilla, who works at another company, also commented on the integrations that are made in Slack: "It was not me [who did the integration], it was internally. (...) I more or less know where to go [to integrate], but I never did." In Michael's case, he tailored something that ended up having influence over the entire company and Priscilla was influenced by an end-user tailoring performed by someone else. In fact, 100% of the companies had Slack integrated with another system. The ability to integrate other systems to Slack allows users to adapt the application according to work team routines.

It is also important to mention tailorings that did not work. During interviews it was asked if some end-user tailoring had to be undone or redone for not meeting expectations, and six respondents reported that this came to happen in their daily use. Robert reports that he had tailored to receive Slack notifications on his smartphone, but he had to redo the action for a new configuration: "I always try to pay attention to the notifications on the phone, but the way it was configured the first time, I was receiving many notifications. Soon after I reconfigured to just let me know in mentions." Priscilla also reported that she tailored Slack interface view, hiding the avatars' visualization—thumbnails of team images – in conversations because she thought they took up too much space. After some

---

[5] https://zapier.com/ System that allows the integration of diverse computational applications.

time, she undid this tailoring because, as she reports, "I started to confuse people into groups, so I put their 'little heads' back." In addition to the tailorings that have been undone or redone, James and Mark also have examples of tailorings that have never been used, even being executed, such as integration with another system in the case of James, and the programming of at chatbot in Mark's case.

Interaction is a continuous and evolving process and the interest in end-user tailoring arises as contexts and social groups require. It is what Grudin and Poltrock [25] comment that, over time, use evolves as technology is better understood or used along with other new technologies or processes.

4.4 Implications Reported

This section shows the implications related to communication systems and end-user tailoring. Consequences, effects and/or results reported by interviewees from Slack and WhatsApp are therefore discussed here. In many cases, these consequences are appropriations, which will be specifically addressed in the next section.

During interviews, it was noticed that people had very distinct views about systems studied. Positive or negative perceptions of systems in general were related to how features facilitated or made difficult communication in the context of use. In the case of Slack, Robert comments that he likes the system because: "Sometimes it would be difficult to reconcile the conversations if it were to use another medium of communication." Louise attributes the advantages of WhatsApp to "It's easier. Sometimes the person cannot answer [a call] and we end up sending Whats..." In a opposite view, Priscilla reports that Slack has negative aspects like: "I think one of the things that is bad is not having the history." Marcela, commenting on the changes that WhatsApp reports that she sees damages in personal communication: "People have a medium of communication that is easy and end up no longer having a human contact, like visiting, since the person is always there available, we just lost some of that personal touch, right?." Perceptions about systems are often ambiguous, and depending on point of view and context of analysis, different perceptions emerge. In the above quotes, it is noted that people's perception of Slack and WhatsApp is relative to specific situations.

Among the consequences reported, we observed situations in which people saw the results of tailorings as positive. In both WhatsApp and Slack, users experienced improvements in experience, efficiency, or overall satisfaction after tailoring. In percentages, 100% of WhatsApp respondents and 83% of Slack realized gains in productivity, organization, usage experience, or overall satisfaction after tailoring. This perception that a problem has been solved or that the situation has improved is required for an appropriation to occur through end-user tailoring.

In the questionnaire, respondents could inform how often each tailoring functionality was used. It should be noted here that most of the tailoring functionalities available on both systems were unknown to the interviewees. Among the tailoring functionalities available in Slack, most respondents reported having **never** done: changes in side menu (83%), in accessibility (100%), preferences of searching (100%), of reading (83%), of message input (67%), of keyboard (83%), and change in system appearance (83%). This is consistent with the results of Mackay [26] research, which had reported that unless the user is bored or just learning a new system, customizations that make the software aesthetically pleasing or more interesting are generally avoided. Among tailoring functionalities available in WhatsApp, most respondents reported not having used: disabling the read receipt (67%), changing the visibility of the current location (67%), and setting use of data (67%).

Based on the literature, it was previously known that social context influences end-user tailoring, however, it was perceived that the perception of utility of the resource itself is also a determining factor. In her study of triggers and barriers in customizing, Mackay [26] commented that among the individual factors that prevented users from performing a customization, 12% was attributed to a lack of interest. An example of this is Robert, when asked about not performing the simplest tailorings, reported his experience as: "The only time I saw the Slack settings was when I installed it. Then I never looked it again." In this sense, Mackay [26] had already commented in her work that, in the beginning, many users tailor as a way to explore and learn about the system. After a certain time, most users establish a usage pattern, influenced by tailorings already done, and interrupt this exploration process.

End-user tailoring is not always advantageous, and have ambiguities and contradictions. The first negative aspect is its complexity of implementation and development in technologies. Tchounikine [5] comments that this difficulty is attributed to two reasons: first, designing an tailorable system presents an additional cost and challenge for designers, and secondly, and more important, tailorability can directly compromise the ease of use and simplicity of the systems. Creating tailorable systems, in some cases, means creating more complex systems. In Slack's case, approximately 55% of the tailoring functionalities available in the system were never used by respondents. However, it does not mean that they should not exist, but the opposite, each use context motivates different modes and actions of appropriation, and possibly the tailoring functionalities available in the application that were not used by participants of this research make sense in different contexts.

The second negative aspect is that end-user tailoring functionalities do not always bring benefits to people, but they may also increase the power of control of some people over others. In fact, in questionnaire, 83.3% of WhatsApp respondents and 50% of Slack reported having had some loss in experience or use after tailoring. Trigg and Bødker [9] had already commented that certain tailorings are not unanimous, especially when their effects have repercussions on the group of users.

4.5   Contextual Factors Motivate and Condition Appropriation Through End-User Tailoring in Communication Systems

People assume authority over technology after appropriating it. Some appropriations observed in this research are related to the way in which people attribute new meanings to technologies by end-user tailoring. In this sense, the same end-user tailoring, performed by different people in different contexts, ends up assuming different meanings.

Example of this is the change of the Last Seen functionality in WhatsApp, as shown in Fig. 2 where the image on the left the last seen functionality is visible and the image on the right it is hidden. Victor, for example, said he knew he could turn off the Last Seen time, but he chose to leave it active as a way of communication with his mother: "I let this visualization active, because my mom knows that I'm alive (laughs). When she sees the Last Seen time, she knows I'm fine even though I didn't answer." Here, he appropriates using a tailoring functionality to create a channel of communication with people close to him. The context in which he is inserted and the social group he is part allow this kind of meaning to be attributed to the functionality. If Victor's mother, for example, was used to her son regularly responding to her messages, she might be worried if he would not answer her anytime, even with the Last Seen feature active. In a different scenario this kind of communication would not be possible, what exemplifies how appropriation only happens according to the context of use.

Fig. 2. Last Seen in WhatsApp (v.2.18.60)

On the other hand, Andrea reported that she had a bad experience with this same functionality. She deactivated the Last Seen feature because, according to her, her boyfriend was a jealous person: "I had to change it because I felt like this, watched. In a few moments, okay?." If in Victor's example this end-user tailoring assumed the meaning of a communication channel, here, in Andrea's case, assumes a meaning related to privacy. In another context, for example, if Andrea's boyfriend was not jealous, perhaps this tailoring was not necessary, and even if it was executed, it would assume other meanings than Andrea's privacy or security.

In general, people tailor when they want to change the state they are, something is a problem for them, and seek a better condition where an issue is mitigated. Mørch [4] argues that when a problem is associated with a certain use, there will be the motivation to understand the problem and learn to customize the system to solve it. In this sense, appropriation examples from interviews and questionnaires were performed by people who would like to improve their condition, solve a problem, adapt the system to their personal preferences, or obtain some type of positive result about something.

Expecting for something to be improved or resolved was a reason for some of the interviewees to tailor. Broadcast Lists is a feature of WhatsApp that enables people to create contact lists and send messages that are delivered individually to each member of the list (Fig. 3). Louise coordinates the basketball team at the college where she studies, and comments that she had initially created a WhatsApp group to communicate with teammates. However, she reported that of the 18 members of the group, only 4 or 5 answered the schedule when they were available to train, or other matters that needed to be decided based on individual opinions. Given the lack of communication and participation in the group of basketball team, it was difficult to decide important issues via WhatsApp.

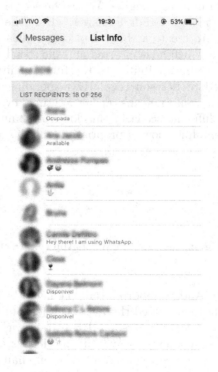

Fig. 3. Broadcast Lists in WhatsApp (v.2.18.60)

To change this situation Louise set up a Broadcast List and sent messages that were delivered individually to each athlete, as she reports: "When I had to schedule trainings, no one answered me. I had to beg. So I did it [Broadcast List] and everyone answers now, almost everyone." With this tailoring, she says that now only one or two teammates do not respond, and that the WhatsApp group started to be used only for minor issues. She appropriated the system so it would meet her wants and needs. The context appears intrinsically related to appropriation, by making clear factors that would impel an action to be taken in relation to a given situation. If Louise and her colleagues had more free time or more engagement in WhatsApp group, possibly the setup of the Broadcast List would not be necessary. But tailoring was one of the ways she made technology appropriate for her.

It is also interesting to note that users' behavior also changed in Louise's context. When an information or question was communicated to the whole group, the common behavior was not to answer or to wait for someone to answer before. When the message was delivered individually, people began to answer more, possibly because they were less influenced by the behavior of the other members of the group. In these examples, after tailoring, WhatsApp has become more appropriate to people's needs. The application assumed a new meaning, in a more efficient scenario and becomes suited to who uses it. As mentioned earlier, the notion of appropriation can be interpreted as people empowerment [6].

Harrisson, Tatar and Sengers [15] present as a matter of interest of the third wave of HCI to realize how we can support interaction without constraining it by what a computer can do or understand. The authors also mention that in this wave, designing interaction moves from attempting to establish one correct understanding, to studying the situated practices of users, taking into account but not adjudicating the varying and perhaps conflicting perspectives of users.

In the case of Slack, it was noticed that people appropriate in a way to adapt it to their work routine. An example is the company where Priscilla works. As a member of the product development team, she reported having a high number of documentation requests. People from other teams were requesting documentation so often that overwhelmed her to respond demands. Given this scenario, she reported that she selected keywords that would identify those requests and configured for each one an automatic response with these documentation files attached in Slack (Fig. 4). This tailoring provided her the conditions to automate a repetitive process, as she says: "I created these shortcuts so people would receive those files automatically, without me having to respond." The end-user tailoring in this example is motivated by a contextual factor (the excess of demand) that resulted in a change in Slack to better fit the needs of use (automation of repetitive tasks), and also changed the teams' work routine (instead of repeatedly replying to the messages requesting the same documents, she now only cares about keeping the attached documents in the automatic replies up to date). Not only for efficiency, but the attribution of a new meaning to the application emerges, as it is no longer seen as a space for information exchange, but also for process automation and as a reference to find files and data. The context of use is central to the appropriation, because in a different scenario, possibly other alternatives would emerge or even be unnecessary.

Appropriation impacts several spheres, from the artifact itself to the interaction and context of use. In these examples end-user tailoring articulates the intentions of designers and developers and the appropriations that people do in their context of use. It is also interesting to note that most appropriations through end-user tailoring happened in WhatsApp. In fact it is a tool used

Fig. 4. Slackbot - Automatic responses in Slack (v.3.1.1)

in various contexts of people's lives, which increases the variation of groups involved, activities, environments, and so on. The variability of influencing factors for tailoring is greater, compared to Slack for example, which, although used also by large groups, is usually restricted to the work environment. Within the understanding of the third wave of HCI, appropriation is becoming increasingly important, especially as it becomes increasingly difficult for artifacts to meet the demands of all users. As Harrisson, Tatar, and Sengers [15] commented, one of the objectives of the third wave is to deal with all the complexity around the system, with the context, and that often, what happens around the system is more important than what appears in the interface. Contexts of use are rich and complex, especially when they involve systems for personal use.

5   Conclusion

In this study we investigated ways in which people tailor technologies in order to appropriate them. Through semi-structured interviews and questionnaires, we collected data that was later coded. From coding results, we found evidence that contextual factors influence and motivate appropriation through end-user tailoring in communication systems. This means that people appropriate because the context influences in some way, and contexts are so diverse that each situation is singular when it comes to appropriation. There are factors that come from many different spheres, and to understand appropriation it is necessary to understand social and environmental relations from a broad perspective. On the other hand, each case of appropriation is a combination of specific factors that make it unique.

Our study was conducted with systems directed to the use in both professional and personal contexts. It was noticed that in some aspects, the personal and professional contexts have different characteristics but, in others, they are close and even confuse themselves. In professional contexts we realized that end-user tailoring is closely associated with work processes and other systems used in the company. In this context, appropriation through end-user tailoring was especially related to the optimization of work processes. In the case of the system for personal context, we realized that end-user tailoring was strongly associated with aspects related to communication and to personal preferences. The appropriation through end-user tailoring, in this context, is related to facilitate communication and to make their experience better suited to their reality.

We also found evidence that personal and professional contexts intersect, and the purposes and moments in which people use these systems are intertwined.

People use systems in a way that builds, elaborates, and suits them according to their wishes. And this is the great contribution of systems designed for appropriation. Regardless of whether it is through end-user tailoring or not, it is important to think systems that increase the users' agency, so that they have less restrictions to assign new meanings and develop uses appropriate to their realities.

Along with the understanding of appropriation comes the understanding of the context and of people as part of it. Our purpose was to look for cases where people were empowered and played central role in technology appropriation. Appropriation shows new possibilities, opens up alternative dimensions that can enhance experience, and enrich the ways we interact with systems.

References

1. Dourish, P.: The appropriation of interactive technologies: some lessons from placeless documents. J. Comput. Support. Coop. Work **12**(4), 465–490 (2003)
2. Kahler, H., et al.: Computer supported cooperative work. J. Collab. Comput. **9**(1), 1–4 (2000). Computer Supported Cooperative Work (CSCW)
3. Oppermann, R., Rashev, R., Kinshuk, R.: Adaptability and adaptivity in learning systems. Knowl. Transf. **2**, 173–179 (1997)
4. Mørch, A.: Three levels of end-user tailoring: customization, integration, and extension, pp. 51–76. MIT Press, Cambridge (1997)
5. Tchounikine, P.: Designing for appropriation: a theoretical account. Hum.-Comput. Interact. **32**(4), 155–195 (2017)
6. Lindtner, S., Anderson, K., Dourish, P.: Cultural appropriation: information technologies as sites of transnational imagination. In: Proceedings of the ACM 2012 Conference on Computer Supported Cooperative Work, pp. 77–86 (2012)
7. Henderson, A., Kyng, M.: There's no place like home: continuing design in use. In: Greenbaum, J., Kyng, M. (eds.) Design at Work: Cooperative Design of Computer Systems. Lawrence Erlbaum Associate Publishers, Hillsdale (1991)
8. Slagter, R., Biemans, M., ter Hofte, H.: Evolution in use of groupware: facilitating tailoring to the extreme. Proceedings - 7th International Workshop on Groupware, CRIWG 2001, pp. 68–73 (2001)
9. Trigg, R.H., Bødker, S.: From implementation to design: tailoring and the emergence of systematization in CSCW. In: Proceedings of the 1994 ACM Conference on Computer Supported Cooperative Work - CSCW 1994, pp. 45–54 (1994)
10. Feenberg, A.: Do essencialismo ao construtivismo: A filosofia da tecnologia numa encruzilhada, vol. 20, 01 (2010)
11. Balka, E., Wagner, I.: Making things work: dimensions of configurability as appropriation work. In: Proceedings of the 2006 20th Anniversary Conference on Computer Supported Cooperative Work, pp. 229–238 (2006)
12. Grudin, J., Poltrock, S.: Computer Supported Cooperative Work, pp. 1–51 (2013)
13. Pipek, V.: From Tailoring to Appropriation Support: Negotiating Groupware Usage. University of Oulu (2005)
14. Greenberg, S.: Personalizable groupware: accommodating individual roles and group differences. In: Bannon, L., Robinson, M., Schmidt, K. (eds.) ECSCW 1991. Springer, Dordrecht (1991). https://doi.org/10.1007/978-94-011-3506-1_2

15. Harrison, S., Tatar, D., Sengers, P.: The three paradigms of HCI. In: Alt. Chi. Session at the SIGCHI Conference on Human Factors in Computing Systems, San Jose, California, USA (2007)
16. Lakatos, E.M., de Marconi, M.: A Metodologia Científica. 4th edn. Atlas, São Paulo (2004)
17. Bødker, S.: Third-wave HCI, 10 years later - participation and sharing. Interactions **22**(5), 24–31 (2015)
18. Gil, A.C.: Métodos e Técnicas de Pesquisa Social, 2nd edn. Editora Atlas S.A, São Paulo (1989)
19. Strauss, A., Corbin, J.: Grounded theory, procedures, canons and evaluative criteria. Qual. Sociol. **13**(1), 3–21 (1990)
20. Gibbs, G.: Analise de dados qualitativos: Coleção Pesquisa Qualitativa. Bookman Editora, [S.l.] (2009)
21. Charmaz, K.: Constructing Grounded Theory: A Practical Guide Through Qualitative Analysis. SAGE Publications, Thousand Oaks (2006)
22. Dix, A., et al.: Human-Computer Interaction, 3rd edn. Prentice-Hall Inc., Upper Saddle River (2003)
23. Spinuzzi, C.: Tracing Genres Through Organizations. MIT Press, Cambridge (2003)
24. da Silva, T.T., Hall, S., Woodward, K.: Identidade e diferença: A perspectiva dos Estudos Culturais, 12th edn. Editora Vozes, Petropolis - RJ (2012)
25. Grudin, J., Poltrock, S.: Taxonomy and theory in computer supported cooperative work, pp. 1323–1348 (2012)
26. Mackay, W.E.: Users and Customizable Software: A Co-Adaptive Phenomenon. 203 p. Massachussetts Institute of Technology (1990)

Social Network Analysis

Automating Instagram Activities and Analysis: A Survey of Existing Tools

Asma Alsaeed[✉], Ola Alotaibi, Norah Alotaibi, and Meznah Almutairy

Department of Computer Science,
Al Imam Mohammad Ibn Saud Islamic University,
Riyadh, Saudi Arabia
{azalsaeed,osalotiby,nmgalotaibi}@sm.imamu.edu.sa, mrmutairy@imamu.edu.sa

Abstract. Instagram serves as a modern advertising channel for many business sectors. For a business Instagram account to be effective in advertising, they need to be active and reach the current and potential clients constantly. A common way to achieve that is to hire workers to keep the accounts active by, for example, liking and commenting on photos and video. However, this process is time and money consuming. In addition, data associated with accounts present a valuable information to guide business plans. Since the data usually large, data analysis has to be completed in an automated fashion. Therefore, it is important to automate both Instagram activities and data analysis. However, it is not clear if such tools are available. In this paper, we survey the existing tools within the context of automations. We investigate the capability of the current tools to perform Instagram activities and data analysis in an automated fashion. An important factor we added to our investigation is whether the tools are free and open source. We found that there is an urgent need for both free and open source tools to support especially small emerging business. This paper should serve as a reference about current tools for business companies at different scale. Also, it helps tools? developers to design and implement tools that are better serve the current business needs. To understand the automation in Instagram, we proposed a simple automation layered architecture. This should help in understanding current tools and develop new ones.

Keywords: Instagram · Automation · Tasks automations · Data analysis · Open source tools · Web-based tools

1 Introduction

Social media has grown tremendously in the last few years and captured millions of users in just a few years. According to the statistic published on the official website of Instagram, for example, the number of monthly active users has reached one billion [1]. As a term, Instagram consists of two words; the first word is "insta" come from "instant". But in the history of using the cameras, "Instant" is another name for the type of camera that can instantly print

© Springer Nature Switzerland AG 2019
G. Meiselwitz (Ed.): HCII 2019, LNCS 11578, pp. 267–277, 2019.
https://doi.org/10.1007/978-3-030-21902-4_19

photos after the shot, which is a Polaroid camera. The second word is "gram" which comes from "telegram", that is an attribute in an application to send and exchange messages quickly [2].

Automating Instagram is to achieve some activities of Instagram using computer software. These activities could include interaction tasks such as logging and following people [3–8] or analysis tasks such as flowers or hashtag analysis [5–7,9] In business, with the increase of social media users, maintaining and influencing users behaviors become one of the task in social marketing. Automating Instagram is very significant to those businesses, because it saves their staff time and effort. In addition, social media networks, including Instagram, contain a huge amount of data that could reveal interesting information about users. Thus, analyzing data in social media networks becomes a valuable information source.

Exploring and monitoring data on Instagram is an important task in social sciences and business intelligence at the present time. Despite the exiting of many social media analysis tools, the tools suffer from limited capacity in collecting, monitoring, and analyzing data in an automated fashion. In these tools, most of the tasks require human interactions to perform simple tasks.

In this paper, we surveyed the existing tools within the context of automation of Instagram. We investigated the capability of the current tools to perform Instagram activities and data analysis in an automated fashion. We found that there is no free or open source tools that support such automation, especially for small emerging business. This paper aims to collect, organize, describe the current tools for business companies at different scale. Also, it should encourage software developers to collaborate with business sector to implement useful and goal oriented programs.

The paper is organized as the following. First, we describe the instagram framework. Second, we give a brief description about system automation, in general, and Instagram automation, in particular. Then we conduct a comparison between the state of the art tools in Instagram automation. We conclude with comparison results and possible future extension of this work.

2   Instagram Framework

Instagram is a social network service (SNS) [10] that allow the user to upload and share pictures and videos with their followers or with selected group of friends. Instagram support two account types: personal account and business account. Business account is a personal account but with some limitations and extra functionality that help entrepreneur users. Instagram provides many functionalities to support picture and videos sharing [11]. We classify these functionalities into the following:

Profile functions: allow to manage accounts and edit profile information such as name, username, bio, and email.

Targeted functions: allow interacting with targeted users that are defined by specific user account. This include liking, commenting, and sending private messages to a specific account.

None-targeted functions: allow the interacting with none-targeted user. This includes discovering photos, videos and stories.

Profile functions are unlikely to be called frequently. Thus no automation is needed for these functions. However, both targeted and none-targeted functions are called frequently. Thus, it is crucial to automat both targeted and none-targeted functions. In this study we investigate the ability of the current tools to automate these functions.

3   System Automation Applications

Software automation means software development with the assistance of tools as most as possible. Software automation aims to improve software productivity and quality. There are many applications where software automation is successfully applied. These applications are mainly in software development and testing. There is hardly any work have been propped to automate "tasks" on social media, including Instagram.

The applications that benefit greatly from software automation differ in the purpose of the automation. This includes: automation for software testing, automating PC tasks, and automating for programming. Some automation tools may combine more than on purpose. In this section we limit our investigation to the free and open-source tools. We show that most of the mature automation tools are not designed, developed, or studied to automate necessary functions in social media, in general, and Instagram, in particular. This is expected since social media is a relatively new phenomenon in most companies, but, it is rapidly turning into a vital part of the modern marketing.

The first and the major application for automation is Software testing, which is mainly refer to the execution of an automation Software to find all bugs or error in the program, to produce error-free software. Software automation testing is usually used to check if a software performs all the requirements, define by the Software designer, under different scenarios and still gives correct output. It also test and measure the ability to complete tasks with an acceptable time and to run correctly in different environments. There are various testing strategies used to describe the testing approach such as unit testing and Integration testing [12]. Sneha and Malle [12] classify testing tools into different categories based on the area of testing. The first is testing management tools such as TET (Test Environment Toolkit) and TETware. The second is functional testing tools such that Selenium and Junit. The last category is load testing tools like JMeter and WebLoad.

The second application for automation is running PC tasks. In this case an automation tool is used to automate repetitive tasks on your PC such as launching applications, checking email, moving or backing up files for uploading or downloading, and sending email. Also, some complex automation can be done such as conditional IF/ELSE statements, loops, custom variables and other advanced options. RoboTask [13] is one of the best software to automate PC tasks. It uses the visual interface to view tasks and select action for each.

Another feature of RoboTask is to execute task automatically if certain conditions apply, such as file movement.

The third application fro automation is programming. This is usually completed by a combination of an artificial Intelligence and a compilers techniques. The end-user assign certain high- level specifications (easily understandable by human) then the program converts it into machine code executable. There are two categories for automatic programming. The first category is Generative Programming where it is done using libraries that contain prebuilt functions such as graphics library for C++ "glut.h". The second category is Source Code Generation, where the code is powerful enough to understand incomplete instructions and generate complete source codes [14].

Although, automation is heavily used in Software testing and applied for program generations, it is not clear if automation can be used for social media activities. In this project, we propose to automate performing Instagram tasks. Mainly, we would like to automate firstly the major activities in Instagram and secondly automate the process of analyzing Instagram data.

4   Automating Instagram

In the business market, the social marketing is a very important, especially with increasing social media users. This is because it allows the company to reach large number of customers quickly and make a significant influence compared to the traditional marketing ways, such as advertisements in the street or on TVt. Many of brands in, for example, fashion, food, fitness, travels and beauty have Instagram accounts to serve their clients. To maintain their current clients and attract new ones, their accounts need to be active constantly. Therefore, they hire staff just to maintain an active account, by performing constantly some Instagram activities such as "like" and "comment" to posts of their clients' posts.

Automating Instagram applications/tools is very significant to those companies, because they save money by avoid hiring people for logging into clients accounts, like photos, commenting, and following other accounts. They complete all these tasks by hand eight hours a day. Alternately, a well automated application or tool could do all of these tasks accurately and efficiently. Automating tasks is usually one-time effort, and one might have to make only slight adjustments later [3].

In the next subsections, we first proposed an automation architecture to illustrate the process of designing an automation tools. Next, we described the major automation tools for both Instagram activities or data-analysis.

4.1   Instagram Automation Layered Architecture

In order to design and develop an automated Instagram tool, an architecture has to be designed and followed to ensure the proper development of the automation tool. This architecture also helpful when comparing different tools, where the tools can be compared at different layers according to some architecture.

The key value of layered architecture is that each layer is dedicated and separated for a particular aspect of a computer program. This dedication allows more concrete designs and better interpretation of each aspect. Also, it fasciate easier integration of different layers' designs. Therefore, it is important for tools developers to choose the layers that isolated the most important concrete design aspects.

Based on the current literature, there is no architecture has been proposed for automating Instagram activities and analysis. Therefore, we propose the following four layered architecture for automating Instagram: Business, Logical, Physical, and Application/website layers. The Fig. 1 depicts the suggested Instagram automation architecture.

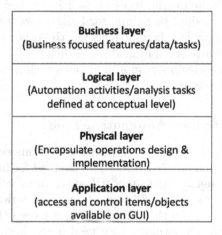

Fig. 1. Instagram automation architecture.

The *Business layer* provides the user with business oriented features and data need to be collected or tasks need to be completed. These features/data/tasks are defined regardless of how it could be completed from programming perspectives. For example, a business goal could be define and monitor business competitors, or send special promotions to potential customers.

The *Logical layer* Define, design, and lists the automation activities/analysis tasks, at conceptual level. These tasks should be organized and used to archive the goals listed in business layer. Automation tasks are usually defined for different stories, scenarios, and corner cases rely on the same piece of code in the layer below, the only difference is in parameters or test data representing different cases. Foe example, one could track and record a user activities, in terms of his/her liking and commenting, to check if he/she is a potential customer to be reached.

The *physical layer* provides users with automation capabilities to support the activities/analysis defined in logical ayer. In this layer, the real framework really lives, and it deals with providing low-level API to communicate with tested application, which is Instagram in our case. It encapsulate operations design and implementation to automation Instagram. This includes the use an API and/or a generic programming language to perform for example, url concatenation, xml/html parsing, GUI/browser control.

Finally, the *application/website layer* lists and defines the items/objects available on Instagram GUI that are supported by Instagram. This include, for example, the login box and liking button. In our study, we classified the functions, that needed to be automated, to targeted and none-targeted functions.

In this paper we compare the tools based on the logical layer. That is we compare weather tools support certain activities/analysis tasks. These tasks are independent from both the business motivations and the implementation details. It will be helpful to compare the tools at each layer. For example, comparing tools at business layer, would be helpful for business owner and decision maker to pick the suitable tools for their benefit. On the other hand, comparing the tools based on their logical and physical layers, helps to tools developers in how to improve the design and support more functions with a careful selection of the best technologies and languages.

4.2   Instagram Activities Automation Tools

To the best of our knowledge, the following are the major tools used for task automation and/or data analysis automation designed for Instagram specifically, or for social media in general and support Instagram as well. We describe these tools in tow contexts. First, the ability to automate activities, Second, the ability to automate data analysis. In this study we usually used the term automation, however, an alternative term that is also used is the bot. We use these terms interchangeably.

InstaPy (2017): It is a very customizable bot that can be used for either personal or business accounts. It is an open source tool and it allows the user to comment, follow and like other user in an automatic way [3]. The tools is available at https://github.com/timgrossmann/InstaPy.

Instbot (2017): It is a bot that can be used for either personal or business account [4]. It is an open source tool. It provides users with the ability to perform certain functions automatically such as likes, comments, follow and unfollow users. The tools is available at https://instagrambot.github.io.

Sprout-Social (2009): It is a tool that provides users with the ability to manage their content and analyze its performance with high accuracy. One of the most important features in Sprout-Social is post scheduling. It provides the user with time management and planning capability, so that users can schedule contents and publish them automatically at a later times [5]. The tools is available at https://sproutsocial.com.

Hootsuite (2009): It supports scheduling and publishing posts automatically and provide information regarding the user interaction at all times [6]. The tools is available at https://hootsuite.com.

Sendible (2008): Similar to Hootsuite, Sendible allows for automatic scheduling and posting of posts. It provides the user with the frequency of posts at the time the audience interacts. The user selects the posts that he/she wants and publishes them automatically according to the time where public interaction is large enough [7]. It also support for another social media such as Twitter and Facebook. The tools is available at https://www.sendible.com.

Buffer (2010): This tool helps, in particular, businesses and marketing teams for managing their account on many social media not only in Instagram but also in Twitter, Facebook, Pinterest, etc. With Buffer, you can schedule posts in one place for different social networks, other than Buffer, and it publish them automatically. The Buffer is available as an application for IOS, Android and as a browser extension on Chrome, Firefox, Safari, and Opera [8]. The tools is available at https://buffer.com.

4.3 Instagram Data Analysis Tools

The analysis of data in computer science is interpreted as the extraction of data or the discovery of new knowledge [15]. In this subsection, we will review some studies that analyze Instagram data.

Instagram-Insight. It is a web-based tool this is provided and hosted by Instagram and available for business accounts only. The system supports Windows, IOS, Android and web-based. This tool has the ability to analyze data, posts, and stories and provide information about followers (such as gender, age and geographical location). Instagram-Insight especially focuses on analysis of stories such as the number of times their post or story was seen, the total number of users who saw it posted, the number of users who either liked commented on or saved the post. The total number of times a video or story was viewed. Also it reports the top post: all of their posts sorted by their number of impressions (viewing) from top to bottom within the last 30 days and the number of times a user skipped your story or exited out while viewing it [9]. Instagram-Insight supports analysis visualization using the Charts. This tools is free but not open source, which limits the flexibility to use the tool.

Sprout-Social. It is a web-based tool hosted on a server and requires businesses account. The system supported Windows, IOS, Android and the web- based It is a tool that provides users with the ability to manage their content and analyze its performance. This tool allows to mange multiple accounts simultaneously (e.g. publishing images in all accounts at one time). It has three main functionalities publishing, engagement, and analytics. Analytics are typically shown as a charts. Some of Analytics includes reporting the top post which has the maximum number of impressions (viewing) within the last 30 days, It also reports the number of times posts or stories were seen, the number of users who either liked or commented-on or saved a post, and the total number of times a video or story was viewed [5]. This tool consider one of the best tools for content analysis and management. However, it is a commercial tool, and thus not open source, limiting its usability to well established business companies.

Hootsuite. It is a tool that measures and analyzes the performance of a user account. It generates charts, for examples, about the interaction of the public with a post, the number of likes on each post, and the number of additions during a period of time [6]. Hootsuite supports other social media such as Twitter and Facebook.

Sendible. It also support analyzing the data and measuring of the interactions on a user account. Sendible analyzes an account then suggests the best time to publish the posts according to the interaction of the public at certain times. To provide a clear vision for the interaction of the account [7], it provides chart of the like and followers rates and comments. Similar to Hootsuite, Sendible supports other social media.

5   Tools Comparison Framework and Discussion

We compare the automation tools for Instagram at two levels: abstract and detail levels. In the abstract level we look into basic automation usability features that we suggest are critical for the designing and development of Instagram automation tool. At the detail level, we investigate the major automation functions supported by the current tools. We focus only on the major functions to be able to compare the tools.

To compare the tools at an abstract level, we focus on the following usability feature: Does the tool support tasks/activity automation? Does the tool support automatic data analysis? Is the tool open source? Is the tool built using Instagram API? Does the tool support major platforms? The results of our comparisons is shown in Table 1.

In our compassion, we check if a tool is an open source. This is because open source tool gives the user the flexibility to customize the tools for its own need. We also check if a tools is built using Instagram API, because tools built using this API usually limit the ability to add more feature to the program, even if it is an open source. Finally, we think supporting the major platform is a good feature for business sector, since tools could be used in widen range of machines.

Table 1. Major tools for automating Instagram

Tool	Activity	Analysis	Commercial	Open-source	Insta. API	Cross-Platform
InstaPy	✓			✓		✓
Instabot	✓			✓		✓
Sprout-Social	✓	✓	✓		✓	✓
Hootsuite	✓	✓	✓		✓	✓
Sendible	✓	✓	✓		✓	✓
Instagram-Insight		✓		✓	✓	✓
Buffer	✓	✓	✓		-	✓

To compare the tools at a detail level, we focus on the major tasks automation functions supported by the current tools (see Table 2). In our study, we classified the functions to targeted and none-targeted functions. For targeted functions, we check the ability of a tool to automatically follow and unfollow other accounts, to like and unlike a post, and to comment on a post. For none- targeted functions we check if a tool supports scheduling to post images and videos. The scheduling usually includes the option to save a post, set a time for posting, and give the option to send a reminder for posting or automatically complete posting process.

Another detail information that supports data analysis is to the ability of a tool to produce statistics about data. This include statistics about followers (e.g. gender, age and geographical location) and posts/stories (e.g. number of times the post was viewed, seen, liked, commented, or saved, skipped).

Table 2. The automation of targeted and non-targeted functions

Tool	(Un)follow	(Un)like	Commenting	Scheduling	Followers stat.	Posts stat.
InstaPy	✓	✓	✓			
Instabot	✓	✓	✓			
Sprout-Social				✓		✓
Hootsuite				✓		✓
Sendible				✓		✓
Instagram-Insight					✓	✓
Buffer				✓		

After conducting the comparisons, we found that there is a limited work proposed for automating activities and data analysis on Instagram, in particular, and social media, in general. This is expected since social media is a relatively new phenomenon. However, it is rapidly turning into a vital part of the modern marketing.

We can see from the Table 1 that there is a need for open source program that could do both task and data analysis automation. Most of the current tools that enable task and data analysis automation are only commercial. There is no free/open-source tool that can do both task and data-analysis automation. There is no free/open-source tools that perform even data-analysis alone. Also, even if the tool perform some automation, it uses Instagram API. This limit the ability to enhance the tools and customize it.

Looking into more depth, we can see from the Table 2 that the functions supported in the current tools is very limited. The open source program, only support simple tasks such following accounts and linking posts. A slightly advance tasks are only supported by commercial tools such as post scheduling.

The data analysis functions are provided by only commercial tools. These analysis functions are simple just statistics such as counting and rating based on these counts.

To conclude, there is no free powerful tool that perform both activities and data-analysis. It is important to design and develop an open-source tool that can allow for integrating multiple functions and allow for large flexibility to add new functions.

6   Conclusion and Future Work

In this paper, we surveyed the current tools that perform Instagram activities and data analysis in an automated fashion. We found that there is no free or open source tools that could automate the activities and tasks. Most of the existing tools that provide this service are commercial and pricey for small emerging business.

We compared the tools at an abstract level, where it focus on major usability features. It will be useful to expand the current list to study the security aspects of these tools. We compared the tools based on the logical layer in our proposed layered architecture. However, it will be more comprehensive to compare the tools in business, physical, and application layers as well.

References

1. Instagram-INFO-CENTER: Our story, August 2018. https://instagram-press.com/our-story/. Accessed 1 Nov 2018
2. Sudrajat, R., Si, M., Rosadi, R., Si, S., Kom, M., Muhammad, H.: Implementation of data mining in analyzing social media users personality with Naïve Bayes classifier: a case study of instagram social media. Int. J. Comput. Sci. Issues (IJCSI) **13**(4), 76 (2016)
3. Grossman, T.: My open source Instagram bot got me 2,500 real followers for 5$ in server costs, April 2017. https://medium.freecodecamp.org. Accessed 1 Nov 2018
4. Okhlopkov, D.: Instabot (2017). https://instagrambot.github.io/. Accessed 1 Nov 2018
5. Sprout-Social: Social media management solutions. https://sproutsocial.com. Accessed 1 Nov 2018
6. Hootsuite: Scheduling - social media marketing & management dashboard. https://hootsuite.com/platform/scheduling. Accessed 1 Nov 2018

7. Sendible: Streamlined scheduling & social media publishing tools. https://www.sendible.com/features/social-media-publishing. Accessed 1 Nov 2018
8. Buffer: Social media management platform. https://buffer.com/. Accessed 25 Nov 2018
9. Instagram: Instagram help center. https://help.instagram.com/. Accessed 1 Nov 2018
10. Gong, X.: Strategic customer engagement on Instagram: a case of global business to customer (B2C) brands. Masters thesis, KTH Royal Institute of Technology (2014)
11. Riaz, F., Alam, M., Ali, A.: Filtering the big data based on volume, variety and velocity by using Kalman filter recursive approach. In: Engineering Technologies and Social Sciences (ICETSS), pp. 1–6. IEEE, August 2017
12. Sneha, K., Malle, G.M.: Research on software testing techniques and software automation testing tools. In: International Conference on Energy, Communication, Data Analytics and Soft Computing (ICECDS), pp. 77–81. IEEE, August 2017
13. Robotask: Robotask features. https://robotask.com/features/. Accessed 30 Nov 2018
14. Fatima, S.: Automatic programming... yes, it exists!. https://www.linkedin.com/pulse/automatic-programming-yes-exists-sarosh-fatima. Accessed 30 Nov 2018
15. Chen, J., Jiang, Q., Wang, Y., Tang, J.: Study of data analysis model based on big data technology. In: IEEE International Conference on Big Data Analysis (ICBDA), pp. 1–6. IEEE, March 2016

User Motivation and Personal Safety
on a Mobile Dating App

Vanessa Breitschuh$^{(\boxtimes)}$ iD and Julia Göretz$^{(\boxtimes)}$ iD

Heinrich Heine University, Universitätsstr. 1, 40225 Düsseldorf, Germany
vanessa.breitschuh@hhu.de

Abstract. With mobile dating apps taking over the lives of millions, researchers have become more interested in the subject in recent years. Tinder is often perceived as a dangerous place, where users are only interested in one-night stands, while collecting your data for blackmail. Prior research also showed that Tinder collects and stores a variety of information about their users. To see whether or not users are motivated to protect their data from misuse, and why they do so specifically, as well as why they use Tinder in general, a survey was conducted. Results showed that the majority of the 346 participants are more truthful when providing information than not, and usually only change their names. The main reasons for doing so were to protect their privacy and for personal safety. They mostly use Tinder out of boredom, to find a steady relationship, or as a joke. Casual sexual encounters were only the fourth most common reason for using Tinder.

Keywords: Mobile dating app · Personal safety · User motivation · Tinder

1 Introduction

1.1 Mobile Dating Apps

Social media influences most peoples' lives, including how we meet people. Online dating has been around and studied for much longer than two decades, but really gained more popularity in the early 2000s [1]. As mobile apps are taking over, providing a constant stream of information directly to our phones, the way is paved for location-based real-time mobile dating apps like Tinder[1], Bumble[2], Grindr[3] and Hinge[4] to be introduced to millions [2]. This study focuses on Tinder, which has received a lot of attention in prior research, as well as in mainstream media.

---

[1] https://tinder.com/.

[2] https://bumble.com/.

[3] https://www.grindr.com/.

[4] https://hinge.co/.

© Springer Nature Switzerland AG 2019
G. Meiselwitz (Ed.): HCII 2019, LNCS 11578, pp. 278–292, 2019.
https://doi.org/10.1007/978-3-030-21902-4_20

When signing up for Tinder each user is presented with two options: Logging in using Facebook[5] or logging in via phone number. By signing up with a phone number one can set all information manually, meaning birthday, gender, name and pictures. One has to provide an email address, password and access to the phone's location. The sexual orientation can also be defined via the settings. Once all the information is gathered the user can start *swiping* straight away to create *matches*: They are presented with the pictures, names and ages of other users, as well as optional additional information. Once a match has occurred the users can start messaging each other. If either of the two swipes left, a match will not occur. Messaging is similar to most other messaging services, with the exception that the sending of pictures is prohibited.

Based on these functionalities, the question arises, what motivates users to use a service like Tinder? According to Koch, Ott and Oertelt [3] motivation is the willingness to perform an action as well as the totality of all the reasons that caused it. In particular, the human need for social inclusion and the associated striving for recognition and acceptance by other people represents a decisive motivational aspect for human action [4]. In addition to social interaction, McQuail [5] identifies three other reasons for using media: entertainment, information and personal identity. The following studies show how these motivational aspects are addressed by Tinder and how they influence self-expression and appearance on a dating app.

1.2 Related Research and the Current Situation

Location-based real-time dating apps have been studied in general [6–8], although predominantly with a focus on men who have sex with men [9, 10]. Looking into the study Lemke and Merz [11] published in 2018 sparked ideas regarding the app Tinder. Their paper focuses on "the prevalence of nude pictures and gratifications sought while displaying them" [11]. However, Tinder does not allow the sending of pictures and the amount of nude self-presentation in profile pictures seems minor.

In their paper, Farnden, Martini, and Choo [12] state that they "recover a number of data types from these apps that raise concerns about user privacy." The researchers have studied eight different dating apps regarding the data each one stores. After gathering the information in a five step process, they created a table to evaluate their findings. Tinder stores the messages, profile images and precise location of a user, among other data.

Additionally, not only may the data collected by the app itself be a potential threat: "Unfortunately, the hopeful optimism and convenience of sharing in-depth, personal information online with strangers can put the user's safety and well-being in jeopardy" [13]. This statement is based on information given in an article in the British newspaper 'The Telegraph'. "Crimes linked to dating apps Tinder and Grindr, including rape, child sex grooming and attempted murder, have increased seven fold in just two year [sic]" [14]. Murphy [13] has studied the misconducts linked to mobile dating apps,

---

[5] https://www.facebook.com/.

focusing on "Crimes of Sexual Violence and Assault" and "Stalking and Harassment", as well as "Cyber Crimes". During her research, the following was found by Murphy [13]: "If a crime is committed, as a recourse, information can be extracted and used against a fellow user of a mobile dating app. [...] Probable cause is not required because the user lacks a reasonable expectation of privacy in his or her geolocation and such data can be obtained without a warrant."

This raises the question whether or not Tinder users are concerned for their privacy or personal safety, and if users are motivated to take measures to protect themselves, like using false information. "Profiles are essential for online daters because they constitute a gateway for future [Face to Face] dating" [15].

Other papers [16, 17] have already focused on the reasons people have for using Tinder. Sumter et al. [16] found six motivations: "Love, Casual Sex, Ease of Communication, Self-Worth Validation, Thrill of Excitement, and Trendiness." This particular research, however, was conducted on a limited amount of people, who all fit a tight age range (18–30) and all come from the same country (Netherlands).

Lastly, it is necessary to gather data about the participants to see if there are any demographic differences between their answers. Tinder asks their users for a variety of data. Following this, the research model will be presented, outlining the approach chosen for this research, to fill the current research gap.

1.3   Research Model and Research Questions

The research model consists of three dimensions. Dimension 1 focused on the usage of the application. It was to be studied if the frequency with which participants use the app relates to other factors. Additionally, it was also interesting to see which different reasons a user may have for using the dating app. This dimension aimed to answer the first research question (RQ):

RQ1: Why do people use Tinder?

The second dimension regarded the personal safety online, studying whether or not users of Tinder use real information regarding their name, age, location and appearance. Additionally, if the users gave false information, Dimension 2 aimed to find out why they do so, and then answer the second research question:

RQ2: What motivates users to protect their data on Tinder?

The third dimension regarded the personal data that may have value when trying to assess possible demographic differences, and therefore was kept close to the data which users disclose publicly on Tinder, with the exception of the name (Fig. 1).

Next follow the methods, showing how the questionnaire was developed and explaining how the research was conducted specifically.

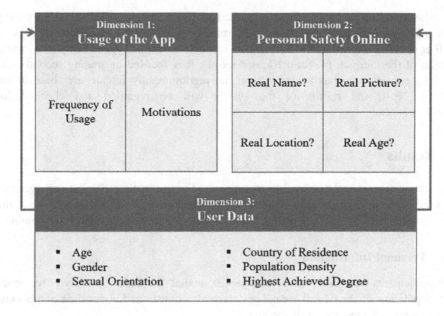

Fig. 1. Research model.

2 Methods

2.1 Building the Questionnaire

The survey consisted of the three dimensions mentioned previously, two dimensions which are excluded from this paper and two additional filter questions. It was modelled in English and then translated into German and French. Firstly, participants were asked whether they use Tinder or not and only those who use Tinder were brought to the second filter question, which checked that only participants above the age of 18 partake in the rest of the survey. Apart from these two questions, every question gave the option to not provide an answer.

The first block of questions regarded the personal safety online, enquiring whether or not the participants used true in their Tinder profile. If they indicated that they did not provide true information they were led to two sub-questions (or three in the case of age), where they were asked why they use wrong information.

Following some questions which were excluded from this paper, the participants were asked how often and why they use Tinder.

Lastly, the survey concluded in questions about the participants' demographic data. They were firstly asked about their age, to check if the age groups for Tinder are similar to those of the general online dating community: "Some 22% of 25–34 year olds and 17% of 35–44 year olds are online daters" [18]. The participants were then also asked about their gender, sexual orientation on Tinder, country of residence and the population of their local area, to monitor whether population density has an influence on the other dimensions.

After conducting a pretest which resulted in minor changes of wording, the survey was posted on multiple social media platforms, websites designed to spread surveys, as well as reddit[6], a forum in which members can discuss anything, and lastly to a forum-section of the German platform Kleiderkreisel[7]. It is focused on trading second-hand clothing articles, and has a very active, but predominantly female user base in the forums. Next, the results of the survey will be regarded and checked for co-occurrences.

3   Results

The survey was completed by 346 participants. Firstly, in Sect. 3.1 the demographic data the participants were asked to give will be presented, as well as their usage of the app. Secondly, Sect. 3.2 will record the participants' view of personal safety online.

3.1   Personal Information

The participants were asked about age, gender, sexual orientation, country of residence and population of their local area. They were also questioned about their educational background and their usage of the app.

Firstly, the participants were asked about their age, which was then sorted into five groups. 110 participants (31.79%) were between the ages of 18 and 22. 151 participants (43.64%) were between the ages of 23 and 27, this was also the majority of participants for this question. Another 54 participants (15.61%) were between the ages of 28 and 32.

Next, the participants were asked with which gender they identify. 272 participants (78.61%) said they identified as female, 73 participants (21.1%) indicated they identified as male and one participant (0.29%) stated that they identify as non-binary.

The participants were then asked about their sexual orientation on Tinder. 278 participants (80.35%) chose heterosexual, while eleven participants (3.18%) answered with homosexual. 47 participants (13.58%) disclosed that their sexual orientation is bisexual and four participants (1.16%) chose pansexual. Eight participants (2.31%) either chose not to give an answer or chose 'other'.

When it came to their country of residence, 79.19% (274 participants) of the 346 participants who were asked said that they live in Germany. Another 5.49% (19 participants) come from the United States of America and 4.91% (17 participants) are from Great Britain. Overall 21 countries were chosen from a drop-down menu by the participants.

The participants were then asked how well populated their local area is. 67 participants (19.36%) stated that they live in a Metropolis or city with more than one million inhabitants. 173 participants (50%) are living in a city that has between 100,000 and 1,000,000 inhabitants. 58 participants (16.76%) are living in a suburban area, which has more than 10,000 inhabitants, but less than 100,000. 34 participants (9.83%)

---

[6] https://www.reddit.com/.
[7] https://www.kleiderkreisel.de/.

live in an exurban area, which has between 1,000 and 10,000 inhabitants, and lastly 14 participants (4.05%) live in a rural area with less than 1,000 inhabitants.

Lastly, the participants were asked what their highest achieved degree was. The results of the educational levels were compared to the other results, showing no significant outliers.

3.2 Usage of the App

When asked about how often they use the app, 153 of the 350 participants (43.71%) stated they use it a couple of times a day. Another 63 participants (18%) said they use it once a day. 59 participants (16.86%) use the app a couple times each week. The remaining 56 participants (16%) who gave an answer use the app once a week or less. None of the remaining intervals given were chosen by more than 10% of the participants, as can be seen in more detail in Fig. 2.

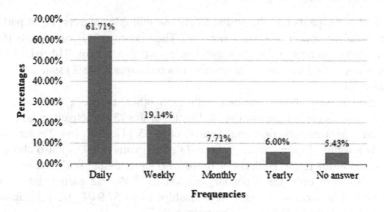

Fig. 2. Frequencies of using Tinder. N = 350

When checking how often the different age groups use Tinder, most values were close to the general data gathered, with the exception of participants between the ages of 33 and 37. Here 60% of the 25 participants use Tinder a couple of times a day, compared to the average of 43.71%. Also within the age group of 28 to 32, only one participant (1.85%) indicated that they use Tinder a couple of times per week.

Afterwards, the participants were asked about their reasons for using the app, as shown in Fig. 3 below. This question was aimed to answer the first research question:

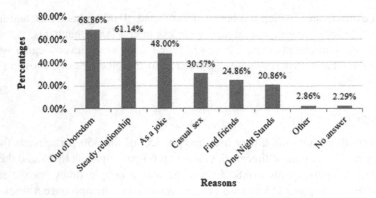

Fig. 3. Motivations for using Tinder. N = 350

RQ1: Why do people use Tinder?

The 350 participants had the option to choose multiple answers. Eight participants (2.29%) chose the option 'I'd rather not say'. The majority, 241 participants (68.86%) for this question, indicated that they use Tinder out of boredom. 214 (61.14%) stated that they use it to find a steady relationship. 168 participants (48%) stated that they use Tinder as a joke.

The groups were then compared with each other, to check for co-occurrences within answers, as can be seen in Fig. 4. Firstly, of the 73 participants who gave 'one-night stands' as a reason for using Tinder, only 35 (47.95%) use Tinder 'to find a steady relationship'. However, 62 of those 73 participants (84.93%) also chose 'casual sex' as a reason for using Tinder. For those who gave 'casual sex' as a reason, 'one-night stands' were only the secondary reason (57.94%, 62 participants) for using Tinder, alongside 'finding a steady relationship' (also 57.94%, 62 participants) and after 'out of boredom' (73.83%, 79 participants).

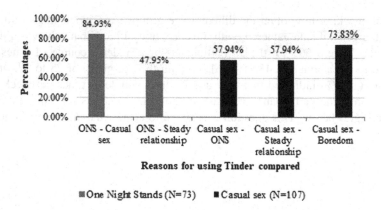

Fig. 4. Co-occurrences of reasons for using Tinder.

The reasons for use for female participants mirrored the overall distributions quite closely, and most men (47 participants, 64.38%) gave boredom as a reason for using Tinder, which is close to the average. The second most given reason for using Tinder among the 73 men was casual sex, as indicated by 38 male participants (52.05%).

When looking into the age groups for this question, the distributions were again close to the average, and between the ages of 18 to 32, the top three reasons were always boredom, using Tinder as a joke, and to find a steady relationship, in varying orders. For those participants aged between 33 and 37, the first two reasons were also boredom and finding a steady relationship, yet the third most common reason, which was selected by 10 participants (40%), was casual sex. Additionally, of the five participants who were older than 37, only one participant (20%) disclosed that they use Tinder to find a steady relationship, while using Tinder to find friends, one-night stands, casual sex and out of boredom were each given three times (60%).

3.3 Personal Safety Online

The following is focused on personal safety online, as well as how and why users try to protect their data. The questions posed here were aimed to answer the second research question:

RQ2: What motivates users to protect their data on Tinder?

Truthfulness of a Tinder Profile. Firstly, users were asked about the truthfulness of their profile, specifically if they use a real or fake name, picture and age, and whether they disclose their location to other users (distance to them). Figure 5 shows how many participants use true information regarding the aforementioned aspects in their Tinder profiles. Of the 392 participants who were asked about their name, 277 (70.66%) stated that they use their real name on Tinder, 109 (27.81%) said that they do not use a real name on Tinder and six (1.53%) chose not to answer the question. In comparison, of 390 participants asked, 375 (96.15%) indicated that they use a real photo on Tinder. Only 0.51% (two participants) use a fake photo, however, 2.8% (eleven participants)

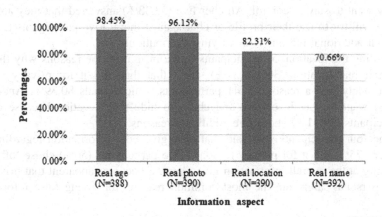

Fig. 5. Truthfulness of information in Tinder profiles.

use a picture in which they are unidentifiable and 0.51% (two participants) are shown with a group of friends. The same 390 were asked about their location and 82.31% (321 participants) stated that they have their real location disclosed, whereas 13.59% (53 participants) disabled the information. 4.1% (16 participants) chose not to respond. When asked whether or not they use their real age on Tinder, 382 (98.45%) of the 388 participants who were asked confirmed that they use their real age. Four (1.03%) stated that they use a fake age and two (0.52%) chose not to answer.

Comparing the truthfulness of information in the participants' Tinder profiles with the population of the participants' local areas showed some disparities. For example, 64.71% of participants from exurban areas (22 participants) use a real name, in comparison to the average of 70.66%. Also, ten out of 14 participants from rural areas (71.43%) use a real photo, whereas the average is 96.15%. Lastly, ten participants from rural areas (71.43%) and 42 participants from suburban areas (72.41%) use a real location, the average here is 82.31%.

Participants who chose 'homosexual' as their sexual orientation all use their real names, photos and ages in their profiles, and only one participant (9.09%) stated that they do not disclose their real location. In comparison, all four participants who chose 'pansexual' do not use a real name, even though for their ages, locations and photos they provided true information.

Reasons for Wrong Data. If participants stated that the data they give on Tinder is not entirely truthful, they were then asked for their reasoning behind this.

Of the 106 participants that were asked why they do not use their real name, 92 participants (86.79%) use a different name due to privacy reasons. 69 participants (65.09%) indicated that they use a different name as a measure of personal safety. 28 participants (26.41%) have a fake name on Tinder, because they want to stay in control. 50 additional answers spread over five other reasons were given by 37 participants (34.91%).

Truthfulness varied greatly amongst the different aspects of picture, location and age, compared to their name. Of the 15 participants asked why they use a photo in which they cannot be identified, eight (53.33%) chose 'privacy'. Another eight (53.33%) chose their 'personal safety' as a reason. Five participants (33.33%) stated that they want to stay in control. Another five (33.33%) answered that they are afraid someone will try to use their profile or chat against them. Five participants (33.33%) chose four additional reasons with varying distributions.

Regarding the location, 51 participants[8] gave insight on the reasons why they disabled their real location. 36 (70.59%) stated that they did it for privacy reasons. Personal safety was a reason for 41 participants, which equals 80.39%. Another 20 (39.22%) want to stay in control and chose to hide their location because of that. 15 participants (29.41%) chose five additional reasons.

Of the four participants who said that they give false information regarding their age, three (75%) did it for privacy reasons. Two participants (50%) chose 'other'.

Looking at the overall information given here, it becomes apparent that privacy, as well as personal safety are the most common reasons for giving false information.

---

[8] One participant was excluded due to inconclusive data.

Additionally, some participants have concerns regarding misuse of their personal data, and some wish to stay in control of the situation. The distributions for each aspect can be seen in Fig. 6.

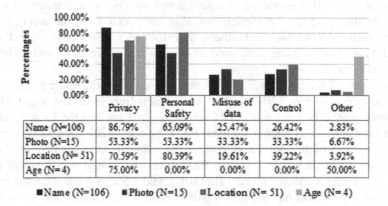

	Privacy	Personal Safety	Misuse of data	Control	Other
Name (N=106)	86.79%	65.09%	25.47%	26.42%	2.83%
Photo (N=15)	53.33%	53.33%	33.33%	33.33%	6.67%
Location (N= 51)	70.59%	80.39%	19.61%	39.22%	3.92%
Age (N=4)	75.00%	0.00%	0.00%	0.00%	50.00%

■ Name (N=106) ■ Photo (N=15) ■ Location (N= 51) ■ Age (N= 4)

Fig. 6. Reasons for using false information in Tinder profiles.

The least given answers were a variation of individual reasons, a fear for consequences if they did give the correct info, or the fact that the participants did not want to be in a relationship.

Seven out of twelve participants (58.33%) from exurban areas stated that they are afraid someone might use their profile or chat against them.

Finally, the same goes for comparing reasons for providing wrong location information when it comes to participants from rural areas. Two participated for this question and both chose only privacy (100%). On the other hand, when looking into the reasons for participants from suburban areas, eight (66.67%) indicated that they use a fake location for privacy and eleven (91.67%) stated that they use a fake location for personal safety. The average, regarding privacy as a reason for using fake location information, is 70.59% and the average for personal safety is 80.39%, meaning that people from suburban areas are a little less concerned about their privacy in this sample. Then again, they are a little more concerned about their personal safety.

4 Discussion

4.1 Reasons for Using Tinder

Sumter et al. [16] stated in their paper that their "study identified six Tinder motivations, namely Love, Casual Sex, Ease of Communication, Self-Worth Validation, Thrill of Excitement, and Trendiness." Though their sample size was smaller than the one used in this study (n = 266, of which 163 had used Tinder) [16], there are some commonalities found in both studies. For example they found that "the Love motivation was stronger than the Casual Sex motivation" [16], which is in line with the findings presented in this paper. The participants of this study use Tinder mainly out of boredom, an aspect which was not studied by Sumter et al. [16]. However, their results showed that "[...] Trendiness was a main motivation [...]" [16], which might be similar to the aspect of boredom. If there is nothing else to be done, one might look into the most recent trends. It is important to note that boredom is a common reason not only for mobile dating apps like Tinder, but also for Social Live Streaming Services (SLSSs), such as YouNow[9] and others, as Friedländer [19] found: "Most of [the streamers] appear to be using these services out of simplistic reasons, such as boredom (21.8%) and fun (13.5%)."

Mainstream media portraits Tinder as the hook-up network, where people only go to find the next best thing [20–22]. And while this is true for almost one-third of the participants, a little under two-thirds of the participants are looking for a steady relationship on Tinder. The aforementioned article by Sales [20] features various interviews with users of the app. It is correct that while more than half of the male participants of this study use Tinder to find partners for casual sex, it is still not the most common reason amongst them. That being said, 65% of women are interested in finding a steady relationship, yet this is only true for 47% of men. One has to keep in mind, though, that the survey was completed by a lot more women than men, and therefore these results may be due to a lack of data. The article by Sales [20] suggests that men are mostly interested in sex when using Tinder. "They all say they don't want to be in relationships" [20]. The present study suggests that while men do have a higher interest in casual sex than women, sex is neither their main nor their only motive. The picture of women on dating apps painted by the article is quite one-sided as well. Towards the end of the article a different opinion is given, which is closer to what the present study found as well. As Sales [20] writes: "'Women do exactly the same things guys do,' said Matt, 26, who works in a New York art gallery. 'I've had girls sleep with me off OkCupid and then just ghost me' – that is, disappear, in a digital sense, not returning texts. 'They play the game the exact same way'".

The most important sentence regarding the women's attitudes featured in this article is mentioned at the very beginning: "'Tinder sucks,' they say. But they don't stop swiping" [20]. This also perfectly summarizes the answer for the first research question: Most participants use Tinder out of boredom. Some are looking for casual sex; but not nearly as many as mainstream media portraits it to be. The majority are still interested in finding a steady relationship and use Tinder to do so.

Deci and Ryan [23] established "that integral to intrinsic motivation are [...] the needs for autonomy and competence." They also found that "choice and the acknowledgment of their internal perspective have been found to increase people's sense of autonomy, [...] positive feedback tends to affirm people's sense of effectance, thus satisfying their need for competence and enhancing their intrinsic motivation [...]." This shows two key aspects of Tinder and may be another clue as to why it is so successful. Users are presented with an abundance of choice, and even if they are limited by their lightly populated area, they can increase the displayed radius and will in turn receive more possible matches, thus giving them a lot of choices. By receiving

---

[9] https://www.younow.com/.

matches, which serves as positive feedback on their appearance or their profile in general, they feel validated, and their "competence" [23] in dating strengthens their intrinsic motivation.

4.2   Protectiveness of Data on Tinder

Truthfulness. The study shows that participants are mostly motivated to protect their name, with just under 30% of participants using a false name on Tinder. Following this, users are most protective of their location, which is a paradox given that Tinder is a location-based application. Farnden et al. [12] also found that they "were able to recover messages sent or received by the user." Since Farnden et al. [12] conducted their research, several new features have been added to the app, and the additional data collected through these features can likely be accessed as well. In her article in 'The Guardian', Duportail [24] shares which data specifically she received from Tinder, when invoking her right to retrieve the information. Duportail [24] writes: "Some 800 pages came back containing information such as my Facebook 'likes', links to where my Instagram photos would have been had I not previously deleted the associated account, my education, the age-rank of men I was interested in, how many Facebook friends I had, when and where every online conversation with every single one of my matches happened ... the list goes on."

When looking into the demographic data for these questions, it was interesting to see that participants from bigger cities and metropolitan areas are more truthful in their profile than those from less populated areas. It is important to note, though, that the number of participants for each category varied greatly, which is also the case when regarding sexual orientations. This is due to the fact, that especially for users whose sexual orientation is homosexual, other apps dominate the market.

Protectiveness of Data on Tinder. The two most common reasons for using false information on Tinder are privacy and personal safety for each aspect, except for age. This is in line with the research by Farnden et al. [12]: "It is also problematic that many users are not aware how much data is being sent, stored and what their data is being used for. Many users would not appreciate their privately shared images and conversations being seen by third parties that they had not consented to."

As an important note: With the current legal situation in the EU, Tinder is required to grant insight about the data stored to their users. "Every European citizen is allowed to do so under EU data protection law, yet very few actually do, according to Tinder" [24]. The fourth most picked reason for using false data by the participants was being afraid that their profile or chat will be used against them. Given that the information in a Tinder profile can be accessed easily by anyone, this fear is understandable. As blackmail is a threat in online dating apps [14], and Tinder users can provide information on their jobs, potential repercussions have to be considered.

Conclusion. To really assess what motivates users to protect their data is difficult. The participants showed protectiveness for their name and location, but not so much for their picture and age. The majority uses true information for all four aspects, which can result in issues caused through potential data breaches, or misuse of data from potential matches. The majority of those who use false information seem to be aware of the potential problems, which is why the most picked reason for providing false data is privacy. It has not been established though whether those who use their real names, ages, locations and pictures are not aware that Tinder stores this data or not, neither has it been confirmed that those who provide false information truly are aware of Tinder storing all their data.

4.3   Limitations

When considering the reasons of use, most demographic data showed interesting results. However, all groups that can be distinguished (male and female participants, different age groups, sexual orientations, population densities) were imbalanced in number of participants, which means that many of the findings need to be checked against more balanced groups of participants to reliably confirm the differences that were found.

It is not certain whether the participants who stated that they use a different name due to privacy reasons mean that they are scared that Tinder will be hacked or their data sold, or that they want to protect their private data from other users.

4.4   Future Research

Several interesting new aspects for future research came to light when analyzing the results. A variety of research papers and articles in the mainstream media discuss why Tinder is so popular, while painting the app in a poor light; in Nancy Sales' article in Vanityfair, one interviewee stated: "I call it the Dating Apocalypse" [20].[10] And even the most common reason for using Tinder given in this study, boredom, does not really explain Tinder's popularity. While other studies seem to have found reasons [16, 25], it has not been studied whether or not users actually enjoy the experience. Pages like tindernightmares[11] on Instagram suggest otherwise. Additionally it would be important to utilize some of the more recent models to study the behavior and motivation of Tinder users, such as the one created by Zimmer, Scheibe and Stock [26], who developed "a heuristic theoretical model for the scientific description, analysis and explanation of users' information behavior on [Social Live Streaming Services] in order to gain better understanding of the communication patterns in real-time social media." Even though Tinder is not a live streaming platform, the model might still be relevant, as "it is (with small changes) suitable for all kinds of social media" [26].

It would be interesting to see if the results are similar when the sample includes more participants who are more mature, male, homosexual or pansexual, or from suburban, exurban, and rural areas, in order to then compare it to the data gathered in this survey.

Another revealing aspect regarding the personal safety online would be to see which information the users find most important. At first one only sees the picture, name and age of a potential match. What do the participants feel when their match does not provide true information? A comparison between different dating apps could help

---

[10] Which influenced the title of the article: "Tinder and the Dawn of the 'Dating Apocalypse'".

[11] https://www.instagram.com/tindernightmares/?hl=de.

to gather more data on this when it comes to different sexual orientations. Also, are users aware of how much data Tinder stores and do they care? Is that what the participants who use false information in their profile due to privacy reasons want to prevent?

References

1. Valkenburg, P.M., Peter, J.: Who visits online dating sites? Exploring some characteristics of online daters. CyberPsychol. Behav. **10**(6), 849–852 (2007). https://doi.org/10.1089/cpb. 2007.9941
2. Bilton, N.: Tinder, the fast-growing dating app, taps an age-old truth. New York Times. https://www.nytimes.com/2014/10/30/fashion/tinder-the-fast-growing-dating-app-taps-an-age-old-truth.html?referrer=&_r=0. Accessed 15 Sept 2018
3. Koch, M., Ott, F., Oertelt, S.: Gamification von business software - Steigerung von motivation und partizipation. http://d-nb.info/1046737929/34. Accessed 20 Jan 2017
4. Deci, E.L., Ryan, R.M.: The "What" and "Why" of goal pursuits: human needs and the self-determination of behavior. Psychol. Inq. **11**(4), 227–268 (2000). https://doi.org/10.1207/S15327965PLI1104_01
5. McQuail, D.: Mass Communication Theory. SAGE, London (1983)
6. Fitzpatrick, C., Birnholtz, J., Brubaker, J.R.: Social and personal disclosure in a location-based real time dating app. In: 2015 48th Hawaii International Conference on System Sciences (HICSS), pp. 1983–1992. IEEE (2015)
7. Eichenberg, C., Huss, J., Küsel, C.: From online dating to online divorce: an overview of couple and family relationships shaped through digital. Contemp. Fam. Ther. **39**(4), 249–260 (2017). https://doi.org/10.1007/s10591-017-9434-x
8. Enomoto, C., Noor, S., Widner, B.: Is social media to blame for the sharp rise in STDs? Soc. Sci. **6**(3), 78 (2017). https://doi.org/10.3390/socsci6030078
9. Landovitz, R.J., et al.: Epidemiology, sexual risk behavior, and HIV prevention practices of men who have sex with men using Grindr in Los Angeles. California. J. Urban Health **90**(4), 729–739 (2013). https://doi.org/10.1007/s11524-012-9766-7
10. Blackwell, C., Birnholtz, J., Abbot, C.: Seeing and being seen: co-situation and impression formation using Grindr, a location-aware gay dating app. New Media Soc. **17**(7), 1117–1136 (2015). https://doi.org/10.1177/1461444814521595
11. Lemke, R., Merz, S.: The prevalence and gratification of nude self-presentation of men who have sex with men in online-dating environments: attracting attention, empowerment, and self-verification. Cyberpsychol. Behav. Soc. Networking **21**(1), 16–24 (2018). https://doi.org/10.1089/cyber.2016.0691
12. Farnden, J., Martini, B., Choo, K.K.: Privacy risks in mobile dating apps. In: Proceedings of 21st Americas Conference on Information Systems (AMCIS 2015). Association for Information Systems (2015)
13. Murphy, A.: Dating dangerously: risks lurking within mobile dating apps. Catholic Univ. J. Law Technol. **26**(1), 7 (2018)
14. The Telegraph. https://www.telegraph.co.uk/news/2016/03/16/crimes-linked-to-tinder-and-grindr-increase-seven-fold/. Accessed 06 Sept 2018
15. Ellison, N.B., Hancock, J.T., Toma, C.L.: Profile as promise: A framework for conceptualizing veracity in online dating self-presentations. New Media Soc. **14**(1), 45–62 (2012). https://doi.org/10.1177/1461444811410395

16. Sumter, S.R., Vandenbosch, L., Ligtenberg, L.: Love me Tinder: Untangling emerging adults' motivations for using the dating application Tinder. Telematics Inform. **34**(1), 67–78 (2017). https://doi.org/10.1016/j.tele.2016.04.009

17. Timmermans, E., De Caluwé, E.: Development and validation of the Tinder motives scale (TMS). Comput. Hum. Behav. **70**, 341–350 (2017). https://doi.org/10.1016/j.chb.2017.01. 028

18. Smith, A., Duggan, M.: Online dating & relationships. Pew Research Center. http://www. pewinternet.org/2013/10/21/online-dating-relationships/. Accessed 06 Sept 2018

19. Friedländer, M.B.: Streamer motives and user-generated content on social live-streaming services. J. Inf. Sci. Theory Pract. **5**(1), 65–84 (2017). https://doi.org/10.1633/JISTaP.2017. 5.1.5

20. Sales, N.J.: Tinder and the dawn of the "dating apocalypse". Vanityfair. https://www. vanityfair.com/culture/2015/08/tinder-hook-up-culture-end-of-dating. Accessed 12 Sept 2018

21. Kivanc, J.: Why young women on Tinder have 'no hook-ups' in their bios. VICE. https:// www.vice.com/sv/article/8ge4kz/we-asked-young-women-who-do-no-hookup-tinder-about-why-they-do-it. Accessed 12 Sept 2018

22. Jones, A.: Hookups, sexting and unwanted threesomes: first-time dating in the age of Tinder. The Guardian. https://www.theguardian.com/lifeandstyle/2017/nov/04/hookups-sexting-unwanted-threesomes-first-time-dating-age-tinder. Accessed 12 Sept 2018

23. Deci, E.L., Ryan, R.M.: Self-determination theory. In: Wright, J.D. (ed.) International Encyclopedia of the Social & Behavioral Sciences, 2nd edn, pp. 486–491. Elsevier, Amsterdam (2015). https://doi.org/10.1016/B978-0-08-097086-8.26036-4

24. Duportail, J.: I asked Tinder for my data. It sent me 800 pages of my deepest darkest secrets. The Guardian. https://www.theguardian.com/technology/2017/sep/26/tinder-personal-data-dating-app-messages-hacked-sold. Accessed 13 Sept 2018

25. Aretz, W.: Match me if you can: Eine explorative Studie zur Beschreibung der Nutzung von Tinder. J. Bus. Media Psychol. **6**(1), 41–51 (2015)

26. Zimmer, F., Scheibe, K., Stock, W.G.: A model for information behavior research on social live streaming services (SLSSs). In: Meiselwitz, G. (ed.) SCSM 2018. LNCS, vol. 10914, pp. 429–448. Springer, Cham (2018). https://doi.org/10.1007/978-3-319-91485-5_33

An Empirical Analysis of Rumor Detection on Microblogs with Recurrent Neural Networks

Margarita Bugueño[1], Gabriel Sepulveda[2], and Marcelo Mendoza[1(✉)]

[1] Departamento de Informática, Instituto Milenio Fundamentos de los Datos,
Universidad Técnica Federico Santa María, Santiago, Chile
margarita.bugueno.13@sansano.usm.cl, mmendoza@inf.utfsm.cl
[2] Departamento de Ciencia de la Computación,
Pontificia Universidad Católica de Chile, Santiago, Chile
grsepulveda@uc.cl

Abstract. The popularity of microblogging websites makes them important for information dissemination. The diffusion of large volumes of fake or unverified information could emerge and spread producing damage. Due to the ever-increasing volume of data and the nature of complex diffusion, automatic rumor detection is a very challenging task. Supervised classification and other approaches have been widely used to identify rumors in social media posts. However, despite achieving competitive results, only a few studies have delved into the nature of the problem itself in order to identify key empirical factors that allow defining both the baseline models and their performance. In this work, we learn discriminative features from tweets content and propagation trees by following their sequential propagation structure. To do this we study the performance of a number of architectures based on recursive neural networks conditioning for rumor detection. In addition, to ingest tweets into each network, we study the effect of two different word embeddings schemes: Glove and Google news skip-grams. Results on the *Twitter16* dataset show that model performance depends on many empirical factors and that some specific experimental configurations consistently drive to better results.

Keywords: Rumor detection · Propagation trees · Empirical factors

1 Introduction

A rumor, according to Allport and Postman [3], involves the communication of information that has not been confirmed by a reliable source. More specifically, it is a proposition or belief, passed along from person to person, usually by word of mouth, without secure standards of evidence. Our society is a structure in which the dissemination of messages is often convoluted and uncontrollable. This circulation of information produces twisted facts which, depending on the

© Springer Nature Switzerland AG 2019
G. Meiselwitz (Ed.): HCII 2019, LNCS 11578, pp. 293–310, 2019.
https://doi.org/10.1007/978-3-030-21902-4_21

parties involved, may have a protean impact on the significance a human being places on information.

Currently, the popularity of microblogging websites and social networks makes them important for information dissemination where millions of users could spontaneously post messages to release news or share opinions about various information everyday. The diffusion of large volumes of fake or unverified information could emerge and spread producing enormous damage to social stability such as occurred during the 2016 U.S. presidential election. Candidates and their supporters were actively involved on Facebook and Twitter to do campaigns and express their opinions. However, as many as 529 different rumor stories pertaining to presidential candidates Donald Trump and Hillary Clinton were propagated on social media during the election [2]. These rumors reached millions of voters via social network promptly and potentially influenced the election[1].

The scenario described above encourages the development of more effective methods for verifying the veracity of information on social media. The methods of automatic detection of rumors can be of great value. Rumor detection methods may provide early precautions on rumor's spread minimizing its negative influence. Nevertheless, this is a challenging task due to the ever-increasing volume of data and the complex nature of information diffusion.

A number of studies have faced the task of rumor detection in order to identify the veracity of the exposed news. These studies have covered a range of rumor detection variants as the binary case (rumors and non rumors) [4,11,24], and the fine-grained case that works using four classes (non-rumor, true rumor, false rumor and unverified) [14]. These works have been of great help, reaching competitive performances in the identification of rumors. However, only a few studies have explored the impact of empirical factors in performance. This is the reason why in the present work we discuss the impact of empirical factors in rumor detection performance, diving into the definition of an appropriate architecture and its variants. In addition, we will study the impact of data preprocessing techniques.

To compare the exposed variants, we conduct experiments on Twitter16 [14], a public dataset for rumor detection, showing that both the complexity of the models in terms of number of parameters, as well as the strategy used to ingest data in the network are key empirical factors to deal with this problem. Accordingly, the contributions of this paper are:

- To provide a better understanding of the impact of empirical factors in the detection of rumors, assessing the performance of different deep learning architectures as well as two word embeddings approaches (Glove and Google word2vec).
- To study the impact of data ingest in the learning process, i.e. how different data ingest strategies affect the performance in the detection of rumors.

---

[1] "Where Donald Trump got his real power" by Kara Alaimo, available at: https://edition.cnn.com/2016/11/15/opinions/social-media-facebook-twitter-trump-alaimo/index.html.

The paper is organized as follows. Section 2 presents related work. Section 3 discusses the data used in this study. Section 4 introduces our experimental methodology. Sections 5 and 6 show the models explored and empirical performance results, respectively. We discuss findings in Sect. 7. We conclude in Sect. 8 presenting our remarks and outlining future work.

2   Related Work

The first papers that addressed the problem of rumor detection did so using binary classifiers [4]. Whereas often a rumor begins with an unverified information, later it turns out to be true or false [24]. This is the reason why recent works consider this problem as a fine-grained classification problem. Currently, the problem of rumor detection is addressed using four classes: non-rumor, false rumor, true rumor and unverified [14].

Automatic rumor detection methods can be organized into three approaches: handcrafted features-based approaches, propagation-based approaches and deep learning-based approaches. Now we are going to describe each of these three approaches.

2.1   Handcrafted Features-Based Approaches

Despite the fact that the manual annotation of rumors has become feasible thanks to initiatives based on fact checking, manual labeling is labor intensive and expensive in time [12]. Due to the above, the methods of automatic detection of rumors have gained popularity in recent years. Within the main challenges faced by automatic methods of rumor detection it should be considered the unstructured, incomplete and noisy nature of social media data. Despite these difficulties, supervised classification has been widely used to detect rumors in social media.

The first works based on supervised learning for rumor detection made use of a wide range of handcrafted features retrieved from post contents, user profiles and propagation patterns [4]. Each rumor was characterized by constructing a feature vector. Then, different learning strategies based on feature vectors were studied. Support vector machines (SVM) showed good results in binary rumor detection tasks [5]. Other studies focused on the analysis of lexical features of posts. Using lexical expressions such as "not true", "unconfirmed" or "really?", Zhao et al. [23] showed that questioning and denying tweets are key data units for debunking rumors. The positions of the people in front of a given post has showed to be helpful in rumor detection. This specific task is known as stance detection [17].

2.2   Propagation-Based Approaches

Subsequently, further studies were conducted to detect rumors using temporal features. Kwon et al. [11] introduced time-series to explore how the volume of tweets over time behaves during rumor spreading. In the same line, Friggeri *et al.* [8] tracked the propagation of thousands of rumors appearing in Facebook to infer the rates at which rumors were uploaded and reshared. In [9], the authors examined the contexts and consequences of fact-checking interventions in the post stream. Ma *et al.* [13] studied the lifecycle of rumors using kernel-based methods modeling propagation patterns in social networks. Wu *et al.* [22] proposed a SVM classifier which combines a radial-basis function kernel and a random-walk-based graph kernel capturing complex propagation patterns of rumor detection in Sina Weibo.

2.3 Deep Learning-Based Approaches

Currently the most active approach in rumor detection is based on deep learning. Ma *et al.* [12] use recurrent neural networks (RNN) to detect rumors on sequences of tweets. The idea is to detect the veracity of a post from its sequence of related posts (retweets and comments of the original post). Sequence learning strategies as the ones based on long short-term memory (LSTM) and gated recurrent units (GRU) architectures are studied showing good performance in this task. In the same line, Rath *et al.* [20] use RNN sequence learning for the automatic detection of the users that more rumors spread.

Recently, Ma *et al.* [15] proposed a joint learning architecture for stance detection and rumor classification showing that both tasks can be used to improve the performance of each specific task. In [16], the authors used the propagation tree structure to train a recursive neural network model. Two learning approaches were explored named bottom-up and top-down ingest strategies.

This paper can be considered as an extension of [12], where sequential learning was studied for first time in rumor detection. In this work we focus the efforts on measuring and evaluating the impact of a number of empirical factors related to sequential learning considering architectural aspects of the models as also different data ingest strategies. In addition, we study for first time in this type of models how different word embeddings behave, as prior work was only based on bag-of-words (BOW) vector representations. We will show that some specific empirical configurations consistently drive to a better performance, showing that a deep discussion of empirical factors is crucial to provide a better understanding of the problem.

3   Data Description

3.1 Twitter16

For experimental evaluation, we use a publicly available Twitter dataset released by Ma *et al.* [14], named Twitter16. A previous version of the dataset was released for binary classification of rumor and non-rumor. The current version of the dataset, Twitter16, comprises a collection of wide spread tweets along with their propagation threads (i.e. replies, comments and retweets) provided as a tree structure. Each propagation tree is annotated into one of the four NTFU classes.

In this work, we removed the retweets from the trees since they do not provide any additional information. Moreover, we note that the proportion between tweets and retweets is highly unbalanced (almost 1 to 10). Then, to prevent over-fitting we provided only distinct tweets to each model.

Table 1 shows basic statistics of the dataset used in this study.

Table 1. Basic statistics of the dataset. As table shows, the number of claims (original tweets) is 818 but the interaction produced in each of them is important.

Statistic	Twitter16
# of users	173,487
# of original tweets (claims)	818
# of tweets (including RT)	348,646
# of RTs	317,499
# of threads	204,820
# distinct tweets (without RTs)	31,147
# of non-rumors	205
# of false rumors	205
# of true rumors	207
# of unverified rumors	201
Avg. # of posts/tree	251
Max # of posts/tree	2,765
Min # of posts/tree	81
Tree min depth	1
Tree max depth	18
Tree avg depth	5

3.2 Data Preprocessing

As social media data sources are unstructured, incomplete and noisy, we require a careful preprocessing procedure to ingest the data in a neural network. Most rumors are deliberately fabricated to confuse public opinion. Fake information is mixed and disguised in a rumor story. Then, it is very difficult for a machine to detect rumor patterns as they tend to be mixed with patterns of true news. In addition, rumors can cover all kinds of topics taking different language styles. This is the reason why algorithms trained on limited labeled data would probably fail detecting rumors on new unseen data.

It is a well-known fact that text preprocessing save space and computational time during the learning stage. In addition, text preprocessing prevents the ingest of noisy data, limiting the effect of artifacts during the learning process. Then, after text preprocessing, data becomes into a logical representation including the most representative and descriptive words.

The normalization procedure applied to the dataset is composed by the following steps:

○ Stopwords removal
○ Punctuation marks and digits removal
○ Transform to lowercase
○ IT jargon processing rules:
  • HTML marks are replaced by 'URL'
  • Replacement of '#word' with the term 'hashtag'
  • '@word' is replaced by the term 'username'
○ Text tokenization

4   Experimental Methodology

Since we will use propagation trees as training data and since our main objective is to study the performance of recurrent neural network models in rumor detection, we must transform the data according to the restrictions imposed by these models. Therefore, the main restriction with which we must work is to ingest the data in the form of a sequence.

As was mentioned by Castillo *et al.* [4], there are measurable differences in the way messages propagate that can be used to infer credibility. For this reason, we analyze the effects that are observed when applying two different approaches with respect to the strategy used to ingest the data during the learning process. One of these approaches, named time-based sequencing, corresponds to the serialization of the propagation trees with respect to the timestamp of each post in the tree. The second method corresponds to a graph traversal of the structure. Note that a graph traversal serialization of a tree breaks the temporal sequence. There are a number of alternatives for graph traversal. We study in-depth traversal strategies which we called branching-based sequencing. The idea behind branching-based sequencing is to ingest data according to the different threads triggered by the original claim.

4.1   Time-Based Sequencing

The first of the approaches corresponds to the transformation of the propagation trees into a sequence ordered by the timestamp of such posts. The proposal allows to serialize the structures which we have originally while it justify the use of recurrent neural networks. It should be noted that this order allows us to observe the order in which interactions occur with respect to the root but discarding the branching structure of the propagation tree. Figure 1 presents an example of serialization for a particular propagation tree using time-based sequencing.

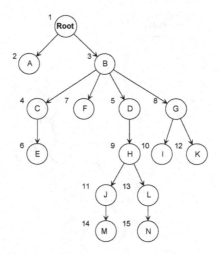

Fig. 1. Time-based sequencing. The alphabetical order of the nodes indicates the temporal order that they follow according to the timestamp of each post.

4.2   Branching-Based Sequencing

The second proposal corresponds to the serialization of propagation trees based on a graph traversal named branching-based sequencing. This strategy allows to show to the neural network the dependency between nodes keeping the order in which each message was disseminated within the network. When carrying out an in-depth traversal of the propagation trees, the partial branches of this tree are recovered and joined in a single great sequence. It should be noted that this new representation handle just one training example for each propagation tree.

Figure 2 presents an example of branching-based sequencing for a given propagation tree.

Regarding the flow of data within the proposed models, it should be noted that there are two levels of processing: the first corresponds to obtaining a vector representation for each post (tweet) determined from its characteristics, and the second level corresponds to the final classification model which will define the level of veracity of a publication.

For the first level of processing, we derive a dense vector representation for the tweets using word2vec vector embeddings, which are averaged producing Average Word Embeddings (AWE). AWE vectors has proven to be effective in document modeling [1]. In order to get these vectors, we studied two approaches:

o The freely-available word2vec word embedding Google News[2] which has a 300-dimensional vector embedding for 3 million words and phrases obtained using skip-grams. The phrases were obtained using a data-driven approach described in [18].

---

[2] https://drive.google.com/file/d/0B7XkCwpI5KDYNlNUTTlSS21pQmM.

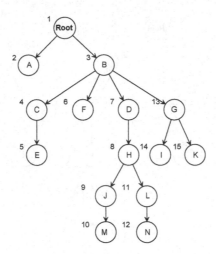

Fig. 2. Branching-based sequencing. The alphabetical order of the nodes indicates the order induced from the timestamps of each post.

○ Global Vectors for word representation (GloVe) [19] which used an unsupervised learning algorithm (Non Negative Matrix Factorization, NNMF) for obtaining vector representations of words. Training is performed at global level of aggregation using in this case a Twitter corpus. This approach produces 200-dimensional vectors from 27B tokens covering a vocabulary composed by 1.2M words[3].

Words that are not included in the pre-computed word embeddings (a.k.a. out-of-vocabulary words) were not considered in the AWE computing phase.

The second (and last) level of processing corresponds to the phase in charge of carrying out the training of the recurrent neural networks with the purpose of classifying seed posts (claims) based on its level of veracity, i.e. to predict the correct label among the four classes of veracity considered in this study (Non-rumor, True rumor, False rumor, and Unverified).

5   Model Definition

To face the challenge presented in this paper, we need a model that allows the classification of propagation trees, and that in turn, takes advantage of the sequential nature of interactions between users.

Based on these considerations, and aiming to establish a simple architecture that helps us to obtain reproducible results, we have defined a model based on recurrent neural networks (*RNNs*) for sequence analysis, plus a dense layer (softmax) to perform the classification stage.

---

[3] https://nlp.stanford.edu/projects/glove.

Our basic architecture is represented by the diagram in Fig. 3. In that diagram, the AWE embeddings of each tweet inside a propagation tree are represented by the vectors x_k. These embeddings are passed to the recurrent network as an input, according to a specific type of serialization. Once the last tweet of the sequence is ingested into the network, which is represented by the vector x_n, the output of the recurrent network (the hidden vector) feeds a dense neural network (feed-forward) composed by one layer and four neurons that implements a softmax classifier, which allow obtaining a probability distribution over each of the four possible classes.

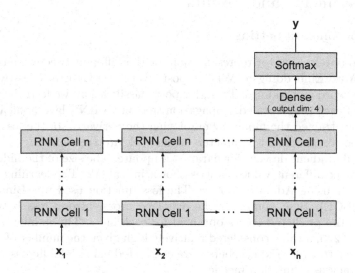

Fig. 3. Basic RNN architecture used in our study. The model considers n sequential layers.

To perform our experiments, we chose two variants for the cells considered in the architecture explained above: Long short-term memory cells (LSTM) [10] and gated recurrent unit cells (GRU) [6]. Both approaches have proven to be succesful in sequence modeling due to their ability to handle long sequences and due to its robustness against vanishing and exploding gradient problems. Therefore, we will study the impact of the number of layers (n-layers) and the size of the hidden vector in model performance. We summarize the explored variants in Table 2.

Table 2 shows that for each type of cell studied in this paper, we will evaluate architectures with one or two stacked layers. For each of these configurations, we will test 6 different hidden vector sizes. In summary, 24 distinct architectural configurations will be evaluated in this study.

Table 2. Selected parameters for sensitivity analysis

Cell type	Layers	Hidden units
LSTM	1	128, 256, 512, 1024, 2048, 3072
	2	128, 256, 512, 1024, 2048, 3072
GRU	1	128, 256, 512, 1024, 2048, 3072
	2	128, 256, 512, 1024, 2048, 3072

6   Experiments and Results

6.1   Experimental Settings

In order to obtain a vector representation for the different tweets, we computed Average Word Embeddings (AWE) at post-level using Google News (word2vec) and GloVe word embeddings. Then, for post classification, we feed the sequence of tweets of each preprocessed propagation tree into a RNN layer, one at-a-time, and then we trained the model by employing the derivative of the loss function with respect to the model parameters using back propagation.

We used gradient descent for parameter update. The size of the hidden units varies into six different values as it is shown in Table 2. The learning rate was set at 0.0001 using Adam optimizer. The loss function used was Binary Cross Entropy (BCE). BCE computes the averaged cross-entropy loss between the target and the predicted scores obtained for each class. The number of epochs was fixed at 200, a value considered relatively high given the number of examples that we have to train. Experiments were conducted using 5-fold cross validation with accuracy as evaluation metric.

6.2   Results

Now we provide a detailed description and analysis of the experimental results for Twitter16 in the following two subsections. These subsections present the performance of two recurrent neural network architectures comparing our two sequencing methods using Google News and GloVe embedding techniques.

LSTM Models

The results obtained using LSTM-based models are presented in Tables 3 and 4 for one and two layers networks, respectively. Best results for each row (number of units of the RNN) are depicted using bold fonts. Best results for each column (word embedding) are depicted using stars.

Table 3 shows that as the number of hidden units increases, model performance also increases as the results depicted with stars show. For a fixed number of units, the results are varied, as the values depicted with bold fonts indicate. Differences between both data ingest strategies are small. In this configuration,

Table 3. Results obtained using a single-layer LSTM-based model.

| | Branching-based sequencing | | Time-based sequencing | |
| | Accuracy | | Accuracy | |
RNN units	Google news	GloVe Twitter	Google news	GloVe Twitter
128	0.4350	0.4339	0.4351	**0.4412**
256	**0.4485**	0.4388	0.4290	0.4302
512	0.4449	**0.4461**	0.4351	0.4400
1024	0.4596	**0.4644**	0.4633	0.4560
2048	0.4755*	0.4620	**0.4805**	0.4646
3072	0.4681	0.4877*	**0.4903***	0.4817*

Table 4. Results obtained using a two-layers LSTM-based model.

| | Branching-based sequencing | | Time-based sequencing | |
| | Accuracy | | Accuracy | |
RNN units	Google news	GloVe Twitter	Google news	GloVe Twitter
128	0.4436	0.4376	0.4204	**0.4559**
256	0.4474	**0.4805**	0.4547	0.4707
512	0.4755	0.5087	0.4927	**0.5233**
1024	0.5369*	**0.5454**	0.5245	0.5320
2048	0.5050	**0.5577**	0.5037	0.5356
3072	0.5332	**0.5698***	0.5455*	0.5466*

the best result is achieved using word2vec (Google news) with 3072 hidden units and a time-based sequencing strategy for data ingest.

When we use a two-layers LSTM-based model, as it is shown in Table 4, the results improve. In fact it should be note that the best result achieved for this configuration corresponds to a branching-based sequencing data ingest with AWE vectors built over Glove using 3072 hidden units, reaching an accuracy performance equal to 56%, almost 7% accuracy points over the best result achieved using a single-layer LSTM-based model. As in the case of single-layer models, the differences between both data ingest strategies are small.

We show in Figs. 4 and 5 accuracy and loss evolution along epochs for branching-based sequencing and time-based sequencing, respectively.

Figures 4 and 5 show a small gap between training and testing performance. A relevant variance can be observed around the epoch 150 for both models.

GRU Models

The results obtained using GRU-based models are presented in Tables 5 and 6 for one and two layers networks, respectively. These results show that, as was

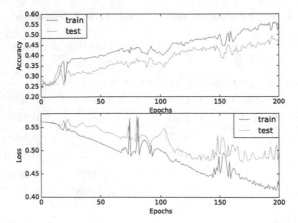

Fig. 4. Accuracy and loss evolution during training time for LSTM two-layers model using branching-based sequencing using 2048 hidden units.

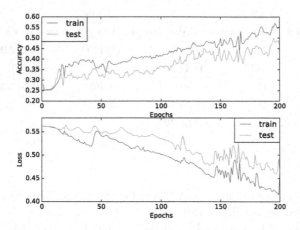

Fig. 5. Accuracy and loss evolution during training time for LSTM two-layers model using time-based sequencing using 2048 hidden units.

seen in the results achieved using LSTM models, the performance improves when the number of hidden units increases. Note that the single-layer model (with 128 hidden units) reaches an accuracy of only 45.23%, while more complex models as the ones built using 1024 or 2048 hidden units, reach results around 55%.

As in the case of LSTM-based models, models based on two layers perform better than models based on a single layer architecture. In fact, the best results using GRU models make use of Google word2vec embeddings and time-based sequencing, using a two-layers model with 2048 hidden units. The performance of this model reaches 67% accuracy points. Results obtained using GRU models show a difference in favor of time-based sequencing. In fact, the best result achieved using branching-based sequencing reaches 64% accuracy points, almost 3% accuracy points below the best result achieved using time-based sequencing.

We show in Figs. 6 and 7 accuracy and loss evolution along epochs for branching-based sequencing and time-based sequencing, respectively.

As in the case of LSTM-based models, Figs. 6 and 7 show a small gap between training and testing performance. However, in this case, the difference between training and testing curves is smaller than in the case of LSTM-based models. In addition, a significant variance can be observed around the epoch 180 for both models.

7 Discussion of Results

The experiments carried out in this work allow us to deepen both the performance of the models and the nature of the rumor detection problem with regard to three empirical factors:

Table 5. Results obtained using a single-layer GRU-based model.

| | Branching-based sequencing | | Time-based sequencing | |
| | Accuracy | | Accuracy | |
RNN units	Google news	GloVe Twitter	Google news	GloVe Twitter
128	0.4241	0.4265	**0.4523**	0.4290
256	**0.4866**	**0.4866**	0.4670	**0.4866**
512	**0.5160**	0.5159	0.4829	0.5037
1024	0.5209	0.5307*	**0.5564***	0.5539*
2048	0.5124	0.5196	0.5171	**0.5478**
3072	**0.5403***	0.4621	0.5208	0.5099

Results marked with * are the best per column. Bold fonts indicate the best results per row.

Table 6. Results obtained using a two-layers GRU-based model.

| | Branching-based sequencing | | Time-based sequencing | |
| | Accuracy | | Accuracy | |
RNN units	Google news	GloVe Twitter	Google news	GloVe Twitter
128	0.5049	0.5110	0.5135	**0.5209**
256	0.5723	0.5857	0.5589	**0.6103**
512	0.6041	**0.6042**	0.5919	0.5980
1024	**0.6434***	0.6054*	0.6250	0.6250*
2048	0.6323	0.5894	**0.6703***	0.6029
3072	**0.5884**	0.5724	0.5013	0.5724

Results marked with * are the best per column. Bold fonts indicate the best results per row.

Hidden Units

Regarding the number of hidden units that must be used, our results show that for an LSTM the best option is to use 3072 hidden units. The same observation arises when using a single-layer or a two-layers model because these neural networks are complex models that seek to extract information from a limited number of training examples. Accordingly, the most effective strategy for extracting information patterns from data was achieved using a high number of hidden units.

On the other hand, working with simpler models (e.g. GRU), as it is well known and discussed in previous work [7], allow us to face the problems of vanishing gradient and exploding gradient achieving much more stable models, avoiding the use a large number of hidden units or many epochs. This observation can be deduced from Tables 5 and 6, where the best results are reached by models that use 1024 hidden units (or 2048 units in specific cases).

Word Embeddings

As mentioned in previous sections, the embeddings used in this study have different dimensionalities. Google News corresponds to embeddings of high dimensionality resulting in a considerable amount of parameters to infer. Thus, for complex models, such as the two-layer LSTM, the use of Google News embeddings impose a huge amount of parameters to tune, and then due to the limited amount of training examples its performance is poor. On the other hand, the performance of GRU models (both one layer and two layers) are benefited by the use of a more enriched embedding technique since they have a high dimensionality.

Notice that the results obtained by making use of Glove Twitter embeddings do not move away significantly from the results reported using Google News

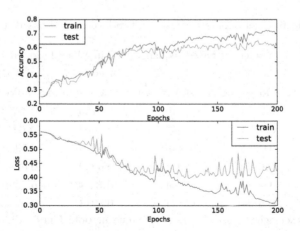

Fig. 6. Accuracy and loss evolution during training time for GRU two-layers model using branching-based sequencing using 2048 hidden units.

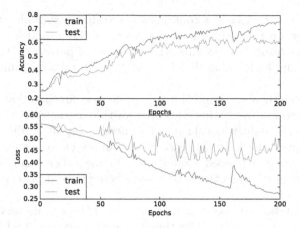

Fig. 7. Accuracy and loss evolution during training time for GRU two-layers model using time-based sequencing using 2048 hidden units.

vector embeddings. This representation has 100 extra attributes which could be a determinant factor when training our recurrent neural networks. Moreover, in some cases GloVe Twitter achieves better performance than Google's vectors, as can be seen in Table 4.

Sequencing Techniques

LSTM-based models have a great capacity to extract information from the data since they work over a high number of parameters. However, as the amount of examples showed to the network in this study is small, it is not possible to take advantage of all its capabilities. This is the reason why GRU models outperforms LSTM in this study. We note that time-based sequencing is a good choice when GRU models are used. The difference in performance between both data ingest strategies is very small in the case of LSTM-based models.

Which Model Is Better?

As the reader can see, this study explores an important number of experimental configurations. However, each representation and learner allows to exploit certain specific aspects of the problem. As was discussed in this section, time-based sequencing turns out to be the best option when training a LSTM neural network of a single layer with 1024, or higher, hidden units using Google News-based embeddings. On the other hand, branching-based sequencing appears as a good choice when the number of hidden units is lower than 1024. In the case of GloVe Twitter embeddings, no conclusive results were observed using single layer or two layers model variants.

As was mentioned above, these types of models have a large number of parameters to tune. Because of this, they operate at a fairly high level of complexity and given that the dataset just contains a few training examples, they are more prone to overfit. In this way, the performance of these models yields valuable but inconclusive results to recognize the existence of patterns. On the contrary, these models could be learning the observed data after a large number of epochs, as in our case.

Likewise, from the Figs. 4 and 5, it is possible to appreciate that both sequencing techniques exhibit overfitting. However, for the case of time-based sequencing the phenomenon is slightly less abrupt but it needs to apply regularization to deal with such inconveniences. In this case, the accuracy curve depicts more abrupt changes than branching-based sequencing. On the other hand, the loss curve depicts a low variance when time-based sequencing is used instead of branching-based sequencing.

A similar situation can be seen in Figs. 6 and 7. Once again we can appreciate a small overfitting but much milder than the one observed in LSTM-based models [21]. Therefore, time-based sequencing shows the best accuracy accompanied by a fairly low level of loss where it is possible to notice that after 200 epochs, the model continues to learn.

8   Conclusions

Currently, the popularity of microblogging websites and social networks makes them important for the dissemination of information. The dissemination of large volumes of false or unverified information could arise and spread, causing enormous damage. Because of this, several studies have faced the task of detecting rumors covering a wide range of variants of rumor detection. In the present work we discussed the impact of empirical factors on the performance of rumor detection. We studied the performance of a number of architectures based on recursive neural networks for the detection of rumors and we studied the effect of two different schemes: Glove and Google News. Experimental results show that the performance of the model depends on the number of model parameters, and depending on the sequencing technique used, different patterns will be recognized. We show that when the number of training samples is limited, the best option will be a GRU model using time-based sequencing over Google News embeddings.

It is clear that there is enough room for improvement in rumor detection methods. To better understand how deep learning helps rumor detection, more extensive experimentation is required since it has been shown that little changes in the models may produce important changes in performance, among them, the dimensionality of vectors embeddings. GloVe Twitter achieves similar performances to Google News vectors even though it has a considerably smaller dimensionality. Thus, experiments like these are proposed as future work regarding rumor detection.

Acknowledgements. Mr. Mendoza and Ms. Bugueño acknowledge funding from the Millennium Institute for Foundational Research on Data. Mr. Mendoza was partially funded by the project BASAL FB0821.

References

1. Adi, Y., Kermany, E., Belinkov, Y., Lavi, O., Goldberg, Y.: Fine-grained analysis of sentence embeddings using auxiliary prediction tasks. arXiv preprint arXiv:1608.04207 (2016)
2. Allcott, H., Gentzkow, M.: Social media and fake news in the 2016 election. J. Econ. Perspect. **31**(2), 211–36 (2017)
3. Allport, G.W., Postman, L.: The Psychology of Rumor. Henry Holt & Company, New York (1947)
4. Castillo, C., Mendoza, M., Poblete, B.: Information credibility on twitter. In: Proceedings of the 20th International Conference on World Wide Web, pp. 675–684. ACM (2011)
5. Castillo, C., Mendoza, M., Poblete, B.: Predicting information credibility in time-sensitive social media. Internet Res. **23**(5), 560–588 (2013)
6. Cho, K., et al.: Learning phrase representations using RNN encoder-decoder for statistical machine translation. In: Proceedings of the 2014 Conference on Empirical Methods in Natural Language Processing (EMNLP), pp. 1724–1734, Doha, Qatar, October 2014. Association for Computational Linguistics (2014)
7. Chung, J., Gulcehre, C., Cho, K., Bengio, Y.: Empirical evaluation of gated recurrent neural networks on sequence modeling. arXiv preprint arXiv:1412.3555 (2014)
8. Friggeri, A., Adamic, L.A., Eckles, D., Cheng, J.: Rumor cascades. In: ICWSM (2014)
9. Hannak, A., Margolin, D., Keegan, B., Weber, I.: Get back! you don't know me like that: the social mediation of fact checking interventions in twitter conversations. In: ICWSM (2014)
10. Hochreiter, S., Schmidhuber, J.: Long short-term memory. Neural Comput. **9**(8), 1735–1780 (1997)
11. Kwon, S., Cha, M., Jung, K., Chen, W., Wang, Y.: Prominent features of rumor propagation in online social media. In: 2013 IEEE 13th International Conference on Data Mining, pp. 1103–1108. IEEE (2013)
12. Ma, J., et al.: Detecting rumors from microblogs with recurrent neural networks. In: IJCAI, pp. 3818–3824 (2016)
13. Ma, J., Gao, W., Wei, Z., Lu, Y., Wong, K.-F.: Detect rumors using time series of social context information on microblogging websites. In: Proceedings of the 24th ACM International on Conference on Information and Knowledge Management, pp. 1751–1754. ACM (2015)
14. Ma, J., Gao, W., Wong, K.-F.: Detect rumors in microblog posts using propagation structure via kernel learning. In: Proceedings of the 55th Annual Meeting of the Association for Computational Linguistics (Volume 1: Long Papers), vol. 1, pp. 708–717 (2017)
15. Ma, J., Gao, W., Wong, K.-F.: Detect rumor and stance jointly by neural multi-task learning. In: Companion of the Web Conference 2018, pp. 585–593. International World Wide Web Conferences Steering Committee (2018)
16. Ma, J., Gao, W., Wong, K.-F.: Rumor detection on twitter with tree-structured recursive neural networks. In: Proceedings of the 56th Annual Meeting of the Association for Computational Linguistics (Volume 1: Long Papers), vol. 1, pp. 1980–1989 (2018)
17. Mendoza, M., Poblete, B., Castillo, C.: Twitter under crisis: can we trust what we RT? In: Proceedings of the 1st Workshop on Social Network Mining and Analysis, SOMA, Wshington, USA, 2010, pp. 71–79 (2010)

18. Mikolov, T., Sutskever, I., Chen, K., Corrado, G.S., Dean, J.: Distributed representations of words and phrases and their compositionality. In: Advances in Neural Information Processing Systems, pp. 3111–3119 (2013)
19. Pennington, J., Socher, R., Manning, C.: Glove: Global vectors for word representation. In: Proceedings of the 2014 Conference on Empirical Methods in Natural Language Processing (EMNLP), pp. 1532–1543 (2014)
20. Rath, B., Gao, W., Ma, J., Srivastava, J.: From retweet to believability: utilizing trust to identify rumor spreaders on Twitter. In: Proceedings of the 2017 IEEE/ACM International Conference on Advances in Social Networks Analysis and Mining 2017, pp. 179–186. ACM (2017)
21. Tang, Z., Shi, Y., Wang, D., Feng, Y., Zhang, S.: Memory visualization for gated recurrent neural networks in speech recognition. In: 2017 IEEE International Conference on Acoustics, Speech and Signal Processing (ICASSP), pp. 2736–2740. IEEE (2017)
22. Wu, K., Yang, S., Zhu, K.Q.: False rumors detection on sina weibo by propagation structures. In: 2015 IEEE 31st International Conference on Data Engineering (ICDE), pp. 651–662. IEEE (2015)
23. Zhao, Z., Resnick, P., Mei, Q.: Enquiring minds: early detection of rumors in social media from enquiry posts. In: Proceedings of the 24th International Conference on World Wide Web, pp. 1395–1405. International World Wide Web Conferences Steering Committee (2015)
24. Zubiaga, A., Liakata, M., Procter, R., Hoi, G.W.S., Tolmie, P.: Analysing how people orient to and spread rumours in social media by looking at conversational threads. PloS one 11(3), e0150989 (2016)

Detection of Bots and Cyborgs in Twitter: A Study on the Chilean Presidential Election in 2017

Samara Castillo[1], Héctor Allende-Cid[1(✉)], Wenceslao Palma[1], Rodrigo Alfaro[1],
Heitor S. Ramos[4], Cristian Gonzalez[2], Claudio Elortegui[3],
and Pedro Santander[3]

[1] Escuela de Ingeniería en Informática,
Pontificia Universidad Católica de Valparaíso, Valparaiso, Chile
hector.allende@pucv.cl
[2] Instituto de Ciencias del Lenguaje y Literatura,
Pontificia Universidad Católica de Valparaíso, Valparaiso, Chile
[3] Escuela de Periodismo,
Pontificia Universidad Católica de Valparaíso, Valparaiso, Chile
[4] Instituto de Computação, Universidade Federal de Alagoas, Maceio, Brazil

Abstract. The increase of content in social networks, and specially its use in the political environment, has led to the creation and proliferation of autonomous entities commonly known as bots. Bots are programs that performs an automated task over the internet. In this study these entities were initially detected based on a manual analysis carried out on the activity produced by electoral candidates in Chile during the presidential election in year 2017. As a result of this, the need to identify these accounts in an automatic way arose, in order to asses the impact of these accounts in the social network activity during the presidential election in 2017. Various features were extracted in order to train Machine Learning algorithms for the automatic classification task using a set of publicly available data, and other semi-automatic approaches. The models obtain over 80% in the training stage, but less than 60% in the testing stage, thus encouraging us to continue to work in other types of representations and models in order to improve the results.

Keywords: Bots · Machine learning · Twitter · Social networks

1 Introduction

Social networks have become an increasingly important tool when it comes to the communication and interaction between users. Even more, when companies and political parties, take advantage of this media to interact and transmit thousands (even millions) of messages in very short periods of time. The main issue in question arises, when the sender of the message is not an "ordinary" person, but an automated and/or false account. The so-called "social" bots (in

© Springer Nature Switzerland AG 2019
G. Meiselwitz (Ed.): HCII 2019, LNCS 11578, pp. 311–323, 2019.
https://doi.org/10.1007/978-3-030-21902-4_22

Twitter) are accounts controlled by software that can generate content (Tweets) and establish interactions (RT, Likes, Follows) algorithmically without (or minimum) intervention of humans. These entities can be used in different ways, on the one hand, they can be used for the dissemination of news and publications or the coordination of volunteers for activities; and on the other hand, they can be used to emulate human behavior in a negative way, in order to increase the political support that a candidate/party can receive [20]. It is also possible that these bots can contaminate the discussion that occurs in the network by granting false credibility to their messages and influencing other users [1,10]. During the investigation carried out by Deep PUCV, consisting of a predictive model of electoral results [18], which is based on the communicative interaction of users in social networks applying computational intelligence techniques and Big Data, that it was discovered that some messages were repeated among different users at the same time stamp, which led to the suspicion of bots and/or cyborgs. From this, arose the need to detect those false accounts (bots) related to the candidates who applied for the Chilean presidential office, in order to automatically identify them during the course of the campaign period. In order to develop this research, we based our work on [22], which provided Machine Learning methodology, to identify certain characteristics that reveal whether an account is a bot or not. In this paper, at first we show the results of some manual analysis of bot detection, and then we propose to automatically detect this accounts by means of an automated way by using a heterogeneous representation of the accounts and machine learning classification models. The structure of the paper is as follows: In the next section, we present related work and an analysis of the social activity regarding years 2017 election year in Chile. In the following section we present the dataset and the proposed methodology. In Section 4 we show the results of the experiments carried out with several machine learning classification models. In the last section we present some concluding remarks and delineate future work.

2   Related Work and Forensic Analysis of Social Media Events in Chile 2017

In the last years the computing community has been developing complex and advanced techniques to detect social bots in an accurate way. According to [14] it is possible to classify the approaches into three classes: (1) bot detection systems based on the social network topology, (2) systems based on feature-based machine learning methods and (3) systems based on crowdsourcing on user posts and profile analysis.

- Structure-Based (Social Network-Based) Bot Detection
  Sybil accounts are the multiple accounts controlled by an malicious user [8]. Structure-based detection techniques focus on detecting Sybil accounts. These accounts are used to infiltrate Social Networks, steal private data, disseminate misinformation and malware. That is why, Sybil attacks are a fundamental

threat for social networks [9,11,16]. For instance, it was reported in 2015 that around 170 million fake Facebook accounts were Sybil accounts [17]. Whereas this type of bots can be generated intentionally by users for benign purposes such as preserving anonymity; they are mainly considered as malicious. Knowing how Sybil accounts spread on the network is crucial to identify them specially for this type of detection techniques.

– Machine Learning-Based Bot Detection
The more sophisticated social bots are (with Artificial Intelligence (AI)), the more risk they pose. That is why, detecting them has become a difficult challenge. The rise of AI leads has increased the sophistication but also the techniques to detect them. The main idea behind them is to find out key features of social bots to find the patterns that differentiate the bots with humans. Chu et al. [5] carried out a study in order to profile human, bot, and cyborgs. They characterized the difference among them in terms of tweet content, tweeting behaviour, and account properties like external URL ratio. Lee et al. [19] present a study for social honeypots for profiling and filtering of content polluters in social media by using their profile features.

– CrowdSourcing-Based Bot Detection
Wang et al. [23] proposed a new approach of applying human effort (crowdsourcing) to the detection of bots. Their insight is that careful users can detect even slight inconsistencies in account profiles and posts. They propose a two-layered system containing filtering and crowdsourcing layer. They offer to use prior automation techniques such as community detection and network-based feature selection, and user reports in filtering layer to obtain suspicious profiles. Then, they apply crowdsourcing for final decision on classifying accounts either legitimate or bot.

During the three Chilean elections that took place in 2017 (primary, first and second presidential round), a total of 12 candidates were running for the presidential candidacy, from which, for the purposes of the present research, we worked with the data of the 8 candidates participating in the first presidential round. 2017 was a year of intense electoral activity and, consequently, a period of high use, of both traditional media and social networks among Chilean users and presidential candidates. That is why the traditional media events (television and radio interviews/debates) that occurred during the elections were used to analyze the activity on Twitter. Twitter is the most used social network in political campaign contexts to publicize their opinions and electoral preferences [4,13,15]. In this way it was possible to analyze and detect the activity of candidates running for the presidency.

As a first attempt to adopt an automated bot detection approach, a detailed analysis has been carried out before the two debates held on September 14 and 28, respectively, thus being able to obtain possible indicators of suspicious activity on social networks. From this analysis we observed, analyzing the debate of September 14, suspicious activities related to one candidate, which obtained a very high peak of participation in the hours of the debate, as shown in Fig. 1.

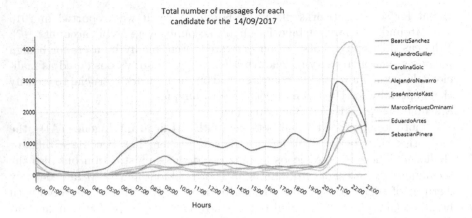

Fig. 1. Messages issued for each candidate on Twitter through September 14

One of the first indicators of possible suspicious activity of the accounts related to this candidate, corresponded to an unusual high activity regarding the mentions and retweets, compared to the other candidates, with the exception of Sebastián Piñera, who constantly generated more activity. During the previous moments of the debate, it is to be expected that the mentions to the candidates will increase. But the drastic increase in mentions for Ominami, who obtained his peak at 22:00 h, with 4172 messages (between 21:00 and 22:00), was a sign of abnormality. Moreover, the next day a peak of messages was again presented between 19:00 and 20:00 (Appearance of candidates Kast and Ominami on CNN [6]), with a total of 2710 messages, presenting the same message decline behavior for the later hours, as shown in Fig. 2.

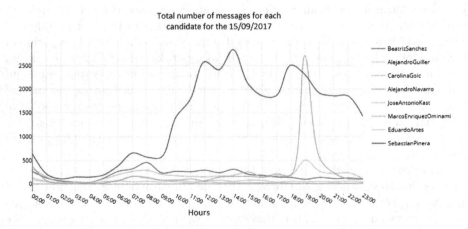

Fig. 2. Messages issued for each candidate on Twitter through September 15

Given the above, we proceeded to review the volume of original tweets versus retweets (RT) for each of the candidates, on the established dates and times, resulting in Ominami being one of the candidates with the lowest proportion of original tweets vs RT, with a ratio of 1/6.23 and 1/6.76 for days 14 and 15 respectively. In contrast to other candidates: Beatriz Sánchez with 1/2.02 and 1/2.53; José Antonio Kast with 1/3,35 and 1/3,77; Sebastián Piñera with 1/1.95 and 1/2.70; Alejandro Guillier with 1/4 and 1/2.08; and finally Carolina Goic with 1/2.46 and 1/2.58 respectively for the aforementioned dates, as seen in the following Fig. 3.

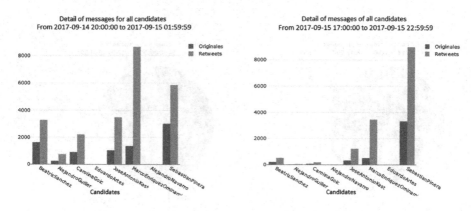

Fig. 3. Detail of Original messages versus RT for both dates

Another analysis, consists in monitoring the applications used to upload the messages, which indicate if there may be a certain level of automation in the generation of messages and simulation of behaviors. At this point, it was detected that the third most used application for Ominami corresponds to TweetDeck [21], which within all its characteristics, allows as a main function, the management of multiple accounts at the same time, being able to operate simultaneously and coordinate the actions of the accounts. Figures 4, 5 and 6 show the composition of the applications for the candidates at the dates and times described above, where the proportion of messages made through TweetDeck versus other applications for each candidate:

While most of the messages generated came from Android, followed by iPhone, it should be noted that for the day of the debate (September 14), Ominami presents a similar proportion between TwitterDeck and Iphone. Presenting situations in which suspicious behavior can be evidenced in different accounts, where two accounts perform RTs to the same tweets, in the same order and at similar times. We could find this behaviour in various accounts.

In the dates discussed before, the presence of bots and/or cyborgs was so evident, that several users noticed the situation. Despite having not appeared at the time in the interview, he was already generating a great number of positive tweets (Fig. 7).

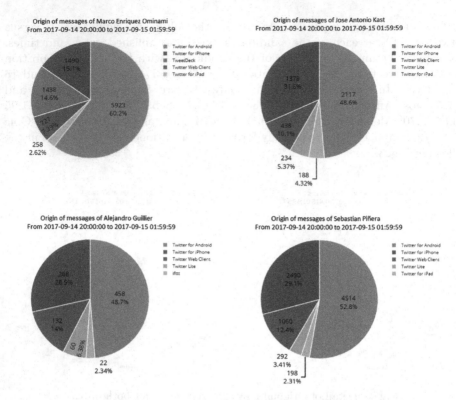

Fig. 4. Origins of the messages for the candidates Alejandro Guillier, Marco Enriquez Ominami, Jose Antonio Kast, Sebastián Piñera during the indicated days

One of the main reasons that made us suspect that Ominami is using bots to generate these behaviors, lies mainly in the use of the TweetDeck application. Although it allows the automation of certain tasks for several accounts, still requires a human user to perform these actions. So instead of defining all these accounts as bots, we will proceed to call them Cyborgs, which, unlike bots, work with a human which occupies computing tools and is no longer 100% autonomous. On the other hand, in the annex the graphs for the event of September 28 are shown, where a similar behavior occurs for Ominami.

2.1 Data Collection and Analysis

For the present study, 9, 367, 127 tweets were collected, from 372, 665 users, following three search criterias:

(a) Mention of a candidate's account.
(b) Mention of the name of the candidate.
(c) Mention of a hashtag related to an event of the candidates.

After the collection and storage procedure, we proceed to perform the tweet classification stage, carried out manually by 6 experts who tagged a total of

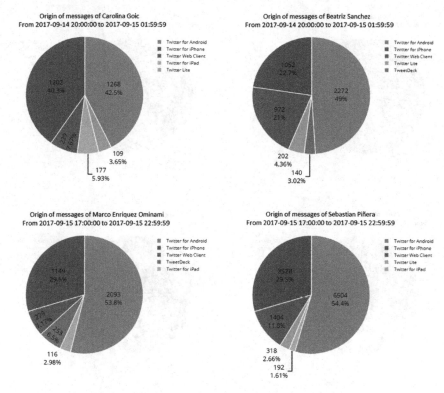

Fig. 5. Origins of the messages for the candidates Carolina Goic, Marco Enriquez Ominami, Beatriz Sánchez, Sebastián Piñera during the indicated days

640, 224 tweets in three sentiment categories (positive, neutral and negative). It was during this stage of manual classification that it was discovered that several tweets were repeated frequently between different users at the same time. The messages were identical, but they were not retweets. Consequently, the suspicion of possible false accounts arose, which led to creating a new tag, tagging them as bots or not bots, based on the messages, name of accounts, etc. In this manual tagging process we collected a total of 2472 bots accounts, which were used for the validation stage.

Regarding the repeated tweets between different users, 4091 tweets were found, from 3072 different users.

3 Automated Detection

For the automated detection of bots, we based our procedure on [22]. In said article the authors proposed the use of supervised automatic learning techniques for the automatic classification of bot accounts.

Regarding the characteristics of a user, data and metadata were extracted from the Twitter users, namely the number of followers and followings,

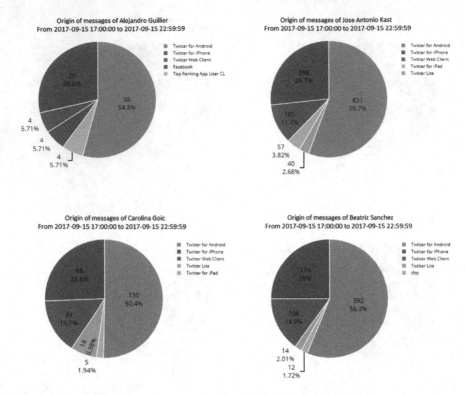

Fig. 6. Origins of the messages for the candidates Carolina Goic, Marco Enriquez Ominami, Beatriz Sánchez, Sebastián Piñera during the indicated days

publications (related to the primaries), date of creation of the account, number of tweets generated, number of favorites and others.

In order to train a model for the detection of bots, we trained the model with the results obtained with a known application called botometer [3] and samples of Twitter accounts that were detected manually.

In conjunction with the aforementioned, friendship relations and the flow of information among users showing behavioral of different nature were characterized: humans and bot. According to Varol [22]:

- Human beings tend to interact with more human accounts than bot ones, on average.
- The reciprocity of the bonds of friendship is greater among human beings.
- Some bots target more or less random users, others can choose targets based on their intentions.

3.1 Description of Extracted Characteristics

To perform the feature extraction process, we can establish 6 different groups:

Fig. 7. User noticing strange behavior on Twitter. "Tell the MEO bots, that he has not intervened yet"

- **Based on the user:** features corresponding to the user characteristics. With them it has been possible to classify the users and the patterns they possess. Among them you can find the number of friends and followers, description of the profile and configuration, number of tweets produced by users, among others. (20 features)
- **Friends Features:** on Twitter, interconnection is actively encouraged. Users are linked by follower-friend relationships (tracking). The content travels from person to person through retweets. In addition, tweets can be directed to specific users through mentions. So it has been considered four types of links: retweeting, mentions, retweeted, and being mentioned. For each group separately, features are extracted about the use of the language, local time, popularity, etc. Bearing in mind that, due to the Twitter API limits, we do not use follower/tracking information beyond these aggregated statistics. (9 features)
- **Network Features:** within a network structure, relevant information to characterize different types of communication can be obtained. Where the use of them, helps in the tasks of political astroturf. For this work, three different networks are recognized: Retweet networks, mentions and hashtag. (7 features)
- **Temporal characteristics:** Here several temporal characteristics related to user activity are measured, including the average rates of tweet production over several time periods and distributions of time intervals between events. (3 features)

- **Content and language features:** In this work the quality of tweets in terms of informal or deceptive language is not analyzed. Instead, certain statistics related to the length and entropy of the body of a tweet are extracted, identifying also the different categories of POS-tags (verbs, predicate, adjective, adverbs, etc.). (4 features)
- **Sentiment characteristics:** with the analysis of feeling you can get the emotions that the user transmits when publishing a tweet, with this it is possible to know the mood of a conversation and in this case the intention of support by part of a user towards a particular candidate. (18 features)

The total of features extracted from the users were 61. For the details of these features please refer to [22].

4   Experimental Results

Different Machine Learning classification algorithms were used to compare results, these correspond to Random Forest, AdaBoost (Gaussian Naive Bayes as weak learner), Decision Trees and Support Vector Machines. Each algorithm was trained with a quantity of 2241 users, dataset obtained through Botometer [3], of which 731 correspond to bots and 1510 to no bots, in terms of testing the data, an amount of 1078 users was tested, of which half were classified manually as bots and the other as non-bots. The results obtained during the training and testing stages are shown in the Tables 1 and 2. The parameters for the Random Forest Classifier were the following: number of estimators (5, 10, 50, 100, 200, 500, 1000), criteria (giny and entropy), maximum number of features (1–6) and maximum depth (1, 5, 10, 15, 20). In the case of the AdaBoost Classifier we trained with different number of weak learner (1, 5, 10, 50, 100, 200, 500, 1000, 2000, 3000), and Guassian Naive Bayes as a weak classifier. In the case of the Decision Tree classifier the parameters were the following: number of estimators (1, 5, 10, 50, 100, 200, 500, 1000, 2000, 3000), as splitting criteria (best and random), maximum depth (1, 5, 10, 15, 20), maximum number of features (1–6) and minimum number to split (0.0001, 0.001, 0.1, 0.2 and 0.5). In the case of the Support Vector Machines we used the following parameters: kernel (linear, polynomial, radial basis function, sigmoid) and degree (1, 3, 5, 10, 50, 100, 200, 500, 1000, 1500, 2000, 3000).

Table 1. Results obtained during the training stage

Algorithm	Accuracy	Precision	Recall	F1-score
Random Forest	0.83	0.83	0.83	0.83
AdaBoost	0.83	0.83	0.83	0.83
Decision Tree	0.82	0.82	0.82	0.82
Support Vector Machines	0.83	0.83	0.83	0.83

In Table 1 we can observe that all classifiers obtained similar results in the training stage. The experiments were carried out with 10 experimental runs, and Grid Search approach was used to find the best combination of parameters. The results shown are the average values of the experiments. Also, dimensionality reduction techniques were used in order improve the results, but the best results were obtained with the original features.

Table 2. Results obtained during the prediction stage

Algorithm	Accuracy	Precision	Recall	F1-score
Random Forest	0.55	0.57	0.55	0.52
AdaBoost	0.53	0.53	0.53	0.50
Decision Tree	0.53	0.54	0.53	0.50
Support Vector Machines	0.56	0.58	0.56	0.53

In Table 2 we can see the results of the testing stage. The best results in all performance measures were obtained with the Support Vector Machine model.

5   Conclusions and Future Work

The main objective of this research is the detection of bots, which correspond to accounts controlled by hybrid or automated methods that create content and interact with other accounts. In this work, different models of bots identification methods are presented, together with an Machine Learning-based method for automated detection. To carry it out, different characteristics of Twitter users are extracted through the Api provided by said social network, complementing it with the public dataset that has bots already identified on Twitter. From these data the different models are trained and the evaluation of their performance is obtained, obtaining an average training accuracy of 0.83. Although the testing results are not optimal (at best 0.58 accuracy), we will continue to work to improve the results and achieve greater precision, through a more complex Graph representation of the user network and its features. In this way it will be possible to detect new features that allow identifying a user as a bot or not bot, and adding these to the already defined models.

References

1. Aiello, L., Deplano, M., Schifanella, R., Ruffo, G.: People are strange when you're a stranger: impact and influence of bots on social networks. In: Proceedings 6th International AAAI Conference on Weblogs & Social Media (ICWSM) (2012)
2. Aparaschivei, P.A.: The use of new media in electoral campaigns: analysis on the use of blogs, Facebook, Twitter and YouTube in the 2009 Romanian presidential campaign. J. Media Res. 4(2), 39–60 (2011)

3. Botometer: Dataset: varol-2017. https://botometer.iuni.iu.edu/bot-repository/datasets.html

4. Ceron, A., Curini, L., Iacus, S.M., Porro, G.: Every Tweet counts? How sentiment analysis of social media can improve our knowledge of citizens' political preferences with an application to Italy and France'. New Media Soc. **16**(2), 340–58 (2014). http://journals.sagepub.com/doi/10.1177/1461444813480466

5. Chu, Z., Gianvecchio, S., Wang, H., Jajodia, S.: Detecting automation of twitter accounts: are you a human, bot, or cyborg? IEEE Trans. Dependable Secure Comput. **9**, 811–824 (2012)

6. CNN Chile. http://www.cnnchile.com/noticia/2017/09/15/. Accessed 27 Nov 2018

7. Escolar, L.D., Claes, F., Osteso López, J.M.: Audiencias Televisivas y Líderes de Opinión En Twitter. Caso de Estudio: El Barco. Estudios Sobre El Mensaje Periodístico **19**(1) (2013). http://revistas.ucm.es/index.php/ESMP/article/view/42526

8. Douceur, J.R.: The sybil attack. In: Druschel, P., Kaashoek, F., Rowstron, A. (eds.) IPTPS 2002. LNCS, vol. 2429, pp. 251–260. Springer, Heidelberg (2002). https://doi.org/10.1007/3-540-45748-8_24

9. Gong, N.Z., Frank, M., Mittal, P.: Sybilbelief: a semisupervised learning approach for structure-based sybil detection. IEEE Trans. Inf. Forensics Secur. **9**, 976–987 (2014)

10. Ferrara, E., Varol, O., Davis, C., Menczer, F., Flammini, A.: The rise of social bots. Commun. ACM **59**(7), 96–104 (2016)

11. Gao, P., Gong, N.Z., Kulkarni, S., Thomas, K., Mittal, P.: Sybilframe: a defense-in-depth framework for structurebased sybil detection. arXiv preprint arXiv:1503.02985 (2015)

12. Hansen, D.L., Shneiderman, B., Smith, M.A.: Analyzing Social Media Networks with NodeXL: Insights from a Connected World. Morgan Kaufmann, Los Altos (2010)

13. Jaidka, K., Ahmed, S., Skoric, M., Hilbert, M.: Predicting elections from Social Media: a three-country, three-method comparative study. Asian J. Commun. 1–21 (2018). https://www.tandfonline.com/doi/full/10.1080/01292986.2018.1453849

14. Karataş, A., Şahin, S.: A review on social bot detection techniques and research directions. In: ISCTurkey 10th International Information Security and Cryptology Conference, At Ankara, Turkey (2017)

15. Kreiss, D.: Seizing the moment: the presidential campaigns' use of twitter during the 2012 electoral cycle. New Media Soc. **18**(8), 1473–90 (2016)

16. Mulamba, D., Ray, I., Ray, I.: SybilRadar: a graph-structure based framework for sybil detection in on-line social networks. In: Hoepman, J.-H., Katzenbeisser, S. (eds.) SEC 2016. IAICT, vol. 471, pp. 179–193. Springer, Cham (2016). https://doi.org/10.1007/978-3-319-33630-5_13

17. Parsons, J.: Facebook's war continues against fake profiles and bots, 2015 September 12. http://www.huffingtonpost.com/james-parsons/facebookswar-continues-against-fake-profiles-andbots-b_6914282.html. Accessed 31 Jan 2019

18. Santander, P., Elórtegui, C., González, C., Allende-Cid, H., Palma, W.: Redes sociales, inteligencia computacional y predicción electoral: el caso de las primarias presidenciales de Chile 2017. Cuadernos. Info **41**, 41–56 (2017)

19. Lee, K., Eoff, B.D., Caverlee, J.: Seven months with the devils: a long-term study of content polluters on Twitter. In: ICWSM (2011)

20. Ratkiewicz, J., Conover, M., Meiss, M., Goncalves, B., Flammini, A., Menczer, F.: Detecting and tracking political abuse in social media. In: 5th International Conference on Weblogs & Social Media, pp. 297–304 (2011)

21. TweetDeck. https://tweetdeck.twitter.com/. Accessed 27 Nov 2018
22. Varol, O., et al.: Online human-bot interactions: detection, estimation, and characterization. arXiv preprint arXiv:1703.03107 (2017)
23. Wang, G., Mohanlal, M., Wilson, C., Wang, X., Metzger, M., Zheng, H., et al.: Social turing tests: crowdsourcing sybil detection. arXiv preprint arXiv:1205.3856 (2012)

A Computational Model of Dynamic Group Formation on Social Media

Nick V. Flor[✉] ⬤ and Erin D. Maestas

University of New Mexico, Albuquerque, NM 87131, USA
{nickflor,emaestas00}@unm.edu

Abstract. We need process theories of how groups form dynamically on social media in response to news events. We perform an analytic ethnography of a case where groups formed on social media in response to incomplete news of an incident. The groups framed the incident in terms of existing narratives and called for action against those actors they perceived as the aggressors. Later, footage showed this framing to be inaccurate. Based on the analytic ethnography, we propose a computational model of how groups form in response to incomplete or inaccurate reports on social media.

Keywords: Dynamic group formation · Viral messages · Analytic ethnography

1 Introduction

We lack both process theories [1] and computational theories about how groups form dynamically on social media. A better understanding of this dynamic formation will allow developers of policy, information assurance, or security to better leverage the beneficial capabilities of such groups, or to design interventions that constrain the formation and activity of groups with detrimental capabilities.

To help us craft such a theory, we studied viral messages surrounding a contentious event on the social media platform Twitter known as the Covington Catholic controversy [2]. In this event, Twitter users widely distributed and criticized a picture of a high school student, wearing a red cap with President Trump's campaign slogan Make America Great Again ("MAGA"), who appeared to be smirking at an elder Native American man with a drum (refer to Fig. 2). Behind the smirking student was a large group of students many of whom were also wearing MAGA caps. Early tweets (postings) framed the students as disrespecting the Native American elder, and many users called for identifying the students, and also for punishing the students, their parents, and their school in various ways. This criticism continued for several days, until later investigation by the news media revealed that this early framing was incorrect and that much of the criticism was unwarranted [3].

What allowed this incorrect narrative to persist for several days? To help answer this question we performed an analytic ethnography of viral messages surrounding the Covington Catholic event on Twitter, with the goal of understanding the different kinds of groups spreading messages on Twitter and their dynamic formation. Distributed cognition [4] forms the theoretical foundation for this research.

© Springer Nature Switzerland AG 2019
G. Meiselwitz (Ed.): HCII 2019, LNCS 11578, pp. 324–335, 2019.
https://doi.org/10.1007/978-3-030-21902-4_23

2   Analytic Ethnography

Our specific analytic ethnography consisted of identifying and characterizing the top five to six shared postings (retweets) over a period of six hours that contained the hashtag #CovingtonCatholic. To triangulate our characterizations, we performed frequency analyses on the words, users, mentions, and hashtags, and then used word clouds to depict these frequencies.

2.1   Hour 2PM–3PM (18-Tweets)

Figure 1-left depicts the very first tweet our scraper returned that contained the hashtag #CovingtonCatholic by user @KaySch10. This tweet criticized the school's slogan and insulted a student, while hash tagging the state of Kentucky, and Kentucky Senator Mitch McConnell who serves as the Senate Majority Leader.

Fig. 1. The first tweet containing the hashtag #CovingtonCatholic (left), and an expanded view of the embedded tweet (right).

While this tweet did not have many shares, it contained an embedded quote ("quote-tweet"), requesting the identity of the student and berating the student as "a POS disrespectful MAGA loser that is gleefully bothering a Native American Student" (see Fig. 1-right), where MAGA is an acronym for President Trump's 2016 campaign slogan Make American Great Again, and where people who wear these hats are viewed as supporters of the President.

The quote-tweet was shared times 6,055 times, which represented 12.08% of @IndivisibleNet's followers. In turn, this quote-tweet contained itself a quote-tweet by user @2020fight (see Fig. 2-left), who identified the boy as a "MAGA loser gleefully bothering a Native American protestor".

This quote-tweet was retweeted 14,490 times, which represented 36% of @2020Fight's total followers. Finally, @2020Fight's tweet contained a reply thread that was shared 3,931 times, which represented 605% of @lulu_says2's followers (see Fig. 2-right). The reply thread reframes the situation from an individual bothering a Native American protester, to an entire mob displaying "ignorance, racism & disrespect" towards the Native American protestor (see Fig. 3).

Fig. 2. User @2020Fight's Quote Tweet (left), and the first reply in the response thread (right). (Color figure online)

Fig. 3. A portion of @lulu_says2's response thread

The reply thread also called for identifying the individuals in the picture, the school they were from and, lastly, who their chaperones were.

Thus, the very first tweet containing the hashtag #CovingtonCatholic, if you follow the quote-tweets and responses contained a complex set of emotions, information, intent, attribution, and requests for action, the latter calling for the identification of the minors, their chaperones, and the school they attended.

Figure 4 depicts a word cloud of the tweets, the participants, and the most viral tweet for the hours of 2PM–3PM UTC (Coordinated Universal Time). Our Twitter scraper collected 18 tweets during this time. The tweet word cloud suggested that users discussed topics including the participants going to the March for Life, the kids, and their chaperones. The most active user was @PiattPatti, and the most shared tweet was a threat to reevaluate a user's grandson going to the school, and a request for apologies and comments from @CovCathColonels—the school's Twitter account.

Fig. 4. Wordclouds of the tweets, the users, and the most viral tweet from 2–3 PM

2.2 Hour 3PM–4PM (182-Tweets)

By analyzing the top-5 tweets shared (retweets) during this time period, we can infer not only the topics discussed but how the topics were evolving relative to the previous hour (refer to Fig. 5). The top retweet by @KAZurcher provided a reason for the students being in DC, and as subtext blamed the chaperones for not supervising the students during the incident. The #2 retweet portrayed the school as anti-gay, and unlikely to discipline the students. The #3 retweet contained three calls to action: release the names of the students, make parent information public and, for colleges, to reject admission to the students. Retweet #4 noted that the topic had gone viral, embedding a tweet from an influencer (blue checkmark near their name) that linked to @2020Fight's tweet (see Fig. 2-left). Retweet #5 is the top tweet from the previous hour.

Fig. 5. Top-5 Retweets for the 3–4 PM time period, from left-to right, top-down.

Figure 6 depicts the word clouds for tweet words, users, mentions, and hashtags. The words and the hashtags suggest that the focus of the discussion for the 3PM–4PM h is on exposing the school, and Christian schools in general, as places where students learn to hate, and that there must be consequences for this behavior. The users who tweeted the most were @blinksup and @chileman55. The most mentioned users were @covcathcolonels, who the users were directing their outrage towards, and @2020fight who users were either retweeting or replying to.

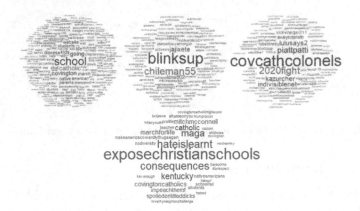

Fig. 6. Word clouds for words, users, mentions, and hashtags (3 pm–4 pm).

2.3   Hour 4PM–5PM (605 Tweets)

The top retweets for the 4PM–5PM time slot (see Fig. 7) indicated that users were discussing the mocking behavior of the boys towards the Native America elder (#1, #3), while questioning the school's ability to teach students higher values such as respect (#4–#6). User @PiattPatti contrasted the students' behavior towards the elder, with the same behavior towards a priest, asking users to imagine what would happen to the students if they behaved this way during mass.

Fig. 7. Top-5 Retweets for the 4–5 PM time period, from left-to right, top-down.

The word clouds (see Fig. 8) corroborate the top retweets, with the terms *school, boys, man,* and *elder* being in the top-tier of most frequent words, and in the second tier, *respected, veteran, ritual,* and *mass.* The most common hashtag was #ExposeChristianSchools, indicating topics similar to top retweets #4–#6 (Fig. 7) that suggest alleged hypocrisy in Christian schools.

Fig. 8. Word clouds for words, users, mentions, and hashtags (4 pm–5 pm).

The most active user was @cathypromotesu, with the previous timeslot's most active user, @blinksup, falling into the second tier of most active users. The main user mentioned was @CovCathColonels who users continued to direct their outrage towards, and @PiattPatti who had two of the top three retweets for this timeslot.

2.4 Hour 5PM–6PM (798 Tweets)

Four of the top six retweets from the 5PM–6PM timeslot (see Fig. 9) were repeats from previous timeslots, suggesting that some of the discussion was stabilizing around those topics. Retweet #4 labels the students racist and an embarrassment to the religion. Of particular note is retweet #5, which provides phone numbers to Covington Catholic High School, and to the area's diocese, as well as an e-mail and a physical address for the school:

RT @kyblueblood: Their school\nCovington Catholic High School\nPhone (859) 491-2247\nFax (859) 448-2242\n\nTheir diocese.\nCovington Catholic Diocese \nPhone: (859) 392-1500\nEmail: info@covdio.org\n1125 Madison Ave.\nCovington, KY 41011-3115\n#CovingtonCatholic — Top Retweet #5, Deleted.

[see text for #5]

Fig. 9. Top-6 Retweets for the 5–6PM time period, from left-to right, top-down.

Both the words cloud and the hashtags cloud, indicate the main topic focus was the school (see Fig. 10). The most mentioned user was once again @CovCathColonels, the school's social media account, with user PiattPatti—who had several top retweets—in the second tier. The user who spread the tweet with the phone and the contact numbers (@KyBlueBlood) was the most active user.

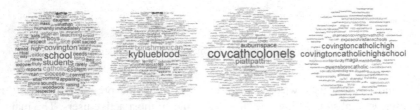

Fig. 10. Word clouds for words, users, mentions, and hashtags (5 pm–6 pm).

2.5   Hour 6PM–7PM (1315 Tweets)

The 6PM–7PM timeslot indicated a shift in main topic, where the top-retweet contained contact information for Covington Catholic High School and the Covington Diocese, including phone numbers, e-mails, and mail addresses. Three of the top-6 retweets were from the previous timeslot (#2, #5, #6), showing overlap in discussion. Retweet #3 described another activist group @LPJLeague that confronted the students at the rally. Finally, retweet #4 contained an embedded tweet of the Native American elder giving his account of what happened at the rally (Fig. 11).

Fig. 11. Top-6 Retweets for the 6 pm–7 pm time period, from left-to right, top-down.

The words cloud (see Fig. 12) aligned with the content of the top retweet. The most prominent word was Covington, with the phone numbers in the lower tiers suggesting the spread of these numbers to other users so that they could contact the school with their complaints. A new most-active user emerged, @AnitaThom57, with the previous most active-user falling into the second tier. Hashtags about Covington Catholic are the

Fig. 12. Word clouds for words, users, mentions, and hashtags (6 pm–7 pm)

most prominent in the hashtags cloud, but several "march" hashtags gained promi-
nence, specifically *MarchForLife* and *MarchForActualLives*.

2.6   Hour 7PM–8PM (1590 Tweets)

The first three most viral retweets were the same as the previous time slot. Retweet #5
had appeared in several timeslots in the past and re-emerged after not being in the top 5
in the previous time slot. Retweet #4 was a unique call to action from a Twitter
influencer, which suggested Covington Catholic teachers should be fired for not
watching their students (Fig. 13).

Fig. 13. Top-5 Retweets for the 7 pm–8 pm time period, from left-to right, top-down.

The words cloud again aligned with the top retweet, with *Covington School* in the
first tier of words, *859*, the area code of the school and the diocese in the second tier,
and the phone numbers in the later tiers. There was a new most active user, and
@CovCathColonels remained the most mentioned user (Fig. 14).

Of note in the hashtags cloud is the appearance of MAGA in the top-tier. While this
hashtag could signal the arrival of MAGA supporters in the discussion, an examination
of the tweets containing #MAGA show that non-MAGA supporters were using the
hashtag to criticize MAGA supporters (Fig. 15).

Fig. 14. Word clouds for words, users, mentions, and hashtags (7 pm–8 pm).

Fig. 15. A sample of critical Tweets containing #MAGA (7 pm–8 pm).

3 Towards a Computational Model

We summarize the results above using both a UML use case diagram and a UML communication diagram. First, we defined the different kinds of actors in the system, based mainly on: (a) the type of information posted; (b) the source of this information, which is largely inferred from the posting; (c) the target for the information, determined by mentions, hash tags, or posting content; and (d) any beliefs intended by the actor who posted the information. We refer to this as a *functional-intentional* categorization of actors.

3.1 Actors

Based on function and intention, we identified at least 9 different kinds of actors in our analytic ethnography. Given a news event consisting of people or groups in which a user can identify ideological allies or enemies, these actors are:

- Instigators—users who first comment on a news event, frame the event in terms of existing narratives, and include a unique hashtag for organizing further discussion of the event. An instigator can also provide links to more information about the event.
- Investigators—users who collect information on the web about the people or the groups in a news event, then post their findings along with any questions that arise during their investigations so that others can search for the answers. They may also post predictions about the behaviors of the people in the event based on their findings.
- Attributers—users who add specific information about people or groups in an event, as well as their actions at the event, intended to make self-identified allies in the

event appear more sympathetic, and to make enemies appear more immoral. They do so by confirming stereotypes about allies and enemies.

- Doxxers—users who post contact information about people or groups in an event who the user identifies as enemies.
- Punishers—users who post descriptions about the people in the event who should be punished, what their punishments should be, and who should execute the punishments.
- Confronters—users who send messages directly to the people or the groups at an event who they identify as enemies. Such messages include telling the people what they must do to atone for their actions; and demanding apologies or answers while mentioning potential consequences for actions.
- Debaters—users who post about the hypocrisy between a group's stated beliefs and their actions.
- Counterfactualists—users who post imaginary scenarios, typically to make immoralities in behaviors explicit.
- Eyewitnesses—users at the event who post their experiences.

3.2 Use-Case Analysis

Figure 16 depicts the nine different actors described previously, and their primary actions.

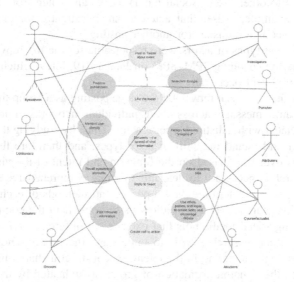

Fig. 16. Use case analysis for the nine actors.

3.3 Communication Diagram

Figure 17 depicts the communication diagram for the nine actors. Also included is an object for the event, which contains both ally and enemy objects.

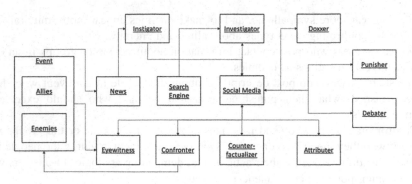

Fig. 17. Communication diagram.

4   Discussion

Based on an analytic ethnography, we identified nine distinct types of actors responsible for the volume of tweets surrounding the #CovingtonCatholic controversy on the
Twitter social media platform. The nine actors are: instigators, investigators, doxxers,
punishers, debaters, attributers, counterfactualizers, confronters, and eyewitnesses. We
based the actor categories on function—the type of information posted, the source of
the information, and the target for the information—as well as intent, viz., beliefs the
posting conveyed to other users. Social media users can switch from any of the nine
actor roles. For example, a user that acted as an investigator for one posting, may
switch roles and act as a punisher for another posting.

The nine different types of actors were responsible for the top retweeted messages
in the six-hour period spanning 2PM–8PM on January 19, 2019, which is the day after
the March for Life event occurred.

We can view the users that retweeted the same posting as a group that are all trying
to spread the same message across their individual networks. Furthermore, each
message is associated with a distinct type of actor. Thus, by studying the change in top
retweets, we can understand the shift in actor types, and therefore the dynamic formation of groups over time based on the function and intent of the viral messages.

Further research is necessary to determine a more comprehensive set of use cases
and set of actors, and to determine the properties and methods of each actor-object in
the communication diagram. This will allow us to implement the computation model,
perhaps developing social media bots that execute the different actor roles.

Another important research area is to understand the process through which the
community of users participating in the event, co-construct a shared understanding of
the event through the dynamic formation of groups as indicated by the shifts in actor
roles for the top shared messages over time. These shifts, and perhaps specific patterns
of shifts, can be viewed as an attempt by the community to construct a consistent and
defensible shared understanding of the individuals, the groups, and the behaviors
exhibited in the event.

Finally, an understanding of the dynamic formation of groups around specific messages may generalize and help us create sociotechnical systems for spreading scientific or technical information across social media.

Acknowledgments. This material is based partly upon work supported by the National Science Foundation (NSF) under CMMI–1635334. Any opinions, findings, and conclusions or recommendations expressed in this material are those of the author and do not necessarily reflect the views of the NSF.

References

1. Mohr, L.B.: Explaining Organizational Behavior. Jossey-Bass, New York (1982)
2. Miller, M.E.: Viral standoff between a tribal elder and a high schooler is more complicated than it first seemed. New York Times, 22 January 2019. https://www.washingtonpost.com/local/social-issues/picture-of-the-conflict-on-the-mall-comes-into-clearer-focus/2019/01/20/c078f092-1ceb-11e9-9145-3f74070bbdb9_story.html. Accessed 14 Feb 2019
3. Soave, R.: The media wildly mischaracterized that video of covington catholic students confronting a native american veteran. Reason, 20 January 2019. https://reason.com/blog/2019/01/20/covington-catholic-nathan-phillips-video. Accessed 14 Feb 2019
4. Hollan, J., Hutchins, E., Kirsh, D.: Distributed cognition: toward a new foundation for human-computer interaction research. ACM Trans. Comput.-Human Interact. **7**, 174–196 (2000)

Emojis in Textual-Based Communication Among College Students: A Study in Perception and Frequency

Hannah Kabir[✉] and David W. Marlow

University of South Carolina-Upstate, Spartanburg, SC 29303, USA
hkabir@email.uscupstate.edu, dmarlow@uscupstate.edu

Abstract. Emojis have revolutionized text-based communication as we know it as users employ this personal utility to add nuance and avoid miscommunication in inflectionless text. Emojis express a more diverse and deeper span of emotions than traditional text-based communication. This study will focus on frequency and perception of emojis in traditional-aged college students (ages 16–28). As a young and technologically heavy-user generation, who see themselves as drivers of personal technology trends, college students make a good population study in this area. This interdisciplinary study applies Linguistics to HCI to further technological advances in emoji development and maintenance.

Keywords: Emojis · Text-based communication · College students

1 Introduction

The advent of technology has brought with it a myriad of developments with one of the most notable advancements being the introduction of social media. Social media has been used over the past decade for a broad range of activities from communication through to the mobilization of masses for a cause. Communication has been streamlined to a point in which people rely heavily on their mobile phones for updates on everything. In order to keep the users interested in their services, developers introduced emojis to represent users' emotions. With emojis, one can be more expressive in the conveying what and how they feel through text-based communication.

The history of emojis dates to the end of the 20th century, with the first case of the emoji being integrated in Japan. Gradually social media companies integrated emoticons into their platforms with the main benefit being the rich set of a graphical representation of activities, animals, emotions addenda to other things (Hakami 2017). Emojis have become vital in helping the reader comprehend the message as traditional text messages are often misconstrued. Summations drawn from research demonstrate that nearly 15% of tweets analyzed from the year 2014 through to 2015 had emojis in them (Chen 2017).

The efficacy of emojis has been a subject of debate for Human-Computer Interaction specialists with most trying to decipher the sentiment lexicon that helps in determining which emojis users choose. Research by Hakami (2017) indicates that the use of emojis helps in the determination of the kind of mood or attitude. Additionally,

G. Meiselwitz (Ed.): HCII 2019, LNCS 11578, pp. 336–344, 2019.
https://doi.org/10.1007/978-3-030-21902-4_24

sentimental analysis has become key to understanding emojis with an influx in emoji usage leading the decrease in the use of abstruse short words like "lol" or "rofl" which hinder the process of human-computer interaction.

Furthermore, additional research by Hakami (2017) exploring the frequency of emoji use found that emojis account for at least 19.6% of messages transmitted over social media by 37.6% of social media users. These figures derive from a dataset comprised of 8,489 Twitter users with a reported 62.4% of users not implementing the use of emojis. Additionally, distribution statistics from Chen (2017) show that 2% of Twitter users employ emojis in nearly every tweet without an emoji while 5% insert emoticons in half tweets. Therefore, while emojis users are a minority of Twitter users, those who do use emojis tend to use them heavily.

From a global perspective, the emojis are used most frequently in Indonesia, where emojis accompanied tweets by Twitter users 46.5% of the time with South Africa having a comparable 36.7% usage rate. Comparatively, the United States, which developed pictograms has a higher percentile of 11%. Hakami's large dataset, covering multiple nations, clearly points to the cultural impact on user's inclination to use emojis. While this study focuses on the United States, we plan to extend the research to other nations in the near future, extending beyond Twitter to include culture-specific Platforms such as WeiBao in China.

2 Literature Review

Emoji are text-sized graphics used in digital, text-based communications platforms used on personal computers, tablets, and smartphones for text messaging, Facebook, Instagram, Twitter, etc. Furthermore, emojis can be found in the more traditional tools such as Microsoft Suite and email, providing options to include facial gestures, animals, objects, and a wide variety of other symbols and expressions in text. They are much like emoticons, however, emojis consist of pictures instead of typo-graphics. Japanese designer Shigetaka Kurita invented emojis in 1999 (Lebduska 2014) while working on the i-mode mobile internet platform of NTTDoCoMo (Blagdon 2013). The inspiration for the invention was symbols, which are used in weather forecasts, Chinese characters, as well as Manga street signs. Emojis gained significant popularity and were included in the Unicode system, with the Unicode consortium approving new sets of emoji, followed by Apple's support for emojis in their 2012 iOS 6 platforms. Now, emojis are strongly integrated into nearly every platform of today's communication spectrum.

It is important to also note that emojis have carved a niche into pop culture as well. In 2015, the Oxford Dictionary hailed emoji as the "word of the year." Emoji is currently considered the fastest growing language in the world. It is estimated that about 90% of the online population in the world tends to use emojis as they can convey irony, wit, joy, sarcasm, etc. They have evolved from flat images into 2D and 3D models and different forms which can include human faces and gifs. While there has been substantial evidence completed on emojis focusing on meanings and interpretations, our research takes a deeper and more comprehensive dive into perception and frequency of emoji use among college students—including attention to variation between females and males.

Stanford linguist, McWhorter (2013) observed that cell-phone contained, text-based communication was then emerging as a fingered speech in which abbreviated syntax, acronyms, and typographic replace traditional non-verbal communicative features such as tone and facial expression. As text-based communication technology has evolved, swipe keyboards, predictive text, and speech-to-text functionalities have lessened, to a degree, the struggles that early texters had with syntax and spelling. However, the need for aesthetic contributions to fingered speech remain—and so, the emoji appears likely to endure in text-based communication.

Previous research from Barron and Ling (2011) investigated the use of emoticons in electronically-mediated communication (EMC, which includes digital and computer-mediated communication, such as online chats) through analyzing adolescents' focus group data of text messages. New EMC tools, including emoticons and similar cues "lend an oral tone to the messages" and that approximate "intonation features or facial features" are comparable to face-to-face conversations (Baron and Ling 2011). The study suggests that using emojis and the like have a structure and purpose—to fulfill non-verbal and intonation gaps in digital communication.

Additionally, research regarding perceptions of the emoji in textual-based communication of female listeners from Kabir (2018) found that women use emojis in accordance with gender norms and cultural practices. Furthermore, this was an indication of how society maintains communication styles.

3 Methodology

To begin to understand the behavior and usage of emojis by college students in the United States, a simple cluster survey consisting of seventeen questions was distributed to ninety-one respondents. The survey was specific to frequency, usage, and perception and was unbiased as well as representative of the university. Based on the findings from the survey, we conducted open-ended interviews with two couples, one same-sex couple and one heterosexual couple and studied secondary data on the subject from various sources including websites and relevant research articles done in the past. The open-ended interview was conducted on two couples in a romantic relationship. Additionally, both couples are college students in the United States between the ages of 16–28 and both couples consented to research conducted on their usage and perception of emojis.

We were able broaden our understanding of how emojis are used in interpersonal communication and how emojis and text can vary within gender regarding relationship and age. Furthermore, by conducting the interviews we were able to get a better understanding of emojis as a universal language in terms of communication and how users (using textual-based communication methods) communicate more extensively and in greater detail based on context and relationship.

3.1   Analysis

Interview. From the open-ended interview, we found that the couples each communicated multiple times per day. Couple one (Respondent 1 and Respondent 2) estimated that they sent roughly 150 messages per day while couple 2 (Respondent 3 and Respondent 4) estimated that they sent roughly 200 messages per day. Each message consists of one "send," including at least a single word or an emoji. When asked whether they use emoji consistently with each other in textual-based messages, couple one comprised of Respondent 1 and Respondent 2 both mentioned that they did, and that "Emojis make it easier to understand each other and interact. It is easier to be clear with each other" (Respondent 1 and Respondent 2, personal communication, 2019). Additionally, couple two comprised of Respondent 3 and Respondent 4 mentioned that they also felt as though emoji created a clearer understanding of the intended messages. In terms of whether the couples felt that emojis should be considered a universal language, Respondent 4 was quick to agree to state that his "cousins in Japan were able to understand his meaning, even though he is not very good at Japanese as he is American" (Respondent 4, personal communication, 2019).

Additionally, both couples (Respondents 1–4, personal communication, 2019) all agreed that emoji are the language of technology and thus, should be considered a universal language in that emoji are easier to understand, even when the sender is not entirely sure of how to send a clear message. Furthermore, the listener or receiver of the message is less likely to misinterpret the intended meaning if they have a clearer picture of what is intended. Furthermore, Respondent 1 noted that he used emoji approximately every 1 in 3 textual-based messages, while Respondent 2 mentioned that he used emoji an estimated 1 in 5 times. When asked for their usage, Respondents 3 and four said that they used emoji an estimated 1 in 3 times (Respondents 1–4, personal communication, 2019).

The couples in the real-life examples confirm the findings in the Literature Review that they express and understand digital messages more clearly with emojis. If they added an emoji "facepalm" (Fig. 1) (Respondent 3, personal communication, 2019) then it would be interpreted as a possible sign of exasperation. Similarly, if they add the emoji "face with rolling eyes" (Fig. 2) (Respondent 4, personal communication, 2019) then it would be interpreted as sarcasm or annoyance. Without emojis, the receiver may not be able to interpret the text accurately and respond properly as well. An interesting aspect of perceiving emojis is how the structure evolves and varies through usage. Baron and Ling (2011) noted from their study that EMC visual images are "punctuations" that are not taught in formal schooling. Instead, users "work out patterns themselves or adopt the punctuation style of their interlocutors" (62). I can see this formation of punctuations that change and differ across digital channels and groups. For instance, one of the subjects used mostly the "smiling face with smiling eyes" with their parents, which implies that they (the respondent) was happy (Respondent 3, personal communication, 2019). Formalization in communication structure according to an audience is comparable to FTF (Face to Face) communication. Furthermore, different kinds of emoji use indicate creativity and variation in use. Wijeratene (2017) studied the similarity of emoji use and determined that many people use the same emojis when they want to convey specific meanings and/or feelings. The same trend was noticeable with real-life examples. One subject would use and receive numerous expressions of happiness, such as "beaming face with smiling eyes" and "tears of joy" from their friends, which are different than what is received from older family members (Respondent 3, personal communication, 2019). Emojis are live cues that can change alongside their users who drive their recognition and use.

Emoticons increased engagement and depth of conversations through boosting the interexchange of emotional experiences (Daud and McLellean 2016). Additionally, they react more emotionally when emojis are used, as if they could imagine the face of the other, and seeing these non-verbal expressions stimulated their emotional engagement (Respondent 2, personal communication, 2019). Anecdotal studies then illustrated how emojis could help increase participation and not necessarily simplify or make conversations less intimate (Participant 1, personal communication, 2019). The findings can be related to how college-aged students in the United States would perceive emojis with greater reaction as they mean something in regard to showing politeness and social connections. If they use emojis, it would suggest closeness and allows them to interpret sender intentions as accurately as possible for clearer, engaging EMC conversations and better relationship maintenance. As in, the more they used emojis, the more profound and extensive their conversations can become. Emoji use debunks the idea that chatting plus emojis is inferior to FTF conversations.

Since emojis enrich meaning and improve emotional interactions, the user interface is worth noting here since as previously mentioned, Stanford linguist McWhorter (2013) observed that cell-phone contained, text-based communication was then emerging as a fingered speech in which abbreviated syntax, acronyms, and typographic replace traditional non-verbal communicative features such as tone and facial expression. This makes it imperative to note that as text-based communication technology has evolved, swipe keyboards, predictive text, and speech-to-text functionalities have lessened, to a degree, the struggles that early texters had with syntax and spelling. Additionally, this has made the user interface of emojis much more simplified and user-friendly. However, the need for aesthetic contributions to fingered speech remain—and so, the emoji appears likely to endure in text-based communication and will continue to make a profound impact on user interface. Emojis are not only the whole way of expressing identity, but for users who see them as part of their "self," it underlines the importance of thee visual cues and grammatical structures to define the relationship between EMC and identity.

Fig. 1. "Facepalm"   **Fig. 2.** "Rolling eyes emoji"

Survey. Firstly, to understand the behavior of college students and their usage and frequency of emojis; a questionnaire was generated with approximately eighteen questions. Approximately ninety-one responses were acquired from users between the ages of 16–28 years of age that were college students in the United States. The questions consisted of simple demographical information, frequency, usage, and inquiries about the communication efficiency that were impacted by emojis. Additionally, the survey was distributed on the University of South Carolina Upstate's campus in Spartanburg, South Carolina as well as electronically on social media, organization-based chat applications, classroom distribution and through word of mouth. From the survey, fifty-nine females and thirty-one males were surveyed, with one respondent preferring not to disclose gender. From the genders that were surveyed, the age results were oddly skewed in response, with most of the female respondents being between the ages of 20–23 and 28 and older, which indicates that female students 20 and older are heavy users of emojis (Fig. 3).

Age Group * Gender Crosstabulation

Count

		Gender			
		Female	Male	NA	Total
Age Group	16 to 19	8	7	0	15
	20 to 23	25	15	0	40
	24 to 27	6	3	1	10
	28 or older	20	6	0	26
Total		59	31	1	91

Fig. 3. Age group gender crosstabulation

From the gender crosstabulation results (Fig. 3), we analyzed the perception of emojis based on age. Approximately 93% of users between the ages of 16–19 felt that the interpretation and usage of emojis vary slightly from person to person, whereas 47% of users 16–19 felt that it is easier to express feelings with emojis. Comparatively, users ages 20–23 had similar results with 75% of respondents believing that interpretation and usage of emojis varying slightly from person to person. However, perhaps the most surprising results came from respondents ages 24–27. Approximately 70% of respondents ages 24–27 believe that it is easier to express feelings with emojis with 40% believing that interpretation and usage of emojis varies slightly from person to person.

Perception, a key concept in the utilization of emojis was arguably the most important component of the survey distributed. As noted in Fig. 4, respondents ages 16–19 and 20–23 were the majority in the belief that emojis help alter the perception of the intended meaning. More interestingly, 40% of users between the ages of 24–27 believed that emojis do not alter the intended perception of a message. It is important to note that users aged 28 or older that were surveyed only had an 11% difference in beliefs that emojis alter perception.

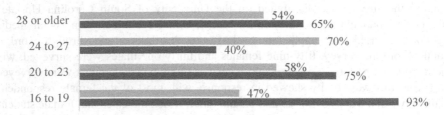

Fig. 4. Perception vary by age group

Emojis as a universal language is crucial to HCI development as it creates the understanding that emojis are a graphical tool that can be "spoken" and understood on a universal language, without having to learn the language as it is self-taught and interpreted. Respondents of the survey were asked if they felt that emojis were a universal language. Depending on their frequency of usage, they were rated on a sliding scale of 1–10 (Fig. 5). Respondents, when asked how often they used emojis, would respond "Always," "Usually," "Sometimes," and "Rarely." The respondents would then rate on a scale of 1–10 whether they felt that emojis were a universal language. Surprisingly, respondents who answered that they "always" use emojis responded that on an average of 8.7, they believe that emojis are a universal language. Respondents who answered that they "rarely" use emojis were the lowest in ratings, having an average 6.7 in their belief that emojis are a universal language. However, this is still important as even though they aren't heavy users of emojis, they still believe on a small scale that emojis are a language.

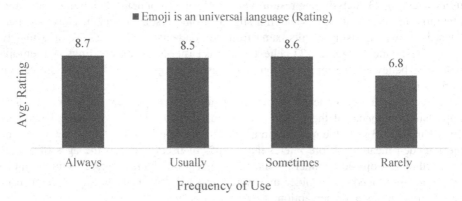

Fig. 5. Emojis as a universal language (rating)

Respondents were also asked about the top three emojis that they most frequently used. The respondents were surveyed on approximately 100 emojis that are currently in the Unicode Consortium. Of the 100 emojis featured in the survey distributed, the top three choices were "Face with Tears of Joy," "Face Blowing a Kiss," "Smiling Face with Heart Eyes" (Fig. 6). Additionally, an overwhelming 65% of respondents chose "Face with Tears of Joy" as their most frequently used emoji while an underwhelming 27% and 24% of respondents chose "Face Blowing a Kiss Emoji Name" and "Smiling Face with Heart Eyes."

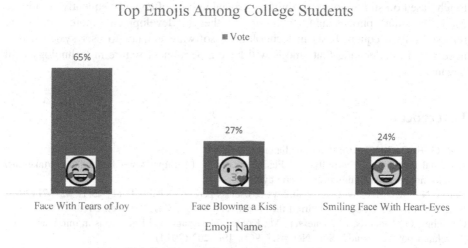

Fig. 6. Top emojis among college students

4 Conclusion

College students use emojis in accordance with their gender norms and cultural practices, an indication of how society maintains communication. The prevalence of using emojis as a form of increasing emotionality in language and to compensate for the absence of nonverbal cues in digital text underscores how college students speak through emojis. Furthermore, culture shapes gender and communication beliefs and practices. If the culture is collective and values communication that is respectful and emotion-laden, then women would tend to use emoticons accordingly. Culture and gender intersect in shaping how college students use and perceive emojis. Additionally, the most surprising data that was received from the respondents was that an over-whelming 85% of respondents rated an 8 or higher on a scale of 1–10 that emojsi are a universal language, which changes the perception of how emojis are used to communicate. The perception of emojis will not only alter the perception of emojis, but how user interface is developed and evolves to better use emojis.

With better communications comes better relationships, therefore proper and frequent emoji use may also boost individual/couple happiness and relationship satisfaction. College students can use emojis with confidence that their real intended message meaning is getting across, even if other communication skills are lacking. Additionally, people do not have to guess what the sender intends to say if emojis are present. Moreover, emojis can enhance politeness and help people avoid wording that may instigate conflict. They can be used for saving face or interpreted as saving face, a new grammar for emotional, but controlled, EMC expressions. Emoji use and prevalence can bridge the gap between absences of non-verbal cues in EMC and the desire to be adequately understood, resulting in possibly greater communication effectiveness as well as happy individuals and relationships.

HCI, while constantly in an evolving and developmental state has a profound impact on how emojis are used from a user-interface standpoint. Since emojis are often touch based on smartphones, usability is crucial in how often and frequently emojis are used. As smart phones and technology further in development, more emojis are released on a frequent basis in technological software updates to user systems. It is necessary to understand that emojis will have a permanent fixture in technology as it advances.

References

A & G: FAQ (2015). http://emojipedia.org/faq/

A digital downside: cyberbullying - Flatlandkc.org (n.d.). https://www.flatlandkc.org/takenote/take-note-season-2/digital-downside-cyberbul

Baron, N.S., Ling, R.: Necessary simleys & useless periods. Visible Lang. 45(1), 45–671 (2011)

Blagdon, J.: How emoji's concurred the world. The Verge. Vox, 4 March 2013

Churches, O., Nicholls, M., Thiessen, M., Kohler, M., Keage, H.: Emoticons in mind: an event-related potential study. Soc. Neurosci. 9(2), 196–202 (2014)

Chen, Z., Lu, X., Shen, S., Ai, W., Liu, X., Mei, Q.: Through a gender lens: an empirical study of emoji usage over large-scale Android users (2017)

Daud, N., McLellan, J.: Gender and code choice in Bruneian Facebook status updates. World Englishes 35, 571–586 (2016). https://doi.org/10.1111/weng.12227

Davis, M., Edberg, P.: Unicode emoji, November 2016. http://unicode.org/reports/tr51/

Hakami, S.A.A.: The importance of understanding emoji: an investigative study. University of Birmingham (2017). http://www.cs.bham.ac.uk/*rjh/courses/ResearchTopicsInHCI/2016-17/Submissions/hakamishatha.pdf

Kabir, H.: Female listener perceptions of the emoji in textual-based communication. In: 14th Annual Conference Proceedings on SC Upstate Symposium (2018)

Lebduska, L.: Emoji, Emoji, What for Art Thou? Harlot (2014). http://harlotofthearts.org/index.php/harlot/article/view/186/157

McWhorter, J.: "Texting." TED Blog, 21 January 2013. https://blog.ted.com/the-linguistic-miracle-of-texting-john-mcwhorter-at-ted2013/

Wijeratne, S., Balasuriya, L., Sheth, A., Doran, D.: A semantics-based measure of emoji similarity. In: 2017 IEEE/WIC/ACM International Conference on Web Intelligence (WI). ACM, Leipzig (2017). https://doi.org/10.1145/3106426.3106490

Clustering Help-Seeking Behaviors in LGBT Online Communities: A Prospective Trial

Chen Liang[1(✉)] , Dena Abbott[1] , Y. Alicia Hong[2] ,
Mahboubeh Madadi[1] , and Amelia White[1]

[1] Louisiana Tech University, Ruston, LA 71272, USA
{cliang,dabbott,madadi,asw018}@latech.edu
[2] George Mason University, Fairfax, VA 22030, USA
yhong22@gmu.edu

Abstract. Online Lesbian, Gay, Bisexual, and Transgender (LGBT) support communities have emerged as a major social media platform for sexual and gender minorities (SGM). These communities play a crucial role in providing LGBT individuals a private and safe space for networking because LGBT individuals are more likely to experience social isolation and family rejection. However, the emergence of these online communities introduced new public health concerns and challenges. Since LGBT individuals are vulnerable to mental illness and risk of suicide as compared to the heterosexual population, crisis prevention and intervention are important. Nevertheless, such a protection mechanism has not yet become a serious consideration when it comes to the design of LGBT online support communities partially because of the difficulties of identifying at-risk users effectively and timely. This pilot study aims to explore the potential of identifying LGBT user discussions related to help-seeking through natural language processing and topic model. The findings suggest the feasibility of the proposed approach by identifying topics and representative forum discussions that contain help-seeking information. This study provides important data to suggest the future direction of improving data analytics and computer-aided modules for LGBT online communities with the goal of enhancing crisis suicide prevention and intervention.

Keywords: LGBT · Suicide · Mental disorders · Topic model ·
Natural language processing

1 Introduction

1.1 LGBT Internet Support Communities

Online Lesbian, Gay, Bisexual, and Transgender (LGBT) communities have emerged as a major social media platform for sexual and gender minorities (SGM). Due to family rejection, isolation, stigma, and discrimination, many LGBT individuals choose to engage with LGBT online communities where they can network with peers in a relatively private and safe space. Notably, however, LGBT individuals experience high rates of mental illness (e.g., mood disorders, anxiety, personality disorders, etc.) as well as high risk of suicide as compared to heterosexual population [1]. Recent studies also

© Springer Nature Switzerland AG 2019
G. Meiselwitz (Ed.): HCII 2019, LNCS 11578, pp. 345–355, 2019.
https://doi.org/10.1007/978-3-030-21902-4_25

indicated an increasing number of LGBT youth in these online communities [2]. The Centers for Disease Control and Prevention (CDC) have reported that suicide is the third leading cause of death for youth ages 10 to 14 and the second leading cause of death for youth ages 15 to 24 in the US [3].

These LGBT support communities have been an ideal venue for LGBT users to expose themselves and to seek advises, but thus far most of the communities are missing the function to protect this vulnerable population from high-lethality suicide risk. More specifically, there is a missing module to identify at-risk users in a timely manner, in which those users may expose signs of urgent needs of support, severe suicidal ideations, or suicidal behaviors. As a result, timely prevention and intervention are barely possible.

1.2   Identifying Help-Seeking Behaviors from Users' Written Speech

Help-seeking behaviors are an observable measure for the state of users' psychosocial functioning, which may be used for identification of at-risk users. The proactive intervention will become feasible if at-risk users and their posts can be accurately identified in a timely manner. In the traditional research environment in which researchers gain direct interactions with participants, such behavioral data is collected through interviews, surveys, and clinical observations. Although it is a less challenging data collection process, studies reported that many participants are reluctant to provide information about their needs [4, 5]. When it comes to the online environment, user-generated written speech is the key data source that enables indirect observation of users' help-seeking behaviors.

Users in LGBT online support communities raise a variety of help-seeking topics such as identity confusion, networking, crises in relationships, mental disorders, etc. Many topics do not necessarily relate to suicide risks, but some others deserve immediate investigation and intervention, e.g., those express depression and suicidal ideations. Unfortunately, there is only a very small number of LGBT support communities, e.g., TrevorSpace, that recruited specialized forum administrators to provide referral information and interventions to those who are at risk. Even so, the service is not provided in a timely manner due to the costly labor. Most LGBT support communities are only able to share the suicide referral information in the announcement column. Hence, there is a pressing need to improve the timely identification of critical help-seeking topics for proactive intervention.

Presently, there is a limited number of studies that focus on help-seeking behaviors of online LGBT users through their written speech. Among published work, most studies adopted content analysis in which human judges are performed on coded free text [6]. The content analysis presents unique advantages of disclosing detailed and clinically valuable information about users' psychobehavioral states but is also criticized for intensive labor and questionable inter-rater reliability [7]. In recent years, computer-aided data processing and analyses have been increasingly used in social, behavioral, and health sciences. Computational methods that were originally developed from computer and information sciences are now used in psychological studies, such as natural language processing (NLP) and machine learning [8]. For example, topic modeling has also been used as a replacement or supplement of content analysis in processing written speech that contains mental health-related information [9, 10]. One of the unique advantages of these computational methods is the efficiency and enhanced capability of processing large-scale data.

1.3 Approach

The primary aim of this study is to identify signs of help-seeking behaviors by analyzing LGBT online users generated written speech. These help-seeking behaviors are important data valuable to identify at-risk users.

To achieve this aim, we employed natural language processing (NLP) to assist in automated analysis of textural data and clustering of topics of posts. In specific, we developed topic models [11] to automatically cluster various topics of help-seeking posts. Our approach allows us to distinguish different posts by clusters of lexical information a thread carries. Recent advances in clinical psychology, NLP, and machine learning have already demonstrated the feasibility of automated identifying suicide-risk related clues through analyzing linguistic information such as individuals' written speech on social media [12–16] and electronic health records [17]. We analyzed the historical posts from LGBT Chat & Forums, an anonymous LGBT online community consisting of ten thousand of threads. The experimental procedures are as follows. (1) We employed standard NLP preprocess to clean the free text data. (2) We implemented the Latent Dirichlet Allocation (LDA) algorithm to construct topic models. (3) We used the trained topic models to cluster posts by topics. Based on the model output, we examined topics, keywords representing the topics, and associated posts relevant to help-seeking behaviors. Discussion of potential design of an interactive module to timely identify at-risk users followed.

Our study provided important data to demonstrate the efficiency and effectiveness of identifying critical help-seeking behaviors by users generated written speech. The findings will serve as the preliminary data to our future plan of developing computational tools for the emerging LGBT online support communities. Our study also provided data to inform potential changes in public health policy that benefits the SGM population.

2   Methods

2.1   Materials

We used historical data of LGBT users' written speech communications from LGBT Chat & Forums (https://lgbtchat.net/). This is an open-registration and anonymized forum that allows LGBT users for networking, chatting, and experience sharing. Historical data refers to data that was generated six months before data collection.

Data were extracted by web crawling technique. We employed the *Python3* wrapped package of *Boilerpipe3* to fetch the data. A corpus consisting of 65,120 forum posts generated from December 2012 to June 2018 was created. Data collection was completed in January 2019.

Although researchers do not need to comprehend forum posts during the automated data collection and processing, it is still possible for observing any adverse events or suicidal behaviors that still have any influence at present. In case any of these adverse events and suicidal behaviors are observed during the study, researchers were instructed to report immediately to forum administrators and local crisis intervention agencies.

2.2   Procedures

We performed standardized NLP procedures to prepare the corpus before it could be used to generate the topic model. Below we described the NLP pre-processing and topic modeling, respectively.

NLP Pre-processing. The motivation of pre-processing the corpus is to extract the bag-of-words (BOW) representation of free text. In the corpus, each post is in the free text format, which can be represented by a multiset of words disregarding the sequence and grammatical rules, i.e., BOW. Topics can be extracted from such a BOW representation. We followed the procedures below. The resulting dataset was in the BOW representation with indexes and word frequency that were ready for topic modeling.

Cleaning-Up Text. We used regular expressions to remove text irrelevant to the users' written speech (e.g., HTML heading and tagged text), new-line characters, and symbols.

Tokenization. This step was to tokenize sentences into words, removing punctuations. We used the tokenization module built in the *Gensim* package.

Removing Stop Words. Stop words (e.g., "the", "a", "an", etc.) are interfering when included in the BOW representation. To remove the stop words, we used the list of stop words included in the *nltk* package as a dictionary.

Bigram Modeling. We considered words frequently occurring together in the corpus to be bigram words (e.g., "Southern Europe"). The identification of bigrams and words combining were performed by employing the *Gensim* package.

Lemmatization. This step was to convert the words into the root format. For example, the word "laughing" should be converted to "laugh" and the word "students" is converted to "student". Lemmatization was performed by employing the *spaCy* package.

Topic Modeling. The topic model we used was built on LDA algorithm and was implemented in the Gensim package. LDA develops probabilistic graphical modeling based on BOW representation. To discover an optimized topic model, we considered a balance between the coherence of words captured by topics and the interpretability of topics.

Building LDA Topic Models. We built the models by employing the *Gensim* package. We used default parameters including *chunksize* (the number of posts in each training chunk), *passes* (total number of training passes), and *alpha* and *eta* (control of sparsity of topics). The only parameter we manipulated was *num_topics*, which represents the number of topics the model generated, discussed next.

Finetuning the Model with Optimized Coherence Score. We conducted an experiment in which we trained topic models with different numbers of topics (i.e., *num_topics*). The number of topics ranged from 5 to 100 with an increment of 5, resulting in 20 different values for *num_topics*. These models were measured by the coherence score [18] ranging from 0 to 1. A higher score represents a better coherence. Models with outperformed coherence scores were used to generate topics for further analysis.

Visualization. We created an interactive 2D visualization for generated topics. The *pyLDAvis* package was used for creating visualization.

Topic Analysis and Interpretation. We first identified topics relevant to help-seeking behaviors by examining the set of topic keywords. Second, we retrieved the most representative posts for relevant topics. This procedure enabled a detailed observation by establishing a direct interaction between topics and posts.

3 Results

3.1 Experimental Results for Optimized Models

We tested 20 different topic models with different a number of topics (*num_topics*). Figure 1 shows the convergence scores for every run of the test. In general, the coherence scores drop slowly when we increased the number of topics. The best coherence (0.47) was recorded when there were 5 topics specified. Moreover, in order to identify an optimized model, we also need to evaluate the interoperability of the topics the model produced, detailed in the next section.

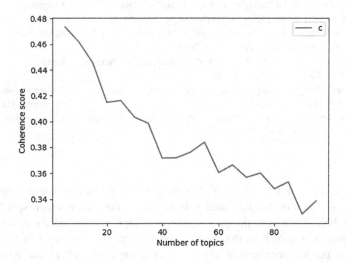

Fig. 1. Coherence scores for models with different number of topics.

3.2   Topic Interpretation

We started to identify an optimized topic model that can generate meaningful topics from the model with *num_topics* = 5 with an increment of *num_topics* each time. Models with comparatively high convergence scores often trade off with the number of meaningful topics. To balance between these two factors, we generated a model with 35 topics (coherence score = 0.4) for downstream analysis.

Examining Relevant Topics. In Table 1, we selected the interpretable topics and the corresponding keywords. Each topic is represented by a set of 10 keywords that have the highest contribution to the topic.

Table 1. Topics and keywords.

Topic	Keywords	Interpretation
#7	"meet" + "welcome" + "people" + "talk" + "old" + "friend" + "new" + "be" + "join" + "chat"	Welcoming
#8	"gender" + "male" + "tran" + "female" + "body" + "transgender" + "doctor" + "identify" + "hormone" + "question"	Gender & sexual identify
#9	"friend" + "come" + "tell" + "family" + "accept" + "father" + "sister" + "scared" + "step" + "know"	Out; family rejection
#10	"girl" + "guy" + "date" + "friend" + "crush" + "boyfriend" + "straight" + "kiss" + "relationship" + "never"	Dating; relationship
#11	"woman" + "man" + "attract" + "bisexual" + "pansexual" + "attraction" + "sexual" + "husband" + "bisexuality" + "straight"	Gender & sexual attraction
#12	"sex" + "relationship" + "partner" + "sexual" + "wife" + "marry" + "romantic" + "married" + "orientation" + "desire"	Relationship
#13	"gay" + "sexuality" + "straight" + "lgbt" + "sin" + "religious" + "community" + "people" + "homophobic" + "homophobia"	Religion
#14	"love" + "wonderful" + "dream" + "god" + "believe" + "heart" + "fight" + "beautiful" + "together" + "lover"	Relationship
#15	"parent" + "mom" + "child" + "mother" + "daughter" + "therapist" + "kid" + "dad" + "live" + "brother"	Family
#22	"country" + "sign" + "die" + "kill" + "cry" + "dog" + "visit" + "cat" + "water" + "dead"	Self-harm; mental problems; help-seeking
#30	"voice" + "pain" + "angry" + "apart" + "pull" + "worker" + "lay" + "sexy" + "gf" + "card"	Mental problems; help-seeking

Among the 35 topics, Topic #22 is relating to posts that contain help-seeking behaviors. As shown on the left-hand side of Fig. 2, the bubbles represent topics. The area of a bubble represents the prevalence of a topic. Semantically close topics are close, or even overlapped, in the figure. The bar chart on the right-hand side of the figure shows the top represented keywords of a topic as well as the frequency and proportion of the keywords. For Topic #22, it was distributed over a number of salient keywords including "die", "kill", "cry", and "dead". Most of these keywords were unique to Topic #22 except for "medical", "would", and "alone".

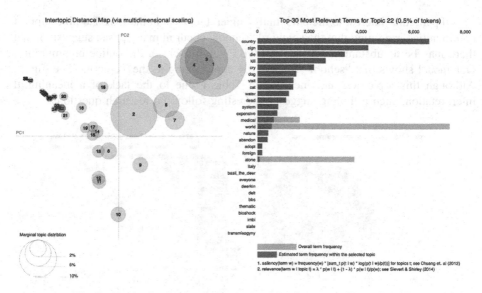

Fig. 2. Topic distribution and representative keywords for topic #22.

Topic #30 is also relevant to help-seeking posts. It was represented by "pain", "angry", "apart", etc. See Fig. 3. All of the keywords made unique contributions to topic #30. Overall, both topics are less prevalent as compared to topics #1, #2, #3, #4, etc.

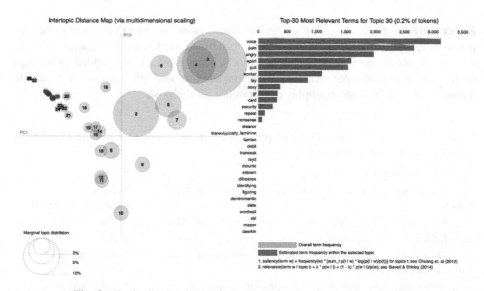

Fig. 3. Topic distribution and representative keywords for topic #30.

Of particular interest to the potentially vulnerable users in the LGBT online support communities, we found that the keyword "school" occur in many posts, suggesting that there may be a substantial number of LGBT youth users in the online communities. Our model shows that "school" is primarily contributing to the Topic #5. See Fig. 4. Although this topic was not included in Table 1 due to the lack of a meaningful interpretation, such a finding suggests interesting follow-up research questions.

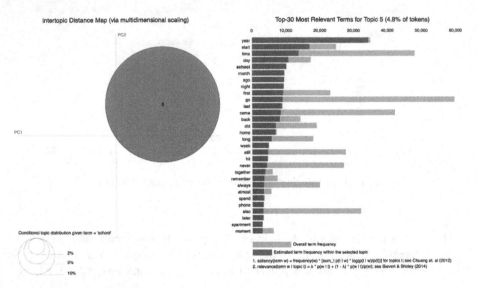

Fig. 4. Contribution of keyword "school" to topic #5.

Representative Posts over Topics. We explored further on identifying representative posts for a topic of interest. Posts relating to help-seeking behaviors contain shared-experience about depression, hopeless, pain, self-harm, etc. Users tended to be supportive and provided emotional support, social support, and information about suicide hotlines. See Table 2 for examples of discussion in the posts.

Table 2. Examples of help-seeking and peer-support related posts. Contents are modified to remove less important information.

Fractions of discussion in the posts	Notes
…… *I wake up every morning so miserable and so tired, I feel hopeless.* ……	Negative mental/physical status
…… *I self harm which is something I never thought I would do.*	Self-harm
…… *I drink excessively every night just to take the pain away.*	Pain
…… *This year is the last year as u all move forward into {year} I will stay in {year}.* ……	Suicidal ideation
…… *My dreams were to have a nice wife and children, just to be loved and share my life with the woman of my dreams. It's never going to happen.* ……	Shared experience
…… *Please talk to us. We understand.* …….	Peer support

4   Discussion

4.1   Major Findings

In this study, we explored the potential of identifying LGBT forum posts that are relating to help-seeking behaviors by topic models. One premise of this approach is that topics of posts are represented by multisets of words. Our findings suggested that a spectrum of meaningful topics can be identified by developing topic models over LGBT forum posts. This finding is in line with a number of studies leveraging topic models to discover topics of interest from textual social media data [19–21].

In a number of topics that we found, we would like to underscore help-seeking topics with the scope of this study. Help-seeking behaviors exist in the LGBT online support communities. Such posts are often associated with shared negative emotion and experience, mental/physical pain, suicidal ideations, and even signs of attempts. Causes include rejection, self-disappointment, gender & sexual identity-related confusion, etc. Based on our observation, users from the LGBT forum are supportive, especially those who have been in the same or similar situations before.

In addition to the help-seeking related topics, we also identified a number of meaningful topics that are widely discussed in the community. These topics are equally interesting to research questions with regard to gender and sexual identity, isolation, rejection, bully, and a number of contributing factors to mental disorders. These research questions are traditionally studied in a face-to-face setting such as interview and questionnaire. Our approach holds potentials to provide an innovative alternative to collect data from LGBT users generated written speech. As compared to the content analysis, which is commonly used to analyze data collected from interview and narrative data, NLP and topic modeling can overcome shortcomings such as less efficiency.

4.2   Implications for LGBT Online Support Communities

In this study, we strived to collect preliminary data to contribute to the improvement of LGBT online communities. LGBT population is vulnerable to mental health problems and suicide. Presently, most of the LGBT online support communities have limited protective mechanism for proactive suicide intervention and prevention, remaining to be a significant public health concern. Since the findings suggest the feasibility of automated identification of at-risk posts, we recognized the potential to develop a real-time monitoring module to identify users who need immediate assistance.

4.3   Limitations and Future Direction

The present study is less valuable without the discussion of its limitations. First, outcomes of the topic model are limited in terms of interpretability. As it has been recognized as a common problem of topic modeling, in our study, only 11 out of 35 topics carry obvious meanings. The rest of the topics are either less salient or containing implicit meanings. Second, identifying meaningful topics requires domain knowledge. The process is less objective, but it was compromised by calculating the coherence score of the model. Third, the corpus of LGBT forum posts contains a considerable portion of noisy information. We noticed that meaningful topics are generally less prevalent, whereas many less-meaningful topics are not. It is probably because the discussion in the LGBT forum involves a broad range of mixed themes, including lyrics, movies, and jargons that are less suitable to be captured by a BOW based model, i.e., topic model.

In the future study, we aim to develop further on the present approach to improve the accuracy, interoperability, and generalizability of NLP methods. For example, we believe that a specialized language system can provide references for the machine to understand contextual semantic information from LGBT users generated narratives. Presently, there is no published tool for that purpose. In addition, a customized NLP pipeline may improve the text pre-process and, further, the performance of the model. Our next step is also to develop data processing tool specialized for LGBT online communities with the goal of improving proactive intervention through data science.

References

1. Haas, A.P., et al.: Suicide and suicide risk in lesbian, gay, bisexual, and transgender populations: review and recommendations. J. Homosex. **58**, 10–51 (2010)
2. GLSEN, CiPHR, & C.: Out online: the experiences of LGBT youth on the internet, New York (2013)
3. Xu, J., Murphy, S.L., Kochanek, K.D., Arias, E.: Mortality in the United States, 2015 (2016)
4. Provini, C., Everett, J.R., Pfeffer, C.R.: Adults mourning suicide: self-reported concerns about bereavement, needs. Death Stud. **24**, 1–19 (2000)
5. Prescott, T.L., Gregory Phillips, I.I., DuBois, L.Z., Bull, S.S., Mustanski, B., Ybarra, M.L.: Reaching adolescent gay, bisexual, and queer men online: development and refinement of a national recruitment strategy. J. Med. Internet Res. **18**, e200 (2016)
6. Griffiths, K.M., Calear, A.L., Banfield, M., Tam, A.: Systematic review on Internet Support Groups (ISGs) and depression (2): what is known about depression ISGs? J. Med. Internet Res. **11**, e41 (2009)
7. Lombard, M., Snyder-Duch, J., Bracken, C.C.: Content analysis in mass communication: assessment and reporting of intercoder reliability. Hum. Commun. Res. **28**, 587–604 (2002)
8. Kern, M.L., et al.: Gaining insights from social media language: methodologies and challenges. Psychol. Methods **21**, 507 (2016)
9. Nguyen, T., Phung, D., Dao, B., Venkatesh, S., Berk, M.: Affective and content analysis of online depression communities. IEEE Trans. Affect. Comput. **5**(3), 217–226 (2014)
10. Carron-Arthur, B., Reynolds, J., Bennett, K., Bennett, A., Griffiths, K.M.: What's all the talk about? Topic modelling in a mental health internet support group. BMC Psychiatry **16**, 367 (2016)
11. Steyvers, M., Griffiths, T.: Probabilistic topic models. In: Handbook of Latent Semantic Analysis. A Road to Meaning, vol. 55, pp. 424–440 (2007)
12. Zhang, L., Huang, X., Liu, T., Li, A., Chen, Z., Zhu, T.: Using linguistic features to estimate suicide probability of chinese microblog users. In: Zu, Q., Hu, B., Gu, N., Seng, S. (eds.) HCC 2014. LNCS, vol. 8944, pp. 549–559. Springer, Cham (2015). https://doi.org/10.1007/978-3-319-15554-8_45

13. De Choudhury, M., Kiciman, E., Dredze, M., Coppersmith, G., Kumar, M.: Discovering shifts to suicidal ideation from mental health content in social media. In: Proceedings of the 2016 CHI Conference on Human Factors in Computing Systems, CHI 2016, pp. 2098–2110 (2016)
14. Burnap, P., Colombo, W., Scourfield, J.: Machine classification and analysis of suicide-related communication on Twitter. In: Proceedings of the 26th ACM Conference on Hypertext & Social Media, HT 2015, pp. 75–84 (2015)
15. O'Dea, B., Wan, S., Batterham, P.J., Calear, A.L., Paris, C., Christensen, H.: Detecting suicidality on Twitter. Internet Interv. **2**, 183–188 (2015)
16. Braithwaite, S.R., Giraud-Carrier, C., West, J., Barnes, M.D., Hanson, C.L.: Validating machine learning algorithms for Twitter data against established measures of suicidality. JMIR Ment. Health **3**, e21 (2016)
17. Walsh, C.G.: Predicting risk of suicide attempts over time through machine learning. Clin. Psychol. Sci. **5**(5), 457–469 (2017)
18. Newman, D., Lau, J.H., Grieser, K., Baldwin, T.: Automatic evaluation of topic coherence. In: Human Language Technologies: The 2010 Annual Conference of the North American Chapter of the Association for Computational Linguistics, pp. 100–108 (2010)
19. Kumar, M., Dredze, M., Coppersmith, G., De Choudhury, M.: Detecting changes in suicide content manifested in social media following celebrity suicides. In: Proceedings of the 26th ACM Conference on Hypertext & Social Media, pp. 85–94 (2015)
20. Resnik, P., Armstrong, W., Claudino, L., Nguyen, T., Nguyen, V.-A., Boyd-Graber, J.: Beyond LDA: exploring supervised topic modeling for depression-related language in Twitter. In: Proceedings of the 2nd Workshop on Computational Linguistics and Clinical Psychology: From Linguistic Signal to Clinical Reality, pp. 99–107 (2015)
21. Huang, X., Li, X., Liu, T., Chiu, D., Zhu, T., Zhang, L.: Topic model for identifying suicidal ideation in Chinese microblog. In: Proceedings of the 29th Pacific Asia Conference on Language, Information and Computation, pp. 553–562 (2015)

Estimating Ground Shaking Regions
with Social Media Propagation Trees

Marcelo Mendoza[1]($\boxtimes$), Bárbara Poblete[2], and Ignacio Valderrama[2]

[1] Millennium Institute for Foundational Research on Data,
Universidad Técnica Federico Santa María, Valparaíso, Chile
`marcelo.mendoza@usm.cl`
[2] Millennium Institute for Foundational Research on Data,
Department of Computer Science, Universidad de Chile, Santiago, Chile
`{bpoblete,ivalderr}@dcc.uchile.cl`

Abstract. The Mercalli scale of quake damages is based on perceived effects and it has a strong dependence on observers. Recently, we proposed a method for ground shaking intensity estimation based on lexical features extracted from tweets, showing good performance in terms of mean absolute error (MAE). One of the flaws of that method is the detection of the region of interest, i.e., the area of a country where the quake was felt. Our previous results showed enough recall in terms of municipality recovery but a poor performance in terms of accuracy. One of the reasons that help to explain this effect is the presence of data noise as many people comment or confirm a quake in areas where the event was unperceived. This happens because people get awareness of an event by watching news or by word-of-mouth propagation. To alleviate this problem in our earthquake detection system we study how propagation features behave in a region of interest estimation task. The intuition behind our study is that the patterns that characterize a word-of-mouth propagation differ from the patterns that characterize a perceived event. If this intuition is true, we expect to separate both kinds of propagation modes. We do this by computing a number of features to represent propagation trees. Then, we trained a learning algorithm using our features in the specific task of region of interest estimation. Our results show that propagation features behave well in this task, outperforming lexical features in terms of accuracy.

Keywords: Social networks · Disaster management ·
Mercalli intensity · Social media during emergencies · Propagation trees

1 Introduction

Richter and Mercalli scales measure the level of impact of an earthquake in a given region. Whilst Richter measures the energy released during an earthquake, Mercalli represents the level of damages produced during an earthquake. Both scales are related but may differ due to several factors as the quality of the

© Springer Nature Switzerland AG 2019
G. Meiselwitz (Ed.): HCII 2019, LNCS 11578, pp. 356–369, 2019.
https://doi.org/10.1007/978-3-030-21902-4_26

buildings, the type of ground where the quake happens or the depth of the epicenter, i.e., the distance of the epicenter to the ground surface.

Mercalli reports are prepared by observers who record the effects of an earthquake on humans and man-made structures. However, these reports may be released even hours or days after an earthquake, as the strong dependence on local observers makes difficult to provide fresh information. Recently we proposed a method for fast estimation of Mercalli intensities using social media [9]. Our method is based on the observation of Twitter and it computes lexical features on a set of messages related to the event. We showed that there are lexical features that are useful for Mercalli intensity estimation. However, one of the difficulties found during the study was the estimation of the ground shaking region. As many people get awareness of an event watching news or by word-of-mouth, these comments are mixed with comments of observers who are placed in the region of interest, introducing noise during the region of interest estimation step of our method. With a good recall but a poor accuracy in the region estimation step, our method shows enough room for improvement.

In this paper we study how propagation features can be used to mitigate the effect of noise during the region of interest estimation process. We extend our method providing better features for ground shaking region estimation. To do this we compute eight propagation features showing how useful they are to alleviate the effect of noise in our system.

Main Contribution of the Paper: In this paper we address the problem of ground shaking region estimation using social media propagation features. Our method starts extracting propagation trees from propagation graphs, detecting seeds and measuring a number of features that characterize spreading patterns. To the best of our knowledge, this is the first work that addresses the problem of ground shaking region estimation using propagation network features. Our intuition indicates that there are measurable differences in propagation patterns between perceived and unperceived events. We sustain this intuition in our previous findings on rumor detection [8]. The intuition behind our study is that the patterns that characterize a word-of-mouth propagation differ from the patterns that characterize a perceived event. If this intuition is true, we expect to separate both kinds of propagation modes. To study this hypothesis we compute a number of features to represent propagation trees. We will show that our features are useful for ground shaking region estimation, giving support to our hypothesis.

This paper is organized as follows. Related work is discussed in Sect. 2. Preliminaries are discussed in Sect. 3. Ground shaking region estimation based on propagation features is introduced in Sect. 4. Experiments are discussed in Sect. 5. Finally, we conclude in Sect. 6.

2   Related Work

The relation between physical events and its correspondence in Twitter has been an active research area during the last years [6]. These efforts have shown interesting results. For instance, a research found that during the Tohoku earthquake in 2011 there were a number of high correlations between the amount of tweets and the intensity of the disaster in some locations [4]. Recently, Poblete *et al.* [10] provided a system for the early detection of earthquakes using social media features. The system dubbed "Twicalli"[1] detects worldwide earthquakes in real time, illustrating the consonance between physical events and social media trends.

There are more quake alert systems based on social media around the world. Systems as the ones placed in Australia [11] or Italy [1] use burst detection algorithms to report earthquakes, where a burst is defined as a large number of occurrences of tweets within a short time window [13]. In addition to the detection of an event, the estimation of the intensity of a quake has also aroused interest. Sakaki *et al.* [12] showed that it is possible to estimate the epicenter of an earthquake event using only information recovered from Twitter as tweets counts and tweets rates. Burks *et al.* [2] proposed an approach to estimate the Mercalli intensity of an earthquake performing a cross match between seismological recording stations and tweets that mention the word 'earthquake'. Computing a number of lexical features in each areal disc centered around each seismograph, the authors studied the correlation of these features with the Mercalli intensity. Using linear regression models, the authors showed good results in terms of accuracy for Mercalli intensity estimation tasks.

The estimation of the maximum intensity of an earthquake using Twitter was studied by Cresci *et al.* [3]. Using linear regression models over a huge collection of aggregated features (45 features were tested in that proposal), the authors showed that Twitter has enough predictive power to infer the maximum intensity of an earthquake in the Mercalli scale. Recently, we showed that it is possible to provide an early estimation of the maximum intensity of an earthquake (just 30 min after the event) using only 12 lexical features, performing well in this specific task [9]. However, one of the limitations of that work relies on the poor accuracy achieved during the estimation of the ground shaking region. As many people get awareness of an event watching news or by word-of-mouth, these comments are mixed with comments of observers who are placed in the region of interest, introducing noise during the estimation process.

To alleviate the effect of noise during the ground shaking estimation process, we study the effectiveness of eight features that characterize the propagation of the event across the network. Propagation features has succeeded in predictive tasks as rumor detection [8] and research output forecasting [7]. The intuition behind this study is to check if there is a consonance between the impact of a perceived event and propagation traces. If this intuition is true, we expect to measure and use the correspondence of the event in the network improving the accuracy on the region of interest estimation task.

The estimation of the ground shaking region of an earthquake using social media has gained attention in last years. Systems based on crowd-sourcing tools[2]

---

[1] http://www.twicalli.cl.

[2] "Did you feel it?" website located at https://earthquake.usgs.gov/data/dyfi/.

or based on geolocated tweets as TwiFelt [5], have revealed the interest of government agencies as the US Geological Survey (USGS) on the use of social media for these tasks. In this paper we will show that propagation features are key event descriptors of earthquakes to address this challenging task.

3 Preliminaries

We proposed a method for the early estimation of the intensity of an earthquake in the Mercalli scale [9]. In that method, we used information gathered from Twitter. Our method works in a tandem with Twicalli [10], the system for detection of earthquakes based on Twitter. Once an earthquake is detected by Twicalli, the event is characterized at municipality level, the finer level of geolocation considered in our system. Then we conduct a regression process to infer the region of interest of a given earthquake. Finally, our method takes the collection of point estimates to infer the maximum intensity in the Mercalli scale for a given quake.

In our system, posts are collected to extract features of the event that characterize the social perception of the earthquake. Each perceived event is characterized at a level of aggregation that describes the perception of the earthquake in a municipality. For each municipality batch, a set of features is computed to describe the earthquake.

Municipality batches are built as follows. After each earthquake, a set of tweets that matches the keywords "quake", "earthquake" or "seismic" are retrieved from Twitter. The time considered to collect the data is a parameter of our system, with a window length of 30 min by default. Shorter windows can be considered but at the cost of less accurate Mercalli predictions. Tweets that are mapped to municipalities are aggregated into municipality batches.

We map tweets to municipalities using the user location field. We were forced to use this field as only a very small fraction of the tweets in our country is geolocated. In order to geolocate tweets we use the following steps: (1) if available, we extract the exact GPS coordinates from the tweet's *location* field, (2) if the location field was not provided by the user in their tweet, we then process the tweet's textual content. This is, we analyze the message's text (e.g., *"Earthquake in Valparaiso!!!"*) to extract, using a fuzzy string matching procedure, any location mentions, or (3) if all else fails, we apply the same procedure as in (2) but this time on the text provided by the user in their profile information.

Our method starts detecting the region of interest from where municipality data batches will be used to infer Mercalli intensities. This step of the method separate municipalities into two classes. We do this using a 0/1 classifier trained over municipality-seismic data batches pairs. These data batches were labeled according to the actual Mercalli intensity reported into two disjoint classes. The 0 class represents an earthquake that was not perceived (not reported in the Mercalli scale) and the 1 class represents an earthquake that was effectively perceived by people with an intensity value in the Mercalli scale. Each data batch is represented by a vector of features. Once the 0/1 classifier was trained, our method is ready to detect the region of interest on new earthquakes at county level.

After the estimation of the region of interest, our method estimate the maximum intensity of the event. Further details of this process are provided in Mendoza *et al.* [9].

4   Region Estimation Based on Propagation Features

4.1   Features

Eleven lexical features are considered at this level of aggregation as is shown in Table 1. In addition, eight propagation features are computed for this task. We also consider the inclusion of the municipality population as a feature. These features are calculated in each municipality data batch, characterizing the set of tweets mapped to each specific county for a given seism.

Table 1. Features used in our study.

	Feature	Description
LEXICAL	NUMBER OF TWEETS	Number of tweets in the data batch
	TWEETS NORM	Fraction of tweets over county population
	AVERAGE WORDS	Average length of tweets in number of words
	AVERAGE LENGTH	Average length of tweets in number of chars
	QUESTION MARKS	Fraction of tweets with question marks
	EXCLAMATION MARKS	Fraction of tweets with exclamation marks
	UPPER WORDS	Fraction of tweets with uppercase words
	HASHTAG SYMBOLS	Fraction of tweets containing the hashtag symbol
	MENTION SYMBOLS	Fraction of tweets containing the mention symbol
	RT SYMBOLS	Fraction of tweets containing the "RT" symbol
	CONTAINS EARTHQUAKE	Fraction of tweets containing the word *earthquake*
	POPULATION	Number of inhabitants in the county
PROPAGATION	NUMBER OF SEEDS	Number of seeds in the data batch
	NUMBER OF TREES	Number of trees in the data batch
	AVG USERS IN TREES	Average number of users across trees
	AVG USERS IN TREES (NI)	Average number of users across not isolated seeds
	BIGGEST TREE SIZE (U)	Size of the biggest tree in number of users
	BIGGEST TREE SIZE (I)	Size of the biggest tree in number of interactions
	AVG TREE SIZE	Average number of interactions across trees
	AVG TREE SIZE (NI)	Average number of interactions across ni seeds

To compute propagation features we need to process the propagation graph recovered for each event. The propagation graph is a graph of message sharing and replaying. In a propagation graph, each node represents a post. Each post can be read by the followers of the post owner. If a follower decides to share (to retweet in Twitter jargon), reply or mention a post, a new node is recorded in the graph, linking both nodes with an arc. Original posts (posts that are not retweets, replies or mentions) are seeds of claims. If a seed post is shared in the network, the propagation graph records an information cascade. As each interaction with the original post produces a new message, the cascade is cycle-free and it compounds a tree.

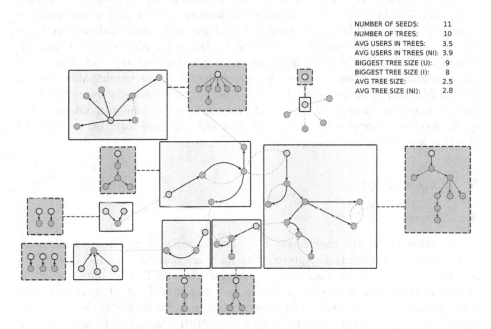

NUMBER OF SEEDS:	11
NUMBER OF TREES:	10
AVG USERS IN TREES:	3.5
AVG USERS IN TREES (NI):	3.9
BIGGEST TREE SIZE (U):	9
BIGGEST TREE SIZE (I):	8
AVG TREE SIZE:	2.5
AVG TREE SIZE (NI):	2.8

Fig. 1. How propagation features are computed. Graphs inside grey boxes represent the original propagation graph. Each node represent a message. Black edges represent RTs or mention posts. Grey edges represent inactive following links. Inferred trees are depicted in green boxes. Seeds are depicted with pink nodes. At the top of the figure we show the eight propagation features that correspond to this example. (Color figure online)

We show in Fig. 1 how propagation features are computed. Black edges show message sharing between posts. Gray edges show followers/followees relationships that do now share a message during the claim. Note that the propagation graph is a subgraph of the social network graph. Each propagation tree is boxed by a grey shaded rectangle. Inferred propagation trees are bounded in green boxes. The example shows eleven seeds (shaded in pink) and ten trees (note that the example shows an isolated seed).

4.2   Estimation of a Region of Interest

The next stage of our approach is estimating which municipalities were affected by the earthquake. We refer to these municipalities as the *region of interest* or *ground shaking region* of an earthquake. To estimate the geographical subdivisions that were affected by the seismic event, we use a supervised classification model. This model separates municipalities into two classes: *unaffected* by the earthquake and *affected* by the earthquake.

To create this model we used a 0/1 classification algorithm, which we trained using municipality-level data modeled as feature vectors (using the features shown in Table 1). The labels that we used for each municipality were class "0" if the earthquake was not perceived by the population (i.e., the municipality had no official Mercalli intensity value associated to it), and class "1" if the earthquake was perceived by the population (i.e., the municipality had an official Mercalli value associated to it). The Mercalli intensity values that we used to label the municipality-level data corresponded to values in official earthquake reports. More details on the technical and empirical aspects of the model creation are presented in Sect. 5.

5   Experiments

5.1   Dataset

A collection of 825310 tweets was retrieved from Twitter. These tweets were collected using keywords as "quake", "earthquake" and "seismic movement" (in Spanish). The collection comprises a year and a half of Twitter data, matching the keywords during 2016 and the first semester of 2017. From these tweets, only 2200 include the geolocation field, representing only the 0.26% of the data. The collection was posted by 309749 users where 207015 records a location field in their profiles, representing the 66.8% of the users recorded in the data. From the set of 207015 users with user location in our dataset, 57546 matched Chile in the country field. Then we used approximate matching to associate this field with a Chilean municipality using *Fuzzy wuzzy*[3]. Using an 80% of fuzzy confidence level, a total of 41885 Chilean users were mapped to Chilean counties. These users record in the dataset a total of 190249 tweets mapped to the 345 different counties in Chile.

We used data collected by the National Seismological Center of Chile, comprising 331 records of earthquakes in Chile during the observation period, ranging magnitudes in Richter from 2.2 Mw to 7.6 Mw. The cross match between our tweet collection and the Mercalli earthquake records was conducted over the municipality field. Only municipality batches that record tweets until 30 min after an earthquake were studied, accounting for a total of 6790 municipality-Mercalli pairs with Twitter activity. A total amount of 6548 municipality batches unmatched a Mercalli report, indicating the presence of tweets that mention earthquake keywords in counties where it was unperceived. In summary, our Twitter-Mercalli dataset comprises 331 earthquakes with 187317 tweets

---

[3] Fuzzy wuzzy is a Python string matching library that uses the Levenshtein Distance to calculate differences between string sequences. It is available in: https://github.com/seatgeek/fuzzywuzzy.

distributed over 345 Chilean counties during 18 months of Twitter activity, with county-earthquake pairs separated into 6790/6548 perceived/not-perceived earthquake data batches.

From the total amount of 331 earthquakes, 264 were selected for training and exploratory issues, reserving the remaining 68 earthquakes for testing and validation tasks, representing a training/testing split of 80/20%. The training/testing splitting process was conducted using stratified sampling over earthquakes according to each Mercalli level. Training/testing proportions of instances according to the maximum Mercalli intensity report of each earthquake are shown in Table 2. Data and its description are available at https://doi.org/10.6084/m9.figshare.c.4206689.

Table 2. Training/testing instance partitions according to the maximum Mercalli intensity of each quake

Partition	II	III	IV	V	VI	VII
Training	11	105	103	39	4	2
Testing	3	26	26	10	2	1
Overall	14	131	129	49	6	3

5.2   Exploratory Analysis

We first performed a data exploration process to analyze the relationship between municipality-level features and Mercalli values. We studied the existence of correlations, which are shown in Table 3.

Table 3 shows correlations in terms of the Spearman coefficient, as the variables studied are skew. All the coefficients found are statistically significant with p-values equal to $2.2e-16$. The correlation between propagation features is strong. Note that the correlation between MERCALLI and the other variables is not as strong. The table shows a strong correlation between size features. Interestingly, the correlation between NUMBER OF SEEDS and NUMBER OF TREES is not as strong, showing that there are a number of isolated seeds that do no achieve a spread in the network.

A strong correlation was also detected between some lexical features as NUMBER OF TWEETS and TWEETS NORM, AVERAGE WORDS and AVERAGE LENGTH and MENTION SYMBOLS and RT SYMBOLS. In general, the correlation between lexical features was weak, except for the indicated cases. A more detailed analysis of the correlation between lexical features can be checked in [9].

5.3   Estimating the Region of Interest

Training/testing municipality data batches accounts for 10491/2847 instances at municipality level. To study the problem of perceived/not-perceived earthquakes

Table 3. Spearman ranked correlation coefficient of the propagation features considered in our study.

MERCALLI	NUMBER OF SEEDS	NUMBER OF TREES	AVG USERS IN TREES	AVG USERS IN TREES (NI)	BIGGEST TREE SIZE (U)	BIGGEST TREE SIZE (I)	AVG TREE SIZE	AVG TREE SIZE (NI)
ρ	0.15	0.18	0.21	0.21	0.20	0.21	0.21	0.21
	ρ	0.55	0.50	0.56	0.56	0.56	0.51	0.55
		ρ	0.96	0.97	0.97	0.97	0.96	0.97
			ρ	0.99	0.98	0.99	0.99	0.99
				ρ	0.99	0.99	0.99	0.99
					ρ	0.99	0.99	0.99
						ρ	0.99	0.99
							ρ	0.99

at county level, we train a 0/1 classifier. In the training fold 5021 instances accounts of the 0 class (unreported Mercalli) and 5470 for the 1 class (reported Mercalli). Training was conducted using 5 folds cross validation, using an SVM of C-SVC type for classification with a radial basis function as a kernel implemented in Weka 3.7. As the focus of the problem is the detection of the 1 class, we used cost sensitive learning, penalizing false negatives in the 1 class to maximize the recall, at the cost of a high FP rate. More learning algorithms were tested among them naive Bayes or a Multilayer Perceptron but SVM was the one with the best results. The detailed accuracy by class using lexical features is shown in Tables 4 and 5 for training and testing partitions, respectively. Tables 6 and 7 show the results achieved using propagation features. The results achieved using the whole set of features considered in this study are shown in Tables 8 and 9 for training and testing partitions, respectively.

Table 4. Training accuracy by class using lexical features

Class	FP Rate	Precision	Recall	F-measure	ROC area
0 (unreported)	0.189	0.736	0.575	0.646	0.693
1 (reported)	0.425	0.675	0.811	0.737	0.693
Weighted avg.	0.312	0.705	0.698	0.693	0.693

Table 5. Testing accuracy by class using lexical features

Class	FP Rate	Precision	Recall	F-measure	ROC area
0 (unreported)	0.184	0.765	0.517	0.617	0.666
1 (reported)	0.483	0.593	0.816	0.687	0.666
Weighted avg.	0.323	0.685	0.655	0.649	0.666

Tables 4 and 5 show a good performance in terms of recall for the class of interest but a poor performance in terms of precision. Accordingly, the F-measure has a performance around 68% for the class of interest on testing data, achieving a ROC value around 0.666.

Table 6. Training accuracy by class using propagation features

Class	FP Rate	Precision	Recall	F-measure	ROC area
0 (unreported)	0.195	0.763	0.683	0.721	0.744
1 (reported)	0.317	0.734	0.805	0.768	0.744
Weighted avg.	0.259	0.748	0.746	0.745	0.744

Table 7. Testing accuracy by class using propagation features

Class	FP Rate	Precision	Recall	F-measure	ROC area
0 (unreported)	0.207	0.771	0.603	0.677	0.698
1 (reported)	0.397	0.633	0.793	0.704	0.698
Weighted avg.	0.295	0.707	0.691	0.690	0.698

The classifier based on propagation features performs better than the one based on lexical features, as it is shown in Tables 6 and 7. These results show that the classifier achieves a precision around 63% on testing data and a F-measure over the 70%, as well as a ROC value near 0.7. These improvements show that the use of propagation features is helpful for this task.

When lexical and propagation features are combined in a single classifier, the results get worse. As Tables 8 and 9 show, the 0/1 classifier increases the presence of false positives, and as a consequence, it decreases its performance in terms of precision and F-measure. These results show that it is better to address this specific task using propagation features, confirming the intuition behind the consonance between propagation patterns and the physical coverage of earthquakes.

The results show that each region of interest is over-estimated as the low precision for class 1 shows but achieving a good coverage of the actual region as

Table 8. Training accuracy by class using lexical and propagation features

Class	FP Rate	Precision	Recall	F-measure	ROC area
0 (unreported)	0.187	0.744	0.591	0.659	0.702
1 (reported)	0.409	0.684	0.813	0.743	0.702
Weighted avg.	0.303	0.713	0.707	0.703	0.702

Table 9. Testing accuracy by class using lexical and propagation features

Class	FP Rate	Precision	Recall	F-measure	ROC area
0 (unreported)	0.180	0.769	0.519	0.619	0.669
1 (reported)	0.481	0.595	0.820	0.690	0.669
Weighted avg.	0.320	0.689	0.658	0.652	0.669

its high recall shows. To better understand how the 0/1 classifier behaves, we disaggregate matching/mismatching testing instances according to the actual level of Mercalli intensity.

Table 10. Matching/mismatching instances according to the actual Mercalli intensity using lexical features

Actual	Predicted	-	I	II	III	IV	V	VI	VII
0	0	790	-	-	-	-	-	-	-
0	1	737	-	-	-	-	-	-	-
1	0	-	66	85	62	25	5	-	-
1	1	-	130	234	351	198	65	95	4
Instances		1527	196	319	413	223	70	95	4
Error rate		0.48	0.33	0.26	0.15	0.11	0.07	-	-

As Tables 10, 11 and 12 show, the false negative rate is very low, and as long as the intensity of the earthquake increases, the error rate decreases. High intensity earthquakes (V to up) show an almost perfect performance. The thick part of this error occurs in low intensity earthquakes (III to down), which is natural for this kind of phenomena as in this part of the Mercalli scale many people do not recognize the event as an earthquake, being felt only under very favorable conditions (for instance, on upper floors of buildings). When the classifier based on propagation features is used for this task, the error in level IV events decreases and it achieves a perfect performance in level V earthquakes. The global error rate using propagation features goes to 0.39 points, almost 10 points below the error rate achieved using lexical features. When both types of features are used,

Table 11. Matching/mismatching instances according to the actual Mercalli intensity using propagation features

Actual	Predicted	-	I	II	III	IV	V	VI	VII
0	0	921	-	-	-	-	-	-	-
0	1	606	-	-	-	-	-	-	-
1	0	-	83	85	65	40	-	-	-
1	1	-	113	234	348	183	70	95	4
Instances		1527	196	319	413	223	70	95	4
Error rate		0.39	0.42	0.26	0.15	0.17	-	-	-

Table 12. Matching/mismatching instances according to the actual Mercalli intensity using lexical and propagation features

Actual	Predicted	-	I	II	III	IV	V	VI	VII
0	0	792	-	-	-	-	-	-	-
0	1	735	-	-	-	-	-	-	-
1	0	-	71	88	50	25	4	-	-
1	1	-	125	231	363	198	66	95	4
Instances		1527	196	319	413	223	70	95	4
Error rate		0.48	0.36	0.27	0.12	0.11	0.05	-	-

as it is shown in Table 12, the performance get worse, confirming that the use of lexical features in this specific task introduces noise during the estimation process.

6 Conclusion

In this paper we have studied the performance of propagation features in a ground shaking region estimation task. Our results show that the use of propagation features is useful for this task outperforming classifiers based on lexical features. The intuition behind this finding sustains that lexical features are unable to hand noise during the inference process, as many observers comment unperceived events getting awareness of earthquakes watching news of by word-of-mouth propagation effects. The use of propagation features allows building robust classifies for ground shaking region estimation tasks, corroborating the presence of a consonance between how actual events spread in social media and how physical events are perceived in the physical world.

Currently, we are extending our method to work with more features. The inclusion of time-based features helps to characterize the tweet stream (e.g. tweet interval rate), a valuable source of information for earthquake detection task. We think that these features will also be helpful in the elaboration of spatial intensity reports.

At last but not least, the design of a system for early tracking of earthquake damages is the next step of this project. How to efficiently use our method to provide spatial real-time damage reports is one of our most challenging tasks in the near future. The pursuit of this goal involves efforts in data integration and visualization, among other challenging tasks for our group.

Acknowledgements. This work was supported by the Millennium Institute for Foundational Research on Data. M. Mendoza was also funded by Conicyt PIA/Basal FB0821.

References

1. Avvenuti, M., Cresci, S., Marchetti, A., Meletti, C., Tesconi, M.: EARS (earthquake alert and report system): a real time decision support system for earthquake crisis management. In: Proceedings of the 20th ACM SIGKDD International Conference on Knowledge Discovery and Data Mining, pp. 1749–1758. ACM (2014)
2. Burks, L., Miller, M., Zadeh, R.: Rapid estimate of ground shaking intensity by combining simple earthquake characteristics with tweets. In: 10th US National Conference on Earthquake Engineering Frontiers of Earthquake Engineering, Anchorage, AK, USA, 21–25 July 2014 (2014)
3. Cresci, S., La Polla, M., Marchetti, A., Meletti, C., Tesconi, M.: Towards a timely prediction of earthquake intensity with social media. IIT TR-12/2014. Technical report. IIT: Istituto di Informatica e Telematica, CNR (2014)
4. Doan, S., Vo, B.-K.H., Collier, N.: An analysis of Twitter messages in the 2011 Tohoku earthquake. In: Kostkova, P., Szomszor, M., Fowler, D. (eds.) eHealth 2011. LNICST, vol. 91, pp. 58–66. Springer, Heidelberg (2012). https://doi.org/10.1007/978-3-642-29262-0_8
5. D'Auria, L., Convertito, V.: Real-time mapping of earthquake perception areas in the Italian region from Twitter streams analysis. In: D'Amico, S. (ed.) Earthquakes and Their Impact on Society. SNH, pp. 619–630. Springer, Cham (2016). https://doi.org/10.1007/978-3-319-21753-6_26
6. Earle, P., et al.: OMG earthquake! Can Twitter improve earthquake response? Seism. Res. Lett. **81**(2), 246–251 (2010)
7. Guevara, M.R., Hartmann, D., Aristarán, M., Mendoza, M., Hidalgo, C.A.: The research space: using career paths to predict the evolution of the research output of individuals, institutions, and nations. Scientometrics **109**(3), 1695–1709 (2016)
8. Mendoza, M., Poblete, B., Castillo, C.: Twitter under crisis: can we trust what we RT? In: Proceedings of the First Workshop on Social Media Analytics, SOMA 2010, pp. 71–79. ACM (2010)
9. Mendoza, M., Poblete, B., Valderrama, I.: Early tracking of people's reaction in Twitter for fast reporting of damages in the mercalli scale. In: Meiselwitz, G. (ed.) SCSM 2018. LNCS, vol. 10914, pp. 247–257. Springer, Cham (2018). https://doi.org/10.1007/978-3-319-91485-5_19
10. Poblete, B., Guzman, J., Flores, J.A.M., Tobar, F.A.: Robust detection of extreme events using Twitter: worldwide earthquake monitoring. IEEE Trans. Multimed. **20**(10), 2551–2561 (2018)
11. Robinson, B., Power, R., Cameron, M.: A sensitive twitter earthquake detector. In: Proceedings of the 22nd International Conference on World Wide Web, pp. 999–1002. ACM (2013)

12. Sakaki, T., Okazaki, M., Matsuo, Y.: Earthquake shakes twitter users: real-time event detection by social sensors. In: Proceedings of the 19th International Conference on World Wide Web, WWW 2010, pp. 851–860. ACM (2010)
13. Zhang, X., Shasha, D.: Better burst detection. In: 2006 Proceedings of the 22nd International Conference on Data Engineering, ICDE 2006, pp. 146–146. IEEE (2006)

Multimodal BigFive Personality Trait Analysis Using Communication Skill Indices and Multiple Discussion Types Dataset

Candy Olivia Mawalim[1(✉)], Shogo Okada[1,3], Yukiko I. Nakano[2,3], and Masashi Unoki[1]

[1] Graduate School of Advanced Science and Technology,
Japan Advanced Institute of Science and Technology,
1-1 Asahidai, Nomi, Ishikawa 923-1292, Japan
{candyolivia,okada-s,unoki}@jaist.ac.jp
[2] Seikei University, Musashino, Tokyo, Japan
y.nakano@st.seikei.ac.jp
[3] RIKEN AIP, Tokyo, Japan

Abstract. This paper focuses on multimodal analysis in multiple discussion types dataset for estimating BigFive personality traits. The analysis was conducted to achieve two goals: First, clarifying the effectiveness of multimodal features and communication skill indices to predict the BigFive personality traits. Second, identifying the relationship among multimodal features, discussion type, and the BigFive personality traits. The MATRICS corpus, which contains of three discussion task types dataset, was utilized in this experiment. From this corpus, three sets of multimodal features (acoustic, head motion, and linguistic) and communication skill indices were extracted as the input for our binary classification system. The evaluation was conducted by using F1-score in 10-fold cross validation. The experimental results showed that the communication skill indices are important in estimating agreeableness trait. In addition, the scope and freedom of conversation affected the performance of personality traits estimator. The freer a discussion is, the better personality traits estimator can be obtained.

Keywords: Multimodal analysis · Multiple discussion ·
BigFive personality traits · Communication skill · Task type

1 Introduction

Personality traits are important in reflecting the way humans think, feel and act. In many cases, knowing the personality traits of an individual can give several advantages. For instance, in hiring new staff, someone with a good personality is more preferable. Consequently, having a general measurement of personality

G. Meiselwitz (Ed.): HCII 2019, LNCS 11578, pp. 370–383, 2019.
https://doi.org/10.1007/978-3-030-21902-4_27

traits is crucial. The BigFive factors [1] are well-known as the most general personality traits measurement. This measurement consists of five traits, including openness, conscientiousness, extraversion, agreeableness, and neuroticism. Psychologists usually evaluate these traits by using standardized factor analysis of personality description questionnaires. However, this manual personality traits evaluation is time-consuming and expensive. Therefore, measuring these traits automatically has become a great interest in the computing field.

In recent years, prior studies focus on using automatic nonverbal analysis for numerous sorts of applications, including the estimation of personality traits. The nonverbal features were obtained from audio and visual data based on the knowledge of social science. For instance, in [2], personality trait was modeled by using audiovisual data of intrapersonal communication. In addition, modeling personality trait by dyadic interactions from body language and speech information was also conducted in [3].

As the time slipped by, investigation on interpersonal communication has been considered to predict either the personality traits or the other functional roles of the participant. It has been reported that using interpersonal communication (such as a group discussion), in which there exists group interaction, can achieve promising performance for detecting some speaker-related variables. For instance, [4] investigated the speaker role in group discussion. [5] attempted to detect the functional roles of each participant in group conversation. Furthermore, personality traits have also been investigated by using co-occurrent multimodal event discovery approach [6]. In this research, we conducted a multimodal analysis from multiple discussion datasets to estimate the BigFive personality traits. The group discussion approach was used since the way a person expresses their opinion and their response in group discussion have a close relationship with their personality traits.

This paper has two novel points. First, we investigated the effectiveness of the communication skill for predicting BigFive personality traits. As we know, social communication skill helps humans exchange their thought in a more convincing way. Furthermore, people with good communication skill tend to have an impressive personality. Second, we investigated whether the discussion task type affected the personality traits of the participants. MATRICS corpus introduced in [7] which consists of three discussion tasks were employed in this research. The discussion tasks were varied with regard to the scope and freedom on dialog structure of the conversation.

2 Related Work

The aim of automatic personality computing is to model the relationship between stimuli (everything observable people do) and the outcomes of the social perception processes (how we form impressions about others). There have been many studies of on a multimodal analysis of the personality trait inference. For instance, Pianesi et al. [8] conducted a personality prediction for each participant using self-reported questionnaires. Aran et al. [9] presented an analysis of personality prediction in small groups on the basis of trait attributes from external observers. Jayagopi et al. [10] proposed a mining approach for finding context features to link to group performance and personality traits. Okada et al. [6] proposed another mining approach to extract co-occurrent events between multimodal time-series data for personality classification. Batrinca et al. [11] conducted a comparative analysis to investigate the difference in the recognition accuracy of personality traits between a human-machine interaction (HMI) setting and a human-human interaction (HHI) setting. Valente et al. [12] conducted personality modeling using dialog acts with speaking activity, prosody, and n-gram distributions.

Besides, several works also focused on improving the accuracy of BigFive prediction. Fang et al. [13] conducted BigFive prediction by using three different nonverbal feature categories, i.e intrapersonal features, dyadic features, and one-vs-all features. On the other hand, Lin et al. [14] attempted to predict the BigFive by modeling vocal behaviors of participants using the interaction-based mechanism in BLSTM.

According to literature [15], several experiments have successfully confirmed the influence of personality traits towards numerous human behavior aspects, such as leadership and job performance. communication skill is also one of the most important human behavior aspects which can lead to creating a successful global relationship. Hence, the association between communication skill and human personality trait has not been investigated yet. Utilizing the communication skill indices for the personality trait inference is one of the main differences between this research and the previous works.

In addition, a comparative analysis of task types varied in the scope and freedom of conversation was conducted for classifying the personality traits. This is also the distinctive point of this research. The prior work of Okada et al. [16] suggested that depending upon the assessed task, people show different manner (different effective multimodal features) in group communication. In contrast, this research aims to investigate the relationship between the assessed task type and the predictive level of BigFive personality traits.

3   Multimodal Data Corpus

The MATRICS multimodal data corpus presented in [7] was employed in this research. This corpus consists of head motion data, audio data, and video data. The head motion data was obtained by an accelerometer and the recorded audio were used to form the acoustics and linguistic features. Previously, in [16], the communication skill indices which assessment by human resource management experts by using video data was the target of the inference. As for now, we aim to confirm how is the relationship between these indices and the BigFive personality traits. The BigFive personality traits scores were annotated by using the self-questionnaire survey (as the standard method in physiology domain).

The MATRICS corpus is a Japanese group discussion corpus which contains 10 discussion groups with 4 participants each. For every discussion groups, three tasks were set for the discussion. The tasks were varied in regards to the scope and freedom on dialog structure of the conversation. The first task is defined as an in-basket task. In this task, the participants acted as the executive committee members who required to select an invited guest for a school festival. Most prior information was provided in this task. The second task is defined as a case study with prior information. In this task, the participants required to create a food and beverage booth for a school festival. Some information was provided with regard to the booth. Lastly, the third task is defined as a case study without prior information. In this task, the participants had to create a two-day itinerary plan in Japan for their foreign friends. Every participant can express their thought freely without time limit per each individual.

4   Feature Representation

We extracted self-context features, including three sets of multimodal features (acoustic features, linguistic features, and head motion features) and communication skill indices. The acoustic features and linguistic features were extracted from audio data and the manual transcription of the discussion dialog. The head motion features were extracted from head accelerator data. The communication skill features were assessed manually by human resource management experts. All the features were normalized by using z-score normalization. The feature sets were summarized in Table 1.

Table 1. Summary of feature sets for the BigFive personality traits estimation

	Variables
Acoustic feature (AFs)	4 energy related LLDs
	54 spectral LLDs
	6 voicing related LLDs
Linguistic features (LFs)	5 PoS tags (number of noun, verb, new noun, interjection, filler)
	12 dialog tags
	3 speech act tags
	2 semantic tags
Head motion (HMs)	Mean of movement
	Deviation of movement
	Mean of movement while speaking
	Deviation of movement while speaking
	Difference of movement while speaking
Communication skill (CSs)	Listening attitude
	Smooth interaction
	Aggregation of opinions
	Communication own claim
	Logical and clear presentation
	Total communication skill

4.1   Acoustic Features

The acoustic features were extracted from each participant speech by using the speech features extractors openSMILE [17]. The unified test-bed for perceived speaker traits configuration file [18] were used to obtain 6,125 features. These features were derived from 64 low-level descriptors (LLDs) (the detail is shown in Table 2). We used these features since these features are considered as the baseline in speaker trait research [19].

Table 2. 64 LLDs of the INTERSPEECH 2012 speaker trait challenge [18]

4 energy related LLDs
Sum of auditory spectrum (loudness)
Sum of RASTA-style filtered auditory spectrum
RMS energy
Zero-crossing rate
54 spectral LLDs
RASTA-style auditory spectrum, bands 1–26 (0–8 kHz)
MFCC 1–14
Spectral energy 250–650 Hz, 1–4 kHz
Spectral roll off point 0.25, 0.50, 0.75, 0.90
Spectral flux, entropy, variance, skewness, kurtosis
Slope, psycho-acoustic sharpness, harmonicity
6 voicing related LLDs
F0 by SHS + viterbi smoothing, probability of voicing
logarithmic HNR, jitter (local, delta), shimmer (local)

4.2   Linguistic Features

The linguistic features consist of part of speech (PoS), dialog act, and semantic tag. These features were extracted using the same approach in [16]. The PoS features were extracted from the manual transcription by using a Japanese morphological analysis tool, MeCab [22]. The number of nouns, verbs, new nouns (the nouns which are spoken for the first time in the discussion), interjection (the word or phrase to convey emotion or feeling of the speaker), and filler (the word or phrase for filling an interlude in an utterance of conversation) belonged to this feature set. The dialog act and semantic tag set consist of 17 tags. Twelve tags came from DAMSL (Dialog Act Markup in Several Layers) [20] and MRDA (Meeting Recorder Dialog Act) [21] tag set, including "conversational opening", "open question", "suggestion", "backchannel", "open opinion", "partial accept", "accept", "reject", "understanding check", "other question", "WH-question", and "y/n question". the other five tags were defined in [16], which consist three speech act tag ("plan", "agreement", and "disagreement") and two semantic tags ("describe fact" and "reason").

4.3 Head Motion Features

We utilized five features to represent head motion, i.e. mean and deviation of head movement, mean and deviation of head movement while speaking, and the range of movement while speaking. The head movement was calculated as the norm of the head acceleration at one duration of time. On the other hand, the head accelerator data were joined with the speaking time data to obtain the head movement while speaking.

4.4 Communication Skill Indices

We employed six features for representing the communication skill, i.e. listening attitude, smooth interaction, aggregation of opinions, communicating one's own claim, logical and clear presentation, and total communication skill. Listening attitudes reflect the participant listening manner towards other participants. Smooth interaction captures the efficiency of information exchange of the participant in the group discussion. Aggregation of opinions represents how well a participant could organize and summarize other opinions. Communicating one's own claim reflects how the participant could express appropriate information in every kind of situations. The logical and clear presentation reflects the logic and coherence of a participant in expressing their opinions. Finally, the total communication skill is the total of all five other features.

5 Experimental Setting

The objectives of this experiment are: (1) to clarify the effective features multimodal (verbal and nonverbal) features and communication skill indices to predict the BigFive personality traits and (2) to identify the relationship among multimodal features, discussion type, and the BigFive personality traits. Since the acoustic features were designed in binary classification environment, we also performed binary classification tasks for achieving the objectives. We used 99 out of 120 data samples since there were some missing values in head motion features or the problem with audio files. The target for inference is the BigFive personality traits, including neuroticism, openness, conscientiousness, agreeableness, and extraversion. The assessment scores from experts were classified into high or low (with threshold $= 50$).

Comparative Tasks
In this experiment, we also compared four tasks [16]. Task 1 is defined as the in-basket task (32 samples). Task 2 is defined as a case study with prior information (36 samples). Task 3 is defined as a case study without prior information (31 samples). All tasks (99 samples) is defined as a combination of task 1, task 2,

and task 3. The utilized dataset for classifying the BigFive personality traits in each task refers to the task type explained in Sect. 3.

Comparative Feature Sets
The 15 feature sets shown in Table 3 were compared to analyze the contribution of each feature set in estimating BigFive personality traits.

Table 3. Comparative feature sets for classifying BigFive personality traits

Unimodal
AFs: Acoustic Features
HMs: Head Motion Features
LFs: Linguistic Features
CSs: communication skill
Bimodal
AF_HM: Fusing AFs and HMs
AF_LF: Fusing AFs and LFs
AF_CS: Fusing AFs and CSs
HM_LF: Fusing HMs and LFs
HM_CS: Fusing HMs and CSs
LF_CS: Fusing LFs and CSs
Multimodal
AF_HM_LF: Fusing AFs, HMs, and LFs
AF_HM_CS: Fusing AFs, HMs, and CSs
AF_LF_CS: Fusing AFs, LFs, and CSs
HM_LF_CS: Fusing HMs, LFs, and CSs
All: Fusing all features (AFs, LFs, HMs, CSs)

5.1   Classification Techniques

In this study, several classification algorithms implemented in scikit-learn [23] were utilized to investigate the effectiveness of the identified features. Scikit-learn is an open-source machine learning library built in python programming language environment. We investigated the support vector machine (SVM), random forest, Naïve Bayes, and decision tree algorithms. The brief explanation for these algorithms is presented below.

- Support Vector Machine (SVM)
  SVM is considered one of a good classification algorithm in any kind of tasks, for example, text categorization problem and face detection [24]. This technique applies kernel trick (finding optimal hyperplane) for separating or classifying the data. In this experiment, we used the SVM classifier with radial basis function (RBF) kernel.

- Random Forest (RF)
  RF is also considered as an alternative to deal with a big number of features. Since it creates a set of decision trees from randomly selected training subset, it can reduce overfitting and produce a very robust, high-performing model [25]. In this experiment, we used RF classifier with maximum depth = 3.
- Gaussian Naïve Bayes (GNB)
  Naïve Bayes classifier is well-known for its simpleness because it requires less training data to perform classification task [26]. The main disadvantage from this classifier is that since it holds NB conditional independence assumption, it cannot learn the relationship among the features (may causes oversensitivity to redundant features). Although it has some disadvantages, it was reported can achieve good performance for some domains. In this experiment, we used Gaussian NB.
- Decision Tree (ID3)
  This algorithm is also utilized in this experiment because it is also easy to use (no need a big effort on preprocessing the data). In this experiment, we use the CART algorithm of the decision tree with the default parameters.

5.2 Evaluation Criteria

F1-score is used to evaluate the performance of our estimators. F1-score conveys the balance between precision and recall since it is calculated as the harmonic mean of these two parameters. In this research, we performed k-fold cross-validation with $K = 10$ to confirm the performance is not overfitting to the testing data. In the result section, we refer the F1-score as the average of this 10-folds performance, defined as follows:

$$\overline{F_1} = \frac{1}{K} \sum_{k=1}^{K} F_1(k) \times 100\%. \tag{1}$$

6 Result

From Tables 4 and 5, the overall experimental results (for all tasks) show that random forest technique achieved the best F1-score for estimating neuroticism (68.07%), openness (63.84%), and agreeableness (73.75%) traits. On the other hand, Gaussian NB could estimate well the extraversion (64.32%) and SVM for estimating conscientiousness (65.84%). The best estimators for neuroticism, extraversion, openness, agreeableness, and conscientiousness were obtained by using AFs, HMs, HM_CS_LF (combination of HMs, CSs, and LFs), AFs, and HMs, respectively. Our experimental results also showed that the agreeableness is the most predictive trait which achieved the best F1-score in almost all cases. Although AFs has the best contribution as unimodal feature set, CSs played a slightly less important role compared to AFs in estimating the agreeableness trait. Compared with the previous research (Okada et al. [6]), these results are better in estimating neuroticism, openness, agreeableness, and conscientiousness traits. However, for estimating extraversion trait, the research of Okada et al. [6] by using co-ocurrent event discovery could obtain better accuracy (up to 69.61%).

Figure 1 shows the highest classification F1-score with regards to the task types. The average of F1-scores from each task shows that order from less predictive task to more predictive task is from All_Tasks (0.672), Task 1 (0.693),

Table 4. BigFive personality traits estimation using all tasks dataset with regards to machine learning technique

Technique	BigFive personality traits (%)				
	Neuroticism	Extraversion	Openness	Agreeableness	Conscientiousness
SVM	59.26	62.14	56.07	67.96	65.84
RF	68.07	62.81	63.84	73.75	64.32
GNB	59.94	64.32	56.30	64.94	65.60
ID3	63.34	63.96	61.20	65.62	62.88
Best	68.07	64.32	63.84	73.75	65.84
	GNB	RF	RF	SVM	HMs

Table 5. BigFive personality traits estimation using all tasks datasets with regards to feature sets

Feature set	BigFive personality traits (%)				
	Neuroticism	Extraversion	Openness	Agreeableness	Conscientiousness
AFs	68.07	55.28	52.19	73.75	53.91
HMs	59.94	64.32	47.22	52.18	65.84
CSs	48.23	46.19	53.13	66.78	52.93
LFs	57.64	63.96	58.17	62.25	61.92
AF_HM	54.54	59.84	56.40	62.13	62.61
AF_CS	51.44	59.25	59.32	64.30	60.55
AF_LF	53.76	59.64	52.84	60.32	57.04
HM_CS	60.26	58.50	59.83	67.96	65.44
HM_LF	63.34	60.42	61.83	62.69	62.88
CS_LF	58.45	62.11	62.36	62.72	64.32
AF_HM_CS	55.33	59.77	57.32	63.45	59.47
AF_HM_LF	52.97	62.81	59.40	62.02	58.40
AF_CS_LF	56.08	56.70	61.20	61.63	63.69
HM_CS_LF	62.09	62.06	63.84	61.40	62.49
All	63.82	54.76	53.10	66.29	55.79
Best	68.07	64.32	63.84	73.75	65.84
	AFs	HMs	HM_CS_LF	AFs	HMs

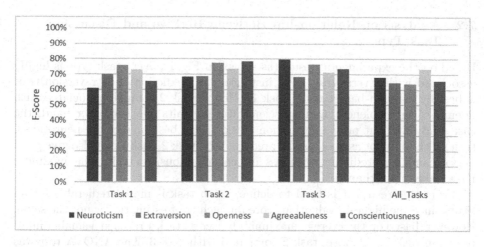

Fig. 1. BigFive personality classification results of depending upon task type (as described in Sect. 5) in term of best F1-score. The order from the less to the most predictive task is from All_Tasks, Task 1, Task 2, and Task 3.

Task 2 (0.733), and Task 3 (0.739), respectively. In addition, we figured out that there are similarities between Task 2 and Task 3. The performance estimators for several personality traits (extraversion, openness, and agreeableness) from Task 2 and Task 3 achieved almost the same F1-score.

7 Discussion

This section contains the discussion of our experimental results. The discussion mainly consists of three parts, i.e. analysis on the relationship between the BigFive personality traits with the multimodal feature sets and analysis on the relationship between the BigFive personality traits with discussion task type.

7.1 Analysis on Relationship Between BigFive and Multimodal Feature Sets

In this section, we discuss the effectiveness of the multimodal features. The overall experimental result in Table 5 shows that for unimodal feature sets, AFs and LFs are highly correlated with the BigFive personality traits (the average F-score for all traits estimation could reach around 60%). This result suggests that the way and the content of speaking play the most important role in estimating the speaker personality traits. Fusing the feature sets can also give a promising result, especially for estimating the openness trait (fusing HMs, CSs, and LFs).

Although the correlation between the personality traits and HMs and CSs feature sets are not as high as AFs and LFs, utilizing them implies better estimation for several traits. For instance, utilizing HMs is best in estimating extraversion and conscientiousness traits. This verified the previous finding that extraversion is positively associated with gesturing [27].

7.2   Analysis on Relationship Between BigFive and Discussion Task Type

Based on the experimental result (as shown in Fig. 1), every task type is highly associated with several traits. For instance, the prediction of extraversion trait is best by using in-basket task (Task 1). Hence, task 2 is highly associated with openness, agreeableness, and conscientiousness traits. On the other hand, the case study without prior information (task 3) can best predict the neuroticism trait. Although not as good as the prediction by task 2, task 3 can also give good performance for predicting openness and conscientiousness traits (the maximum F1-score is more than 60%).

From this result, it is hard to define which task is more predictable for all traits since the highest evaluation score for each trait estimation is not the same. However, based on the average maximum F1-score, task 1 reached a smaller number than task 2. Likewise, task 2 compared with task 3. The ANOVA test was also conducted to check the statistical significance of the result of predicting each trait. From the test, we obtained that only agreeableness trait estimation could reach p-value less than 0.05 (0.0006). Moreover, the estimation of extraversion trait could reach $p\text{-value} = 0.0713$ (weak statistically significant). From this result, we conclude that having free or non-strict conversation dataset may lead to a better automatic BigFive personality traits estimation, especially for estimating the agreeableness trait.

In the case of employing all tasks, the BigFive prediction became more difficult (the average maximum F1-score is the smallest). This was probably because of the characteristics of each task is different. Moreover, this may also be caused by the different manner of the target when the different discussion task was assigned (conclusion from Okada et al. [16]). In other words, we suggest that the homogeneous dataset (unvaried task type) is more predictive than the heterogeneous dataset (varied task type) for predicting BigFive personality traits.

7.3   Analysis on Relationship Between BigFive and Communication Skill Indices

The experimental result shows that taking the CSs indices is useful for estimating agreeableness trait (reached 66.78% F1-score). The high association between CSs and agreeableness may because a good communicator is usually a broad-minded and friendly person. Furthermore, the one who can express an opinion well on a decision affects how he/she can agree or disagree on something. Alternatively, the CSs indices did correlate with the openness and conscientiousness traits. However, we could not conclude that the CSs indices did correlate significantly with BigFive (since the F1-score was not higher than 60%). In addition, because the F1-score for neuroticism and extraversion traits estimation by using CSs indices did not even reach 50%, we conclude that these traits did not correlate with CSs indices.

8   Conclusion and Future Work

This paper presented multimodal analysis in multiple discussion types dataset to estimate the BigFive personality traits, which consists of neuroticism, extraversion, openness, agreeableness, and conscientiousness. This research aimed to clarify the effectiveness of multimodal (verbal and nonverbal) features and communication skill indices to predict the BigFive personality traits and to clarify the relationship among multimodal features, discussion type, and BigFive personality traits. Based on the results shown in Sect. 6, the best estimators for neuroticism, extraversion, openness, agreeableness, and conscientiousness were obtained by using AFs, HMs, HM_CS_LF, AFs, and HMs, respectively. The agreeableness was also reported as the most predictive trait. Although AFs has the best contribution, CSs played a slightly less important role compared to AFs in estimating the agreeableness trait. With regards to the task types, we figured out that the scope and freedom of conversations affected the performance of personality traits estimator. The experimental results suggested that having free or non-strict conversation dataset may lead to a better automatic BigFive personality traits estimation, especially for the agreeableness trait.

As the future work, we would like to investigate not only self-context features but also other-context features (the relationship between the multimodal features of other participants and the personality trait of the speaker). Another important future direction for this work is to consider the dynamics of the features. Zhu et al. [28] suggested that the temporal amplitude modulation played an important role in emotion perception. This implies that utilizing dynamic features instead of static features may lead to a better personality traits inference result. Furthermore, in the current result, we figured out that there may be a non-linearity effect. For instance, as unimodal feature set, AFs were relatively good features compared to HMs for predicting openness trait. However, fusing HMs, CSs, and LFs (HM_CS_LF) resulted in best prediction score. To deal with this issue, the non-linear model will be employed to account for BigFive as the future direction.

References

1. McCrae, R.R., John, O.P.: An Introduction to the five-factor model and its applications. J. Pers. **60**, 175–215 (1992)
2. Celiktutan, O., Eyben, F., Sariyanidi, E., Gunes, H., Schuller, B.: MAPTRAITS 2014 - the first audio/visual mapping personality traits challenge - an introduction: perceived personality and social dimensions. In: 16th International Conference on Multimodal Interaction, ICMI 2014, New York, NY, USA, pp. 3–9 (2014)
3. Metallinou, A., Katsamanis, A., Narayanan, S.: Tracking continuous emotional trends of participants during affective dyadic interactions using body language and speech information. J. Image Vis. Comput. **31**(2), 137–152 (2013)
4. Vinciarelli, A.: Speakers role recognition in multiparty audio recordings using social network analysis and duration distribution modeling. J. IEEE Trans. Multimed. **9**(6), 1215–1226 (2007)

5. Zancanaro, M., Lepri, B., Pianesi, F.: Automatic detection of group functional roles in face to face interactions. In: 8th International Conference on Multimodal Interfaces, ICMI 2006, Banff, Alberta, Canada, pp. 28–34 (2006)
6. Okada, S., Aran, O., Gatica-Perez, D.: Personality trait classification via co-occurrent multiparty multimodal event discovery. In: ACM on International Conference on Multimodal Interaction, ICMI 2015, New York, NY, USA, pp. 15–22 (2015)
7. Nihei, F., Nakano, Y.I., Hayashi, Y., Hung, H.H., Okada, S.: Predicting influential statements in group discussions using speech and head motion information. In: Proceedings of the ACM ICMI, pp. 136–143 (2014)
8. Pianesi, F., Mana, N., Cappelletti, A., Lepri, B., Zancanaro, M.: Multimodal recognition of personality traits in social interactions. In: Proceedings of ACM ICMI, pp. 53–60 (2008)
9. Aran, O., Gatica-Perez, D.: One of a kind: Inferring personality impressions in meetings. In: Proceedings of ACM ICMI, pp. 11–18 (2013)
10. Jayagopi, D.B., Sanchez-Cortes, D., Otsuka, K., Yamato, J., Gatica-Perez, D.: Linking speaking and looking behavior patterns with group composition, perception, and performance. In: Proceedings of ACM ICMI, pp. 433–440 (2012)
11. Batrinca, L., Mana, N., Lepri, B., Sebe, N., Pianesi, F.: Multimodal personality recognition in collaborative goal-oriented tasks. IEEE Trans. Multimed. **18**(4), 659–673 (2016)
12. Valente, F., Kim, S., Motlicek, P.: Annotation and recognition of personality traits in spoken conversations from the AMI meetings corpus. In: Proceedings of INTERSPEECH, pp. 1183–1186 (2012)
13. Fang, S., Achard, C., Dubuisson, S.: Personality classification and behaviour interpretation: an approach based on feature categories. In: Proceedings of the 18th ACM International Conference on Multimodal Interaction, pp. 225–232. ACM (2016)
14. Lin, Y., Lee, C.: Using interlocutor-modulated attention BLSTM to predict personality traits in small group interaction. In: Proceedings of the 2018 on International Conference on Multimodal Interaction, pp. 163–169. ACM (2018)
15. Lepri, B., Pianesi, F.: Computational approaches for personality prediction. In: Burgoon, J., Magnenat-Thalmann, N., Pantic, M., Vinciarelli, A. (eds.) Social Signal Processing, pp. 168–182. Cambridge University Press, Cambridge (2017)
16. Okada, S., et al.: Estimating communication skill using dialogue acts and nonverbal features in multiple discussion datasets. In: ACM on International Conference on Multimodal Interaction, ICMI 2016, Tokyo, pp. 169–176 (2016)
17. Eyben, F., Wöllmer, M., Schuller. B.: OpenSMILE: the munich versatile and fast open-source audio feature extractor. In: Proceedings of the 18th ACM International Conference on Multimedia, MM 2010, pp. 1459–1462. ACM, New York (2010)
18. Schuller, B., et al.: The INTERSPEECH 2012 speaker trait challenge. In: INTERSPEECH (2012)
19. Schuller, B., et al.: A Survey on perceived speaker traits: personality, likability, pathology, and the first challenge. Comput. Speech Lang. **29**(1), 100–131 (2015)
20. Core, M.G., Allen, J.: Coding dialogs with the DAMSL annotation scheme. In: AAAI Fall Symposium on Communicative Action in Humans and Machines, pp. 28–35 (1997)
21. Shriberg, E., Dhillon, R., Bhagat, S., Ang, J., Carvey, H.: The ICSI meeting recorder dialog act (MRDA) corpus. In: Proceedings of SIGDIAL, pp. 97–100 (2004)

22. Kudo, T., Yamamoto, K., Matsumoto, Y.: Applying conditional random fields to Japanese morphological analysis. In: EMNLP, vol. 4, pp. 230–237 (2004)
23. Pedregosa, F., et al.: Scikit-learn: machine learning in python. J. Mach. Learn. Res. **12**, 2825–2830 (2011)
24. Hearst, M.A.: Support vector machine. J. IEEE Intell. Syst. **13**(4), 18–28 (1998)
25. Breiman, L.: Random forest. J. Mach. Learn. **45**(1), 5–32 (2001)
26. Ratanamahatana, C.A., Gunopulos, D.: Scaling up the naive Bayesian classifier: using decision trees for feature selection (2002)
27. Ethier, N.A.: Paralinguistic and nonverbal behaviour in social interactions: a lens model perspective. UWSpac (2010)
28. Zhu, Z., Miyauchi, R., Araki, Y., Unoki, M.: Modulation spectral features for predicting vocal emotion recognition by simulated cochlear implants. In: INTER-SPEECH, pp. 262–266 (2016)

Analysis of Review Text on a Golf Course Reservation Site

Shin Miyake[1]($\boxtimes$), Kohei Otake[2], and Takashi Namatame[3]

[1] Graduate School of Science and Engineering, Chuo University, 1-13-27,
Kasuga, Bunkyo-Ku, Tokyo 112-8551, Japan
a15.66cc@g.chuo-u.ac.jp
[2] Faculty of Science and Engineering, Tokai University, 2-3-23, Takanawa,
Minato-Ku, Tokyo 108-8619, Japan
otake@tsc.u-tokai.ac.jp
[3] Faculty of Science and Engineering, Chuo University, 1-13-27, Kasuga,
Bunkyo-Ku, Tokyo 112-8551, Japan
nama@indsys.chuo-u.ac.jp

Abstract. On EC site, customer's reviews (product review) have a gat influence on other customer's purchase. Rating points for products and evaluation on review itself are expected to be utilized for marketing. In this study, we analyze reviews and rating points of a golf courses reservation site. Moreover, we evaluate positive points for golf courses and we clarified the characteristics of their reviews. Concretely, we performed logistic regression to discriminate evaluation for golf course by using the genre of review sentences.

Keywords: Natural language processing · Logistic regression analysis

1 Introduction

Along with the spread of the EC (Electronic Commerce) market, we became easier to order or to make a reservation the products and services on EC site. Compared with purchasing at a conventional store, the purchase via EC site has no time and place limitation. From these kinds of reasons, the market size of EC is increasing. In many cases, EC site not only purchases products but also has a meaning of place for sharing information such as product review and evaluation of product. Moreover, there is also a service that evaluates the product and service by scores.

The rating service numerically expresses the customer's evaluation. The contents of the review and the evaluation score may have strong influence for the purchase decision of other customers. Especially, consumers cannot examine the purchase by picking up the actual products, the contribution has a huge influence. Further, reviews based on actual experiences are valuable information for consumers who have not been purchased yet.

Therefore, the review plays an important role at EC site and it is important for analyzing consumer behavior. On the other hand, the evaluation criteria differ depending on each customer in the rating service. Even if scores which evaluated by two customers of a product are same, it may be the result of comparison with the past

© Springer Nature Switzerland AG 2019
G. Meiselwitz (Ed.): HCII 2019, LNCS 11578, pp. 384–395, 2019.
https://doi.org/10.1007/978-3-030-21902-4_28

purchasing and using the experience of the customer. Therefore, the viewpoint is different on each customer. In other words, compared with the evaluation criteria of each customer, it is necessary to consider whether a review based on positive evaluation or a review based on the negative evaluation.

2 Purpose of This Study

First, we related some previous studies. Nishikawa, et al. showed a method for automatically classifying the traveler's travel purpose by using the review of travel sites [1]. In addition, Nakayama and Fujii introduced the analysis method of review focusing on words that receive subjective expressions that show useful evaluations [2]. Comparing these studies, we use the review's evaluation point and classify the reviews which are good contents or bad contents.

Then in this study, we clarify the characteristics of the review that satisfied in the evaluation criteria of each customer, using natural language processing and logistic regression.

3 Dataset and Analysis Method

First, we summarize the items of data in Table 1. Then, we explain the detail of them.

Table 1. Data description

Data	Reservation data in the golf course
Duration of data	November 13, 2013–November 13, 2016
Master data in the golf course (total of 3054)	Data in the golf course that treated at the site • Average evaluation score in the golf course golf course information • Golf course's name, address, etc.
Review data (total of 14684)	Data about customer who posted the review • Contributor ID • Review texts • Evaluation score in the golf course • Attributes in customer

3.1 Extraction of Target Reviews

The reviews using in this study were written about golf courses and these are posted on a golf portal site. Also using points that site members assessed with a score of the 5-point scale. As a preprocessing for analysis, we deleted the empty review sentences and extracted by using the golf courses that received over 100 evaluations.

Moreover, we selected customers who are posting reviews 20 to 30 times during the duration. Then in this study, we used 319 contributor's reviews that concerned about 496 golf courses.

3.2 Classification of Reviews

First, we extracted 1000 reviews from the targeting user's review data by random sampling and these used for tagging about categories.

The review is composed of some category sentences. So, we divided 1000 reviews into sentences one by one and gave the 12 genres by the review contents i.e., Golf Course, Nature Environment of the Golf Course, Facilities, Meals, Weather, Game results, other clientele, Game Price, Caddies, Golf Course Staff, Road Condition to Golf Course and Other. In addition, against the genres included in each review sentence, we divided into a positive (P) or negative (N) sentence. Therefore, we tagged the 24 categories to a part of review data.

3.3 TF-IDF Method

We collected reviews belonging to each of the 24 categories and made one sentence in each category. After that, we tried to identify important words that characteristically express each category. Specifically, we extracted words that had appeared in each category by using the TF-IDF method. TF-IDF method was adopted by the following Eqs. (1) to (3).

$$TFIDF_{i,j} = tf_{i,j} \times idf_i \tag{1}$$

$$tf_{i,j} = \frac{n_{i,j}}{\sum_s n_{s,j}} \tag{2}$$

$$idf_i = \log \frac{|D|}{|\{d : d \in t_i\}|} \tag{3}$$

Here, $n_{i,j}$ is the number of appearing frequency about word i in the sentence j. $\sum_s n_{s,j}$ is the number of appearing frequency of all words in the sentence j, $|D|$ is the total number of all sentences. $|\{d : d \in t_i\}|$ is the number of sentences containing word i.

3.4 Logistic Regression Analysis

In preview section, we identified words (characteristic words) that characteristically express each category. We fractionated the individual reviews to good review (1: higher than average evaluation score) or bad review (0: lower than the average evaluation score). Next, for each review, we counted the numbers that include the characteristic words of each 24 categories. Counted result set as the explanatory variables. We identified the characteristics by using logistic regression analysis (Eq. (4)) that has $\beta_0, \beta_1, \cdots, \beta_n$ as parameters.

$$p_y = \frac{\exp\{\beta_0 + \sum_{i=1}^n \beta_i x_i\}}{1 + \exp\{\beta_0 + \sum_{i=1}^n \beta_i x_i\}} \tag{4}$$

Where p_y is the probability which occurs objective event y.

We selected reviews from the targeting user's review data and these used as learning data in the logistic regression model (7,550). The objective variable y show in Eq. (5).

$$y = \begin{cases} 1 \cdots \text{ higher than the average point} \\ 0 \cdots \text{ lower than the average point} \end{cases} \tag{5}$$

In estimating the parameter β in the logistic regression model, estimation was performed by using the maximum likelihood method. The maximum likelihood function of the logistic regression analysis is expressed in Eq. (6) as a function about β.

$$L(\beta) = \prod_{i=1}^{n} \Pr(Y = y_i | x_i) = \prod_{i=1}^{n} p_i^{y_i} (1 - p_i)^{1-y_i} \tag{6}$$

In general, we use a loglikelihood function performing logarithmic transformation likelihood as in the expression (7).

$$\log L(\beta) = \sum_{i=1}^{n} \log \left\{ p_i^{y_i} (1 - p_i)^{1-y_i} \right\} = \sum_{i=1}^{n} \left\{ \log(1 - y_i) + y_i \log \left(\frac{p_i}{1 - p_i} \right) \right\} \tag{7}$$

3.5 Model Selection Criteria

It is necessary to set the criteria to select the best model from a lot of models. One of these criteria is the information reference amount, and in this study, we used Akaike's Information Criterion proposed by Akaike. AIC method was adopted by the following Eq. (8) [3].

$$AIC = -2 \ln L + 2M \tag{8}$$

The second item of an equation expresses the penalty for the complexity of the model as $2M$ which is proportional to the number of parameters. L makes it possible to preferentially select a simple model as a model.

3.6 Confusion Matrix

Confusion matrix is a performance measurement for machine learning classification problem in two classes. It is a table with 4 different combinations of predicted and actual values. We introduce Confusion matrix and numerical calculation method below using for model accuracy verification.

Table 2. Confusion matrix

		Predicted value	
		Positive	Negative
Actual value	Positive	True positive (TP)	False negative (FN)
	Negative	False positive (FP)	True negative (TN)

ACC (accuracy) is the correct classifications divided by all classifications.

$$ACC = \frac{TP + TN}{FP + FN + TP + TN} \tag{9}$$

PRE (Precision) is the correct classifications penalized by the number of incorrect classifications.

$$PRE = \frac{TP}{TP + FP} \tag{10}$$

REC (recall) is the number of correct classifications penalized by the number of missed items.

$$REC = \frac{TP}{TP + FN} \tag{11}$$

F-measure is a derived effectiveness measurement. The resultant value is interpreted as a weighted average of the precision and recall.

$$F\ measure = 2 \times \frac{PRE \times REC}{PRE + REC} \tag{12}$$

4   Results

4.1   Result of Logistic Regression Analysis

In this section, first we show the result of logistic regression without interaction terms.

Next, we show the results with interaction terms of analysis. Then, we compare the accuracy among these results. First, we summarize the characteristic words of each 24 categories at Table 1. The words selected as the characteristic words are the top 10 of the words with high TF-IDF value in each category (Table 3).

Table 3. Characteristic words of each category

Golf Course (P)	course, green, good, maintenance, broad, fun, distance, play, golf, way
Golf Course (N)	green, course, ball, difficult, grass golf, bunker, many, and, distance, hole
Nature Environment of the Golf Course (P)	landscape, course, autumn leaves, good, scenery, entry, tract, Mount Fuji, resort, broad
Nature Environment of the Golf Course (N)	landscape, Mount Fuji, shadow, harm, hill, superior, front, windshield, wild, monkey
Facilities Golf Course (P)	bathroom, hot spring, clubhouse, training, facility, meals, beautiful, nature, course, a place to stay
Facilities Golf Course (N)	cart, hot spring, and, training, locker, field, remote control, bad luck, road, facility
Meals (P)	meals, delicious(a Chinese character), delicious, buffet, menu, branch, good, dish, staff, noon
Meals (N)	menu, meals, buffet, lunch, amount, amount of goods, and, drinks, lonely, piled
Weather (P)	weather, good, play, rain, hot, weather, cold, wind, forecast, round
Weather (N)	rain, good, course, weather, strong, wind, cold, forecast, day, play
Game Price (P)	low price, price, fee, value, reasonable, cost performance, bargain, course, a yen, kos
Game Price (N)	fee, low price, add, yen, price, high, money, towsome, consideration, Fujioka
other clientele (P)	smooth, good, play, round, thing, not, though, start, weekday, in front and behind
other clientele (N)	group, time, manner, and, hole, minute, people, in front, wait, player
Game results (P)	score, revenge, bardie, update, good, best score, short, best, fairway keep, challenging
Game results (N)	score, green, revenge, pat, sinking, putter, arm, score-, fault, myself
Caddies (P)	caddy-, Mr., caddy, accurate, advice, good, course, reception, attender, fun
Caddies (N)	give guidance, caddy-, caddy, play, rainy season, apprentice, private talk, newcomer, before last, appearance
Golf Course Staff (P)	staff, reception, customer service, good, smile, course, everybody, polite, member, nice
Golf Course Staff (N)	and, staff, start, Marshall, cart, in front, pointing out, claim, need, attention
Road Condition to Golf Course (P)	close, inter, close, house, city center, access, traffic jam, train, own house, course
Road Condition to Golf Course (N)	traffic jam, route, nine, drive, accident, night, path, around, be supposed to, return
Other (P)	chance, play, course, challenge, challenging, fun, use, round, hindrance, golf
Other (N)	bad luck, ku, course, bag, order, red, cancel, improvement, and, cart

Within the same category, duplication of words was seen.

We can see that many words are expressing the own category's definition from the result of Table 2. At the result of the Golf course positive category, words such as "green", "road" and "distance" were selected for expressing the feature of the Golf Course. As a word for expressing emotions, a word such as "fun" was selected. Also, in contents of the same category's negative result, words such as "distance", "wind" and "bunker" were selected for expressing the feature of the Golf Course. In addition, words such as "difficulty" was selected as a word that express the emotions. Words such as "green", "course", "distance", etc. were duplicated among categories.

Moreover, at the result of the game price's positive category, words such as "low price", "performance", "bargain" and "reasonable" were selected for expressing the feature of the Game price. The words such as "high" and "consideration" were selected featuring the negative category. Words "Fujioka" expressing the location name of the golf course were selected to words featuring the negative category too. As the duplicated words among the categories, words such as "low price" and "fee" were.

Some of the selected words were due to differences in notation, like "caddy-" or "caddy. Using the result of the words, we perform the logistic regression. The results of the analysis are shown in Table 4.

Table 4. Result of logistic regression analysis $(p < 0.1)$

Categories	Regression coefficient	Pr $(> z|)$
Caddies (P)	0.157	***
Golf Course Staff (N)	0.121	**
Other (P)	0.266	***
Other clientele (N)	−0.178	***
Road Condition to golf course (P)	−0.139	*

$^{***}p < 0.001$, $^{**}p < 0.01$, $^{*}p < 0.05$

Table 4 shows that positive contains about caddies and Other, negative contains about Golf Course Staff tend to get good rating points.

Even though the contents are negative like the staff at the golf course, there was also the case which the evaluation points are high due to the inclusion of the contents in the review sentence. Therefore, we considered interaction effect by using combination variable among 2 or 3 categories.

4.2 Results with Interactive Terms

The number of target reviews is 7550. For model construction, we perform random sampling which the number of reviews of high and low evaluation are same.

Furthermore, in order to verify the prediction accuracy of the model, we divided these data into 70% for learning data and 30% for verification data.

Then the number of each data is shown in Table 5.

Table 5. Data used for logistic regression analysis

	Train data	Test data	Total
High evaluation review	2579	1105	3684
Low evaluation review	2579	1105	3684
Total	5158	2210	7368

From Table 4, 5158 reviews were used for logistic regression analysis in this study.

In addition, in order to confirm the model discrimination accuracy constructed, we verified the hold-out verification by using the learning data and data set above.

Like the first logistic regression model, we use stepwise method. Additionally, we use 13 variables that selected from 24 variables that selected by first stepwise model for next model. As the total variables, we use the 377 variables include 78 variables combined with 2 variables and 286 variables combined with 3 variables.

The results of the analysis are shown in Tables 6 and 7.

Table 6. Combination of category's interaction between 2 categories ($p < 0.1$)

Categories	Regression coefficient	Pr (>z|)
Golf Course (P) & Caddies (P)	−0.189	*
Golf Course (P) & Golf Course Staff (P)	1.361	***
Nature Environment of the Golf Course (P) & Golf Course Staff (N)	0.241	***
Meals (P) & Other clientele (N)	0.754	***
Meals (P) & Caddies (P)	0.656	**
Meals (P) & Golf Course Staff (N)	−0.632	***
Meals(P) & Road Condition to Golf Course (N)	0.327	*
Game Price (N) & Caddies (P)	3.031	**
Game Price (N) & Road Condition to Golf Course (N)	−0.796	*
Other clientele (N) & Golf Course Staff (P)	0.718	*
Other clientele (N) & Golf Course Staff (N)	−0.128	*
Caddies (P) & Golf Course Staff (N)	−0.223	**

$***p < 0.001$, $**p < 0.01$, $*p < 0.05$

Table 6 shows that combination which has the largest partial regression coefficient in positive was "Nature Environment of the Golf Course (N) and Game Price (P)". This combination has the largest partial regression in the model. "Game Price (P)" considered to have produced a satisfying evaluation. "Nature Environment of the Golf Course (N) & Game results (N)" has the largest partial regression coefficient in negative. From this result, we found that the combination result with "other clientele (N)" has led to a negative evaluation. Only one out of five that contain the "other clientele (N)", the combination with "Caddies (P)" had a positive partial regression coefficient. It seems that "Caddies (P)" led to a satisfying evaluation.

Table 7. Combination of category's interaction between 3 categories ($p < 0.1$)

Categories	Regression coefficient	Pr(>z|)
Golf Course (P) & Nature Environment of the Golf Course (P) & Game Price (N)	−0.336	*
Golf Course (P) & Meals (P) & Caddies (P)	0.144	**
Golf Course (P) & Meals (P) & Golf Course Staff (P)	−0.391	*
Golf Course (P) & Meals (P) & Other (P)	−0.211	**
Golf Course (P) & Meals (N) & Road Condition to Golf Course (N)	0.149	**
Golf Course (P) & Game Price (N) & Caddies (P)	−0.429	**
Golf Course (P) & Game Price (N) & Other (P)	1.122	**
Golf Course (P) & Caddies (P) & Golf Course Staff (P)	0.391	*
Nature Environment of the Golf Course (P) & Meals (P) & Caddies (P)	−0.262	***
Nature Environment of the Golf Course (P) & Meals (P) & Road Condition to Golf Course (N)	−0.338	***
Nature Environment of the Golf Course (P) & Meals (N) & Game Price (N)	0.625	**
Nature Environment of the Golf Course (P) & Meals (N) & Other clientele (N)	0.134	**
Nature Environment of the Golf Course (P) & Meals (N) & Golf Course Staff (P)	−0.693	***
Nature Environment of the Golf Course (P) & Game Price (N) & Road Condition to Golf Course (N)	0.642	*
Nature Environment of the Golf Course (P) & Other clientele (N) & Golf Course Staff (N)	−0.062	*
Nature Environment of the Golf Course (P) & Caddies (P) & Golf Course Staff (P)	−1.025	**
Nature Environment of the Golf Course (P) & Caddies (P) & Road Condition to Golf Course (N)	0.277	**
Meals (P) & Meals (N) & Caddies (P)	−0.157	**
Meals (P) & Meals (N) & Golf Course Staff (P)	0.826	***
Meals (P) & Meals (N) & Golf Course Staff (N)	0.107	**
Meals (P) & Game Price (N) & Other clientele (N)	−1.034	**
Meals (P) & Game Price (N) & Golf Course Staff (N)	0.894	**
Meals (P) & Caddies (P) & Golf Course Staff (N)	0.125	*
Meals (P) & Golf Course Staff (P) & Road Condition to Golf Course (N)	0.605	*
Meals (P) & Golf Course Staff (P) & Other (P)	−0.594	*
Meals (N) & Game Price (N) & Golf Course Staff (N)	−0.663	**
Meals (N) & Other clientele (N) & Road Condition to Golf Course (N)	−0.141	**
Game Price (N) & Other clientele (N) & Golf Course Staff (P)	−2.423	*

(*continued*)

Table 7. (*continued*)

Categories	Regression coefficient	Pr(>z|)
Game Price (N) & Caddies (P) & Golf Course Staff (N)	−1.090	**
Game Price (N) & Golf Course Staff (P) & Golf Course Staff (N)	1.940	**
Game Price (N) & Golf Course Staff (P) & Road Condition to Golf Course (N)	2.381	**
Game Price (N) & Golf Course Staff (N) & Other (P)	1.251	**
Game Price (N) & Road Condition to Golf Course (N) & Other (P)	−0.990	*
Other clientele (N) & Caddies (P) & Golf Course Staff (P)	−0.477	*
Other clientele (N) & Caddies (P) & Other (P)	−0.270	*
Other clientele (N) & Golf Course Staff (N) & Road Condition to Golf Course (N)	0.086	*
Golf Course (P) & Nature Environment of the Golf Course (P) & Game Price (N)	−0.336	*

*** $p < 0.001$, ** $p < 0.01$, * $p < 0.05$

All combination contain with "Facilities Golf Course (P)" has positive partial regression coefficient without the combination result with "other clientele (N)".

Table 7 shows that combination which has the largest partial regression coefficient in positive was "Nature Environment of the Golf Course (N) & other clientele (P) & Game results (N)". Combination of "Nature Environment of the Golf Course (N) & Golf Course Staff (N) & other clientele (P)" has the largest partial regression coefficient in negative.

Even if three positive contents are combined like "Caddies (P) & Facilities Golf Course (P) & Game Price (P)", "Facilities Golf Course (P) & other clientele (P) & Road Condition to Golf Course (P)" and "Caddies (P) & Game Price (P) & other clientele (P)", the result showing negative contents was seen. "Caddies (P)" and "Facilities Golf Course (P)" when these are solo represents positive, but positive elements do not work much if combined with three variables. Looking at the content with the second largest partial regression coefficient in positive and negative, these are "Nature Environment of the Golf Course (N) & other clientele (P) & other clientele (N)" and "Nature Environment of the Golf Course (N) & Game Price (P) & other clientele (N)". As a difference of this, it is an element of other clientele (P) or Game Price (P). Both categories are positive, but the values of partial regression are very different.

The results of confusion matrix using train data show in Table 8.

Table 8. Confusion matrix using train data

		Prediction result	
		Low	High
Actual result	Low	1590	988
	High	922	1586

The confusion matrix to the train data and the evaluation values of the model are as shown in Table 9.

Table 9. Evaluation values for logistic regression using train data

ACC	PRE	REC	F-measure
0.615	0.616	0.615	0.615

The results of confusion matrix using test data show in Table 10.

Table 10. Confusion matrix using test data

		Prediction result	
		Low	High
Actual result	Low	600	506
	High	520	586

The confusion matrix to the test data and the evaluation values of the model are as shown in Table 11.

Table 11. Evaluation values for logistic regression using test data

ACC	PRE	REC	F-measure
0.529	0.536	0.529	0.533

5   Discussion

First, we discuss about the model that takes interaction in two categories.

From the result of Table 6, we found that "Game Price (P)" considered to have produced a satisfying evaluation. We found that "Caddies (P)" led to a satisfying evaluation too.

When "Facilities Golf Course (P)" is included, partial regression coefficient in positive does not become so large, but it turned out that the evaluation tends to be slightly higher. About this result, we think that is why facility is not the main but attached to the golf course. In addition, we found that the combination result with "other clientele (N)" has led to a negative evaluation

Next, in order to perform a more elaborate analysis, we considered the result that was 3 combination categories. In combination with "Caddies (P)", three out of four results with positive partial regression coefficients had two negative categories. From this result, "Caddies (P)" is considered to give a strong impression for contributor when "Caddies (P)" combined with other negative factors. Also, as with "Caddies (P) & Game Price (P) & other clientele (P)", all three elements are positive, but the evaluation was negative. It seems that have a good impression on a part leads to high evaluation better than have totally good impression.

6 Conclusion

We found that "Caddies (P)" and "Game Price (P)" tend to red to a satisfying evaluation. In order to give a good evaluation, it seems that have a good impression on a part leads to high evaluation better than have totally good impression.

In this study, we defined some categories using the contents included in the review but individual attributes of customers did not use. As own future study, it is desirable to analyze more fully in consideration of customer attributes like age, sex, place of residence.

Acknowledgment. We thank Golf Digest Online Inc. for permission to use valuable datasets and for useful comments. This work was supported by JSPS KAKENHI Grant Number 16K03944 and 17K13809.

References

1. Nishikawa, T., Okada, M., Hashimoto, K.: Verification of text preprocessing method in automatic classification of review sentences. In: Proceedings of the 18th Annual Meeting of the Association for Natural Language Processing, pp. 246–251 (2012). (in Japanese)
2. Nakayama, Y., Fujii, A.: Extracting evaluative conditions from online reviews: toward enhancing opinion mining. In: Proceedings of the 6th International Joint Conference on Natural Language Processing (IJCNLP), pp. 878–882 (2013)
3. Akaike, H.: Information theory and an extension of the maximum likelihood principle. In: Petrov, B.N., Csaki, F. (eds.) Proceedings of the 2nd International Symposium on Information Theory, pp. 267–281. Akademiai Kidao, Budapest (1973)
4. Tango, T., Yamaoka, K., Takagi, H.: Logistic Regression Analysis, Asakura Publishing (1996). (in Japanese)

Gender-Specific Tagging of Images
on Instagram

Julia Philipps[✉] and Isabelle Dorsch

Department of Information Science, Heinrich Heine University Düsseldorf,
Düsseldorf, Germany
julia-philipps@gmx.net, isabelle.dorsch@hhu.de

Abstract. Instagram is widely known and used as a social media application
for visual content. In order to categorize and describe their posted content as
well as to make it retrievable, users can assign hashtags to each posting. What
kind of hashtags do female and male Instagram users assign to their picture
postings? Which differences and similarities exist? This study analyzes gender-
specific image tagging behavior on Instagram. Therefore, a content analysis of,
in total, 14,951 hashtags from 1,000 Instagram pictures (respectively 500 pictures posted by female and male users) was performed. The subjects of the 1,000
Instagram pictures belong to overall ten picture categories (100 pictures per
category): Activity, Architecture, Art, Captioned Photo, Fashion, Food, Friends,
Landscape, Pet, and Selfie. Seven categories exist for the coding of the hashtags:
Content-relatedness, Emotiveness, Fakeness, "Insta"-Tags, Isness, Performativeness, and Sentences. On average, women assigned 14 hashtags to their
postings, whereas men used one hashtag more. For both genders, hashtags
belonging to the category Content-relatedness were the most used (over 55% of
assigned hashtags). Second most assigned (over 17%) were Isness related
hashtags. Generally, females used slightly more emotional hashtags, whereas
men assigned Isness and "Insta"-Tags in a higher frequency than females.
"Insta"-Tags were assigned in high frequencies (over 22%) to Pet pictures by
both genders. With under 2%, females and males did not use many Sentences
hashtags. As a chi-square test of independence shows, there exists a small
statistical association between hashtag and picture categories for male and
female Instagram users, respectively.

Keywords: Content analysis · Folksonomy · Gender-dependent differences ·
Image indexing · Instagram · Knowledge organization

1 Introduction

The well-known phrase "men are from Mars, women are from Venus" [1] exemplifies
the impression that several people have regarding the degree of differences between
both genders. Can distinct practices also be observed in a social media context with the
primary focus on image tagging behavior? If yes, to what extent do these differences
occur? What hashtags do men and women choose to describe their uploaded content
and to what kind of content do they assign these hashtags?

© Springer Nature Switzerland AG 2019
G. Meiselwitz (Ed.): HCII 2019, LNCS 11578, pp. 396–413, 2019.
https://doi.org/10.1007/978-3-030-21902-4_29

The objective of this study is to answer these questions. In the field of knowledge representation, collaborative services allow the use of tags to index a document and make it retrievable. Tags can be applied by human indexers or automatically by the services and some need to follow rules [2]. The ones that are freely assigned constitute folksonomies [3] which play an important role in the Web 2.0 and for platforms like Twitter and Instagram. Instagram is a popular mobile social photo and video sharing application which allows its users to apply up to 30 different hashtags to their postings.

We found out that in several picture categories (e.g. Activity, Friends, or Pets) there are indeed significant differences, but similarities as well, in how male and female Instagram users apply different kinds of hashtags to their postings (for instance, tags related to the content, Emotiveness, or Fakeness).

1.1   Social Tagging and Gender-Specific Tagging on Social Media

When internet users advanced from consumers to prosumers of knowledge [4], they started to "index" their produced content by means of social tagging to make it retrievable for other users in the respective collaborative online environment [5]. These indexing terms are called "tags" which do not follow any guidelines [2] and form a folksonomy "[...] for each collaborative information service comprised of each individual user's tags" [3, p. 1]. The concept "folksonomy" consists of "folk" as well as "taxonomy," and originates from Vander Wal who was quoted by Smith in a blog entry [6]. The term "taxonomy" is misleading though [2]; unlike a taxonomy, folksonomies have no hierarchical structure [7].

In addition to tags, hashtags exist which have the same function as tags. A hashtag begins with the # symbol, followed by a string of characters, e.g. #guineapig. "Initially, the hashtag was used within Internet chat rooms" [8, p. 4]. On August 23th in 2007, Chris Messina suggested in a tweet: "how do you feel about using # (pound) for groups. As in #barcamp [msg]?" [9] and thus, for the first time, used the hashtag in a different context [8] which helped to establish it in various social network systems subsequently [10]. Both, tags as well as hashtags function as user-generated metadata for posted content (for example, visual media like photos).

Since the first tagging systems emerged in 2003 [11], user tagging behavior and motivation was analyzed by various researchers [e.g. 12–14]. Gender-specific tagging behavior in folksonomies was studied especially on Twitter. For instance, Cunha, Magno, Almeida, Gonçalves, and Benevenuto [15] examined if male and female Twitter users applied different hashtags when talking about the same topic. Women tended to use more common hashtags for all topics chosen by the researchers. In the political debate, females chose more personal hashtags (first person singular), while males used more persuasive hashtags (third person imperative forms).

Holmberg and Hellsten [16] researched gender tweeting behavior in the climate change debate. They noted that "[m]any of the hashtags represent[ed] a very general level of metadata describing the content or context of the tweet" [16, p. 816]. Male twitter users employed politics-related hashtags, but rarely used tags related to climate change or to general environmental issues. Furthermore, they used more descriptive tags. Females employed hashtags connected to campaigns and online movements associated with climate change. They used more specific hashtags, e.g. by referring to a specific event, campaign, or person.

Shapp [17, para. 1–2] differentiates two hashtag categories in Twitter: tag hashtags, which "are used to connect with a larger discussion and/or community" and commentary hashtags which "are not intended to affiliate widely, and are meant to be interpreted within the local context of the tweet." The results of the study show that female twitter users choose commentary hashtags more often than men. Contrarily, men use tag hashtags to a greater extent.

1.2   Instagram

Instagram is a mobile picture and video sharing application created by Kevin Systrom and Mike Krieger. Since April 2012 it is owned by Facebook [18]. Launched in the beginning of October 2010 for iOS exclusively [19], an Android version of the app was released in April 2012 [20]. Since then, Instagram became a very popular social network, has over 1 billion users as of January 2019, and is still growing. Over 500 million active users are online daily [21]. Instagram enables its users to upload pictures and videos, as well as to share stories or create slideshows while using photo filters and applying hashtags and geotags to their posts.

1.3   Research on Instagram

Topics investigated on Instagram include for example hashtag utilization, content analyses, or motivation to use the social network. The following section presents an overview of works conducted by numerous researchers on Instagram.

Sheldon and Bryant [22] surveyed 239 college students to figure out the main motivations for using Instagram. A comparison between Croatian and American students suggested that motivation for using Instagram is culture-independent, although the app was employed for different reasons [23]. Evaluating 212 Instagram users, Lee, Lee, Moon, and Sung [24] concluded that there are five social and psychological motives for using the app: social interaction, archiving, self-expression, escapism, and peeking.

Online expression of six emotions and their perceived appropriateness on Instagram and three other platforms was analyzed by Waterloo, Baumgartner, Peter, and Valkenburg [25]. Instagram scored as the least appropriate platform to express negative emotions and highly appropriate to express positive emotions. Men and women differed in their rating. Psychological subjects were investigated on Instagram as well. Holland and Tiggemann [26] studied eating disorders and compulsive exercises in women. Lup, Trub, and Rosenthal [27] pointed out that Instagram use may lead to psychologically feeling unwell because of negative social comparisons, amongst other things. Non-suicidal self-injury behavior was examined by Brown et al. [28].

Olympic athletes' self-presentation by gender was investigated by Geurin-Eagleman and Burch [29] to research their use of Instagram as a communication and personal brand marketing tool. Analyzing 2,017 images of two football teams by categorizing them into product and non-product-related brand attributes, Anagnostopoulos, Parganas, Chadwick, and Fenton [30] also investigated how Instagram is used as a tool for branding and how fans reacted in the comments to gain new insights for sport marketing. Lavoie [31] examined the branding strategy of Dunkin' Donuts on Instagram. The text captions and the image content of 12 postings were analyzed by sorting them into categories like presence of a call to action in the textual data and color, products, or people information in the image data. Coelho, de Oliveira and de Almeida [32] measured five post types against their likes and comments (advertising, fan, events, information, and promotion). They explored business profiles promoting food, hairdressing, ladies' footwear, body design, and fashion gym wear.

Fitness inspiration and body images are also Instagram research topics. Carrotte, Prichard, and Lim [33] observed gender differences after a content analysis of 415 Instagram, Facebook, Twitter, and Tumblr postings, e.g. women were more likely to be sexualized than men. The postings derived predominantly from Instagram (360 posts in total). Talbot, Gavin, van Steen, and Morey [34] inspected 734 pictures tagged with #thinspiration, #fitspiration, and #bonespiration as well as their top five alternative hashtags. 600 pictures were categorized in the context for body type, activity, objectification, and textual data in a content analysis conducted by Tiggemann and Zaccardo [35]. Santarossa, Coyne, Lisinski, and Woodruff [36] analyzed 10,000 posts and 122 images tagged with #fitspo.

Researchers observed political debates on Instagram. For example, Schmidbauer, Rösch, and Stieler [37] examined postings collected by crawling 16 hashtags related to Clinton/Trump supporters and opponents during the 2016 US presidential election. 9,000 multilingual hashtags were studied by Lee and Chau [38] in the context of the Umbrella Movement in Hong Kong in 2014. Coding them into the categories language, fact, opinion, and emotion, the researchers found that, in addition to stating facts and opinions, Instagram users also were quite emotional about the political movement.

Santarossa, Coyne and Woodruff [39] investigated 18,366 images with the hashtag #nofilter and concluded that 12 percent of these in fact used a filter. Mostly, women applied this hashtag and the subject of these pictures was mainly a person. Giannoulakis and Tsapatsoulis [40] studied the descriptive power of hashtags by analyzing 1,000 images. They concluded that 66% of the hashtags their study participants chose were identical with the ones the picture owner used. Moreover, half of these hashtags referred to the depicted image content. Oh, Lee, Kim, Park, and Suh [41] explored the use of participatory hashtags on Instagram in context with the Weekend Hashtag Project (#WHP). Participatory hashtags are recommended by some users to their followers to promote uploading pictures using these certain hashtags.

A content analysis of 1,382 Instagram posts tagged with #Malaysianfood showed gender-specific utilization of hashtags [42]. Female users employed more often than men emotional and positive hashtags, while male users showed higher use in informative and negative hashtags for pictures. Additionally, the researchers found a positive correlation between the number of hashtags and followers as well as likes.

The following studies form the base of this work. The first in-depth analysis about Instagram was conducted by Hu, Manikonda, and Kambhampati [43]. This empirical study's results encompassed eight popular image categories (friends, food, gadget, captioned photo, pet, activity, selfie, fashion) and five distinct types of users. Almost half of the analyzed photos belonged to the categories friends and fashion.

Dorsch [44] researched tagging behavior of Instagram users in a wider scope. She distinguished between ten picture categories, namely Activity, Architecture, Art, Captioned Photo, Fashion, Food, Friends, Landscape, Pet, and Selfie, and seven hashtag categories (Content-relatedness, Emotiveness, Isness, Performativeness, Fakeness, "Insta"-Tags, and Sentences). The results showed that Instagram users predominantly tag images with hashtags relating to the content, followed by hashtags relating to Isness [44, 45].

1.4 Gender-Specific Tagging of Images on Instagram

Research that takes gender-specific image tagging on Instagram into account is still at its beginning. This study aims to contribute to the limited research on gender-specific Instagram tagging behavior in a broader scope. Conducting a content analysis [46], hashtags of images from ten different picture categories are coded into seven distinct hashtag categories. The research questions of this work are:

RQ1. Are there any gender-specific differences in the relative hashtag frequencies in the picture categories?

RQ2. Given a picture category, what is the gender-specific distribution of hashtag categories; and given a hashtag category, what is the gender-specific distribution of picture categories?

RQ3. Are there any gender-specific associations between picture categories and hashtag categories?

2 Methods

Content analysis [46] is a technique originating from the social sciences and investigates content of any form, e.g. texts, images (as in this study), recordings, or movies. It utilizes different procedures that conceptualize content depending on its context – a process called coding which produces new understanding and data to analyze. The content analysis in this study was performed on posts of Instagram images to analyze gender-specific tagging behavior. As a result, the pictures and hashtags were coded into specifically designed picture and hashtag categories, based on Dorsch's two codebooks [44].

2.1 Codebooks

Generally, codes map the content of the text to the model that the analyst constructed and therefore generate new information that can be analyzed. The process of coding needs to fulfill explicit guidelines that define text boundaries identifying with a specific code [47]. Such guidelines and codes form a codebook. Thereby, a codebook "[…] always reflects the analyst's implicit or explicit research questions" [46, p. 2013]. As mentioned, the two existing codebooks, one for categorizing pictures and one for classifying hashtags were used for this content analysis. The structure of the codebooks is simple and consists of six distinct components: the code, a brief description of the code, the full definition, guidelines when and when not to use it as well as examples. In addition to the six mentioned components, a seventh one exists in the picture categories codebook, namely the corresponding hashtag for the specific category. This format is based on MacQueen et al.'s [47] recommendations.

Picture Categories. In total, ten Instagram picture categories were used, and each category has their respective hashtag. This study only considered pictures that were tagged with the corresponding picture category hashtags (Table 1). Another requirement to be included in the content analysis was that the picture predominantly shows one category or fits the preference rules [44, 45]. The picture categories are based on research of Hu et al. [43]. The authors conducted a cluster analysis and used computer vision techniques in combination with two coders to identify popular Instagram photo categories and user types. Seven of the eight photo categories were chosen for the codebook, namely Activity, Captioned Photo, Fashion, Food, Friends, Pet, and Selfie. Four of these categories were modified as well, namely Activity, Captioned Photo, Friends, and Selfie. Three supplementary categories (Architecture, Art, and Landscape) were added. The category Gadget was omitted because pictures of this category overlapped with the other categories due to its broad definition [44].

Table 1. Picture categories and their respective hashtags

Category	Hashtag
Activity	#activity
Architecture	#architecture
Art	#art
Captioned photo	#quote
Fashion	#fashion
Food	#food
Friends	#friends
Landscape	#landscape
Pet	#pet
Selfie	#selfie

The pictures in the category Activity depict indoor and outdoor activities (e.g. climbing, biking), as well as locations where activities take place (e.g. concerts). The photos in architecture show subjects related to the categories' name like buildings, structures, and cityscapes. Art is the category for pictures showing art-related content in all forms, e.g. paintings, sculptures, tattoos, or crafted art. Pictures that show graphics with quotes belong to the Captioned Photo category. As the name indicates, the category Fashion depicts fashion-related matters like makeup or clothes. The category Food includes photos displaying food, drinks, or recipes. Images in the Friends category depict at least one person that is a friend of the user who uploaded the picture; group of friends fall into this category, too. Pictures with landscapes and nature-related content are sorted into the Landscape category. The images in the Pet category show cats, dogs, and similar animals. Self-taken pictures (selfies) belong to the category Selfie [44, 45].

Hashtag Categories. Coding Instagram hashtags into categories which were designed to represent specific concepts [44, 45], can lead to new results about gender-specific image tagging behavior. Overall, seven categories exist for the coding of hashtags: Content-relatedness, Emotiveness, Fakeness, "Insta"-Tags, Isness, Performativeness, and Sentences.

There are nine common coding rules: A hashtag can only be assigned to one of these categories. It must originate from the picture's caption and be in English (proper names are excluded from this rule). The picture's caption may be used to obtain additional information about the content of the picture. Spelling mistakes can be ignored. Hashtags with only one or more emojis and special characters are excluded from the analysis. Hashtag abbreviations need to be figured out by the coders. Detached tags, for example #Belgian #Shepherd, are categorized separately. If the same hashtag is assigned multiple times, it is counted only one time [44].

The category Content-relatedness is assigned to hashtags that refer "[…] in any form to content-related aspects in the picture" [44, p. 3]. This includes the concepts ofness and aboutness [48] which are based on Panofsky's [49] three levels of art interpretation. For example, if the picture depicts a dog, the hashtags #pet, #dog, or #animal refer to the content and would therefore be coded into the category Content-relatedness. Hashtags which are emotional or describe feelings, are coded into the category Emotiveness, e.g. #love or #sad. Considered basic emotions (love, happiness, fun, surprise, aspiration, sadness, anger, disgust, fear, and shame) originate from Siebenlist [50]. Fakeness is the category for "[…] intentionally wrongly chosen statements" [44, p. 7], e.g. when the tag #cat was assigned to a photo of a dog. Hashtags with any form of "insta," "gram," or other abbreviation of these terms, are sorted into the category "Insta"-tags, e.g. #instalike or #petstagram. These kinds of hashtags are a phenomenon specific to Instagram [44, 45]. Isness is the category for hashtags which represent technical aspects of the picture that are not depicted, like #landscapephotographer, #selfie, or #throwbackthursday. The concept of isness was introduced by Ingwersen [51]. Hashtags that call for actions are coded into the category Performativeness, e.g. #followforfollow, #explore, or #kickit [52]. Performativeness derived from Austin [53]. Hashtags with a participatory function are for example used in various projects on Instagram [41]. Complete sentences are coded into the category Sentences, for example #lifeisgood or #thisislondon. Abbreviations of sentences like #tgif – thank God it's friday, are coded into this category as well [44, 45].

2.2 Data Collection

Instagram pictures were mainly collected from November 2017 to January 2018. The dataset for the content analysis consists of 1,000 Instagram pictures, 500 from male users and 500 from female users, respectively. A multimethodological approach was chosen to collect these pictures. Due to the official Instagram API's access limits, the JSON response of the Instagram website was automatically downloaded and processed with a PHP-script. The script takes a top picture category hashtag and the number of pictures to be downloaded as parameters and saves the most recent pictures of the declared hashtag with metadata.

After the automatic data collection, the picture subject and gender of the picture's owner needed to be identified manually. For checking if the picture conformed to the category, the Instagram picture category codebook [44] was used (by two persons). Pictures that failed to comply with the codebook rules, e.g. a picture tagged with #selfie but depicting more than one person and therefore not matching the requirements, were deleted. The gender of the picture's owner was obtained with the help of the profile picture, the user biography, and the posts. The profile picture, full name, and biography are optional information a user can add to his or her profile. The biography can contain the user's full name and a statement about the gender. For example, in Fig. 1, Annika is the full name of the user *rufinchenx3* and the expression *Gamergirl* in the biography, as well as the profile picture, indicate that this user is female.

Fig. 1. Profile of Instagram user rufinchenx3

There might be special cases a gender is difficult to identify or can't be identified. For example, the gender is harder to determine when pet owners create a profile for their pet and pretend to post and write as their pet. In such situations, it must be determined if the gender of the owner can be derived from the profiles' information. If not, the profile has to be excluded from the analysis.

The replacing of pictures cleaned the automatically crawled data, hence reducing the dataset. Due to the stated data cleansing process, more than 100 pictures for a category were downloaded first. If the manual verification of the data did not result in the number of needed pictures for this analysis (50 pictures of male users, 50 pictures of female users), more data was downloaded and processed in the described way.

All final datasets consist of the following metadata and information: the downloaded picture, the URL to the picture on Instagram, the picture owner's username, full name, biography and gender, all hashtags written in the picture description, the total number of these hashtags, the full caption of the post, the picture category name (e.g. Activity, Pet, etc.), and an ID for naming the picture file, containing the picture owner's gender, the picture category name, and the unique Instagram picture code.

2.3 Coding Process

Coding is the process of assigning specified codes to a text. In this work, the hashtags of the Instagram images were coded into seven different categories by using a codebook. After the data collection, the categorization of the 1,000 pictures took place from

January to March 2018. Two coders classified the hashtags first separately, following a 4-eyes principle. After that, the intercoder-reliability was estimated using Krippendorff's alpha [54]. For every category, the alpha value was >.800 in the initial round and >.880 in a second round (which has to be performed due to interpretational inconsistencies in the category Fakeness).

After the calculation of the Krippendorff's alpha, the coders needed to recode the hashtags that they classified into different categories. They discussed these differences and agreed to one category. A PHP-script takes the file with the recoded hashtags and one of the coder's files as input parameters. For every picture that was tagged with hashtags which need to be corrected, all hashtag categories are scanned. If the hashtag is in the wrong category, it gets deleted from this category and is written to the right category.

3   Results

This chapter presents the results of the content analysis while answering the three research questions.

RQ1. Are there any gender-specific differences in the relative hashtag frequencies in the picture categories?

In total, 14,951 hashtags from 1,000 Instagram photos were coded into the seven hashtag categories. The average number of hashtags per pictures owned by female users was approximately 14 hashtags, whereas males applied over 15 hashtags (Fig. 2, Table 2). Men used significantly more hashtags in the categories Captioned Photo (∅ 21.8 to 12.74 hashtags) and Landscape (∅ 18.84 to 14.52 hashtags). A great difference

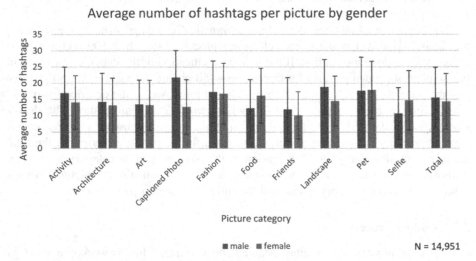

Fig. 2. Average number of hashtags per picture by gender and standard deviation, sorted by picture category.

Table 2. Summary of the significant t-test results for the hashtag frequencies in the picture categories, p ≤ .05.

	Hashtag category		Male (n = 50)	Female (n = 50)	P	t	df	Cohen's d
Captioned photo	Content-relatedness	M	12.64	7.12	<.001	5.166	98	1.03
		SD	5.914	4.702				
	"Insta"-Tags	M	2.36	.7	.001	3.583	98	0.72
		SD	2.926	1.474				
	Isness	M	2.28	1.32	.03	2.208	72.372	0.44
		SD	1.99	2.343				
	N	M	21.8	12.74	<.001	5.446	98	1.09
		SD	8.283	8.351				
Food	Content-relatedness	M	6.36	8.54	.039	-2.093	98	-0.42
		SD	4.733	5.643				
	N	M	12.34	16.18	.028	-2.23	98	-0.45
		SD	8.794	8.422				
Landscape	Fakeness	M	.72	.04	.02	2.404	49.969	0.48
		SD	1.99	.198				
	Isness	M	6.08	3.66	.001	3.355	71.285	0.67
		SD	4.58	2.246				
	N	M	18.84	14.52	.009	2.68	98	0.54
		SD	8.464	7.635				
Selfie	Emotiveness	M	.44	.86	.047	-2.016	98	-0.4
		SD	.861	1.195				
	N	M	10.72	14.78	.019	-2.387	96.092	-0.48
		SD	7.882	9.083				
Total	Emotiveness	M	.61	.75	.05	-1.964	998	-0.13
		SD	1.021	1.103				
	"Insta"-Tags	M	1.33	1.04	.029	2.191	969.422	0.14
		SD	2.218	1.865				
	Isness	M	2.94	2.52	.023	2.28	974.646	0.14
		SD	3.145	2.691				
	N	M	15.53	14.37	.04	2.056	990.239	0.53
		SD	9.324	8.532				

of approximately nine hashtags was observed for captioned photos. For females, these images received the lowest number of hashtags. In the categories Food (⌀ 16.18 to 12.34 tags) and Selfie (⌀ 14.75 to 10.72 tags), female users tagged a picture with a significantly higher number of tags.

For male users, the category Selfie (⌀ 10.72 tags) had the least hashtags. The mean values ranged from around 10 to almost 21 hashtags for males, and from over 10 to roughly 18 for females. This shows that the span of hashtag counts by gender varied noticeably in specific picture categories. The standard deviation lay between 7 and 10 for males, and between 7 and 9 for females. Even though this indicates that the number of hashtags was almost the same for each picture and for both genders, it points out that the male data was more spread out than the female data, specifically in the Pet category with a standard deviation of over 10.

RQ2. Given a picture category, what is the gender-specific distribution of hashtag categories; and given a hashtag category, what is the gender-specific distribution of picture categories?

In total, male users applied 7,766 and female users 7,185 hashtags to their postings (Tables 2 and 3). Over half of these assigned hashtags were classified as Content-relatedness tags for both genders (over 55%). The second most assigned category with about 18% was Isness for men and women alike, just like the least assigned category Sentences (under 1.5%). Females tagged pictures with Performativeness tags third most (7.85%) and with "Insta"-Tags (7.25%) fourth most, whereas males did the opposite (8.54% and 7.39%, respectively). Significant differences existed in the hashtag categories Emotiveness, Isness, and "Insta"-Tags. Emotiveness hashtags were assigned more often by females (5.19% in contrast to 3.95%), whereas Isness (18.93% to 17.52%) and "Insta"-Tags (8.54% to 7.25%) more often by men.

Table 3. Relative frequencies of hashtag categories by picture categories and gender (N = 1,000 posts; 100 posts per picture category, and respectively 50 posts per gender for each picture category).

	Content-relatedness		Emotiveness		Fakeness		"Insta"-Tags		Isness		Performa-tiveness		Sentences		%	
Gender	m	f	m	f	m	f	m	f	m	f	m	f	m	f	m	f
Activity	67.61	67.52	4.26	4.96	2.13	2.13	2.01	2.27	18.44	14.75	4.85	7.09	0.71	1.28	100.00	100.00
Architecture	49.37	51.97	1.68	2.88	1.54	0.60	6.45	6.36	28.75	26.06	11.64	11.21	0.56	0.91	100.00	100.00
Art	70.37	71.99	1.19	2.56	5.04	3.16	5.04	4.52	15.70	15.21	2.67	2.41	0.00	0.15	100.00	100.00
Captioned Photo	57.98	55.89	4.59	8.16	6.97	8.63	10.83	5.49	10.46	10.36	8.17	10.05	1.01	1.41	100.00	100.00
Fashion	58.03	57.31	1.85	2.50	7.63	6.90	6.24	6.54	15.95	18.79	8.09	6.42	2.20	1.55	100.00	100.00
Food	51.54	52.78	2.43	3.09	4.21	5.07	10.37	7.29	23.99	23.36	6.32	6.55	1.13	1.85	100.00	100.00
Friends	49.58	57.87	8.21	9.84	9.72	5.91	6.70	4.13	16.25	14.17	8.88	5.91	0.67	2.17	100.00	100.00
Landscape	44.69	55.37	2.76	3.72	3.82	0.28	5.10	4.55	32.27	25.21	10.62	10.33	0.74	0.55	100.00	100.00
Pet	49.72	53.46	8.25	9.38	4.52	2.34	22.82	20.31	7.57	5.25	3.95	7.03	3.16	2.23	100.00	100.00
Selfie	49.63	47.23	4.10	5.82	4.85	5.55	7.46	6.50	25.19	22.60	8.58	11.64	0.19	0.68	100.00	100.00
Total	55.03	56.87	3.95	5.19	5.03	4.01	8.54	7.25	18.93	17.52	7.39	7.86	1.12	1.29	100.00	100.00

The distribution of picture categories to the hashtag category Content-relatedness was between almost 45% to over 70% for both genders. Female users assigned the lowest value of this hashtag category to the picture category Selfie (47.23%). With 44.69% of all hashtags, male users assigned Content-relatedness hashtags the least to

Landscape images which was the overall lowest assigned value of this hashtag category as well. Both genders tagged pictures related to art subjects the highest with those tags (over 70%). In the categories Captioned Photo, male users assigned Content-relatedness tags in a significantly higher frequency than female users. On the other hand, women assigned significantly more of these tags to pictures depicting food (Table 2). Noticeably, Isness tags reached high values in the picture categories with the least assigned Content-relatedness tags by both genders. For example, the category Landscape scored with 32.27% the highest Isness value assigned by men, which is significantly different to the value assigned by women (25.21%). Furthermore, men assigned significantly more Isness hashtags to captioned photos. Males and females both added "Insta"-Tags to the category Pet the most and to the category Activity the least. Men (22.82%) were more likely to use those tags for Captioned Photo (10.83%). This likeness is statistically significant (Table 2). The highest percentage of the category Performativeness male users assigned to Architecture is the same value that female users assigned to the category Selfie for those hashtags (11.64%). Both genders distributed performative tags the least to images depicting art-related subjects. The picture categories Pet and Selfie were tagged with those tags more by women, whereas Friends obtained more of those tags by men.

Emotions were not expressed by men regarding the category Art (around 1%), while women assigned the least of these hashtags for Fashion (2.50%). Females tagged pictures of Selfies significantly more emotionally than men (5.82% and 4.1%, respectively). Usually, men got higher values for Fakeness hashtags. The category with the highest percentage of Fakeness hashtags assigned by male users is Friends (9.72%). The category Captioned Photo (8.63%) received the highest frequency of fake tags by women. They tagged Landscape (0.28%) and Architecture (0.60%) pictures very rarely with fake tags, too, in contrast to men who added more of those tags to pictures of the category Landscape (3.82%). This difference is statistically significant (Table 2). Images showing Architecture (1.54%) got the least Fakeness hashtags assigned by men. The hashtag category Sentences was not distributed much among the picture categories. Both genders gave the lowest percentages of those tags to images about art. Mostly, Sentences tags were assigned to Pet and Captioned Photo by men and women alike. Women also tagged pictures depicting Friends with those tags. Nearly all of the Sentences hashtags from both genders in the Pet category were emotional and positive, like e.g. #ilovemypet.

RQ4. Are there any gender-specific associations between the picture categories and hashtag categories?

A chi-square test of independence was conducted to investigate if an association between the hashtag categories and picture categories for each gender (male and female) exists. The following hypotheses were formulated:

H0: No gender-specific association between picture categories and hashtag categories exists.

HA: A Gender-specific association between picture categories and hashtag categories exists.

All expected cell frequencies were greater than five. A significant association between hashtag categories, picture categories, and both genders was found. For male users, the chi-square test result was $\chi^2(54, 500) = 970.993$, p < .001 with an effect size of Cramer's V = .144 which indicated a small association [55]. Likewise, female users ($\chi^2(54, 500) = 814.440$, p < .001) showed a small association (Cramer's V = .137) as well. The alternative hypothesis can be accepted, because the null hypothesis has been rejected.

4 Discussion

This research study examined the tagging of images by male and female Instagram users. The number of investigated Instagram picture postings was 1,000 (500 for each gender). The pictures and the text captions of the respective postings were analyzed to answer three research questions about the gender-specific distribution of hashtag and picture categories, as well as hashtag frequencies.

Usually, the number of hashtags differs from picture to picture and, for some image categories, by gender. Males assigned 15 hashtags on average to their postings, whereas women used one hashtag less. Notable categories where men tagged their images with at least 4 hashtags more on average were Captioned Photo and Landscape. A great difference of approximately 9 hashtags was observed for captioned photos. Women tagged Selfie and Food pictures with more hashtags on average. These differences are statistically significant. Both genders applied around 18 hashtags to the Pet category on average, but the male data was more dispersed.

When indexing non-textual content, internet users tend to mix together ofness, aboutness, as well as isness aspects [2]. The same process has been observed in this Instagram study, where users indexed their postings with hashtags. Those tags were coded into Content-relatedness, Isness, and five other kinds of hashtag categories. Content-relatedness was the most important hashtag category for male and female Instagram users alike (over 55%). This category specified the subject of a picture by referring to its ofness and aboutness. Second most assigned category by both genders was Isness, indicating the importance of hashtags relating to isness elements of an image as well as further emphasizing the mentioned mixing together of ofness, aboutness, and isness aspects. Females assigned slightly more emotional hashtags to all image categories than men; this difference is statistically significant. Generally, men assigned Isness and "Insta"-Tags in a higher frequency than females. Furthermore, "Insta"-Tags were assigned in high frequencies by both genders to Pet. Generally, both genders did not use many Sentences as hashtags. A chi-square test of independence showed a small statistical association between hashtag and picture categories for male and female Instagram users, respectively.

The high frequency of Content-relatedness tags in this work are in accordance with two other studies which have shown that a high number of hashtags relate to the depicted content of the picture [40, 44]. Hashtags that refer mostly to the content or context of a document were also observed for tweets [16]. It is possible that male and female Instagram users describe the content and context of their pictures to make them findable for other users. They want their images to be visible in the social network community. Men use informative hashtags more than women when tagging food pictures according to Zhang et al. [42]. Informative hashtags contain information and non-emotional descriptions of an image. Content-relatedness hashtags could be considered as informative and non-emotional, because emotions were classified as Emotiveness hashtags. The hashtag category Isness might be considered as informative as well, since it relates to technical aspects of the picture that are not depicted. In this study, the male Content-relatedness hashtag frequencies only exceed the female ones in four out of ten picture categories. Nevertheless, the difference in the total tag frequency is very small (about 1.5%). In the Isness category, men assign a higher percentage of tags to all image categories except Fashion (about 2.5% difference). The total frequency of Isness hashtags assigned by men is significantly higher when compared to women. If only the category Food would be considered, like in Zhang et al.'s work [42], females tag food pictures significantly more with Content-relatedness tags. The results of this study would differ from Zhang et al.'s findings in this point when isolating this specific picture category.

Various studies concluded that women express more feelings and emotions than men in social networks (e.g. [42, 56, 57]). This study's results support those findings. Even though Emotiveness tags are not highly represented by both genders (<10%), significant differences exist. Women assign more emotional hashtags than men to all picture categories. Women's selfies are tagged with more Emotiveness tags than men's. Pictures depicting friends and pets received the most emotional feedback by both genders, probably because of the bond that users can form with a person or an animal and thus, being able to feel emotions towards them than towards lifeless objects.

Sheldon and Bryant [22] found a positive relationship between regular hashtag use and the motive "Coolness" in a study with college students. It could be speculated that "Insta"-Tags imply, in a way, coolness due to their abbreviation or full inclusion of the application's name (Instagram). These tags are a phenomenon that occurs only on Instagram [44]. Males make more frequently use of "Insta"-Tags, especially in the picture category Captioned Photo. Both genders assign "Insta"-Tags a lot when posting Pet pictures. Is there a specific reason for that? Instagram is especially favored by young adults aged 18 to 24 in the U.S. [58]. Is it young adult slang that introduced these tags to Instagram? Further studies are needed to investigate "Insta"-Tags and motivation for their application.

Another question that needs to be asked is why do male users assign Fakeness tags in significantly greater amounts to Landscape pictures? For this question, apps and websites[1] that provide top hashtags to gain more likes and followers on social media platforms could be relevant. Sometimes, top tags are assigned which only fit in the category Fakeness, e.g. when a picture of an older dog is tagged with #puppy. Nevertheless, these hypotheses require proof.

The tagging behavior of men and women on Instagram is described in this study. Future studies could investigate the motivation of male and female users for applying a specific hashtag to a specific picture motive. With help of uses and gratification theory [59] for social media [60], the motivations behind tagging could be determined. Uses

---

[1] e.g. https://www.hashtagsforlikes.co/.

and gratification theory is about what people do with the media. In context of social media, it investigates motivations for content creation and how the activities in social media are affected by the gratifications of content generation. To the authors knowledge, only one study exists that applied uses and gratification theory to gender-specific hashtag application [42]. It noted that female users gratify needs of expressing feelings by using positive and emotional hashtags, whereas male users gratify needs of giving information by using informative hashtags. Questionnaires and qualitative interviews are possible ways to explain male and female tagging intentions and motivations further. This study could act as base to elaborate these surveys.

The picture categories in this investigation do not cover every potential picture motive. They exemplify possible motives in a broader scope and thus, make no claim to be a complete overview of all image motives on Instagram. Social media data sampling itself also has some limitations, as there often is a fixed time-frame for studies that should not be exceeded. The data for this study was also collected in a specific time-frame. Therefore, not all images that are conform to the picture categories have been included in the content analysis. Another related aspect is that not every Instagram user specifies his or her gender. In conclusion, this work is a case study, as it is impossible to generalize the results for the entire population.

In addition to analyzing pictures, videos could be examined. Do men and women show tagging differences in this media category as well? Would the differences be the same as the ones observed for the picture categories? Furthermore, a content analysis in regard to "hashtags for likes" websites could be conducted, to figure out if men and women make use of the provided hashtags in different frequencies for specific picture motives. In addition to gender, parameters like age, nationality, and lifestyle could be taken into account to research tagging behavior. Do younger Instagram users assign more "Insta"-Tags than older ones? Which lifestyle enables the use of performative tags? It would be interesting to determine if the opinion about a picture category is positive or negative by conducting a sentiment analysis on the Emotiveness hashtags. What kinds of emotions are shown only by men or by women?

The tagging behavior of certain user groups like for example influencers could be investigated as well. Influencers are individuals who can affect purchase decisions of others due to their high reputation and prestige on social media platforms. Do male and female influencers tag their postings differently, and which gender is more successful to which audience? Are there any differences when comparing influencer's and non-influencer's tagging behaviors? Success could be measured by the number of followers and likes. Marketing strategies to target a specific customer group could be enabled.

Finally, examining the image tagging behavior of men and women on a different social media platform may bring further insights to this subject.

This study analyzed gender-specific tagging of images on Instagram. It concludes that in several picture and hashtag categories there are indeed significant differences, but similarities as well, in the tagging behavior of male and female Instagram users.

References

1. Gray, J.: Men are from Mars, Women are from Venus. HarperCollins, New York (1992)
2. Stock, W.G., Stock, M.: Handbook of Information Science. De Gruyter Saur, Berlin (2013)
3. Peters, I.: Folksonomies: Indexing and Retrieval in Web 2.0. De Gruyter Saur, Berlin (2009)
4. Toffler, A.: The Third Wave. Morrow, New York (1980)
5. Trant, J.: Studying social tagging and folksonomy: a review and framework. J. Digit. Inf. **10**, 1–44 (2009)
6. Vander Wal, T.: Folksonomy (2007). http://www.vanderwal.net/folksonomy.html. Accessed 26 Jan 2019
7. Laniado, D., Eynard, D., Colombetti, M.: Using WordNet to turn a folksonomy into a hierarchy of concepts. In: Semeraro, G., Di Sciascio, C., Morbidoni, H., Stoermer, H. (eds.) Semantic Web Application and Perspectives: Proceedings of the 4th Italian Semantic Web Workshop (SWAP 2007). CEUR Workshop Proceedings, vol. 314, pp. 192–201. CEUR Workshop Proceedings, Bari (2007)
8. van den Berg, J.A.: The story of the hashtag (#): a practical theological tracing of the hashtag (#) symbol on Twitter. HTS Theol. Stud. **70**, 1–6 (2014)
9. Messina, C.: How do you feel about using # (pound) for groups. As in #barcamp [msg]? @chrismessina (Twitter) (2007). https://twitter.com/chrismessina/status/223115412. Accessed 26 Jan 2019
10. Halavais, A.: Structure of Twitter: social and technical. In: Weller, K., Bruns, A., Burgess, J., Mahrt, M. (eds.) Twitter and Society, pp. 29–41. Peter Lang, New York (2014)
11. Peters, I., et al.: Social tagging & folksonomies: indexing, retrieving… and beyond? In: Bridging the Gulf: Communication and Information in Society, Technology, and Work. Proceedings of the 74th ASIS&T Annual Meeting, pp. 1–4. Wiley, Hoboken (2011)
12. Daer, A.R., Hoffman, R.F., Goodman, S.: Rhetorical functions of hashtag forms across social media applications. Commun. Des. Q. Rev. **3**, 12–16 (2015)
13. Dubinko, M., Kumar, R., Magnani, J., Novak, J., Raghavan, P., Tomkins, A.: Visualizing tags over time. ACM Trans. Web **1**, 1–22 (2007)
14. Golder, S., Huberman, B.: Usage patterns of collaborative tagging systems. J. Inf. Sci. **32**, 198–208 (2006)
15. Cunha, E., Magno, G., Almeida, V., Gonçalves, M.A., Benevenuto, F.: A gender based study of tagging behavior in Twitter. In: Proceedings of the 23rd ACM Conference on Hypertext and Social Media, HT 2012, pp. 323–324. ACM, New York (2012)
16. Holmberg, K., Hellsten, I.: Gender differences in the climate change communication on Twitter. Internet Res. **25**, 811–828 (2015)
17. Shapp, A.: Gender variation in the pragmatic uses of Twitter hashtags. Poster session presented at the 89th Annual Meeting of the Linguistic Society of America, Portland, Oregon (2015). https://www.nyu.edu/projects/shapp/Shapp_LSA2015.html
18. Instagram: Instagram + Facebook (2012). https://instagram-press.com/blog/2012/04/09/instagram-facebook/. Accessed 26 Jan 2019
19. Instagram: Instagram launches (2010). https://instagram-press.com/blog/2010/10/06/instagram-launches-2/. Accessed 26 Jan 2019
20. Instagram: Instagram for Android (2012). https://instagram-press.com/blog/2012/04/03/instagram-for-android-available-now/ Accessed 26 Jan 2019
21. Instagram: Instagram Statistics. https://instagram-press.com/our-story/
22. Sheldon, P., Bryant, K.: Instagram: motives for its use and relationship to narcissism and contextual age. Comput. Hum. Behav. **58**, 89–97 (2016)

23. Sheldon, P., Rauschnabel, P.A., Antony, M.G., Car, S.: A cross-cultural comparison of croatian and American social network sites: exploring cultural differences in motives for Instagram use. Comput. Hum. Behav. **75**, 643–651 (2017)
24. Lee, E., Lee, J.-A., Moon, J.H., Sung, Y.: Pictures speak louder than words: Motivations for using Instagram. Cyberpsychology Behav. Soc. Netw. **18**, 552–556 (2015)
25. Waterloo, S.F., Baumgartner, S.E., Peter, J., Valkenburg, P.M.: Norms of online expressions of emotion: comparing Facebook, Twitter, Instagram, and WhatsApp. New Media Soc. **20**, 1813–1831 (2018)
26. Holland, G., Tiggemann, M.: "Strong beats skinny every time": disordered eating and compulsive exercise in women who post fitspiration on Instagram. Int. J. Eat. Disord. **50**, 76–79 (2017)
27. Lup, K., Trub, L., Rosenthal, L.: Instagram #Instasad? Exploring associations among Instagram use, depressive symptoms, negative social comparison, and strangers followed. Cyberpsychology Behav. Soc. Netw. **18**, 247–252 (2015)
28. Brown, R.C., Fischer, T., Goldwich, A.D., Keller, F., Young, R., Plener, P.L.: #cutting: non-suicidal self-injury (NSSI) on Instagram. Psychol. Med. **48**, 337–346 (2018)
29. Geurin-Eagleman, A.N., Burch, L.M.: Communicating via photographs: a gendered analysis of Olympic athletes' visual self-presentation on Instagram. Sport Manag. Rev. **19**, 133–145 (2016)
30. Anagnostopoulos, C., Parganas, P., Chadwick, S., Fenton, A.: Branding in pictures: using Instagram as a brand management tool in professional team sport organisations. Eur. Sport Manag. Q. **18**, 413–438 (2018)
31. Lavoie, K.A.: Instagram and branding: a case study of Dunkin' Donuts. Elon J. Undergrad. Res. Commun. **6**, 79–90 (2015)
32. Coelho, R.L.F., De Oliveira, D.S., De Almeida, M.I.S.: Does social media matter for post typology? Impact of post content on Facebook and Instagram metrics. Online Inf. Rev. **40**, 458–471 (2016)
33. Carrotte, E.R., Prichard, I., Lim, M.S.C.: "Fitspiration" on social media: a content analysis of gendered images. J. Med. Internet Res. **19**, e95 (2017)
34. Talbot, C.V., Gavin, J., van Steen, T., Morey, Y.: A content analysis of thinspiration, fitspiration, and bonespiration imagery on social media. J. Eat. Disord. **5**, 1–8 (2017)
35. Tiggemann, M., Zaccardo, M.: "Strong is the new skinny": a content analysis of #fitspiration images on Instagram. J. Health Psychol. **23**, 1003–1011 (2016)
36. Santarossa, S., Coyne, P., Lisinski, C., Woodruff, S.J.: #fitspo on Instagram: a mixed-methods approach using Netlytic and photo analysis, uncovering the online discussion and author/image characteristics. J. Health Psychol. **24**(3), 376–385 (2016)
37. Schmidbauer, H., Rösch, A., Stieler, F.: The 2016 US presidential election and media on Instagram: who was in the lead? Comput. Hum. Behav. **81**, 148–160 (2018)
38. Lee, C., Chau, D.: Language as pride, love, and hate: archiving emotions through multilingual Instagram hashtags. Discourse Context Media **22**, 21–29 (2018)
39. Santarossa, S., Coyne, P., Woodruff, S.J.: Exploring #nofilter images when a filter has been used. Int. J. Virtual Communities Soc. Netw. **9**, 54–63 (2017)
40. Giannoulakis, S., Tsapatsoulis, N.: Evaluating the descriptive power of Instagram hashtags. J. Innov. Digit. Ecosyst. **3**, 114–129 (2016)
41. Oh, C., Lee, T., Kim, Y., Park, S., Suh, B.: Understanding participatory hashtag practices on Instagram: a case study of weekend hashtag project. In: Proceedings of the 2016 CHI Conference Extended Abstracts on Human Factors in Computing Systems, pp. 1280–1287. ACM, New York (2016)
42. Zhang, Y., Hashim, N.H., Baghirov, F., Murphy, J.: Gender differences in Instagram hashtag use. J. Hosp. Mark. Manag. **27**, 386–404 (2018)

43. Hu, Y., Manikonda, L., Kambhampati, S.: What we Instagram : a first analysis of Instagram photo content and user types. In: Proceedings of the 8th International AAAI Conference on Weblogs and Social Media, ICWSM 2014, pp. 595–598. AAAI Press, Palo Alto (2014)

44. Dorsch, I.: Content description on a mobile image sharing service: hashtags on Instagram. J. Inf. Sci. Theory Pract. **6**, 46–61 (2018)

45. Dorsch, I., Zimmer, F., Stock, W.G.: Image indexing through hashtags in Instagram. In: Erdelez, S., Agarwal, N. (eds.) Diversity of Engagement: Connecting People and Information in the Physical and Virtual Worlds. Proceedings of the 80th ASIS&T Annual Meeting, pp. 658–659. Wiley, Somerset (2017)

46. Krippendorff, K.: Content Analysis: An Introduction to Its Methodology. Sage Publications Inc., Thousand Oaks (2004)

47. MacQueen, K.M., McLellan, E., Kay, K., Milstein, B.: Codebook development for team-based qualitative analysis. In: Krippendorff, K., Bock, M.A. (eds.) The Content Analysis Reader, pp. 211–219. Sage Publications Inc, Thousand Oaks (2009)

48. Shatford, S.: Analyzing the subject of a picture: a theoretical approach. Cat. Classif. Q. **6**, 39–62 (1986)

49. Panofsky, E.: Meaning in the Visual Arts. Doubleday Anchor Books, Garden City (1955)

50. Siebenlist, T.: Emotionale Suche – Emotionales Information-Retrieval. In: Lewandowski, D. (ed.) Handbuch der Internet-Suchmaschinen 3: Suchmaschinen zwischen Technik und Gesellschaft, pp. 299–327. Akademische Verlagsgesellschaft, Heidelberg (2013)

51. Ingwersen, P.: Cognitive perspectives of document representation. In: Bruce, H., Fidel, R., Ingwersen, P., Vakkari, P. (eds.) Emerging Frameworks and Methods: CoLIS 4: Proceedings of the 4th International Conference on Conceptions of Library and Information Science, pp. 285–300. Libraries Unlimited, Greenwoord Village (2002)

52. Peters, I., Stock, W.G.: Folksonomy and information retrieval. In: Joining Research and Practice: Social Computing and Information Science. Proceedings of the 70th ASIS&T Annual Meeting, pp. 1510–1542. Wiley, Hoboken (2007)

53. Austin, J.L.: How to do Things with Words. Clarendon, Oxford (1963)

54. Krippendorff, K.: Computing Krippendorff's alpha reliability. Departmental papers (ASC) (2011). https://repository.upenn.edu/asc_papers/43. Accessed 26 Jan 2019

55. Cohen, J.: Statistical Power Analysis for the Behavioral Sciences, 2nd edn. Psychology Press, New York (1988)

56. Kivran-Swaine, F., Brody, S., Diakopoulos, N., Naaman, M.: Of joy and gender: emotional expression in online social networks. In: Proceedings of the ACM 2012 Conference on Computer Supported Cooperative Work Companion, pp. 139–142. ACM, New York (2012)

57. Vikatos, P., Messias, J., Miranda, M., Benevenuto, F.: Linguistic diversities of demographic groups in Twitter. In: Proceedings of the 28th ACM Conference on Hypertext and Social Media, HT 2017, pp. 275–284. ACM, New York (2017)

58. Smith, A., Anderson, M.: Social media use in 2018 (2018). http://www.pewinternet.org/2018/03/01/social-media-use-in-2018/. Accessed 26 Jan 2019

59. Katz, E., Blumler, J.G., Gurevitch, M.: Utilization of mass communication by the individual. In: Blumler, J.G., Katz, E. (eds.) The Uses of Mass Communications: Current Perspectives on Gratifications Research, pp. 19–33. Sage Publications, Beverly Hills (1974)

60. Leung, L.: Generational differences in content generation in social media: the roles of the gratifications sought and of narcissism. Comput. Hum. Behav. **29**, 997–1006 (2013)

Implications of a Psychodynamic Discourse Analysis Study of Aggression in the Online Body Positive Community

Heather Michelann Quimby[(⊠)]

University of Texas at Austin, Austin, TX 78712, USA
mquimby@utexas.edu

Abstract. This study places online aggression within the larger context of human development research. Existing literature identifies a need for a nuanced approach to the study of online aggression that considers potentially adaptive functions. Psychodynamic ego defense theory provides a framework through which to analyze aggressive online discourse. The study provides insight into the complex psychological function of aggressive online interaction. Results fall primarily within the neurotic and immature categories of defense and include a significant number of adaptive or mature comments. The method created for this study, Online Psychodynamic Discourse Analysis, offers a useful addition to existing methods of online research. Thematic analysis provides insight into the psychosocial sources of conflict.

Keywords: Online aggression · Cyberbullying · Human development · Developmental psychology

1 Introduction

Defense mechanisms are ways we distort reality to protect ourselves from disturbing thoughts, feelings, and the memory of trauma. Some examples of defensive behaviors are observable in social media body positive (BOPO) discourse in negative statements that predict an individual's attractiveness to others, potential lifespan, or evaluate the target's overall intelligence, or their belief system based on sparse interaction. *Cyberbullying*, a term used frequently to describe online aggression, is often characterized as a one-way exchange between aggressor and victim, but this study examines the complex adaptive functions of aggressive online discourse. Using psychodynamic ego defense research as an analytical framework provides insight into the complex psychological, and potentially social, function of aggression on social media.

Defense mechanisms can function developmentally. Mature defenses such as *altruism* can have positive individual and social effects. Defense mechanisms on a scale from psychotic (most distorted) to adaptive (least distorted) can be extrapolated to evaluate online behavior. See examples in Table 1.

© Springer Nature Switzerland AG 2019
G. Meiselwitz (Ed.): HCII 2019, LNCS 11578, pp. 414–433, 2019.
https://doi.org/10.1007/978-3-030-21902-4_30

Table 1. Defense mechanisms in online behavior (Derived from [45])

Defense mechanism	Adaptation level	Function	Associated behavior	Online behavior example
Delusional projection	Psychotic	Extreme distortion to protect ego from trauma or violent impulses	Invents fictional relationship or event to distract from trauma	Direct threats of physical and/or sexual violence, cyber-stalking, revenge porn, and swatting
Projection	Immature	Indirect experience of trauma/impulse	Sees one's flaws or fears in another and attacks the object of projection	Verbal denigration such as directly criticizing others' appearance, beliefs, race, etc. Name-calling, degrading language
Isolation	Neurotic	Partial experience of trauma/desire	Experiences the thoughts associated with trauma but not the emotions. Intellectualization, detachment	Pseudo-rational behavior such as citing sources of perceived authority to denigrate the target while claiming a neutral or helping viewpoint
Humor	Adaptive	Regulated experience of trauma/desire	Expresses emotions associated with trauma/desire without focusing on pain	Blogging that deals with trauma or oppressive social norms through humor and joining with others in shared experience

The perception of anonymity online, combined with limited legal safeguards and social norms that control online behavior, can reinforce aberrant behavior [9]. This phenomenon is termed the *Online Disinhibition Effect* [15, 40]. While existing research explores negative effects of online aggression [17, 24, 39], the potential for positive outcomes has largely been overlooked.

This study examined the effects of aggression in the online Body Positive (BOPO) community. BOPO refers to a social justice movement that combats restrictive and discriminatory social norms around physical beauty and health [37]. On BOPO social media, tropes of body normativity are challenged, counter-challenged, and sometimes transformed through grassroots, online activism and discourse. By extension, social norms around the expression of aggression are also challenged and transformed. People who engage in conflict online challenge existing beliefs and norms about their topic;

they also challenge the ways in which society expresses emotions like anger, rage, disgust, fear, and love. These negotiations of expression clearly merits deeper observation.

Defense mechanisms have been studied from a developmental perspective since their inception by Freud [21], and more fully by his daughter Freud [20]. George Vaillant has studied the ways defense mechanisms transform over the lifespan [28, 44–46].

Existing social media and online interaction research may be biased towards pathological rather than developmental interpretation. Social norms change rapidly (as does the technology driving online communication). Perhaps online aggression and defense should be examined with the goal to contextualize, rather than pathologize.

This study seeks to examine of online aggression within the context of human behavior and development research, including the adaptive functions of aggressive online discourse. Using psychodynamic ego defense research as a framework through which to analyze aggressive online discourse offers insight into the complex function of aggression on social media. Additionally, this study utilizes thematic analysis to explore how larger psychosocial forces may be engaged in contentious online discourse.

2   Related Work

A body of research that fails to examine adaptive psychological development as a possible outcome of online conflict fails to capture the human experience. While there is a growing body of literature on the adaptive aspects of relational aggression in children and youth [3, 8], there is scant research on positive outcomes in online conflict. There is instead a pervasive belief that online behavior is innately disinhibited and potentially aberrant and dangerous [39]. Negativity bias—a tendency for the human brain to retain negative information over positive—affects both cognition and retention of positive information [11]. This may be a factor in the way online conflict is reported by the media and studied in the scientific community.

While significant violence takes place online, its frequency is exaggerated by media attention [32]. A more nuanced examination of the dynamics of online aggression is needed to explore the full range of behavior.

2.1   Unpacking Cyberbullying

Aggressive behavior online is referred to in multiple ways, some of which overlap considerably. These terms are often imprecise and frequently change in meaning and usage. In this paper, *online aggression* is the general term used for aggressive behavior on the internet. Much of the literature uses the term *cyberbullying*. Other terms include *cyber-aggression* [16], *cybercrime*, which generally refers to theft and illegal use of private information; and *trolling*, which is online harassment consciously intended to cause emotional distress.

Cyberbullying, a modified version of bullying, is frequently used to describe aggressive online behavior. Cyberbullying derives from existing definitions of bullying, which include three main elements: (1) the intention to cause harm, (2) repetition, and (3) an imbalance of power between bully and victim [29]. Cyberbullying definitions vary slightly, but generally include at least two of these elements, performed in an electronic or digital media setting [34, 42].

In spite of these limitations, *cyberbullying* is used to describe a wide range of phenomena. Bullying-based definitions for online behavior are problematic as they imply a lack of fluidity between roles of aggressor and target. The targets of bullying are not always victims. Online, physical strength and social status have little relevance, unless the online aggression is an extension of face-to-face aggression. Even then, the relative parity in agency between aggressor and target may change the bullying dynamic significantly [23].

Targets of online aggression have considerable agency and may engage in various kinds of defense, counter-aggression, and escalation. Examples include publicly exposing cyberbullying through blogging [30], sending copies of sexually abusive messages from male teenage gamers to the gamer's mothers [43], and engaging in public discourse with online aggressors [21, 27] These examples are difficult to classify under existing cyberbullying definitions. Are these targets still considered victims, in spite of the effectiveness of their counter-aggression? The cyberbullying model seems inadequate when the targets' responses are examined with the same level of scrutiny as the agents'.

2.2 Other Approaches

Taking an ethnographic approach to the causes of online aggression, Phillips [33], a digital ethnographer, embedded herself within the highly aggressive 4chan trolling community as a qualitative researcher, both observing and interacting with participants. She also examined the relationship between the trolling community and the corporate media, adding insight into the cultural forces that create or reinforce psychologically violent online behavior. Asking why trolls consciously violate cultural norms to the detriment of others, Phillips draws a connection between the ways sensationalized media regularly violates taboos (such as showing disturbingly violent or exploitative videos) in the name of information freedom, while trolls who exhibit similar behavior are considered social deviants. Phillips places those who troll into a social context where their behavior is not as deviant (or at least non-normative) as it first appears. Phillips' relationships within the 4chan community allowed her to look more critically at assumptions about why people engage in this form of online aggression.

Applied psychoanalysis, the study of existing texts using psychoanalytic methods, provides further insight into the underlying causes of online aggression. Suler's essay on the psychology of online behavior "The Online Disinhibition Effect" [40] posits several unconscious reasons for disinhibited behavior on the internet. Although it is not associated with a study, Suler's essay is frequently cited as a model for disinhibited behavior and other unique aspects of online participation.

Like Suler, Balick's research [6, 7] uses applied psychoanalysis. In his examination of psychological phenomena in the online world [7], his experience as a therapist provides a deeper look into the potential motivations of participants. He is neither too eager to frame all online phenomena within an existing model (such as bullying), nor is he convinced that all online interaction is entirely new. His primary interest is, "The way in which the disruptive nature of technology operates alongside the ways that social media mediates the basic human dynamics of relating" [6, p. xvi]. Balick is interested in how online interaction fits into and changes the way people relate.

Balick claims that the psychoanalytic perspective on online interaction can benefit therapists, who erroneously see online interaction as false. It can also inform public policy, which may ignore the complexity of online interpersonal dynamics. Balick seeks to understand why people engage in various forms of online interaction and performance of identity; answering these questions more fully could fundamentally change how we look at participants in cyber-aggression. Balick also examines the differences between online interactions that objectify others and interactions that increase connection and intimacy [6, 7].

Projection, or perceiving one's repressed feelings as enacted by someone else, is one of the defense mechanisms that psychiatrist Vaillant outlines in his work on adaptive ego defense [46]. People have the capacity and proclivity to mature beyond psychotic and immature defense mechanisms. Through externalizing repressed material by projecting it onto others, it may be recognized and re-integrated into the core personality—a basic tenet of psychodynamic psychology. Defensive behaviors are required for repressed feelings, desires, and urges to become conscious and for mal-adaptive behavior to be replaced with adaptive [46]. Online aggression can be examined for the seeds of this development. When participants show a shift from objectification to connection, there is the possibility of maturation and growth.

2.3   Summary

In the eyes of researchers and reporters, the roles of bully and victim have become archetypes inhabited by people enacting and receiving aggressive behaviors. These simplistic reductions ignore the complexity of aggressive human behavior, particularly on the internet where there are limited parallels with face-to-face bullying. While aggression is universal, differences in power, proximity, and structure online profoundly influence how aggression is enacted, received, and responded to. Social media allows targets of aggressive acts to respond in varied public and private ways.

The research question for this study is: *What types of ego-defensive behavior occur in aggressive online forum discussions?*

It is equally important to draw attention to adaptive and reparative outcomes of online aggression and conflict. We must examine both the psychological dynamics of the participants and the social-technological system in which they interact if we are to understand how online aggression fits into the larger context of human development.

3   Background

This study examines social media forum comments under posts by prominent Body Positive (BOPO) activists. Such exchanges are frequently contentious and attract participants from outside the BOPO movement who direct aggression at the creators of the posts and other participants.

This study focuses on the response to a disparaging video titled *Dear Fat People*, which went viral in September of 2015 [2] and then was widely discussed in the body positive community and in mainstream media [12, 14, 18, 35, 41, 48]. The study's three samples are drawn from the public comment forums on commentary pieces by body positive activists who addressed the video: an online article from *The Guardian* by Lindy West [38], an Instagram post by Holliday [25], and a video on YouTube by Thore [41].

4   Method

The study uses Online Psychodynamic Discourse Analysis, a new approach that includes elements of Discourse Analysis, Applied Psychoanalysis, and descriptive statistics.

4.1   Online Psychodynamic Discourse Analysis

Discourse analysis examines communications to identify and interpret hidden assumptions and norms; it is concerned with how meaning is made on personal, interpersonal, and structural levels. Discourse analysis has been used in both psychodynamic research [1] and online research [26].

Balick [7] and Suler [40] use *applied psychoanalysis* to analyze the psychodynamics of online interaction. Originally used to examine fictional works and characters [10], recent research reimagines it as a way of understanding the ways people use social media to meet emotional needs, connect to others, and be known [7]. The analytical framework used in this study has clear similarities, as it applies a psychodynamic analytical framework to existing documents.

However, researchers can fall prey to confirmation bias in online aggression. Due to the corporate media's focus on cybercrime and online hate crimes, researchers may be conditioned to ignore adaptive or neutral online behavior in favor of aggression [7, 32]. Descriptive statistics are used to graphically compare the proportions of adaptive behavior with defensive behavior.

4.2   Delimitations

The study sample is derived from online discourse stemming from issues concerning the Body Positive community. Sample discourse is extracted from online forums under posts, videos, or articles written by prominent BOPO activists. While issues of structural inequality and intersectionality are certainly germane to the discussion of online aggression in the BOPO community, this study specifically addresses psychodynamic motivations for engaging in aggressive discourse, an identified gap in research of online aggression. Examining intrapsychic functions adds nuance to existent research on the interpersonal and structural [33] aspects of online discourse.

4.3 Data Organization

Social media outlets have different ways of organizing and monitoring public discussion. All three samples were organized from most recent to oldest before the data were extracted.

YouTube allows subthreads, where commenters respond to one another in an indented section of the page. I chose a subthread that consisted of 52 comments posted around the time of the release of the video in August of 2015 and continued for about a month. YouTube is difficult to study from a discourse perspective because users can change their usernames. This did not affect my ability to examine the comments for defense mechanisms but made following the discourse challenging at times.

Instagram comments were displayed chronologically so I chose the first 50 posted comments. However, many of these comments were in response to a commenter who had since deleted his or her account. This did not impede my ability to analyze the data but did create challenges in examining the flow of the discourse.

I used the first 50 comments in the *Guardian* sample. However, several comments were blocked by moderators. These comments were not counted as part of the 50 selected comments. Since this discourse was to some degree censored, it may have been less representative than the other two samples. Non-English comments were also excluded.

4.4 Coding

Comments first were coded by phrase, statement, or sentence for speech acts, such as disparaging, testifying, explaining, attacking, relating, etc. After these codes were applied, the discourse was re-examined for instances of cognitive distortion, for example, predicting future outcomes; exaggeration; minimization; and over-generalization [13]. When these codes were completed, I looked for constellations of distortions that identify specific defense mechanisms. A final layer of thematic analysis was added, identifying polarities in the topics of discourse, such as health-sickness, civility-rudeness, and life-death.

5 Findings

Thematically, the discourse centered primarily on the health and social acceptability of fatness and the ethics of shaming or trolling people for being fat. However, this study examines adaptiveness in online discourse, not the validity of a particular position.

Out of the 150 comments, 139 were coded with defense mechanisms. Some comments were too brief to provide enough material for psychological analysis. However, all 150 comments were coded for speech acts, and a majority were coded for cognitive distortion.

Overall, the predominant defense mechanisms were *projection* (immature) at 32% and *displacement* (neurotic) at 30%. See Fig. 1:

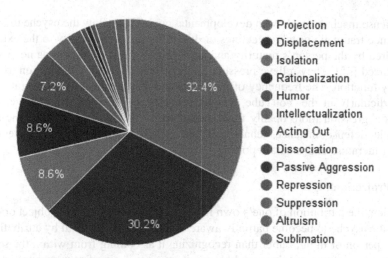

Fig. 1. Distribution of defense mechanisms by category across full sample (N = 139)

However, despite the slightly larger proportion of projection to displacement, comments indicating a neurotic level of defense were dominant, with a smaller proportion of immature comments, and a small number of adaptive comments. There were no psychotic comments. See Fig. 2:

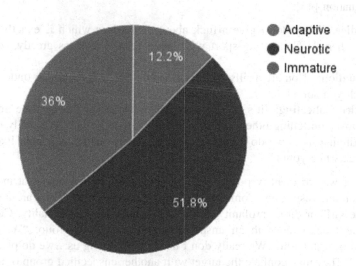

Fig. 2. Distribution of defense mechanisms across full sample (N = 139)

5.1 Dominant Defense Mechanisms

The main levels of ego defense found in the sample were neurotic and immature, while the two most common defense mechanisms were projection and displacement. Adaptive defense mechanisms were also present, particularly humor in *the Guardian* sample.

Defense mechanisms have a developmental goal: They allow the psyche to partially experience traumatic or taboo feelings or desires by distorting reality to the extent that is required by the person's maturity and according to the level of trauma he or she has experienced [45]. They relieve pressure on the psyche and allow the person to at least partially function. The frequency of projection and displacement in the overall sample, and particularly in the YouTube sample, suggests that there is a pervasive need to express aggression more openly than is allowed by face-to-face society. The lack of psychotic defense instances challenges the pathologizing of online aggression in existing literature and media reporting.

5.2 Projection

Projection, the attribution of one's own feelings or traits to an external object or person, allows the psyche to become partially aware of unconscious material by attributing it to another person or thing, rather than recognizing it as coming from within the self. It is an immature defense mechanism because it requires a significant amount of reality distortion for the unconscious desire or feeling to manifest. Comments were coded for projection if they displayed a level of distortion that (a) demonstrated strong irrational feelings, and (b) directed these feelings at a person with whom the commenter had no prior relationship or knowledge.

Each defense mechanism has certain behavioral hallmarks that are identifiable through discourse. The hallmarks of projection include prejudice, injustice collecting, and devaluation [45]:

Prejudice: "They don't give a fuck about themselves which is exactly why they judge others." "Comparing sport with being a lazy, feckless greedy, self-entitled fatty?"

Devaluation: "You are a silly mean nasty little girl." "I doubt you understand how childish you sound."

Injustice Collecting: "it's bad for the population in general because you lazy fat fucks insist on telling other fat fucks that it's OK to be fat. "We really don't need you bullying us... we do plenty of it to ourselves thanks to people like you and comments like yours."

Another way to identify projection is to look for certain words that indicate personalization and distortion. Commenters call the target names, "You are a silly mean nasty little girl" or direct profanity at the target, indicating irrationality. Commenters may group themselves with an unspecified assumed target group, "We know the dangers of our situation...We really don't need you bullying us...we do plenty of it to ourselves." They may conflate the target with another unspecified group of aggressors, "thanks to people like you." The specificity of the comments towards the target identifies them as examples of projection rather than displacement.

Rejecting a person's beliefs by calling him stupid or ignorant may temporarily relieve the discomfort caused by having one's own perspective challenged. Many of the comments coded as projection include name-calling and profanity, behaviors that appear childish or immature. This is regressive, as Anna Freud claims it is common in adolescents who tend to swing between extremes of behavior [20].

The YouTube sample scored the highest rate of projection. People who habitually express superiority to fat people may be motivated by the source video (which disputes this viewpoint) to denigrate those who agree with it. Comments coded as projection rarely demonstrate the ability to consider multiple perspectives. Projection creates objectification: the inability to relate to the target. This may be particularly true online, due to the lack of non-textual information or feedback [6].

5.3 Displacement

Displacement redirects the commenter's feelings towards a less important object or person. The online environment may facilitate this particular defense—being unable to see or hear the object of displaced impulses depersonalizes them. Substituting strangers for emotionally important people is a feature of displacement [45]. Like projection, displacement allows for partial expression of repressed material by directing it away from the original source. It is different from projection because the unconscious material is not directed at a single person. It is instead diffused; the object is more general and less threatening than the original source [45].

Hallmarks of displacement include phobias, harmful humor, and prejudice [45]. These hallmarks of displacement were illustrated in the sample:

Sarcasm/Wit: "OMG! You changed my life! How was I to ever know this will work? You should be crowned royalty and teach us all! You are the Dr. Oz of Fatties!"

Prejudice: "To think that people worry about kids doing drugs, or the "example" legalization would set, when one and a half million Americans die of heart disease each year, because it's perfectly acceptable to eat until you croak."

Comments were coded for displacement if they contained some of the features of projection, such as attributing one's feelings to something else, but were more indirect or rational in their language, indicating that the intensity of the emotion was diffused, rather than transferred directly to an alternative object. Diffusion indicates a higher level of adaptation; adaptive defense mechanisms succeed in at least partial expression of the impulse with potentially less harm to self or others. Displacement may still cause harm to the target, but it is not as direct as projection.

- "Lets be honest, obesity that you actually have is a disease!" (YouTube, 2015)
- "People who think its all about calories in/out are defunct. Look at the science ppl."

Comments coded as displacement often debated the legitimacy of the correlation between health and weight. The second comment could also be coded for isolation—being unaware of emotions underlying seemingly rational arguments. However, the fact that he or she is commenting on the legitimacy of people who hold different views, rather than the views themselves, indicates displacement. The first comment would be coded as projection if it had been directed at a specific target (on Instagram the use of @username means it is directed at a specific person). In this case, the use of "you" seems to be generally directed towards people who do not believe that obesity is universally indicative of poor health.

Like projection, displacement may temporarily relieve the discomfort associated with having one's assumptions or biases challenged. *The Guardian* sample provided the highest number of examples of displacement, in the form of argument about the value, health, and validity of fat people. Rather than personal attacks, as in the You-Tube sample, commenters argued about whether or not shaming fat people is effective or moral:

- It's a really interesting turn of phrase. 'There's something wrong with' fat people. They are fat, is what's wrong. It's a health issue, at most. But there's nothing 'wrong' with them and I wish we'd stop behaving as if it's a sign of moral weakness.
- I'm not usually one to criticize people for issues of individual freedom or indulgence, but when a group such as the obese try to carve out a space in society immune from criticism, they deserve a friendly fuck no.

Neither of these commenters identify themselves or a specific object (person) in their arguments; their comments are general, not personal. Even when the discourse becomes more direct, it is still about the strength of the argument, not the person making the argument:

- You now give three new responses: an argument from different risks, an argument from 'fairness', and an argument from disgust. Of these three, the third has the most intellectual content. You may want to reflect on that.

Ironically, these commenters objectify a larger swath of people than those who attack individuals. While the YouTube commenters are direct in their attacks of one another, *The Guardian* commenters use third person to discuss the validity of a group that is not actively participating in the discussion. Displacement is a more mature, less distorting defense mechanism than projection, but may be more prejudicial in the online context because of its tendency to diffuse intense feeling through reinforcing social biases.

5.4   Implications of Levels of Defense

Much of the existing literature on online aggression, often referred to as trolling or cyberbullying, focuses on maladaptive behavior and negative outcomes [19, 36, 38]. As in this sample, online aggression often includes denigration, name calling, profanity, and vociferous personal attacks. On the surface, these results seem to support the claim that online behavior is significantly disinhibited [40]. However, the results of this study call into question the idea that online behavior is more frequently aberrant and harmful than face-to-face aggression. Certainly, criminal online aggression, such as revenge porn, cyber stalking, swatting, and impersonation, can be harmful and are likely pathological. However, no comments in this study were coded indicated a level of distortion necessary to enact these crimes.

5.5   Lack of Psychotic Defense

The online Body Positive community frequently engages in arguments about the validity of its goals of self-acceptance [4, 5]. It espouses a narrative of self-acceptance that contradicts social views of obesity and social norms of attractiveness, making it a magnet for online debate. What is remarkable about the findings, then, is that the most frequent codes were neurotic, second most frequent were immature, and third most frequent were mature/adaptive. No comments were coded as psychotic. Through a psychodynamic lens, the comments examined in this study, while often angry, immature, or disparaging, were not particularly pathological or violent. The one violent comment in the sample wished for another's death but did not threaten. The death wish indicates a lack of ability to control one's speech (*acting out*), not the intent to commit murder (*delusional projection*). Online hate crimes exist, but the bulk of online discourse may fit within the larger picture of normal (not psychotic) human behavior.

These results suggest that further research is needed to examine the Online Disinhibition Effect [40]. While the perception of anonymity on the internet may allow people to more openly express their feelings and beliefs, the textual nature of online discourse is also a factor [27]. Studies have suggested that anonymity does not have a significant effect on disinhibition [29]. In the YouTube sample, one of the commenters claimed to know another personally, and came to her defense:

- Just want to say u have some nerve talking to [username redacted] like that. I'll have you known I have known her my whole life and she is one amazing person. For ur info it is not her choice that she is the way she is. It's not because she's lazy or because she over eats or doesn't care. She has a fucking medical condition. She does care about her self and she is trying to loose weight.
- So you sitting here running your mouth and trying to look like a bad ass is just fucking wrong and stupid. Not everyone in this world is fat by their own choice. There are people out there who can't control how they look or weigh. You are just luck I don't know who you are because I would run ur ass into the damn ground.

This commenter is not shy about expressing his or her feelings, in spite of the fact that anonymity may be compromised. He or she expresses a desire to break anonymity to exact retribution for the attack on his or her friend.

5.6   Defense and Growth

Vaillant's research shows those with distinct disadvantages in early life can overcome them by midlife [28]. Even immature defense mechanisms may function as building blocks towards greater adaptivity. If the only function of defense mechanisms was temporary relief of discomfort, it would be easy to dismiss contentious online discourse as a pointless, immature circus. But people of opposing viewpoints *choose* to engage in textual debate over issues that can be upsetting. These debates may have developmental functions just as in the face-to-face world. While those who seek out conflict are probably not consciously looking to expand their worldviews, the effects in some cases are compassion, understanding, or consideration.

Each of the three samples had examples of either adaptive turns in the conversation, adaptive comments, or positive changes in the level of adaptation in response to negative comments. In this Section I will excerpt small sections of the discourse in sequence to show where and how adaptive change occurred.

5.7   YouTube: From Denigration to Protection

The YouTube sample was highly immature. The most frequent defense mechanism was projection, and it was the only sample that had comments coded as *acting out*. However, in the midst of some of the worst personal attacks, a commenter who had previously criticized a self-identified fat person came to her defense (in an attempt to show this interaction, some peripheral comments are left out):

Commenter 3 (to Commenter 1) literally kill yourself tbh [to be honest] irl [in real life]

Commenter 3 (to Commenter 1) how does it feel knowing that this "fat acceptance" bs you're pushing for is just a way of making people feel bad for your sorry fat ass for not doing any thing about your condition. you deserve to be made fun of and ridiculed you disgusting sack of lard and excuses:) go take that butthurt out on some food now you self defeating bovine

Commenter 2 (to Commenter 3) fuck off. never tell someone to kill them self. thats too far

Commenter 1 (to Commenter 2) He's just a stuck up asshole who doesn't think before he speaks. An if he does he probably has issues.. I'm not taking it personal.

Commenter 2 begins by contradicting Commenter 1's assertion that a medical condition prevents her from losing weight. However, when Commenter 3 makes violent and disparaging comments to Commenter 1, Commenter 2 defends her and she acknowledges the defense, reassuring him or her that she is unaffected. This indicates that Commenter 2 is capable of regarding Commenter 1 with compassion and recognizes that Commenter 3's vitriol may be destructive to her. This moves the conversation away from objectification and towards relating.

5.8   The Guardian: Flexibility and Humor

The Guardian sample is predominantly coded as displacement. However, in the middle of a fierce debate over the validity of the body positivity, the commenters break into clowning.

Commenter 1 Arbour, I quickly gathered, is a Canadian YouTuber on that information alone anyone with a brain would avoid her.... (not the canadian bit, i like canadians)

Commenter 2 (to Commenter 1) Not enough to capitalise them.

Commenter 1 (to Commenter 2) as a devotee of k.d. lang i never capitalise.

Commenter 3 (to Commenter 1) I suspect that you employ someone to do that type of thing? 3;)

Commenter 4 (to Commenter 2) So Ottowan Canadians are ok?

The discourse then returns to debating the validity of fat-shaming, but humor and non-harmful satire are woven into the rest of the sample. This sample demonstrates some flexibility and playfulness that is not apparent in the other two. While not without immature discourse, the overall tone is more inquisitive and playful.

5.9   Instagram: Defensiveness and Altruism

The Instagram sample shows isolated sparks of compassion. While most of the discourse is consumed with debating the health and validity of fatness (and attacking or refuting a deleted user), some participants express solidarity with one another or reveal their own journey to self-acceptance.

- are they really saying that? I mean I'm fat, and I am heathy but that doesn't mean I am blind to statistics. I don't know if you are familiar with health literacy research but it's a fascinating topic. If knowing that something is a risk was enough to change behaviour then why would anyone smoke for example? Behaviour change is complex and difficult. If you want to encourage people to change their behaviour you need to work with their intrinsic motivation. Fat shaming and similar tactics only work to entrench the patterns that have lead someone to get fat in the first place.
- I think there is nothing more beautiful than to feel good in your own skin. We need more people like Tess [the original poster] no matter what your size. Her beauty shines from within.
- I am 5'10" and wear a size 24. My Dr. does blood work yearly. I do not have high blood pressure, heart disease, high cholesterol or diabetes. I work out in the water daily. Not all plus size people are unhealthy. I know 30 years ago I thought I would always be a size 13 but life changes. I love myself my husband, children and grandchildren love me. I have learned to accept myself in a society that doesn't accept me. I used to have to make a lot of my own clothes. It is nice to have so many choices now days.

Rather than resorting to extremes, these commenters refute negative comments without being drawn into displacement or projection. The first commenter describes the complexity of the science behind fatness, rather attacking those with whom he or she disagrees. The second emphasizes the importance of self-acceptance rather than approval. Both of these comments were coded as *altruism*, taking care of an internal need by serving this need on others. The third commenter shares her own journey to self-acceptance in the midst of a contentious debate about whether self-love is acceptable. This is coded as *sublimation*—gratifying needs through substitution of healthy relationships or activities—as she describes how having loving relationships has led her to self-acceptance. In the midst of discourse that contains frequent denigration, these comments stand out.

All three samples consistently showed a majority of comments coded as neurotic (n = 72) or Immature (n = 50). A significant number of comments were coded as adaptive or mature (n = 17). No comments were coded as psychotic. While the tone of the discourse varied across the three segments, the overall themes were similar: the health, validity, and social acceptability of fat people.

5.10   Thematic Analysis

An additional layer of coding was added to examine thematic polarities in discourse. The most frequent polarities were health-sickness (30), knowledge-ignorance (28), and civility-rudeness (21). Examples are below.

Health-sickness

- Not all plus size people are unhealthy.
- There's nothing wrong with being slightly overweight, obviously not everyone is going to have a 'perfect' body. But when that becomes obesity (non-genetic), it shouldn't be 'normalised' or encouraged. Obesity causes so many health problems, from type 2 diabetes to knee problems, that result in an early death.

Knowledge-ignorance

- I am doing something about it. You don't know that so you can't tell me shit. You are the dumbest person on here yet.. You cant tell me there isn't any disease that causes weight gain. you can ask any doctor and they'll tell you..
- You are either moronic or mentally blank if you think I will believe you. Being black is immutable and fat isn't. I'm just going to assume you are being extremely lazy. I would be willing to say that don't even know where to beginning, but why bother any further.

Civility-rudeness

- Obesity absolutely should be mocked and ridiculed. Its called societal pressure. And not being obese.
- You're not really a very nice person, are you?

Within the context of ego defense, these comments demonstrate the level of ire and cognitive distortion that occurs in heated exchanges. However, the pervasiveness of these polarities warrants future exploration, as the underlying themes suggest deeper insecurities and fears about death, identity, worthiness, and morality.

6   Discussion

This study was conceived to contextualize aggressive online discourse within human development, thereby filling a significant gap in existing literature derived primarily from behavioral, face-to-face bullying studies. Moments of generosity or humor, within largely contentious discourse, point to the potential for personal growth, understanding, and connection. Even discourse rooted in anger and invalidation sometimes visibly moves towards mature relationships.

While the sample was specific to the body positive movement and the controversy it engenders, the method and findings have implications for other divisive social issues. Public discussion of fatness, obesity, and weight, in general, can be contentious, but might seem less significant than police shootings, gun control, free speech, civil rights, rape culture, abortion, and immigration. Yet, these issues engender similar ego defense responses. The lens of Online Psychodynamic Discourse Analysis allows us to observe behavior uncoupled from our opinions and beliefs. Additionally, an examination of the embedded polarities hints at deeper intrapsychic and social conflicts that play out in online forums that could be explored in future studies.

6.1 Significance of Study

Combining discourse analysis with applied psychoanalysis offers a systematized approach to the examination of online discussions, named Online Psychodynamic Discourse Analysis. While the sample is derived from a discussion of reactions in the Body Positive community to a viral video, the method used to identify ego defense mechanisms in online discourse can be used in any environment that engenders habitual conflict.

The psychodynamic framework adds nuance to discussion of online conflict. Instead of separating participants into bullies and victims, examining the defense responses of all participants allows for a greater sense of what participants are co-creating. Applying the defense mechanism spectrum to online conflict places it within the larger context of human behavior, particularly acknowledging capacity for growth.

Though the main focus of this study was not thematic, one macro-theme emerged, nonetheless: All three samples discussed the right of fat people to take up space or resources, through addressing the polarities of health-sickness, civility-rudeness, and knowledge-ignorance. The video that all three samples discussed, *Dear Fat People*, explicitly disparages a fat child for taking up too much space in an airplane seat, and this theme is echoed in the data. This visceral reaction to the potential denial of emotional and physical space or resources could be explored in online forums dealing with the Black Lives Matter movement and its counter-movements; the current debate on illegal immigration and asylum seekers; and environmental issues such as the North Dakota Pipeline protests, fossil fuels and climate change. Whether viewed from an intrapsychic or social perspective, the ability and right to occupy space seems to foment conflict and aggression.

The most prominent theme, health-sickness, may also indicate deeper forces in a species that is struggling with environmental sickness and social unease. It would be beneficial to further develop this approach to the data and apply it to other online environments to determine whether or not there are similarities in polarities.

This research also contributes to understanding the social function of aggression online. Just as Phillip's work examines the cultural context of extreme trolling this study adds a psychological (micro) dimension to the reasons why people attack one another online, enhancing Phillip's social (macro) observations [33]. Balick's applied psychoanalysis research examines the ways in which people connect with or objectify one another through social media [6, 7]. Adding the systematized method used in this study may allow researchers to study related phenomena (such as aggression) in more detail. Finally, using an archival sample allows for deep textual analysis, which can complement the ethnographic approach taken by Phillips [33] and others in this discipline.

Vaillant's work, the cornerstone of this study, shows how maturation is incremental, messy, and slow. If researchers and reporters continue to assume that individual instances of dysfunction indicate mass psychosis (or at least neurosis), the study of online aggression will suffer from myopia. Vaillant says of his work,

> But the quality of the whole journey is seldom changed by a single turning…What makes or breaks our luck seems to be the continued interaction between our choice of adaptive mechanisms and our sustained relationships with other people. [44, p. 368].

Just as Vaillant points out it is folly to think that a single event shapes the trajectory of one's life, it is also folly to imagine that aggressive discourse is devoid of adaptive outcomes; of signs of slowly growing compassion, relationship, and understanding.

6.2 Limitations

The size of this sample limits the ability to draw broad conclusions about social trends. Because the study is archival, demographic information is unavailable, making it difficult draw conclusions about applicability across demographics. As a new method, Online Psychodynamic Discourse Analysis will need to be reproduced and tested in multiple environments. This study examined small samples from three sources on a similar topic, limiting generalizability for other topics or types of samples. Larger or broader samples may yield different results. Combining Online Psychodynamic Discourse Analysis with interviews or surveys may be helpful for future studies, so assumptions and interpretations can be examined alongside the lived experiences of online participants.

7 Conclusion

Although the focal point of this study was conflict, each sample has moments of beauty —an older woman sharing how she has come to accept herself; a group of people engaged in a contentious debate devolving into a Monty-Python-esque humor break; a critic standing up for a target when a troll tells her to kill herself.

Each of these moments provides a window into the complexity of human interaction. Redemption does not come easily. Human development is not immediate or dramatic. People mature over decades, not months. Online interaction, while relatively new, should not be oversimplified because it appears different from other kinds of human contact. It is more explicit than face-to-face interaction—not necessarily less mature.

This study shows that the seeds of maturation—of compassion and growth—are being planted in aggressive online conversations. Online aggression must be placed in the context of human behavior and development. It should not be considered an anomaly or an unreal form of human interaction. The environment is new; the behavior is not. Adults continue to develop, learn, and grow throughout the lives. The birth of the internet has not changed our ability to mature; in fact, it may offer us more opportunities for connection and growth.

References

1. Anderson, D.K.: A psychodynamic analysis of discourse theory: understanding the influence of emotions, regression, and change. Adm. Theory Prax. **24**(1), 3 (2002)
2. Arbour, N.: Dear fat people (2015). https://www.youtube.com/watch?v=CXFgNhyP4-A
3. Archer, J., Coyne, S.M.: An integrated review of indirect, relational, and social aggression. Pers. Soc. Psychol. **9**(3), 212–230 (2005). https://doi.org/10.1207/s15327957pspr0903_2
4. Baker, J.T.M.: Body hate on the internet: How to cope (2015). http://www.themilitantbaker.com/2015/08/body-hate-on-internet-how-to-cope.html
5. Baker, J.T.M.: The militant baker: why people hate Tess Munster (and other happy fat people (2015). http://www.themilitantbaker.com/2015/01/why-people-hate-tess-munster-and-other.html
6. Balick, A.: The Psychodynamics of Social Networking: Connected-up Instantaneous Culture and the Self. Karnac Books, London (2015)
7. Balick, A.: TMI in the transference LOL: psychoanalytic reflections on Google, social networking, and "virtual impingement". Psychoanal. Cult. Soc. **17**(2), 120–136 (2012). https://doi.org/10.1057/pcs.2012.19
8. Banny, A.M., Heilbron, N., Ames, A., Prinstein, M.J.: Relational benefits of relational aggression: adaptive and maladaptive associations with adolescent friendship quality. Dev. Psychol. **47**(4), 1153–1166 (2011). https://doi.org/10.1037/a0022546
9. Barlett, C.P.: Anonymously hurting others online: the effect of anonymity on cyberbullying frequency. Psychol. Popul. Media Cult. (2013). https://doi.org/10.1037/a0034335
10. Baudry, F.: An essay on method in applied psychoanalysis. Psychoanal. Q. **53**, 551–581 (1984)
11. Bebbington, K., MacLeod, C., Ellison, T.M., Fay, N.: The sky is falling: evidence of a negativity bias in the social transmission of information. Evol. Hum. Behav. **38**(1), 92–101 (2017). https://doi.org/10.1016/j.evolhumbehav.2016.07.004
12. Boone, J.: YouTuber behind "Dear Fat People" says critics must be "really f***ing slow" to be offended. Entertainment Tonight Online. (2015). http://www.etonline.com/news/171471_youtuber_called_out_for_fat_shaming_over_dear_fat_people
13. Burns, D.: Feeling Good: The New Mood Therapy. HarperCollins, New York (1999)
14. Bussel, R.: "Dear Fat People" isn't satire: Despite the backlash publicity, it's unlikely to make Nicole Arbour a star. Salon. http://www.salon.com/2015/09/08/dear_fat_people_isnt_satire_despite_the_backlash_publicity_its_unlikely_to_make_nicole_arbour_a_star/
15. Chaikin, D.: Network investigations of cyber attacks: the limits of digital evidence. Crime, Law Soc. Change **46**(4/5), 239–256 (2007). https://doi.org/10.1007/s10611-007-9058-4
16. Corcoran, L., Prentice, G., McGuckin, C.: Cyberbullying or cyber aggression?: A review of existing definitions of cyber-based peer-to-peer aggression. Societies **5**(2), 245 (2015). ISSN 2075-4698
17. Corbett, P.E.: Cyberbullying and other high-tech crimes involving teens. J. Internet Law **12**(3), 1–20 (2008)
18. Edelman, J.: Response #7431 to the "Dear Fat People" lady. The Huffington Post (2015). http://www.huffingtonpost.com/joni-edelman/response-7431-to-the-dear-fat-people-lady_b_8155576.html
19. Eksi, F.: Examination of narcissistic personality traits' predicting level of internet addiction and cyber bullying through path analysis. Educ. Sci.: Theory Pract. **12**(3), 1694–1706 (2012)
20. Freud, A.: The Ego and the Mechanisms of Defence. International Universities Press, New York (1966/1937)

21. Freud, S.: A general Introduction to Psychoanalysis. (G. S. Hall, Trans.) Horace Liveright, New York (2011/1920)
22. Glass, I.: If You Don't Have Anything Nice to Say, SAY IT IN ALL CAPS. This American Life (2015). http://www.thisamericanlife.org/radio-archives/episode/545/if-you-dont-have-anything-nice-to-say-say-it-in-all-caps?act=1#play
23. Heatherington, W., Coyne, I.: Understanding individual experiences of cyberbullying encountered through work. Int. J. Organ. Theory Behav. **17**(2), 163 (2014)
24. Hinduja, S., Patchin, J.W.: Bullying, cyberbullying, and suicide. Arch. Suicide Res. **14**(3), 206–221 (2010). https://doi.org/10.1080/13811118.2010.494133
25. Holliday, T.: Instagram photo by plus model—Mom—Feminist (2015). https://www.instagram.com/p/7TjsTpPObR/
26. James, L., Nahl, D.: A discourse analysis technique for charting the flow of interactions in online activity. Webology **11**(2), 1–36 (2014)
27. Johnson, A.N.: Disinhibition and the internet. In: Gackenback, J. (ed.) Psychology and the Internet: Intrapersonal, Interpersonal and Transpersonal Implications, pp. 75–92. Academic Press, Burlington (2006)
28. Landes, S.D., Ardelt, M., Vaillant, G.E., Waldinger, R.J.: Childhood adversity, midlife generativity, and later life well-being. J. Gerontol. Ser. B: Psychol. Sci. Soc. Sci. **69**(6), 942–952 (2014)
29. Lapidot-Lefler, N., Barak, A.: The benign online disinhibition effect: could situational factors induce self-disclosure and prosocial behaviors? Cyberpsychology: J. Psychosoc. Res. Cyberspace **9**(2) (2015). https://doi.org/10.5817/CP2015-2-3
30. Menesini, E.: Cyberbullying: the right value of the phenomenon. Comments on the paper "Cyberbullying: an overrated phenomenon"? Eur. J. Dev. Psychol. **9**(5), 544–552 (2012). https://doi.org/10.1080/17405629.2012.706449
31. Mina, C.: A plus size woman's open letter to the internet trolls, haters, and all those who have something to say about fat bodies. Bustle (2015). http://www.bustle.com/articles/83265-a-plus-size-womans-open-letter-to-the-internet-trolls-haters-and-all-those-who-have
32. Olweus, D.: Cyberbullying: an overrated phenomenon? Eur. J. Dev. Psychol. **9**(5), 520–538 (2012). https://doi.org/10.1080/17405629.2012.682358
33. Phillips, W.: This is Why We Can't Have Nice Things: Mapping the Relationship Between Online Trolling and Mainstream Culture. The MIT Press, Cambridge (2015)
34. Rafferty, R., Vander Ven, T.: "I hate everything about you": a qualitative examination of cyberbullying and on-line aggression in a college sample. Deviant Behav. **35**(5), 364–377 (2014). https://doi.org/10.1080/01639625.2013.849171
35. Ross, A.: "Dear Fat People" Comedian Nicole Arbour: "I'm not apologizing". Time (2015). http://time.com/4028119/dear-fat-people-nicole-arbour/
36. Runions, K.: Toward a conceptual model of motive and self-control in cyber-aggression: Rage, revenge, reward, and recreation. J. Youth Adolesc. **42**(5), 751–771 (2013). https://doi.org/10.1007/s10964-013-9936-2
37. Sastre, A.: Towards a radical body positive. Fem. Media Stud. **14**(6), 929–943 (2014). https://doi.org/10.1080/14680777.2014.883420
38. Schenk, A.M., Fremouw, W.J., Keelan, C.M.: Characteristics of college cyberbullies. Comput. Hum. Behav. **29**, 2320–2327 (2013). https://doi.org/10.1016/j.chb.2013.05.013
39. Seiler, S.J., Navarro, J.N.: Bullying on the pixel playground: Investigating risk factors of cyberbullying at the intersection of children's online-offline social lives. Cyberpsychology **8**(4), 37–52 (2014). https://doi.org/10.5817/CP2014-4-6
40. Suler, J.: The online disinhibition effect. CyberPsychology Behav. **7**(3), 321–326 (2004). https://doi.org/10.1089/1094931041291295

41. Thore, W.: What I want to say to fat people: Response to Nicole Arbour – YouTube (2015). https://www.youtube.com/watch?v=r2YYZBrPwwU
42. Tokunaga, R.S.: Following you home from school: a critical review and synthesis of research on cyberbullying victimization. Comput. Hum. Behav. **26**, 277–287 (2010). https://doi.org/10.1016/j.chb.2009.11.014
43. True, E.: The gaming journalist who tells on her internet trolls – to their mothers. The Guardian (2014). http://www.theguardian.com/culture/australia-culture-blog/2014/nov/28/alanah-pearce-tells-on-her-internet-trolls-to-their-mothers
44. Vaillant, G.E.: Adaptation to Life. Harvard University Press, Cambridge (1977)
45. Vaillant, G.E.: Ego Mechanisms of Defense: A Guide for Clinicians and Researchers. American Psychiatric Press, Washington, D.C. (1992)
46. Vaillant, G.E.: The Wisdom of the Ego. First Harvard University Press, Cambridge (1993)
47. West, L.: Don't ignore the trolls. Feed them until they explode (2013). http://jezebel.com/dont-ignore-the-trolls-feed-them-until-they-explode-977453815
48. West, L.: The "Dear Fat People" video is tired, cruel and lazy – but I still fight for the woman who made it. The Guardian (2015). http://www.theguardian.com/commentisfree/2015/sep/08/dear-fat-people-vrial-video-canadian-comedian-nicole-arbour

From Social Media to Expert Reports: The Impact of Source Selection on Automatically Validating Complex Conceptual Models of Obesity

Mannila Sandhu[1], Philippe J. Giabbanelli[2(✉)], and Vijay K. Mago[1]

[1] Department of Computer Science, Lakehead University, Thunder Bay, ON, Canada
{msandhu3,vmago}@lakeheadu.ca
[2] Computer Science Department, Furman University, Greenville, SC, USA
giabbanelli@gmail.com

Abstract. Models are predominantly developed using either quantitative data (e.g., for structured equation models) or qualitative data obtained through questionnaires designed by researchers (e.g., for fuzzy cognitive maps). The wide availability of social media data and advances in natural language processing raise the possibility of developing models from qualitative data naturally produced by users. This is of particular interest for public health surveillance and policymaking, as social media provide the opinions of constituents. In this paper, we contrast a model produced by social media with one produced via expert reports. We use the same process to derive a model in each case, thus focusing our analysis on the impact of source selection. We found that three expert reports were sufficient to touch on more aspects of a complex problem (measured by the number of relationships) than several million tweets. Consequently, developing a model exclusively from social media may lead to oversimplifying a problem. This may be avoided by complementing social media with expert reports. Alternatively, future research should explore whether a much larger volume of tweets would be needed, which also calls for improvements in scalable methods to transform qualitative data into models.

Keywords: Conceptual modeling · Network analysis ·
Social web mining · Theme mining · Twitter mining

1 Introduction

Overweight and obesity is now a global phenomenon, found in economically developed or developing countries (e.g., United States [1], European countries [2], South Africa [3], China [4]) as well as in regions that experience a double burden with the concomitant problem of malnutrition [5]. While there are ongoing

Research funded by MITACS Globalink Research Award, Canada.

debates on a possible plateau or even decrease of overweight and obesity in the next generation, updated prevalence data for children suggests that severe obesity is on the rise [6]. There is a plethora of interventions to prevent overweight and obesity in both children [7] and adults [8], and an equally impressive number of interventions for treatment [9,10]. Yet, individual struggles to achieve a health weight over a sustained period of time. For example, a review of weight management interventions found a weight loss over two years of 1.54 kg [11], which is far from the 5% weight loss recommended to produce health benefits [12]. These challenges have led to the realization that a simple solution would not suffice [13]: the health system needs to cope with the *complexity* of obesity [14–16].

The notion of complexity covers multiple characteristics, such as the vast individual differences (or *heterogeneity*) between weight-related factors [17,18], or the nonlinear ways in which factors interact to form a system. The obesity system has been the subject of numerous studies [19–22]. This system involves factors from a broad array of sectors (e.g., built environment, eating disorders, weight stigma [23,24]), with interactions within as well as across sectors. Accurately modeling this system facilitates the development of integrated policies building on cross-sectoral efforts [25,26]. If policies are developed separately along traditional themes (e.g., public planning works on the environment, doctors work on diseases and physiology, mental health experts work on psychology), then we have a heavily fragmented approach to obesity (Fig. 1a). Efforts such as the Foresight Obesity Map [20,27], or the Public Health Services Authority's series of maps [24,28,29] thus support the development of synergistic policies working on integrated thematic clusters (Fig. 1b).

Given the importance of developing accurate models of the obesity system, the modeling process often seeks to be comprehensive by including experts and community members [19,24,30–34]. While many qualitative modeling processes can produce models in the form of maps [35] (e.g., cognitive/concept mapping, causal loop diagrams), they are generally conducted with a facilitator. Some of the limitations (e.g., costs, trained facilitator) may be addressed through emerging technologies [36]. However, one limitation remains: participants may not openly express their beliefs (e.g., weight discrimination) when perceiving that they may not be well received by a facilitator or the research team. In contrast, the naturally occurring exchange of perspectives in social media provides an unobtrusive approach to collecting beliefs on causes and consequences of obesity. Mining social media may thus provide the views of community members [37–40].

While obtaining a model via social media can inform policymakers about popular support for possible policies [41], the model may stand in stark contrast with an expert-based model [34]. Identifying and reconciling these differences is an important step to integrate social computing (and specifically social web mining) with policy making. In this paper, we contrast how mining social media instead of expert reports affects the validation of a large conceptual model of obesity. This overarching goal is achieved through three consecutive steps. First, we assemble a social media dataset (consisting of several million tweets) and several expert reports (totaling hundred of pages). Second, we employ an innovative

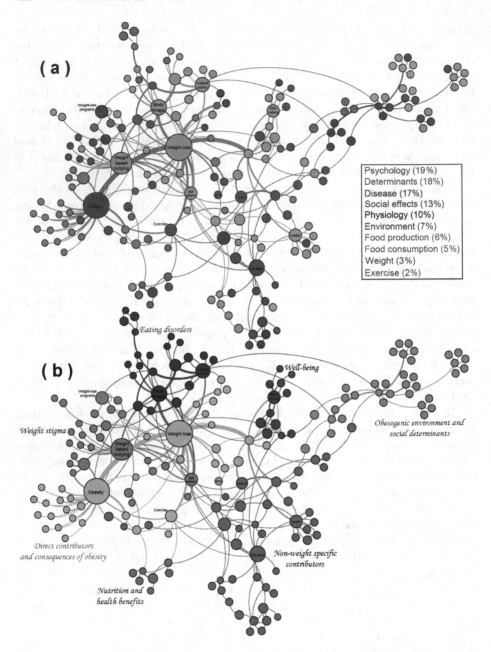

Fig. 1. The Public Health Services Authority's series of maps [24, 28, 29] suggests that typical categories lead to fragmented approaches (a) whereas themes specific to overweight and obesity can support more integrated options (b). These maps are *conceptual maps* as they articulate how concepts (labeled circles) are related (curves).

multi-step process to examine a conceptual model using both the social media dataset and the expert reports. Finally, we contrast the structure of these models using network methods.

The remainder of this paper is organized as follows. In Sect. 2, we provide background information on the application of social web mining to health, and on the use of conceptual models in obesity research. In Sect. 3, we briefly explain our approach to validate a conceptual model from text. In Sect. 4, we perform this inference on both expert reports and tweets, and we examine how the conceptual models differ. Finally, these differences are discussed and contextualized in Sect. 5.

2 Background

2.1 Social Web Mining for Health

The social media of interest in this paper is Twitter, in which users post and interact through short messages known as 'tweets'. Twitter has been used for many studies on obesity and weight-related behaviors. For instance, Harris and colleagues collected 1,110 tweets and read them to understand how childhood obesity was discussed [42], while Lydecker *et al.* read 529 tweets to identify the main themes related to fatness [43]. Similarly, So and colleagues analyzed the common features of 120 tweets that were most frequently shared (i.e., retweets) to understand what information individuals preferred to relay when it came to obesity [37]. Reading the tweets to identify themes (i.e., content analysis) is a typical task to understand the arguments that a specific population uses on a subject of interest. Broader examples in health include the content analysis of 700 tweets [44] and 625 tweets [45] to examine the type of claims that health professionals make online, or an examination of 8,934 tweets documenting cyber-incivility among nurses and nursing students [46]. While such content analyses make a valuable contribution to the body of knowledge on arguments in public health[1], they do not employ computational methods to automate (parts of) the analysis and thus scale it to a larger dataset. Automation can be as simple as counting how many times keywords of interest appear across tweets. Turner-McGrievy and Beets used Hashtagify.me to automatically count keywords in tens of thousands of tweets on weight loss, health, diet, and fitness. By dividing the analysis across time periods, they were able to examine if there are times of the year when individuals would be likely to consider weight loss, thus contributing to the timing of interventions [48]. Similarly, Sui *et al.* used the intensity of topics on Twitter as part of an effort to identify the public interest in intensive obesity treatment [49]. Such studies illustrate the important shift from having

---

[1] While our focus is on analyzing the *text* provided by tweets, studies on Twitter that are primarily human- rather than computer-based are not exclusively content analyses. In the study of May and colleagues, the researchers created twitter accounts for fictional obese and non-obese characters. They evaluated whether the weight status mediated how other users would interact with them [47].

humans read and code all tweets to relying on a machine to handle most of a (much larger) dataset. The latter is the focus of data mining applied to the 'social web' (i.e. social web mining) which includes social networking sites such as Twitter but also encompasses blogs and micro-blogging. As Twitter has been the social platform of interest for many studies, the term of 'Twitter mining' has also emerged to refer specifically to the application of social web mining to Twitter [50].

Social web mining started to garner attention in the late 2000's to early 2010's. The application of social web mining to health was discussed in 2010 by Boulos *et al.* [51] and in 2011 by Paul and Dredze [52], showing how a broad range of public health applications could benefit from mining Twitter. Studies have been able to mine a staggering volume of data, going well over what a team of humans could handle. For example, Eichstaedt *et al.* mapped 148 million tweets to counties in an effort to relate language patterns to county-level heart disease mortality [53]. At an even larger scale, Ediger and colleagues used a Cray computer to approximate centrality within two hours on a dataset of interactions between Twitter users comprising 1.47 billion edges [54]. While these cases are noteworthy by their volume of data, studies employing social web mining for obesity research typically involve millions of tweets[2]. Using 2.2 million tweets, Chou and colleagues found that tweets (as well as Facebook posts) often stigmatized individuals living with overweight and obesity [38]. In two studies on obesity and weight-related factors, Karami analyzed 6 million [39] and 4.5 million tweets [40]. In a study of health-related statistics, Culotta mined 4.3 million tweets and found that the data was correlated with obesity [56]. Given that obesity is driven by many factors (e.g., eating behaviors, physical activity behaviors), there is also a wealth of large-scale studies on such factors, such as the work of Abbar *et al.* on 503 million tweets regarding food [57]. Finally, the value proposition of several new platforms is not the analysis of one particular dataset, but rather the ongoing ability to monitor diet or physical activity. This is particularly the case for the Lexicocalorimeter, which measures calories in each US state via Twitter [58], and to a lesser extent for the National Neighborhood Dataset of Zhang *et al.* which tracks diet and physical activity through Twitter [59].

Several commentaries [60] and reviews [61–63] have explored whether this abundance of studies has contributed to public health. Findings depend on what specific aspect of health is concerned. Social media has yet to impact practices in public health surveillance [62], but a review centered on chronic disease found a benefit on clinical outcomes in almost half of the studies [61], and a review specific to obesity highlighted a modest impact on weight [63].

---

[2] There are several exceptions of studies employing smaller dataset. However, their objectives may not be to identify themes (which necessitates a large volume of tweets), thus they can accomplish their goals with a smaller dataset. A case in point is the work of Tiggemann and colleagues, who used 3,289 tweets to examine interactions between Twitter communities that promoted either a 'thin ideal' or health and fitness [55].

2.2   Conceptual Models in Obesity Research

Although our work will involve the identification of themes, we have a very different endeavor from studies reviewed in the previous section, which focused on identifying themes and their variations across time, places, or communities of users. Our objective is to contrast *conceptual models* that have been automatically extracted from tweets and expert reports. As evoked in the introduction, models of complex systems such as obesity support several important policy-making and analytical tasks. In this section, we briefly review the features that models often seek to capture when it comes to complex health systems, and how models are used in obesity research specifically. Penn detailed key characteristics of complex health systems that justify the development of models (emphases added):

> "Many problems that society wishes to address in population health are clearly problems of *managing complex adaptive systems.* They involve making interventions in systems with *multiple interacting causal connections*, which *span domains* from physiological to economic. Additionally, of course, the individuals whose health we ultimately wish to improve adapt and *change their behavior* in response to medical or policy interventions." [64]

Several of these points were echoed by Silverman in justifying the use of systems-based simulation for population health research [65]. Modeling changes in the heterogeneous health behaviors of individuals often uses the simulation technique of Agent-Based Modeling, and has been done in obesity research on multiple occasions [66–70]. Such models can be very detailed and use widely different architectures to capture the cognitive processes of the agents. Validating them using text is thus an arduous task. Modeling interacting causes across domains has been achieved in obesity research through a variety of techniques. System Dynamics (SD) allows to represent nonlinear interactions between weigh-related factors over different time scales and at different strengths [71, 72]. However, much like agent-based modeling, the great level of details supported by SD makes it difficult to derive or validate such models from text. Fuzzy Cognitive Maps (FCM) are a simpler alternative that eliminates the notion of time to focus on the different strengths of causal relations [34, 73–75]. Such models can be compared [34], but validating them from text still requires a trained analyst [76]. An even greater simplification is to use conceptual rather than simulation models. Conceptual models cannot run scenarios or what-if questions, and cannot 'generate' numbers. Instead, their focus is to capture relevant factors and whether they are connected [77]. Conceptual models can be compared [78] and validated using text as shown in our previous work [77].

There are several types of conceptual models [35]. We recently detailed the differences between causal maps, mind maps, and concept maps [36]. In short, this paper focuses on concept maps (Fig. 1), which are undirected networks representing concepts as nodes and relationships as edges. Similarly to the other forms of conceptual models aforementioned, a concept map supports policy-oriented

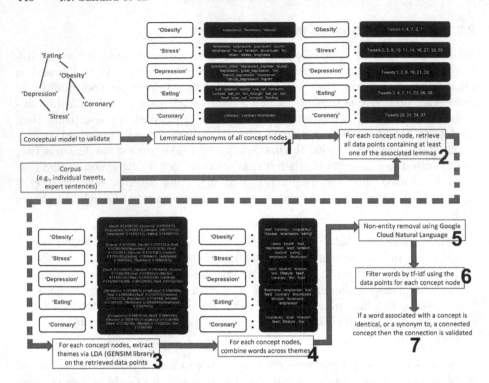

Fig. 2. Our process in seven steps to validate a conceptual model using textual data. *The high-definition figure can be zoomed in for details.*

tasks such as identifying clusters [27] (e.g., to coordinate actors across domains on one problem such as food) or finding feedback loops [24,28,29] (e.g., to use as leverage points in an intervention).

3   Validating a Conceptual Model from Text

The process starts with a conceptual model that we seek to validate, and the text corpus is used to validate. Intuitively, our process uses the concepts' names to find relevant parts of the corpus and find which concepts tend to co-occur. Technical aspects include handling variations in language (as we cannot rigidly assume that a concept's name will appear as such), identifying themes, and mapping themes from the corpus back to concepts in the conceptual model. Our process uses seven steps, illustrated on a theoretical example in Fig. 2. The first two steps are performed for each concept node:

(1.a) We replace all concepts' names and words from the corpus with their base form (i.e., lemma). This is accomplished through *lemmatization*, which uses a morphological analysis to remove inflectional endings. This step ensures that minor variations of a term are all mapped to the same one (e.g., 'flooding' and 'floods' are all mapped to 'flood').

(1.b) Each lemmatized concept names is expanded with derivationally related forms. For instance, instead of only searching for 'flood' in the corpus, we will also accept words such as 'deluge'.

(2) For each concept (i.e., the expanded lemma), we retrieve all parts of the corpus that contain it. For instance, the concept 'flooding' will lead to retrieving all tweets include the lemmas 'flood' or 'deluge'.

Upon completion of step 2, we have related a portion of the corpus to each concept node. We then find the themes in each portion of the corpus using three parameters:

(3) We apply the Latent Dirichlet Accuracy (LDA) model to find prevalent themes. The two parameters for this step are the number of themes and number of words per theme.

(4) We gather words across themes into a single set of words. This set is cleaned by removing words that are already present in the set of derivationally related form of the node. In other words, we only look for concepts that the node could be *associated* with but not *equivalent* to.

(5) Since concepts' names are entities, a concept can only be associated with an entity. Consequently, we remove all non-entities from the words.

(6) At this step, we have a set of entities that a concept node could be associated with. However, some of the entities may be noise rather than meaningful associations. We thus sort the entities by tf-idf (term-frequency inverse-document-frequency) computed over the set of tweets in which each word appears. We use a threshold parameter to identify which entities have a sufficient tf-idf to be selected.

Upon completion of step 2, we found entities that a concept node could be associated with. The final step goes back to the conceptual model to see if the association exists:

(7) For each node, we compare its associated entities with its connected nodes and derivationally related forms. If there is a match, then the text corpus has confirmed an association between the two concepts. If no match is found, the association is not confirmed. Note that associated entities that do not match any connected nodes suggest additional connections, which is a different from validation as we seek to confirm existing connections.

This process is also depicted in Fig. 3, listing the libraries that can be used for each step. The specific versions of the libraries used in our experiments are included in Sect. 4.

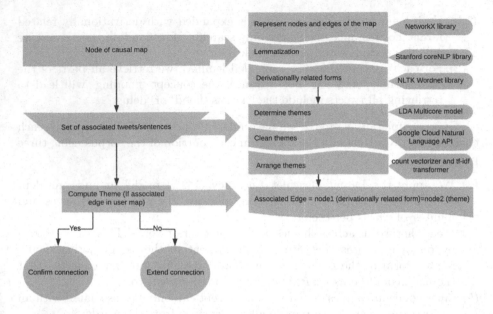

Fig. 3. Alternative view of our process, including libraries and APIs.

4   Comparing Conceptual Models from Twitter and Expert Reports

4.1   Datasets and Pre-processing

The conceptual model that we seek to validate was developed with the Provincial Health Services Authority (PHSA) of British Columbia to explore the interrelationships involved in obesity and well-being. The model was presented in 2015 at the Canadian Obesity Summit [24] and tested with policy makers in 2016 [29]. The model is now part of the `ActionableSystems` tool [28] can be downloaded at https://osf.io/7ztwu/ within 'Sample maps' (file *Drasic et al (edges).csv*). The model consists of 98 nodes and 177 edges. From here on, we will refer to it as 'the PHSA map'.

To validate the PHSA map, we used two datasets. Our first dataset ('the twitter dataset') consists of 6,633,625 tweets in the English language on obesity collected from Oct. 2, 2018 to Oct. 4, 2018. The number of tweets was chosen to be in line with comparable studies at the interface of natural language processing and obesity research [38–40]. The keywords to collect the tweets included each of the 98 concept names in the PHSA map as well as their synonyms automatically retrieved through WordNet. For instance, we used not only 'obesity' but also words such as 'fatness', 'corpulent', 'embonpoint' and 'fleshiness'. Similarly, physical activity was expanded to include many forms such as calisthenics, isometrics, jogging, jump rope, and so on. The rationale is that the map contains abstract concepts, but individuals may speak of specific instances or use a variety of words to describe the same abstraction. After collecting a large number of tweets, natural language applications require extensive pre-processing. The impact of each options (and their interactions) on results obtained from Twitter has been extensively described when performing sentiment analysis [79–81] and in more generic tasks such as classification [82]. Some of these options are summarized in Fig. 4 and include the removal of parts deemed unnecessary for analysis (e.g., hashtags, URLs, numbers, non English words) or the mapping of data into forms that can be more conveniently processed (e.g., expanding acronyms and abbreviations, replacing emojis, spell checking). The pre-processing options used for our dataset are depicted in Fig. 5. These options are chosen specifically for our research question: for instance, we remove stop words because they cannot be meaningful concept names in a model, but other analyses (e.g., attributing tweets to specific writers) may have kept such words. The order of the steps also matters: for instance, we cannot perform part-of-speech tagging and lemmatization (step 5) before ensuring that all the words have been corrected (step 3). After pre-processing, our dataset included 1,791,333 tweets.

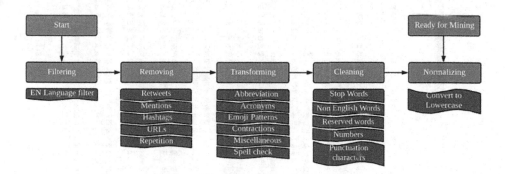

Fig. 4. Typical pre-processing techniques applied to tweets.

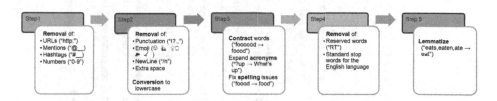

Fig. 5. Pre-processing techniques applied to our tweeter dataset in a specific order. We used a Spell Checker library in step 3, the Natural Language Toolkit (NLTK) for steps 1–4, and the Stanford coreNLP library for step 5.

The second dataset is formed of three reports on obesity: the 2010 report from the white house task force on childhood obesity [83], the 2013 report to the Provincial Health Services Authority [84] and its 2015 update (whose findings

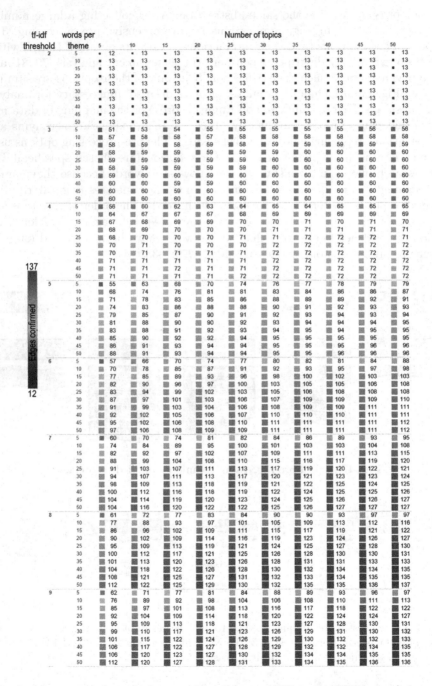

Fig. 6. Average number of edges confirmed (out of 177 in the PHSA map) for each combination of parameter values over ten experiments.

are published in [24]). We combined the three reports with the PyPDF2 library, leading to 310 pages, and we kept 247 pages after removing those that were either blank or only contained images. Pages were then transformed into raw text using the pdftotext library and divded into 4,302 sentences using the full point ('.'). Pre-processing was finally applied, using the same script as for tweets while noting that several options such as removing emojis would not be triggered. The resulting dataset had 3447 sentences.

4.2 Validating the Model for Each Dataset

The methods introduced in Sect. 3 are implemented in Python, relying on libraries as listed in Table 1. While our implementation was able to cope with millions of tweets, we note that a larger volume of data may also require a distributed database architecture and an efficient search engine such as Elastic-search [85].

Table 1. Libraries used in each step (Sect. 3) of our experiments.

Step	Library	Used for
	NetworkX	Conceptual model (accessing node labels and edges)
1a	Stanford coreNLP	Lemmatization
1b	WordNet	Derivationally related forms
3	[86]	Parallel, multi-core Latent Dirichlet Allocation (LDA) model for big data
5	Google Cloud Natural language API	Entity identification
6	scikit-learn (CountVectorizer, TfidfTransformer)	Sorting words by tf-idf

Our approach has three parameters: number of themes, number of words per theme, and tf-idf threshold to eliminate noise. Hyperparameter optimization was thus necessary to use each dataset most efficiently, and fairly compare their potential in validating a model. To optimize performances with expert reports, we performed a grid search by varying the number of topics and words per topic from 5 to 50 in increments of 5, and we varied the tf-idf from 2 to 9 by increments of 1. This resulted in 800 combinations of parameter values. As there is randomness in the LDA model, we performed ten experiments per combination of parameter values, leading to a total of 8,000 experiments. At most, our process validated an average of 136.5 edges (77.11% of the map) using 50 topics, 50 words per topic, and a td-idf threshold of 8 (Fig. 6).

A grid search was also performed on the Twitter dataset. However, our current implementation takes approximately five days to compute the results for one combination of parameter values (single experiment), using a server-grade workstation (Dual Xeon Gold 6140). Given this limitation, we used single experiments and a coarser grid. At most, our process validated 101 edges (57.06%) using 50 topics, 50 words per topic, and a tf-idf threshold of 9.

5   Discussion

A focus group with a few participants may only discuss some of the interrelationships at work in overweight and obesity, and may avoid sharing opinions that are potentially disapproved by others. In contrast, social media such as Twitter provide access to a massive number of participants who can use conditions of anonymity to share opinions more freely. Social web mining applied to Twiter thus comes with the potential to explore many interrelationships in an unobtrusive fashion. In particular, crowdsourcing over Twitter holds the promise of easily building large conceptual models, under the assumption that at least some groups of users will touch on each part of the model. Our study questions this potential and promises by analyzing whether millions of tweets are more useful to develop a conceptual model of obesity than a handful of reports.

Although conceptual models can be automatically compared [78], developing a model from each dataset (tweets vs. reports) and comparing them would not be able to tell us which one is 'better'. Our study question thus requires a referential. We use a previously developed conceptual model of obesity and well-being to serve as referential, and we establish how much of this model would have been obtained if we used either tweets or reports. In other words, we measured the percentage of the model's structure that is confirmed with each dataset.

While both datasets were able to cover over half of the model, we note that it only took three expert reports compared to using millions of tweets. In addition, despite the abundance of tweets, the three expert reports touched on more relationships. Within our application context, these results suggest that an exclusive reliance on social media may result in oversimplifying a complex system, thus limiting the potential to automatically develop models using such a source. We note that a comprehensive analysis across subjects and using a variety of maps would be needed to assess whether our results produced on one model (the Provincial Health Services Authority map) and one application subject (obesity) can be generalized to other models and subjects.

There are several limitations to this study, which we intend to address in our future research. First, one of the premises of big data research is that a large volume may compensate for many imperfections in the individual data points. Although we used a similar number of tweets to other studies at the interface of natural language processing and obesity research [38–40], it is possible that some of the interrelationships of the model we seek to validate are rare and thus only detectable in even larger datasets. Repeating this study with significantly larger datasets could elucidate this question. However, we then run into the second issue: our process to validate a causal map against textual data is very computational intensive. The search space to optimize the result is defined by three parameters which involve randomness, thus requiring several experiments for each combination of parameter values. On a server-grade workstation, a single combination with a CPU-based implementation requires in the order of days. Optimizing results and using larger datasets will thus require implementations that scale, with a particularly promising option consisting of a GPU-based implementation. Alternatively, we may reduce the search space if we can better characterize the impact that parameters generally have on the results and then devise more computational efficient processes. For instance, the tf-idf threshold plays an essential role in driving performances (Fig. 6) but may be replaced by additional pre-processing steps preventing the inclusion of noise, such as classifiers removing unwanted documents [87].

6 Conclusion

Both social media data and expert reports may be used to take into account popular perspectives and expert opinions when creating large conceptual models. In the case of obesity, we found that three expert reports discussed 77% of all possibilities while millions of tweets on obesity and its cognates covered fewer interrelationships. Creating models using social media only may thus result in an oversimplification of complex problems.

Acknowledgments. The authors are indebted to Mitacs Canada for providing the financial support which allowed MS to perform this research at Furman University, while mentored by PJG (local advisor) and VKM (home advisor). Publication costs are supported by an NSERC Discovery Grant for VKM. We thank Chetan Harichandra Mendhe for gathering the tweets under supervision of VKM.

Contributions. MS wrote the scripts to generate the results and analyzed them. PJG wrote the manuscript and designed the methods. MS was advised by PJG and VKM, who jointly initiated the study. All authors read and approved of this manuscript.

References

1. Centers for Disease Control and Prevention (CDC): Selected health conditions and risk factors, by age: United states, selected years 1988–1994 through 2015–2016
2. Peralta, M., et al.: Prevalence and trends of overweight and obesity in older adults from 10 European Countries from 2005 to 2013. Scand. J. Public Health **46**, 522–529 (2018). https://doi.org/10.1177/1403494818764810
3. Lubbe, J.: Obesity and metabolic surgery in South Africa. S. Afr. Gastroenterology Rev. **16**(1), 23–28 (2018)
4. Wang, Y., Wang, L., Qu, W.: New national data show alarming increase in obesity and noncommunicable chronic diseases in China. Eur. J. Clin. Nutr. **71**(1), 149 (2017)
5. Ng, M., et al.: Global, regional, and national prevalence of overweight and obesity in children and adults during 1980–2013: a systematic analysis for the global burden of disease study 2013. Lancet **384**(9945), 766–781 (2014)

6. Skinner, A.C., Perrin, E.M., Skelton, J.A.: Prevalence of obesity and severe obesity in US children, 1999-2014. Obesity **24**(5), 1116–1123 (2016)
7. Bleich, S.N., et al.: Interventions to prevent global childhood overweight and obesity: a systematic review. Lancet Diabetes Endocrinol. **6**(4), 332–346 (2018)
8. Hutchesson, M., et al.: eH ealth interventions for the prevention and treatment of overweight and obesity in adults: a systematic review with meta-analysis. Obes. Rev. **16**(5), 376–392 (2015)
9. Rajjo, T., et al.: Treatment of pediatric obesity: an umbrella systematic review. J. Clin. Endocrinol. Metab. **102**(3), 763–775 (2017)
10. Teixeira, P.J., et al.: Successful behavior change in obesity interventions in adults: a systematic review of self-regulation mediators. BMC Med. **13**(1), 84 (2015)
11. National Institute for Health and Care Excellence: Managing overweight and obesity in adults-lifestyle weight management services. NICE Public Health Guideline, **53** (2014)
12. Blackburn, G.: Effect of degree of weight loss on health benefits. Obes. Res. **3**(S2), 211s–216s (1995)
13. Fink, D.S., Keyes, K.M.: Wrong answers: when simple interpretations create complex problems. In: Systems Science and Population Health, pp. 25–36 (2017)
14. Frood, S., et al.: Obesity, complexity, and the role of the health system. Curr. Obes. Rep. **2**(4), 320–326 (2013)
15. Finegood, D.T.: The complex systems science of obesity. In: The Oxford Handbook of the Social Science of Obesity (2011)
16. Rutter, H., et al.: The need for a complex systems model of evidence for public health. Lancet **390**(10112), 2602–2604 (2017)
17. Giabbanelli, P.J.: Analyzing the complexity of behavioural factors influencing weight in adults. In: Giabbanelli, P.J., Mago, V.K., Papageorgiou, E.I. (eds.) Advanced Data Analytics in Health. SIST, vol. 93, pp. 163–181. Springer, Cham (2018). https://doi.org/10.1007/978-3-319-77911-9_10
18. Deck, P., Giabbanelli, P., Finegood, D.T.: Exploring the heterogeneity of factors associated with weight management in young adults. Can. J. Diabetes **37**, S269–S270 (2013)
19. Giabbanelli, P.J., Torsney-Weir, T., Mago, V.K.: A fuzzy cognitive map of the psychosocial determinants of obesity. Appl. Soft Comput. **12**(12), 3711–3724 (2012)
20. Jebb, S., Kopelman, P., Butland, B.: Executive summary: foresight 'tackling obesities: future choices' project. Obes. Rev. **8**, vi–ix (2007)
21. Xue, H., et al.: Applications of systems modelling in obesity research. Obes. Rev. **19**(9), 1293–1308 (2018)
22. Frerichs, L., et al.: Mind maps and network analysis to evaluate conceptualization of complex issues: a case example evaluating systems science workshops for childhood obesity prevention. Eval. Program Plan. **68**, 135–147 (2018)
23. Johnston, L.M., Matteson, C.L., Finegood, D.T.: Systems science and obesity policy: a novel framework for analyzing and rethinking population-level planning. Am. J. Public Health **104**(7), 1270–1278 (2014)
24. Drasic, L., Giabbanelli, P.J.: Exploring the interactions between physical well-being, and obesity. Can. J. Diabetes **39**, S12–S13 (2015)
25. Dubé, L., Du, P., McRae, C., Sharma, N., Jayaraman, S., Nie, J.-Y.: Convergent innovation in food through big data and artificial intelligence for societal-scale inclusive growth. Technol. Innov. Manag. Rev. **8**, 49–65 (2018)
26. Jha, S.K., Gold, R., Dube, L.: Convergent innovation platform to address complex social problems: a tiered governance model. In: Academy of Management Proceedings, Volume 2016, Academy of Management Briarcliff Manor, NY 10510 (2016)

27. Finegood, D.T., Merth, T.D., Rutter, H.: Implications of the foresight obesity system map for solutions to childhood obesity. Obesity **18**(S1), S13–S16 (2010)
28. Giabbanelli, P.J., Baniukiewicz, M.: Navigating complex systems for policymaking using simple software tools. In: Giabbanelli, P.J., Mago, V.K., Papageorgiou, E.I. (eds.) Advanced Data Analytics in Health. SIST, vol. 93, pp. 21–40. Springer, Cham (2018). https://doi.org/10.1007/978-3-319-77911-9_2
29. Giabbanelli, P., et al.: developing technology to support policymakers in taking a systems science approach to obesity and well-being. Obes. Rev. **17**, 194–195 (2016)
30. Owen, B., et al.: Understanding a successful obesity prevention initiative in children under 5 from a systems perspective. PloS one **13**(3), e0195141 (2018)
31. McGlashan, J., et al.: Quantifying a systems map: network analysis of a childhood obesity causal loop diagram. PloS one **11**(10), e0165459 (2016)
32. McGlashan, J., et al.: Comparing complex perspectives on obesity drivers: action-driven communities and evidence-oriented experts. Obes. Sci. Pract. **4**, 575–581 (2018)
33. Allender, S., et al.: A community based systems diagram of obesity causes. PLoS One **10**(7), e0129683 (2015)
34. Giles, B.G., et al.: Integrating conventional science and aboriginal perspectives on diabetes using fuzzy cognitive maps. Soc. Sci. Med. **64**(3), 562–576 (2007)
35. Voinov, A., et al.: Tools and methods in participatory modeling: selecting the right tool for the job. Environ. Model. Softw. **109**, 232–255 (2018)
36. Reddy, T., Giabbanelli, P.J., Mago, V.K.: The artificial facilitator: guiding participants in developing causal maps using voice-activated technologies. In: International Conference on Augmented Cognition (2019)
37. So, J., et al.: What do people like to "share" about obesity? A content analysis of frequent retweets about obesity on twitter. Health Commun. **31**(2), 193–206 (2016)
38. Chou, W.Y.S., Prestin, A., Kunath, S.: Obesity in social media: a mixed methods analysis. Transl. Behav. Med. **4**(3), 314–323 (2014)
39. Shaw Jr., G., Karami, A.: Computational content analysis of negative tweets for obesity, diet, diabetes, and exercise. Proc. Assoc. Inf. Sci. Technol. **54**(1), 357–365 (2017)
40. Karami, A., et al.: Characterizing diabetes, diet, exercise, and obesity comments on twitter. Int. J. Inf. Manag. **38**(1), 1–6 (2018)
41. Giabbanelli, P.J., Adams, J., Pillutla, V.S.: Feasibility and framing of interventions based on public support: leveraging text analytics for policymakers. In: Meiselwitz, G. (ed.) SCSM 2016. LNCS, vol. 9742, pp. 188–200. Springer, Cham (2016). https://doi.org/10.1007/978-3-319-39910-2_18
42. Harris, J.K., et al.: Communication about childhood obesity on twitter. Am. J. Public Health **104**(7), e62–e69 (2014)
43. Lydecker, J.A., et al.: Does this tweet make me look fat? A content analysis of weight stigma on twitter. Eat. Weight. Disord.-Stud. Anorex. Bulim. Obes. **21**(2), 229–235 (2016)
44. Lee, J.L., et al.: What are health-related users tweeting? A qualitative content analysis of health-related users and their messages on twitter. J. Med. Internet Res. **16**(10), e237 (2014)
45. Alnemer, K.A., et al.: Are health-related tweets evidence based? Review and analysis of health-related tweets on twitter. J. Med. Internet Res. **17**(10), e246 (2015)
46. De Gagne, J.C., et al.: Uncovering cyberincivility among nurses and nursing students on twitter: a data mining study. Int. J. Nurs. Stud. **89**, 24–31 (2019)

47. May, C.N., et al.: Weight loss support seeking on twitter: the impact of weight on follow back rates and interactions. Transl. Behav. Med. **7**(1), 84–91 (2016)
48. Turner-McGrievy, G.M., Beets, M.W.: Tweet for health: using an online social network to examine temporal trends in weight loss-related posts. Transl. Behav. Med. **5**(2), 160–166 (2015)
49. Sui, Z., et al.: Recent trends in intensive treatments of obesity: is academic research matching public interest? Surg. Obes. Relat. Dis. (2019). https://www.sciencedirect.com/science/article/pii/S1550728918311948
50. O'Leary, D.E.: Twitter mining for discovery, prediction and causality: applications and methodologies. Intell. Syst. Account. Financ. Manag. **22**(3), 227–247 (2015)
51. Boulos, M.N.K., et al.: Social web mining and exploitation for serious applications: technosocial predictive analytics and related technologies for public health, environmental and national security surveillance. Comput. Methods Programs Biomed. **100**(1), 16–23 (2010)
52. Paul, M.J., Dredze, M.: You are what you tweet: analyzing twitter for public health. Icwsm **20**, 265–272 (2011)
53. Eichstaedt, J.C., et al.: Psychological language on twitter predicts county-level heart disease mortality. Psychol. Sci. **26**(2), 159–169 (2015)
54. Ediger, D., et al.: Massive social network analysis: mining twitter for social good. In: 2010 39th International Conference on Parallel Processing, pp. 583–593. IEEE (2010)
55. Tiggemann, M., et al.: Tweeting weight loss: a comparison of# thinspiration and# fitspiration communities on twitter. Body Image **25**, 133–138 (2018)
56. Culotta, A.: Estimating county health statistics with twitter. In: Proceedings of the SIGCHI Conference on Human Factors in Computing Systems, pp. 1335–1344. ACM (2014)
57. Abbar, S., Mejova, Y., Weber, I.: You tweet what you eat: studying food consumption through twitter. In: Proceedings of the 33rd Annual ACM Conference on Human Factors in Computing Systems, pp. 3197–3206. ACM (2015)
58. Alajajian, S.E., et al.: The lexicocalorimeter: gauging public health through caloric input and output on social media. PloS One **12**(2), e0168893 (2017)
59. Nguyen, Q.C., et al.: Building a national neighborhood dataset from geotagged twitter datafor indicators of happiness, diet, and physical activity. JMIR Public Health Surveill. **2**(2), e158 (2016)
60. Eke, P.I.: Using social media for research and public health surveillance. J. Dent. Res. **90**(9), 1045 (2011)
61. Patel, R., et al.: Social media use in chronic disease: a systematic review and novel taxonomy. Am. J. Med. **128**(12), 1335–1350 (2015)
62. Charles-Smith, L.E., et al.: Using social media for actionable disease surveillance and outbreak management: a systematic literature review. PloS One **10**(10), e0139701 (2015)
63. Waring, M.E., et al.: Social media and obesity in adults: a review of recent research and future directions. Curr. Diabetes Rep. **18**(6), 34 (2018)
64. Penn, A.: Moving from overwhelming to actionable complexity in population health policy: Can alife help? (2018)
65. Silverman, E.: Bringing alife and complex systems science to population health research. Artif. Life **24**(3), 220–223 (2018)
66. Giabbanelli, P.J., Crutzen, R.: Using agent-based models to develop public policy about food behaviours: future directions and recommendations. Comput. Math. Methods Med. (2017). https://www.hindawi.com/journals/cmmm/2017/5742629/abs/

67. Giabbanelli, P., Crutzen, R.: An agent-based social network model of binge drinking among Dutch adults. J. Artif. Soc. Soc. Simul. **16**(2), 10 (2013)
68. Khademi, A., Zhang, D., Giabbanelli, P.J., Timmons, S., Luo, C., Shi, L.: An agent-based model of healthy eating with applications to hypertension. In: Giabbanelli, P.J., Mago, V.K., Papageorgiou, E.I. (eds.) Advanced Data Analytics in Health. SIST, vol. 93, pp. 43–58. Springer, Cham (2018). https://doi.org/10.1007/978-3-319-77911-9_3
69. Zhang, D., et al.: Impact of different policies on unhealthy dietary behaviors in an urban adult population: an agent-based simulation model. Am. J. Public Health **104**(7), 1217–1222 (2014)
70. Giabbanelli, P.J., et al.: Modeling the influence of social networks and environment on energy balance and obesity. J. Comput. Sci. **3**(1–2), 17–27 (2012)
71. Verigin, T., Giabbanelli, P.J., Davidsen, P.I.: Supporting a systems approach to healthy weight interventions in British Columbia by modeling weight and well-being. In: Proceedings of the 49th Annual Simulation Symposium, Society for Computer Simulation International, p. 9 (2016)
72. Fallah-Fini, S., et al.: Modeling us adult obesity trends: a system dynamics model for estimating energy imbalance gap. Am. J. Public Health **104**(7), 1230–1239 (2014)
73. Mago, V.K., et al.: Fuzzy cognitive maps and cellular automata: an evolutionary approach for social systems modelling. Appl. Soft Comput. **12**(12), 3771–3784 (2012)
74. Giabbanelli, P.J., Jackson, P.J., Finegood, D.T.: Modelling the joint effect of social determinants and peers on obesity among Canadian adults. In: Dabbaghian, V., Mago, V. (eds.) Theories and simulations of complex social systems. ISRL, vol. 52, pp. 145–160. Springer, Heidelberg (2014). https://doi.org/10.1007/978-3-642-39149-1_10
75. Giabbanelli, P.J., Crutzen, R.: Creating groups with similar expected behavioural response in randomized controlled trials: a fuzzy cognitive map approach. BMC Med. Res. Methodol. **14**(1), 130 (2014)
76. Pillutla, V.S., Giabbanelli, P.J.: Iterative generation of insight from text collections through mutually reinforcing visualizations and fuzzy cognitive maps. Appl. Soft Comput. **76**, 459–472 (2019)
77. Giabbanelli, P.J., Jackson, P.J.: Using visual analytics to support the integration of expert knowledge in the design of medical models and simulations. Procedia Comput. Sci. **51**, 755–764 (2015)
78. Giabbanelli, P.J., Tawfik, A.A., Gupta, V.K.: Learning analytics to support teachers' assessment of problem solving: a novel application for machine learning and graph algorithms. In: Ifenthaler, D., Mah, D.-K., Yau, J.Y.-K. (eds.) Utilizing Learning Analytics to Support Study Success, pp. 175–199. Springer, Cham (2019). https://doi.org/10.1007/978-3-319-64792-0_11
79. Jianqiang, Z., Xiaolin, G.: Comparison research on text pre-processing methods on twitter sentiment analysis. IEEE Access **5**, 2870–2879 (2017)
80. Singh, T., Kumari, M.: Role of text pre-processing in twitter sentiment analysis. Procedia Comput. Sci. **89**, 549–554 (2016)
81. Symeonidis, S., Effrosynidis, D., Arampatzis, A.: A comparative evaluation of pre-processing techniques and their interactions for twitter sentiment analysis. Expert. Syst. Appl. **110**, 298–310 (2018)

82. Keerthi Kumar, H.M., Harish, B.S.: Classification of short text using various pre-processing techniques: an empirical evaluation. In: Sa, P.K., Bakshi, S., Hatzilygeroudis, I.K., Sahoo, M.N. (eds.) Recent Findings in Intelligent Computing Techniques. AISC, vol. 709, pp. 19–30. Springer, Singapore (2018). https://doi.org/10.1007/978-981-10-8633-5_3

83. Barnes, M.: Solving the problem of childhood obesity within a generation. White House Task Force on Childhood Obesity Report to the President, Washington, DC (2010)

84. Daghofer, D.: From weight to well-being: time for shift in paradigms. Technical report, a discussion paper on the inter-relationships among obesity, overweight ... (2013)

85. Shah, N., Willick, D., Mago, V.: A framework for social media data analytics using Elasticsearch and Kibana. Wirel. Netw., 1–9 (2009)

86. Rehurek, R., Sojka, P.: Software framework for topic modelling with large corpora. In: In Proceedings of the LREC 2010 Workshop on New Challenges for NLP Frameworks. Citeseer (2010)

87. Robinson, K., Mago, V.: Birds of prey: identifying lexical irregularities in spam on twitter. Wirel. Netw. 1–8 (2018). https://doi.org/10.1007/s11276-018-01900-9

Beware of the Fakes – Overview of Fake Detection Methods for Online Product Reviews

Simon André Scherr[(⊠)], Svenja Polst, and Frank Elberzhager

Fraunhofer Institut für Experimentelles Software Engineering,
Fraunhofer Platz 1, 67663 Kaiserslautern, Germany
simon.scherr@iese.fraunofer.de,
{svenja.polst,frank.elberzhager}@iese.fraunhofer.de

Abstract. Online reviews about products and services, such as reviews in stores, are a valuable source of information for customers. Unfortunately, reviews are contaminated by fake reviews, which may lead to wrong conclusions when including them in the analyses of user feedback. As these fake reviews are not marked as advertisement, they might lead to wrong conclusions for customers. If customers are trusting fake reviews their user experience is significantly lowered as soon as they find out that they were betrayed. Therefore, online stores and social media platforms have to take countermeasures against fake reviews. Thus, we performed a systematic literature review to create an overview of the available methods to detect fake reviews and relate the methods to their necessarily required data. This will enable us to identify fake reviews within different data sources easier in order to improve the reliability of the used customer feedback. We have analyzed 141 methods for fake detection. As the reporting quality of a substantial part lacked understandability in terms of method description and evaluation details, we have provided recommendations for method and evaluation descriptions for future method proposals. In addition, we have performed an assessment in terms of detection effectiveness and quality of those methods.

Keywords: User feedback · Online review · Fake review · Spam · Spammer · Literature study

1 Introduction

Online reviews exist for a tremendous number of products and services, and this number has been growing steadily for years. These reviews are a valuable source of information for customers. The reviews express the current product reputation and they contain requests for improvement. Platforms such as Amazon or app stores provide different ways to let people express their feedback, for example, by star ratings or written text. Such feedback can be valuable for a company to improve their products or to convince other users of using their products or services. However, in case the products or services are of bad quality, users provide critical feedback. In other words, the power of users providing feedback via a review has increased in recent years and can have a big influence on the business success of a company.

© Springer Nature Switzerland AG 2019
G. Meiselwitz (Ed.): HCII 2019, LNCS 11578, pp. 453–467, 2019.
https://doi.org/10.1007/978-3-030-21902-4_32

In the scope of our research activities, we developed Opti4Apps as a quality assurance approach that allows developer to include feedback into their quality assurance and development activities [1]. In previous work, we concentrated on different kinds of text analyses [2]. However, we observed that a certain amount of feedback were fake reviews. In general, more than 10% of reviews are assumed to be fake, for some products this is up to 30% [3, 4]. Reviews for apps are also not free of fakes. Including fake reviews (in the following just called fakes) in a feedback analysis of customers has the risk to lead to wrong conclusions. If customers are trusting fake reviews their user experience is significantly lowered as soon as they find out that they were betrayed. This poor user experience will negatively influence their future visits to a website. To prevent such poor user experiences, online stores and social media platforms have to take countermeasures against fake reviews. Detecting and eliminating the fake reviews will lead to an improved reliability of the user feedback and prevent bad user experience. Therefore, our aim was to get an overview of methods that can find such fake reviews, but also fake reviewers. For this, we performed a systematic literature review.

The paper is structured as follows: Sect. 2 presents the foundations in terms of necessary concepts and definitions for our work. Section 3 continues with describing the systematic literature review process, which we have followed. Our results are described in Sect. 4 and discussed in Sect. 5 followed by our threats to validity. We provide conclusions and possible future work in Sect. 7.

2 Foundations

We consider a review to be fake if the review was written for the purpose of promoting or downgrading a product, service or company [5]. It is possible to distinguish between three types of fake reviews [6]: (1) false opinions, (2) reviews on brands only, and (3) non-reviews. We consider the person or bot that is writing fake reviews to be a faker. The place where the fake review was published is called data source. There are two perspectives to identify fakes. It is possible to identify fake reviews, or to identify fake reviewers. We call these perspectives "review view" or "reviewer view". The reviewer view assumes that reviews posted by a fake reviewer are likely to be fake reviews.

As methods for detecting fakes work on different data, multiple levels can be identified: (1) review level (2) product level and (3) source level. The first level is the review level. Part of this level are methods that work by checking one review. The product level (2) contains the information from all reviews written about a product on a feedback source and the information about the product. The source level (3) contains the information on the data source. This includes information about all products and the profile information, such as the name of the reviewer being available there.

We have defined a model for classifying fake detection. This data model makes use of the different levels being used for fake detection and the two perspectives on fake data. In addition, we have added the information aspects to the model. The model is described in Fig. 1. The data categories mentioned in the model are building blocks of online platforms who offer the review of products. The building blocks are supposed to ease the identification of available data in a data source and to select appropriate methods for these data.

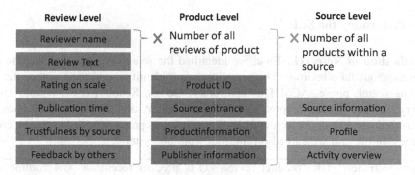

Fig. 1. Data model for method classification

3   Methodology

To capture the state of the art in fake detection in the context of online product and service reviews we have performed a systematic literature review (SLR). The procedure is based on the guidelines provided by Kitchenham [7].

3.1   Planning the SLR

We did not find a review that was conducted systematically, considers all kinds of methods, and covers the most recent ones. A complete and comprehensive description of the methods is necessary to enable us to apply them. Several literature reviews have been published, so far. The study by Sheibani [8] focusses on general terms and definitions rather than methods. Ma and Li put their focus on the challenges and opportunities in the field [9]. Crawford et al. [10] are just covering machine learning methods. The work of Xu is focused on the behavior of fakers that have been identified before [11]. This topic was also investigated in a study of Mukherjee et al. [12]. Heydari et al. provide a comprehensive analysis of fake detection methods [13]. Unfortunately, they have only investigated methods until 2014. Even though the survey of Rajamohana et al. is from 2017 [14] they just analyzed seven methods. They concluded that the field still required future research.

Our goal is to get an understanding of fake detection methods and how these approaches can be applied to different data sources. Therefore, we decided to identify methods, how they work, and how they were evaluated. We considered the data that was used for evaluation as especially important since the characteristics of the data determine whether a method can be applied to another data set. Such characteristics are the language, source of the data set, the domain and the data attributes being used. In addition, we want to analyze how good those fake detection methods are reported. We came up with the following research questions for our SLR:

RQ1: On which aspects do fake detection methods focus on?
RQ2: Which data is used for fake detection?
RQ3: How is the reporting quality of the methods?

3.2   Performing the SLR

Identification of Research. First, we identified the search engines that include publications about fake reviews. These engines were identified and used within the prototyping search phase: ACM Digital Library, Google Scholar, IEEE Xplore Digital Library, Science Direct, Scopus, and Springer Link. Within the prototyping phase we constructed a search query for the SLR. The query was prototyped and revised a couple of times. In the end we agreed on the following query term:

> ("online review" OR "product review" OR "product recension" OR "online reviews" OR "product reviews" OR "product recensions" OR write-up) AND (fake OR spam OR spammer OR fraud OR deceptive OR manipulation OR "opinion spam")

Our term contains two different major subjects that are connected by a logical 'and'. Each of the major subjects contained various synonyms connected by logical 'or' operators. The first block was used to restrict the results to elements mentioning online reviews and different synonyms. The second one was used to restrict the results to elements mentioning fake or faker and their synonyms.

We decided to apply the query to the title, keyword, and abstract in our prototyping phase. As Google Scholar is not able to offer the abstract field, we executed the search based on the title. Springer Link does not offer a restriction to fields therefore we have not made any restriction. In our prototyping phase it turned out that ACM Digital Library was not able to handle the complexity of our query. Due to this issue, we used this library only for a cross check with our systematically derived sources. We checked after our formal search phase the first 100 results of the result set but did not find new studies to include. An explanation could be that we have used Scopus and Google Scholar, which include the search for ACM content.

We performed our searches in January 2018. In total, the engines found 667 results. An overview of the results per search engine can be seen in Table 1. Google Scholar provided 295 and Scopus 192 results.

Table 1. Data sources, fields and number of results that we have considered

Data source	Field	Number of results
Google Scholar	Title	295
IEEE Xplore Digital Library	Abstract	54
Science Direct	Abstract	77
Scopus	Abstract	192
Springer Link	All	49
Total results		667

Study Selection. In the beginning, we eliminated duplicates from the results and defined inclusion and exclusion criteria. We considered a result as duplicate if it was included multiple times. We also considered results as a duplicate if we have found a more recent version of the result. The inclusion criteria are described in Table 2. Our exclusion criteria were the opposite the inclusion criteria. A publication had to fulfill all the inclusion criteria to be considered for our SLR. We required a publication to be published from 2007 (T) onwards as the ground-breaking paper for fake detection in online reviews was published in this year [6]. The publication language was required to be fully English (L). The publication type (PT) had to be an article, conference proceeding, journal paper, book chapter, or thesis documents. We required the studies to be focused on online product reviews (OnR). In addition, they had to focus on fake content or spammer (FaSp). Moreover, the papers must present and explain one or multiple methods for detecting fake reviews, fake reviewers, spam or spammers (Me). In the initial version of our criteria, the criteria FaSp and Me were combined to one criterion. In the prototyping phase, we had quality assured our criteria and found out that a distinction into two criteria is necessary to assure a high quality.

Table 2. Inclusion criteria for the selection study phase

Code	Criterion	Definition
T	Time Period of publication	Publication since 2007
L	Language	English
PT	Publication type	Article, Conference Proceeding, Journal Paper, Book Chapter, Thesis
OnR	Online	The paper is focused on product reviews published online
FaSp	Fake or Spammer	The paper is focused on fake reviews, Review Spam or Spammers publishing reviews
Me	Method	The paper has to mention and explain methods or approaches how to identify fake reviews or fake reviewer

We defined the following strategy for the study selection: each paper had to be reviewed by two selectors independently from each other. If one selector decided to include the paper and the other one decided for exclusion, they had to discuss this conflict and come to an agreement. In our selection protocol, we wrote down the selectors' decision, based on which inclusion respectively exclusion criteria the decision was made and to what extent the selector has read the paper.

We defined the following reading strategy for the selection phase (see Fig. 2). First the researchers had to check the meta data, if the result was fitting at all. Then, they should read the title. If the title did not include enough information about the inclusion criteria, they had to read the abstract, then the introduction and conclusion and finally they had to (cross-) read the full paper. We decided to report exclusions by the furthest reading step on which one of the readers excluded it, i.e. if reader one excluded the paper by the abstract and reader two excluded it by reading introduction and conclusion, we reported the paper as excluded by reading introduction and conclusion. In the end, we had a total number of 139 included results for our extraction phase[1]. Our readers had a very good agreement when selecting the papers. In total, we had only 23 conflicts when selecting the 549 different duplicate-free papers.

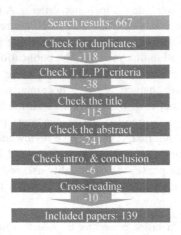

Fig. 2. Reading strategy for selection and number of excluded studies per step

Quality Assessment. We performed a quality assessment for the studies we have included. To be able to extract the methods in a suitable way we defined the following three criteria. (1) We required a result to cover primary research in the area of detection methods. This means that the authors had to present a new or improved method and not just applied a method existing (quality criterion Pri). (2) In addition, we only extracted the methods if they were described in a comprehensible way (quality criterion MethodDec). (3) Furthermore, we required a method evaluation (quality criterion MethodEval) to be present and written in an understandable way providing information of how the method was evaluated, which data was used and what the result was. If the result only fulfilled the first two criteria and not the third one, we did extract it, but marked the impact as low. If it was not fulfilling the first two criteria, we have not performed an extraction. Two persons took decisions for whether a paper not fulfilled the quality criteria. The first proposed a mismatch between our quality criteria and a second researcher had to check if the result really does not fulfill them. We used the second two criteria as a minimum standard for a paper to fulfill. Achieving these criteria does just assure a quality baseline and cannot act as seal of quality. 33 results did not completely fulfill our quality criteria for the extraction. 21 of those results have not provided a new method for fake detection (quality criterion Pri). Five additional results have not described a fake detection method (quality criterion MethodDec). Therefore, these 26 results were not extracted at all. Additional seven results have not fulfilled our quality criterion for method evaluations (MethodEval).

---

[1] Due to the large amount of results being found our selection phase results are available to download from http://opti4apps.iese.de/fakes/downloads.html and not listed in the paper.

Data Extraction. We performed the data extraction with the help of a data extraction guideline and an extraction form that was made available to all extractors[2]. The guideline contained the extraction procedure, information for extraction, and our quality assessment criteria as well as a detailed description of each field from our extraction form. To assure the quality of the guideline and the extraction form each extractor should perform one test extraction and give feedback on the guideline and the form. Based on this we improved the guideline in terms of clarity and added additional information that was missed by extractors in the trial phase. The improved guideline was given to the extractors to review the guideline again to maximize the quality. After that, the data extraction took place. Our extraction form and the fields being used are described in the online material. In our extraction phase it turned out that we were not able to access, even with the help of a document retrieval service, five full papers that seemed promising from their descriptions.

Data Synthesis. We investigated how many selected papers were published per year. Then, we calculated the total number of identified methods and the number of papers that describe more than one method. We counted the number of methods that report an assumption for the method and investigated the degree of automation, whether the method detects fake reviewers or fake reviews and which level the method addresses. Moreover, we analyzed how many methods were applied for a certain domain and in which natural language the reviews were written. When extracting the domain, we identified several domains that were overlapping, such as hotel and service or product and book. There are data sets that refer only to books but data sets that included reviews to several different products on Amazon cannot be assigned to a specific domain. As we realized that the domains were not as distinct as we expected, we categorized the domains into the two main domains 'product' and 'service'. We also analyzed the language of the data set and whether the language was mentioned at all.

We investigated the quality of the method descriptions, evaluation descriptions and results regarding completeness and comprehensibility. We created a checklist on how aspects should be reported by authors proposing fake detection methods. The checklist can be seen in Table 3, our results per method are available online. Aim of the checks is to distinguish methods being presented and evaluated in a detailed and clear manner from those being insufficiently presented and evaluated from the perspective of a person that is seeking for fake detection methods in order to apply them. The checklist is not suitable to rank methods in terms of detection quality or performance and should more serve as requirements of elements that should be checked when analyzing methods. Core aspects of the checklist are the description details and the applicability of the method, as well as the reported evaluation steps and results. If a method did not fulfil the criteria, we reported a 0, if the method fulfilled the criteria, we reported a 1. If a criterion like the reporting of assumptions was not applicable to the method, we have not reported a value to keep it neutral. We calculated a score in percent of the fulfilled and applicable criterions to provide a ranking of the methods.

---

[2] We have made the extraction guideline, results and form downloadable from http://opti4apps.iese.de/fakes/downloads.html.

Table 3. Checklist for method description and evaluation assessment

Name	Definition
View	Is it clear if the method tries to detect spam or spammers?
Level	Can we map the method to our data levels?
Assumptions	If assumptions are made, are they explained? Do they preserve a realistic scenario?
Language	Is the natural language named for which the method was proposed
Data categories	Are the used data attributes described in a way that we can classify the methods within our classification scheme?
Degree of automation	Is the degree of automation clear?
Data source	Is the data source for the data to be analyzed named?
Domain	Is the domain of reviews named?
Replicable	Could a third party create an evaluation for a different method, which can be compared if they have access to the data set?
Results	Are the results clearly reported and backed by evaluation metrics?
Own fake data	If manually inserted fake data is used, is it explained how this data has been created?
Data set	Is the data set described clearly i.e. which elements were used and how they got there?

4 Results

In total, we identified 141 methods from 108 papers. 22 of these papers described more than one method. The maximum number of methods described in a single paper was seven. Since the number of identified methods is big, we do not describe the identified methods in this publication. The method descriptions are available under the download link mentioned above. Figure 3 shows the number of selected papers per year. In the year 2007, only the initial paper by Jinadal about fake detection methods was published [6]. The figure shows that the importance of fake detection methods has greatly increased since then.

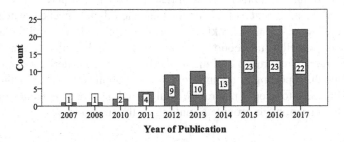

Fig. 3. Number of extracted studies per year

4.1   Aspects of Methods (RQ1)

We have analyzed the distribution of the domains. The reviews were in 32.6% of the methods about products, in 20.6% about a service and in 3.5% about products as well as services. Most methods (43.3%) did not report the domain.

In 2011, 2013 and 2014 data sets with fake and non-fake reviews were developed by Ott [15, 16], Li [17] and their colleagues. They collected reviews from various hotel rating sites (Expedia.com, Hotels.com, Orbitz.com, Priceline.com, TripAdvisor.com and Yelp.com) and extended them with self-created fake reviews. These sets were made available to the public and later used by other authors. Nine studies used the data set of Ott et al. and seven the one by Li et al. Reviews from Amazon were used for the evaluation of 34 methods. Next to Amazon, Yelp.com was the most often used source of reviews (21 methods). TripAdvisor was used seven times. Twenty-three methods used reviews from various sources, three of them used even seven different sources. However, the majority (84 methods) uses only one source.

More than the half of the methods (56.0%) address the detection of fake reviews, about one-third of the methods (53 methods, 37.6%) aim at detecting fake reviewers and only six (4.3%) address reviews as well as reviewers. Methods for fake reviews investigate, for instance, the review length the appearance of duplicates, the sentiment, readability scores and inclusion of hyperlinks in a review test. For the identification of fake reviewers, the source level is required by 45 out of 53 methods (88.2%). The level required by the methods about fake reviews is more divers; the review level is the most often used level (45.6% of fake reviews methods), the product level the second most (35.4%) and the source level is used by 19.0%. None of the methods addressing fake reviews as well as fake reviewers uses the product level. These methods used equally either review or source level.

4.2   Data Used for Fake Detection (RQ2)

One goal of the systematic literature review was to map methods to required data (see Fig. 1. for data model). The idea is to have a list of all data necessary to apply a method. This list could be matched with the data available in a certain data source, such as Amazon or Google Play Store. For 17 methods (12.1%) we were not able to identify data. For one more method, we could identify only one data, however, it was obvious that more, but unidentifiable data were required.

Reviews mostly consist of the review text, a rating on a defined scale, the name of the reviewer, trustfulness information added by other reviewers (e.g. helpfulness rating), trustfulness ratings by the system (e.g. verified purchase) and publication date of the review. Most methods (89 methods, 63.1%) use the review text as input. These kinds of methods perform linguistic analyses such as readability analyses (e.g. [18]) or they use the text to identify duplicates. There are methods that consider exact duplicates, but also partially related reviews. In 53 methods (37.6%), the text is the only data required for the method. The rating on a rating scale and the publication date are also often subject of a method, the rating in 32 methods and the publication date in 15 methods. The ratings given by a reviewer could be compared to the average ratings to the reviewed products. If the ratings often diverge from the average, the reviewer is considered suspicious. The publication date could be used in several ways, too. It could be compared to the date a product enters a source (i.e. a product is set on an online platform). If the publication date is shortly after the product entrance date, the review is suspicious by several methods (e.g. [19]). The publication date could also be used to analyze the number of reviews a reviewer writes within a certain time.

Three methods used the trustfulness rating provided by the source. In all three cases the rating was the verified purchase information. The feedback added by other reviewers was used in two methods. For nine methods it was clear that an identification of the reviewer was needed, however, it was not clear which type of data was used for the identification.

According to our data model, on the product level, there are four types of data; a product ID (required by 13 methods), information about the publisher respectively the product brand (6 methods), the information added by the publisher (e.g. product description) (2 methods), date of entering the source (1 method).

The methods aiming at identifying fake reviewer often require the activity overview of a user. This mostly contains all reviews written to all products by a specific reviewer. The methods often extract the time of publishing a review and the rating on a rating scale. Often more information of the product is required, such as the brand and the rating of other reviewers. The methods then consider a reviewer suspicious if his ratings often diverge from the ratings of other reviewers or when he mostly reviews product of a certain brand. The activity overview of a reviewer was used in 31 methods. The profile of a reviewer was required for nine methods.

4.3   Reporting Quality Assessment (RQ3)

We applied our checklist for fake detection method description and evaluation assessment to the methods. Figure 4 shows the results how well the methods have been evaluated according to our checklist. On average the methods achieved a score of 64%. 101 methods achieved a score being higher than 50%, but only 56 achieved more than 70%. The criteria which were fulfilled mostly were the view (97%) and level (96%) description. On the opposite we only got the natural language mentioned in 16% of the methods. In 4.9% of the methods the review language was Chinese and in 9.8% it was English. Methods that reported the use of a data set by Ott et al. [16] or Li et al. [17] were considered to have reported English reviews even if the language was not directly mentioned in the study.

35% of the evaluations contain a description which data was used, which goes beyond mentioning the data source and some general remarks. 37 methods did not mention any data source of the reviews. 24% of the method evaluations use self-created fake data describe in a reproducible way how this data was inserted. The number of these methods does not include the self-created fake reviews by Li et al. [17] and Ott et al. [16]. Adding the methods that rely on these data sets, a total of 22 methods were evaluated on self-created fakes. Most of the methods did not report an assumption (68.8%). Methods that detect fake reviewers had more often an assumption (39.6% of fake reviewer methods) compared to methods that address fake reviews (24.1% of fake review methods). The degree of automation of the methods is high as 62.4% of the methods are fully automated and 7.8% are semi-automated. However, there are many methods that do not report the automation degree (28.4% of all methods).

Three method proposals achieved a score of 100%. These methods were namely presented by Ahsan et al. [20], Heydari et al. [19] and Sandulescu and Ester [21].

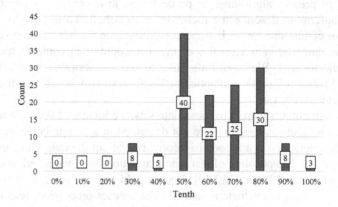

Fig. 4. Quality assessment results grouped by tenths

5 Discussion

We identified required data for 88% of all methods but we assume that the list of identified data is not complete. It seems reasonable that several methods need to somehow distinguish users. However, the identification of users is mostly not described. Methods aiming at identifying fake reviewer by their activities in the source platform often do not describe how they obtain the activities. The activities could be obtained by a publicly available activity overview linked to a profile or by generating a large set of data within the source.

We identified three major problems: (1) documentation of the method, (2) documentation of the evaluation, and (3) description of the evaluation data. This implies that there is still a lot of improvement potential not only for better methods but also for better reporting and evaluation of them.

Methods are documented in very different levels of detail. The publications range from detailed algorithms and theoretical mathematical background for the method like in Ye and Akoglu [22] to just mentioning that the method solves fake detection with machine learning [23]. Many methods do not report information that is necessary for applying the method to an own data set. Authors need to mention the data source for which the method is designed, as it might use unique characteristics of that source. We also noticed that authors frequently do not describe the target language for their detection method. This is a problem especially if the method uses linguistic approaches for the detection. Recently publications in the field of natural language processing methods actively investigate the problem that usually those methods are highly depending on the language being used and cannot be just adapted to new languages [24].

Our results lead to several recommendations about how to report a fake detection method. The method should be described in a way that other people get an understanding of the process of detecting the fakes. This means finding a balance between a high-level description not providing any details and a description being full of complex mathematical formulas which require comprehensive expertise in this subject area. We recommend to present algorithms or processes as flow charts, activity diagrams or sequence diagrams to describe the methods in a nutshell. To identify if a method is applicable for certain use case it is important to mention the natural language, domain, source of the data and characteristics of the data source that could restrict the applicability of the method. We would also like to see a description how automated the method is. In case of semi-automatic methods, it should be clear which parts are automated and which not.

Even though authors started to reuse data sets, we identified six methods that were not evaluated by their authors or were not described in a comprehensible way and 37 evaluation descriptions did not contain information about the data set or even the data source being used. The problem of test data generation was mentioned as critical issue in the SLR of Ma and Li in 2012 [9]. Recent publications in the field posed several standard metrics how to evaluate a method. The metrics precession, recall, F-measure and accuracy have been widely accepted [25]. This in connection with a gold standard for data is a step forward in enabling evaluations to be comparable.

As mentioned above it was not always clear which data was used for the evaluation. Some authors used a mixture of real data from websites enriched with self-made fake data, e.g. Banerjee et al. [26]. This data generation is a challenge. As Zhang et al. [25] reported it is complex to generate realistic fake data. Also, the literature survey of Heydari et al. [13] complained about lack of gold standard data sets. Recent years showed an improvement in that area. In addition, the source data itself might contain fake data that might or might not be detected by the method. We consider the artificial creation of fake data to evaluate a method as a threat to validity for the methods. First methods might be optimized to detect the artificial fake data sets, which might be different to real data.

6 Threats to Validity

While preparing and performing our SLR we have identified and mitigated several possible threats to validity. To capture the relevant sources for establishing a state of the art in fake and spam detection in the context of online reviews it is crucial to not miss relevant sources. We tried to achieve this by prototyping our search term in an iterative way, adding a lot of synonyms, to keep the result set relatively broad. Within our selection phase we put emphasis on only deselecting obviously not matching results within the title stage. In addition, every selection decision was performed by two independent people. This should prevent that the opinion of one single researcher is able to influence the selection decision.

Another identified threat is that errors might occur while searching. This might be entering a malformed search term, using the wrong field codes or copying not all the results. Therefore, we checked the search results with our trial searches to ensure not having a wrong term entered.

To perform SLR the extraction phase is crucial. A wrong extraction guideline or a not matching extraction sheet reduces the quality a lot. Therefore, we quality assured and prototyped our guideline as well as the extraction form. In addition, we focused in our extraction phase on copying citations from our results into our forms. This should prevent the addition of personal interpretation or opinion of the primary research. Our listing of methods faces the problem that it was up to the authors to define what a method exactly is. It might be the case that an author proposes a set of methods that would be proposed by a different author as a single method.

7 Conclusion and Future Work

We performed a systematic literature review on the topic of fake detection methods within online reviews. Our search led to initially 139 papers being included. 141 methods were extracted from a result set of 108 different papers. These methods tried to detect fakes with various approaches ranging from analyzing the content of a review to analyzing the entire user behavior. We have mapped the methods to two different views. Identifying fakes and identifying fakers. Furthermore, we classified the data level and data categories the methods are using. We observed that most methods were using the review level, followed by the product level. This seems naturally as more methods were focused on detecting fakes compared to detecting fakers.

Our analysis of the method descriptions and evaluations revealed that the descriptions lack information, which is necessary to apply the methods to other data sets. The fact that data sources and review language was missing quite frequently is a huge problem in reproducing the evaluation. The current status of available fake detection methods makes it hard to prevent poor user experience as untruthful reviews cannot be detected easily. This lowers significantly the potential of online reviews as source of trustful information. We were clearly able to identify Amazon, Yelp, and TripAdvisor as leading platforms of investigation. The data set provided by Ott et al. [16] and Li et al. [17] became powerful standard data sets to be used.

Despite the found shortcomings the results show many promising opportunities to continue our investigation. In the context of user feedback analysis removing fake reviews is the first step to raw data quality assurance. The second step would be to identify indicators how reliable or trustworthy the different feedback entries are. Measuring reliability and trustworthiness is yet a huge challenge for the research community that has just been addressed in some smaller focus areas.

Acknowledgments. The research described in this paper was performed in the project Opti4Apps (grant no. 02K14A182) of the German Federal Ministry of Education and Research. We would like to thank the students Selina Meyer, Lisa Müller, Sadaf Alvani, Phil Stüpfert and Lukas Zerger, who contributed to the systematic literature review.

References

1. Elberzhager, F., Holl, K.: Towards automated capturing and processing of user feedback for optimizing mobile apps. Procedia Comput. Sci. **110**, 215–221 (2017)
2. Scherr, S., Elberzshager, F., Holl, K.: An automated feedback-based approach to support mobile app development. In: Proceedings - 43rd Euromicro Conference on Software Engineering and Advanced Applications, SEAA 2017, Vienna (2017)
3. Tuttle, B.: 9 Reasons Why You Shouldn't Trust Online Reviews. http://business.time.com/2012/02/03/9-reasons-why-you-shouldnt-trust-online-reviews/. Accessed 03 Feb 2012
4. Weise, K.: A Lie Detector Test for Online Reviewers. https://www.bloomberg.com/news/articles/2011-09-29/a-lie-detector-test-for-online-reviewers. Accessed 29 Sept 2011
5. Jindal, N., Liu, B.: Opinion spam and analysis. In: WSDM 2008 Proceedings of the 2008 International Conference on Web Search and Data Mining, Palo Alto, California, USA (2008)
6. Jindal, N., Liu, B.: Analyzing and detecting review spam. In: IEEE International Conference on Data Mining, Omaha, NE, United States (2007)
7. Kitchenham, B.: Guidelines for performing systematic literature reviews in software engineering (2007)
8. Sheibani, A.: Opinion mining and opinion spam: a literature review focusing on product reviews. In: 6th International Symposium on Telecommunications (IST 2012), Shiraz (2012)
9. Ma, Y., Li, F.: Detecting review spam: challenges and opportunities. In: 8th International Conference Conference on Collaborative Computing: Networking, Applications and Worksharing, Collaboratecom, Pittsburgh (2012)
10. Crawford, M., Khoshgoftaar, T., Prusa, D., Richter, N., Al Najada, H.: Survey of review spam detection using machine learning techniques. J. Big Data **2**, 24 (2015)
11. Xu, C.: Detecting collusive spammers in online review communities. In: International Conference on Information and Knowledge Management, Proceedings, San Francisco (2013)
12. Mukherjee, A., Venkataraman, V., Liu, B., Glance, N.: What yelp fake review filter might be doing? In: Seventh International AAAI Conference on Weblogs and Social Media, Cambridge (2013)
13. Heydari, A., Tavakoli, M., Salim, N., Heydari, Z.: Detection of review spam: a survey. Expert Syst. Appl. **42**(7), 3634–3642 (2015)
14. Rajamohana, S., Umamaheswari, K., Dharani, M., Vedackshya, R.: A survey on online review SPAM detection techniques. In: 2017 International Conference on Innovations in Green Energy and Healthcare Technologies (IGEHT), Coimbatore (2007)
15. Ott, M., Cardie, C., Hancock, J.: Estimating the prevalence of deception in online review communities. In: WWW 2012 Proceedings of the 21st International Conference on World Wide Web, Lyon (2012)
16. Ott, M., Cardie, C., Hancock, J.: Negative deceptive opinion spam. In: NAACL HLT 2013 - 2013 Conference of the North American Chapter of the Association for Computational Linguistics: Human Language Technologies, Proceedings of the Main Conference, Atlanta (2013)
17. Li, J., Ott, M., Cardie, C., Hovy, E.: Towards a general rule for identifying deceptive opinion spam. In: 52nd Annual Meeting of the Association for Computational Linguistics, Baltimore (2014)
18. Banerjee, S., Chua, A.: A linguistic framework to distinguish between genuine and deceptive online reviews. In: Proceedings of the International Multi Conference of Engineers and Computer Scientists, Hong Kong (2014)

19. Heydari, A., Tavakoli, M., Salim, N.: Detection of fake opinions using time series. Expert Syst. Appl. **58**, 83–92 (2016)
20. Ahsan, M.N.I., Nahian, T., Kafi, A., Hossain, M., Shah, M.: An ensemble approach to detect review spam using hybrid machine learning technique, Dhaka, Bangladesh (2016)
21. Sandulescu, V., Ester, M.: Detecting singleton review spammers using semantic similarity, Florence (2015)
22. Ye, J., Akoglu, L.: Discovering opinion spammer groups by network footprints. In: Appice, A., Rodrigues, P.P., Santos Costa, V., Soares, C., Gama, J., Jorge, A. (eds.) ECML PKDD 2015. LNCS (LNAI), vol. 9284, pp. 267–282. Springer, Cham (2015). https://doi.org/10. 1007/978-3-319-23528-8_17
23. Xi, Y.: Chinese review spam classification using machine learning method. In: 2012 International Conference on Control Engineering and Communication Technology, Liaoning (2012)
24. Hogenboom, A., Bal, M., Frasincar, F., Bal, D.: Towards cross-language sentiment analysis through universal star ratings. In: Uden, L., Herrera, F., Bajo Pérez, J., Corchado Rodríguez, J. (eds.) Knowledge Management in Organizations: Service and Cloud Computing. AISC, vol. 172, pp. 69–79. Springer, Heidelberg (2013). https://doi.org/10.1007/978-3-642-30867-3_7
25. Zhang, D., Zhou, L., Kehoe, J., Kilic, I.: What online reviewer behaviors really matter? Effects of verbal and nonverbal behaviors on detection of fake online reviews. J. Manag. Inf. Syst. **33**(2), 456–481 (2016)
26. Banerjee, S., Chua, Y., Kim, J.: Let's vote to classify authentic and manipulative online reviews: the role of comprehensibility, informativeness and writing style. In: 2015 Science and Information Conference (SAI), London (2015)

Claim Behavior over Time in Twitter

Fernanda Weiss[1], Ignacio Espinoza[1], Julio Hurtado[2], and Marcelo Mendoza[1(✉)]

[1] Millennium Institute for Foundational Research on Data,
Universidad Técnica Federico Santa María, Valparaíso, Chile
{fernanda.weiss.13,ignacio.espinozav}@sansano.usm.cl,
marcelo.mendoza@usm.cl
[2] Millennium Institute for Foundational Research on Data,
Pontificia Universidad Católica de Chile, Santiago, Chile
jahurtado@uc.cl

Abstract. Social media is the primary source of information for many people around the world, not only to know about their families and friends but also to read about news and trends in different areas of interest. Fake News or rumors can generate big problems of misinformation, being able to change the mindset of a large group of people concerning a specific topic. Many companies and researchers have put their efforts into detecting these rumors with machine learning algorithms creating reports of the influence of these "news" in social media (https://www.knightfoundation.org/reports/disinformation-fake-news-and-influence-campaigns-on-twitter). Only a few studies have been made in detecting rumors in real-time, considering the first hours of propagation. In this work, we study the spread of a claim, analyzing different characteristics and how propagation patterns behave in time. Experiments show that rumors have different behaviours that can be used to classify them within the first hours of propagation.

Keywords: Fake news · Early detection · Social media · Rumor detection

1 Introduction

With the massive use of social networks we can quickly inform ourselves and at the same time, it is easy for us to broadcast news, which can reach a large audience due to the connections that exist between people. For example, on Twitter, when someone tweet an information, it reaches his/her followers if the information produces an emotional response in that group of people. This scenario has led to an increase of false and malicious news that have been spread by news media. We take the definition of rumor from [1] as *"an item of circulating information whose veracity status is not yet verified"*.

We had seen news where, by a false rumor spread through Whatsapp, people burned two men because it was reported that they were kidnapping a children. However, this information was false[1]. This phenomena has arisen in the political

---

[1] https://www.bbc.com/news/world-latin-america-46145986.

© Springer Nature Switzerland AG 2019
G. Meiselwitz (Ed.): HCII 2019, LNCS 11578, pp. 468–479, 2019.
https://doi.org/10.1007/978-3-030-21902-4_33

sphere, where a group of fake news against a presidential candidate were used to polarize citizens in Brazil[2].

The first approach to verify the veracity of a story, without appeal to an external source is to use common sense and sources of information. This process is not always carried out due to several factors as emotional reactions or ideological biases. Another option is to get help from a committee of journalists so they can conduct fact-checking. Salient fact checking sites such as Politifact[3] have addressed the problem from this perspective. The problem with this solution is that it is too expensive both in time and in human effort, and then the level of truthfulness could take hours or days to be determined. Investigations in machine learning has being conducted to address this problem using automatic detection systems, modeling the information created by the users. Thus a machine can learn to differentiate between rumor and non-rumor doing this process as soon as possible.

The goal of this work is to study the behaviour of claims over time on Twitter, focusing on different features that a news propagation network has. We explore both time based and full claim analysis to discover if there are relevant characteristics that could permit us differentiating between levels of veracity during the first hours of the spread of a rumor.

This paper is organized as follows. In Sect. 2 we start with a review of investigations in time series on social media, what approaches on rumor detection have been researched, giving special attention to those works which explore the capacity of their model to make early detection of rumors. In Sect. 3 we discuss in detail the methodological approaches taken to study the behavior of the evolution of a rumor in two levels: using the complete structure of propagation and the serialization over time. Then, in Sect. 4 we explain the data that we use in this study. Then we discuss experiments and results. Finally, we conclude in Sect. 5 giving our conclusion about our findings outlining future work.

2   Related Work

Information credibility has been an important research area in the last years. There are several works where the main task is to classify news or claims in a binary way (True or False) [5]. Over the years, these two classes has been expanded to 4 categories (*True rumor, False rumor, Non-rumor* and *Unverified*) [9]. In those works the classifier uses the entire information of the claim (e.g. all tweets linked to an original tweet), without taking care of which features are essential for rumor detection.

Accordingly, we show different investigations focused on time sensitive detection. Two research lines arise: time sensitive analysis on social media and early detection of rumors.

---

[2] https://bit.ly/2ET80Qg.
[3] www.politifact.com.

2.1   Time Sensitive Analysis on Social Media

In general, rumor detection is made over an entire claim; this means that it considers all the events associated with the spread of a rumor making a classification among different classes of veracity. However, in real world contexts, it is necessary to detect rumors at the beginning of its spread. For this reason, it is essential to know how rumors evolve over time, making it possible to identify rumors before viralization. In this line, Ma *et al.* [3] work using microblogging services (Twitter and Sina Weibo) to classify claims into two classes, rumor, and non-rumor. The authors used three types of features for this task: content-based, user-based and propagation-based features. They explain the process of early detection between rumor and non-rumor with machine learning, but they do not show which specific features were most useful for early detection.

In [4], Kwon *et al.* used different features of claims that have a temporal evolution, like linguistic, user and propagation factors, observing the impact that they have on news spread. They classified each event into two classes, rumor and non-rumor. The collection of claims studied was made mixing trustworthy sources like CNN[4] and rumors selected from a dataset of Twitter where they picked the most remarkable tweets for each claim.

Leaving aside the detection of rumors, Lukasik *et al.* [6] proposed a process for the task of stance classification, assuming that the occurrence of a tweet will influence the rate at which future tweets will arrive, taking into account time-sensitive information as well as the text of the tweets.

2.2   Early Detection of Rumors

In the last years a number of works [9–11] have focused their efforts on creating datasets, extracting events from social media with related posts. Some works [10, 11] model user interactions for credibility verification, classifying the original post as Rumor or Non-Rumor. Due to the nature of the problem, in [12] the authors proposed a different setting, creating a dataset with four classes (True Rumor, False Rumor, Non-Rumor and Unverified) including information from the propagation structure, leveraging two datasets.

Many works have used machine learning algorithms [15,16] to address this problem but only a few of them have maked use of propagation trees. Ma *et al.* [13] use a tree structure with recursive neural networks to identify supporting, denying or questioning posts. In [14], the authors included stance classification as an auxiliary task during the training of a model by sharing weights in recursive layers with a rumor detection layer in a joint learning schema.

Most of the previous studies have focused their efforts on detection tasks conducting batch analysis over tweets. We believe that a more natural approach to address this problem is to use time series to extract the inherent timeliness information of the propagation of a rumor. Time series modeling will help to study early detection in a more natural fashion.

---

[4] https://edition.cnn.com/.

Combining both network and text information, Ruchansky *et al.* [15] proposed a model with three levels of analysis: capture of textual information, scoring of users according to trust and integration of the previous steps to classify rumors. In [2], the authors created a new model based on verification features. That model is one of the first models that include the stance of individual tweets, rather than one associated with the entire claim. Zhao *et al.* [7] created a detection scheme based on clustering of tweets using these clusters to compare intra-cluster properties. Liu *et al.* [8] propose a time series classifier that incorporates both user and text information. That model uses a combination of recurrent and convolutional networks that focus on capturing the variations of user characteristics along with propagation patterns.

3   Methods

We will study the behavior of claims over time in social media, specifically on Twitter. These events or claims are news or sentences that a user asserts in a post and that is spread in a network due to interactions between users including replies and retweets. The evolution of the claim is finished when no more interactions are recorded, obtaining a propagation tree where each node corresponds to an interaction (retweet or reply) that belongs to a user and each edge between a couple of nodes represent a causal relationship.

Rumors can spread due to many reasons as personal beliefs, political propaganda or ideological biases. However, most of the rumors spread according to specific propagation characteristics, making it possible to classify rumors into four classes: **True-rumor** (T), **False-rumor** (F), **Non-rumor** (N) and **Unverified-rumor** (U).

In the case of non-rumors we know that these claims correspond to factual information. In the case of true rumors, the information is potentially accurate, then its spread is not dangerous. Ideally, if a rumor is false it is necessary to detect it before spreading, avoiding the reaching of many people. False rumors can have terrible consequences depending on the content. Unverified rumors are claims from which it is potentially unfeasible to determine its truthfulness or deceitfulness. In most situations something that can not be proven tends to be false.

In this work, we will analyze three types of sources of features: (1) User-based sources that corresponds to explicit information from the user (e.g. the amount of posts or the amount of favorites), (2) Post-based sources, that corresponds to information extracted from tweets (e.g. It contains a hashtag?), and (3) Propagation-based features, that correspond to characteristics obtained from propagation trees (for example, the average length of the branches). These features are useful to detect rumors using batch analysis [5]. The design criteria behind these features is to provide a set of language-agnostic features.

We will conduct two analysis. In the first one, we will detect rumors retroactively, using the whole batch of information gathered for the event. In the second one, we will identify a real-time review of claims taking different characteristics over time.

3.1   Batch Analysis of Claims

By considering the whole propagation tree, the complete information from users and posts will be in disposal to a classifier that can determine the level of veracity of the original claim. One might think that by having this information the classification could perform better than just having a few hours of data.

We obtained information from different sources for every type of feature, and for each one, we got the mean value for the batch. For example, the "length description" related to an specific event corresponds to the mean of the "length description" of all users profiles that interacted with that claim. Posts-based features were computed in the same way whilst propagation-based features were obtained directly from the tree.

These features can be used as a ground truth for the study because it is going to tell us what are the most relevant characteristics for each type of claim. If no feature excels when we have the full propagation tree, this could mean that there are not patterns able to help in rumor detection tasks. We firmly believe that a reduced amount of features could help us in the analysis.

After identifying these features we will use them to study the behavior of each type of claim over time, generating patterns of behavior in time series.

3.2   Claims over Time

We will analyze claims over time with the idea of cutting the spreading of the rumor at the early stages of the spread. Using representative features found within the batch analysis, we will analyze the behavior of those features over time detecting patterns that can help us to identify the level of veracity.

We will show in the batch analysis part of this study that the most relevant features for each source of information are: (1) The ratio between followers and followees of the users, (2) the average amount of hashtags used in each post, and (3) the number of interactions over time. We will represent each feature over time analyzing the first stages of the spread. Then we will apply logarithmic transformations over the data to visualize these time series in a log-log curve.

4   Experiments and Results

4.1   Data

We will use two datasets based on Twitter, Twitter 15 y Twitter 16, introduced in [12]. Both datasets have four classes for classification: True rumor, False rumor, Non rumor and Unverified. Table 1 shows the details for the datasets. These datasets are different from the original ones because when retrieving the tweets some original posts and users were deleted. In any case a huge amount of the original data was recovered.

Both datasets have similar characteristics as it is shown in Tables 1 and 2. Although the amounts of events in Twitter 15 is greater, both datasets have well-balanced classes.

Table 1. Information of datasets

	Twitter 15	Twitter 16
# claim	1490	818
# users	447495	265286
# posts	45696	21741
# false rumor	370	205
# true rumor	372	207
# non-rumor	374	205
# unverified rumor	374	201
Avg. time/claim [h]	1487	829
Avg. # unique posts/claim	37	33
Avg. # unique users/claim	402	425

In our experiments, we used a complete set of features from different sources. Table 2 shows the mean values for both datasets. For each feature it can be observed that both datasets exhibit similar values. The ratio (see the second row in Table 2) corresponds to the proportion between the number of followers and the number of followees that a user has. Table 2 also shows the favorites (the amount of favorites posts that a user has), if the account is geo-enabled, *lists count* (amount of lists in which the user appears), *statuses count* (amount of posts posted by a user) and *verified* (number of users with verified accounts in the tree).

Post-based features refer to the length of the text of the post, the number of hashtags, mentions, and URLs in the tweet of the current claim batch. Propagation-based features are the number of unique tweets that appear in each event, time refers to the time elapsed between the first and last post of the claim, and branch length is the average depth of the branches in the claims.

4.2 Batch Analysis of Claims

We start this section analyzing claim data batches. In Figs. 1, 2 and 3 we show box-plots for each type of claim according to the source of information. When we observe only the information extracted from user-based features (see Fig. 1), non rumors and true rumors tend to be very similar. This observation is consistent with the fact that both types of events are related to confirmed truths. The ratio feature gives good information for a binary classification. The number of verified users in these claims tend to be higher than in true rumors. Users with verified accounts usually help to spread true rumors.

Post-based features can be observed in Fig. 2. We can observe that most events do not have hashtags, but true rumors have more claims with a higher mean value of hashtags per post. Similar to the number of URLs used, non-rumors usually have an URL in their tweets.

Table 2. Information extracted from claims. Each value was computed across claim batches.

	Twitter 15	Twitter 16
User-based features		
Ratio	32	37
Favourites	19179	22154
Geo enabled	214	220
Lists count	92	100
Description length	66	65
Length name	11	10
Statuses count	46892	48584
Verified	5.8	6.2
Post-based features		
Text length	106	104
Mentions	0.3	0.3
Hashtags	0.35	0.34
URLs	0.6	0.6
Propagation-based features		
Unique post	37	33
Re-Tweet	364	390
Time [min]	77295	49737
Unique users	399	423
Average branch depth	2.3	2.3

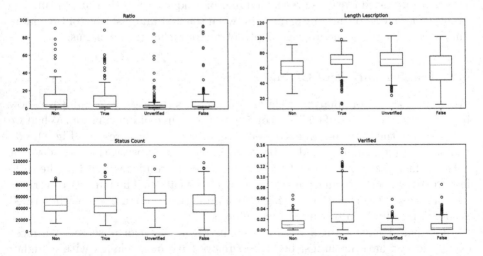

Fig. 1. User-based features. Some features are useful to differentiate between classes. For example, the ratio and the amount of verified users are helpful for this task.

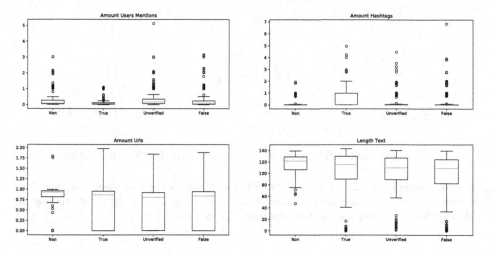

Fig. 2. Post-based features. Each value represents the mean across batches.

Propagation-based features can be shown in Fig. 3. Non-rumors usually have a greater median than the rest of the claims. Non-rumors register also more interactions recording more replies and retweets. True rumors typically finish before other type of claims, possibly because they produce less discussions. This is confirmed with the low amount of unique posts.

4.3   Claims over Time

Each time series was computed using a time-based window of fixed length and in each window we measured the corresponding feature. For example, in Fig. 4(a)

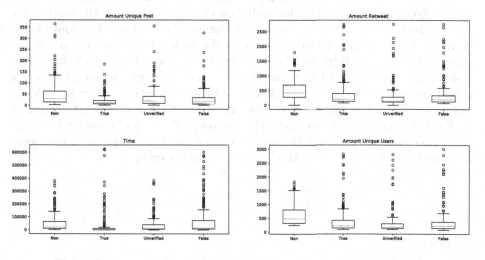

Fig. 3. Propagation-based features. Non rumors show greater values.

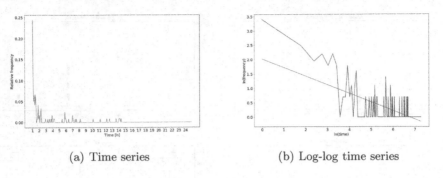

(a) Time series   (b) Log-log time series

Fig. 4. Example of a true rumor claim. Figure (a) shows the time series for this claim during its first 24 h using a time-based window of 5 min. Figure (b) shows the log-log plot of the time series and its linearization. (Color figure online)

the time series shows the interactions during the first 24 h of a claim using time-based windows of 15 min. Accordingly, the x-axis represents a hourly-based timeline and the y-axis represents the volume of interactions within the event.

Then, we applied a logarithmic transformation in both axes. The log-log plot is useful to look spread velocities and then to find out if there is any difference among different types of rumors. To find this velocity we computed a linear regression of the log-log plot, whilst in the slope of this curve we will observe the speed with which each feature was spread over time. Figure 4(b) shows the log-log curve (blue) and the linearization (green).

We computed the slope of the log-log linearization of interactions, hashtags, and the ratio between followers and friends in each claim of each dataset. Figure 5 shows the behaviors over time using these features. Figure 5(a) shows propagation-based features. We can see that non-rumors have a particular behavior regarding other classes, showing that in factual claims the interactions arrive faster. True rumors have a similar behavior than non-rumors at the start of the spread. In Fig. 5(b) we show post-based features as hashtags. The four classes converge together and the variance across classes is wide, then we can not discover any particular behavior over time in this scenario. Figure 5(c) shows that non-rumors are again below than the other types of rumors. True rumors, in the beginning of the spread, reach people faster but after a while its velocity decreases. From that point of view it looks similar to false or unverified rumors. In Fig. 5 we can observe a similar behavior both in false and unverified rumors, observing only a small gap between both curves. This behavior makes sense because both classes are very similar in terms of meaning.

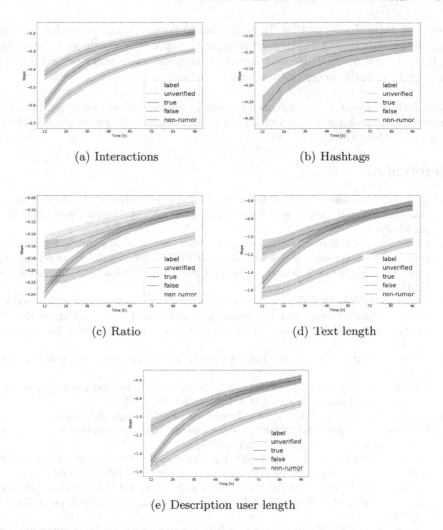

(a) Interactions

(b) Hashtags

(c) Ratio

(d) Text length

(e) Description user length

Fig. 5. The mean slope of log-log linearization every 12 h for every feature selected (a) Propagation-based features: thos figure shows the mean slopes for interactions amount with the claims, including comments and re-tweets. (b and d) Post-based features: this figure shows the mean slopes for hashtags amount used in different interactions with the claims, and the mean slopes for text post length. (c and e) User-based features: this figure shows the mean slopes for the ratio between followers and followees who interact with the claims, and the mean slope for the description user length.

5   Conclusions

In this work, we presented a study of claims veracity type on Twitter comparing two approaches: batch analysis and claim behavior over time. In the time-sensitive analysis, we find some interesting findings. Non-rumors have different behavior than the other classes in most features, due to the fact that they are based on factual information. In rumor-based posts (true rumors, false rumors and unverified claims), in the beginning of the spread true rumors behave similarly to factual posts. False and unverified rumors have similar behavior due to the fact that both classes are semantically close.

Acknowledgements. The authors acknowledge funding support from the Millennium Institute for Foundational Research on Data. Mr. Mendoza was partially funded by the project BASAL FB0821.

References

1. Zubiaga, A., Aker, A., Bontcheva, K., Liakata, M., Procter, R.: Detection and resolution of rumours in social media: a survey. ACM Comput. Surv. **51**, 32:1–32:36 (2018)
2. Liu, X., Nourbakhsh, A., Li, Q., Fang, R., Shah, S.: Real-time rumor debunking on twitter. In Proceedings of the 24th ACM International on Conference on Information and Knowledge Management (CIKM 2015), pp. 1867–1870. ACM, New York (2015)
3. Ma, J., Gao, W., Wei, Z., Lu, Y., Wong, K.F.: Detect rumors using time series of social context information on microblogging websites. In: Proceedings of the 24th ACM International on Conference on Information and Knowledge Management, pp. 1751–1754. ACM (2015)
4. Kwon, S., Cha, M., Jung, K.: Rumor detection over varying time windows. PLOS ONE **12**, 1 (2017)
5. Castillo, C., Mendoza, M., Poblete, B.: Predicting information credibility in time-sensitive social media. Internet Res. **23**(5), 560–588 (2013)
6. Lukasik, M., Srijith, P.K., Vu, D., Bontcheva, K., Zubiaga, A., Cohn, T.: Hawkes Processes for continuous time sequence classification: an application to rumour stance classification in twitter. ACL (2016)
7. Zhao, Z., Resnick, P., Mei, Q.: Enquiring minds: early detection of rumors in social media from enquiry posts. In: Proceedings of the 24th International Conference on World Wide Web (WWW 2015), International World Wide Web Conferences Steering Committee, Republic and Canton of Geneva, Switzerland, pp. 1395–1405 (2015)
8. Liu, Y., Wu, Y.B.: Early detection of fake news on social media through propagation path classification with recurrent and convolutional networks. AAAI (2018)
9. Ma, J., et al.: Detecting rumors from microblogs with recurrent neural networks. In: IJCAI, pp. 3818–3824 (2016)
10. Mitra, T., Gilbert, E.: CREDBANK: a large-scale social media corpus with associated credibility annotations. In: ICWSM, pp. 258–267 (2016)
11. Shu, K., Sliva, A., Wang, S., Tang, J., Liu, H.: Fake news detection on social media: a data mining perspective. ACM SIGKDD Explor. Newsl. **19**(1), 22–36 (2017)
12. Ma, J., Gao, W., Wong, K.F.: Detect rumors in microblog posts using propagation structure via kernel learning. In: Proceedings of the 55th Annual Meeting of the Association for Computational Linguistics, (Volume 1: Long Papers), vol. 1, pp. 708–717 (2017)
13. Ma, J., Gao, W., Wong, K.F.: Rumor detection on twitter with tree-structured recursive neural networks. In: Proceedings of the 56th Annual Meeting of the Association for Computational Linguistics (Volume 1: Long Papers), vol. 1, pp. 1980–1989 (2018)

14. Ma, J., Gao, W., Wong, K.F.: Detect rumor and stance jointly by neural multi-task learning. In: Companion of the The Web Conference 2018 on The Web Conference 2018, pp. 585–593. International World Wide Web Conferences Steering Committee (2018)
15. Ruchansky, N., Seo, S., Liu, Y.: CSI: a hybrid deep model for fake news detection. In: Proceedings of the 2017 ACM on Conference on Information and Knowledge Management, pp. 797–806. ACM (2017)
16. Kumar, S., Shah, N.: False information on web and social media: a survey. arXiv preprint arXiv:1804.08559 (2018)

Community Engagement and Social Participation

Towards Understanding Negative Votes in a Question and Answer Social Network

Ifeoma Adaji[(⊠)], Kiemute Oyibo, and Julita Vassileva

University of Saskatchewan, Saskatoon, Canada
{Ifeoma.adaji,Kiemute.oyibo}@usask.ca,
jiv@cs.usask.ca

Abstract. Online community question answering (CQA) social networking sites thrive when community members actively participate in the network. To influence participation, some CQA sites such as Stack Overflow reward members with incentives such as reputation, badges, and privileges. One way people earn such rewards is by posting helpful question and answers which get upvoted. An upvote is an indication of how useful a post is to the reader. An increase in a post's upvotes could lead to the user who created the post accruing reputation and earning rewards in the community. To encourage people to write good posts, Stack Overflow has guidelines on their site for writing good question and answer posts. Despite these measures by Stack Overflow to encourage quality posts from community members, there are still several posts in the community with negative scores. A negative score indicates that the post received more downvotes than upvotes. If one consistently receives negative scores on their posts, it could influence them to stop using the network. Thus, it is important to identify the characteristics of posts with negative scores and explore how they differ from posts with positive scores. To contribute to research in this area, we identified the time of day posts were created, the sentiments and emotions used in writing the posts, the length of posts, and the topics that the posts were tagged with for posts with negative scores and those with positive scores. The result of our analysis on these two groups of posts suggests that posts created between 6.01 pm and 12 am received significantly higher scores than posts written at other times of the day. In addition, posts with positive scores were significantly longer in length than posts with negative scores. Furthermore, posts with positive scores were significantly more analytical and clout and less authentic compared to posts with negative scores.

Keywords: Community question answering · Sentiment analysis · Stack overflow

1 Introduction

In online community question answering (CQA) sites, active participation is essential in keeping the network active [7]. Stack Overflow, a popular CQA[1], is an online social networking site where users can ask specific computer programing questions and other

---

[1] https://stackoverflow.com/.

© Springer Nature Switzerland AG 2019
G. Meiselwitz (Ed.): HCII 2019, LNCS 11578, pp. 483–498, 2019.
https://doi.org/10.1007/978-3-030-21902-4_34

users can post answers to the questions. Because quality posts are essential in keeping the network active [7], if people who post questions do not receive quality answers, they could be discouraged from returning to the site. Similarly, if the questions are not well written or are of poor quality, this could discourage people who often post answers from doing so. Thus, it is important for the network's users to continuously post quality content. To influence users to do so, Stack Overflow has a voting system where community members can vote for questions and answers depending on the perceived quality of such posts. According to Stack Overflow[2], *"Voting up a question or answer signals to the rest of the community that a post is interesting, well-researched, and useful, while voting down a post signals the opposite: that the post contains wrong information, is poorly researched, or fails to communicate information. The more that people vote on a post, the more certain future visitors can be of the quality of information contained within that post – not to mention that upvotes are a great way to thank the author of a good post for the time and effort put into writing it!"*. Voting is central to the model of Stack Overflow because voting is one of the ways users who consistently post useful content are rewarded with reputation points, privileges, and badges. Reputation shows how much the community trusts a user and it can be earned by posting quality questions and answers[3]. The more reputation points earned by a user, the more privileges they have in the network. For example, a user who has earned at least 10,000 reputation points earns "access to moderator tools" privilege which gives them access to reports exclusive to site moderators and the ability to delete questions[4]. Badges are rewarded to users in the network who are especially helpful in the community[5]. Some badges are rewarded as a result of the votes earned by users on their question and answer posts. For example, the "nice question" badge is rewarded to users whose question post has earned 10 scores. Scores are computed based on the number of upvotes and downvotes a post has earned.

To encourage users to write quality posts (that can earn upvotes), Stack Overflow provides guidelines on how to write good questions[6] and answers[7]. For example, Stack Overflow recommends proofreading before posting a question. Despite these guidelines and the rewards in place for quality posts, there are still several posts in Stack Overflow with negative scores. This suggests that such questions received more downvotes than upvotes. Negative votes on posts could be discouraging to the users who make such posts. Thus, it is important to explore the characteristics of posts with negative scores to identify what makes a post receive negative votes. This could inform users on why their posts could receive negative votes and what can do to increase the chances of receiving upvotes on their posts.

---

[2] https://stackoverflow.com/help/why-vote.

[3] https://stackoverflow.com/help/whats-reputation.

[4] https://stackoverflow.com/help/privileges.

[5] https://stackoverflow.com/help/badges.

[6] https://stackoverflow.com/help/how-to-ask.

[7] https://stackoverflow.com/help/how-to-answer.

The quality of posts in CQAs is an ongoing research area. Bazelli et al. [12] explored the relationship between the personality traits of users and the votes received by the users' posts in order to determine if people of particular personality traits received only certain types of votes. Gantayat et al. [19] explored the difference in the *accepted answer* to a question and the answer with the highest number of *upvotes* in order to determine if the post voted by the asker as the answer to their question was also the post with the highest number of *upvotes* from the community. Yao et al. [39] studied high-quality posts in Stack Overflow using the votes received by the post. They developed an algorithm to identify high-quality posts soon after they are posted on Stack Overflow. Although these researchers explored the quality of posts in the community, they did not consider the emotions or sentiments expressed in the posts in addition to other features of the post such as the length of post and time of day the post was created. To fill that gap, we aim in this study to investigate the difference in (1) sentiments and emotions, (2) length of posts, (3) creation time of posts, and (4) the subject area posts were tagged with between posts with positive scores and those with negative scores.

The sentiments and emotions expressed by users in their posts in online communities have been shown to influence the popularity of such posts [18, 23]. We thus hypothesize that the emotions and sentiments expressed by users in their posts could have an effect on the type of votes received by such posts. In addition, research has shown that the length of a post and the time it was created in CQAs influence people's attitude towards the post [11, 24]. We, therefore, hypothesize that the length of posts and time when posts were created in Stack Overflow could influence the votes the posts receive in the community. Furthermore, the subject areas questions are tagged with have been shown to influence the response time of answers posted in response to the questions [14]. We further hypothesize that the subject areas posts are tagged with could influence the scores received by the posts.

To validate our hypotheses, we compared the posts that have earned high negative scores to those that have earned high positive scores and explore the differences in variance in the timing of the posts, the emotions and sentiments used in writing the posts, the length of the posts and the tags/subject areas of the posts between these two groups. We analyze posts with high positive scores and those with negative scores to determine if there are any significant differences in these factors between both groups of posts. In addition, we developed a predictive model using these factors to predict if a post will likely receive a positive or negative score.

The results of our analyses suggest that posts created at night received significantly higher scores than posts written at other times of the day. In addition, posts with positive scores were significantly longer in length than posts with negative scores. Furthermore, posts with positive scores were significantly more analytical and clout and less authentic compared to posts with negative scores. To predict if a post will receive a positive or negative score, we developed and tested a predictive model using the word count of posts, sentiment and time of day the post was created. Using random forest machine learning algorithm, our model had a classification accuracy of 73%.

Our study contributes to the domain of CQAs in several ways. First, the results presented here explain how positive posts differ from negative ones and what features could differentiate positive posts from negative ones. Second, our study shows that the emotions and sentiments expressed by users in their posts should be considered in explaining the type of votes received by a post. Finally, our predictive model suggests that sentiments and emotions in addition to the length of posts, time of day of post and score are able to predict the score of posts with high accuracy.

2 Related Work

2.1 Stack Overflow

Stack Overflow[8] is a CQA platform where users can ask and answer specific IT related questions. Authors of questions can earn reputation and rewards when their posts get upvoted. Stack Overflow currently has over 5 million users with over 11 million questions. Stack Overflow is an active research area for CQAs with researchers studying the effect of rewards on the community and exploring voting patterns of users. While the former has received a lot of attention in recent times [4–10] there is still room for more research on the latter.

Research on voting patterns could be in the form of understanding what makes a good post in the community. For example, Nasehi et al. [29] explored the features that make a good code example in Stack Overflow. In Stack Overflow, questions are often accompanied with code examples if the asker needs help with their code. Nasehi et al. concluded that the quality of the code example accompanying a question is as important as the question itself. By analyzing posts with high scores, the authors determined the characteristics of good code examples; this could explain why posts received upvotes. Similarly, Asaduzzaman et al. [11] investigated why some questions in the community go unanswered. They concluded that questions that go unanswered failed to attract experts, were too short, were sometimes a duplicate and often times such questions were too hard or time consuming. Bazelli et al. [13] also investigated voting patterns in the community by exploring the personality of users on Stack Overflow based on their reputation. Their results suggest that the users who have high reputation are more extroverted compared to the users who have low reputation. They also concluded that the authors of posts with positive votes showed fewer negative emotions compared to authors of posts with negative votes. Our research differs from theirs because in addition to the emotions of the users, we also explored their sentiments. Furthermore, we developed a predictive model using sentiment and emotion in addition to length of post, time of day post was made and score of post.

2.2 LIWC

In this paper, we identify sentiments and emotions of users in Stack overflow using the Linguistic Inquiry Word Count tool (LIWC) [33]. The LIWC tool reads text and determines what percentage of words in the text reflect various dimensions of sentiments and emotions of the writer. LIWC works by calculating the percentage of given words that match its built-in dictionary of over 6,400 words for different dimensions of

---

[8] https://stackoverflow.com/.

sentiment and emotions. The LIWC tool has several dimensions for sentiments and emotions which include (1) *analytic* which refers to how analytical a user's text is, (2) *clout* which refers to the social status, confidence and leadership displayed in the text by the author, (3) *authentic* which shows how authentic the author is and (4) *tone* which describes the emotional tone of the author.

LIWC has been used extensively in identifying personality of users in online social communities with success. Bazelli et al. [13] used the LIWC tool in exploring the personality traits of users in a Stack Overflow. Their research suggests that top contributors in the community are extroverts. Romero et al. [36] also used the LIWC tool in their study of social networks. The authors explored how the personality traits and behavior of decision makers in a large hedge fund change based on price shocks. Adaji et al. [3] developed a personality based recipe recommendation system for a popular recipe social site, allrecipes.com. In their study, the authors used the LIWC tool to identify the personality of users. In investigating low review ratings in Yelp based on the personality of users, Adaji et al. [2] used the LIWC tool to identify users' personality.

The LIWC tool has also been used in natural language processing for the analysis of sentiment and emotions of users from their text. Kacewicz et al. [22] investigated the use of pronouns to reflect standings in social hierarchies by analyzing the text of users using the LIWC tool. Their research suggests that people with higher status use fewer first-person singular pronouns such as "I". In addition, people with higher status also use more first-person plural pronouns such as "we" and more second-person singular pronouns such as "you". Newman et al. [30] also used the LIWC tool to explore the linguistic style of writers in order to identify deception. Their research suggests that people who are deceptive showed lower cognitive complexity and use fewer self-references.

Based on the popularity and success of the LIWC tool as reported by other researchers, we chose to use it in this research in identifying the sentiments and emotions displayed by users in their posts.

3 Methodology

The aim of this study is to investigate the difference in (1) sentiments and emotions, (2) length of posts, (3) creation time of posts, and (4) the subject area posts were tagged with between posts with positive scores and those with negative scores. In this section, we describe the methodology used in the study.

3.1 Data Collection

To carry out this study, we used data from Stack Overflow's data explorer[9]. The data explorer allows one to directly query Stack Overflow's publicly available dataset. We extracted question and answer posts that were created within the last one year with a

---

[9] https://data.stackexchange.com/stackoverflow/query/new.

score of −5 or less which we termed *negative_posts* and posts with a score of at least 20 which we called *positive_posts*. These values were chosen based on the average score of posts on Stack Overflow. We had a total of 10,005 posts with negative scores and 4,714 posts with positive scores.

3.2 Predictive Model

To predict if a post will get a positive score or a negative score, we developed a predictive model using the following features:

- word count: the length of the post
- sentiments and emotions identified from post
- time of day the post was made: morning, afternoon or night.

We applied various classification algorithms to predict if a post will receive a positive or negative final score. These include logistic regression, random forest, k-nearest neighbor, Naïve Bayes, support vector machine, and neural networks. These algorithms were selected based on what other researchers have used in the past [7, 11, 39].

In developing and testing our model, we used Python's Scikit-learn machine learning module[10]. We chose this module because of its ease of use, performance, documentation and API consistency [32]. In addition, several researchers have successfully used it for supervised and unsupervised learning [17].

The following section briefly describes the classifiers we used and how they were implemented using Pythons' Scikit-learn machine learning module

Logistic Regression
Logistic regression is a classification model used to predict the outcome of a dependent variable using one or more predictors. It can be used when a model has one nominal dependent variable and two or more measurement variables. Logistic regression has been used extensively in predictive analysis [27, 28, 38] and research has shown that it is effective in producing quick and robust results [28]. Logistic regression was implemented using the *LogisticRegression* class of Scikit-learn.

Random Forests
Random forests is a well-researched classification algorithm that is known to be robust against over-fitting [26]. The algorithm does not consider all the predictors [25] which is necessary in a case where there is a very strong predictor in the data set along with several moderately strong predictors. Random forests will not consider the strong predictor, so other predictors will have more of a chance. Random forests was implemented using the *RandomForestClassifier* class of Scikit-learn.

K-nearest Neighbor
K-nearest neighbor classifies data based on a "majority vote" of the nearest neighbors of each point. K-nearest neighbor is non-parametric, thus the structure of the model is determined from the data. K-nearest neighbor is known to be highly intuitive with low

---

[10] https://scikit-learn.org/stable/.

classification errors [15]. K-nearest neighbor was implemented using *KNeighborsClassifier* class of Scikit-learn with 5 neighbors.

Naïve Bayes
Naïve Bayes is an efficient and effective learning algorithm that uses Bayes theorem. Bayes theorem describes the probability of an event based on previous information about the event; the probability is revised given new or additional knowledge. Naïve Bayes assumes strong independence between predictors [1]. Naïve Bayes was implemented using *GaussianNB* class of Scikit-learn.

Support Vector Machine
Support vector machine represents variables as points in space, mapped in such a way that the variables are divided into classes by a clear gap that is as wide as possible; new variables are easily assigned to a class based on which side of the gap they fall [21]. Support vector machine was implemented using the *SVC* class of Scikit-learn.

Neural Networks
Neural networks are nonlinear regression techniques inspired by theories about the central nervous system of animals, in particular the human brain. In this algorithm, hidden variables model the outcome of neural networks. These hidden variables are a linear combination of all or some of the original predictors. A linear combination of the hidden variables form the output or prediction [25]. Neural networks was implemented using the *MLPClassifier* class of Scikit-learn and five hidden layers.

3.3   Evaluating the Algorithms

The algorithms were evaluated by computing their classification accuracy, precision, recall and *F*-score. Classification accuracy is calculated as the sum of correct classifications divided by the total number of classifications. While precision is the fraction of items retrieved by the algorithm that are relevant, recall is a fraction of all relevant items that were retrieved by the algorithm. The *F*-score is the average of precision and recall [16]. The closer these metrics are to 1, the higher the performance of the algorithm. The closer they are to 0, the lower the performance of the algorithms.

4   Analyses and Results

We used four main factors in comparing posts with negative scores to those with positive scores: (1) the creation time of posts, (2) the sentiments and emotions used in writing posts, (3) the length of the posts, and (4) tags/subject areas of the posts.

4.1   Creation Time of Posts and Scores

A two-way ANOVA was conducted to determine if the average score received by posts was (1) different based on the time of day the post was created and (2) significantly different between the two groups of post: *negative_posts* and *positive_posts*. The time of day was classified into three: morning - between 12:01 am to 12:00 pm ($n = 2205$), afternoon - between 12:01 pm and 6:00 pm (n = 1418), and night - between 6:01 pm and 12:00 am (n = 992). There were no outliers, as assessed by boxplot; data was normally distributed for each group, as assessed by Shapiro-Wilk test ($p > .05$); and there was homogeneity of variances, as assessed by Levene's test of homogeneity of variances ($p = .120$). Data is presented as mean ± standard deviation.

There was a statistically significant interaction between the groups of post (negative_posts and positive_posts) and time of day the posts were made, $F(2,14713) = 3.117$, $p = 0.044$, partial $\eta^2 = .01$. Therefore, an analysis of simple main effect for negative_posts and positive_posts was carried out. There was a statistically significant difference in mean score of posts between the different times (morning, afternoon and night) and positive_posts $F(2,14713) = 4.662$, $p = .009$, partial $\eta^2 = .001$. The average score for positive posts as shown in Fig. 1 decreased from morning to afternoon from (57.44 ± 353.49), to (49.50 ± 258.92), and increased significantly in the night to (73.21 ± 400.49). This suggests that posts created at night receive significantly higher votes compared to those created in the morning or afternoon. Thus, users who receive negative scores on their posts could consider creating their posts at night instead of during the day.

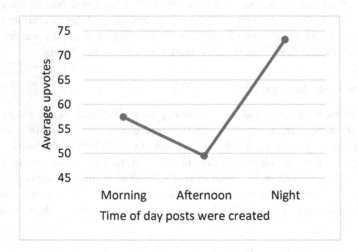

Fig. 1. Average upvotes posts received based on the time of the day they were created

4.2   Sentiments and Emotions

To understand the sentiments and emotions shown in posts, we carried out sentiment analysis of the posts in our dataset using the Linguistic Inquiry Word Count (LIWC) tool [37]. We chose this tool because it has been used extensively in research for analyzing user generated content in online systems [2, 3, 13]. The results displayed in Fig. 2 show the average sentiment and emotions for posts with negative score and posts with positive score for the different dimensions of sentiment and emotion. Our results suggest that posts with positive scores have a higher mean score for *analytic, clout,* and *tone.* Several emotions and sentiments had very low scores such as *affect, positive* and *negative emotion.* We attributed this to the type of social network Stack Overflow is. Compared to a social networking site such as Facebook which is meant for building friendship, Stack Overflow is mainly for learning. Thus, Stack Overflow posts will likely be more analytical and less emotional. We therefore excluded the sentiments and emotions with low mean scores and continued our analysis using only *analytic, clout, authentic* and *tone* because of their high mean scores.

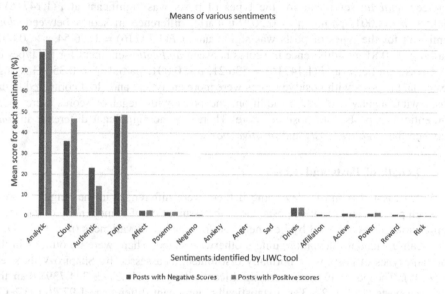

Fig. 2. Sentiments identified by LIWC tool

According to the LIWC tool[11], the dimension *analytic* represents the extent to which people use formal words, and how logical and hierarchical their thinking patterns are. The dimension *clout* is an indication of the social status, confidence or leadership displayed by an individual through their writing or speaking. *Authenticity*, according to the LIWC tool, reveals how honest people are through their writing. People high in authenticity are more personal, humble and vulnerable. *Tone* indicates the emotions displayed by users in their posts.

To determine if there were any statistically significant differences in the mean sentiments between the posts with positive scores and those with negative scores, we carried out a two-way mixed ANOVA with sentiments: *analytic, clout, authentic* and *tone* as our within-subject factors and the type of score received by posts: *negative_posts* and *positive_posts* as our between-subject factors.

Mauchly's test of sphericity indicated that the assumption of sphericity was not met for the two-way interaction, $\chi2(2) = 4979.784$, $p < .01$, therefore degrees of freedom were corrected using Huynh-Feldt estimates of sphericity ($\varepsilon = 0.86$) as suggested

---

[11] http://liwc.wpengine.com/interpreting-liwc-output/.

by [20], since ε is greater than 0.75. There was statistically significant interaction between the sentiments and the type of posts: *negative_posts* or *positive_posts*, F (2.579, 37958) = 494.056, $p < .0005$, partial $\eta^2 = 0.32$, $\varepsilon = 0.86$. To determine where the differences were, we carried out testing for simple main effects to identify any differences between the two groups of posts for each sentiment.

There was statistically significant difference between the sentiments: *analytic, clout, authentic* and type of posts: *negative_posts* and *positive_posts*. Difference in scores between *analytic* sentiment for the types of posts was significant at $F(1,14716) = 400.58$, $p < 0.001$, partial $\eta^2 = 0.26$. Similarly, difference in scores between *clout* sentiment for the types of posts was significant at $F(1,14716) = 1296.54$, $p < 0.001$, partial $\eta^2 = 0.81$ and difference in scores between *authentic* sentiment for the types of post was significant at $F(1,14716) = 536.21$, $p < 0.001$, partial $\eta^2 = 0.35$. This suggests that the posts with positive scores were more analytical and clout compared to the posts with negative scores. In addition, the posts with negative scores were more authentic than posts with positive score. There was no significant difference in *tone* between the *negative_posts* and *positive_posts*.

4.3   Length of Posts and Tags

A Welch t-test was run to determine if there were differences in the length of posts between positive and negative posts due to the assumption of homogeneity of variances being violated, as assessed by Levene's test for equality of variances ($p < .001$). Data are mean ± standard deviation, unless otherwise stated. There were no outliers in the data and types of posts were normally distributed, as assessed by Shapiro-Wilk's test ($p > .05$). The positive posts were significantly longer (249.27 ± 344.739) than the negative posts (152 ± 2.8.33), a statistically significant difference of 97.26 (95% CI, 86.61 to 107.92), $t(6383.718) = 17.892$, $p < .001$.

We also compared the tags used in the posts with positive votes and those used in posts with negative votes to determine if both groups of posts had different tags. Figure 3 shows that there are similarities in the popularity of tags for both groups of posts; for example, both categories include several posts about Python, Java, JavaScript and Android. Both groups have similar top 10 tags. This suggests that popularity of tags was similar for both types of posts.

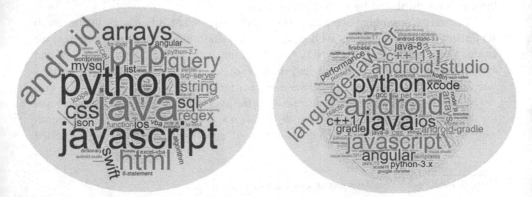

Fig. 3. Word cloud of tags used in posts with negative scores and positive scores

4.4   Predictive Model

We used the predictors word count, sentiment (*analytic, clout, and authentic*) and time of day (morning, afternoon and night) to predict if a post will have positive or negative scores. We excluded tags because there was no difference in *negative_posts* and *positive_posts* groups based on tags. Our data set was randomly split into 75% training and 25% test sets. We tested our model using six algorithms: logistic regression, random forest, k-nearest neighbor, Naïve Bayes, support vector machine, and neural networks. The results of these algorithms are presented in Table 1.

Table 1. Classification accuracy, precision and recall of the classification algorithms

Algorithms	Classification accuracy	Precision	Recall	F-score
Logistic regression	0.71	0.73	0.91	.812
Random forest	0.73	0.77	0.87	0.820
K-nearest neighbor	0.68	0.74	0.83	0.783
Naïve Bayes	0.72	0.76	0.85	0.810
Support vector machine	0.69	0.69	0.99	0.820
Neural networks	0.71	0.73	0.91	0.810

Of the six algorithms used, random forest had the highest classification accuracy, precision and *F-score*.

4.5   Discussion

To better understand why some posts receive negative scores and others receive positive scores, we set out to investigate any differences in posts with positive scores and those with negative scores based on the following criteria: (1) the time of day the post was created, (2) sentiments and emotions used in writing the posts (3) the length of the post and (4) topics that the posts were tagged with. We further developed and tested a model to predict if a post will receive positive or negative scores using these criteria and six machine learning algorithms.

Our results show significant differences in the scores received by posts based on the time of day the posts were created. Our results suggest that posts with positive scores created between 6:01 pm and 12:00 am had significantly higher scores on average than posts created at other times of the day. Thus, in order to avoid negative scores on their posts and possibly receive higher positive scores, authors could consider posting questions and answers between 6:01 pm and 12:00 am.

According to the LIWC tool[12], the dimension *analytic* represents the extent to which people use formal words, and how logical and hierarchical their thinking patterns are. People low in analytical thinking typically write in more narrative ways, use less of formal logic and rely on knowledge gained from personal experiences [31]. On

---

[12]   http://liwc.wpengine.com/interpreting-liwc-output/.

the other hand, people high in analytical thinking use formal logic, are more detailed in their explanations and avoid contradiction [31]. Our results show that the posts with negative scores are less analytical than those with positive scores. This suggests that posts with negative scores are written with less formal words, little logic and fewer explanations. Thus, in order to avoid low scores, authors should post questions and answers in Stack Overflow using more logic, detailed explanations and more formal technical words.

The dimension *clout*, as defined by the LIWC tool, is an indication of the social status, confidence or leadership displayed by an individual through their writing or speaking. People with higher clout typically use more first-person plural (such as "we") and second-person singular pronouns (such as "you"). In addition, they use fewer first-person singular pronouns (such as "I") [22]. People in this category tend to focus their attention outwards, towards the people they are interacting with. On the other hand, people low in clout are more self-focused and use more first-person singular pronouns (such as "I") [22]. Our results show that posts with positive scores are written by people who have high clout. This suggests that posts with positive scores are written in a way to focus attention outwards and not in words on the writer. Such posts are also written with less use first-person singular pronouns and more use of first-person plural (such as "we") and second-person singular pronouns (such as "you"). We therefore suggest that authors who post questions and answers in Stack Overflow should use fewer first-person singular pronouns.

People that are high in the dimension *authenticity*, according to the LIWC tool, reveal themselves to others (through their writing) in a more honest way. Such people are more personal, humble and vulnerable. On the other hand, people that are lower in authenticity use words that show lower cognitive complexity and more negative emotion words [30]. Our results show that posts with positive scores display less authenticity compare to posts with negative scores. Thus, in order to avoid negative scores, authors should post questions and answers using words that show less of their personal side and their vulnerability. These could include using words with higher cognitive complexity and positive emotions [30].

There was significant difference in the average length of posts between posts with positive scores and those with negative scores; the former had an average word count of 231 while the latter had an average word count of 152. This suggests that users who create posts with negative scores could improve their posts by writing more words that better explain their questions/answers. This is in line with other researchers that suggest that the length of a post is an influencing factor of the score the post will receive [11, 35].

We developed a predictive model using word count, the dimensions of sentiment and emotions: *analytic, clout, authentic, tone,* and time of day to predict if a post will receive a positive or negative score. We tested our model using six classification algorithms: logistic regression, random forest, k-nearest neighbor, Naïve Bayes, support vector machine, and neural networks and evaluated them using the classification accuracy, precision, recall. Random forest performed best with a classification accuracy of 73%, a precision of 77% and recall of 87%. Changing the number of trees from 5 to 100 had no effect on the accuracy of classification. This result is in line with previous research on prediction in Stack Overflow [7, 11]. Our results suggest that users could predict if their posts will receive a positive or negative score using the features length of the post, the dimensions of sentiment and emotions: *analytic, clout, authentic, tone,* and time of day the post was created using random forest algorithm.

5 Conclusion and Future Work

Voting is central to the model of providing quality posts in Stack Overflow. According to Stack Overflow, an upvote indicates that a post is interesting, well researched and useful, while a down vote indicates the opposite. People can earn rewards such as reputation, privileges and badges when their posts get upvoted. To encourage people to write good posts (which could lead to upvotes), Stack Overflow has a "How to ask" guide with suggestions on how to write good question posts and a similar one, "How do I write a good answer" with suggestions on how to write good answer posts. Despite these measures by Stack Overflow to ensure quality of posts, there are still several posts with negative scores. A post with a negative score indicates that the post received more down votes than upvotes. Negative scores could have a negative influence on users' participation; if a user keeps getting negative scores on their posts, they could be discouraged from using the network. To better understand the scores received by posts, we investigated differences in some features of posts with positive scores and negative scores. In particular, we compared the time of day the post was created, sentiments and emotions used in writing the posts, the length of the post, and the topics that the posts were tagged with for posts with negative scores and posts with positive scores. The result of our analysis suggests that posts between 6.01 pm and 12 am received significantly higher scores than posts written at other times of the day. In addition, posts with positive scores were significantly longer in length than posts with negative scores. Furthermore, posts with positive scores were significantly more analytical and clout and less authentic compared to posts with negative scores. To predict if a post will receive a positive or negative score, we developed and tested a predictive model using length of post, sentiment and time of day post was created. Using random forest machine learning algorithm, our model had a classification accuracy of 73%.

Our research is limited in a few ways. First, the sentiment and emotions expressed in posts were identified using the LIWC tool. Thus, the accuracy of the sentiments identified depends on the accuracy of the tool. The tool has been used widely by researchers who attest to its accuracy [34, 37]. Second, the number of posts we used in this study (over 14,000) only represents a small fraction of the number of all the posts in Stack Overflow. We plan to re-run this study on a larger scale.

In the future, we plan to re-run this study on a larger scale using different datasets for training and testing. In addition, we plan to explore if the number of negative votes people receive influence their participation in the network. For example, if their participation has any correlation with number of negative votes over time.

References

1. Zang, H.: The optimality of naive Bayes. Am. Assoc. Artif. Intell. **1**(2), 3 (2004)
2. Adaji, I., Oyibo, K., Vassileva, J.: Understanding low review ratings in online communities: a personality based approach. In: CEUR Workshop Proceedings (2018)
3. Adaji, I., Sharmaine, C., Debrowney, S., Oyibo, K., Vassileva, J.: Personality based recipe recommendation using recipe network graphs. In: Meiselwitz, G. (ed.) SCSM 2018. LNCS, vol. 10914, pp. 161–170. Springer, Cham (2018). https://doi.org/10.1007/978-3-319-91485-5_12
4. Adaji, I., Vassileva, J.: Modelling user collaboration in social networks using edits and comments. In: UMAP 2016 - Proceedings of the 2016 Conference on User Modeling Adaptation and Personalization (2016)
5. Adaji, I., Vassileva, J.: Personalizing social influence strategies in a Q&A social network. In: UMAP 2017 - Adjunct Publication of the 25th Conference on User Modeling, Adaptation and Personalization, Bratislava, pp. 215–220 (2017)
6. Adaji, I., Vassileva, J.: Persuasive patterns in Q&A social networks. In: Meschtscherjakov, A., Ruyter, B., Fuchsberger, V., Murer, M., Tscheligi, M. (eds.) PERSUASIVE 2016. LNCS, vol. 9638, pp. 189–196. Springer, Cham (2016). https://doi.org/10.1007/978-3-319-31510-2_16
7. Adaji, I., Vassileva, J.: Predicting churn of expert respondents in social networks using data mining techniques: a case study of stack overflow. In: 2015 IEEE 14th International Conference on Machine Learning and Applications (ICMLA), Florida, pp. 182–189, December 2015
8. Adaji, I., Vassileva, J.: Susceptibility of users to social influence strategies and the influence of culture in a Q&A collaborative learning environment. In: Gutwin, C., Ochoa, S., Vassileva, J., Inoue, T. (eds.) CRIWG 2017. LNCS, vol. 10391, pp. 49–64. Springer, Cham (2017). https://doi.org/10.1007/978-3-319-63874-4_5
9. Adaji, I., Vassileva, J.: Towards understanding user participation in stack overflow using profile data. In: Spiro, E., Ahn, Y.-Y. (eds.) SocInfo 2016. LNCS, vol. 10047, pp. 3–13. Springer, Cham (2016). https://doi.org/10.1007/978-3-319-47874-6_1
10. Adaji, I., Vassileva, J.: Towards understanding users' motivation in a Q&A social network using social influence and the moderation by culture. In: UMAP 2017 - Proceedings of the 25th Conference on User Modeling, Adaptation and Personalization, pp. 349–350 (2017)
11. Asaduzzaman, M., Mashiyat, A.S., Roy, C.K., Schneider, K.A.: Answering questions about unanswered questions of stack overflow (2013)
12. Bazelli, B., Hindle, A., Stroulia, E.: On the personality traits of stackoverflow users. In: 2013 IEEE International Conference on Software Maintenance, pp. 460–463, September 2013
13. Bhat, V., Gokhale, A., Jadhav, R., Pudipeddi, J., Akoglu, L.: Min(e)d your tags: analysis of question response time in stackoverflow. In: IEEE/ACM International Conference on Advances in Social Networks Analysis and Mining, pp. 328–335 (2014)
14. Bousquet, O., Boucheron, S., Lugosi, G.: Introduction to statistical learning theory. In: Bousquet, O., von Luxburg, U., Rätsch, G. (eds.) ML -2003. LNCS (LNAI), vol. 3176, pp. 169–207. Springer, Heidelberg (2004). https://doi.org/10.1007/978-3-540-28650-9_8
15. Buckland, M., Gey, F.: The relationship between recall and precision. J. Am. Soc. Inf. Sci. **45**(1), 12–19 (1994). https://doi.org/10.1002/(SICI)1097-4571(199401)45:1%3c12:AID-ASI2%3e3.0.CO;2-L
16. Buitinck, L., Louppe, G., Blondel, M., Pedregosa, F.: API design for machine learning software: experiences from the scikit-learn project. In: European Conference on Machine Learning and Principles and Practices of Knowledge Discovery in Databases (2013)

17. Filipczuk, J., Pesce, E., Senatore, S.: Sentiment detection for predicting altruistic behaviors in Social Web: A case study. In: 2016 IEEE International Conference on Systems, Man, and Cybernetics (SMC), pp. 004377–004382, October 2016
18. Gantayat, N., Dhoolia, P., Padhye, R., Mani, S., Sinha, V.S.: The synergy between voting and acceptance of answers on stackOverflow - or the lack thereof. In: 2015 IEEE/ACM 12th Working Conference on Mining Software Repositories, pp. 406–409, May 2015
19. Girden, E.R.: ANOVA: Repeated Measures. SAGE, Beverley Hills (1992)
20. James, G., Witten, D., Hastie, T., Tibshirani, R.: An Introduction to Statistical Learning. Springer, New York (2013). https://doi.org/10.1007/978-1-4614-7138-7
21. Kacewicz, E., Pennebaker, J.W., Davis, M., Jeon, M., Graesser, A.C.: Pronoun use reflects standings in social hierarchies. J. Soc. Psychol. 33(2), 125–143 (2014). https://doi.org/10.1177/0261927X13502654
22. Khobzi, H., Lau, R., Cheung, T.: Consumers' sentiments and popularity of brand posts in social media: the moderating role of up-votes. In: Hawaii International Conference on System Sciences, Hawaii (2017)
23. Kucuktunc, O., Cambazoglu, B.B., Weber, I., Ferhatosmanoglu, H.: A large-scale sentiment analysis for Yahoo! answers. In: Proceedings of the fifth ACM international Conference on Web Search and Data Mining, pp. 633–642 (2012)
24. Kuhn, M., Johnson, K.: Applied Predictive Modeling. Springer, New York (2013). https://doi.org/10.1007/978-1-4614-6849-3
25. Liaw, A., Wiener, M.: Classification and regression by random forest. Newslett. R Project. 2(3), 18–22 (2002)
26. Lima, E., Mues, C., Baesens, B.: Domain knowledge integration in data mining using decision tables: case studies in churn prediction. J. Oper. Res. Soc. 60(8), 1096–1106 (2009)
27. Migueis, V.L., van den Poel, D., Camanho, A.S., e Cunha, J.F.: Modeling partial customer churn: on the value of first product-category purchase sequences. Expert Syst. Appl. 39(12), 11250–11256 (2012). https://doi.org/10.1016/j.eswa.2012.03.073
28. Nasehi, S.M., Sillito, J., Maurer, F., Burns, C.: What makes a good code example?: A study of programming Q& a in StackOverflow. In: 2012 28th IEEE International Conference on Software Maintenance (ICSM), pp. 25–34, September 2012)
29. Newman, M.L., Pennebaker, J.W., Berry, D.S., Richards, J.M.: Lying words: predicting deception from linguistic styles. Pers. Soc. Psychol. Bul. 29(5), 665–675 (2003). https://doi.org/10.1177/0146167203029005010
30. Nisbett, R., Peng, K., Choi, I., Norenzayan, A.: Culture and systems of thought: holistic versus analytic cognition. Psychol. Rev. 108(2), 291 (2001)
31. Pedregosa, F., et al.: Scikit-learn: machine learning in Python. J. Mach. Learn. Res. 12, 2825–2830 (2011)
32. Pennebaker, J. Linguistic inquiry and word count: LIWC 2001 (2001). downloads.liwc.net.s3.amazonaws
33. Pennebaker, J.W., Chung, C.K., Frazee, J., Lavergne, G.M., Beaver, D.I.: When small words foretell academic success: the case of college admissions essays. PLoS ONE 9(12), e115844 (2014). https://doi.org/10.1371/journal.pone.0115844
34. Ponzanelli, L., Mocci, A., Bacchelli, A., Lanza, M., Fullerton, D.: Improving low quality stack overflow post detection. In: Software Maintenance and Evolution, pp. 541–544 (2014)
35. Romero, D.M., Uzzi, B., Kleinberg, J.: Social networks under stress. In: Proceedings of the 25th International Conference on World Wide Web - WWW 2016, New York, USA, pp. 9–20 (2016)
36. Tausczik, Y.R., Pennebaker, J.W.: The psychological meaning of words: LIWC and computerized text analysis methods. J. Language Soc. Psychol. 29(1), 24–54 (2010). https://doi.org/10.1177/0261927X09351676

<caption>498   I. Adaji et al.</caption>

37. Thorleuchter, D., Van den Poel, D.: Predicting e-commerce company success by mining the text of its publicly-accessible website. Expert Syst. Appl. **39**(17), 13026 (2012). https://doi.org/10.1016/j.eswa.2012.05.096
38. Verbeke, W., Martens, D., Mues, C., Baesens, B.: Building comprehensible customer churn prediction models with advanced rule induction techniques. Expert Syst. Appl. **38**(3), 2354–2364 (2011). https://doi.org/10.1016/j.eswa.2010.08.023
39. Yao, Y., Tong, H., Xie, T., Akoglu, L., Xu, F., Lu, J.: Detecting high-quality posts in community question answering sites. Inf. Sci. **302**(2015), 70–82 (2015). https://doi.org/10.1016/j.ins.2014.12.038

From the Street to the Tweet: Applying Task Technology Fit to Examine the Information Technology Role in Revolutionizing Social Movements

Fadi Almazyad$^{(\boxtimes)}$ and Eleanor Loiacono$^{(\boxtimes)}$

Worcester Polytechnic Institute, Worcester, MA 01609, USA
{falmazyad, eloiacono}@wpi.edu

Abstract. The aim of this paper is to examine the role of social media technologies in revolutionizing consumer activism by applying the theory of Task Technology Fit (TTF) model. Due to the affordability of getting internet connection, there has been a surge in the use of social media platforms which simplify the communication and interaction between people around the world. People now are more enthusiastic to join and use social media platforms to exchange information with people who share same interests. Social media did not just change how people communicate with each other, but it changed how businesses and corporations communicate with their customers. Another common application of social media is activism. With the help of social media platforms, activists can start a social movement immediately and reach a global audience. In the case of activism, the Task Technology Fit is evaluating whether the technology's functionality meets the task requirements or not. The technology in this context is social media platforms.

Keywords: Social media · Task Technology Fit · Activism ·
Social movements

1 Introduction

The aim of this paper is to examine the role of social media technologies in revolutionizing consumer activism by applying the theory of Task Technology Fit (TTF) model. The case that this paper uses is the SURGE movement. In 1997, Coca Cola introduced SURGE, a citrus flavored soft drink. However, in 2002 the SURGE brand was discontinued due to falling sales and a change in the company's strategy. Some SURGE consumers were infuriated with Coca Cola's decision. So, on December 23, 2011 these enthusiastic, brand loyalists started a social media movement on Facebook called the Surge Movement (see Fig. 1) and later added a less popular Twitter account for the movement (see Fig. 2). The "SURGE Movement" is a centralized community of SURGE fans, whose mission was and continues to remain "the return of SURGE Soda and... making SURGE a sustainable brand (The SURGE Movement). The movement received support from more than 352,000 Facebook

© Springer Nature Switzerland AG 2019
G. Meiselwitz (Ed.): HCII 2019, LNCS 11578, pp. 499–505, 2019.
https://doi.org/10.1007/978-3-030-21902-4_35

followers. The movement leaders were communicating with Coca Cola for two years before Coca Cola capitulated and re-introduced SURGE back into the market in 2014.

Fig. 1. Surge movement Facebook page

Fig. 2. Surge movement Twitter account

2 Literature Review

The internet enables people to easily communicate with each other (Thomsen et al. 1998). Specifically, people are able to connect over the internet using chat rooms, bulletin boards, forms and blogs (De Valck et al. 2009). The rapid development of Information Technology (IT) and communication produced the Web 2.0, which is defined as a collection of technological artifacts that allow instant communication between people around the world at a low cost (Habibi et al. 2013). Due to the affordability of getting an internet connection, there was a surge in the use of social media platforms which simplify the communication and interaction between people around the world.

Kaplan and Haenlein (2010) define social media as "a group of Internet-based applications that build on the ideological and technological foundations of Web 2.0, which allows the creation and exchange of user-generated content". Social Media platforms are viewed as a new trend which can impact businesses and people's social life (Lin and Lu 2011). Facebook, one of the most popular social media platforms has 2.19 billion active users at the end of the third quarter of 2018 (Facebook 2018). Another Social Media platform that is attracting people is Twitter, which has 336 million active users by the end of the third quarter of 2018. People now are more enthusiastic to join and use social media platforms to exchange information with people who share same interests (Powell 2009). Social media did not just change how people communicate with each other, but it also changed how businesses and corporations communicate with their customers.

Today, Facebook is the most used Social Media platform to create online brand communities. Companies such as Coca Cola, Nike, Apple, Microsoft and Samsung all have fans pages on Facebook with more than 400 million followers together (Social-bakers.com). Through these fan pages, companies can interact with their followers (customers) by posting photos or videos (Vries et al. 2012, p. 84). In addition to that, social media pages are rich in information that is critical in understanding customers' needs and thoughts (Luo et al. 2013). However, social media fan pages can work the other way as well. Instead of being sponsored by the business, these fan pages could be created and controlled entirely by customers to communicate with other customers to share product experience and services.

Another common application of social media is activism. With the help of social media platforms, activists can start a social change movement (see Fig. 3) immediately and reach global audience. Social media provides activists with information and news that were not available through mainstream media (Valenzuela 2013). From the Arab Springs to Occupy Wall Street to Me too movements, all these social and political movements would not reach a global audience if it was not for the use of social media.

This model is borrowed from the book "A Social Change Model of Leadership". Change here is the goal of activists who are not satisfied with the status que. Activists at the individual level must be consciousness of self which means aware of what makes one enthusiastic to act. Congruence means thinking consistency about others with honesty. Commitment here means a person who has the commitment to act and serve his/her own believes about the change. At the group level, there are characteristics that are shred among activists. Collaboration is to work in harmony within the group toward a common goal which is the common purpose. Controversy with civility means the ability to accommodate the different viewpoints within the group and talk about them to bring them close to the common goal. At the society level, citizenship means the ability to be member of the community and work toward bringing positive change to the community (Higher Education Research Institute 1996).

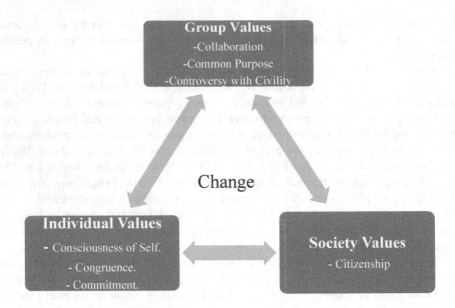

Fig. 3. Social change model

3 Task Technology Fit Theory

Task Technology Fit (TTF) theory is a model developed by Goodhue and Thompson (see Fig. 4). The goal of the TTF model is to assess the impact of using IT on individual performance. To assure the success of the technology utilization, the technology must fit the task for which it is intended to be used.

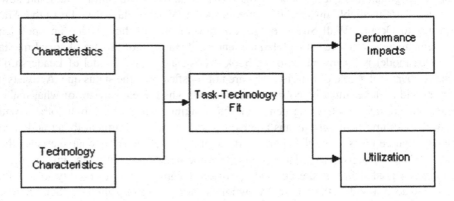

Source: Goodhue and Thompson, (1995)

Fig. 4. Task technology fit model

The TTF model shows that to have high performance impact and high utilization, technology characteristics must meet task characteristics in the technology fit. If the gap between task characteristics and technology characteristics increases, the model will produce low score in task technology fit, which will result in low performance impact and utilization (Goodhue and Thompson 1995). In the TTF model, technologies are defined as "tools used by individuals in carrying out their tasks" (p. 216, Goodhue and Thompson 1995). In the context of information technology, social media platforms are referred to as technology in the model. Task is defined as "the actions carried out by individuals in turning inputs into out puts" (p. 216, Goodhue and Thompson 1995). In the context of activism, an individual expressing his or her opinion to start a movement is considered a task. This task has characteristics such as mission and goals.

Task Technology Fit is defined as "the degree to which a technology assists an individual in performing his or her portfolio tasks" (p. 216, Goodhue and Thompson, 1995). In the case of activism, the Task Technology Fit is evaluating whether the technology's functionality meets the task requirements or not. The technology in this context is social media platforms.

Although Goodhue and Thompson stated that the utilization construct is not well explained and understood, they defined it as "the behavior of employing the technology in completing tasks. Measures such as the frequency of use or the diversity of applications employed" (p. 218, Goodhue and Thompson 1995). In activism, utilization would be considered as the reuse frequency of the same social media to start an activism. In the TTF model, utilization includes both mandatory and voluntary utilization. However, in activism, the use and utilization of social media platforms is completely voluntary. The last construct in the model is performance impact, and it is used to assess the accomplishment of the task performed by the individual. In the context of activism, it will assess whether the activism movement accomplished its goal or not.

The SURGE movement has a mission which is "the return of SURGE Soda and… making SURGE a sustainable brand (The SURGE Movement). This mission is the task and social media represented by Facebook is the technology, the TTF construct is used to determine the degree of fitness. The purpose of the task must be considered carefully in the construct of task technology fit. When combining tasks with the selected technology in the task technology fit construct, the technology (Facebook) must meet the task characteristics (SURGE Movement mission and goal). For example, the SURGE movement's mission was to bring the product back and keep the community connected regarding the product, so the use of Facebook as the technology was appropriate. This fit is due to the popularity of Facebook and the many features it provides for its users such as creating pages and connecting with others who share same interests. Performance impact and utilization are in the model to examine how successful was the technology characteristic meeting the task characteristic. The output of the selected social movement measures the performance impact and utilization.

TTF theory has been studied in many IT research; Dishaw and Strong (1998) applied TTF theory to asses software maintenance which titled as "Assessing software maintenance tool utilization using task-technology fit and fitness-for-use models" (Dishaw and Strong 1998). D'Ambra and Wilson applied the TTF theory to explain World Wide Web performance with uncertainty (D'Ambra and Wilson 2004). Ferratt and Vlahos evaluated how computer-based information systems (CBIS) help managers in decision making; their research titled as "An investigation of task-technology fit for managers in Greece and the US." (Ferratt and Vlahos 1998). However, to our knowledge, there is no study that applied TTF theory to social media platforms to validate the model. TTF has not been applied to examine how IT represented by social media platforms transformed activism.

4   Research Method and Data Collection

We have collected data from the SURGE Movement fan page to analyze what people are posting, commenting and sharing. We extracted all posts and comments that have been posted by the organizers or followers. These posts and comments will be analyzed using Nvivo 12 Plus.

In addition, we will collect data using online surveys and interviews. For the online survey, we will invite people who are part of the SURGE Movement fan page to participate in the survey; the survey will solicit data about their opinions on participating in this consumer activism by using the social media platform. In addition, we will contact organizers of this movement to ask them to participate in this survey and conduct an interview with them to understand their decision about using social media platforms for consumer activism. We are planning to perform factor analysis on data collected from the survey and qualitative analysis from the interview. Quantitative data from the survey will measure people's view of social media platforms as a tool for consumer activism. Qualitative data from interviews with the organizers will examine their tool selection and how they evaluated their selection against alternative options.

5   Discussion

Since the task is consumer activism in this context, through this research we will better understand how consumer activism works. There is a need to integrate a theory that explains social movement and consumer activism with TTF theory. Applying the theory will help evaluate the task characteristic and ease the selection for the fit technology that will meet task characteristic. Since there are many social media platforms, each one having a different set of features and limitations that will influence the decisions of people selecting one over the others in the context of consumer activism. For example, Facebook is a popular platform for fans pages whereas Twitter is popular in the use of customer experience and boycott movements. Depending on the task and the movement mission, selecting the right platform for the task is critical for achieving activists goals'.

6 Implication and Conclusion

The results of this study will help both academics and practitioners. For academics, it will bridge the gap regarding the role that social media plays in transforming social media movements. It will enlighten designers of future social media platforms that there might be other uses of their tool in the future than initially projected. Facebook was intended as an entertainment and relationship platform for college students. Designers must consider how social media now is used by social movements to deliver their messages to a large global audience.

References

Austin, H.S., Austin, A.: A Social Change Model of Leadership. Higher Education Research Institute-University of California, Los Angeles (1996)

De Valck, K., Van Bruggen, G.H., Wierenga, B.: Virtual communities: a marketing perspective. Decis. Support Syst. **47**(3), 185–203 (2009)

De Vries, L., Gensler, S., Leeflang, P.S.: Popularity of brand posts on brand fan pages: an investigation of the effects of social media marketing. J. Interact. Mark. **26**(2), 83–91 (2012)

Goodhue, D.L., Thompson, R.L.: Task-technology fit and individual performance. MIS Q. **19**, 213–236 (1995)

Kaplan, A.M., Haenlein, M.: Users of the world, unite! The challenges and opportunities of Social Media. Bus. Horiz. **53**(1), 59–68 (2010)

Laroche, M., Habibi, M.R., Richard, M.-O.: To be or not to be in social media: how brand loyalty is affected by social media? Int. J. Inf. Manag. **33**(1), 76–82 (2013)

Lu, H.-P., Yang, Y.-W.: Toward an understanding of the behavioral intention to use a social networking site: an extension of task-technology fit to social-technology fit. Comput. Hum. Behav. **34**, 323–332 (2014)

Luo, X., Zhang, J., Duan, W.: Social media and firm equity value. Inf. Syst. Res. **24**(1), 146–163 (2013)

Powell, J.: 33 Million People in the Room: How to Create, Influence, and Run a Successful Business with Social Networking. Que Publishing, London (2009)

Thomsen, S.R., Straubhaar, J.D., Bolyard, D.M.: Ethnomethodology and the study of online communities: exploring the cyber streets. Inf. Res. **4**(1), 4-1 (1998)

Valenzuela, S.: Unpacking the use of social media for protest behavior. Am. Behav. Sci. **57**(7), 920–942 (2013). https://doi.org/10.1177/0002764213479375

The Olympic Games as a Multicultural Environment and Their Relationship with Social Media

Devena Haggis[1][✉] and Simona Vasilache[2]

[1] Faculty of Health and Sport Sciences, University of Tsukuba, Tsukuba, Japan
haggis.devena.pen.gf@u.tsukuba.ac.jp
[2] Graduate School of Systems and Information Engineering,
University of Tsukuba, Tsukuba, Japan
simona@cs.tsukuba.ac.jp

Abstract. 'Multicultural' can be defined as relating to or containing several cultural or ethnic groups within a society and is used to encompass different cultures, groups, and relationships within a specific context. The sporting context of the Olympic Games could be considered a multicultural environment in addition to being a multi-sport environment and a mega sporting event. It is also an arena for intercultural adaptation as the athletes, event staff, visitors and audience are exposed to social media at the event. The athletes establish and maintain relationships among each other and with others in their own countries and the international audience also interacts and communicates with the athletes and the Games via social media. This communication and interaction affect and reinforce the intercultural adaptation and the multi-cultural environment of the Olympic Games.

Much has been made of the preparations for the Tokyo 2020 Olympic and Paralympic Games, with the media dubbing the games the most 'futuristic' yet, given the advanced technology and innovation of Japan. Social media is considered an important component of the Olympic games, in the lead up to and at each edition of the games. These aspects of sport and social media at the Olympic Games are of interest due to their interaction and the creation and reinforcement of a multicultural environment. This paper will explore the social media impact and the multicultural environment of the Olympic Games through a review of social media usage leading up to the Tokyo 2020 games.

Keywords: Social media · Olympic games · Multicultural environment

1 Background

In ancient Greece the Olympic Games represented an event that focused on the educational, religious, athletic and self-development aspects of the human condition. It promoted the integral development of body and mind, in tandem, to produce an athlete whose performance at the games would match this ideal as well as contribute to the development of society. In addition, the period of travel to and from the games, the event itself and the city of Olympia were protected by the 'Olympic Truce', when all

© Springer Nature Switzerland AG 2019
G. Meiselwitz (Ed.): HCII 2019, LNCS 11578, pp. 506–523, 2019.
https://doi.org/10.1007/978-3-030-21902-4_36

armed conflict between warring states was suspended and as such represent early Olympism and unique peace building efforts [1]. The unity of the body and mind, the development of human beings and self-improvement through participation in sport are the components that Pierre de Coubertin would later focus on in his efforts to revive the Olympic Games [2]. Therefore, the Olympic Games were not just a sporting event, but they also served socio-cultural purposes and provided a multi-cultural, educational, religious and sporting environment in which the athletes, protagonists and public interacted. Elements of these concepts have been implemented within the Olympic movement since the first modern Olympic Games in 1896. Media was used in 1896 to report on the Games, but the limited technology of the written press and newsreels meant the impact of the medium was distant from the actual events of the Games. However, the development of media had an incremental effect on engagement and connectiveness of the public and the athletes with the Games, culminating in the present with social media positioning itself as an influential medium of communication and significant contributor to the creation of a global multicultural environment within the context of the Olympic Games.

2 Introduction

Much has been made of the preparations for the Tokyo 2020 Olympic and Paralympic Games in the media, which have dubbed the games the most 'futuristic' yet, given the advanced technology and innovation expected to be on show for the global audience [3]. It is assumed that the Games will use cutting-edge technology to "ensure the security of contestants and the public, to bring unprecedented coverage to a global audience, and to provide seamless convenience for visitors" [4]. Continuing the tradition of media innovation at the Olympics "Tokyo 2020 will use new technology and media platforms to ensure Olympic fans everywhere can take part in the Olympic atmosphere" [5]. These initiatives follow on from the increasing and diversified use of media platforms in previous Olympics. Very few people have the opportunity to attend the Olympic Games in person, therefore the dissemination of the Olympic Games, the Olympic atmosphere and the Olympic values is necessary to bridge the engagement gap between the Olympics as a mega sports event and the public as the watchers, consumers, associates or participants. The sheer size and scope of the Olympic Games, hosting athletes from various countries (206 countries for Rio 2016) and hosting an audience of billions via various forms of media suggest that it could be considered the largest multicultural event in the world.

Culture has always been an integral part of the ancient and modern Olympic Games; the culture and traditions derived from the Greek games; the culture of the hosting city and country; the athlete culture of the participants; and since the advent of media, the culture of engagement and interaction during the Olympic Games by the public as consumers and social participants. Prior to the advent of media, public exposure to the Olympic Games was less diverse. In this sense, the Olympic Games can be considered a sporting and a social event [6] not only for the athletes, but also for the public who are socially and culturally engaged for the duration of the games. The rapid and extensive changes in broadcasting forms for Athens (2004), Beijing (2008) and

London (2012) onwards highlight the impact of social media on the Olympic games as a cultural and multicultural sporting event [7]. The term 'socialympics', used initially in relation to London 2012, has been used to define the rapid proliferation and use of social media at the Olympic Games and the facilitation of communication and interaction between the diverse global communities.

Similarly, the preparations for Tokyo 2020 also represent aspects of the incorporation and adaptation of social media for sporting events and a recognition of its significance. The importance of social media within the Olympic context is shown by the creation of guidelines related to social media and the Olympics by the International Olympic Committee (IOC) initially for the London 2012 Olympics [8] and later amended for other editions of the Games. The IOC can, to some extent, control the images of the Games that are disseminated around the world; however, technology develops so quickly that, in order to have some input into the process of dissemination, it must also relinquish some control. Social media therefore is considered an important component of the Olympic games, both during the lead up to and at each edition of the games itself.

Social media interactions provide the basis for communication and adaptation within the multicultural and intercultural environment of the Olympic Games which must be acknowledged. Thomas Bach, the president of the International Olympic Committee (IOC) stated: "People today are connecting with the Olympic Games in more ways than ever before, they are doing so digitally, and they are doing so on mobile. This is not a challenge to overcome. This is a huge opportunity to reach even more people with the values of sport and the magic of the Olympic Games" [9]. Therefore, the digitalization of the Games and by extension the adaptation, implementation and focus on portable media use highlight the importance of social media within this environment. The extent to which athletes, the audience, the public and the community interact and communicate via social media in relation to the Olympic Games is becoming increasingly important.

Considering this mega sport event environment and its relationship with social media, these interactions are played out within a multicultural global context. The sport event reflects a multicultural environment due to the combination and interaction of the athletes, associates and the social participants from various nations. For the period of the Games, different cultures are mixed, merged, blended and dispersed via the personal and interpersonal contact of social media. During the Olympic Games, all those who connect with the Games in some way, however brief, become a part of the Olympic family, and media, and more recently social media, have played a dominant role. Sugden and Tomlinson suggest that global sporting events such as the Olympic Games are unique in that they play a distinct role in the creation, management and mediation of cultural meanings [10]. This is especially true within the context of connecting with the Games. These myriad ways of creating and maintaining engagement, connections and interactions provide the mechanism by which the Olympic Games mediate and reflect multiculturalism as a core component of the social milieu and outreach of the event.

3   Multiculturalism

In its broadest sense, the term 'multicultural' is defined as "relating to or containing several cultural or ethnic groups within a society" [11]. As such, the term can be used to encompass different cultures, groups and relationships within a specific context. This assumes the acceptance and integration of diverse groups within a nation or cultural group. If the Olympic Games is considered a cultural group (i.e. sport) as well as a multicultural environment, the interactivity and integration between the participants and the public must also be understood within the sport event and social media context. According to Traganou [12], although based on a universal narrative, the Olympics also reflect the idea of 'nation' and of the world being divided into nations. Despite the competitive aspect of the Games, it is an interesting juxtaposition, given its aim of inclusiveness and the multicultural environment represented, disseminated and reinforced by the use of media to connect people with the games and provide opportunities for interaction. This multicultural aspect of the games is advanced through media and reinforced by the use of social media, as it removes the engagement/interaction gap between the Olympic Games, the athletes and the public.

4   Intercultural Adaptation

This gap creates an environment whereby connections are brought closer, made, enhanced, re-made, redefined, extended or cut, as people come together either physically or digitally, by connecting with the Olympic Games. Involvement with the Games, within the context of social media, therefore, does not necessitate the presence of the actor (although presence is possible) at the Olympic Games, given that the interactions that help create this multicultural environment are dispersed. This creates an environment of interculturalism and intercultural adaptation between the different groups. Interculturalism refers to the interaction, understanding and communication of people from different cultural and ethnic backgrounds when they associate with each other. Within the context of the Games, this can be understood to mean the connection or association of people via social media.

Due to the myriad of interactions that occur between people of diverse cultural and social backgrounds and geographical distances, social media becomes one vehicle through which people engage with each other at the Games. This engagement also requires intercultural adaptation to mitigate the multicultural aspects of engagement at the event. The Olympic Games is a unique event held every four years and provides a challenging competitive environment for the participating athletes who must adapt to often strange conditions. Athlete or sport cultures may vary between nations, teams or groups of athletes within the same team, creating circumstances whereby adaptation is necessary. Social media provides a medium for athletes to communicate and interact with others from their own cultural, ethnic and national communities, facilitating long-distance intercultural adaptation through communication. Likewise, the audience gains access to the multicultural environment via their interaction with the various media.

5 Multiculturalism at the Olympic Games

The proliferation of social media has ensured that during the brief period of the Olympic Games, this mega sport event encompasses a multi-cultural global environment which extends beyond usual geographical and community interactions. As such, the sporting environment, specifically the Olympic Games, could be considered a manifestation of a multicultural environment in addition to being a multi-sport environment and a mega sporting event. It is an event that facilitates and exhibits Verkuytens's [13] contention that the fostering of multiculturalism requires a necessary understanding and appreciation of ethnic diversity as well as the inclusion of minority cultures and identities. A recent example of this in relation to the Games is the creation of the 'Refugee Olympic Team' for the Rio 2016 Olympic Games and its reconstitution for the Tokyo 2020 Olympic and Paralympic Games [14].

This action reinforces the multiculturalism inherent in the Olympic Games as an event and the associated ethics of equality that are implied in the Olympic values of *friendship, respect* and *excellence*, the Paralympic values of *determination, inspiration, courage* and *equality*, and the UN Sustainable Development Goals of *gender equality* (Goal 5) and *reduced inequality* (Goal 10) [15]. These values provide the ethical and philosophical foundations of universal principles that are applied together with multiculturalism and diversity within the context of the Olympic Games in order to foster the same in lives and society. As well as being a multicultural environment, the Olympic Games is also an arena for intercultural adaptation as the athletes, event staff, visitors and even the audience are exposed to social media as a vehicle to learn about the host country's culture and vice versa. The athletes also establish and maintain relationships among each other and stay in touch with events in their own countries and conversely the international audience also interacts and communicates with the athletes and the Games through the provision of media and social media. As such, the communication and interaction occurring through the influences of media and social media also affects and reinforces the intercultural adaptation and the multicultural environment of the Olympic Games.

6 Media and the Olympic Games

The IOC broadcast policy is described in Rule 48 of the Olympic Charter as, "the IOC takes all necessary steps in order to ensure the fullest coverage by the different media and the widest possible audience in the world for the Olympic Games." [16]. Table 1 shows the progression, media type, content and first usage of the various media since the revival of the modern Olympic Games in 1896. Looking at the adoption and adaptation of new technology in successive Games, it is clear that the IOC from its inception sought to engage and encourage participation in the Olympic Games by the public audience. A milestone in media provision occurred with the creation of the Olympic Broadcasting Service in 2001 to serve as the host broadcaster for all Olympic editions, thereby negating the need to rebuild the broadcast operation for each new edition of the Games [17]. In recent times, the level of engagement has increased exponentially through the proliferation of digital platforms and content, emphasizing that the IOC has adapted well to the new media environment launching its own YouTube channel, the Olympic news channel and Olympic video player app.

Table 1. Development and implementation of media at the Olympic Games.

Olympics (*denotes winter Games)	Year	Media type, content and first usage
Athens	1896	Written press Newsreels (screened within weeks) [18]
Stockholm	1912	Newsreels (screened within days), Film [18]
Paris	1924	Limited live radio [18]
Berlin	1936	Full length feature film Television broadcast via closed circuit TV Live radio in 28 languages and 2,500 broadcasts [18]
London	1948	Worldwide radio broadcast Television broadcast up to 200 km from the Games venue [18]
Rome	1960	Live broadcast to 18 European countries [17]
Tokyo	1964	Satellite broadcast relays images overseas [17]
Mexico	1968	Slow motion footage available live [17]
*Sapporo	1972	Television feed provided to broadcasters [17]
*Lillehammer	1994	Satellite broadcasts to Africa begin [17]
*Nagano	1998	Video on demand and 3-D high definition [17]
Sydney	2000	Internet provision of specific news and results [19]
*Salt Lake City	2002	All winter events covered live [17]
Athens	2004	Internet streaming [18]
*Turin	2006	HDTV coverage Coverage available on mobile phones [17]
Beijing	2008	High definition broadcast Global digital coverage Digital platforms provide live and VOD access VOD, internet coverage & highlight clips for mobile phones IOC launches Beijing YouTube internet channel [20]
*Vancouver	2010	Full coverage on digital media coverage Debut of 24-h Olympic News Channel Mobile phone feed [21]
London	2012	Internet, mobile and other digital platforms exceed TV coverage for the first time Live 3-D coverage of opening and closing ceremonies and selected events [22]
*Sochi	2014	Digital coverage exceeds traditional broadcasting (winter games context) Launch of Olympic video player app. [17]
Rio	2016	Most consumed Games ever Digital coverage exceeds traditional broadcasting (summer games context) [17]
*Pyeong Chang	2018	Increased digital coverage over multiple platforms Biggest games ever on social media platforms [17]

6.1 Social Media and the Olympic Games

Despite the IOC's uptake and implementation of technology as shown in Table 1, a clear distinction needs to be made between more traditional forms of media and social media when considering media engagement at the Olympic Games in relation to the creation of a multicultural environment. This is because social media removes the gap between the audiences, the Games and the athletes, as these actors can respond immediately to digital interaction by tweet, post, blog, photo or other means. Therefore, for the purposes of this paper, social media is defined as the "digital platforms, services and apps that are built around the convergence of content sharing, public communication and interpersonal connection" [23].

Table 2 shows the development of media broadcast at the Olympic Games from Sydney 2000 until Pyeong Chang 2018. Sydney 2000 is considered to be the first Olympic Games where limited digital content was made available. The change in technology, its affordability and immediate accessibility are the prime reasons for the explosion in the use of social media at the Olympic Games from London 2012 onwards. According to the communications director of the London Organizing Committee of the Olympic Games (LOCOG), this reflects the fact that there was limited fast internet in Sydney (2000), limited access to smart phones in Athens (2004) and limited membership of social networks in Beijing 2008. As such, London 2012 is considered the first social media games because "…everyone has all that and will be consuming the games in a different way" [24]. As technology changed and it was incorporated into the Olympic Games, the way of measuring the engagement of the audience also changed.

Table 2. Olympic Games broadcast audience.

Olympic Games	Year	Television audience (billion)	Digital platforms		Social media platforms
			Unique user (billion)	Video views (billion)	Video views (billion)
Sydney [26]	**2000**	**3.7**	**0.23 page views**		
Salt Lake City [17]	2002	2.1			
Athens [17]	2004	3.9			
Turin [30]	2006	3.1			
Beijing [17]	**2008**	**3.5**	**0.4**	**0.7**	
Vancouver [17]	2010	1.8	0.13	0.3	
London [28]	2012	3.6	1.2	1.9	0.376 [27]
Sochi [17]	2014	2.1	0.3	1.4	
Rio de Janeiro [17]	**2016**	**3.2**	**1.3**	**4.4**	>7 [29]
Pyeong Chang [25]	2018	1.92	0.67	3.2	1.6

The provision of media and digital media content in relation to Table 2 can therefore be broken down into three distinct periods: Sydney 2000 until Beijing, Beijing 2008 until Rio and Rio 2016 onwards. For the Sydney 2000 Olympic Games, internet content/access became more widely available, although speeds were relatively low. The Sydney Olympics website received over 230 million page visits during a 17 day period [31]. This data is shown for reference only, as the data measurement and assessment for Salt Lake City, Athens and Turin varied. In addition, the IOC introduced Total Viewer Hours (TVH), a new method of measuring the Olympic television audience levels [31]. The figures in the Television Audience column represent the net number of people who saw at least one minute of the Olympic Games coverage [17]. From Beijing 2008, viewers were divided into television and digital audiences. Platform 'unique users' represent the number of different individuals who visit a site within a specific time frame and video views represent the number of times a video is watched [17]. From Rio 2016 onwards, viewership of the social media platforms was considered. The social media platforms 'video views' represent the official content viewed across platforms. The latter two editions of the Games, Pyeong Chang (winter) and Rio (summer) have the largest numbers of engagement via social media platforms.

6.2   Use of Social Media at the Olympic Games

Social media platforms encompass and celebrate the diversity of the multicultural environment that is the Olympic Games and actively promote and encourage association with the event. Social media facilitates and allows the integration of the user with the hosting community (the Olympic Games) [32]. The proliferation of mobile platforms like Twitter, Snapchat, Facebook and Instagram provide a way of linking people together through knowledge and behaviors, thereby creating a sense of belonging to a greater (global) network, larger than the local community [33]. Figure 1-left [34] shows Australian cross-country skier Phil Bellingham taking a selfie on Thursday, Feb. 8, at the Pyeong Chang Olympic Village in South Korea, during a welcoming ceremony. Figure 1-right [35] acknowledges the public and social perception of London 2012 being the 'social' Games or the 'twitter' Games. The icons associated with the athletes are instantly recognizable – their faces (who the athletes are does not matter) blocked out to represent the encompassing nature of the social media influence at the Games.

Fig. 1. Representation of social media and the Olympic Games: Pyeong Chang 2018 (left) and London 2012 (right).

This environment is created by official social content from the IOC, International Federations, rights holders and sponsors as well by 'unofficial' content from athletes and attendees and those not at the event but active on social media. The iconography also speaks to the less structured aspects of social media – the IOC increasingly has less control over the content and interactions between the athletes and their online/social media fans or communities.

7 Watchers, Consumers, Associates and Participants and the Extension of the Multicultural Environment

In considering the engagement of people with media and the Olympic Games and the creation and reinforcement of their multicultural environment, it is also necessary to define the different groups who make up the overall extended multicultural community and their relationship with each other. These groups, despite their distance from the Games, are connected with each other via media and social media and they create and reinforce the concept that the Olympic Games is a multicultural environment. Watchers comprise the audience that views the Olympic Games through any type of media. This audience consists of groups or individuals who are the most distant in terms of space to the event. *Consumers* are those at the Games, who experience the events first hand, but who are not participants. This group is present at the Games, therefore their social media profile is different from other types of audience, due to their immediacy with the event. *Associates* are the relatives, friends and communities associated or directly connected to the athlete participants; they have immediacy with the participants and reflect a different interaction. *Participants* comprise the athletes and national teams competing in the Games. All these groups interact and contribute to the intercultural adaptation and multiculturalism of the Olympic Games through their interactions. Community has evolved from being place-based to being space-based [36], as virtual communities have no constraints in relation to how, when and why they interact. The relationships of each of these groups to each other are shown in Figs. 2 and 3.

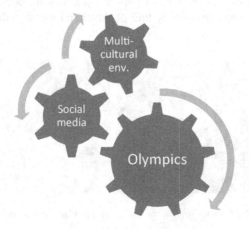

Fig. 2. Relationships between groups: components

Figure 2 shows the Olympics as the core component by which the multicultural environment of this global sporting mega event is formed and reinforced. Without the event to provide the context, 'social media' and 'multicultural' environment are disparate entities. Figure 3-left shows how social media connects the different groups to the Olympic Games, providing the impetus for engagement and closing the gap between the event, participants, audience, consumers and the associates. Chen [37] suggests that the distinctive nature of new media (e.g. social media) has facilitated the development of human interaction in an interconnected and complex way. Likewise, in Fig. 3-right the multicultural environment is created, maintained and reinforced by the connections made between the different groups. These include connections within the multicultural environment of the Olympic Games itself and within the virtual multicultural environment created and fostered through interactions on social media.

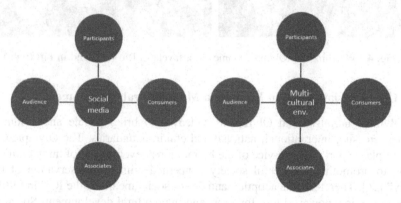

Fig. 3. Relationships between groups: social media (left), multicultural environment (right)

Figure 4-left shows people in a favela in Rio de Janeiro watching the Olympic Games on television as Rafaela Silva, also from the favela, is presented with a gold medal in judo [38]. Figure 4-right shows the public in Fiji watching the final of the rugby sevens match of Rio 2016 [39]. These images reflect Jacobsen's [36] view that the Olympics is a profoundly social event, as people gather around various forms of technology in groups and settings to view the Games. Traditional media provides the means and social media provides the digital space or place where people around the world can feel connected to an event such as the Olympic Games, regardless of the distance that separates them. In this instance, the favela is right next to some of the Olympic Games venues, whereas Fiji is geographically distant from the same venues. The athletes and consumers at the Games are present in the existent and virtual multicultural environments of the event. This represents a multicultural environment by default – respect and recognition of other diverse cultures within the arena of digital platforms is necessary also, given the immediacy of viewing, comment and response. Television, for example, is one-dimensional in that the connection and interaction between the audience and the event is limited. The audience can choose to watch or not - turn the television off and the event becomes a recent memory. Conversely, social media provides the impetus for continued association but also acknowledgment that the digital presence is pervasive – just one click or swipe away. This immediate access promotes engagement, but also inherent acceptance of the multicultural aspects of communication and of the environment that the Games represent.

Fig. 4. Watching the Olympic Games in a favela in Rio (left) and in Fiji (right)

7.1   Use of Social Media to Promote a Multicultural Environment

The Olympic narrative and Olympism endeavor to bring people and communities together, crossing international, national and ethnic boundaries. The Olympic Charter aims "to place sport at the service of the harmonious development of human-kind, with a view to promoting a peaceful society concerned with the preservation of human dignity" [16]. Therefore, the adoption and use of social media by the IOC in fulfillment of these aims is a powerful tool for sport and intercultural development. Social media provides the platform and thus contributes and reinforces the Olympic narrative that the Games should bring people together. Any person can experience, interact and contribute to the Games by blogging, liking, tweeting, photographing and following social media. In this instance technology provides the means to develop and expand the multicultural and intercultural interactions of the Games – expanding it beyond the confines of physical stadia.

The choice to engage with social media within the context of the Olympic Games is a communicative and social choice, but by doing so, social media users and their interactions reflect and reinforce the realities and discourse of the Olympic Games that are defined by the implementing organizations. This opportunity for engagement also reflects a sphere of influence to be utilized as the public respond and interact with social media.

This association with the social aspects of spreading information continues beyond the closing ceremony of an Olympic Games. In the context of the Tokyo 2020 Olympics, the extent to which social media has an impact on the dissemination of 'correct' information within an intercultural and multicultural context is considered important, as is the use and monitoring of social media [40]. These aspects of sport and social media at the Olympic Games and in respect to Tokyo 2020 are of interest from the viewpoint of their interaction and the creation, maintaining and reinforcement of a multicultural environment.

8 Social Media and Fast Forward Towards Tokyo 2020

Other aspects must be addressed when considering the impact of social media and the multicultural environment of the Olympic Games. The multicultural environment engendered by the Games has two distinct periods: the mega event and its associated competition schedule and the Olympiad. In ancient times, the Olympiad meant the span between the Olympics, but in modern times various definitions and usages have occurred. Taken in its historical and ritual context, it could also mean the time spanning the ending of one Games (e.g. the conclusion of the closing ceremony of Rio 2016) and the ending of the next Games (the conclusion of the closing ceremony of Tokyo 2020) (Alexis Lyras, personal communication, 11 March 2019). It is useful within the context of the Olympic Games, social media and multiculturalism to consider the period after one Olympic Games and the beginning of the next and to consider whether people maintain their connection with the Olympic movement in relation to their social media interactions.

At present, the pervasiveness of social media is exemplified by the fact that it is estimated that there will be around 2.77 billion social media users around the globe at some point in 2019, an increase from 2.46 billion in 2017 [41]. This phenomenon, when considered form the viewpoint of an engaged multicultural community, has implications for how people interact pre, during and post Olympic Games. Liu and Guo [33] indicate that the interaction and interconnectedness of people with social media is a result of their sense of belonging with a particular brand of social media that also engenders their loyalty as this sense of connectedness and interaction is supported and maintained. From a mega sport event perspective, it is important to retain the interest of the public in the Olympic Games during the period between each edition of the Games. The association with the social and educational aspects of spreading information is important pre, during and post Games as are maintaining and enhancing the connection between the public and the Olympic movement (or family).

Table 3 details the numbers of followers for selected social media platforms (Facebook, Twitter, Instagram and You Tube) for the Olympic Federations from 2016 to 2018 [43–45]. TSE Consulting produced the first Social Media Ranking of International Sports Organizations in 2016 [42] and provides an overview of how the international sports organizations are performing on social media. The reports for 2017 and 2018 include other social media platforms than the four mentioned above, but for the purposes of this paper and comparison the benchmark platforms of 2016 will be utilized for uniformity. The release of this report in 2016 is a timely reminder of how connected and engaged the Rio Olympics were and indicates the increasing influence of social media in the past three years. Future work will consider comparison of the additional platforms. In Table 3, the counts for the various platforms were recorded in a slightly different way during the three-year period. For Facebook, in 2016 the designation counted was 'followed', but for 2017–2018 it was 'most liked'. For Twitter and Instagram in 2016–2018 the counts represent the 'most followed' designation. For YouTube, in 2016 the category counted was 'most followed', which changed to 'most subscribed' in 2017–2018.

Table 3. Olympic federations and selected social media platforms 2016–2018.

Platform	Organization	Year 2016 [43]	Organization	Year 2017 [44]	Organization	Year 2018 [45]
Facebook	Olympics	15,080,245	Olympics	19,048,216	Olympics	19,149,424
	FIBA	3,334,657	FIBA	4,513,721	FIBA	5,945,217
	FIFA	3,165,937	FIFA	3,471,960	FIFA	3,985,621
	Olympic Channel	1,783,807	Olympic Channel	2,616,333	Olympic Channel	3,065,109
	Hockey	1,001,238	Hockey	1,078,242	FIBA 3x3	1,504,046
	Cycling	758,743	FIBA 3 × 3	1,053,725	Hockey	1,906,640
	Judo	697,379	IAAF	814,361	IAAF	850,373
	IAAF	679,041	Judo	751,058	Volleyball	800,902
	Paralympics	581,515	Volleyball	657,271	Judo	778,670
	Volleyball	524,414	Rugby 7s	620,996	Rugby 7s	716,277
Twitter	FIFA	9,567,158	FIFA	19,309,646	FIFA	21,063,758
	Olympics	5,628,977	Olympics	8,143,842	Olympics	8,749,100
	FIBA	327,417	World Rugby	495,866	World Rugby	596,114
	Cycling	310,586	FIBA	428,480	FIBA	468,824
	World Rugby	267,408	Cycling	363,207	Cycling	406,449
	IAAF	113,156	WBSC	245,325	WBSC	251,623
	Volleyball	104,579	Paralympics	217,866	Paralympics	236,249
	Hockey	104,004	IAAF	206,985	IAAF	233,219
	Skiing	100,638	Volleyball	132,832	Volleyball	190,310
	Triathlon	84,842	World wrestling	131,655	Badminton	151,377
Instagram	FIFA	3,799,463	Olympics	1,640,082	Olympics	2,000,232
	Olympics	1,534,336	World Rugby	832,179	World Rugby	1,022,783
	World Rugby	690,171	FIBA	521,717	FIBA	707,310
	FIBA	440,863	Volleyball	381,897	Cycling	534,386
	Volleyball	268,146	Cycling	350,678	Volleyball	496,385
	Cycling	213,369	Equestrian	185,158	Judo	386,443
	World Triathlon	121,431	World Triathlon	172,990	Equestrian	280,728
	Skiing	115,458	IAAF	166,128	IAAF	273,096
	Hockey	100,686	Karate	156,796	Wrestling	266,799
	Equestrian	99,051	Olympic Channel	155,196	Olympic Channel	255,216

(*continued*)

Table 3. (*continued*)

Platform	Organization	Year 2016 [43]	Organization	Year 2017 [44]	Organization	Year 2018 [45]
You Tube	Olympics	1,602,630	Olympics	1,945,275	FIFA	7,424,590
	FIFA TV	1,495,663	FIFA TV	1,908,307	Olympic	3,085,799
	FIBA World	257,610	FIBA World	367,460	Badminton	789,700
	Cycling	214,170	Volleyball	317,348	FIBA	565,445
	Volleyball	170,348	World Rugby	264,382	World Rugby	428,303
	ITTF	160,054	Cycling	251,444	Volleyball	394,804
	Gymnastics	142,309	ITTF	202,364	Cycling	316,627
	Archery	80,738	FIG channel	195,511	Karate	305,813
	Hockey	79,843	FIBA 3 × 3	110,648	ITTF	287,303
	Judo	77,837	Judo	108,833	Gymnastics	273,711

The figures for 2016 indicate that the International Olympic Committee (IOC) and its associated International Sports Federations are well represented on social media and continue to maintain a presence across the four platforms. The IOC (Olympics) tops the rankings on YouTube and Facebook, with the Facebook page having in excess of fifteen million likes. The International Football Federation (FIFA) is dominant on Twitter and Instagram. The top three organizations over all platforms for 2016 are the IOC, FIFA and FIBA (International Basketball Federation). For 2017, the numbers again show that the IOC is top for Facebook, Instagram and YouTube, whereas FIFA maintains its dominance on Twitter. The IOC Olympics page is the most liked of any international organization, with over nineteen million likes. For 2018, the IOC is dominant on Facebook and Instagram, with FIFA being top on YouTube and Twitter; FIFA's YouTube presence increased dramatically, most probably due to the holding of the Football World Cup. Likewise, the IOC's presence on Facebook might be due to the Youth Olympic Games and the Pyeong Chang Winter Olympic Games. In general, since 2016, all the international federations have increased their presence on social media, with the top five organizations remaining fairly constant and positional changes in the 6–10 rankings amongst the smaller federations. It is interesting to see the increase in social media presence of the smaller federations as they endeavor to engage further with their fans. Of note is the rise in karate in 2018, presumably linked to Tokyo 2020 where it is a competitive sport for the first time.

The Tokyo Organizing Committee of the Olympic and the Paralympic Games (TOCOG) presence on social media is extensive and complements the IOC's offerings. As of 9 March 2019, the official TOCOG social media platforms of Facebook (607,741 followers) [46], Twitter (2,687 tweets and 140,000 followers) [47], Instagram (192 posts and 129,000 followers) [48], Weibo (10,533 fans) [49] and YouTube (26,777 subscribers) [50] represent a significant presence more than 500 days out from the Games [51] and is likely to increase as the Tokyo edition of the games draws nearer. The social presence of the IOC, the international federations and TOCOG reflect a high self-presentation/self-disclosure and 'medium' presence as defined by Kaplan and Heinlaen [52] in Table 4.

Table 4. Classification of social media by social presence/media richness and self-preservation/self-disclosure.

		Social presence/media richness		
		Low	Medium	High
Self-presentation/self-disclosure	High	Blogs	Social networking sites (e.g., Facebook)	Virtual social worlds (e.g., second life)
	Low	Collaborative projects (e.g., Wikipedia)	Content communities (e.g., YouTube)	Virtual game worlds (e.g., world of warcraft)

Perhaps the next step in the development of a virtual multicultural environment mirroring Kaplan and Heinlaen's [52] 'high' classification would be the development of integrative technology – using virtual reality and augmented reality, as in the Japanese National Broadcaster's (NHK) virtual trip back to the 1964 Tokyo Olympics in the lead up to the 2020 Games [53].

9   Conclusion

Various terms including 'networked spectators' have been used to describe the nature of social media in relation to the Olympic Games and the dispersed nature of the interaction during this mega sporting event. The nature of social media encourages active participation in the Olympic Games by the various communities and contributes towards the establishment of virtual spaces where the different actors can communicate in contrast with the physical places usually associated with an edition of the Games. These types of interactions create virtual communities manifesting a multicultural and intercultural environment associated with the Olympic Games on a physical and virtual level. This environment is reinforced, extended and maintained by the IOC and the international federations before, during and after each edition of the Olympic Games. The increase in social media usage has facilitated an increase in the number of people interacting on social media with the various sporting organizations, creating a level of interest and engagement that is growing year by year, reinforcing the social and educational aspects of Olympism. The advent of new technology is also redefining the way people can interact and utilize social media in the lead up to Tokyo 2020.

References

1. International Olympic Academy. http://ioa.org.gr/the-legacy-of-ancient-olympic-games/. Accessed 25 Feb 2019
2. Naul, R., Binder, D.: Olympic Education: An International Review. Routledge, London (2017)
3. Business Insider. http://www.businessinsider.com/the-2020-tokyo-olympics-may-be-the-most-high-tech-yet-2016-3/#hydrogen-cars-could-transport-athletes-1. Accessed 13 Jan 2019

4. Ryall, J.: Games changer: technology that will innovate the Olympics in 2020. https://japantoday.com/category/tech/games-changer-technology-that-will-innovate-the-olympics-in-2020. Accessed 15 Jan 2019
5. International Olympic Committee: Tokyo 2020 to Organise Innovative and Engaging Games. https://www.olympic.org/news/tokyo-2020-to-organise-innovative-and-engaging-games. Accessed 19 Jan 2019
6. Savic, Z.: The Olympic Games as a Cultural Event. Acta Universitatis Palackianae Olomucensis. Gymnica. **37**(3), 7–13 (2007)
7. Liu, Y.: The development of social media and its impact on the intercultural exchange of the Olympic movement, 2004–2012. Int. J. Hist. Sport **33**(12), 1395–1410 (2016)
8. International Olympic Committee: IOC Social Media, Blogging and Internet Guidelines for participants and other accredited persons at the London 2012 Olympic Games. https://stillmed.olympic.org/Documents/Games_London_2012/IOC_Social_Media_Blogging_and_Internet_Guidelines-London.pdf. Accessed 13 Jan 2019
9. International Olympic Committee: IOC President Bach Outlines Digital Future of the Olympic Games. https://www.olympic.org/news/ioc-president-bach-outlines-digital-future-of-the-olympic-games. Accessed 27 Feb 2019
10. Sugden, J., Tomlinson, A.: Watching the Olympics: Politics, Power and Representation. Routledge, London (2011)
11. Oxford University Press Homepage. https://en.oxforddictionaries.com/definition/multicultural. Accessed 14 Jan 2019
12. Traganou, J.: Designing the Olympics: Representation, Participation, Contestation. Routledge, New York (2016)
13. Verkuyten, M.: Multicultural recognition and ethnic minority rights: a social identity perspective. Eur. Rev. Psychol. **17**(1), 148–184 (2006)
14. International Olympic Committee: IOC Creates Refugee Olympic Team Tokyo 2020. https://www.olympic.org/news/ioc-creates-refugee-olympic-team-tokyo-2020. Accessed 14 Jan 2019
15. United Nations: About the Sustainable Development Goals. https://www.un.org/sustainabledevelopment/sustainable-development-goals/. Accessed 14 Jan 2019
16. International Olympic Committee: The Olympic Charter. https://stillmed.olympic.org/Documents/olympic_charter_en.pdf. Accessed 01 Mar 2019
17. International Olympic Committee: Olympic Marketing Fact File 2019 Edition. https://stillmed.olympic.org/media/Document%20Library/OlympicOrg/Documents/IOC-Marketing-and-Broadcasting-General-Files/Olympic-Marketing-Fact-File-2019.pdf. Accessed 28 Feb 2018
18. International Olympic Committee: Broadcasting the Olympic Games. https://stillmed.olympic.org/media/Document%20Library/Museum/Visit/TOM-Schools/Teaching-Resources/Broadcasting-the-Olympic-Games/FicheInfoDiffusionJO_historique_ENG.pdf. Accessed 21 Feb 2019
19. International Olympic Committee: The Sydney 2000 Olympic Games. https://stillmed.olympic.org/media/Document%20Library/OlympicOrg/IOC/How_We_Do_It/Broadcasters/EN_Sydney_2000_Broadcast_Report.pdf. Accessed 28 Feb 2019
20. International Olympic Committee: IOC Marketing Report Beijing 2008. view.digipage.net/?id=iocbeijing2008. Accessed 28 Feb 2019
21. International Olympic Committee: IOC Marketing Report Vancouver 2010. http://view.digipage.net/?id=iocvancouver2010. Accessed 28 Feb 2019
22. International Olympic Committee: IOC Marketing Report London 2012. https://stillmed.olympic.org/Documents/IOC_Marketing/London_2012/LR_IOC_MarketingReport_medium_res1.pdf. Accessed 28 Feb 2018

23. Burgess, J., Marwick, A., Poell, T.: Introduction. In: The SAGE Handbook of Social Media, pp. 1–10. Sage Publishing, London (2018)
24. Sydney Morning Herald: London Games to be first social media Olympics. https://www.smh.com.au/technology/london-games-to-be-first-social-media-olympics-20120620-20n0l.html. Accessed 04 Mar 04
25. International Olympic Committee: IOC Marketing Report Pyeong Chang 2016. iocmarketingreport.touchlines.com/pyeongchang2018. Accessed 25 Feb 2019
26. International Olympic Committee: Final Sydney 2000 Marketing Overview. Marketing Matters. https://stillmed.olympic.org/Documents/Reports/EN/en_report_274.pdf. Accessed 24 Feb 2019
27. International Olympic Committee: London 2012 Olympic Games Global Broadcast Report. https://stillmed.olympic.org/media/Document%20Library/OlympicOrg/Games/Summer-Games/Games-London-2012-Olympic-Games/IOC-Marketing-and-Broadcasting-Various-files/Global-Broadcast-Report-London-2012.pdf. Accessed 27 Feb 2019
28. International Olympic Committee: IOC Marketing Report London 2012. https://stillmed.olympic.org/Documents/IOC_Marketing/London_2012/LR_IOC_MarketingReport_medium_res1.pdf. Accessed 25 Feb 2019
29. International Olympic Committee, IOC Marketing Report Rio 2016. touchline.digipage.net/iocmarketing/reportrio2016/. Accessed 25 Feb 2019
30. International Olympic Committee: Marketing Report Torino 2006. https://stillmed.olympic.org/Documents/Reports/EN/en_report_1143.pdf. Accessed 20 Feb 2019
31. Commonwealth of Australia: Olympic Games a Huge Broadcasting and Online Event. https://www.communications.gov.au/departmental-news/olympic-games-huge-broadcast-and-online-event. Accessed 20 Feb 2019
32. Sawyer, R., Chen, G.-M.: The impact of social media on intercultural adaptation. Intercult. Commun. Stud. 21(2), 151–169 (2012)
33. Liu, C.-T., Guo, Y.M.: The role of sense of belonging in social media usage: a tale of two types of users. Asia Pac. J. Inf. Syst. 25(2), 211–233 (2015)
34. Daytona Beach News Journal: Photos Getting Ready for the 2018 Winter Olympics. Online Image. AP Photo/Charlie Riedel, Thursday February 8, 2018. https://www.news-journalonline.com/photogallery/LK/20180208/NEWS/208009989/PH/1. Accessed 28 Feb 2019
35. Carey, B.: Do the Olympics earn a gold medal in social media marketing? http://tik-talk.com/do-the-olympics-earn-a-gold-in-social-media-marketing/. Accessed 20 Feb 2018
36. Jacobson, J.: Networked spectators: social media conversation and moderation at the Olympic opening ceremony. Online Inf. Rev. 40(6), 746–760 (2016)
37. Chen, G.-M.: The impact of new media on intercultural communication in global context. China Media Res. 8(2), 1–10 (2012)
38. The Irish Times: City of God. https://www.irishtimes.com/sport/other-sports/city-of-god-1.2750386. Accessed 27 Feb 2019
39. Ryall, J.: This is how people watched the Olympics around the world. https://mashable.com/2016/08/21/rio-olympics-photos-watch/#bFia_Zu4Nkqy. Accessed 27 Feb 2019
40. Mainichi Newspaper: Tokyo 2020 organizing committee watching social media over fear of fake news. https://mainichi.jp/english/articles/20171114/p2a/00m/0na/021000. Accessed 29 Jan 2019
41. Statista: Number of Social Media users worldwide from 2010 to 2021 (in billions). https://www.statista.com/statistics/278414/number-of-worldwide-social-network-users/. Accessed 30 Jan 2019

42. Around the Rings: First-Ever Social Media Ranking of International Sports Organizations. http://aroundtherings.com/site/A__58318/Title__First-Ever-Social-Media-Ranking-of-International-Sports-Organizations/292/Articles. Accessed 01 Mar 2019

43. TSE Consulting: The 2016 Social Media and Olympic Sport Ranking. http://www.tseconsulting.com/wp-content/uploads/2016/12/2016OlympicRanking.pdf. Accessed 09 Mar 2019

44. TSE Consulting: The 2017 Social Media and Olympic Sport Ranking. https://www.insidethegames.biz/media/file/91475/2017%20Olympic%20Sports%20Social%20Media%20Ranking.pdf. Accessed 09 Mar 2019

45. TSE Consulting 2018: The 2018 Social Media and Olympic Sport Ranking. https://www.insidethegames.biz/media/file/131473/The-2018-Olympic-Sports-Ranking.pdf. Accessed 09 Mar 2019

46. Tokyo Organising Committee of the Olympic and Paralympic Games, Tokyo 2020. https://www.facebook.com/tokyo2020/. Accessed 09 Mar 2019

47. Tokyo Organising Committee of the Olympic and Paralympic Games, Tokyo 2020. https://twitter.com/Tokyo2020. Accessed 09 Mar 2019

48. Tokyo Organising Committee of the Olympic and Paralympic Games, Tokyo 2020. https://www.instagram.com/tokyo2020/. Accessed 09 Mar 2019

49. Tokyo Organising Committee of the Olympic and Paralympic Games. 2019, Tokyo 2020_official. https://www.weibo.com/tokyo2020official. Accessed 09 Mar 2019

50. Tokyo Organising Committee of the Olympic and Paralympic Games. 2019, Tokyo 2020. https://www.youtube.com/tokyo2020. Accessed 09 Mar 2019

51. Tokyo Organising Committee of the Olympic and Paralympic Games (2019). https://tokyo2020.org/en/. Accessed 09 Mar 2019

52. Kaplan, A.M., Haenlein, M.: Users of the world, unite! The challenges and opportunities of social media. Bus. Horiz. **53**, 59–68 (2010)

53. Frater, P.: SXSW: Japan's NHK Offers Pre-Olympic VR Trip Back to 1964 Tokyo. https://variety.com/2019/digital/asia/sxsw-japan-nhk-olympic-vr-tokyo-1203150688/. Accessed 09 Mar 2019

Bridging Between Jewish Ultra-Orthodox and the Start-up Nation: A Case Study

Dalit Levy[(⊠)]

Zefat Academic College, Zefat, Israel
dality@zefat.ac.il

Abstract. The paper describes an innovative undergraduate program aiming to be sensitive to the increasing demand for higher education by the multi-cultural population in north-eastern part of Israel. The program interweaves societal, economical, informational, and technological facets of businesses, organizations, and communities in order to prepare students to successful Information Systems careers. The paper's focus is on a group of ultra-Orthodox students who graduated in 2017, including the unique case of an elderly caregiver who became a startupist. In light of recent calls for increasing the low employment rate of Israeli ultra-Orthodox Jews and for enabling their employment in fields that offer higher-paying jobs, such program might suggest a fruitful path.

Keywords: Community Information Systems · Entrepreneurship · ICT4D · PBL

1 Introduction

In the last three decades we have witnessed an invasion of homes, workplaces, public spaces, and both local and global organizations by information technology tools and systems. The advents of the World Wide Web, wireless communications, and miniaturized computing technology have expanded this invasion into mobile devices and remote communities. The widespread everyday use of mobile devices, computers, and information systems reflects a shift in conceptualizing the technology as more social than it was perceived before. More recently, over the last several years, social information systems have gained significant popularity. Social networking sites, social sharing and tagging systems and social media attract several million users a day all over the globe. These kinds of information systems provide their individual users with increased social presence, much broader access to information and knowledge, and powerful means of communication [1]. At the same time, social information systems emerge as an empowering force for both local and global communities, organizations, and businesses.

Following these changes [2], a new interdisciplinary area of study has evolved, arguing that the social and the technological mutually shape each other. Studies in this area touch several different fields, including computer science, information systems, information science, and some social sciences [3]. By examining the social aspects of computing, the fields of Social Informatics and Community Informatics aim to ensure that technical research agendas and information systems designs are relevant to the

© Springer Nature Switzerland AG 2019
G. Meiselwitz (Ed.): HCII 2019, LNCS 11578, pp. 524–534, 2019.
https://doi.org/10.1007/978-3-030-21902-4_37

lives of people and organizations. Community Informatics aims further at empowering communities through the use of technology, especially those groups who are excluded from the mainstream communication systems [4].

The increasing interest among different communities of practice in integrating human and social considerations into traditional Information Systems (IS) curricula has led to the development of new academic programs around the globe. These are aimed at establishing a framework within which students develop analytical skills to identify and evaluate the social consequences of ICT-based systems and gain experience in the socio-technical process of designing information systems in business, libraries, health, government, education and beyond. While IS curricula have been traditionally targeted to business schools, the latest model curricula for undergraduate degrees in Information Systems [5] recommended reaching beyond the schools of management and business, stating that the discipline provides expertise that is critically important for an increasing number of other domains. In Israel, however, most undergraduate Information Systems programs operate either as part of the faculty of engineering or within the context of the business environment and related activities.

The undergraduate program in Community Information Systems (CIS) has been developed at a college situated in the north-eastern part of Israel in light of the global trends discussed above and, in addition, as a response to the educational gap identified between various population sectors in Israel. The program seeks to prepare and grow local Information Systems workforce by advancing understanding of computing, design, human-computer interaction, digital culture, entrepreneurship and other subjects regarded as critical to developing the needed workforce for the 21st century [6]. The curriculum combines theory and practice while emphasizing subjects that are relevant to the workforce and the organizations surrounding the college, thus creating 'practice of relevance' [7] for its students.

2   The CIS Program Structure

The undergraduate program in Community Information Systems (CIS) has been approved by the national council for higher education at the end of 2010 and the first students started their course of study in the fall term of 2011. The program's main assumption is that the revolutionary development of information technologies in general and of information systems in particular, changes organizational structure and organizational practices. Therefore, the workforce as a whole will benefit from acquiring basic academic knowledge in information systems, not only the engineers or those in managerial positions [8]. The notion of "community" in Community Information Systems is broad, including business communities as well as non-profit organizations, global or local organizations, public communities, cultural communities, and rural communities [3, 4, 9].

Imagining information system as a junction connecting (i) human users, (ii) supporting technologies, and (iii) organizational environment, the curriculum includes (i) psychological and sociological aspects, (ii) information technologies and systems, and (iii) issues of organizational culture. This interdisciplinary approach can be seen also in Community Informatics undergraduate and graduate programs in Canada, USA,

Australia, Italy, South Africa, and other countries [10] as well as in the emerging field of ICT for Development – ICT4D [11, 12]. The interdisciplinary nature of these fields calls for creating interdisciplinary academic programs that will support educating "more capable learners, more innovative teachers, more creative thinkers, more effective leaders and more engaged global citizens" [13, p. 626]. Such programs enable students' specialization both in the technical and the social aspects of information systems. They also expose learners to the breadth of human arenas and communities supported by information systems like public health, economic development, education, and many more.

The three-years curriculum is structured around "Information Technologies and Systems" as a core area of study [14]. Required core courses provide 70 out of 120 credits, where one credit typically equals fifteen class hours. The core curriculum contains foundation courses in Mathematics and Statistics, Programming and Computer Science (CS) [15], and Information Systems (IS). Additional ten credits are offered through elective courses in the core area of study, such as cybersecurity [16], Big Data analytics [17], and Bioinformatics [18] (see details in Table 1).

Table 1. Distribution of courses in different areas of study

Area of study		Year 1	Year 2	Year 3	Sum of credits
Core: Information Technologies and Information Systems	Required credits	25	25	20	70
	Elective credits		6	4	10
Sum of core credits		25	31	24	80
Areas of specialization: (a) The Knowledge Society (b) Information in Organizations	Required credits in area (a)	8	6	4	18
	Required credits in area (b)	8	6	4	18
	Elective credits		2	2	4
Sum of credits in areas of specialization		16	14	10	40

The rest of the credits are equally divided between two supporting areas of study: (a) "The Knowledge Society" and (b) "Information in Organizations". Area (a) includes required courses like digital culture and new media [19], sociology of the internet, online learning strategies, and evaluating digital communities [20]. Area (b) includes required courses like knowledge management and organizational behaviour. The electives include project management, Enterprise Resource Planning (ERP) [21], and an innovative course named "Israel the Start-up Nation" [22] in which students are visiting high-tech companies and start-ups to experience first-hand the organizational culture of the industry they are about to join.

As part of the required core curriculum, 3rd year students are designing, developing, and presenting a real-life project thus combining the knowledge from previous years to construct a digital information system for an organization of their choice (see examples in Fig. 1). Project-Based Learning (PBL) plays an important role in this process. PBL is a powerful pedagogy, thought of as especially appropriate for ICT and business management courses [21, 23]. PBL provides students opportunities to practice cognitive and interpersonal skills, as they work in group projects, cope with complex, real world issues and practices and produce carefully designed products [24]. It is further justified by the CIS program's inherent diversity as well as the learning requirement from students to develop a broader and deeper understanding of how high-tech organizations and entrepreneurs work, and how they utilize technology to improve their products in particular and the society in general [8].

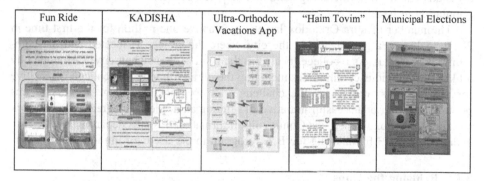

Fun Ride	KADISHA	Ultra-Orthodox Vacations App	"Haim Tovim"	Municipal Elections

Fig. 1. Final projects designed by 2017 graduates of the ultra-Orthodox group

The structure of the Community Information Systems program separates the core of the curriculum from the electives with the intent of supporting the creation of a sound knowledge base of information systems, at a level appropriate for undergraduate students. At the same time, the courses in both areas of specializations mark the social, cultural, organizational, and human aspects as central to the knowledge base of information systems, thus can support the conceptual development of a multi-faceted body of knowledge. As can be seen in Table 1 above, students are exposed to the interdisciplinary nature of the program from Year 1. That way the program provides the multidisciplinary knowledge required for entry-level positions in a wide spectrum of organizations, as well as design experience of real-world information systems.

One of the program's pillars is rooted in the disciplinary foundations of Computer Science (CS) and software development. The core Community Information Systems curriculum proposes a computing track tailored for non-computer-science majors in order to give them an understanding of the principles and practices of computing as well as its potential for transforming the world [25]. As a result of such integrated curriculum, the program envisions graduates which are both information-technology-oriented and social-oriented, and thus can empower the communities within they live and work. Five cohorts have graduated the program so far, and most graduates are now employed as knowledge workers in a wide array of organizations.

3   Opening the CIS Program for Ultra-Orthodox

In parallel to the process of designing and opening the unique B.A. program in Community Information Systems at the college, significant changes have been documented with regard to integrating ultra-Orthodox undergraduates in the Israeli higher education system in [26]. Recent reports expect that within the next decade, the ultra-Orthodox sector will reach 16% of the total population (now 12%), and that more than half of its population will be young (under 20). The Israeli higher education system has joined forces in an effort to prepare for these changes, while the number of ultra-Orthodox students in it has already grown from 1,000 in 2007 to more than 10,000 in 2017. Worth noticing is the fact that the breakdown of B.A. subjects taken by ultra-Orthodox students differs greatly from that among the general population, and that only 8% study engineering (including computer science), compared with 18% of the general population in Israel.

The number of ultra-Orthodox Israelis rose above one million for the first time in 2017, including a growth within the city where the college is located and the communities around it. As a college located at the heart of the ancient city, surrounded by all kinds of religious communities including the ultra-Orthodox, the college is sensitive for the needs as well as for the challenges in opening the college's doors to this population. After a successful initiative of offering an academic degree in social work for ultra-Orthodox women, the Community Information Systems department joined the endeavor in 2013 by tailoring the B.A. program to the needs of ultra-Orthodox men.

3.1   Bridging the Gaps

The ultra-Orthodox class of 15 men from the major cities and the surrounding communities of the eastern Gallilee, was constructed with the aid of external agencies and philanthropies that generously supported the students during four and a half years of study. This support enabled overcoming the income gap, which is only one of the barriers need to be considered. In special, the college needed to construct a program of study that will overcome the knowledge gap, including a lack of general studies and matriculation certificates, as the following quotation clarifies:

"Most members of the ultra-Orthodox sector have never received a basic educational foundation. Ultra-Orthodox elementary schools for boys teach secular subjects for a limited number of hours and at a level that does not provide a suitable basis for the modern labor market. Most of the ultra-Orthodox (both men and women) do not obtain a matriculation certificate, and thus find it difficult to gain entry to regular institutions of higher education" [27, p. 85].

In order to meet the acceptance conditions for the Community Information Systems program, the ultra-Orthodox group began with a first-year general preparatory program emphasizing Mathematic, English, and computer literacy, equivalent to high school matriculation certificate. In the second year, the group was offered a structured program of studying towards the national psychometric exam, and in addition took courses like Academic Literacy and Introduction to Information and Communication Technologies. These credits were later qualified towards the 120 credits of the Community Information Systems program. Only after successfully passing the December 2013 national psychometric exam with a sufficient score, the students could begin their course of study in the B.A. program. Their first semester of the program was the spring semester of 2014.

Another gap needed bridging has been more cultural. The male students in the ultra-Orthodox group were relatively older than the regular college student population and were already fathers in large families. They often were the first in their families to reach the academic world and were not used and sometimes reluctant to study and work in a mixed-gender and multi-cultural environment. It is worth noticing however that the ultra-Orthodox society is changing in this respect as well. For example, a survey from 2013 shows that a growing percentage of the ultra-Orthodox parents support academic studies for their children [28].

The college therefore supported constructing a special learning environment for the Community Information Systems' ultra-Orthodox group, using the college's facilities in less crowded evening hours, leaving Fridays off (unlike the regular program), and offering additional summer semesters. As Table 2 shows, the complete program included 8 semesters over three years, while regular B.A. studies usually spread over 6 semesters with long summer vacation between the first and the second year and then again between the second and the third year. The Community Information Systems' ultra-Orthodox students therefore took part in a challenging non-stop learning journey towards becoming part of the high-tech community and the professional workforce of what is termed "The Startup Nation" [22].

Table 2. Timeline of the ultra-Orthodox CIS program

Part of the program		Dates
Preparatory program		October 2012–August 2013
National psychometric exam		December 2013
B.A. Year 1	1st semester	Spring 2014
	2nd semester	Summer 2014
	3rd semester	Fall-Winter 2014
B.A. Year 2	4th semester	Spring 2015
	5th semester	Summer 2015
	6th semester	Fall-Winter 2015
B.A. Year 3	7th semester	Spring 2016
	8th semester	Summer 2016
Final projects presentation (see examples in Fig. 1)		January 2017
Graduation ceremony		June 2017

3.2   The Case of M.M.

A few days after the holiday of Sukkot in October 2017, only four months after graduating the CIS program and receiving his B.A. diploma, stepped M.M. on to the stage of the college's auditorium to make a pitch presenting his innovative social-technological idea. The presentation was a part of the Demo Day of the newly established center of innovation and entrepreneurship at the college. Following a summer full of design activities and preparations for this ground-breaking event, happening for the first time at the northern periphery of Israel, seven pioneering teams presented their inventive ideas and technological initiatives in front of key figures of the Start-up Nation and potential investors from all around the country (Fig. 2).

Fig. 2. Invitation for the demo day of the 1st cycle of Zefat's entrepreneurship center

Among the teams chosen to participate in the pioneering cycle based on the authenticity and maturity of their initiatives, was M.M. and his classmate from the ultra-Orthodox group. The couple collaborated with an academic advisor who is a user-experience (UX) professional, and also a lecturer teaching in the Community Information Systems program, to design what they termed "Haim Tovim", translated into "Good Life". The initiative grew out in the third year of studying in the program, while the students needed to find an idea for developing an information system that meets a real-life need, and to design a prototype as a final project using what they had learned and experienced throughout the Community Information Systems program. In addition to his academic studies, M.M. was also working part time as a caregiver for Haim, an elderly person with ALS in a complex nursing state. His idea was to develop a comprehensive information system for monitoring the treatment of the nursing patient outside the hospital (at home or protected housing), that will enable the caregiver as well as the patient and the family to make sure that the required treatment has indeed been done. Describing how the idea emerged, M.M. wrote (E-mail communication, September 2017)[1]:

> "My personal encounter with the giving to others while studying Information Systems gave birth to the idea for the project (which is titled 'Haim Tovim' in honor of my patient). I truly hope that the idea will progress from being a prototype in the academy to a real-world application helping so many people who desperately need it!"

Indeed, during their last two semesters (in the summer and fall of 2016) M.M. and his colleague further developed the idea and the prototype of the system and presented the final project in an exciting event in front of the Community Information Systems

---

[1] Although M.M. gave his full consent to publish any detail concerning his project, the paper uses a pseudo name.

department' students and teachers in January 2017. Shortly thereafter, the project got to the finals in a national ultra-Orthodox startups competition. Following the acceptance of the bachelor's degree in June 2017, M.M. received a technological job offer and retired from his work as a caregiver. However, the original idea to develop an information system for caregivers was not abandoned and in July 2017 the "Haim Tovim" project was accepted to the pioneering cycle of the center of innovation and entrepreneurship. As part of participating in the center's activities during the summer of 2017, the team further developed the project and designed a "one pager" briefly describing the aims, the market, and the needs (Fig. 3).

Fig. 3. The top part of the project's one pager (in Hebrew)

In an email correspondence during the preparations for the Demo Day, M.M. provided a few words on himself and the unique and personal path he had been through prior to starting the academic studies. M.M. was severely hurt twice in his left hand, both times in terror attacks, and had to go through complex medical and psychological treatments that disrupted his normal life (September 2017):

> "…We moved to the city of Zefat. After a long time of ups and downs, treatments and personal work, an opportunity arrived for me at the college. In a quick decision that I thank God for, I enrolled in the CIS program. I now realize how much this move improved my life and stabilized them".

A few weeks later, in his Demo Day pitch, M.M. started with this personal story and directed the audience towards realizing the potential contribution of the suggested information system. As a result of the successful presentation, M.M. was invited to present the project in additional professional events, and a window of opportunity was opened for future business development. Currently, the project is being developed by M.M. in collaboration with another graduate of the ultra-Orthodox group and the support of a senior lecturer in the Community Information Systems program. All the three live and work in the high-tech sector at the eastern Galilee, thus serving as a physical bridge between the ultra-Orthodox and the Start-up Nation. In a recent email communication M.M. reflected on their progress stating that "we constantly work on promoting the project, (but) as it often happens, behind each wall there is another one…" (E-mail communication, June 2018). The project's team grows its organizational network hoping to run experimental trials of the information system and attract more investors and supporters.

4 Summary

Accompanying and guiding the ultra-Orthodox group of students throughout their years of studying in the Community Information Systems program has been a unique and rare opportunity for the program's academic staff to assist in closing some of the abovementioned gaps, as well as to open new horizons for future professional success in the knowledge age of the 21st century [29]. This goes hand in hand with the main goal of the national plan to integrate ultra-Orthodox Israelis into higher-quality segments of the labor market [27] or, as the title of this paper suggests, with bridging between the ultra-Orthodox communities and the Startup Nation.

Despite the efforts to keep technology such as computers and televisions out of ultra-Orthodox schools and homes, the mobile revolution of the last decade makes it almost impossible [30, 31]. Since the Community Information Systems program deals with issues connecting social and communal understanding with advanced technological skills, the ultra-Orthodox who have graduated the program might be better able to serve their communities with regard to understanding of both current mobile revolution and future technological developments.

In addition, in light of current trends that call for programming for all and regard coding as the literacy of the 21st century, the Community Information Systems program holds potential to give students majoring in non-Computer-Science fields an understanding of the principles of computing and knowledge about the practices of computing professionals. Although the ultra-Orthodox graduates are not expected to become professional programmers, their exposure to these basic features of software engineering makes them more able to talk to computer scientists, understand these professionals' concerns, collaborate with them in developing and maintaining organizational and communal IT projects, and at the same time to develop their own interdisciplinary career on a proper foundation.

As is hinted in M.M.'s story briefly brought above, the students in the ultra-Orthodox group faced numerous challenges, including a lack of general studies (in special, Mathematics and English); the need to support their large families while studying; the absence of 'role models' – people from their familiar communities who have experienced academic studies in technological fields; resistance to change and to modernity within their close cycle of family, friends, and religious leaders; to name just a few. A recent study of the phenomenon of ultra-Orthodox women who join high-tech organizations raises similar challenges, but also points to the broader change underway in employment patterns [32].

Working at the mixed-gendered, multi-cultural environment of a general academic college, the lecturers, the managers, and the administrative staff needed also to adjust procedures and behaviors to the specific needs of this unique group of learners.

In spite of those and additional challenges not detailed here, the experience has been successful for both the college and the ultra-Orthodox group who graduated in June 2017. In light of recent calls for increasing the low employment rate of Israeli ultra-Orthodox Jews in general and for enabling their employment in fields that offer higher-paying jobs in particular, the Community Information Systems program might suggest a fruitful path.

References

1. Stillman, L., Linger, H.: Community informatics and information systems: how can they be better connected? Inf. Soc. **25**(4), 255–264 (2009)
2. Carr, N.: The Big Switch. W. W. Norton & Company, New York (2008)
3. Kling, R.: What is social informatics and why does it matter? Inf. Soc. **23**(4), 205–220 (2007). https://doi.org/10.1080/01972240701441556
4. Gurstein, M.: What is Community Informatics (and Why Does It Matter)?. Polimetrica, Milan (2008)
5. Topi, H., et al.: IS 2010: curriculum guidelines for undergraduate degree programs in information systems. Commun. AIS **26**(1), 359–428 (2010)
6. The College Board. AP® Computer Science Principles (2017). https://secure-media. collegeboard.org/digitalServices/pdf/ap/ap-computer-science-principles-course-and-exam-description.pdf
7. Benbasat, I., Zmud, R.W.: Empirical research in information systems: the practice of relevance. MIS Q. **23**(1), 3–16 (1999)
8. Levy, D.: Computer science education as part of an undergraduate program in community information systems. In: The 43rd Annual Frontiers in Education Conference, Oklahoma City, OK (2013)
9. Mamba, M.S.N., Isabirye, N.: A framework to guide development through ICTs in rural areas in South Africa. IT Dev. **21**(1), 135–150 (2015)
10. Stillman, L., Denison, T., Anwar, M. (eds.): Proceedings of the 13th Prato CIRN Conference, Prato, Italy (2016)
11. Heeks, R.: ICT4D 2.0: the next phase of applying ICT for international development. Computer **41**(6), 26–33 (2008)
12. Heeks, R.: Information and Communication Technology for Development (ICT4D). Routledge, Abingdon (2018)
13. Bennett, J.K., Sterling, R.: Computer science is not enough. tripleC **9**(2), 624–631 (2011). Special Issue: ICTs and Society - A New Transdiscipline?
14. Shoval, P.: Planning, Design and Analysis of Information Systems, vol. I, II, III. Open University Press, Raanana (1998). (in Hebrew)
15. Zur, I., Muller, O., Haberman, B., Cohen, A., Levy, D., Hotovely, R.: A new computer science curriculum for middle school in Israel. In: Proceeding of the 42nd annual Frontiers in Education Conference, Seattle, WA (2012)
16. von Solms, R., van Niekerk, J.: From information security to cyber security. Comput. Secur. **38**, 97–102 (2013)
17. Chen, H., Chiang, R.H.L., Storey, V.C.: Business intelligence and analytics: from big data to big impact. MIS Q. **36**(4), 1165–1188 (2012)
18. Lesk, A.: Introduction to Bioinformatics. Oxford University Press, Oxford (2014)
19. Bruns, A.: Blogs, Wikipedia, Second Life, and Beyond: From Production to Produsage. Peter Lang, New York (2008)
20. Hine, C.: Ethnography for the Internet: Embedded, Embodied and Everyday. Bloomsbury Publishing, London (2015)
21. Gerogiannis, V., Fitsilis, P.: A project-based learning approach for teaching ERP concepts. Int. J. Learn. **5**(12), 261–268 (2006)
22. Senor, D., Singer, S.: Start-Up Nation: Israel's Economic Growth Engine. Twelve, New York (2009)
23. Janeck, M., Bleek, W.G.: Project-based learning with CommSy. In: CSCL conference, University of Colorado, Boulder, CO, USA (2002)

24. Strand Norman, C., Rose, A.M., Lehmann, C.M.: Cooperative leaning: resources from the business disciplines. J. Acc. Educ. **22**, 1–28 (2004)
25. Harvey, B., Garcia, D.D.: CS10: the beauty and joy of computing (2011). http://inst.eecs.berkeley.edu/~cs10/fa11/
26. Cahaner, L., Malach, G., Choshen, M.: Statistical Report on Ultra-Orthodox Society in Israel. The Israel Democracy Institute, Jerusalem, Israel (2017). https://en.idi.org.il/articles/20439
27. Malach, G., Cohen, D., Zicherman, H.: A Master Plan for Ultra-Orthodox Employment in Israel. Policy Paper 11E, The Israel Democracy Institute, Jerusalem, Israel (2016). https://en.idi.org.il/media/4670/taasukat_karedim_web.pdf
28. Gal, R.: What happens inside the ultra-Orthodox home? Samuel Neaman Institute, Haifa, Israel (2018). (in Hebrew)
29. Barzilai-Nahon, K., Barzilai, G.: Cultured technology: the internet and religious fundamentalism. Inf. Soc. **21**(1), 25–40 (2005)
30. Rosenberg, H., Blondheim, M., Katz, E.: Guardians of the walls: supervision, boundaries and the ultra-Orthodox mobile-phone usages campaign. Israel Sociol. **17**(2), 115–136 (2016). (in Hebrew)
31. Benayon, M.: Special education instruction in the Jewish ultra Orthodox and hassidic communities in Toronto. Ph.D. dissertation. University of Toronto (2012)
32. Gilboa, H.: 'She brings her food from afar': Haredi women working in Israel's high-tech market. Invest. Haredic Soc. **2**, 193–220 (2015). (in Hebrew)

The Effectiveness of Twitter as a Tertiary Education Stakeholder Communication Tool: A Case of #FeesMustFall in South Africa

Nkululeko Makhubu[✉] and Adheesh Budree[✉]

Department of Information Systems, The University of Cape Town, Rondebosch, Cape Town, South Africa
nmakhubu@hsrc.ac.za, adheesh.budree@uct.ac.za

Abstract. Twitter has been a prevailing proxy in activating South Africa's #FeesMustFall student movement. This research explores whether or not, social media enables effective student online activism. In contentious periods, it is crucial to determine an effective means of conflict resolution within tertiary education, via information and telecommunication technology. This case study analyses a gross total of 567,533 tweets, sampling the student movement's inceptional years of 2015 and 2016. Frameworking this enormous engagement using big data requires a mixed research approach. Using a big data conceptual framework, this paper prioritises trend lines over headlines. The findings suggests a methodological problem for South African researchers, university practitioners, and social science scholars to collaborate ensuring long-term success of a microblogging data management value chain within a tertiary education specific ecosystem. A South African higher education microblogging environment which collectively explores local inter-campus microblogging for public engagement. The Big Data V-Model can inform higher education stakeholders of public engagement effectiveness on five different qualitative and quantitative factors. In this process, key big data opportunities and issues can be addressed promptly and appropriately to the respective campus issues.

Keywords: Big data · Higher education · Social media · Twitter · Student activism · #FeesMustFall

1 Introduction

Social media has fundamentally changed how a globalized society communicates. Citizens, students and the international arena can increasingly easily engage on socio economic issues. As an empirical problem, this research is motivated by the #Fees-MustFall public engagement of universities in South Africa, where there is often difficulty in communicating within and beyond necessary campus stakeholders. "In a highly political post-apartheid South Africa, the promise of a truly, non-racialized society remains largely unrealized" (Haffajee 2015: 11). After 25 years of democracy, South Africans still faces a multitude of socio-economic and political challenges. These may include a depressed economy, a growing lack of confidence in the political liberation party of the African National Congress party (ANC) as well as a large youth

© Springer Nature Switzerland AG 2019
G. Meiselwitz (Ed.): HCII 2019, LNCS 11578, pp. 535–555, 2019.
https://doi.org/10.1007/978-3-030-21902-4_38

population demanding better access to their basic rights and jobs (Malala 2015). Big data facilitates with investigating the effect of protestors' online socio-political grievances on campus, the national, and student life arena calls for transformation in the higher education.

Due to application programming interface (API) accessibility, Twitter is the most studied as it differs from other social media platforms for academic research. Williams et al. (2017) further pronounces the platform is the main space for the online citizenry engagement to events. In this case, the hashtag campaign #FeesMustFall. Mentioned empirical and methodological problems are addressed respectively.

Twitter hashtag campaigns allow for rich mixed research worthy data from smartphones to desktops user perspectives. The case of #FeesMustFall serves as lessons learnt to student unity, higher education policy stakeholders, and local campus communities. Should student communities build personalised microblogging platforms, specific for student activism?

Applicable for this study, descriptive science, as Dey (2003) describes a category of science that involves descriptive research; that is, observing, recording, describing, and classifying phenomena.

1.1 Research Question

Was Twitter an effective platform for student engagement during the #FeesMustFall protests in South Africa?

If not, should campus communities build internal microblogging platforms for inter-campus stakeholder communication?

1.2 Research Objective

Case study research is based on an in-depth empirical investigation of a single individual, group or event to explore the causes of underlying principles, in accordance to Yin (1998). Social media has changed how we communicate with each other. Therefore this case study of 2015 and 2016, #FeesMustFall as indicated by its naming, on Twitter, not only as conveyors of information but effectively as decentralised organising platforms. "Moreover, #FeesMustFall represents a new kind of activist politics in the context of post-apartheid South Africa: it was a multi-cultural, multi-racial and multi-class movement; it was multi-partisan, in that frequently the full range of party-aligned national student political organisations were acknowledged according to Brooks (2018). Throughout 2015, comments became centred on #RhodesMustFall, #SONA (State of the Nation Address), #FeesMustFall, and #ZumaMustFall (Findlay 2015).

The study uses an objectivist ontological stance to describe characteristics of the #FeesMustFall twitter population. Descriptive research used focuses not on questions about how, when, why the characteristics occurred. Rather it addresses the "what" question, hence a pragmatic epistemology is appropriate.

The approach to literature deductively moves from exploratory to descriptive nature. In the span of two years, the study collects over half a million tweet data to explore and explain additional information about online student protest culture.

Considering Twitter protestor practice the study interrogates big data constructs if whether or not campus communities should build internal microblogging platforms for inter-campus stakeholder communication.

2   Literature Review

"Daily data" such as comments on Facebook, likes, video and picture posts, tweets, and millions of videos on YouTube are just common examples of the sources of millions and trillions of data that is being stored and uploaded/downloaded every day over the Internet. Tomar et al. (2017) explains the exponential growth of data is challenging for Facebook, Yahoo, Google, Amazon, and Microsoft. The term "Big Data" is used to refer to the collection of data sets that are too large and complex to handle and process using traditional (relational database management) data processing applications.

Big Data, involves the amount of data (volume), timeliness (velocity), diversity (variety), and accuracy (veracity). Tomar et al. (2017) Big Data refers to the huge amount of data that cannot pass through current mainstream software tools. Once captured, managed, processed, and finished, Big Data could help make business decisions within a reasonable time.

A student movement is defined by students' sense of common cause in 'a combination of emotional response and intellectual conviction' (Altbach 1966: 180). Gill and de Fronzo (2009: 207–209) add a social change orientation as a criterion, arguing that student movements represent a collective effort of 'a large number of students to either bring about or prevent change'.

Suggestively, a big data political mechanism is suited for this Digitally Networked Action Segerberg and Bennett (2011) argue that evaluating the relation between transforming communication technologies and collective action demands recognizing how such technologies infuse specific protest ecologies. This includes looking beyond informational functions to the role of social media as organizing mechanisms and recognizing that traces of these media may reflect larger organizational schemes, the FeesMustFall student movement can also be included in this description.

Lei et al. (2014)'s Big Data theoretical framework defines 'Volume', 'Variety', 'Velocity', and 'Veracity' to critically discuss gaps, commonalities and contradictions thereof, deductively arriving to the fifth V-, 'Value'. Each of these framework constructs can consult tertiary education stakeholders, as this literature review will now detail.

2.1   Big Data Volume

'Volume' means Big Data systems need to be able to handle a large volume of data according to Cuicker and Schonberger (2013: 19). This study has big data narratives as a result of what social movement theorists refer to as Contentious Politics. "Contentious Politics involves interactions in which actors make claims bearing on other actors' interests, leading to coordinated efforts on behalf of shared interests or programs, in which governments are involved as targets, initiators of claims, or third parties. Contentious politics thus brings together three familiar features of social life: contention, collective action, and politics" (Tilly and Tarrow 2015).

Asian Protests
Protests "The Umbrella Movement was originally called 'Occupy Central with Peace and Love'. The Umbrella Movement became so named for the yellow umbrellas used by demonstrators as a shield against pepper spray" (Flowerdew 2017: 454). The protest was sparked after Hong Kong was notified that The Standing Committee of the National People's Congress (NPCSC) of mainland China wanted to moderate the position of Hong Kong's Chief Executive by limiting who could run for elections. The protesters took to the streets and the demonstration lasted for 97 days (Flowerdew 2017, p. 455). Social media played a key role. Demonstrators used Facebook to stay informed of the news and to stay in touch (Lee et al. 2015, p. 371).

In a similar student participation study by Qin et al. (2017, p. 139) use a big dataset of blog posts from the main Chinese microblogging platform, Sina Weibo—over a 2009–2013 date range to document how to make sense of the data and what they may imply for protest inducing outcomes, such as corruption, regime stability, local and central accountability, and the central–local balance of power. The platform mimics Twitter and it has also been used to promote social activism amongst users. The People's Republic of China still use Twitter illegally.

Coming back to South Africa, according to Fasiha Hassan (2016), Wits SRC Secretary General: Decolonisation is the umbrella under which we are functioning. #FeesMustFall highlighted the racial disparity in a post-1994 context where people like myself (who are born free) haven't overcome the real wounds of apartheid, colonialism, racism, structural racism and it's clear that there are still biases.

South American Protests
According to the authors of Social Inclusion and Usability of ICT-enabled Services (Choudrie et al. 2018) the United States and Chile have the most active student protests considering that they now have the highest student debt in the world amongst developed nations. Contextual and temporal effects on the social media–participation link, it can be expected that the cycle of protest impacts the effect of Facebook and Twitter in two ways according to Valenzuela et al. (2014).

Middle East Asia and Maghreb Protests
Considering the Middle East, "Social media played a crucial role in the Egyptian revolution, but not an exhaustive one. They were crucial for motivating the core constituency of the movement, the so-called Shabab-al-Facebook and for constructing a choreography of assembly to facilitate its coming together in public space. However, social media alone would have not 'done the trick' without young internet connected activists also engaging in street-level agitation to cross the digital divide and engage with the lower classes" (Gerbaudo 2018: 73). The dawn of the Arab Spring of 2011 brought about a change in how protests are conducted, social media platforms became a space which allowed activism to take place (Tufekci 2017: ix). Indeed 2011 was named "year of the protester" by Times Magazine (Gerbaudo 2018: 2). The quote also shows how users are using the internet to enable activism "…activists have made full use of that 'group of Internet-based applications … that allow the creation and exchange of user-generated content" (Kaplan and Haenlein 2010: 60).

Consequently, the Big Data V Model under 'volume', refers to historical context of this case study. The tweets from the #RhodesMustFall predates #FeesMustFall hashtag campaign by a few months which marked the 'Fall' of the Cecil John Rhodes statue at the University of Cape Town. The idolising of the 1890's Prime Minister of the Cape Colony generated voluminous free decolonised education narratives on Twitter in 2015 and 2016. Bosch (2016) activists argued that it promoted institutionalized racism and promoted a culture of exclusion particularly for black students.

2.2 Big Data Variety

Kitchin (2014a, b), American, described 'variety' big data as being structured and unstructured in nature, and often temporally and spatially referenced. On a Far-East complementary framework, the Lei et al. (2014) Chinese for the Institute of Computing Technology research paper released data 'variety' as the capability of processing data of different types such as un-structured, semi-structured, structured data, and different sources. Cuicker and Schonberger (2013: 73) define datafication, unearthing data from a variety of materials that no one thought held any (digital) value. Digitization, (2013: 85–97) converting analogue information into zeros and ones - so computers formats can handle it. This is true for #FeesMustFall tweets, scholars and press media cited can write based on Twitter Analytics, something that couldn't happen prior Twitter API.

The right to freedom of expression is related to freedom rights, as well as political rights. Section 7(1) of the South African Constitution provides the Bill of Rights as a post-apartheid cornerstone for citizens to contest political legitimacy. For this case study, a mixed research approach is appropriate when considering variety of numerical and non-numerical student protest tweet data constructs. Young people's political involvement is increasingly mediated through new technologies and social media linked to the idea of 'clicktivism' (Pickard 2018).

Tweet Language is mainly in English, just one of South Africa's has 11 official languages. Twitter has few afro centric translation tools, a misrepresentation of end users. Furthermore, studies find that African newsrooms are experiencing the disruptive impact of new digital technologies. Thus appropriate for this study, Mabweazara (2015) says localised new technology appropriations as defined by the complex socio-political structures in which African journalists operate, they are not rigidly confined to Africa.

Tweet sources vary from Android, iOS, desktop apps like Tweetdeck depending on the user. South Africa's growing middle class and the increased affordability of smartphones, has led to a strong Twitter uptake. "This means a big user base coming on board that is keen on a platform where they can express themselves" (World Wide Worx and Fuseware 2015: 2).

According to eNCA, in April 2018 the Higher Education and Training Minister Naledi Pandor has emphasised that meeting academic and progression requirements is still key in getting a bursary under the new scheme administered by the National Student Financial Aid Scheme (NSFAS). eNCA (2018), further states in December 2017, the former President announced free higher education for students from poor and working class families earning below R350 000 per annum.

Each campus student community initially had a unique hashtag, but after October 21, 2015, when student protesters were confronted by police at the Parliament Buildings in Cape Town, these hashtags consolidated into a single hashtag, #Fees-MustFall (Findlay 2015). The importance of this covalence is indicated by the government's short-lived attempts to ban this hashtag (Chunylall 2015). The nature of the movement changed from a protest over student tuition fees to demanding the resignation of then Higher Education and Training minister, Blade Nzimande and finally demanding change to the South African government (Findlay 2015). Ergo, this chapter shows that despite all the 'variety' of culture, language and devices, the online protest was for a certain audience not representative of the entire national stance on higher education.

2.3   Velocity and Veracity

'Velocity' refers to speed of incoming tweet data. According to research, over 554.7 million people actively use the service globally, sending 58 million "tweets" each day. Or, perhaps query one of the 135,000 new users joining the network daily (Statistic Brain 2013). In terms of Big Data Governance Frameworks (Berniz 2017) describes 'veracity', i.e. the correctness and accuracy of information in the midst of dark data.

Fast Paced Communication - No Clear Leadership
When critically discussing activism, a researcher is not only to assess reasons for protesting using an actor-specific perspective, but also the politics within the apparatus of active participation. Here a platform-specific perspective context reveals useful meta-narrative. As a communication platform, Twitter has increasingly infused itself into daily life regardless of user's geographical location, velocity in this regard is the speed of tweet data.

According to research, over 554.7 million people actively use the service globally, sending 58 million "tweets" each day. Or, perhaps query one of the 135,000 new users joining the network daily (Statistic Brain 2013). Further, it could be argued that opinion leaders play a role in influencing the masses. Even more so, these findings seem to negate the idea that Twitter, as (Walck 2013) purports can expand the possibility of how many, and whose, voices pierce through the societal noise loud enough to generate mass attention. Just like student protest issues, Twitter select few users who are driving public opinion and much of this influence is based on their number of followers and to a lesser degree, the subjects they are addressing (Walck 2013). Despite the uncertainty and messiness of the tweet data, 'veracity' in this regard. Operalization of such microblogging platforms allow protests to have increase active participation.

Father of neoliberalism, Milton Friedman writes: "Theoretical models should be tested primarily by the accuracy of their predictions rather than by the reality of their assumptions" (Friedman 1953). Like many other US based apps, Twitter's continued support in South Africa is not guaranteed. In the meantime for research, a tweet is short and harder to put out of context in analysis in this case study. However, known for his controversial tweets, Donald Trump urged US lawmakers to accept fewer immigrants from "shithole countries" – such as Haiti and poorer African nations – and more from the likes of Norway (Skodo 2018). A New York Times article responds, Mr. Trump's remarks came the same day that the United Nations secretary general, António Guterres, gave a speech urging reasoned debate on immigration. "Let us focus on the overwhelming positives of migration and use facts, not prejudice, to address its challenges" as Libell and Porter (2018) quotes.

In conclusion, apart from geographical uncertainty of Tweets, 'veracity' points the need for wider access of smartphones, cheaper data and social media knowhow. Additional user data fields during the #FeesMustFall student uprising contributes to better understanding of soft power influence on Twitter protest culture. Hence, more velocity of Twitter data could potentially contribute to a disruptive microblogging culture representing marginalized student needs (politics) quicker, within a participatory democracy.

2.4 Digital Information and Technology Value in #FeesMustFall

What is the Value of Microblogging?

According to Passant et al. (2008) Microblogging is one of the recent social phenomena of Web 2.0. It fills a gap between blogging and instant messaging, allowing people to publish short messages on the web about what they are currently doing. Moreover, Zhang et al. (2017) say the popularity of social media applications has provided governments, especially in developing countries, new opportunities and challenges associated with the administrative shift toward open innovation.

As a result, the term 'Big Data' over the past decade or so has noticeably become an interesting study in the ICT sector, used first by Francis X. Diebold, an economist at the University of Pennsylvania (Lohr 2013). It refers to our ability to harness, store, and extract valuable meaning from vast amounts of data. It holds the implicit promise of answering fundamental questions, which disciplines such as the sciences, technology, healthcare, and business have yet to answer (Kitchin 2014a, b). In fact, as the volume of data available to professionals and researchers steadily grows opportunities for new discoveries as well as potential to answer research challenges at stake are fast increasing (Manovich 2011).

A Platform-Specific Perspective to #FeesMustFall

In a 2016 chapter, the International Higher Education journal, Africa's top Higher Education researcher based at the Human Sciences Research Council, Luescher (2016) writes: "The truly innovative dimension of the 2015 '#...MustFall' movements is the extent to which student activists and sympathizers took to social media and the Internet". If social movement Theorists Manuel Castells conceptualizes in Networks of Outrage and Hope a new form of Internet-age social movements at the example of Occupy Wall Street and others around the globe (Castells 2015: 10–13), the #Fees-MustFall movements signal the advent of a new way of organizing student power in a networked student movement that occupies simultaneously the cyberspace and public spaces. Students used social media and Internet-based platforms prolifically as means to conscientize and mobilize others, coordinate activism, share pamphlets, readings, pictures, and video-clips, and document in an unending stream what is happening around the country and campus based social media organisations.

However, According to Tufekci (2017) there are activists who do not tweet, yet make impactful rhetoric to the cause. A platform-specific perspective (as opposed to an actor-specific one) is the focus of this paper's Twitter analytics findings. How the platform and its social, regulatory and technical environment has change from 2015 and what this study can say now about Twitter activism.

Twitter or Bespoke Microblogs

Differentiating between microblogging and social networking has become ambiguous as apps attempt to have multiple services, such as WeChat. However according to Murphy (2013) social networking service is an online platform which people use to build social networks or social relations with other people who share similar personal or career interests, activities, backgrounds or real-life connections. Conversely according to Murphy (2013) Microblogging is an online broadcast medium that exists as a specific form of blogging. A microblog differs from a traditional blog in that its content is typically smaller in both actual and aggregated file size. Microblogs "allow users to exchange small elements of content such as short sentences, individual images, or video links", which may be the major reason for their popularity. These small messages are sometimes called micro-posts.

It seems, the Chinese multi-purpose messaging, social media and mobile payment app WeChat is an example that social media use - at its optimal may be socially invasive, and that the data may be used by authorities for complex misuse. This could be an issue on other platforms too. Shobhit (2018) lists other popular microblog platforms namely: Gab, micro.blog, identi.ca, Tout, Twitter, Yammer, Mastodon, Twister, Tumblr, some include even Facebook in this category.

3   Theoretical Framework

3.1   The Big Data V Model

This case study uses a big data framework where #FeesMustFall findings will indicate whether or not dependence on Twitter activism adequately responds to student politics. This response has to satisfy the V Model by being fast, deep, representational, and ease of satisfying additional data fields.

Remember, Big Data is all about seeing and understanding the relations within and among pieces of information that, until very recently, we struggled to fully grasp (Cuicker and Schonberger 2013: 19). Furthermore, Lei et al. (2014) Big Data theoretical framework defines 'Volume', 'Variety', 'Velocity', and 'Veracity' to critically discuss gaps, commonalities and contradictions thereof, to arrive to the fifth V-, 'Value'.

IBM has created the framework for dealing with Big Data, regardless of the type of stakeholder or industry. The American multinational technology company headquartered in Armonk, New York, say "the Four V's break big data into four dimensions: volume, variety, velocity and veracity. For updated figures, please refer to the infographic Extracting business value from the 4 V's of big data" (IBM; 2013). The fifth V- is for the useable 'Value' extracted, this information can be used for various aspects depending on end user requirements. In the case study of student participation online, fits with #FeesMustFall tweets in the month of October 2015 and 2016.

Informing the big data conceptual framework of this paper Lei et al. (2014) "propose novel data generation tools meeting with the requirements of data volume, variety, velocity, and veracity. To cover diverse and representative workloads, we classify big data applications into three types from the user's perspective: online services, offline analytics, and real time analytics." Others use the V Model as a good structure for handling Twitter analytics for critical discourse analysis.

Hilbert (2015) "Big Data for Development: A Review of Promises and Challenges. Development Policy Review" looks at the "V model" to create a framework suitable for this paper. The Four V's for this research are namely, Volume, Variety, Velocity and Veracity. The fifth V is Value, whereas the information goals and principles are for a specific output. Variability is included in other models, where-by "inconsistency of the data set can hamper processes to handle and manage it".

#FeesMustFall has messy data as it was a major trending 2015 hashtag campaign on Twitter (Fairbanks 2015). In this literature review study, disregarding Veracity assumes that the available dataset is clean. That is exactly how (Xiaomeng 2013) conceptual models big data as a simple set theory of three constructs, namely volume (size of data), velocity (speed of change) and variety (data sources) notably, the three V of Big Data. (Lei et al. 2014) Defines this model saying, other companies fill the gap between approaches by releasing all sorts of applications (such as Hadoop) that address different steps of the data processing sequence plus the management and the system configuration.

4 Data Collection Method

4.1 Qualitative Aspect of Mixed Research

Secondary data for this mixed study is based on #FeesMustFall Twitter data which was mined using Twitter's public REST API. The data is aggregated by MeCoDEM Twitter Analysis, powered by Mecodify v1.42 (available on GitHub). The CSV file output of tweets consist of rich date, string and numeric variables based on each Tweet's metadata. Twitter's public REST API has certain representational and operational limitations which will be discussed in greater detail later.

The MeCodify Twitter Analytics dashboard, queried the keyword 'FeesMustFall', a hashtag Twitter campaign with data for this research is aggregated in the following steps:

1. The twitter data was 'mined' using MeCodify on 14 March 2018. Using the search query: "FeesMustFall" with the date range "01 January 2015-to-31 December 2016".
2. The **data export** was a CSV file of (unclean) 567 533 rows of cases, in this case tweet data.
3. For **data processing** the CSV file is default set into the designated 26 columns containing the tweet data variables.
4. Data Analysis - Descriptive statistics (Using IBM SPSS v23). The big data V model places constructs applicable to explained constructs volume, variety, velocity and veracity. Data visualization **and social network analysis** aspect of the data set will have to be explored to add more value to the study.
5. Nvivo 12 - the qualitative aspects are considered after the value of quantitative analysis is justified. A hashtag cloud of veracity variables which contextualise **metanarrative differences** of #FeesMustFall tweets in 2015 and 2016.

4.2 Sample Selection

A longitudinal study is an observational research method in which data is gathered for the same subjects repeatedly over a period of time. Mann (2003) further states in a longitudinal cohort study, the same individuals are observed over the study period. Metadiscourse is self-reflective linguistic material referring to the evolving text and to the writer and imagined reader of that text according to Hyland and Tse (2004). A hashtag cloud guided by metadiscourse, contextualizes the social, political and even geographical rhetoric of #FeesMustFall tweets in the full years of 2015 and 2016. This is how the research justifies the student representational effect of student activists tweets. By ranking variable frequency, within the twitter data, the research can advise.

5 Statistical Design

Big data concepts allows findings for descriptive statistics on what made #FeesMustFall narratives trend daily with rapid protest engagement among users. The research design looks at how each big data construct select variables from the Twitter API dataset (Table 1).

Considering the vastness of the 462,769 tweet metadata, mixed method defines both quantitative and qualitative analysis. The ranking of variables allows meaningful data sampling – measuring the effectiveness of the given matrices. The frequency of big data variables is based on first those with 1000 tweets for string variables, also those with more than 0.1% population for numeric variables.

The logic behind this approach is to describe the effectiveness of Twitter in the student movement. Exploring relevant Twitter metadata by rankings, establishes priority factors. Then to analyze the factors quantitatively on the Big Data V Model framework. After that, qualitative analysis can triangulate how the '#FeesMustFall' Twitter narratives differed in 2015 and 2016 respectively. Thus presenting an array of

Table 1. Shows the variables to be used from the generated #FeesMustFall Twitter Metadata, which includes in total 462,769 rows, and 27 columns of data

Volume - size of data	Variety – data formats
• hashtags(X);	• tweet_language(R); source(Q);
Quantitative Method:	*Quantitative Method:*
• Frequencies	• Frequencies
Velocity – speed of data	**Veracity - dark data**
• retweets (N);	• location_name (T); location_fullname
Quantitative Method:	(U); user_location (V); user_timezone
• Range	(W);
	Quantitative Method:
	• Frequencies

findings to discuss with reference to the research question, and chapter points made in the literature review.

6   Findings and Discussion

6.1   Big Data Volume

Clout baiting is when users jump on a hashtag for no major interest, but fear of missing out. The highest ranked big data volume hashtag metadiscourse as per statistical frequencies on SPSS shows that some users employ multiple hashtags to clout bait their tweets, as #FeesMustFall was trending at numerous periods, especially towards October 2015.

For although it and some very similar terms have some currency in linguistics and discourse analysis, and although the closely related term metacommunication appears fairly often in work on speech communication (Kopple 1985). Figure 1 shows only hashtags within the database that were used more than 1000 tweets. The main point of observation is that tweets which use multiple hashtags in addition to "#FeesMustFall" rank high in terms of retweets. Metadiscourse is a term that is used in philosophy to denote a discussion about a discussion (and so on), as opposed to a simple discussion about a given topic. The term metadiscourse is also used in writing to describe a word or phrase that comments on what is in the sentence, usually as an introductory adverbial clause.

Metadiscourse is self-reflective linguistic material referring to the evolving text and to the writer and imagined reader of that text. The 2552 (0.5%) null entries represent tweets that had no spacing in between, as user attempted to tag multiple hashtags in a Tweet. For example on October 19, 2015, 11:48 by userID "6.56074E+17", when the user tweeted:

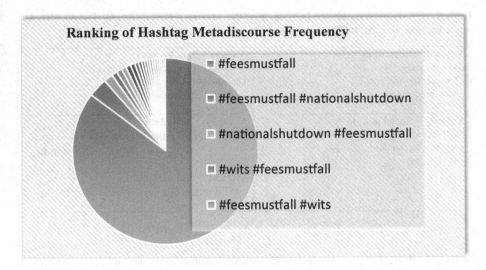

Ranking of Hashtag Metadiscourse Frequency

- #feesmustfall
- #feesmustfall #nationalshutdown
- #nationalshutdown #feesmustfall
- #wits #feesmustfall
- #feesmustfall #wits

Fig. 1. Shows only hashtags within the database that were used more than 1000 tweets.

"These protests should be directed at our corrupt officials in the Union buildings, Parliament and yes eNkandla #FeesMustFall#blademustfall".

Hashtags which the Twitter community could have no hyperlinked conversation for such tweets.

6.2 Big Data Variety

Ranking Fig. 2 is sampled based on the tweet source (instrument or device) type with over 0.1% within the database. Language: Selection of rank size was based upon over a thousand tweets sent in that particular language type within the range of Twitter identifiable language inventory. According to Twitter Developer policy and terms (2019), the following language codes express the following ranked dialects: 'en' is the English language. 'und' are undisclosed languages or vernacular. 'in' language code for Indonesian. 'nl' is for dutch, tl is for Thai, and ht is 'Tagalog'.

Figure 3 ranking selection is based on the tweet source (instrument or device) type with over 0.1% population distribution within the database. On the other hand, Fig. 3 considers the increased use of smartphone adoption over traditional laptop and desktops. It is alarming that the data indicates desktop users (Twitter web Client) rank higher than those on iPhones. Moreso, the multiple platforms and devices show that there was a significant amount of #FeesMustFall tweets that can be safely assumed were at a desk situation, as higher education lecturers, administrators, parents and media collectively played empathizers to the student movement.

The following tweet by user "6.56424E+17", on the October 20, 2015 at 10:57, is an example of the South African student dialect, undetected by Twitter, unifies not only

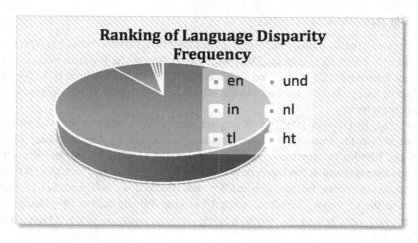

Fig. 2. Ranking selection is based on the tweet source (instrument or device) type with over 0.1% population distribution within the database.

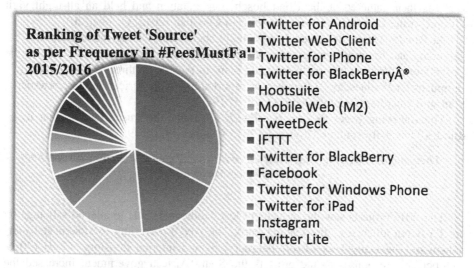

Fig. 3. Considering the increased use of smartphone adoption over traditional laptop and desktops. It is alarming that the data indicates desktop users (Twitter web Client) rank higher than those on iPhones.

metadiscourse with the use of hashtags, but also the unification of isiXhosa and the English language in a single tweet:

"You know students are fed up when they tell Maimane that "Hamba, you fucken sellout" ðŸˆ,ðŸˆ,ðŸˆ, #UCTFeesMustFall #FeesMustFall"

6.3 Big Data Velocity

In the #FeesMustFall dataset there was a sum total of 1,210,150 retweets. Specifically there were 838,974 Retweets in 2015, which is 69.3% of the big data velocity as per retweets. Retweets in 2016 reduced to a mere 371,176 in 2016, which is 30.6% of the big data velocity. Below are the events which became iconic to the #FeesMustFall student movement.

Monday, 19 October 2015: fresh negotiations between students and the university had begun. On the same day similar protests had spread to the University of Cape Town and Rhodes University according to Kekana et al. (2015, October, 19). On the same day management at the University of Cape Town - which had announced a 10.3% fee increase the week before- applied for and received a court interdict to prevent protests at the university. Students started blocking vehicle access by placing rocks, dustbins, and benches on the roads leading into the campus, writes Quintal (2015, October, 19).

Students went ahead and led by the Rhodes Must Fall movement occupied the university's administration building. Riot police were called to forcibly evict the protesters with over 25 students being arrested late at night. Reportedly over a thousand students then gathered at the Rondebosch police station and held an all-night vigil calling for the student's release according to Christian (2015, October 20).

At Rhodes University students reportedly started barricading themselves into the university and forcibly turning away others from entering the campus. Students at the University of Pretoria reportedly initiated plans to lock down three of that university's campuses for Wednesday 21 October, as reported by South African weekly newspaper Mail and Guardian Quintal (2015, October, 19).

The following tweet by user 6.56E+17, illustrates the frustration of what many Rhodes University student activists in 2015 October 19, 05:19:

"They might as well say they want the White privileged to register with R45000 upfront #FeesMustFall"

The 2016 protests saw the movement lose momentum, due to alleged sabotage by the PYA (an alliance of the leading party, the ANC) according to student-led journalism of The Daily Vox (2017, February, 3) and internal divisions. Goba (2016, October, 27) responses to the protests the South African government increased the amount budgeted for higher education by R17-billion over 3 years and stated that government subsidies to universities would increase by 10.9% a year. The protests also increased the use of blended learning by South African universities to assist non-protesting students complete their courses.

In October 27, 2016 the following two tweets illustrate the sentiments shared between national political metadiscourse, from what was a student movement initially:

"#FeesMustFall that simply means tax must rise!! That's where government will get the money....Students are shooting themselves on the leg!"

And

"Don't burden the poor in solving #FeesMustFall. Stop #IFF, abandon nuclear power, spend less on arms, increase corporate tax @TreasuryRSA"

6.4   Big Data Veracity

Geographic information using Twitter API is a challenge as users have an option to stich on their geotagging on their smartphones, also that users can write wherever they reside on their bio's information even fictional locations. More so, the variable 'location_fullname' are void of data entry in the entire dataset.

User Location is also troublesome as these are the GPS based tweets where there are only 13% of the users do not disclose this meta data whilst tweeting. Furthermore, 12.1% only disclose 'South Africa' this is insufficient demographical disclosure also, gender is not disclosed.

Today, it's possible to gather every click of every move of every user who interacts with any software in a database and submit it to a second-degree data-mining operation. Girardin et al. (2008) continues that along with the growing ubiquity of mobile technologies, the logs produced have helped researchers create and define new methods of observing, recording, and analyzing a city and its human dynamics. In effect, these personal devices create a vast, geographically aware sensor web that accumulates tracks to reveal both individual and social behaviors with unprecedented detail.

The selection of an appropriate model for large-scale data analysis is critical. Talia (2013) pointed out that obtaining useful information from large amounts of data requires scalable analysis algorithms to produce timely results. However, current algorithms are inefficient in terms of big data analysis. Therefore, efficient data analysis tools and technologies are required to process such data. Each algorithm performance ceases to increase linearly with increasing computational resources. As researchers continue to probe the issues of big data in cloud computing, new problems in big data processing arise from the transitional data analysis techniques. The speed of stream data arriving from different data sources must be processed and compared with historical information within a certain period of time. Such data sources may contain different formats, which makes the integration of multiple sources for analysis a complex task.

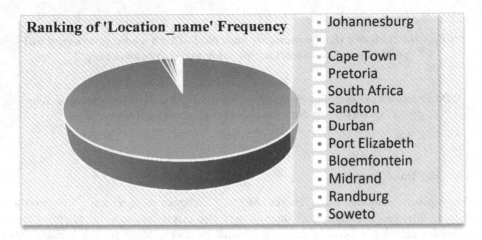

Fig. 4. Shows the representational improbability that 94.2% of 2015 and 2016 #FeesMustFall tweets came from Johannesburg

As seen in Figs. 5 and 4 dark data is not only misleading, but data which is acquired through various computer network operations but not used in any manner to derive insights or for decision making. Tittel (2014) reiterates the ability of an organisation to collect data can exceed the throughput at which it can analyse the data. In some cases the organisation may not even be aware that the data is being collected.

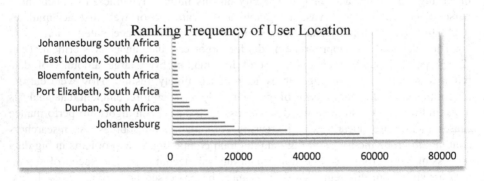

Fig. 5. Difficulty to make geography specific analysis or decisions on this data, expressing 13% as null and 12.1% as South Africa, not assigning an exact "user_location".

As seen on Fig. 6 time zone is yet another way to detect the location of the tweet, even that seems misleading in this 2015 and 2016 #FeesMustFall database. As a result of no mandatory requirement for users to supply time zone, 170,379 tweets have null entries 36.8%, followed by 22.4% which is Pretoria, the correct time zone for South Africa.

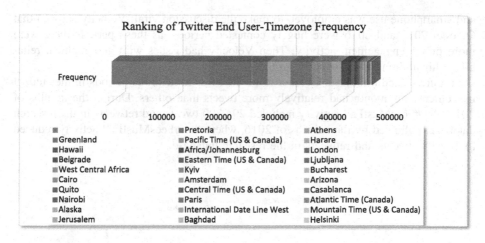

Fig. 6. Time zone is yet another way to detect the location of the tweet, even that seems misleading in this 2015 and 2016 #FeesMustFall database

Nevertheless, despite all the big data geographical veracity, the data validate important points mentioned above, in 2.1. Volume. The discourse in South Africa's student movement, #FeesMustFall, because of Twitter extended the perimeters of the respective campuses, and borders of the African continent.

6.5   Big Data Value

The effectiveness of Twitter using the V Model consults higher education stakeholders that the communication tool can be measured on five factors. Volume attests Metadiscourse amongst Twitter activists; Variety shows unity in language and desktop

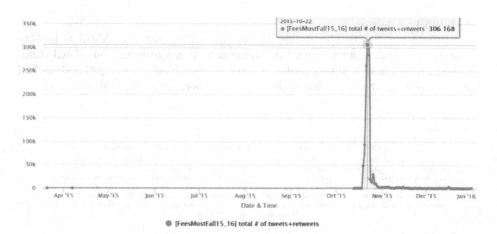

Fig. 7. During the months of 2015, the #FeesMustFall activity included 294 790 tweets and retweets in the research database.

and smartphone use was employed to make the discussion viral; Velocity showed that October 2015 and 2016 were hugely contested periods, as these periods there were more public engagement activity; Then Velocity had issues with geographical reliability, highlighting user concerns around privacy and anonymity.

Figures 7 and 8 indicate October to be the most contentious periods in the student movement, this month had relatively more tweets than others. During the months of 2015, the #FeesMustFall activity included 294 790 tweets and retweets in the research database. Followed by the months of 2016, where the #FeesMustFall activity reduced to 167 983 tweets and retweets in the research database.

Activity of tweets
Detail level: days (click and drag to zoom,
2016-10-04
[FeesMustFall15_16] total # of tweets+retweets: 37 145
40k
30k
20k
10k
0
# of tweets
Jan '16
Feb '16
Mar '16
Apr '16
May '16
Jun '16
Jul '16
Aug '16
Sep '16
Oct '16
Nov '16
Dec '16
Date & Time
[FeesMustFall15_16] total # of tweets+retweets

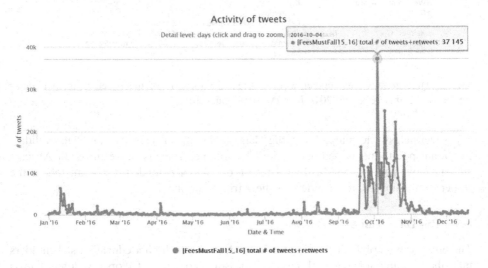

Fig. 8. During the months of 2016, the #FeesMustFall activity reduced to 167 983 tweets and retweets in the research database.

Quantitative Analysis

Furthermore, Fig. 9 ranks that during the months of 2015, the #FeesMustFall hashtag cloud gained metadiscourse centred on higher education transformation related rhetoric. And Fig. 10 ranks hashtags confirming that the months of 2016, the #FeesMustFall hashtag cloud transforms from student focus, to a more national political rhetoric.

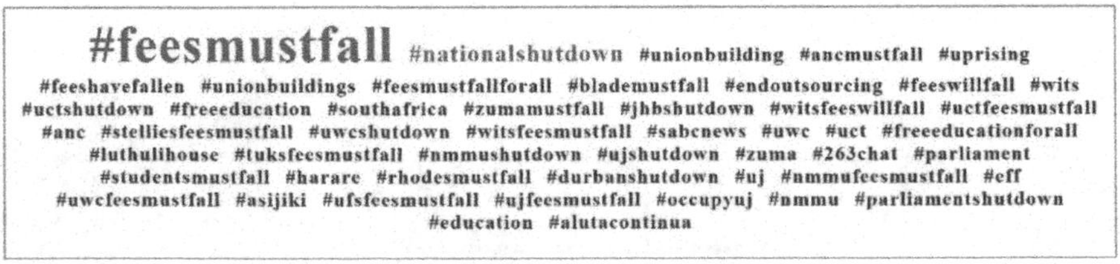

#feesmustfall #nationalshutdown #unionbuilding #ancmustfall #uprising
#feeshavefallen #unionbuildings #feesmustfallforall #blademustfall #endoutsourcing #feeswillfall #wits
#uctshutdown #freeeducation #southafrica #zumamustfall #jhbshutdown #witsfeeswillfall #uctfeesmustfall
#anc #stelliesfeesmustfall #uwcshutdown #witsfeesmustfall #sabcnews #uwc #uct #freeeducationforall
#luthulihouse #tuksfeesmustfall #nmmushutdown #ujshutdown #zuma #263chat #parliament
#studentsmustfall #harare #rhodesmustfall #durbanshutdown #uj #nmmufeesmustfall #eff
#uwcfeesmustfall #asijiki #ufsfeesmustfall #ujfeesmustfall #occupyuj #nmmu #parliamentshutdown
#education #alutacontinua

Fig. 9. During the months of 2015, the #FeesMustFall hashtag cloud gained metadiscourse centred on higher education transformation related rhetoric.

7 Conclusion

The Big Data V-Model can enlighten higher education stakeholders of public engagement effectiveness on five dissimilar qualitative and quantitative factors. In this process, key big data prospects and concerns can be developed or addressed, promptly and appropriately to the respective campus issues. Taking cue from the big data v-model framework, big data volume: the size of "#FeesMustFall" Twitter data at present is huge, and continues to increase every day. The variety of data being generated is also expanding. The velocity of data generation and growth is increasing because of the proliferation of mobile devices and other device sensors connected to the Internet. These data provide opportunities that allow businesses across all industries to gain real-time insights, such as the Future of Work (in the so called, Fourth Industrial Revolution), using Twitter Analytics dashboards such as Mecodify used for this research.

The findings prove that volume, scalability, availability, data integrity, data protection, data transformation, data quality/heterogeneity, privacy and legal/regulatory issues, data access, and governance. Furthermore, the key issues in big data in clouds were highlighted. In the future, significant challenges and issues must be addressed by the academia and industry.

This study is an appropriate contribution for either researchers, commerce, higher education practitioners, and social science scholars should collaborate to ensure the long-term success of a transformed tertiary education landscape in South Africa. Twitter was an effective disruptive platform for student engagement, during the #FeesMustFall protests. Tweeting #FeesMustFall collectively presented a case to explore new local inter-campus microblogging platforms, for student and higher education stakeholder engagement.

References

Altbach, P.G.: Students and politics. Comp. Educ. Rev. **10**(2), 175–187 (1966)

Berniz, A.: Big Data Frameworks – Practical Insights in a Data-Driven World!. Project Managers (2017). https://projectmanagers.org/big-data-frameworks/

Booysen, S.: Fees Must Fall: Student Revolt, Decolonisation and Governance in South Africa. Wits University Press, Johannesburg (2017)

Bosch, T.: Twitter activism and youth in South Africa: the case of #RhodesMustFall. Inf. Commun. Soc. **20**(2), 221–232 (2016)

Chunylall, R.: Thought Leader, #FeesMustFall: a movement of shares, likes, tweets and posts. http://thoughtleader.co.za/rasvanthchunylall/2015/10/29/feesmustfall-a-movement-of-shares-likes-tweets-and-posts/. Accessed 10 Nov 2015

Castells, M.: Networks of Outrage and Hope: Social Movements in the Internet Age, Polity, Malden (2015)

Choudrie, J., Kurnia, S., Tsatsou, P.: Social Inclusion and Usability of ICT-Enabled Services. Routledge, New York City (2018)

Dey, I.: Qualitative Data Analysis: A User Friendly Guide for Social Scientists. Routledge, New York (2003)

Earl, J., Kimport, K.: Digitally Enabled Social Change: Activism in the Internet Age. MIT Press, Cambridge (2011)

Friedman, M.: Essays in Positive Economics 'The Evolution of the Concept'. In: Snook (ed.) University of Chicago Press, Chicago (1953)

Gasson, S.: SSM Rationale: "Soft Systems" Thinking. http://cci.drexel.edu/faculty/sgasson/SSM/ SystemsThinking.htm. Accessed 25 July 2018

Gill, J., de Fonzo, J.: A comparative framework for analysis of student movements. Soc. Mov. Stud. **8**(3), 203–224 (2009)

Haffajee, F.: What If There Were No Whites in South Africa? Picador Africa, Johannesburg (2015)

Hilbert, M., López, P.: The world's technological capacity to store, communicate, and compute information. Science **332**(6025), 60–65 (2011)

Hofmeyr, J., Govender, R.: South African Reconciliation Barometer 2015, Briefing Paper 2, Cape Town: Institute for Justice and Reconciliation, Cape Town (2016)

Kitchin, R.: Big data, new epistemologies and paradigm shifts. Big Data Soc. Digit. Hum. **1**(1), 1–12 (2014a)

Kitchin, R.: The real-time city? Big data and smart urbanism. Geo J. **79**(1), 1–14 (2014b)

Lee, P.S.N., So, C.Y.K., Leung, L.: Social media and umbrella movement: insurgent public sphere in formation. Chin. J. Commun. **8**(4), 356–375 (2015). https://doi.org/10.1080/ 17544750.2015.1088874

Lei, J., et al.: BigDataBench: A Big Data Benchmark Suite from Internet Services. University of Chinese Academy of Sciences, China (2014)

Leif, J.: XMPP as MOM - Greater NOrdic MIddleware Symposium (GNOMIS) (2005). http:// www.gnomis.org/presentasjoner/oslo2005/xmpp.pdf. Accessed 1 Mar 2018

Libell, H.P., Porter, C.: New York Times, From Norway to Haiti, Trump's Comments Stir Fresh Outrage.   https://www.nytimes.com/2018/01/11/world/trump-countries-haiti-africa.html? hp&action=click&pgtype=Homepage&clickSource=story-heading&module=b-lede-package- region&region=top-news&WT.nav=top-news&_r=. Accessed 11 Jan 2018

Luescher, T.M.: Frantz Fanon and the #MustFall movements in South Africa. Int. High. Educ. **85**, 22–24 (2016)

Luescher, T., Klemenčičn, M., Jowi, J.O.: Student Politics in Africa - Representation and Activism, African Minds Higher Education Dynamics Series, Cape Town (2016)

Lohr, S.: The New York Times, The Origins of 'Big Data': An Etymological Detective Story. https://bits.blogs.nytimes.com/2013/02/01/the-origins-of-big-data-an-etymological-detective- story. Accessed 23 July 2018

Mabweazara, H. (ed.): Digital Technologies and the Evolving African Newsroom. Routledge, London (2015)

Malala, J.: We Have Now Begun Our Descent. Jonathan Ball Publishers, Johannesburg & Cape Town (2015)

Mann, C.J.: Observational research methods. Research design II: cohort, cross sectional, and case-control studies. Emerg. Med. J. **20**(1), 54–60 (2003)

Manovich, L.: Trending: The Promises and the Challenges of Big Social Data (2011). http:// manovich.net/content/04-projects/067-trending-the-promises-and-the-challenges-of-big- social-data/64-article-2011.pdf. Accessed 20 Apr 2018

Murphy, B.: The New York Times, Benét's reader's encyclopedia, Harper Collins, New York. https://bits.blogs.nytimes.com/2013/02/01/the-origins-of-big-data-an-etymological-detective- story/. Accessed 25 July 2018

Passant, A., Hastrup, T., Bojars, U., Breslin, J.: Microblogging: a semantic web and distributed approach (2008)

Segerberg, A., Bennett, W.L.: Social media and the organization of collective action: using Twitter to explore the ecologies of two climate change protests. Commun. Rev. **14**(3), 197– 215 (2011)

Shobhit, S.: World's Top 10 Internet Companies. Investopedia. https://www.investopedia.com/articles/personal-finance/030415/worlds-top-10-internet-companies.asp. Accessed 25 July 2018

Skodo, A.: Scandinavia takes plenty of people from Trump's 'shithole countries'. The Conversation. https://theconversation.com/scandinavia-takes-plenty-of-people-from-trumps-shithole-countries-90062. Accessed 15 Jan 2018

Tomar, G., Chaudhari, N.S., Bhadoria, R.S., Deka, G.C.: The Human Element of Big Data: Issues, Analytics, and Performance. CRC Press, Boca Raton (2017)

Tufekci, Z.: Twitter and Tear Gas: The Power and Fragility of Networked Protest. Yale University Press, United States (2017)

Valenzuela, S., Arriagada, A., Scherman, A.: Facebook, Twitter, and Youth Engagement: A Quasi-experimental Study of Social Media Use and Protest Behavior Using Propensity Score Matching. Pontificia Universidad Católica de Chile, Chile (2014)

Walck, P.E.: Twitter: social communication in the twitter age. Int. J. Interact. Commun. Syst. Technol. 3(2), 66–69 (2013)

Willis, N.: StatusNet, Identi.ca, and transitioning to pump.io. LWN.net (2013). Accessed 20 Mar 2018

World Wide Worx and Fuseware: South African Social Media Landscape 2015. Executive Summary (2015) http://www.worldwideworx.com/wp-content/uploads/2014/11/Exec-Summary-Social-Media-2015.pdf. Accessed 5 Dec 2018

Xiaomeng, S.: Introduction to Big Data. Opphavsrett: Forfatter og Stiftelsen TISIP (2013). https://www.ntnu.no/iie/fag/big/lessons/lesson2.pdf. Accessed 20 June 2018

Yin, R.K.: The abridged version of case study research: design and method. In: Bickman, L., Rog, D.J. (eds.) Handbook of Applied Social Research Methods, pp. 229–259. Sage Publications, Inc., Thousand Oaks (1998)

Zhang, N., Zhao, X., Zhang, Z., Meng, Q., Tan, H.: What factors drive open innovation in China's public sector? A case study of official document exchange via microblogging (ODEM). Haining Gov. Inf. Quart. 34(1), 126–133 (2017)

The Use of Social Media as Part
of a Transmedia Storytelling Strategy
in WWE's Professional Wrestling

Eliseo Sciarretta[✉]

Link Campus University, via del Casale di San Pio V, 44, 00165 Rome, Italy
e.sciarretta@unilink.it

Abstract. This paper aims at exploring the ways social media and new technologies are currently used within professional wrestling and how this model is exploited to create transmedia storytelling strategies. The first chapter is an introduction to the world of professional wrestling and its main promotion, World Wrestling Entertainment. In the second chapter, the author focuses on the storytelling within wrestling, introducing the concept of kayfabe, highlighting similarities in narrative between wrestling and serialized drama, but also their differences, bringing out the active role of the audience in wrestling. Then, attention is paid to how WWE in particular has managed to succeed in transmedia storytelling, exporting its content from TV shows and live performances to a wide range of other media and products. Finally, before the conclusions, the author analyzes the different uses of social media within wrestling, arguing that they impact kayfabe and allow the audience to change scenarios and storylines.

Keywords: Professional wrestling · Social media · Transmedia storytelling

1 Introduction

1.1 The World of Professional Wrestling

Professional wrestling is a sport/entertainment where athletes/actors (commonly referred to as wrestlers) play the role of characters, or personas, who mainly aspire to win one or more championship belts.

In other words, pro-wrestling "presents a simulacrum of grappling and combat sport practices with ancient roots, framed by serial narratives of rivalry, jealousy and deceit that present a moral universe often characterized in simplistic way" (Chow 2014).

To achieve their goal, in fact, characters follow different paths, depending on their own attitude: the good guy is called "babyface" and usually fights a "heel", the bad guy. The babyface is therefore the embodied sign of "good" within the conventional "good versus evil" wrestling narrative (Barthes 1972). Following this scheme, wrestlers face rivalries (or feuds) with other characters of the same roster: feuds can arise because of simple dislikes, or because a wrestler has set off on another's path, for example by stealing an opportunity, and generally involve betrayals and subterfuges by the heel.

G. Meiselwitz (Ed.): HCII 2019, LNCS 11578, pp. 556–570, 2019.
https://doi.org/10.1007/978-3-030-21902-4_39

Thus, the narratives behind the rivalries are considered one of the main reasons that can determine the success or failure of wrestling.

Feuds are eventually solved through fight matches in the ring, then wrestlers move on to the next rivalry.

The outcomes of the matches, and therefore of the feuds, are pre-determined by scriptwriters (known as bookers). So, unlike traditional sport, there is no real competition in wrestling. Or at least, the nature of this competition is very different from that found in traditional sports. Fights, as already said, "are woven into an on-going story about the individual wrestler and their interaction with the rest of the wrestling community" (Oliva 2009). In a traditional sport, the stronger fighter would win. In professional wrestling, to be the winner, performers need to show other features: they must play their role in the best possible way, a babyface must be loved by the crowd, while a heel must be hated. Those who succeed at this, usually are "pushed" by the promotion and have better chances to win and get close to the coveted championship belt.

The athletes/actors follow a general script in the spoken segments used to build up the matches, but they keep a significant share of freedom in the fight sequences.

The results of the matches and important events may be ordained by the bookers, but all of the time athletes spend in the ring engaged in a simulation of a competition is a negotiation between wrestlers. This custom is so ingrained that "there is also a certain type of standardized etiquette at work in these negotiations to build the flow of the match and its narrative points" (MacFarlane 2012). In this custom, the most skilled wrestlers generally make decisions while typically heels "call the spots", through an improvised communication based on a shared terminology, and control the general flow of the match within the ring.

To this extent, professional wrestling has been sometimes compared to other forms of choreographed performance, such as dance. What is different, though, is that a wrestling match is responsive to the live audience. People attending the show do not know anything about how it will end, just as if the match was "real". Wrestlers hear if fans cheer or boo and they can tailor the performance to those reactions, for example by speeding up the pace.

Still, fans who crowd the arenas to attend wrestling pay not to see a sport or a challenge, but a staged performance. "This has tended to outrage critics, who judge professional wrestling by its legitimacy as a traditional sport and thus painting professional wrestling as deceptive" (Oliva 2009). As Barthes argued this perspective trivializes the fictionality of professional wrestling: "There are people who think that wrestling is an ignoble sport. Wrestling is not a sport, it is a spectacle, and it is no more ignoble to attend a wrestled performance of suffering than a performance of the sorrows of Arnolphe or Andromaque" (Barthes 1972).

1.2 World Wrestling Entertainment (WWE)

As of 2019, the largest wrestling promotion in the world is Stamford's based WWE, which holds over 500 events a year, and has a roster of athletes divided up into various globally traveling brands. The very name, World Wrestling Entertainment, already shows how important this combination of sport and entertainment is for the company.

Before 2002, the name of the company was World Wrestling Federation, but it was changed to emphasize its focus on entertainment (although mostly because of an unfavorable ruling in its dispute with the World Wildlife Fund regarding the "WWF" initialism).

World Wrestling Entertainment is now a publicly traded global media conglomerate that had an international audience and revenues of more than $800 million in 2017.

The company consists of a portfolio of businesses that create and deliver original content 52 weeks a year to a global audience. WWE is committed to family friendly entertainment on its television programming, pay-per-view, digital media and publishing platforms. The award-winning WWE Network is the first-ever 24/7 direct-to-consumer premium network that includes all live pay-per-views, scheduled programming and a massive video-on-demand library, and is currently available in more than 180 countries.

WWE has also branched out into other fields, including movies, real estate, and various other business ventures.

Revenues reached $188.4 million for the third quarter 2018 and a record $657.7 million for the nine months ended September 30, 2018, representing 12% growth over the prior year period. Through the first nine months of 2018, digital engagement increased with video views up 61% to 22.9 billion and hours consumed up 81% to 842 million across digital and social media platforms (WWE Corporate, Investors).

Most notably, in addition to its original programming watched by more than 800 million homes worldwide in 25 languages (WWE Corporate, Who We Are), WWE's far-reaching social media presence helps augment its programming and enhance the experience for viewers.

2   Professional Wrestling Storytelling

2.1   Kayfabe: What Is Real, What Is Fake

Storytelling is the most important element in decreeing the success or failure of wrestling. If a match doesn't tell a story with a good psychology, the audience won't be engaged and the business will suffer.

"The means by which matches are won fuel rivalries and keep the stories alive; the matches themselves are not the only focal point, but rather devices used to advance an intricately detailed plot" (Vargas 2007).

The whole narrative strategy of WWE is based on mimicking the sports world. Sam Ford calls WWE "the world's biggest alternate reality game", because it bases the story it wants to tell upon the rules of a sports federation, matching the place where the story takes place with the real world.

The glossary from Steel Chair to the Head (Sammond 2005) defines "kayfabe" as follows: "maintaining a fictional storyline, or the illusion that professional wrestling is a genuine contest".

In other words, it is the "illusion of realness" (Smith 2006), the portrayal of competition, rivalries, and relationships between participants as being genuine and not of a staged or predetermined nature of any kind.

In general, anything in a professional wrestling show is subject to kayfabe, even though at times it is portrayed as real-life. Some of the wrestlers compete under their real name, but the character they portray, even if is called like them or incorporates some traits of their personality, does not correspond to the person who interprets it. The line between fiction and reality is very blurred. This is because almost always wrestlers remain "in character" even during their private life.

For this reason, wrestlers can never start completely from scratch in their narration, but are always tied to the progress of their character and their personal ability. In this sense, wrestling "identity" can be constructed, but it cannot necessarily be "faked" (MacFarlane 2012).

The nature of the "fake" in wrestling is complex and controversial. For example, the moves are adapted to minimize the impact and wrestlers know how to give or take a punch (relatively) safely, but the chances of painful injuries remain high. The intentional self-injury in order to draw blood, a common practice called "blading" or "getting color", produces a real wound, even if it's self-inflicted by a wrestler who "makes a small incision in his forehead using a razor hidden in the wrist cuff or taped to the fingers, out of view of the audience (for example, when holding one's head after a blow from a steel chair that is meant to be the actual cause of injury)" (Chow 2014).

Arguably throughout its history and certainly since the 1990s, when wrestlers and promoters began to actively acknowledge kayfabe, everyone in the wrestling event is "keeping kayfabe", cheering and booing as if the bouts were sportive rather than theatrical. However, with the advent of Internet, the pro-wrestling industry has become less concerned about protecting backstage secrets and typically maintains kayfabe only during the shows. Even then, kayfabe is occasionally broken, usually when dealing with genuine injuries during a match or paying tribute to wrestlers.

Nowadays, kayfabe is often broken when wrestlers go on tour. Feuding stars in storylines can be seen being civil to each other when they are not wrestling. Off-ring persona can be strikingly different from the in-ring character with less disapproval.

As a result, "today fans and audiences take pleasure in active collaboration in not only creating the kayfabe world but also in looking for ways of dissecting it" (Mazer 2005; Wrenn 2007).

2.2 Pro-wrestling and Drama

From another point of view, WWE's pro wrestling can be interpreted as a big "soap opera" or dramatic series, and this is somehow confirmed by the management itself, as production studios, such as HBO, Fox and so on are considered as company's main competitors rather than other wrestling federations.

WWE cares that its audience is interested not so much in the outcome of the fight, as in how it is narrated and represented. The importance of the performance is therefore crucial. Storylines are a fundamental part of today's professional wrestling: WWE uses its weekly shows to tell storylines and resolves them or introduces major changes during monthly pay-per-views. "WWE wrestling therefore follows a similar narrative structure to television series, with each match developing the relations between characters and pushing the story forward" (Oliva 2009).

This vision is reinforced by the kayfabe concept itself, since it is often seen as the suspension of disbelief that is used to create feuds, angles, and gimmicks, in a manner similar to other forms of fictional entertainment. In relative terms, a wrestler breaking kayfabe during a show would be likened to an actor breaking character on-camera.

As in a soap opera, the main plot is a continuous rise towards moments of tension that are then solved and pave the way for new climaxes, in cycles that are repeated, from season to season, in a model of "open" seriality.

The basic difference, of course, is that these conflicts in WWE are solved in the ring, and not in a courtroom or in a hospital, for example.

Moreover, as in a soap opera, the audience understands (or at least should) and accepts that what they see is not real. I say "should", however, because, as said before, wrestling characters partly overlap to the people who interpret them, and this adds more realism to the story (or sometimes a sense of confusion).

The other huge difference is that pro wrestling is shot to be broadcast on TV in sports arenas, in the presence of a paying audience. Some soap operas are shot in front of a public, too, but pro wrestling is the only show of this kind in which the audience can be seen and heard and whose presence is acknowledged by performers. WWE's audience can almost be considered as an additional character, since it can influence the course of events through its behavior, and indeed it is the most difficult to manage, because it is the only one that bookers can not fully control, as I am going to address in the following paragraph.

2.3 The Importance of Audience

Henry Jenkins defines fandom as the "social structures and cultural practices created by the most passionately engaged consumers of mass media properties" (Jenkins 2010). WWE broadly refers to its fandom as the "WWE Universe".

Situated between sport and theatre, the WWE Universe and the audience in general have a "large and active role in the wrestling spectacle, participating as if the results of the matches were not determined before the performers enter the ring" (Chow 2014).

To clarify this concept and explain the importance of audience's reactions, I refer to one of the major cases in recent years, occurred in 2014: the rise of the "Yes movement" lead by wrestler Daniel Bryan. At that time, Bryan was starting to gain space in the federation, but was considered by the WWE and by its on-stage bosses, Triple H and Stephanie McMahon (collectively known as "The Authority"), as a good loser or, to use their word, "a B + player", not worthy of the main spotlight.

On the other hand, Daniel Bryan was the absolute favorite by the audience, because he was "a lanky, nervous pale kid with a goofy smile who brushes his hair forward and looks like he's just happy to be there" and a guy everyone can relate to (Oglesby 2017).

People wanted to see Bryan winning the title, but The Authority thought it otherwise, and kept denying him chances.

The situation degenerated at Royal Rumble 2014, one of the major annual pay-per-views, in which thirty professional wrestlers toss each other over the top rope until only one wrestler remains. The winner then goes on to headline WrestleMania, WWE's version of the Super Bowl.

Daniel Bryan, despite expectations, was ousted by the match and barred from the "nano-narrative" constituted within the particular match (Petten 2010; Jenkins 2014), which instead was won by Batista, the musclebound athlete chosen by WWE to be the main babyface.

The plans organized by the bookers were clear: Batista was going to challenge the heel champion Randy Orton at WrestleMania.

What WWE did not foresee, however, was the incessant, overwhelming booing coming from over 15,000 fans within the arena.

That was just the tip of the iceberg: this protest continued for months and its reasons are to be found both inside and outside of kayfabe. In fact, fans were hoping for triumph as a result of the "macro-narrative" involving Bryan (Petten 2010), but they suddenly realized that their underdog hero wouldn't have been able to overcome the odds and eventually carry out the "excessive spectacle of good triumphing over evil" (Barthes 1972).

Thus, the protest began both in the arenas and in virtual spaces, as I am going to explain later, and rapidly became impossible to ignore, leading to a change in the plans of WWE and the subsequent involvement of Daniel Bryan in the title match, which eventually culminated with his victory at WrestleMania.

This example shows how "wrestling audience members see themselves as co-performers. The fans can take action against unacceptable performances, even if it causes a narrative and social breach" (Oglesby 2017).

3 WWE Transmedia Storytelling

3.1 Narrating Kayfabe Across Platforms

WWE's television shows are not broadcast every day like episodes of a soap opera, but the number of shows (different, but with intertwining narratives) is broad and is complemented by live performances not shot on camera, and thus become a daily appointment. And everything that does not go directly on television, promptly ends up on the Internet, on the company's website, on WWE's YouTube channel or on other social platforms, on the new monthly subscription platform called WWE Network.

Due to this, professional wrestling is by its nature a fantastic example of transmedia storytelling, thanks to the unique participation of the audience, which differentiates the product by a TV series or a book, for example.

Kayfabe usually extends beyond the physical space of the ring and the arena to the media around the event but, as I said, in the social media era this process has become difficult to manage.

Transmedia storytelling is the use of multiple platforms to tell a cohesive story, where each piece adds to the story to create a better overall story.

The transmediality (Jenkins 2003; 2004) of wrestling began in the 80 s, when some wrestlers became so popular that they could be compared to movie stars. The admixture became even bigger when some television or film actors became part of the wrestling storylines by competing in some matches.

There is usually a degree of confusion between franchising and transmedia platforms since many franchises use techniques that mimic transmedia storytelling. For example, many large franchises have novel and video games adaptations of films. While this is an example of cross-platform storytelling, none of the pieces expand on the existing story, as it would be proper to transmedia storytelling.

WWE is a good example of both categories: the company produces DVDs, videogames, action figures and merchandise that are useful to amplify the revenues and the market share, but often these products add content to what is shown on TV, allowing storylines to progress, for example through breaking news reported on the website.

Social media has made this shift to transmedia storytelling a lot easier. Early transmedia storytelling was limited to major publishing companies like TV, film, comics, and books and the cost of entry was high. Now with the internet and social media, anyone can have access to content creation.

3.2   Transmedia Storytelling at Its Best

Transmedia storytelling works better in WWE and professional wrestling in general than in other serialized dramas because of the very nature of this sport-entertainment, and its main strength: wrestlers travel from arena to arena performing almost every evening, and during their tours they tell stories (which are conceived by bookers). The contemporaneity thus created between the narrated world and the real world is the secret weapon of WWE compared to other production studios in the entertainment world: during breaks between performances, wrestlers, who keep interpreting their character, can use social media to continue telling the same story, through their own profiles that they manage in real time, in the same space where viewers live, creating a suggestive mix between their real and fictitious life.

By considering wrestling as a serialized fictional product, in fact, "it is possible to analyze the kayfabe as a unique narrative frame, capable of keeping narrative coherence operating with a 1:1 ratio between real time and fictional time" (Oliva 2009).

A character that exists in a narration that takes place in real time at times produces a blurred understanding of the fictional character/real person relation.

WWE wrestlers, also called Superstars, have characters or personas that are carried over all media like their weekly television series, Twitter or any other platform. They can and have to perform their personas in their everyday life through the various social media. They are required to have Twitter handles and they can use them however they want.

By using Twitter, wrestlers are able to carry their on-screen persona off screen and into the real life. Superstars interact with each other and fans, share backstage segments, promote their merchandise. But they can also carry out on-screen feuds on the web, developing them without having to use air time on their televised show. Many times they tweet and interact with other superstars, sending out congratulations or just trash talking. This gives weight to the feuds, as if they really do not get along in their personal lives.

For example, some years ago, during a storyline between Nikki and Brie Bella, Nikki forced her sister to become her personal assistant. A few days after, Nikki posted on Vine (a short-form video hosting service where users could share six-second-long looping video clips, now closed) videos of herself coming up with embarrassing chores for her sister Brie to do. This made it seem as if the storyline continued on outside of the televised shows.

With such a large roster, it is hard to give every superstar the air time they deserve, and that the fans want. By using social media to extend the personas of the wrestlers, the WWE is able to carry out feuds and storylines outside of the television show and into everyday life. This allows every superstar to connect with the fans and audience on a whole new level.

This kind of storytelling was not previously available. Transmedia storytelling allows for the story to be told on multiple platforms, so the story feels real, and as if it was not scripted.

4 WWE Use of Social Media

4.1 Social Media and Kayfabe

Professional wrestling has received many benefits from social media, and this is especially true of independent wrestling, which has exploded in recent years, thanks in large part to the influence of these sites.

Social media have replaced portals and search engines as a starting point for navigation. Therefore, all of the content published on the web finds a great sounding board in being re-launched on social media, since it is important to go where people are nesting.

Social media allow fans to be more involved and personal with the wrestlers than ever before. It is a two-way dynamic between the superstars and the fans: from the perspective of the wrestlers, it allows them to use social media platforms to promote themselves and their promotions.

Social media have made wrestlers three-dimensional. Fans may not just choose who their favorite wrestler is, but they can also verify that real-life behavior matches the one shown on screen and understand if they like who wrestlers are as people.

There are also negative aspects, though: wrestlers are now easy target for criticism. Before social media no fan would have criticized a 2-meter-tall wrestler face-to-face; behind a computer screen, instead, fans easily turn into "keyboard lions" and can say whatever they want, even if not justifiable and dictated by hatred.

WWE Superstar Baron Corbin said: "social media give a bunch of idiots, in reality, an opinion and they don't know how to express it appropriately. The language, the insults, all of those things, and it just makes the world seem so unhappy. If you read the Twitter feed, it seems like everyone in the entire world is beyond miserable. But, I think now, unfortunately, it's a necessity. It's a form of exposure and advertisement. My Instagram, my Twitter, is a form of advertisement for my business and what I do. Yeah, my brand. It is, but it is crazy how negative it is to everything!".

Still, who knows how to use social media to their fullest potential, can make a fortune, since social media have become one of the most powerful tools at anyone's disposal.

Each social media platform has its own benefits and pitfalls. Twitter, for example, allows users to engage with their audience on an unprecedented level. Wrestlers can promote shows, appearances, and new merchandise available. They can tell people where they like to eat. Some wrestlers will host Q&A sessions with a specific hashtag. The fans get to ask a question directly of the performer, and the performers get to build their brand with the hashtag.

But how do social media impact the notion of kayfabe? Social media are just an easier and faster way to expose whatever someone wants to expose.

Wrestlers try to maintain kayfabe as much as possible. On Rey Mysterio's character Twitter page, fans could possibly read posts about how much he hates Randy Orton because he beat up his buddy Jeff Hardy, but on a personal Facebook page fans could see the three of them hanging out watching sports.

Since the arrival of the Internet and social media, keeping kayfabe has been increasingly difficult, but the federations and promotions, as I said, have accepted the idea and are trying to re-negotiate the concept to find a fair compromise between what to keep secret and what to let leaked out.

In addition, some wrestlers use social media to build their own personal brands and promote other projects, whether they are kayfabe or not. For example, during his run with Impact Wrestling (a WWE's competitor federation), Matt Hardy used social media to develop the Broken Universe, and now uses his various platforms to recreate this narrative for the WWE. Meanwhile, Xavier Woods created a new platform for himself via his YouTube channel, Up Up Down Down (UUDD), which gave him and the rest of the New Day, the stable he is part of, increased visibility and allowed them to get over with fans.

WWE routinely encourages interaction during its live shows through hashtags and tweet scrolls, as well as having their wrestlers engage with fans through a variety of social media sites. Even when wrestlers walk down the ramp to the ring, their name appears on television screen along with their Twitter handle. It also tries to exploit social media in new ways.

For instance, WWE Mixed Match Challenge, a tag team tournament featuring intergender pairings, has been launched in 2018 as a web television series that airs exclusively on Facebook Watch, and the company urges fans to interact with the Superstars during the bouts via Facebook's commenting feature. Interactions such as these serve two primary functions. First, as I already said, they allow the WWE to advance transmedia storylines across multiple media platforms (for example, wrestlers can taunt one another on Twitter, and commentators can mention these interactions while calling the in-ring action). In addition, "these interactions can sometimes allow fans a previously-unheard-of peek behind the kayfabe curtain and grant them a glimpse of the personalities that exist behind the characters" (Olson 2018).

Conversely, by demonstrating their true personalities, some wrestlers can break free from the strict oversight exercised by the promotion and thereby get "over" with the members of the WWE Universe. Thus, social media can shape or re-shape kayfabe within pro-wrestling and its main promotion, WWE.

4.2   WWE and Social Media

In 2016 alone, WWE social media had engagements over 739 million different social media accounts, grown to 850 in 2017 and 950 by the end of third quarter of 2018 (WWE Corporate, Key Performance Indicators), numbers that helped them achieve their financial and company goals during broadcasts.

At WWE headquarters in Stamford, CT, the team of marketers and strategists works hard to pump out the content that gets its viewers excited. Social media is a growing part of that process.

WWE considers social media so important, so much they generate post-show reports to analyze the audience's reactions to the events narrated on social platforms such as twitter.

The content creation team, in fact, uses Twitter as a consumer research tool, because of the instant feedback loop that it provides. Usually, at the end of pay-per-views or weekly shows, one of the superstars or one of the matches held is a top trending topic on Twitter. The team keeps an eye on what users are saying about the facts happened and the storylines told and use those insights moving forward.

While watching the show, people can use social media to connect to each other and exchange comments and impressions. They can also stay in touch with wrestlers, who use the system to build up and increase the expectation on their feuds, filling the narrative silence that exist between the airing of two episodes. Superstars use their own social media accounts, at times breaking the audience's perceived interpretation of their characters to interact with fans, both during and between broadcasts.

"You get to see what they're feeling and what they're thinking as they travel around the country and world", noted Corey Clayton (online community leader) during an interview.

WWE live broadcasts are a unique mixture of theatre, entertainment, reality television, and gameshow. They regularly "social cast" during their live and taped broadcasts, taking fans' opinions and suggestions through engagement to help shape the on-air outcomes of the product. In recent years, WWE succeeded in including fan responses in its broadcasts by featuring targeted hashtags in the corner of the screen, as well as occasionally featuring curated fan tweets in a scrolling chyron at the bottom of the screen (Oglesby 2017).

It works so well, in fact, that the company is listed weekly among the top ten social media scores by Nielsen Social Media for series and specials (https://www.nielsensocial.com/socialcontentratings/weekly/), outperforming other events such as Monday Night Football on social media.

It's impressive to see that WWE is one of the world's most popular brands on social media. Klout (now closed) was a service which assigned a score to a brand or person's social media influence, ranking them from one to 100. WWE's Klout last score was an impressive 99.

Moreover, through its mobile app, WWE provides viewers with a "second screen experience", and the chance to continue watching the matches during advertising breaks and get insights, exclusive information directly from the backstage.

WWE has also been a protagonist in the development of social media, although not always with excellent results.

From April 2008 to January 2011, WWE supported its own social network called WWE Universe. It was mildly successful, with 750,000 accounts created, 3.5 million photo uploads, 3 million comments and 400,000 blog posts, all generated from the network's community. The creative team has taken a U turn, though, since it realized that its main Facebook pages were seeing more action than its custom social network. The company shut down WWE Universe and, in preparation, began migrating its audience to its Facebook pages via its television properties, social icons in its website's top navigation.

In 2012 WWE tried again, by investing into the social media platform TOUT which allowed users to record 15 s videos and share them. This started a two-year partnership between the two companies. WWE would promote TOUT by having the commentators urge fans to TOUT their reactions and showcasing TOUTs that WWE superstars had made. This was a transmedia strategy that gave fans a look inside the lives of the superstars by giving the personas more depth. Because of the unpopularity of TOUT, though, the WWE has then moved on to use Vine.

On that principle of going where the people are, WWE has focused its efforts on making sure its content is available on the key social sites where its community is flocking, namely Facebook, Twitter and YouTube.

WWE produces about 1,500 unique pieces of content for its website per week, which it then optimizes across its social sites. Mark Keys (VP, web production) explained "We pick and choose, from our four different shows we produce, or any public events or appearances that the superstars are doing, to any other television relationships that we have".

WWE is leveraging social media to fill in the gaps that occur between TV episodes, by creating a connection via social media.

"Our form of content is really entertainment, it's not sports. So, a lot of news, if you will, is really an extension of the storyline that you're seeing on TV", explained Keys. "One of the things that WWE can do as a program that runs 52 weeks a year that is literally scripted week by week, is that we can augment our storylines with simple feeds to these social networks on a weekly basis. So, with a two-hour show that runs on Monday, we have the ability to, two or three times a week, prompt that something else is happened and that [fans] should see it. [We can] continue the story that ended on Monday night and carry it through to the next Monday night".

Recently, WWE SmackDown Live women's champion Becky Lynch has been ruled out of her Survivor Series showdown against Raw women's champ Ronda Rousey, but their feud has continued through social media, with very hard comments by "The Man" Becky Lynch.

Becky Lynch is not new to this kind of reactions, also due to her character, and she has also been criticized for some of these. In an interview with Yahoo Sports she talked (also) about the much-discussed social media issue.

She admitted that she had actually increased the use of these media and justified herself like this:

"I know a lot of people are getting nervous about how I use my social networks, but it makes people interested and involved. I will do everything in my power to make the most of my skills. If you want to punch me in the face and keep me out, you can not keep my mouth out too.

On TV I have 15 min, if I'm lucky, to tell people what I think, but if I have a platform within reach of my fingers, I can say what I think constantly, so that everyone knows exactly who I am, if they care who I am and against whom I am fighting. I take a look at some people on social media and they all write love letters… I do not have time for this, I do not understand it".

4.3   Social Media Impact Wrestling by Allowing the Audience to Change Storylines

In paragraph 2.3, I explained how audience members can affect wrestling shows and kayfabe, through an example involving Daniel Bryan and the Royal Rumble 2014.

The same example is useful now to explain how it is necessary to consider the behavior of the audience not only in the arenas but also in virtual spaces.

Outside of live events, in fact, WWE's fandom largely organizes in virtual spaces, starting during the years social media campaigns like #HijackRaw, #OccupyRaw, which trended worldwide, and #CancelWWENetwork, which arose a year after Daniel Bryan's Yes Movement, in response to, again, widespread dissatisfaction over the Royal Rumble result (Stout 2015; Oglesby 2017).

After Royal Rumble 2014, the social media reactions were immediate and enormous, with "Daniel Bryan" trending worldwide on Twitter. WWE legend Mick Foley even tweeted asking of his own employer, "Does @WWE actually hate their own audience? I've never been so disgusted with a PPV". Bryan posted the following on Twitter:

"Sorry guys, the machine wanted me nowhere near the Royal Rumble match. But I thank everyone for their support. YOU are the #YESMovement. They try to keep US down and away from the top spots, but they can't ignore the reactions forever. Keep voicing your opinions. #YESMovement".

After that, a spontaneous uprising movement named #HijackRaw has formed. A fan made a Twitter account to disseminate information about the #HijackRaw plan, posting a flyer with four main objectives. The tweet alongside the posted flyer said "Our power is in our coordination. Our objective is to be one. This is how we #HijackRaw".

The plan detailed collective actions to carry out during the live broadcast of Raw, including turning their back to some wrestlers during their segments and directions as to which stipulations for Bryan the crowd should chant "Yes" or "No" for. The plan, however, wasn't immediately successful, but it took to a new evolution.

A few weeks later, in fact, during a Raw episode, Bryan built upon the notion of he and his fandom as a collective as he revealed the plans for what would eventually become known as Occupy Raw:

"Tonight is when it ends, because we are all tired of you. You are not listening to me. You are not listening to these people. You are not listening to any of us! But tonight, we're gonna make it so you have to listen to us. Because tonight, the Yes Movement is in full effect, and tonight, we are going to occupy Raw! You see, I'm not going to leave this ring until I get what I want, which is a match with Triple H at WrestleMania. And I know you've heard people say that all the time, they're not leaving this ring. But tonight, I am not alone".

After that, that, more than 100 fans in Daniel Bryan shirts make their way to ringside.

Until the day of Occupy Raw, countless fans had made predictions and posted dream scenarios on Twitter, among them Daniel Bryan defeating Batista and taking his spot in the championship match, Bryan and Triple H both being inserted into the championship match, and the eventual result – Bryan being added to the championship match if he can defeat Triple H earlier in the same night (Oglesby 2017).

So, fans can effectively use social media to change the way storylines end. On Twitter or Facebook we can express whatever we want about whomever we want, so it would be reasonable to think that there will be some negativity about the WWE.

What emerges, though, is that World Wrestling Entertainment does not fight any Twitter hashtag, trending or not, against them. That is mostly because, as I said before, the audience can't be scripted and engaging the fans is one of the main goals of the company; without the WWE Universe, WWE basically goes out of business.

5   Conclusions

5.1   Audience's Motivation

In the previous paragraphs of this paper I have shown what the main characteristics of storytelling are within the world's biggest wrestling company, WWE, and argued how social media can affect the creative process behind storyline development, allowing on one side the federation to fill the spaces between shows and to obtain a truly transmedia narrative, and on the other hand the audience to assert even more their active role in the representation, coming up to change some choices made by the management.

While the bookers are the main authors of what the outcomes will be, the fans and their social media presence can shape the programming. WWE writers will revise sometimes long-term plans for characters based upon fan reactions on social media. WWE social media has helped grow its outreach and engagement exponentially, and its impact cannot be ignored.

While the activity and impact of WWE social media are widely regarded as a success, the use of this technology is relatively new in the WWE's history. As with any phenomenon of using new communication technology, what requires attention is why users engage with WWE social media (Karlis 2018).

With these technologies, tv viewers can make their voices heard and feel like those who attend the show live in the arena, recovering and relaunching the dimension of audience's interactivity, that constitutes the main strength of pro wrestling.

Professional wrestling fans definitely use social media to "constitute their collective identity and act upon their agency to alter live performances and narratives" (Oglesby 2017).

Audience's rising awareness of their role and of the strength acquired through these tools, raises some questions, which may be investigated in future works: to what extent the WWE and other wrestling promotions are willing to ride the wave of this growing phenomenon, continuing to listen to the voice of fans in the arenas and virtual spaces? In the medium term, is it possible to arrive at a breaking point in which an increasingly "hungry for power" audience comes into a collision course with the decisions made by creative teams and managers? or will it be possible to find a meeting point that will allow a full development of the use of social media within transmedia storytelling strategies in wrestling?

Since it is difficult to predict an early end of the social media era, an important part of the future success of professional wrestling as an entertainment product may depend on the answers to these questions.

References

Barthes, R.: The World of Wrestling. Mythologies. Hill and Wang, New York (1972)

Chow, B., Laine, E.: Audience affirmation and the labour of professional wrestling. Perform. Res. **19**(2), 44–53 (2014). https://doi.org/10.1080/13528165.2014.928516

Jenkins, H.: Transmedia Storytelling. MIT Technology Review (2003). http://technologyreview.com/biomedicine/13052/

Jenkins, H.: Game Design as Narrative Architecture, in "First Person: New Media as Story, Performance and Game". In: Wardrip-Fruin, N., Harrigan, P. (ed.) MIT Press (2004)

Jenkins, H.: Fandom, Participatory Culture, and Web 2.0 - A Syllabus. (2010). http://henryjenkins.org/2010/01/fandom_participatory_culture_a.html

Jenkins, H.: What World Wrestling Entertainment Can Teach Us About the Future of Television (Part One) (2014). http://henryjenkins.org/2014/01/what-the-world-wrestling-federation-can-teach-us-about-the-future-of-television.html

Karlis, J.: "My Guy or Girl in the ring" and on my newsfeed: a study of viewers' uses and gratifications of WWE social media. Popul. Cult. Stud. J. **6**(1), 231 (2018)

MacFarlane, K.: A sport, a tradition, a religion, a joke: the need for a poetics of in-ring storytelling and a reclamation of professional wrestling as a global art. Asiatic **6**(2), 136–155 (2012)

Mazer, S.: "Real" Wrestling/"Real" Life. In: Sammond, N. (ed.) Steel Chair to the Head, pp. 67–87. Duke University Press, Durham (2005)

Oglesby, B.: Daniel Bryan & the Negotiation of Kayfabe in Professional Wrestling. Graduate Theses and Dissertations (2017). http://scholarcommons.usf.edu/etd/6735

Oliva, C., Calleja, G.: Fake rules, real fiction: professional wrestling and videogames. In: Proceedings of the 2009 DiGRA International Conference: Breaking New Ground: Innovation in Games, Play, Practice and Theory, vol. 5, Brunel University (2009). ISSN 2342-9666

Olson, C.: Twitter, Facebook, and professional wrestling: indie wrestler perspectives on the importance of social media. Popul. Cult. Stud. J. **6**(1) (2018)

Petten, A.J.: The narrative structuring and interactive narrative logic of televised professional wrestling. New Rev. Film Telev. Stud. **8**(4), 436–447 (2010)

Sammond, N., (ed.): Steel Chair to the Head: The Pleasure and Pain of Professional Wrestling. Duke University Press, 365 p. ISBN 0822334380 (2005)

Smith, T.: Wrestling With "Kayfabe". Contexts **5**(2), 54–55 (2006)

Stout, D.: Wrestling Fans Lash Out With '#CancelWWENetwork'. Time.com (2015)

Vargas, C.: Professional wrestling: the ultimate storytelling device. Comp. Media Stud. 602 (2007)

Wrenn, M.: Managing doubt: pro-wrestling jargon and the making of "smart fans". In: Sennett, R., Calhoun, C. (eds.) Practicing Culture, pp. 149–170. Routledge, New York (2007)

WWE Corporate, Investors: WWE Reports Q3 2018 Results

Maintains Path to Record Full-Year Performance (2018). https://corporate.wwe.com/~/media/Files/W/WWE/press-releases/2018/3q18-earnings-pr.pdf

WWE Corporate: Who We are (2018). https://corporate.wwe.com/who-we-are/company-overview

WWE Corporate: Key Performance Indicators (2018). https://corporate.wwe.com/~/media/Files/W/WWE/press-releases/2018/3q18-key-performance-indicators.pdf

How Factors that Influence Engagement Impact Users' Evaluations in Mobile App Stores

Leonardo Vasconcelos[1], Raissa Barcellos[1], José Viterbo[1(✉)],
Flavia Bernardini[1], Clodis Boscarioli[2], and Eunice Nunes[3]

[1] Fluminense Federal University, Niterói, RJ, Brazil
{lvasconcellos,viterbo,fcbernardini}@ic.uff.br,
raissabarcellos@id.uff.br
[2] Western Paraná State University, Cascavel, PR, Brazil
boscarioli@gmail.com
[3] Mato Grosso Federal University, Cuiabá, MT, Brazil
eunice@ufmt.br

Abstract. The range of mobile applications and the number of users of those technologies have been steadily increasing in recent years. Today, mobile applications deliver a variety of experiences, encouraging users to engage in tasks that create feelings of satisfaction and fulfillment. In app stores, users' evaluation of these applications directly influence their adoption and stay in the marketplace. In addition, for an application to succeed, users must be engaged into using it. The purpose of this paper is to investigate whether negative comments—related to factors that influence engagement—are able to directly influence user evaluation in app stores. We performed an experiment, in which we selected a set of apps from Android Play Store and analyzed the comments of users to determine the number of complaints involving factors that influence engagement. We then calculated a linear correlation to verify the influence of those factors over the users' rating of the selected apps. We verified that these factors have a real influence, from average to strong, in the evaluation of the user, considering the selected applications.

Keywords: Engagement · Recommendation system · User's evaluation

1 Introduction

The number of mobile technology users has been increasing on a large scale [1]. The features of smartphones have been expanded to meet the different needs of users [2]. Mobile applications are able to offer a vast and distinct set of pleasurable experiences, that often arouse in users the desire to engage for a long time in tasks that generate value, fulfillment and well-being [3]. In today's society, the mobile applications' market is fast growing, causing changes in society. Nowadays, mobile apps are an integral part of everyday life in society, influencing how

© Springer Nature Switzerland AG 2019
G. Meiselwitz (Ed.): HCII 2019, LNCS 11578, pp. 571–584, 2019.
https://doi.org/10.1007/978-3-030-21902-4_40

people interact with the world. With the advent of mobile apps, our lives have become richer, facilitating global social interactions [4].

Among several mobile applications that have been proposed, many follow a crowdsourcing approach. According to Bassi *et al.* [5] "crowdsourcing is a type of participatory online activity in which an individual or organization proposes to a group of individuals of varying knowledge and number, via a flexible open call, the voluntary undertaking of a task". Ghezzi *et al.* [6] affirm that "crowdsourcing is a branch of co-creation practice, which has been made possible through the upsurge of the web, where the "crowd" can help in validating, modifying and improving a company's value - creating idea or the material it posts over the internet". When crowdsourcing is coupled with mobile technology it is usually called mobile crowdsourcing (MC). In a MC app, the crowd of users, through mobile devices, perform various tasks, such as sharing information, results, analyzing data, among others [7]. Mobile applications, made available by most popular mobile devices – smartphones and tablets – provide a number of useful features, making everyday life easier for people in general. For example, if we need location services for roads in the city, the service function in mobile applications is to provide navigation, map and GPS [8].

Jung *et al.* [9] conducted a product survival analysis study for the Apple App Store in Korea. They said customer ratings, ranking, and content size offer a great deal of weight for a product, including apps, to stay in the market, especially if it's free. Therefore, the app ranking, or user rating, influences popularity as it brings more users to use these applications. In addition, for an MC application to succeed, it needs to go beyond being used, it is necessary that the users engage with it [10]. According to Lalmas *et al.* [11], user engagement is about the quality of the user experience, emphasizing aspects of interacting with an online application and, in particular, the desire to use that application more times. Liang *et al.* [12] define engagement as a psychological state where an individual invests his cognitive, physical, and affective energy to solve a task. The existence of factors that influence the users engagement in diverse applications is already explored in the literature, such as usability and confidence [11].

Some types of MC apps involve recommendation systems, benefiting from user evaluations so that they can provide rich information necessary for the app to make more recommendations to the user, in an efficient way [13]. This evaluation covers comments on the services or items recommended by the application. Recommendation systems have always faced the problem of sparse data. In the current era, however, with its demand for highly personalized, context-aware recommendations, real-time, the sparse data problem only threatens to worsen. If the app does not succeed in engaging the user, the user can not get the information needed to make the recommendations. Therefore, applications that involve crowdsourcing allied to recommendation systems have an increased need for engagement [13].

The textual part of the rating mechanism, represented by the comments section, is a free text description, without any predefined structure, and is used to describe, in a totally informal way, impressions, positions, claims, bugs, and desired resources [14]. These comments can provide valuable insight into a number of highly relevant topics, and developers can use this feature to better meet users expectations, by designing ways to engage them [15]. If app developers fail to engage users, and if the relevant suggestions for improving the app are ignored, the app rating will decrease and the app will probably lose market share [16].

In this work, our main purpose was to verify how negative comments—or complaints—, related to factors that knowingly influence engagement, influence the users' evaluation about crowdsourcing apps. We investigated the following hypothesis: the lower the number of complaints related to engagement factors, the higher the app rating. We performed an experiment, in which we selected a set of apps from Android Play Store and analyzed the comments of users to determine the number of complaints involving factors that influence engagement. We then calculated a linear correlation to verify the influence of those factors over the users' rating of the selected apps.

This paper is divided into six sections, including this one. In Sect. 2, we introduce a theoretical reference of all the concepts that will be used in our experiment. In Sect. 3, we present the related works in the literature. In Sect. 4, we describe our methodology and the experiment. In Sect. 5, we present the results. And finally, in Sect. 6, we present our conclusions and future work.

2 Theoretical Reference

In this study it is important to identify concepts such as: mobile applications and how they are made available to the users, the meaning of crowdsourcing and, more specifically, mobile crowdsourcing, conceptualizing recommendation systems - citing examples, and finally elucidating the definition of user - citing some factors that influence the user's real engagement.

2.1 Mobile Applications and App Stores

With the arrival of smartphones, the way users request software services was revolutionized [17]. Consequently, smartphone functionalities have been greatly expanded to meet the different needs of users [2]. Several services were created by the opportunities generated by the increased use of mobile applications [17]. Mobile applications are one of the fastest growing segments in the software application download markets. Several mobile app markets, such as the Amazon App Store, BlackBerry World, Google Play and the Apple App Store, emerged and grew rapidly in a short period of time. These application store markets exhibit characteristics of a "long tail market", as a huge plurality of digital products and low user search costs [18].

Currently, the Android operating system is the most used open source smartphone [19]. Android applications can be found at the Google Play Store that offers a variety of apps to download on any device that has the operating system installed. These applications can be free or paid. Hundreds of thousands of programmers submit applications for Google Play Store. Millions of people create an account on the Google Play Store to use the various apps it offers [20].

Each app in the Play Store has developer information, classifications, ratings, and space where users post comments informing their opinion of the app. Each comment has two characteristics: The first is that they are written in short sentences. The second is that the comment refers only to one version of the application and it may have been updated over time [21]. Evaluations and comments are of great importance to the success of applications [22].

Although having a large number of applications available can be an advantage, choosing the best option to meet a need can be an extremely complex task for the user. Users' reviews provide a way for helping other users in their choices. Reviews are rich repositories of information where multiple users post a rating on a star rating and/or comment on app quality, bugs, human-computer interaction issues such as usability and more. This information helps the user in deciding whether to install or purchase an application, whether to hire a service or not, among other things [23,24]. However, little has been researched on user review on mobile apps [25].

2.2 Crowdsourcing Applications

Crowdsourcing is a distributed model of participatory online activities where an undetermined crowd of people works engaged in solving a given task through an open call [5,26]. Crowdsourcing is, for the most part, a very well structured process by the company or organization that proposes the task, because of this it is able to make the most of the individuals' intelligence and creativity in a targeted way [27].

When crowdsourcing is coupled with mobile technology it is called mobile crowdsourcing (MC). In an MC app, the crowd of users, through mobile devices, perform various tasks, such as sharing information, results, analyzing data, among others [7]. One feature of Mobile Crowdsourcing applications is the active and passive contribution of the crowd. In the active contribution, users generate data such as text translation, user evaluation, performing calculations, or entering input data as a solution. In the passive contribution, the data from the features of the user's smartphone, such as sensors, GPS, triangulation calculations of a position, among others. It should be noted that the passive contribution crowdsourcing tasks are performed transparently for the device owner [26].

MC applications are a new way for commercial crowdsourcing [28]. Mobile crowdsourcing markets have attracted great attention from the industrial and academic community [29]. Several MC applications have stood out in the use by users like: review of films (IMDB[1], Netflix[2]), e-commerce (Google Play[3], Amazon[4]), provision of services (Uber[5], Airbnb[6]), among others.

2.3   Recommendation Systems

A Recommendation System is a system that uses a set of techniques and software tools to generate suggestions for items [30, 31]. Item is the name given to what the recommendation system suggests. Some examples are movies, a product, a news, among others. Recommendation Systems generally are directed to recommending a particular type of item. So your interface, your set of techniques and your algorithms are customized to get a more accurate recommendation. They are considered important in big companies like Amazon, YouTube, Netflix, among others [30].

They can be categorized into three forms: Content Based Recommendation System, Collaborative Filtering Recommendation System, and Hybrid Recommendation System [32]. A Content-Based Recommendation System uses user information such as profile, behavior, and choices to generate recommendations. An example can be considered an online movie rental. In this case, the system will store which movies the user has been watching for a period of time and thus suggest new movies based on what he has watched. If he has ever watched action movies, the system may suggest launching more action. The Collaborative Filtering Recommendation System uses choices that have been made previously by users who have similarities. An example might be a user who wants to buy a book at an online bookstore. When he enters the site when fetching books, he will be recommended by similar books based on the features previously searched for. And a Hybrid Recommendation System makes recommendations using the two previous forms. An example can be a user that connects to Facebook and receives recommendations from friends based on their tastes, preferences and also based on their user profile [32].

2.4   User Engagement

User engagement is an essential concept in application design. We can say that successful applications are not only used, but encourage the user to invest time, attention, and emotion, seeking to meet their needs. User engagement is not a new concept, but has been stimulating an evident number of researchers from diverse areas, such as information science, computing and learning sciences. Currently, we are in a highly connected society, engaging the user has become a

---

[1] https://play.google.com/store/apps/details?id=com.imdb.mobile&hl=pt_BR.

[2] https://play.google.com/store/apps/details?id=com.netflix.mediaclient&hl=pt_BR.

[3] https://play.google.com/store.

[4] https://play.google.com/store/apps/details?id=com.amazon.mShop.android.shopping&hl=pt_BR.

[5] https://play.google.com/store/apps/details?id=com.ubercab&hl=pt_BR.

[6] https://play.google.com/store/apps/details?id=com.airbnb.android.

non-trivial goal and an undeniable need [11]. People indulge emotionally, physically, and psychologically when engaged in performing their role [33].

Measuring user engagement is essential to assess whether applications are able to engage users effectively. User engagement is a complicated phenomenon - this gives rise to several measurement approaches. Existing literature means to assess user involvement include the use of questionnaires, observational methods, and facial expression analysis [11].

From the literature studied, it is known that some factors influence the user's engagement in applications, they are:

- **Usability** - As for the application interface, it is important to perform the tasks without any difficulty.
- **Aesthetic Appeal** - As for the application interface, it is very important that it be aesthetically appealing.
- **Attention** - As for the use of the application, it is important that the user is fully concentrated, without perceiving the passage of time.
- **Endurability** - It is important that the application motivates the user to use it frequently and to share it with friends.
- **User Control** - It is critical that the user realize that he is in control of the application until he reaches his goal.
- **Interactivity** - It is critical that the application promote easy, simple and fluid interaction.
- **Pleasure** - It's important to be fully involved with the application, providing a satisfying and rewarding experience.
- **Sensory Appeal** - It is important that the application uses sensory features, such as: hearing, speech, vision and touch.
- **Confidence** - The application must pass credibility and trust throughout the user experience.
- **Efficiency** - The recommendations suggested by the application should be fully compliant with user preferences.

Typically, recommendation systems were evaluated exclusively through the precision of the algorithms that guide recommendations. However, we have noticed concerns about the importance of identifying the factors that influence users to engage with a recommendation technology, since only a good recommendation does not guarantee an effective, efficient and satisfactory user experience.

3   Related Work

There have been many recent studies that have investigated the factors involved in users' adoption, intent of use and acceptance of apps. However, there have not been many studies that have investigated the engagement factors that influence the users' evaluation in mobile app stores.

In [34], Harris *et al.* investigated the factors that influenced the user to install a mobile application - a model is created, using perceived risk, perceived benefit, confidence and intent to install. Seven antecedents of trust and risk including

Table 1. Some related works

Author	Context	Factors/Theory used	Findings
[34]	Explore the factors that influence a user before installing a app	Perceived risk, Confidence, Perceived benefit, and Intent to install and seven antecedents of confidence and risk	A model explains 50.5% of the variance in the intention to install an app
[35]	Predict use intention of mobile apps	Performance enhancement of tasks, ease, opinions of others, motivation of the entertainment, information seek motivation and motivation of social connection	Ease is the key factor influencing the intention of continuing the use of mobile applications
[36]	Predict the intent and use of mobile applications of young American users	Perceived enjoyment, usefulness, ease of use, subjective norm, perceived behavioral control, usefulness, and mobile Internet	The perceived pleasure, ease of use, utility and subjective norm emerge as significant predictors of their attitudes in mobile applications. The attitudes and intentions of young people predict the use of mobile applications
[37]	Explore the factors that influence consumers' intent to continuously use branded applications	Expectation of effort, social influence and brand identification	The interactivity perceived by consumers positively affects the expectation of effort, which, in turn, contributes to the expectation of performance. The expectation of performance is another direct factor of the intention to use continuity

perceived safety, perceived reputation, application characteristics, familiarity, desensitization, consumer willingness to trust and consumer disposition. The presented model explains 50.5% of the variation in the intention to install an application The results show that the consumers who perceive more security have greater confidence and less perceived risk.

In [35], Kang *et al.* presented as the performance enhancement of tasks, the ease, the opinions of others important, the motivation of the entertainment, the information seek motivation and motivation of social connection could predict the intention to use mobile applications by users. The results of a hypothetical model test show that ease is the key factor influencing the intention of continuing the use of mobile applications.

In [36], Yang *et al.* integrated the Technology Acceptance Model, the Planned Behavior Theory and the Usage and Gratification Theory to predict the intent and use of mobile applications of young American users. The model was tested by a Web search of 555 American college students. The perceived pleasure, ease of use, utility and subjective norm emerge as significant predictors of their attitudes in mobile applications. The results conclude that the attitudes and intentions of such young people predict the use of mobile applications.

In [37], Wu *et al.* conducted an online survey to explore the factors that influence consumers' intent to continuously use branded applications. The results confirm the great importance of application engagement, which is positively influenced by the expectation of effort, social influence and brand identification. Moreover, the interactivity perceived by consumers positively affects the

expectation of effort, which, in turn, contributes to the expectation of performance. The expectation of performance is another direct factor of the intention
to use continuity. The paper suggests that marketers of branded apps need to
emphasize improving consumers' app engagement rather than just providing
useful app functions.

In summary, there were no studies found that investigated the engagement
factors that influence the users' evaluation in mobile app stores, as we can see in
Table 1, but a few studies were found that investigated the factors that influence
adoption and the continuous use of apps.

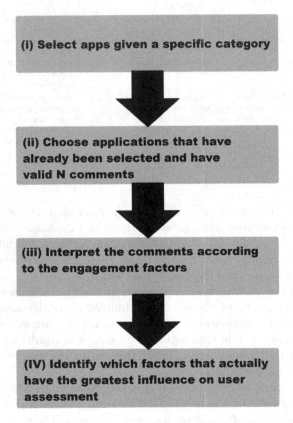

Fig. 1. Each step of our methodology.

4   Methodology

Our methodology was divided into four phases: (i) select apps given a specific
category, (ii) choose applications that have already been selected and have valid
N comments, (iii) interpret the comments according to the engagement factors,

and (iv) identify how the engagement factors induce the evaluation of the users. In Fig. 1 we present each step.

In the execution of this methodology, for data collection, we first select apps about service recommendations from the Android Play Store - chose the android operating system because it is the most used open source in mobile devices [19]. This category - service recommendations - was chosen because it is not well explored in the literature, and has as a principle the recommendation that uses the user's evaluation to make the recommendation more efficient. The applications selected were those that hold the highest amount of comments according to category: recommendation of services. The following applications have been selected:

- Service Touch: Application for users to hire or offer services without intermediaries, such as: painter, day laborer, hairdresser, mechanic, personal trainer, electrician, masseur among others.
- Labor: Application to search for service providers.
- Get Ninjas: Application for professionals to offer their services and for clients to hire them.
- Helpie: Application to search for service providers.
- Service Market: Application to search for service providers.
- Diaríssima[7]: Application to search for domestic service providers.
- Help me cleaning: Application to search for domestic service providers.

Table 2. Examples and responses quantities for each factor

Factor	Response's example	Total citations
Usability	"App is very complicated, I could not finalize nor search for professionals, app was asking for birthday, but did not show the field on screen."	20
Endurability	"The problem is that the advertising is very small, but the app has great potential to grow."	7
Control	"App keeps the location active all the time unnecessarily."	7
Confidence	"If you do not close the order they will not return the deposited coins."	14
Efficiency	"Until today no clients, do they really call?"	16

After this selection, we choose the 10 most recent/really useful comments for each chosen application. 10 comments were chosen because of the limited number of experts on the team in this work. We interpreted each comment manually, in order to identify whether or not some engagement term can be applied to the due complaint. We pointed out all the complaints for each engagement factor - considering each definition already grounded in the literature. That is, when the user made complaints about one of the factors, a complaint was counted. Table 2 shows, for each factor, examples of comments collected and amounts of related comments.

---

[7] Application that assists those who need to contract or provide hourly housekeepers/day laborers.

Table 3. Apps, their ratings and claims quantities by engagement factor

App	Rating	Usability	Endurability	Confidence	Control	Efficiency
Labor	3,2	3	4	0	3	1
Service Touch	3,7	6	3	0	0	3
Diaríssima	3,8	4	0	2	0	4
Helpie	3,8	3	0	2	1	5
Get Ninjas	4,2	4	0	7	0	3
Help me cleaning	4,3	0	0	2	2	0
Service Market	4,4	0	0	1	1	0

Due to the limitation on the amount of data collected, we used five factors of engagement in our study: usability, endurability, control, confidence and efficiency - these factors were the most cited in complaints. The Table 3 provide data for each application, such as: rating and the number of complaints for each engagement factor checked. In the next Section, we present the analysis of our results.

5 Results

In order to verify how the engagement factors induce the evaluation of the users, we performed a linear correlation test evaluation. A numerical measure of linear correlation between two variables, takes values between -1 (perfectly strong and indirect relation) to $+1$ (perfectly strong and direct relation). Values close to zero indicate a lack of linear relationship. An array of these coefficients is called correlation matrix [38].

Table 4. Engagement factors and their respective linear correlation values

Factor	Correlation value	Interpretation
Usability	−0,56	Moderate negative correlation
Endurability	−0,80	Strong negative correlation
Confidence	0,46	Moderate positive correlation
Control	−0,34	Weak negative correlation
Efficiency	−0,30	Weak negative correlation

According to results presented in the Table 4, in Fig. 2 and in Fig. 3, we can observe that:

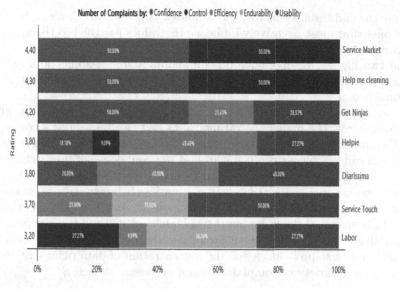

Fig. 2. Composition around the number of complaints of each engagement factor, per app. Rating in descending order.

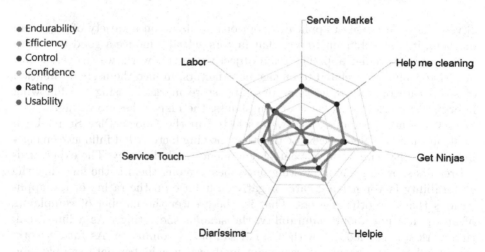

Fig. 3. Radar chart comprising multivariate data (engagement factors per app). Radar chart is used to measure scales, where each variable is "better" in some respect - in our case, in some engagement factor.

- The endurability factor holds the greatest influence on the rating of the applications, presenting strong negative correlation.
- The higher the number of complaints about the endurability, the lower the ratings assigned.

- After the endurability factor, the usability, control and efficiency factors are the ones that most negatively influence the values assigned to the application ratings.
- The two highest ratings have no complaints about usability and efficiency. The predominant complaints about the engagement factors are control and confidence.
- The confidence factor has a positive correlation, where the higher the number of complaints, the higher the ratings. This fact can be seen as a consequence of the success of the application, since applications that hold larger numbers of users can get bigger problems around the confidence of user data.
- In Fig. 3, through the multivariate comparative visualization of the radar chart, we can see that ratings applications with larger data points concentrate fewer complaints about the engagement factors. For example, the right-hand dimension of the radar chart has higher ratings and fewer demarcations than about general engagement factors, while the left-sided dimension - with smaller ratings apps - has a greater concentration of data points, represented by a greater variety of complaints about engagement factors.

6   Conclusions

Given the wide range of application options available on a variety of app store markets, it is still difficult to see what factors actually induce a good user evaluation of a particular app. The main objective, in this work, was to verify how negative comments, related to engagement factors, induce the users' evaluation of some category of applications in a app store market - using the following hypothesis: the lower the number complaints, the higher the app rating.

Seven Android applications were selected in the Google Play Store. Each application was evaluated considering the following factors that influence engagement: usability, endurability, control, confidence and efficiency. The experimental results showed some interesting outcomes. Among them is the fact that the endurability factor has a greater negative influence on the rating of the applications than the other factors. That is, the greater the number of complaints of an application about endurability, the smaller the ratings. As a limitation, this work was carried out with a small sample of comments. As future work, we intend to use automated sentiment analysis on a higher data sample, and also use social networks to check for comments on the applications on different platforms.

Acknowledgement. This study was financed in part by the Coordenação de Aperfeiçoamento de Pessoal de Nível Superior - Brasil (CAPES) - Finance Code 001.

References

1. Yang, D., Xue, G., Fang, X., Tang, J.: Crowdsourcing to smartphones: incentive mechanism design for mobile phone sensing. In: Proceedings of the 18th Annual International Conference on Mobile Computing and Networking, pp. 173–184. ACM (2012)
2. Zhu, H., Xiong, H., Ge, Y., Chen, E.: Mobile app recommendations with security and privacy awareness. In: Proceedings of the 20th ACM SIGKDD International Conference on Knowledge Discovery and Data Mining, pp. 951–960. ACM (2014)
3. Turgeman, L., Smart, O., Guy, N.: Unsupervised learning approach to estimating user engagement with mobile applications: a case study of the weather company (IBM). Expert Syst. Appl. **120**, 397–412 (2019)
4. Laudon, K.C., Traver, C.G., et al.: E-commerce: Business, Technology, Society (2016)
5. Bassi, H., Lee, C.J., Misener, L., Johnson, A.M.: Exploring the characteristics of crowdsourcing: an online observational study. J. Inf. Sci. (2019). https://doi.org/10.1177/0165551519828626
6. Ghezzi, A., Gabelloni, D., Martini, A., Natalicchio, A.: Crowdsourcing: a review and suggestions for future research. Int. J. Manag. Rev. **20**(2), 343–363 (2018)
7. Gong, Y., Wei, L., Guo, Y., Zhang, C., Fang, Y.: Optimal task recommendation for mobile crowdsourcing with privacy control. IEEE Internet Things J. **3**(5), 745–756 (2016)
8. Suh, Y., Park, Y.: Identifying and structuring service functions of mobile applications in Google's android market. Inf. Syst. e-Bus. Manag. **16**(2), 383–406 (2018)
9. Jung, E.Y., Baek, C., Lee, J.D.: Product survival analysis for the app store. Mark. Lett. **23**(4), 929–941 (2012)
10. Lehmann, J., Lalmas, M., Yom-Tov, E., Dupret, G.: Models of user engagement. In: Masthoff, J., Mobasher, B., Desmarais, M.C., Nkambou, R. (eds.) UMAP 2012. LNCS, vol. 7379, pp. 164–175. Springer, Heidelberg (2012). https://doi.org/10.1007/978-3-642-31454-4_14
11. Lalmas, M., O'Brien, H., Yom-Tov, E.: Measuring user engagement. Synth. Lect. Inf. Concepts, Retr. Serv. **6**(4), 1–132 (2014)
12. Liang, H., Wang, M.M., Wang, J.J., Xue, Y.: How intrinsic motivation and extrinsic incentives affect task effort in crowdsourcing contests: a mediated moderation model. Comput. Hum. Behav. **81**, 168–176 (2018)
13. Larson, M., et al.: Activating the crowd: exploiting user-item reciprocity for recommendation (2013)
14. Palomba, F., et al.: User reviews matter! tracking crowdsourced reviews to support evolution of successful apps. In: IEEE International Conference on Software Maintenance and Evolution (ICSME), pp. 291–300. IEEE (2015)
15. Di Sorbo, A., et al.: What would users change in my app? Summarizing app reviews for recommending software changes. In: Proceedings of the 2016 24th ACM SIGSOFT International Symposium on Foundations of Software Engineering, pp. 499–510. ACM (2016)
16. Villarroel, L., Bavota, G., Russo, B., Oliveto, R., Di Penta, M.: Release planning of mobile apps based on user reviews. In: 2016 IEEE/ACM 38th International Conference on Software Engineering (ICSE), pp. 14–24. IEEE (2016)
17. Junior, E.L.L., Rosa, R.L., Rodriguez, D.Z.: A recommendation system for shared-use mobility service. In: 2018 26th International Conference on Software, Telecommunications and Computer Networks (SoftCOM), pp. 1–6. IEEE (2018)

18. Lee, G., Raghu, T.S.: Determinants of mobile apps' success: evidence from the app store market. J. Manag. Inf. Syst. **31**(2), 133–170 (2014)
19. Jisha, R., Krishnan, R., Vikraman, V.: Mobile applications recommendation based on user ratings and permissions. In: 2018 International Conference on Advances in Computing, Communications and Informatics (ICACCI), pp. 1000–1005. IEEE (2018)
20. Viennot, N., Garcia, E., Nieh, J.: A measurement study of Google play. In: ACM SIGMETRICS Performance Evaluation Review, vol. 42, pp. 221–233. ACM (2014)
21. Fu, B., Lin, J., Li, L., Faloutsos, C., Hong, J., Sadeh, N.: Why people hate your app: making sense of user feedback in a mobile app store. In: Proceedings of the 19th ACM SIGKDD International Conference on Knowledge Discovery and Data Mining, pp. 1276–1284. ACM (2013)
22. Palomba, F., et al.: Crowdsourcing user reviews to support the evolution of mobile apps. J. Syst. Softw. **137**, 143–162 (2018)
23. Iacob, C., Harrison, R.: Retrieving and analyzing mobile apps feature requests from online reviews. In: Proceedings of the 10th Working Conference on Mining Software Repositories, pp. 41–44. IEEE Press (2013)
24. Khalid, H., Shihab, E., Nagappan, M., Hassan, A.E.: What do mobile app users complain about? IEEE Softw. **32**(3), 70–77 (2015)
25. Khalid, H.: On identifying user complaints of iOS apps. In: Proceedings of the 2013 International Conference on Software Engineering, pp. 1474–1476. IEEE Press (2013)
26. Chatzimilioudis, G., Konstantinidis, A., Laoudias, C., Zeinalipour-Yazti, D.: Crowdsourcing with smartphones. IEEE Internet Comput. **16**(5), 36–44 (2012)
27. Brabham, D.C., Ribisl, K.M., Kirchner, T.R., Bernhardt, J.M.: Crowdsourcing applications for public health. Am. J. Prev. Med. **46**(2), 179–187 (2014)
28. Wang, Y., Cai, Z., Yin, G., Gao, Y., Tong, X., Wu, G.: An incentive mechanism with privacy protection in mobile crowdsourcing systems. Comput. Netw. **102**, 157–171 (2016)
29. Thebault-Spieker, J., Terveen, L.G., Hecht, B.: Avoiding the south side and the suburbs: the geography of mobile crowdsourcing markets. In: Proceedings of the 18th ACM Conference on Computer Supported Cooperative Work and Social Computing, pp. 265–275. ACM (2015)
30. Ricci, F., Rokach, L., Shapira, B.: Introduction to recommender systems handbook. In: Ricci, F., Rokach, L., Shapira, B., Kantor, P. (eds.) Recommender Systems Handbook, pp. 1–35. Springer, Boston (2011). https://doi.org/10.1007/978-0-387-85820-3_1
31. Beel, J., Gipp, B., Langer, S., Breitinger, C.: Research-paper recommender systems: a literature survey. Int. J. Digit. Libr. **17**(4), 305–338 (2016)
32. Reis, J.R., Viterbo, J., Bernardini, F.C.: Uma análise comparativa de sistemas de recomendação musical para grupos
33. Kahn, W.A.: Psychological conditions of personal engagement and disengagement at work. Acad. Manag. J. **33**(4), 692–724 (1990)
34. Harris, M.A., Brookshire, R., Chin, A.G.: Identifying factors influencing consumers' intent to install mobile applications. Int. J. Inf. Manag. **36**(3), 441–450 (2016)
35. Kang, S.: Factors influencing intention of mobile application use. Int. J. Mob. Commun. **12**(4), 360–379 (2014)
36. Yang, H.: Bon appétit for apps: young American consumers' acceptance of mobile applications. J. Comput. Inf. Syst. **53**(3), 85–96 (2013)
37. Wu, L.: Factors of continually using branded mobile apps: the central role of app engagement. Int. J. Internet Mark. Advert. **9**(4), 303–320 (2015)
38. Usip, E.E.: Glossary of statistical terms, July 2013

Author Index

Printed in the United States
By Bookmasters